Pathways to Tax Reform

Pathways to Tax Reform

The Concept of Tax Expenditures

STANLEY S. SURREY

Harvard University Press

Cambridge, Massachusetts

Contents

Contents

Preface

As the title and subtitle of this book together indicate, I believe that the principal ways to tax reform and improvement of our federal tax system lie in the concept of tax expenditures. The phrase, "tax expenditures" is, as far as I know, a new one in the literature of tax reform. I first used it in a speech in late 1967 given while I was Assistant Secretary for Tax Policy in the Treasury Department, in which I introduced my understanding of the concept. The speech pointed out that those provisions of the federal income tax containing special exemptions, exclusions, deductions, and other tax benefits were really methods of providing governmental financial assistance. These special provisions were not part of the structure required for the income tax itself, but were instead Government expenditures made through the tax system. They were similar in purpose, therefore, to the direct expenditures listed in the regular budget. But since they provided their assistance through the route of tax reduction rather than direct aid, I called them "tax expenditures." In the speech that introduced this term I stressed the need for an accounting of these tax expenditures, since at that point no Government document or private research study listed and quantified this assistance provided through the tax system. In my position as Assistant Secretary I was able in 1968 to conduct the research that provided a "Tax Expenditure Budget," published in the Annual Report of the Secretary of the Treasury in 1968. This Budget is described and furnished in Chapter I.

On my return to Harvard Law School in 1969 I continued the exploration of the concept of tax expenditures. Since tax expenditures involve governmental financial assistance given through the tax system rather than through the direct methods of the regular budget, the question naturally arises as to what criteria Government should use in deciding when to channel needed financial assistance through the tax expenditure route and when to channel that assistance through the direct expenditure route. The use of the word "naturally" in this sentence is hindsight. In the Treasury in the late 1960s I faced the task of articulating why the Treasury opposed the widespread use of the tax incentives, especially tax credits, then being urged as the way to handle our social goals of more housing, more training for the unskilled, more higher education, less pollution — the list of goals and consequent tax incentives seemed almost endless. In working on this task I soon discovered that apparently no one, in or out of Government, had systematically considered the criteria to be used in choosing between tax incentives and direct expenditures. Perhaps there was due retribution in my being forced as a consequence to commence the search for those criteria and to state them in Treasury legislative statements opposing the numerous tax incentive proposals. In 1961 I had been perhaps the principal architect of the new investment tax credit for machinery and equipment, and the adoption of this credit in the tax system was probably the main inspiration for the flock of tax credit incentives proposed thereafter, all of which the Treasury opposed. It urged instead that direct expenditure programs be used to meet those social goals and therefore took on the burden of pushing the White House and the other executive departments to develop the required programs.

At Harvard, with the benefit of hindsight, I sought to develop the criteria I considered applicable, which I described in a February 1970 article in the *Harvard Law Review.* This in turn led to the next step, that of linking tax reform to the concept of tax expenditures. Again, while in the Treasury, I had conducted the preparation of a major study on tax reform that was published early in 1969. This study essentially regarded the task of tax reform as that of restoring "fairness" to the federal tax system by ending both the escape of many well-to-do individuals and large corporations from the burdens of that system and the ironic contrast of placing an income tax on those still in the poverty class. This study, and the proposals it offered, became the basis of the Tax Reform Act of 1969. In reflecting on these developments I came to recognize that most of the matters considered in 1969 — whether they were adopted or rejected in the final legislation — related to items in the Tax Expenditure Budget. This led to the view, developed in a December 1970 article in the *Harvard Law Review,* that the task of tax reform lay in a systematic exploration of the Tax Expenditure Budget. But since that budget is a catalog of *expenditure* items, although the assistance they provide is conveyed through tax reduction, the task of tax reform becomes inseparably linked with the problems of Government expenditures. With this thought stated, one can begin to see the many new avenues of research, exploration, and action that at once are opened: Is the tax assistance really required by national priorities? If so, is tax assistance the preferred route, or should the assistance be given directly? Which method comes closest to the targeted goal of the assistance and does so with fairness and efficiency? If the answer is direct assistance, how structure the direct program and then how bring about the executive branch coordination and, perhaps more important, the coordination among congressional committees required to achieve the switch from tax assistance to direct assistance?

The consideration of these questions — these pathways to tax reform —

are the subject of this book. The title could well have been "New Pathways to Tax Reform," for I believe we are still at the threshhold of the insights and courses of action to be derived from continued study of the concept of tax expenditures. The linkage of tax reform to expenditure analysis provides fertile ground for further research in a great variety of fields, many of which involve pressing social problems. The consequences of that linkage are beginning to be perceived by those in the Government who work on the development of our tax system, and with this perception new courses of action and the errors of existing approaches are becoming evident. Likewise, those who work on the expenditure side of our fiscal system are commencing to see the problems and defects involved in allowing a huge expenditure apparatus, $60 to $65 billion in total amount, to be contained — "buried" is a better word — in the tax system. I believe — or at least one can be hopeful — that through these pathways opened by the concept of tax expenditures a better tax system and a better budget policy will be achieved.

In the desire to have as many and varied talents as possible pursue these new pathways, this book does not require an extensive background knowledge of the tax system. It is hoped that all those concerned with tax and budgetary reform — legislators and other Government officials; business executives; the professions directly involved with these matters and with the social goals that have often prompted tax expenditures, such as lawyers, accountants, economists, journalists, political scientists, sociologists; and many others — will find the material of interest and not burdened by the tax expert's jargon or particular perspectives. At the same time, I also hope that the tax experts will not find technical slippage because of the desire to involve this broader audience.

I am greatly indebted to many lawyers and economists for their assistance in preparing the material. Jerome Kurtz of the Pennsylvania Bar, Stuart E. Seigel of the District of Columbia Bar, Professors Hugh J. Ault and Paul R. McDaniel (my co-authors of *Federal Income Taxation, Cases and Materials,* a law school course book whose parallel preparation was of considerable assistance), and my colleague Richard B. Stewart read various portions of the manuscript. Joseph A. Pechman of the Brookings Institution also read the manuscript and through his studies published with Benjamin A. Okner of the Institution provided important statistical data. The benefits of teaching a seminar on tax policy with my economist colleague, Richard A. Musgrave, are a significant part of the background for the writing, as are the insights obtained through conversations with my legal colleague, William D. Andrews. Harris L. Hartz, of the New Mexico Bar, while a student at the Harvard Law School did the initial research and organization which form the basis for the Appendix to Chapter V.

I have had the assistance of Alicia Munnell in preparing some of the mathematical deferral material and of Paul Barba in the computations for the tables in Chapter III. Steven C. Marshall undertook the task of checking the original manuscript, and Professor George Carey and William D. Luck participated in the final stages of checking and proofing.

I am indebted to Bowne & Co., and especially to Paul S. Hoffman, Vice President of that concern, for contributing to the Harvard Law School the computerized manuscript preparation and type-setting facilities which were used in the production of this book. Kathy Lynch was the indispensable link between the manuscript and the machine. Her indefatigable and careful pursuit of the benefits to be derived from the use of the machine's facilities carried my initial handwriting through to the machine's final product of the printed page.

I wish to express my appreciation for the above assistance. I also wish to underscore my indebtedness to all those who worked with me when I was in the Treasury Department. Their skills and insights educated me so thoroughly that thoughts which I am prone to consider as my own are really in so many unseen ways only the consequences of that education.

August 1973

Stanley S. Surrey

Acknowledgments

I gratefully acknowledge the permission extended by the following authors and publishers to reprint excerpts from the works indicated: Schultze, Fried, Rivlin and Teeters, *Setting National Priorities,* copyrighted 1972 by The Brookings Institution, Washington, D.C.; Presidents Publishing House, Inc.: Reid, *Corporate and Executive Tax Investments* (1972); The Environmental Law Institute, Washington, D.C.: *Effluent Charges on Air and Water Pollution,* copyright 1973; *The New Yorker:* "Talk of the Town," copyright 1970, The New Yorker Magazine, Inc.; American Association of American Universities: *Tax Reform and the Crises of Financing Higher Education* (1973); *National Tax Journal:* Aaron, "What is a Comprehensive Tax Base Anyway?" (1969), Surrey and Hellmuth, "The Tax Expenditure Budget — A Reply to Professor Bittker" (1969), and Fortune, "The Impact of Taxable Municipal Bonds: Policy Simulations With a Large Econometric Model" (1973); *New England Economic Review:* "Restructuring the Municipal Bond Market" (1971), and "Tax Exemption of State and Local Interest Payments: an Economic Analysis of the Issues and an Alternative" (1973); *Harvard Law Review:* Andrews, "Personal Deductions in an Ideal Income Tax" (1972), Surrey, "Tax Incentives As a Device for Implementing Government Policy: A Comparison with Direct Government Expenditures" (1970), and Surrey, "Federal Income Tax Reforms: The Varied Approaches Necessary to Replace Tax Expenditures with Direct Government Assistance" (1970), copyright for respective years by The Harvard Law Review Association; Committee for Economic Development: Social Responsibilities of Business Corporations (1971); *Law and Contemporary Problems:* Vickrey, "Tax Simplification Through Cumulative Averaging" (1969); Halperin, "Capital Gains and Ordinary Deductions: Negative Income Tax for the Wealthy" (1971), and Surrey, "The Tax Reform Act of 1969 — Tax Deferral and Tax Shelters" (1971), copyright 1971, reprinted by permission of the *Boston College Industrial and Commercial Law Review.*

Pathways to Tax Reform

I

The Tax Expenditure Budget

Background

This is the scene: It is September 1967. President Johnson has recommended that a surcharge of 10 percent be imposed on individual and corporate income taxes. The combination of expanded domestic spending under the President's Great Society programs and of increased Vietnam war expenditures is producing a growing budget deficit that in turn threatens to create inflationary conditions. The recommended surcharge is designed to control that deficit. But the Ways and Means Committee of the House of Representatives, which must make the initial legislative judgment on the recommendation, is troubled about a tax increase. Most of its members believe the inflationary potential could better be controlled through a reduction in Government expenditures, or that at least a tax increase must be matched by a decrease in those expenditures. So the Committee in Executive Session is questioning the Director of the Budget and considering ways to reduce expenditures. Some members wish a flat expenditure cut across the board, but others seek to establish priorities for reduction. Some desire to reduce recent programs, others want to reduce "research" expenditures, and some stress reduction of "unpopular" programs.

As a result, for several days the Ways and Means Committee and the Budget Director pore over the Federal Budget, category by category, sometimes stopping to look at minutiae, sometimes trying to get the broad perspective. For the moment the committee, in its desire to see expenditures controlled and thus make a tax increase more palatable if it must be voted, became an Appropriations Committee. But in its scrutiny of the expenditures listed in the budget, the committee had forgotten what it knew as a tax committee. Never once in its examination of the direct expenditures listed in the budget did the committee pause to consider the dollars involved in the tax incentives and tax subsidies contained in the Internal Revenue Code.

It was not for lack of knowledge. The committee members were fully aware that through tax benefits the income tax law provided financial assistance to this or that business, such as the special depletion allowances for the oil and minerals industries or the special tax treatment for the timber industry. They were familiar with the special provisions which financially aided state and local governments through exemption from tax of the interest on their obligations. They were aware of the special tax benefits for the aged, the sick, and the blind which provided assistance to these groups. Some of these provisions, and many others of like nature, had been the occasion for legislative struggles before the committee in the past. But the committee kept the financial assistance furnished by these special tax provisions completely separate and isolated in its mind from the task at hand. Indeed, the connection with that task simply did not occur to the members. They thought of the legislative consideration of those special provisions as raising issues for a tax bill. Such issues are categorized in legislative parlance as a "tax reform" controversy if the provisions are under attack and as a program for the "removal of special tax hardships" if the adoption of such provisions is being sought. But now the committee was engaged in looking at the "budget," and the budget did not list the dollars of financial assistance provided by the special tax provisions. It listed only the direct, traditional expenditures of Government.

So the committee and Budget Director in the search for expenditure control and expenditure reduction did not give thought to those "tax expenditure" dollars. Indeed, if the committee had asked the Director for a list of those tax expenditure dollars he could not have provided one, for neither his agency nor the Treasury Department had compiled such a list. Yet in a number of budget categories — for example, "Community Development and Housing" or "Commerce and Transportation" — the tax expenditure dollars provided more Government financial assistance than did budget expenditures. And in a number of instances the assistance could just as readily have been provided through a budget program instead of a tax provision.

The scene soon ended. The committee saw the futility of detailed expenditure examination on its part, but then held to the view that a budget reduction must accompany any tax increase. There thus ensued a prolonged dispute between the Congress and the President, who wanted his tax increase without any major change in his budget policies. In the end the Congress prevailed. When in June 1968 the Revenue and Expenditure Control Act of 1968 became law, it contained both a 10 percent tax surcharge and a budget reduction of $6 billion in expenditures for the fiscal year 1969 and of $10 billion in new spending authority for that year, enforced through specific ceilings on those categories. The President was charged with making the necessary reductions to keep the actual amounts within those ceilings. But the ceilings, being "budget" ceilings, related only to items in the budget and thus did not affect the dollars "spent" through the special tax provisions. Hence those dollars remained untouched, and the President could not affect them in seeking the places and programs to cut back expenditures to keep within the ceilings.

It was not until 1969, in response to a public desire for "tax reform," that the Congress considered a number of those tax provisions. As a result, some of the provisions were affected by the legislation that resulted, the Tax Reform Act of 1969. But each provision considered was the occasion for a difficult legislative struggle, as those benefited by the provision fought to retain their benefits. In a number of cases the beneficiaries of provisions under attack successfully prevented any change, or at least any material change. The process of achieving a reduction in those tax expenditure programs affected by the 1969 Act, with each provision involving its own battleground, was thus far different from that used in 1968 to control direct budget expenditures, where the Congress set an overall ceiling and the President carried out the reduction in specific programs.

This episode in fiscal history is recounted here because it was responsible for the development by the Treasury Department of a "Tax Expenditure Budget." The scene in the House Ways and Means Committee suddenly illuminated many questions: Just what would a list of the special tax provisions that are comparable to expenditure programs look like? What would be the categories covered and the groups benefited? How many dollars would be involved and how would the amounts compare with direct budget spending in those categories for those groups? Given the existence of such a list, other questions follow: How do you go about comparing the substantive results under the tax benefits with those under budget expenditures? Once it is determined to provide Government financial assistance to a particular group, how does Government decide — and how should it decide — whether to use the tax route or the direct budget route?

The "illumination" prompted a speech by me, in my then capacity as Assistant Secretary of the Treasury for Tax Policy, on November 15, 1967, before the Money Marketeers, a New York financial group, entitled "The United States Income Tax System — the Need for a Full Accounting."[1] The speech developed the concept of "tax expenditures" and a "tax expenditure budget." It stated that:

> ...through deliberate departures from accepted concepts of net income and through various special exemptions, deductions and credits, our tax system does operate to affect the private economy in ways that are usually accomplished by expenditures — in effect to produce an expenditure system described in tax language.

The speech then went on to say:

> When Congressional talk and public opinion turn to reduction and

3

control of Federal expenditures, these tax expenditures are never mentioned. Yet it is clear that if these tax amounts were treated as line items on the expenditure side of the Budget, they would automatically come under the close scrutiny of the Congress and the Budget Bureau. But the tax expenditures are not so listed, and they are thus automatically excluded from that scrutiny. Instead, since they are phrased in tax language and placed in the Internal Revenue Code, any examination to be given to them must fall in the classification of "tax reform" and not "expenditure control." There is a vast difference between the two classifications.

It can be suggested therefore that we need a full accounting for these effects of the tax system. The approach would be to explore the possibility of describing in the Federal Budget the expenditure equivalents of tax benefit provisions. We should not, of course, overlook the difficulties of interpretation or measurement involved here. Thus, just which tax measures can be said to fall in this category — in other words, which tax rules are integral to a tax system in order to provide a balanced tax structure and a proper measurement of net income, and which tax rules represent departures from that net income concept and balanced structure to provide relief, assistance, incentive or what you will for a particular group or activity. Also, once a tax item can be identified as falling in this second category, we must then compute its expenditure equivalent. Presumably this would be the amount of revenue lost, i.e., "spent," under the special tax treatment, and in a number of situations revenue statistics would have to be improved to give us this information.

The Treasury Department tax staff, with the assistance of consultants, especially Professor Henry Aaron of the University of Maryland, proceeded to the preparation of such a budget. The result was published in the Annual Report of the Secretary of the Treasury, Fiscal Year 1968, as the Tax Expenditure Budget for that year.[2] That budget was presented to the Joint Economic Committee by the Secretary of the Treasury in January 1969.[3] With that publication and presentation there became available for the first time a systematic enumeration of these tax expenditures arranged by budget categories, together with the amounts involved and their relationship to the direct expenditures in the respective budget categories. The Treasury Department in 1970 published a similar budget for the fiscal year 1969, using the term "tax aids" rather than expenditures.[4] In 1971 the Conference Committee on the Revenue Act of 1971 agreed that such data should be submitted annually to the tax committees of the Congress, presumably to be published by those committees.[5] A Senate colloquy regarding that agreement included the Joint Economic Committee as a recipient of the material.[6] The latter committee, through its Subcommittee on Economy in Government, had urged the adoption of this tax expenditure analysis as part of a program to expand the comprehensiveness of the material contained in the Federal Budget.[7] Indeed, it would be quite desirable to include the tax expenditure budget in the Federal Budget Document itself, at least as a "Special Analysis." On October 4, 1972, the House Committee on Ways and Means, pursuant to the Conference agreement in 1971, published "Estimates of Federal Tax Expenditures" for the years 1967–1971. On June 1, 1973, the Committee published its estimates for the years 1967–1972. The latter document will be considered further on in this chapter.

Since 1969 the list of these tax expenditures — or tax subsidies — has grown larger with the Treasury Department itself, forces within the Congress, and outside groups pushing new subsidies into the tax system.[8] The major part of the permanent changes in the income tax provided by the 1971 Act — both as to revenue and space in the tax law — involved new tax expenditures. Thus, the 1971 Act introduced the following income tax subsidies: restoration of the 7 percent investment credit; a class life system for depreciation of machinery and equipment, currently based on the use of the thirtieth percentile experience as of 1962 (starting at the shorter pole), abandoning the reserve ratio test which had required, in fixing depreciable lives, a consideration of the taxpayer's own experience, and with permission to the Treasury to grant a 20 percent shorter class life; a preferential treatment of income from exporting (DISC), which in practical operation will exempt one-half of that income from tax; five-year amortization for the cost of construction of employer facilities for employer on-the-job training programs and child care; a large increase in the child care deduction, including household expenses; a tax credit to employers who employ persons certified by the Secretary of Labor as having been placed in employment under work incentive programs (WIN); a tax credit and deduction for political campaign contributions. It should be added, to indicate the extent to which the 1971 bill involved tax expenditures, that the Conference Committee on that bill rejected the following Senate-passed tax subsidies: a system of credits and rebates for post-secondary school education; a tax credit for elderly persons for property taxes on their residences or rent constituting property taxes; an extra personal exemption for disabled persons; a 10 percent credit for investments in rural or central city job development assets.

The 1971 tax legislation was thus dominated by the aspect of tax subsidies. It is not a coincidental but a direct result of this influence that the 1971 Tax Act is one of the least creditable revenue measures in many a decade and one that considerably weakens the fairness and structure of the income tax.

The Treasury is still active in pushing proposals for additional tax credits. In its 1973 Proposals for tax change it recommended a tax credit to provide property tax relief for the elderly, a tax credit for parents paying tuition to

5

private elementary and secondary schools, and tax credits to drillers of new domestic exploratory oil wells.[9]

It can generally be said that less critical analysis is paid to these tax expenditures than to almost any direct expenditure program one can mention. The tax expenditures tumble into the law without supporting studies, being propelled instead by cliches, debating points, and scraps of data and tables that are passed off as serious evidence. A tax system that is so vulnerable to this injection of extraneous, costly, and ill-considered expenditure programs is in a precarious state from the standpoint of the basic tax goals of providing adequate revenues and maintaining tax equity. It is therefore imperative that the process and substance of these tax expenditures be reexamined.

With this background, we may now turn to the Expenditure Budget itself.

The Tax Expenditure Budget

The federal income tax system consists really of two parts: one part comprises the structural provisions necessary to implement the income tax on individual and corporate net income; the second part comprises a system of tax expenditures under which Governmental financial assistance programs are carried out through special tax provisions rather than through direct Government expenditures. This second system is grafted on to the structure of the income tax proper; it has no basic relation to that structure and is not necessary to its operation. Instead, the system of tax expenditures provides a vast subsidy apparatus that uses the mechanics of the income tax as the method of paying the subsidies. The special provisions under which this subsidy apparatus functions take a variety of forms, covering exclusions from income, exemptions, deductions, credits against tax, preferential rates of tax, and deferrals of tax.

These special tax provisions serve ends which are similar in nature to those served in the same or other areas by direct government expenditures in the form of grants, loans, interest subsidies, and federal insurance or guarantees of private loans. The interplay is such that for any given program involving federal monetary assistance, the program may be structured to use the tax system to provide that assistance — where it will usually be called a "tax incentive" — or structured to use a direct Government expenditure. As a consequence of history, design, lack of analysis, and similar factors our present tax system is replete with these special provisions, or tax expenditures, under which many existing Government assistance programs operate through the tax system rather than the direct expenditure route.

The tax expenditure concept in essence considers these special provisions as composed of two elements: the imputed tax payment that would have been made in the absence of the special provision (all else remaining the same) and the simultaneous expenditure of that payment as a direct grant to the person benefited by the special provision. The exemption, deduction, or other type of tax benefit is thus seen as a combined process of assumed payment of the proper tax by the taxpayer involved and an appropriation by the Government of an expenditure made to that taxpayer in the amount of the reduction in his actual tax payment from the assumed payment — that is, the tax reduction provided by the special provision.

The Tax Expenditure Budget, included herein as Table 1.1, identifies and quantifies the existing tax expenditures. This Tax Expenditure Budget is essentially an enumeration of the present "tax incentives," or "tax subsidies," contained in our income tax system.[10] The list of these tax expenditures here used is based on that published by the House Ways and Means Committee in June 1973, and prepared by the staffs of the Treasury Department and the Joint Committee on Internal Revenue Taxation.[11]

The items in this Tax Expenditure Budget total between $60 and $65 billion — equal to around one-fourth of the regular budget. Yet most of these items seem almost to live a life of their own, undisturbed and unexamined. No agency really studies or controls them. The Office of Management and Budget largely neglects them, for the items are not in *its* budget. The executive departments likewise are usually unconcerned, for the items are not in *their* programs. The Treasury is apparently not evaluating them, but rather is adding new and indefensible items. This is no way to run a tax system and no way to run a budget policy.

These tax subsidies constitute by far the largest element in Government subsidy programs, clearly overshadowing the $12 billion in direct cash payment subsidies, $9 billion in benefit-in-kind subsidies, and $4 billion in credit subsidies.[12] Table 1.2, taken from a Joint Economic Committee Report,[13] gives a picture of the relative importance of tax subsidies to other subsidy programs in the various budget categories, though the table considerably understates the amount of the tax subsidies.

Tax expenditure analysis and the construction of a Tax Expenditure Budget involve some important structural aspects. Primary among these is the basic matter of definition: Which income tax rules are special provisions representing Government expenditures made through the income tax system to achieve various objectives apart from that tax, and which income tax rules constitute the basic structure of the income tax itself and hence are integral to having such a tax at all? What is required to answer this central question of definition is a normative model for an income tax structure. That normative model in turn will depend on a definition of "income" for income tax purposes. The original Treasury analysis discussed this matter at some length.[14] It indicated the tax expenditures there listed cover "the major respects in which

Table 1.1* Federal Income Tax Expenditures Calendar Year 1972 (by Budget Function)

	\$Millions		
	Corpora- tions	Indi- viduals	Total
National Defense			
Exclusion of benefits and allowances to Armed Forces personnel		700	700
International Affairs and Finance			
Exemption for certain income earned abroad by United States citizens		50	50
Western Hemisphere Trade Corporations	50		50
Exclusion of gross-up on dividends of less-developed country corporations	60		60
Deferral of income of controlled foreign corporations	300	25	325[b]
Exclusion of income earned in United States possessions	80	10	90
Deferral of export income (DISC)	240		240[a]
Total:	730	85	815
Agriculture			
Farming: expensing and capital gain treatment	50	850	900
Timber: capital gain treatment for certain income	125	50	175
Total:	175	900	1,075
Natural Resources			
Expensing of exploration and development costs	580	70	650
Excess of percentage over cost depletion	1,400	300	1,700
Capital gain treatment of royalties on coal and iron ore	5		5
Total:	1,985	370	2,355
Commerce and Transportation			
Investment credit	3,050	750	3,800
Depreciation on buildings (other than rental housing) in excess of straight-line depreciation	330	170	500
Asset depreciation range system for depreciation	2,100	200	2,300[a]
Dividend exclusion		300	300

8

Table 1.1 (continued)

	\$Millions		
	Corpora-tions	Indi-viduals	Total

Commerce and Transportation (continued)

Capital gains: corporation (other than farming and timber)	400		400
Capital gains: individuals (other than farming and timber)		9,000	9,000[b]
Bad debt reserves of financial institutions in excess of actual	400		400[b]
Exemption of credit unions	90		90
Deductibility of interest on consumer credit		1,100	1,100
Expensing of research and development expenditures	570		570
\$25,000 corporate surtax exemption	2,500		2,500
Deferral of tax on shipping companies	30		30
Five-year amortization of railroad rolling stock	80		80
Total:	9,550	11,520	21,070[b]

Housing and Community Development

Deductibility of interest on mortgages on owner-occupied homes		3,500	3,500
Deductibility of property taxes on owner-occupied homes		3,250	3,250
Depreciation on rental housing in excess of straight-line depreciation	350	250	600
Five-year amortization of housing rehabilitation expenditures	65	100	165[a]
Deferral of capital gain on sale to occupants of certain low-income housing			n.a.
Total:	415	7,100	7,515

Health, Labor and Welfare

Exclusion of employer-provided disability insurance benefits		175	175
Provisions relating to aged: combined cost for additional exemptions, retirement income credit, and exclusion of social security payments		3,550	3,550
Additional exemption for blind		10	10
Exclusion of unemployment insurance benefits		700	700

Table 1.1 (continued)

	$Millions		
	Corpora- tions	Indi- viduals	Total

Health, Labor and Welfare (continued)

	Corpora- tions	Indi- viduals	Total
Sick pay exclusion		225	225
Exclusion of workmen's compensation benefits		375	375
Exclusion of public assistance benefits		65	65
Net exclusion of pension contributions and earnings:			
Plans for employees		4,000	4,000
Plans for self-employed persons		200	200
Exclusion of other employee benefits:			
Premiums on group term life insurance		550	550
Accident and accidental death premiums		35	35
Medical insurance premiums and medical care		2,500	2,500
Privately financed supplementary unemployment benefits		5	5
Meals and lodging		170	170
Exclusion of interest on life insurance savings		1,200	1,200
Deductibility of charitable contributions (other than education)		3,100	3,100[b]
Deductibility of medical expenses		1,900	1,900
Deductibility of child and dependent care and household expenses		180	180
Deductibility of casualty losses		150	150
Standard deduction in excess of minimum standard deduction		1,040	1,040
Five-year amortization of pollution control facilities (pre-1969 plants)	25		25
Credit for employment of public assistance recipients under WIN program	20		20[a]
Five-year amortization of employer child care and on-the-job training facilities	10		10[a]
Total:	55	20,130	20,185

Education

	Corpora- tions	Indi- viduals	Total
Additional parental personal exemption for students		640	640

Table 1.1   (continued)

	$Millions		
	Corpora- tions	Indi- viduals	Total
Education (continued)			
Deductibility of contributions to educational institutions		275	275
Exclusion of scholarships and fellowships		125	125
Total:		1,040	1,040
Veterans Benefits and Services			
Exclusion of certain veterans benefits		480	480
General Government			
Credit and deduction for political contributions		100	100ª
Aid to State and Local Financing			
Exemption of interest on state and local debt	1,900	1,000	2,900
Deductibility of nonbusiness state and local taxes (other than on owner-occupied homes)		5,300	5,300
Total:	1,900	6,300	8,200

Source: Estimates of Federal Tax Expenditures, House Committee on Ways and Means, June 1, 1973. This document stated that the estimates are prepared on a separate basis for each item on the assumption that the item would be eliminated from the law without any other changes in the law with respect to other items. If two or more changes are made, the aggregate effect will frequently not equal the sum of the revenue effects of the individual changes. Accordingly, the costs of the items are not additive. Hence, totals are of quite limited usefulness. (The document does state the totals in a footnote.) The calendar year 1972 estimates roughly reflect the fiscal year 1973.

Notes
ªEstimates so marked are for periods other than calendar year 1972 as explained below.
ᵇEstimates so marked involve special factors as explained below.

Explanation
(a)   The following estimates are for periods other than calendar year 1972:

Deferral of export income (DISC) — estimate when fully effective after transitional period. The estimate is based on that given when the provision was adopted and presumably requires re-examination.

Asset Depreciation Range — estimate is for year when fully effective (calendar year 1977). The figure is lower than that used when the provision was adopted. Calendar year 1972 effect in the document is $860 million. Estimate covers 20% reduction in class lives. No estimate made available on effect of dropping reserve ratio test and using 30th percentile for class lives.

Five-year amortization of housing rehabilitation expenditures — estimate is after end of transition period and is lower than used when the provision was adopted.

Credit for employment of public assistance recipients under WIN program — estimate when fully effective. The figure is lower than that used when the provision was adopted.

11

Table 1.1 (continued)

Five-year amortization of employer facilities – estimate when fully effective. Estimate presumably a guess.

Credit and deduction for political contributions – estimate is for a presidential election year when fully effective. The "checkoff" system is not here included; it is a tax expenditure only in the sense that "votes" of taxpayers to make the expenditure are relevant, but no direct tax reduction is involved.

(b) The following estimates involve special factors:

Deferral of income of controlled foreign corporations – the estimate in the table apparently is based on the assumption of repatriation of around 50% of earnings by foreign subsidiaries if deferral were eliminated; if, as some believe, the assumption is on the high side, then the estimate could be perhaps $100–$200 million higher.

Five-year amortization of coal mine safety equipment – this item could be included under Natural Resources, but the amount is less than $1 million.

Capital Gains – Individuals – the estimate assumes present restrictions on deduction ˙of capital losses is retained. This estimate covers the treatment at death, as did the 1968 Treasury Table. The estimate in the document – $7 billion – apparently neglected to include such treatment.

Bad debt reserves of financial institutions in excess of actual – the amount will decline over time as present law becomes fully effective.

Five-year amortization of railroad rolling stock – this item is being superseded by use of the investment credit.

Charitable contributions – the 1968 Treasury Table included "untaxed appreciation" on contributions in kind under charitable contributions, and also educational contributions. This is apparently not the case for the document, which apparently neglected this aspect. The estimate is thus understated.

The *minimum tax* on individuals and corporations affects a number of items, *i.e.*, those included as preferences, such as accelerated depreciation on buildings, capital gains, percentage depletion, stock option compensation, excess bad debt reserves, and the five-year amortization provisions. But the overall effect is minor. The total collected from individuals in 1970 was $117 million, and from corporations was $218 million.

---

the current income tax bases deviate from widely accepted definitions of income and standards of business accounting and from the generally accepted structure of an income tax."

The Tax Expenditure Budget and underlying analysis drew importantly on the general acceptance of the Haig-Simons approach to the definition of "income," which essentially is based on "gain" or "accretion" and which Simons phrased as follows: "Personal income may be defined as the algebraic sum of (1) the market value of rights exercised in consumption and (2) the change in the value of the store of property rights between the beginning and end of the period in question."[15] This "accretion" approach and the Simons definition cast a very wide net, one reaching in a number of respects further than the coverage of modern income tax systems. The Treasury analysis, while referring to this approach when it spoke of "widely accepted definitions of income," therefore qualified reliance on it by also referring to the "generally accepted structure of an income tax." Thus, contrary to the Simons definition,

The Tax Expenditure Budget

Table 1.2   Major Federal Subsidies, Fiscal Year 1970 (In millions of dollars)

Function	Cash payment	Tax	Credit	Benefits-in-kind	Total
Agriculture	3,879	880	443		5,202
Food				1,593	1,593
Medical care	973	3,150	NA	4,617	8,740
Manpower	1,991	550			2,541
Education	1,976	785	434	409	3,604
International trade	106	420	623	34	1,183
Housing	195	5,680	2,550		8,425
Natural resources	330	1,970	22	712	3,034
Transportation	300	10		362	672
Commerce and economic development	2,051	15,635	59	1,518	19,263
Other		9,400			9,400
Total	11,801	38,480	4,131	9,245	63,657[a]

Source: The Economics of Federal Subsidy Programs: A Staff Study, the Joint Economic Committee, Jan. 11, 1972.

[a]The individual totals of each financial form are rounded up so that the total cost is approximated at $63,000,000,000.

the noncoverage under the United States income tax, and indeed all other income taxes, of imputed rental income on owner-occupied homes was not listed as a tax expenditure. In addition, the analysis indicated that aspects of our income tax, such as the personal exemptions, rate schedules, and income-splitting for married couples are not considered as "variations from the generally accepted measure of net income or as tax preferences, but as part of the structure of an income tax system based on ability to pay." Hence, they were not treated as tax expenditures but instead were considered as outside the scope of the Treasury study of tax expenditures.

While the original Treasury analysis "recognized that these exclusions are to some extent arbitrary," that phrase in the light of hindsight is both too pessimistic and not properly descriptive of the underlying definitional structure for the Tax Expenditure Budget. Further reflection on the definitional task required for that budget leads to the conclusion that the original analysis was well-grounded. The items included are included for valid and defensible reasons; this is equally true of the excluded items. There are of course borderline issues as in any such analysis, but their existence does

13

not basically affect the analysis or the budget. There are also problems involved in the estimates of the various items included in that budget, but most of these problems turn on the lack of adequate data. That lack is itself a reflection of the fact that we earlier did not think in terms of tax expenditure analysis and thus neglected both quantitative and qualitative aspects of these items and that analysis.

These matters, as well as other structural aspects of the Tax Expenditure Budget, are considered at greater length and more technically in the Appendix to this chapter.

APPENDIX

STRUCTURAL ASPECTS OF THE
TAX EXPENDITURE BUDGET

This appendix considers various structural aspects of the Tax Expenditure Budget, such as the analysis supporting the composition of that budget, the problems in estimating the revenue impact of the items included, and the application of the tax expenditure approach to taxes other than the income tax.

Definitional Aspects

Tax expenditure analysis and a Tax Expenditure Budget for the income tax involve a basic definitional question: Which income tax rules are special provisions representing Government expenditures made through the income tax system to achieve various social and economic objectives and which income tax rules are just tax rules, that is, constitute the basic structure of an income tax system and thus are integral to having an income tax at all?[1] The Treasury Department analysis in 1968 used the following guidelines for the Tax Expenditure Budget there presented:[2]

> [The analysis] lists the major respects in which the current income tax bases deviate from widely accepted definitions of income and standards of business accounting and from the generally accepted structure of an income tax. . . .
> The study does not attempt a complete listing of all the tax provisions which vary from a strict definition of net income. Various items that could have been added have been excluded for one or more of several reasons:
> (a) Some items were excluded where there is no available indication of the precise magnitude of the implicit subsidy. This is the case, for example, with depreciation on machinery and equipment where the accelerated tax methods may provide an allowance beyond that appropriate to the measurement of net income but where it is difficult to measure that difference because the true economic deterioration or obsolescence factor cannot be readily determined.[3]
> (b) Some items were excluded where the case for their inclusion in the income base stands on relatively technical or theoretical tax

15

arguments. This is the case, for example, with the imputed rent on owner-occupied homes, which involves not only a conceptual problem but difficult practical problems such as those of measurement.

(c) Some items were omitted because of their relatively small quantitative importance.

Other features of our income tax system are considered not as variations from the generally accepted measure of net income or as tax preferences but as part of the structure of an income tax system based on ability to pay. Such features include personal exemptions and the rate schedules under the individual income tax, including the income splitting allowed for married couples filing joint returns or for heads of households. A discussion of income splitting and the dependent's personal exemption is thus considered outside the scope of this study on tax expenditures.

It must be recognized that these exclusions are to some extent arbitrary and some may prefer to add items that we have omitted or to omit items that we have included. The immediate objective, however, of the study is to provide a list of items that would be generally recognized as more or less intended use of the tax system to achieve results commonly obtained by Government expenditures. The design of the list seemed best served by constructing what seemed a minimum list rather than including highly complicated or controversial items that would becloud the utility of this special analysis.

. . . .

. . . . The assumption inherent in current law, that corporations are separate entities and subject to income taxation independently from their shareholders, is adhered to in this analysis.

The application of these criteria will of course produce definitional problems and the precise contours of the dividing line will present uncertainties. To a considerable extent we are talking about a normative model for an income tax structure. Some questions that here arise are:

— what receipts should be included and what expenses allowed to obtain the proper measure of net income for an income tax — "proper" in the sense that it is an *income tax* for which the measure is being sought;

— in what time periods should includable receipts be included and allowable expenditures be taken (e.g., cash and accrual accounting, expensing or capitalization of expenditures, and if the latter, how written off — the method of depreciation, for example);

— over what interval of time should the measurement itself be made (e.g., averaging and net operating loss questions);

— what is the unit whose income is being measured (e.g., is the family to be taxed as a unit or the members separately taxed);

— how should the income of organizations of individuals be treated (e.g., the relationship of corporate income and the corporate tax to the tax treatment of the shareholders).

The building of an income tax requires two types of provisions that collectively perform the following two functions: *First,* they provide the answers to those aspects of the above, and similar, questions that would essentially be treated in much the same way by any group of tax experts building the structure of an income tax and being governed in that task by all the requirements implicit in such a tax because it is an *income tax.* These answers then become the structural provisions which shape a normative income tax. As an illustration, in this first category fall matters relating to the measurement of net income and the time periods for inclusion of that income. *Second,* they provide the answers to those aspects of the above, and similar, questions that likewise are necessary to building an income tax but could, in the view of such a group of tax experts, conceivably be treated differently from country to country depending on the views and policies shaped by other goals in the particular society, rather than by factors special to an income tax. These answers, in view of these possible differences, are not part of a normative income tax. However, these answers, once they are determined, do become structural parts of an income tax — and essential to the operation of that tax — and therefore are not tax expenditures. For example, as the Treasury analysis indicates, the treatment of the family — e.g., the tax burden on married couples in relation to single persons — is not part of a normative income tax. There is no preordained method of treatment that follows from the decision to adopt an income tax. Countries properly differ in the treatment depending on their attitudes toward marriage or women in the labor force and other such social and economic questions. The levels of personal exemptions and tax rates, and the degree of rate progressivity, are other examples mentioned in the Treasury analysis that would fall in this second category. The treatment of the corporation — as a separate entity or its income integrated with that of the shareholders in some fashion — is still another example. The provisions incorporating the decisions in these areas are not tax expenditures. But the decisions have to be made before the structure of the income tax is complete and the tax is ready to be applied. As a consequence, this set of provisions, while necessary to the construction of an income tax, is shaped by processes different in character from the processes determining the provisions in the first category, also relating to the inherent structure of an income tax. The tax expenditure provisions are, then, the provisions that may be found in an income tax law but that do not serve the two functions set forth above.

Economists have given considerable thought to many of the questions earlier set forth and especially the first question, that of the tax base or measure of net income. Their judgments are often discussed in terms of a "comprehensive tax base" measured by changes in the net economic power of an individual between two points of time plus consumption in that period.[4] But while offering a very large measure of guidance, such an economic definition is not the only criterion used in the Treasury classification. The latter tempers the economic analysis by utilizing "widely accepted definitions of income" and the "generally accepted structure of an income tax" as the governing guidelines.

Thus, although most economists feel comfortable in including in taxable income the imputed income arising from asset ownership (e.g., owner-occupied home) and services performed by individuals for their own benefit (e.g., nonworking spouse),[5] or receipts in the form of gifts and bequests, these items are not within the general understanding of the proper structure of an income tax in the United States or elsewhere. Hence, while people can readily recognize and comprehend most of the tax expenditure classifications in the Treasury analysis, they would in general be puzzled by the inclusion of the exemption of gifts and bequests as a tax expenditure.[6] A standard of general acceptance, of course, results in changes over time as the economists' norm in a particular instance comes more and more to be accepted.

The development of the boundaries of an income tax structure will at many points be an evolutionary matter, as we gain in insight and experience. In this evolution we usually pass through several stages. The first stage is where most people would simply not accept a proposed change, suggested on the basis of the economists' concept or definition above stated, in the existing treatment of an item as being necessary to the determination of a proper income tax base. In other words, the application of the economists' concept is still too novel an approach in the particular area. The second stage is where the economists' approach is accepted and the existing treatment comes to be regarded as at variance with that approach so that a change is proper in terms of the income tax base, but the existing treatment is then defended for the economic or social advantages it is said to provide. Or the other way around, at this stage the existing treatment is defended to prevent the disadvantages that a change in the status of the item, now admittedly a tax preference, is said to entail. When this second stage is reached we certainly have a "tax expenditure." The exemption from the income tax of unrealized appreciation on assets transferred at death may be an illustration of this process, for I believe that for this item

18

we are now at the second stage.[7] But current taxation of the unrealized appreciation as it accrues during lifetime is probably still somewhere between the first and second stage, probably closer to the first stage.[8] We could, if we used the economists' definitions fully, always have a tax expenditure at the first stage. But too rigid an adherence to those definitions is likely, as the Treasury material states, to "becloud the utility of this special analysis" of tax expenditures.

There also can be difficulties in the application of agreed income tax structural concepts, such as the proper line between allowable expenses incurred in trade or business or in the acquisition of income and nondeductible personal consumption expenses (e.g., moving expenses or child care expenses) or nondeductible personal investment expenses (e.g., educational expenses).[9] There are also administrative problems in making agreed concepts operational, such as determining money values for employee compensation received in the form of certain employer-provided services or fringe benefits.

There are, of course, dangers involved in any listing of tax expenditures, since omitted items may either become "lost" or be considered as not in need of reexamination when tax expenditures are under scrutiny. But I believe the understanding to be gained through the tax expenditure approach outweighs this risk by far. The guidelines used in the Treasury analysis readily identify a significant number of provisions in existing law which we can all agree are "special" and represent tax expenditures: tax benefits for the aged, natural resources provisions such as percentage depletion allowances, the investment credit, excessive real estate depreciation, and so on. These provisions are identifiable as tax expenditures for the additional reason that they have been defended, either by their beneficiaries or by Congress in adopting them, on the grounds that they achieve a particular purpose, claimed to be desirable, other than the technical measurement of net income under an income tax.

The dangers of omission are likely to lie in leaving out items excluded under present law but which under a strict adherence to conceptual standards would be included as items of income in the measurement of gross income. An example earlier mentioned is imputed income from asset ownership, at least owner-occupied homes. Another is accrued appreciation in the value of assets. The approach of most economists is to have a wide scope for the income tax as far as the source of income is concerned. The omitted items, though probably few in number, but significant in amount, produce an income tax structure somewhat less comprehensive than the economists' approach would produce.

There do not appear to be similar dangers on the inclusion side, since the items listed as tax expenditures all appear to lie outside the factors that the economists would utilize to measure net income. Indeed, most economists should feel comfortable with the listings in the Tax Expenditure Budget since their talents largely shaped its composition.[10] But there has been criticism of some of the inclusions involving personal expenditures. Thus, Professor Andrews of Harvard Law School has questioned the appropriateness of including the deductions for medical care and charitable contributions as tax expenditures.[11] But the thrust of his criticism is not based on any definitional variance between the economists' concept of an income tax and the items in the Tax Expenditure Budget. Rather, his discussion first premises a model different from that traditionally used by the economists in structuring an income tax, and then sees where those two expenditures, as well as other personal deductions, fit in relation to his own model. Thus, while he starts by discussing an "ideal income tax," the "ideal tax" soon becomes an "ideal personal tax" rather than an ideal income tax, and this ideal personal tax then turns into a tax primarily focused on consumption. Indeed, the ultimate thrust of his approach, as his discussion indicates, favors a personal tax based only on consumption and disregarding saving or accumulation. Essentially, under this approach, whether an item is to be taxed depends on the "use" of funds and whether such use evidences the "consumption" which is the base of the tax. When medical expenses and charitable contributions are so tested, Professor Andrews considers expenditures for such purposes as not constituting the type of consumption which a personal tax so based on "consumption" should reach.[12]

Whether medical expenses and charitable contributions constitute "consumption" are issues that must be debated in structuring taxes on consumption. Thus, it can be argued whether a national sales tax should cover medical services, or indeed legal services and other categories of services — and some governments do reach these services and some do not under their consumption taxes.[13] Also, the proper treatment of charitable enterprises under a value-added tax has engaged the attention of those countries using that form of tax on consumption.[14] Further, if a country desired a graduated tax on expenditures for personal consumption, the type of national personal tax which Professor Andrews seems to advocate, then it would of course require a concept of such "consumption" to determine the base of the tax. Both the framing of that concept and the structure of that tax would have to deal with the two items considered in detail by Professor Andrews, as well as a host of other items on which people spend funds.

But all of this is a far cry from the structure of an *income tax,* a tax which does not focus on "consumption" but on "income" — a tax which focuses on the accretion of funds, i.e. income, rather than on the uses of funds. The customary approach of the economists to defining "income," following Henry Simons, is a comparison of two balance sheets, at the beginning and end of the taxable period, to determine the income for the period. But if funds are spent during the period, i.e., consumption occurs, the funds spent must be added algebraically to the balance sheet difference to determine the total income. Consumption under this definition has a mathematical role in an algebraic definition that simply totals funds spent and the change in the balance sheets. Consumption in this approach is thus all funds spent except where spent in the earning or production of income — since the tax is on net income. The definitional borderline regarding consumption comes only at this point under the Simons definition — is an expenditure incurred in the earning or production of income or is it personal consumption?[15]

Nations must make choices on the kinds of personal taxes they desire, depending on the aspects of "ability to pay" they seek to stress. Under current approaches, if it is a person's "income" that they wish to stress, then an income tax is used; if it is a person's "consumption," then a sales tax (with a number of varieties available such as retail tax, value-added version of a retail tax, and so on) is used today, with some urging further personalization of such a tax through a graduated tax on a person's total expenditures for consumption; if it is a person's "wealth," then an estate or inheritance is used, or, much less frequently, an annual net wealth tax. Nations are not limited to a single choice, and these taxes can be used in various combinations. Nor on the other hand must nations use all three taxes, and a country can well choose to have an income tax and do without a consumption tax.

Each tax has its own appropriate structure and each has its advantages and disadvantages. But the scope of each such tax in actual application must be tested by *its* concepts, which concepts led to its choice in the first instance. The structure of a normative income tax is not to be tested by the values or concepts used by those who prefer that a consumption tax be chosen instead, and vice versa. A tax expenditure budget for an income tax, to be useful in seeing what objectives that tax has been asked to carry in addition to taxing net income, is to be framed by using a normative definiton of "income." Equally, a tax expenditure budget for a sales tax or other form of personal consumption tax must be framed by using a normative definition of "consumption." Nor would nations do well by trying to make all things out of a single tax and seeking to combine elements of the various concepts within a single structure. That structure would soon lose any identity, and critical analysis of the tax system would suffer.[16]

When medical expenses and charitable contributions are tested against the generally accepted definition of income, most economists would classify these items as tax expenditures. Hence their place in the Tax Expenditure Budget.[17]

Another approach that should be mentioned is the view that a medical expense deduction is, shall we say, appropriate under an income tax since the deduction is needed to equalize the "ability to pay" an income tax between a family with an illness and a family without an illness. Proponents of this view would acquiesce in the listing of the medical expense deduction as a tax expenditure, since they both accept the Simons definition of income and recognize that, under that definition, the fact that funds are spent for medical care does not reduce the amount of "income." In this sense the medical expense deduction is not a theoretically necessary deduction in an income tax. But supporters of this view find this particular tax expenditure to be proper on policy grounds since they believe that, in the case of medical care, income is an imperfect measure of ability to pay, or an imperfect measure of horizontal equality between the above two families. This appears, for example, to be Joseph Pechman's tax policy justification for accepting a medical expense deduction.[18]

We will later discuss the implications of using the tax system rather than a direct expenditure to achieve a national policy goal.[19] At this stage, suffice it to say that while I find understandable Pechman's concern about the medical bills of ill family A compared with the lack of such bills in healthy family B, I dislike the end consequences of his using a tax deduction and hence the tax system to equalize the two families. Essentially, he is saying that the Government as a creditor should yield a tax claim against family A — since Pechman accepts the Simons definition — in order that funds otherwise required to pay that tax claim may be used to pay a doctor's bill. But the amount of funds thus made available to pay that doctor's bill depends on the marginal tax bracket of family A. For a 70 percent bracket family, the tax deduction — the yielding of the tax claim — means the Government is in effect paying 70 percent of the doctor's bill. For a 14 percent bracket family, it is through the deduction paying only 14 percent of that bill. This is the inevitable upside-down quality that any tax expenditure phrased as a deduction has under a progressive income tax, and why such a tax expenditure is not as fair or efficient a way of meeting a national goal — here financial assistance in the payment of medical expenses — as is a direct expenditure program. Certainly, no direct program for medical care would have this upside-down effect. There are, in addition, other problems besides this upside-down effect in using the tax system to relieve hardship instead of a direct expenditure program — such as divided consideration in the Congress of a national issue between the tax committees and the committees normally having jurisdiction over the issue, and the differing effects of "budget restraint" on programs lodged in the regular budget and programs lodged in the tax system.

For these reasons, I find it difficult to accept Pechman's use of the income tax to provide financial assistance to the ill family to bring it to equality with the healthy family.[20] Pechman accepts the doctor's bill as given and in the desire to relieve the hardship of medical expense he focuses on the ill family's ability to pay its income tax. He thus shifts the focus from the ability of people to pay their doctors' bills to the ability of people who are burdened with those bills to pay their income taxes. But a direct medical care expenditure program would keep the focus on the main problem — the cost of medical care — and in so doing would provide an entirely different allocation of funds without the upside-down effect that results from the focus on the income tax as the mechanism for relief. Pechman would not worry about the ability to pay income taxes of families with gambling debts or high entertainment expenses or charitable contributions. The fact that it is medical expenses which cause his worry about the income tax indicates the main problem is those expenses themselves. The focus should therefore be kept on those expenses and not be shifted to the income tax.[21]

The tax base used for a tax — any tax — presents problems, but departures from that tax base also present problems, as tax expenditure analysis indicates. However, as indicated later, I can sympathize with the desire — and the policy objective behind the adoption of the medical expense deduction in the tax law — that Government "do something" about medical expense burdens and hence can understand that any change in the medical expense deduction must await the grant of Government assistance through a national health program.[22] In short, there may be both policy reasons for providing Government financial assistance for medical care — and charitable organizations — and reasons, sometimes historical and sometimes more currently pertinent, for using the income tax system to provide that assistance; but those reasons must face the problems which tax expenditure analysis discloses are involved in such a use of the tax system.

It is important that the experts continue the task of analysis and classification that underlies the Tax Expenditure Budget. Thus, the Treasury analysis views the coexistence of the cash receipts and accrual accounting methods as a part of the structure of an income tax system. But consideration should be given to various aspects of accounting that have not been analyzed from this perspective but which operate to defer the inclusion of income items in gross income — for example, installment reporting. Thus, to what extent is a difference, favoring the taxpayer, between tax accounting rules and generally accepted financial accounting concepts a signal that a tax expenditure is present? The original Treasury analysis, quoted earlier, referred to "the respects in which the current income tax bases deviate from widely accepted . . . standards of business accounting," indicating that such a difference does point to the presence of a tax expenditure. Put differently, under what circumstances, if at all, would a properly structured income tax have accounting rules that differ from financial accounting?[23] As another aspect, the Treasury analysis would presumably regard the developing concepts in the averaging and net operating loss areas as within the borders of the search for the proper structural provisions and hence not as involving tax expenditures. But are there aspects here that should be viewed differently?

The Treasury analysis also adheres to the "assumption, inherent in current law, that corporations are separate entities and subject to income taxation independently from their shareholders." It therefore develops the tax expenditure classification against the background of the corporation tax as a separate tax. Thus, the income of a corporation is to be taxed separately, with full taxation of shareholders on distributed income, such as dividends, under the individual income tax. This background departs from the view of many economists, who prefer to see corporate income integrated into the shareholders' income, with a corporation tax, if it is to exist, treated as a withholding tax. Within the Treasury guideline of this separateness of the corporation, however, how should one approach the various provisions that operate to eliminate the corporate tax and on an elective basis tax the corporate income directly to the shareholders, such as Subchapter S for closely held corporations and the real estate trust provisions? And how does one view the intercorporate dividend deduction? In addition, how are the various tax-exempt organizations to be considered? Here a preliminary question is to what extent do these organizations have "taxable income" — i.e., how would their receipts and expenditures be regarded if no tax exemption existed, and would there be a positive net income to be taxed?[24]

Estimates

A number of the tax expenditures have required estimates that in the past have been off the beaten track of customary Treasury estimating areas. Hence the underlying data are not as complete as one would desire. Other estimators have provided higher amounts than the Treasury figures, so that on the whole the estimates used here are presumably conservative.[25] The Treasury analysis, moreover, indicated that the estimates are "first level" figures, i.e., they measure the revenue that would be obtained from a change in the tax expenditure provision involved, without anything else being changed. Thus, the estimates do not involve predictions of what taxpayers would do in the light of change, or what direct expenditure programs would be substituted, or what changes in tax rates, personal exemption levels, and the like would be made. Nor are the estimates cumulative; each item stands by itself so that the inclusion of one item does not push the amount of another item into a higher marginal rate bracket. Hence, the overall combined effect of the changes is not evident.[26]

This approach is in keeping with the regular budget, since budget estimates of direct expenditures do not involve the second-level effects of the expenditure itself, or its absence, and a tax expenditure need not be estimated in a different fashion. The approach is also in keeping with standard Treasury estimating procedure on revenue changes generally, which uses the "first level" and noncumulative approaches. It would be appropriate, nevertheless, to consider the effects of this approach to ascertain, for example, whether further explanatory material is desirable.[27]

The Tax Expenditure Budget allocates the revenue cost of special tax provisions to the different major expenditure categories in the Federal Budget. In the Treasury analysis, it was possible to allocate most of the tax

24

expenditures to the customary expenditure headings in the budget in what seemed a reasonable and consistent way. But it seemed desirable to set up two new headings for tax expenditures beyond those regularly used in the budget summary, one for "Aid to State and Local Government Financing" and the other for "Capital Gains." The first of these indicates the function aided by the exemption from income tax of interest on state and local government debt and the deductibility of state and local taxes other than on owner-occupied homes, which was allocated to the functional heading of Community Development and Housing.

With "Capital Gains" of individuals, the state of development of the data and analysis did not permit an allocation of the large revenue cost of $5.5 to $8.5 billion — perhaps more — to be made to one or more expenditure headings in the original Tax Expenditure Budget. This special provision reflects various activities in several expenditure categories, including Agriculture, Natural Resources, Commerce and Transportation, Housing and Community Development, and Health, Labor, and Welfare. The data did not permit a separation of the revenue cost by function. Allocation of the entire large amount to any single functional category would have overstated the tax expenditures for that function. The solution then chosen of a new separate heading identifies the revenue cost but, lacking any functional allocation, leads to an understatement of each function to which any appreciable amount would be allocated, if the data permitted. In Table 1.1, following the House Ways and Means Committee pamphlet, the total revenue cost of the capital gains treatment for individuals is placed under the heading Commerce and Transportation. This placement probably covers the bulk of the revenue cost, but it does lead to some understatement of the tax expenditures for the other headings and some overstatement for Commerce and Transportation.

The method of computing the amounts of these tax expenditures understates their impact on the revenue side of the regular budget in those cases in which the expenditure operates through deferring a series of tax liabilities into the future. Such a tax expenditure involves a considerable commitment for future budgets. Thus, adoption of five-year amortization for expenditures for rehabilitation of low-income rental housing means reduced taxes over a five-year period as a result of compressing future depreciation deductions into that time span. It has been suggested that the cost of such a tax expenditure would be better understood by policymakers if it were expressed as a "cash grant equivalent." This equivalent would represent the cost of a direct grant to the taxpayers involved equal to the full amount of the subsidy. In the case of rental housing rehabilitation, the grant would be the present value to the taxpayers of the tax benefits under the five-year amortization. This grant could be expressed as a percentage of his investment, here 16.5 percent for a taxpayer in the 50 percent bracket and assuming a before-tax discount rate of 15 percent. These cash grant equivalents would be larger in the initial years than the revenue losses. In the rehabilitation situation, under one estimate, they would have totaled $639.5 million in the first five years compared to the estimated revenue losses of $485.7 million. In the first three years, the figures are $350.7 million and $147.4 million. The suggestion has therefore been made:

> [Revenue] estimates are appropriate for the tax expenditure budget which treats these expenditures on a cash basis analogous to the treatment of direct expenditures in the unified Federal budget. However, for policy making purposes, tax subsidies involving the deferral of taxes should be considered in the context of cash grant equivalents.[28]

This aspect of the appropriate manner in which to express the cost to the Government parallels the problem of how best to express the benefit a taxpayer obtains from a deferral of tax liability. As will be discussed later, legislators often greatly underestimate the advantages of tax deferral.[29]

Application to Other Taxes

The original Treasury analysis considered only the federal income taxes, individual and corporate. Presumably that analysis and the above discussion are applicable to state income taxes. But what can be said regarding other forms of taxation used in the United States, such as the property tax, the retail sales tax, excises generally, and the estate and gift taxes?[30]

To a very large degree the analysis under the income tax flowed from the concept of horizontal equity under the tenets of that tax, an aspect inherent in the Haig-Simons definition of income. Such a concept is clearly relevant to taxes that are applied in terms of an individual's total position, as is the normative model of an individual income tax. Thus, it presumably could also apply to a net wealth tax. But is the equity concept relevant, and is the tax expenditure analysis applicable, where a tax designedly departs from the total approach? Thus, is it relevant to a real property tax, which admittedly seeks to occupy only a portion of the net wealth measure? Or is it relevant to a graduated personal expenditure tax which, while seeking to reach an individual's total consumption, does omit income currently saved and hence is less broad than the income tax? Further, is it relevant to a retail sales tax which, while reaching a broad area of consumption, will probably fall short of the scope of a personal expenditure tax? And so on, down to particular excise taxes such as those on alcohol, automobiles, and the like.

These other forms of taxes — real property tax, retail sales tax, alcohol tax — are deliberately structured to place a burden on only some forms of consumption or wealth, and thus favor other forms. But it would not be useful or appropriate for tax expenditure analysis to assume an imputed revenue figure for the general area not taxed and then list that amount as a tax expenditure for that area. While it may be useful for other purposes to recognize that the customary real property tax is unneutral in taxing only real property, it is not helpful for our purposes. Similarly, it is not helpful here to consider that a real property tax places a heavier burden on businesses with relatively large amounts of real property, even though the economic and other implications of that unneutrality are important — for example, in the heavier taxation, under that tax, of railroad transportation as against motor transportation.

But within a real property tax itself, it would seem there is a concept of horizontal equity or fairness, and that *ab initio* all forms of real property should be assessed in the same way and taxed at the same rate. Any deliberate departures from that approach can then be considered as tax expenditures under that tax. Thus, abatements and exemptions for new buildings in certain areas granted to encourage the development of those areas would be so classified. So would the exemption of educational, charitable, and other nonprofit organizations. In most of these cases the exemption itself is granted and defended on "subsidy" grounds, and the departure from the norm fully recognized. Where the variance is not openly deliberate but stems, say, from practices or attitudes of administration, such as under-assessments for single dwellings compared to multifamily rental units or private housing compared to business buildings, the picture is cloudy. One may not be able to tell whether deliberate encouragement of an activity is involved or unconscious preference that would be corrected if clearly perceived.

In the case of a retail sales tax, if the tax is structured on a broad base, then any exemptions must be examined for our purposes. An exemption for goods consumed in production would be a part of the basic structure of the tax itself and not a tax expenditure. But suppose it is desired to exempt purchases of medicine so as to encourage expenditures on health per se. Here a tax expenditure would seem to be present, though perhaps Professor Andrews' analysis of medical expenses and "consumption" discussed earlier would lead to a different conclusion. If the exemption were extended to athletic goods, in order further to encourage expenditures on health, presumably a tax expenditure would clearly be present. As another example, let us suppose that food and clothing are exempted. If the purpose of the exemption is to make the tax less regressive, and the exemption of food and clothing is thus a proxy for, say, a decreasing overall dollar exemption per person, then it could be said that a tax expenditure would not be present. It would not be present if the dollar exemption approach were directly used (and as it is not present as respects the personal exemptions under the income tax). However, the device of these two items, food and clothing, as the proxy items does involve a preference for those items, and this points to a tax expenditure.

A tax on alcohol or cigarettes is at the other side of the spectrum — i.e., a tax designed to be clearly targeted at a special form of consumption and to place a higher burden on the particular commodity involved. Here the purpose is generally revenue and the disincentive effects are either tolerated or seen as sufficiently proper in the light of revenue needs or urged as strong supporting grounds, depending on one's view of the commodities involved. But a tax may be designed only for its disincentive effect, such as the Federal interest equalization tax on purchases of foreign securities. Presumably in these areas the contours of the tax mark its purposes, and tax expenditures are not involved. An interest equalization tax applied only to foreign bonds and thus not covering foreign stocks does not represent a subsidy for stocks, but simply a disincentive aimed at the purchase of foreign bonds. Presumably this is also true if an alcohol tax excluded beer or wine.

The matter here is one of the initial design of a specific tax. As another example, consider the passenger automobile tax and subsequent changes to exclude camper coaches used primarily as living quarters and accessories in the form of feed, seed, and fertilizer equipment. Here there was an "image" of an automobile or truck; and these particular vehicles and accessories, though close to the line, fell outside that image. But what about three-wheeled trucks, which were also excluded? If the "image" of a truck would encompass an item sold competitively as a small truck, though it had only three wheels, is a tax expenditure involved for this form of equipment? Let us assume that, unlike the camper coach or the farm equipment, the change is recognized as a deliberate departure from the image of a truck, but is made to help promote the sale of three-wheeled trucks. In a sense there is a tax expenditure, for Congress itself basically so considered its action under these assumptions. But it would probably not be desirable to engage in a careful dissection of these special excises since they are special, and for the most part each decision is regarded as itself establishing the basic structure, contours, or image of the intended tax rather than as a recognized departure from a norm. The matter may be one of degree, as we move back along the spectrum to the broad-based sales taxes.[31]

Some excise taxes are levied essentially as user charges, such as the federal gasoline tax or the passenger ticket tax on air travel. Here any nontaxed user does have a subsidy, but it is a direct expenditure subsidy. So also is the subsidy present if federal expenditures are involved for the particular use and no user charge or excise tax is levied at all, such as vessels on inland waterways; or if the use is undertaxed, such as civil aviation. Other excise taxes are levied as regulatory taxes, using the tax system rather than direct regulation, and here also any nontaxed person or transaction simply falls outside the intended coverage of the regulatory goal.[32]

In the case of the estate and gift taxes, we are still in the process of formulating the proper structural contours of these taxes, considered as independent taxes and not within the position that some would take of including gifts and bequests under an income tax. The recent studies of the Brookings Institution, the American Law Institute, and the Treasury Department all point with considerable agreement to an approach that does move toward a model and underscores many weaknesses and preferences in the existing structure. Moreover, many who oppose the proposals in the Treasury Department studies and defend the departures therefrom in the present situation generally do so on grounds that the departures achieve social objectives they consider desirable, such as the encouragement of lifetime gifts or of family trusts.[33] It would thus seem that a tax expenditure analysis could be developed for the estate and gift taxes, as an adjunct of the consideration of their "proper structure."

II

Some Uses of the Tax Expenditure Budget

We turn now from the Tax Expenditure Budget itself to the uses to which such a budget may be put. For what purposes of tax policy is it a useful tool? What questions does it help us to formulate and ask? What questions does it help us to answer?

Overall Consideration of the Income Tax

Tax Revision and Tax Reform

The task of improving the tax system is a constant one. The system must be kept up to date and its workings considered against the changes constantly occurring in business structure and activities, in family patterns of organization and asset holding, in the economic and social objectives of our society. Alongside this work of modernization, of keeping the tax system responsive to current conditions and activities, is the work of correcting past mistakes. Efforts at improvement are often styled "tax revision" or "tax reform." The first expression is generally utilized by those groups seeking new tax benefits in the name of modernization; the latter is used by those seeking to end benefits earlier obtained by certain groups and now attacked by the reformers as loopholes or tax preferences.

In the past, legislative efforts at revision or reform of the income tax have generally looked upon that tax as a unitary structure, a bundle of complex tax provisions making up the income tax. But the Tax Expenditure Budget tells us that the income tax is really composed of two structures. One is the structure necessary to the imposition of the income tax itself and consists of the provisions which in their totality represent our understanding of what is required to construct an income tax. It is the United States understanding of the normative income tax model and its necessary auxiliary provisions. The second structure is that reflecting the Tax Expenditure Budget and contains the provisions carrying out the financial assistance set forth in that budget. It is true that both these sets of provisions exist side by side, or rather are intertwined, and without guidance cannot be told apart. The Tax Expenditure Budget provides that guidance, for it seeks to separate the apparatus of expenditure policy from the inherent structure of the income tax itself. The latter structure is what would remain if we suddenly decided that no governmental financial assistance should be given through the tax system and instead should be handled by direct Government expenditures.

Would an understanding that our income tax system thus consists of two structures serving different functions make a difference in the approach to tax revision or tax reform? I think it should, and I also think that efforts at reform in the past have failed to take this difference into account. Tax reform is one thing if it means looking at a part of the inherent income tax structure that is not working well and asking where the tax experts went wrong in shaping that part. The issues posed and the answers to be explored are considered within the premises of an income tax and can be judged accordingly. But tax reform is quite another matter if it means examining a program of financial assistance to a particular group to decide whether that assistance should be given, in what amount, and on what terms. It really is not tax reform but "expenditure reform," and the issues and answers to be explored both involve different premises and require different experts. The importance of seeing this distinction is underscored by the fact that most of the issues presently involved in "tax reform" concern the items in the Tax Expenditure Budget rather than the provisions making up the inherent income tax structure.[1]

The implications of this use of the Tax Expenditure Budget to divide legislative issues of tax reform, and tax revision, between those addressed to the inherent tax structure and those relating to the tax expenditure apparatus are considered in Chapter VI.

Relationship between Tax Reform and Economy in Government Expenditures

The prime objective of income tax reform is to achieve greater fairness in the federal tax system and thereby restore the confidence of the public in that system. This confidence has been seriously diminished. What we know and read about public attitudes indicates a lack of trust in the tax system, a belief that there are privileged groups escaping taxes while the average person must pay his tax bills. This view of the tax system, and in particular the income tax, is — unfortunately — justified by the actual facts.

A second objective of income tax reform is to restore efficiency and economy in the expenditure of Government funds. To talk of these expenditure goals in the context of tax reform may appear strange at first. The usual image of tax reform focuses upon the persons and individuals escaping payment of their proper share of the tax burden and the steps required to correct that situation. Indeed, that is the aspect of tax reform stressed above in emphasizing the need to restore fairness to the tax system. But the Tax Expenditure Budget enables us to see that wasteful and inefficient expenditure of Government funds is the other side of the tax escape coin. For every escape from tax can be seen as the consequence of what is in reality a Government expenditure program carried out through a special provision in the tax system. These special tax provisions really have nothing to do with the essentials of an income tax, nothing to do with shaping the structural framework necessary to operate an income tax. Instead, these special provisions are methods of spending Government funds. The expenditure in turn is intended to induce or obtain certain responses from the recipients of the funds — who are the beneficiaries under the tax provisions.

Thus, as examples, the very rapid tax depreciation for machinery and equipment under the new Asset Depreciation Range system was urged by the Treasury and adopted by Congress in 1971 not as a device needed to measure real net income as part of the structure of an income tax applied to a business concern. Financial accounting in reporting profits to shareholders and creditors uses far less rapid depreciation schedules to determine business net income. Instead, this rapid tax depreciation was defended as an incentive for the purchases of new machinery and equipment by providing Government assistance for those purchases through tax reduction. This is equally true of the investment credit. The special provisions in the oil and mineral areas are not defended as necessary to measure real net income from natural resource operations. Financial accounting does not use percentage depletion and immediate write-off of intangible drilling expenses in determining business net income from these operations. Instead, these special provisions are defended either as needed financial assistance for the exploration and drilling of oil or as a subsidy to maintain a lower price level for gasoline and fuel oil. Deferral of tax on income from exports — deferral so long deferred it amounts virtually to exemption — was not defended when adopted in 1971 as necessary to measure real net income from exporting. Financial accounting reflects the entire income currently. Instead, this special provision — DISC — was defended as Government assistance to exporters through tax reduction to encourage an increase in exports. Tax exemption for state and local bonds is not defended as necessary to measure net income, but as a method of providing federal assistance to states and localities through inducing investors to accept lower interest rates on those bonds.

These tax subsidies amount in the aggregate to around $60 to $65 billion, and thus are in size equal to about a quarter of the regular federal budget. Yet buried as they are in the tax system, these tax subsidies are immune from scrutiny at a time when the regular budget is being carefully scrutinized for every possible saving. When budget ceilings are discussed, when Congress is seeking new approaches to place expenditures and expenditure procedures under rational control, these tax subsidies are never considered. They are not shown in the federal budget; indeed, they are usually not even mentioned in the special budget analyses annually made of the different program areas.

Spending ceilings and rigid expenditure controls obviously come down to priorities and to a choice among programs and expenditure policies. This examination of priorities and programs is entirely proper and much needed. But it should extend to tax expenditures as well as direct expenditures, to tax subsidies as well as direct subsidies. If direct spending programs for hospitals, housing, agriculture, medical care, community action, urban affairs, and many more are all to be gone over carefully and reduced, why not the tax expenditure programs for exporters, for natural resources, for investment abroad, for real estate, for machinery and equipment, for timber, and the other activities favored by tax subsidies. When Government spending is under close, tough scrutiny, and when Congress is considering new procedures to permit an integrated control over Government spending, a system that excludes a vast amount of expenditures from that scrutiny and those procedures just because the expenditures are clothed in tax language is both bad tax policy and bad budget policy.

These tax subsidies, and questions about their low priorities, their wastefulness and their inefficiencies are thus out of sight and unseen, unless they are examined in the context of tax reform. This is why stress can be laid, as an objective of tax reform, on the restoration of efficiency and economy in the expenditure of government funds. Tax reform means a careful scrutiny of these tax subsidy programs — and it means the only way they can get such a needed scrutiny. Moreover, it is a scrutiny that views the special tax provisions embodying these tax subsidies for what they really are — expenditure programs that must be considered and tested by expenditure standards. Do we as a country really want to spend this much money, in these ways, to assist these activities and these persons? Do our expenditure priorities encompass these spending targets?

A rigorous examination of the items in the Tax Expenditure Budget is therefore a necessary ingredient in any search for efficiency and economy in Government spending. This aspect of the Tax Expenditure Budget is considered in Chapter VI.

Tax Simplification and Tax Complexity

The Tax Expenditure Budget permits us to consider the matter of tax simplification — or tax complexity — in a different manner from that usually followed. The perennial desire for tax simplification always makes that goal one of the objectives of tax revision and tax reform campaigners. Yet the income tax system becomes increasingly more complex as each revision or reform passes into tax history. The efforts at tax simplification are rarely preceded by a consideration of what factors make for tax complexity and whether those factors are inherent in an income tax or instead are the result of faulty policies or faulty techniques. But the Tax Expenditure Budget enables us to perceive that one significant source of complexity is the presence of the tax expenditure apparatus within the income tax system. We are thus led to inquire how much of the complexity of our present tax stems from that apparatus and how much follows just from having an income tax itself.

The tax expenditure apparatus is equal to about one-fourth of the regular federal budget. Moreover, it extends to every budget functional classification except Space Research and Technology, and even here the tax expenditures classified under Commerce and Transportation assist companies engaged in programs under the prior classification. A tax system that is required to contain an expenditure operation of this scope and magnitude is bound to be complex — it has in a sense all the complications that these programs would have if handled as direct expenditure programs in the regular budget. To be sure, the degree of complexity might vary somewhat item by item between the tax expenditure approach and the direct expenditure approach, sometimes probably being more, sometimes less, complex. But in totality, the existence of this expenditure apparatus is a tremendous force for complexity in the tax system viewed as a whole. With capital gains — itself a tax expenditure — probably the tax expenditure apparatus is responsible for more complexity in total than the income tax structure proper. In scanning the list of tax provisions involved in this apparatus we can certainly recognize item after item that has added its impact to the total complexity presented by our income tax structure.

Much of the complexity of the 1969 Act derives from its entanglement with some of these existing tax incentives — for example, assistance to philanthropy, especially private foundations; farm activities; financial institutions; real estate and housing; the new minimum tax; capital gains — and, unfortunately, in adding new incentives, such as five-year amortization of the costs of housing rehabilitation, pollution control facilities, railroad cars, and mine safety equipment. The 1971 Act also has its responsibilities for adding to the tax expenditure list — and to complexity: the indefensible and complicated DISC provision granting, in effect, partial tax exemption to exports as a tax incentive to exporters, and perhaps the most deplorable step taken in recent decades by a Treasury Department charged with responsibility for maintaining a fair tax system; the investment credit; the asset depreciation range system; the five-year amortization for costs of employer-provided training and child care facilities; a tax credit for employers who hire public assistance recipients from the Labor Department's welfare training programs; the credit and deduction for political contributions.

On the income side, these tax preferences establish, in effect, numerous schedular enclaves in what would otherwise be a unitary system. This special schedular treatment — such as that for tax exempt interest, for natural resources income, and for capital gains — makes it necessary to classify a person's receipts among these compartments rather than simply calling all the receipts gross income. Moreover, in many situations these classifications made at one tax level must be traced through distributions to, or other connections made with, another tax level. Thus the separate subclassification of each gross income (and deduction) item in a partnership return must be carried through to the partners, and that in a trust return carried through to the beneficiaries. It is clear that this required subclassification is a serious source of technical complication, which could be avoided if the unitary concept of gross income were not so seriously undercut by these schedular enclaves necessitated by the tax expenditures. On the deduction side for individuals, the availability of the so-called personal expense deductions reflecting tax expenditures — for example, mortgage and other consumer interest, state and local taxes, medical expenses, charitable contributions, and casualty losses — greatly increase the amount of detail needed to reduce gross income to taxable income. The presence of the standard deduction is required to make this detail at all manageable.

An income tax is a complex tax, but we should not fault it as a tax because of the complexities forced on it when it is required also to carry out a whole host of expenditure programs.[2]

Evaluation of the Existing Tax Expenditure Programs

The Tax Expenditure Budget enables us to look at the income tax provisions reflecting that budget in a new light. When these tax provisions are seen not as inherent parts of an income tax structure but as carrying out programs of financial assistance for particular groups and activities, a number of questions immediately come into focus. Once we see that we are not evaluating technical tax provisions but rather expenditure programs, we are able to ask the traditional questions and use the analytical tools that make up the intellectual apparatus of expenditure experts.

We thus can put the basic question of whether we desire to provide that financial assistance at all, and if so in what amount — a stock question any budget expert would normally ask of any item in the regular budget. We can inquire whether the program is working well, how its benefits compare with its costs; whether it is accomplishing its objectives — indeed, what are its objectives? Who is actually being assisted by the program, and is that assistance too much or too little? Again, these are stock questions directed by any budget expert at existing programs. They all equally must be asked of the items and programs in the Tax Expenditure Budget.

The fact that the Tax Expenditure Budget summarizes an "expenditure system described in tax language" adds, however, a new dimension to these traditional questions. Each program in that budget is carried out through a special tax provision. The financial assistance which the program grants is thus determined through the effect of that special provision on the tax liabilities of the persons benefited. And also, since the persons benefited are only those within the ambit of the income tax system, the program's assistance is confined to taxpayers and does not extend to nontaxpayers. Individuals whose income amounts are below personal exemption levels, businesses that are losing money rather than making profits, organizations that are tax exempt, all being nontaxpayers thus do not receive the assistance. As a consequence, before we analyze the tax expenditure program, we must first translate the tax language into expenditure results.

Consider, for example, the tax expenditure program for housing represented by the deductibility of mortgage interest and property taxes paid on owner-occupied homes, listed as an item under Housing and Community Development. This is a program of assistance estimated at about $6.7 billion (calendar 1972). The translation of the tax language in which the program is framed and the assistance provided — a *deduction* in computing taxable income — tells us first that the wealthier the individual the greater is his assistance under the program. This is because the higher the individual's income and thus the higher the individual's income tax rate, the larger is the tax benefit — the tax reduction — brought about by the deduction. A deduction of $100 in mortgage interest or $100 in property tax is "worth" $70 to a taxpayer in the 70 percent top tax bracket — i.e., is financial assistance of $70. But it is "worth" only $14 to a taxpayer in the first tax bracket of 14 percent. As a consequence, 85 percent of the $6.7 billion of financial assistance goes to individuals with incomes of over $10,000.[3] The translation next tells us that an individual or family whose income is so low that they are not required to pay an income tax — their income being below their personal exemptions and low-income allowance — do not receive any financial assistance, for deductions benefit only taxpayers and not nontaxpayers. The translation also tells us that there is no limit placed on the size or value of the homes to be assisted nor on the number of residences for which a taxpayer may receive assistance, for the deduction is simply in terms of mortgage interest and property taxes paid. The process of translation thus gives us the contours of the tax expenditure program for housing — contours that are quite different from the housing assistance programs formulated in direct expenditure terms. But the contrast — and hence the nature of the task of analysis in expenditure terms — can only be appreciated after the translation is made. It is only then that we can really ask the crucial question of how this tax expenditure program measures up as an "expenditure" program. For then we can restate the tax program as a direct expenditure program and ask whether, as such, it represents a desirable policy.

The translation and consequent restatement of a tax expenditure program in direct expenditure terms generally show an upside-down result utterly at variance with usual expenditure policies. Thus, if expressed in direct expenditure language, the present assistance for owner-occupied homes under the tax deductions for mortgage interest and property taxes would appear as follows:

— for a married couple with more than $200,000 in income, HUD would, for each $100 of mortgage interest on the couple's home, pay $70 to the bank holding the mortgage, leaving the couple to pay $30. It would also pay a similar portion of the couple's property tax to the state or city levying the tax.

— for a married couple with income of $10,000, HUD would pay the bank on the couple's mortgage $19 per each $100 interest unit, with the couple paying $81. It would also pay a similar portion of the couple's property tax to the state or city levying the tax.

— for a married couple too poor to pay an income tax, HUD would pay nothing to the bank, leaving the couple to pay the entire interest cost. The couple would also have to pay the entire property tax.

One can assume that no HUD Secretary would ever have presented to Congress a direct housing program with this upside-down effect.

Other illustrations exist — in fact, almost any of these tax expenditures is seen as woefully unfair or inefficient when cast as a direct expenditure program. Thus, the 1969 tax legislation contained a tax incentive for the rehabilitation of low income rental housing, using the device of five-year amortization of capital expenditures which otherwise would be depreciated over a longer period. This device, which was proposed by the Treasury Department, has these interesting effects for individual taxpayers: for a taxpayer in the 70 percent bracket, the benefit is the equivalent of a 19 percent investment credit (assuming an expenditure with a 20-year life and discount rate of 10 percent); for a taxpayer in the 20 percent bracket it is the equivalent of a 5 percent credit. In terms of interest costs on a loan made for rehabilitation purposes, the benefit of five-year amortization is equivalent, for the 70 percent bracket taxpayer, to reducing an 8 percent interest charge to 3 percent; for the 20 percent bracket taxpayer it is equivalent to reducing the 8 percent charge to 7 percent. Besides having this upside-down effect, the rehabilitation incentive is probably a waste of Government money all around. It is not likely to increase the amount of rehabilitated housing over what would be accomplished through the existing HUD direct subsidy alone, so that the tax incentive will simply make some wealthy investors more wealthy.

It is tax expenditures like this rehabilitation provision that produce the various "tax shelters" being marketed by investment houses for upper-bracket individuals. These tax shelters — through fast tax write-offs for investment in low-income housing, oil drilling, leasing of equipment, and farming — are responsible for many of the cases in which these individuals pay little or no income tax. The tax shelters are as inefficient as they are unfair. Thus, the tax benefits for investment in low-income housing result in the Treasury's paying the investor $1 in tax benefits so that he will in turn pay the developer seventy cents. But generous commissions paid by the Treasury are not unusual in this tax subsidy world. The Treasury also pays $1 in tax benefits to a top-bracket taxpayer who buys a tax-exempt bond in order to provide fifty-eight cents in assistance to state and local governments through lower interest rates on their bonds.

These inequities and inefficiencies cannot be avoided when the tax system is being used to pay the financial assistance provided by the Government. A recent example is the 1971 Act provision for political contributions. The $100 deduction (on a joint return) for political contributions, or alternative tax credit of one-half of the contribution up to a maximum credit of $25 (on a joint return), added in 1971, in effect bars individuals below the taxable levels from participating in the allocation of Government funds to their candidates. Thus, the credit approach in effect means that if a taxpayer sends $25 to a candidate, then the Government will also send $25 to the candidate — the effect of allowing a tax credit of $25 for a contribution of $50. But if individuals below the taxable levels — perhaps 25 percent to 30 percent of the electorate — contribute any money to the political process, the Government refuses to match those funds.

This examination and translation of tax expenditure items would force the exploration of possible direct expenditure programs as alternatives to accomplish the same overall financial assistance goal. The exploration would seek to ascertain if such direct expenditure programs would be more desirable and effective vehicles for providing that assistance than the existing tax expenditure program. This process would probably be hastened if the tax expenditure items were placed in the regular budget and the funds involved charged to the agencies having the prime responsibility for the program objectives represented by the items. An agency so charged with these tax expenditure funds in *its* "budget" might well be prompted to see if it likes the results and is willing to stand behind them, in contrast with the present attitude

38

of indifference to the tax expenditure item or perhaps even ignorance of the item or its effects.

In the final analysis, these considerations take us to the basic question that underlies the Tax Expenditure Budget: *given* a Congressional decision to provide financial assistance to a particular group or activity, when should that assistance be furnished through a direct expenditure program — be it a grant, a loan, an interest subsidy, a loan guarantee — and when should it be furnished through the tax system? What are the considerations or criteria that govern the choice between the direct expenditure route or the tax route? Put differently, when is it desirable to use a "tax incentive" to induce action rather than a direct expenditure program and what factors determine the answer? When is it desirable to use tax benefits as relief for personal hardships rather than a direct program?

The comparison between tax incentives and direct expenditures as devices for implementing Government policies of financial assistance is considered in Chapter V.

Evaluation of Newly Proposed Tax Incentives

The Tax Expenditure Budget also provides a tool to evaluate newly proposed tax incentives. The technique is the same as that described above for the existing tax expenditure items. The first step in testing the proposed tax incentive is to translate it from tax language into direct expenditure terms. However, this step, on its face seemingly an obvious necessity, is generally not taken when tax incentives are proposed. Instead, the tax incentive remains cast in its tax language and the legislators who consider it are generally unaware of its direct expenditure meaning. As a consequence, many a tax incentive finds its way into the tax law.

Tax language is dangerously deceptive. It looks so right, with its neat technical wording and its seeming promise of affording proper assistance to everyone needing the assistance. Consider, for example, a Senator desiring to assist elderly people faced with medical expenses. His office drafts an amendment to the tax law to remove for persons over the age of 65 years the 3 percent floor under the medical expense deduction that now applies to all persons. Under the amendment, elderly persons would be able to take a tax deduction for their full medical expenses rather than for only those expenses in excess of 3 percent of their income. The proposal has its obvious appeal — a minor tax change to assist the elderly who are ill, "a matter of equity for millions of older Americans." But let us translate the tax relief into direct expenditure terms: The proposal would cost around $200 million, of which $90 million would go to persons with incomes over $50,000 and only $8 million to persons with incomes under $5,000. It seems clear that no HEW Secretary would ever propose a direct medical assistance program for the aged that would have these results. And yet the tax language looks so appealing and effective — indeed it has several times passed the Senate for just those reasons! Fortunately, the analysis in direct expenditure terms prevailed in the Conference Committee and the legislation was not enacted.[4]

Once translated, the tax incentive — or tax relief — can then be appraised in the same fashion as would a direct expenditure initially proposed in just those terms. It would be appropriate in this appraisal to consider what would be the most desirable direct expenditure program that could be devised. The two programs — tax incentive and direct expenditure — could then be compared and a rational choice made. In many instances the translation itself would probably end the inquiry, for it would show the tax incentive woefully lacking in fairness and effectiveness.

These aspects of the Tax Expenditure Budget and tax incentives are further discussed in Chapter V.

The Effect on Civil Rights and Other Constitutional Issues

The courts have held unconstitutional direct Governmental financial assistance to organizations that maintain racially segregated facilities or discriminate in other ways against blacks and other minority groups. For example, state tuition grants to racially segregated schools would be invalid.[5] This being so, is assistance to such schools through the tax system also invalid? How should a tax deduction for charitable contributions to such schools or a tax exemption for such schools be viewed? Do these tax benefits constitute financial assistance comparable to direct assistance, and are they therefore invalid if available to such schools? Or are these tax consequences simply a part of an income tax system and, while providing indirect benefits to the schools, not to be viewed in the same light as direct benefits?

The Tax Expenditure Budget approach obviously offers answers to these questions. Its premise is that Governmental financial assistance, if made available through the income tax, should be viewed and judged in the same manner as direct assistance. Clearly the Treasury Department is saying this through the publication and description of that budget. The House Ways and Means Committee in publishing its "Estimates of Federal Tax Expenditures" is also calling attention to the parallel with direct expenditures. Some courts are beginning to take the same view, and in some instances have been influenced by tax expenditure analysis.

In *Green v. Kennedy,*[6] parents of black children in Mississippi sued to enjoin the Secretary of the Treasury and the Commissioner of Internal Revenue from granting tax-exempt status to private schools in Mississippi which discriminated against Negroes in admissions and from ensuring donors to such schools the right to deduct their contributions. A three-judge Federal Court in the District of Columbia granted a preliminary injunction in an opinion which said:[7]

> We are aware that the case before us does not involve outright tuition grants to students by the Government, such as were invalidated in the *Coffey* case, but rather tax benefits to the schools, and to persons contributing to the schools.
>
> For reasons we shall now relate we find this difference to be only a difference of degree that does not negative our essential finding, on the evidence presented on the motion, that the tax benefits under the Internal Revenue Code mean a substantial and significant support by the Government to the segregated private school pattern. The pertinent legal conclusion is that there is a substantial question in plaintiffs' claim that this support constitutes a derogation of constitutional rights.
>
> The support which is significant in the context of this controversy is not the exemption of the schools from taxes laid on their income, but rather the deductions from income tax available to the individual, and corporations, making contributions supporting the school.
>
> . . . .
>
> The critical significance of support from tax deductions is in effect recognized by the Commissioner, and in the general context of school segregation, in his denial of deductions to contributions to segregated schools that have significant state involvement. What stops him from extending disallowance to the schools like those involved in the case at bar is not unawareness of the significance of deductions, but rather certain legal conclusions, including conclusions as to the scope of his authority under the Code.

In a subsequent opinion[8] the court granted a final injunction which it supported by holding that the Internal Revenue Code provisions on charitable deductions and tax exemption for educational institutions as a matter of statutory interpretation do not extend to schools practicing racial discrimination in admissions:[9]

> The Internal Revenue Code provisions on charitable exemptions and deductions must be construed to avoid frustrations of Federal policy. Under the conditions of today they can no longer be construed so as to provide to private schools operating on a racially discriminatory premise the support of the exemptions and deductions which Federal tax law affords to charitable organizations and their sponsors.

41

The court fortified this result by the following view on the assistance that would otherwise be afforded by those provisions if interpreted to be applicable to these schools:[10]

> We are fortified in our view of the correctness of [this] construction by the consideration that a contrary interpretation of the tax laws would raise serious constitutional questions, such as those we ventilated in our January, 1970, opinion. Clearly the Federal Government could not under the Constitution give direct financial aid to schools practicing racial discrimination. But tax exemptions and deductions certainly constitute a Federal Government benefit and support. While that support is indirect, and is in the nature of a matching grant rather than an unconditional grant, it would be difficult indeed to establish that such support can be provided consistently with the Constitution. The propriety of the interpretation approved by this court is underscored by the fact that it obviates the need to determine such serious constitutional claims.

A three-judge District of Columbia court in *McGlotten v. Connally*[11] went a step further. Here a black American brought a similar suit against the Secretary of the Treasury and the Commissioner, this time directed against the Benevolent and Protective Order of Elks, a fraternal organization, on the ground that it excluded nonwhites from membership. The plaintiff based his action on three separate grounds: the charitable deduction and tax-exemption Code provisions are unconstitutional if they are interpreted to apply to the Elks; those provisions should be interpreted as not applicable to benefit the Elks; the provisions if applicable are a form of federal financial assistance barred by Title VI of the Civil Rights Act of 1964. That Act states that no person shall on grounds of race, color, or national origin be excluded from participation in, denied the benefits of, or be subjected to discrimination under any program or activity receiving "federal financial assistance." "Assistance" is defined as "assistance to any program or activity by way of grant, loan or contract other than a contract of insurance or guaranty." The court denied the Government's motion to dismiss the action and stated that all three grounds were legally sufficient to support the plaintiff's action.

The decision throughout underlines the similarity to direct expenditures of financial assistance provided through the tax system. On the constitutional effect in this situation of the charitable deduction, the court said:[12]

> To demonstrate the unconstitutionality of the challenged deductions plaintiff must, of course, show that they in fact aid, perpetuate, or encourage racial discrimination. He alleges, subject to proof at trial, both the substantiality of the benefits provided[(37)] and a causal relation to the

discrimination practiced by the segregated organizations. But more is required to find a violation of the Constitution. Every deduction in the tax laws provides a benefit to the class who may take advantage of it. And the withdrawal of that benefit would often act as a substantial incentive to eliminate the behavior which caused the change in status. Yet the provision of an income tax deduction for mortgage interest paid has not been held sufficient to make the Federal Government a "joint participant" in the bigotry practiced by a homeowner. An additional line of inquiry is essential, one considering the nature of the Government activity in providing the challenged benefit and necessarily involving the sifting and weighing prescribed in *[Burton v. Wilmington Parking Authority]*.

The rationale for allowing the deduction of charitable contributions has historically been that by doing so, the Government relieves itself of the burden of meeting public needs which in the absence of charitable activity would fall on the shoulders of the Government. "The Government is compensated for its loss of revenue by its relief from financial burdens which would otherwise have to be met by appropriations from public funds." H.Rep. No. 1860, 75th Cong., 3rd Sess. 19 (1938). And here the Government does more than simply authorize deduction of contributions to any cause which the individual taxpayer deems charitable. The statute, regulations, and administrative rulings thereunder, define in extensive detail not only the purposes which will satisfy the statute, but the *vehicles* through which those purposes may be achieved as well. A contribution, even for an approved purpose, is deductible *only* if made to an organization of the type specified in §170 and which has obtained a ruling or letter of determination from the Internal Revenue Service. Thus the government has marked certain organizations as *"Government Approved"* with the result that such organizations may solicit funds from the general public on the basis of that approval.

. . . .

The public nature of the activity delegated to the organization in question, the degree of control the Government has retained as to the purposes and organizations which may benefit, and the aura of Government approval inherent in an exempt ruling by the Internal Revenue Service, all serve to distinguish the benefits at issue from the general run of deductions available under the Internal Revenue Code. Certain deductions provided by the Code do not act as matching grants, but are merely attempts to provide for an equitable measure of net income.[44] Others are simply part of the structure of an income tax based on ability to pay.[45] We recognize that an additional class of deductions — such as accelerated depreciation for rehabilitated low income rental property, or deductions for mortgage interest — do act as "incentives" favoring certain types of activities. But unlike the charitable deductions before us, these provisions go no further than simply indicating the activities hoped to be encouraged; they do not expressly choose fraternal organizations as a vehicle for that activity and do not allow such organizations to represent themselves as having the imprimatur of the Government. This seems to us a significant difference of degree in an area where no bright-line rule is possible.

(37.) There is no question that allowing the deduction of charitable contributions in fact confers a benefit on the organization receiving the contribution. The court in *Green v. Kennedy, supra* note 11, described "the impact of Federal tax . . . deduction" as a "matching grant," *id.* at 1136, and we agree. *See generally,* Surrey, Tax Incentives as a Device for Implementing Government Policy: A Comparison with Direct Government Expenditures, 83 Harv. L. Rev. 705 (1970); Surrey, Federal Income Tax Reforms: The Varied Approaches Necessary [to] Replace Tax Expenditures with Direct Government Assistance, 84 Harv. L. Rev. 352 (1970); Stone, Federal Tax Support of Charities and Other Exempt Organizations: The Need for a National Policy, 20 So. Calif. Tax Instit. 27 (1968).

(44.) *E.g.,* Int. Rev. Code §§162 (deductibility of trade or business expenses); 172 (net operating loss carryovers and carrybacks); 1301–5 (income averaging).

(45.) *E.g.,* Int. Rev. Code §151 (personal exemptions).

On the status of the charitable deduction as "federal financial assistance" within the meaning of the Civil Rights Act, the court said:[13]

We think there is little question that the provision of a tax deduction for charitable contributions is a grant of federal financial assistance within the scope of the 1964 Civil Rights Act. "The charitable contribution deduction is a special tax provision not required by, and contrary to, widely accepted definitions of income applicable to the determination of the structure of an income tax."[68] It operates in effect as a Government matching grant and is available only for the particular purposes and to the particular organizations outlined in the Code.[69] We see no difference between the provision of Federal property "at a consideration which is reduced . . . in recognition of the public interest to be served by such sale or lease to the recipient," and a tax deduction in the form of a matching grant provided for contributions to causes deemed worthy by the Internal Revenue Code.

(68.) Surrey, Federal Income Tax Reforms: The Varied Approaches Necessary to Replace Tax Expenditures with Direct Governmental Assistance, 84 Harv. Law Rev. 352, 384 (1970).

(69.) *See* note 37 above.

The opinion is of further interest for its effort to determine when the conferring of tax-exempt status under the income tax on an organization operates as a grant of financial assistance and when that exemption serves a different purpose. The Elks apparently could qualify for tax exemption either as a "social club" [section 501(c)(7)] or as a "fraternal organization" [section 501(c)(8)]. The court found that exemption as a social club would confer no benefit upon the organization:[14]

> Unlike the deduction for charitable contributions, the deduction for "exempt function income" does not operate to provide a grant of federal funds through the tax system. Rather, it is part and parcel of defining appropriate subjects of taxation. Congress has determined that in a situation where individuals have banded together to provide recreational facilities on a mutual basis, it would be conceptually erroneous to impose a tax on the organization as a separate entity. The funds exempted are received only from the members and any "profit" which results from overcharging for the use of the facilities still belongs to the same members. No income of the sort usually taxed has been generated; the money has simply been shifted from one pocket to another, both within the same pair of pants. Thus the exclusion of member generated revenue reflects a determination that as to these funds the organization does not operate as a separate entity.
>
> That the Government provides no monetary benefit does not, however, insulate its involvement from constitutional scrutiny. . . . Encouragement of discrimination through the appearance of governmental approval may also be sufficient involvement to violate the Constitution. But here the necessary involvement is not readily apparent. Section 501(c)(7) does not limit its coverage to particular activities; exemption is given to "[c]lubs organized and operated exclusively for pleasure, recreation *and other nonprofitable purposes* . . ." (emphasis added). Thus, there is no mark of Government approval inherent in the designation of a group as exempt. Congress has simply chosen not to tax a particular type of revenue because it is not within the scope sought to be taxed by the statute. And however dysfunctional the "state action" limitation is at a time when the nation has sufficiently matured that the elimination of racial discrimination is a cornerstone of national policy, it still means that Congress does not violate the Constitution by *failing to tax* private discrimination where there is no other act of Government involvement.

For the same reasons, the exemption as a social club did not operate as financial assistance within the meaning of the Civil Rights Act.

However, the court considered exemption as a fraternal organization to have a different impact:[15]

> The exemption given to fraternal organizations under §501(c)(8) stands on different footing. Unlike nonprofit clubs, fraternal organizations are taxed only on "unrelated business taxable income" defined as "any trade or business the conduct of which is not substantially related (aside from the need of such organization for income or funds or the use it makes of the profits derived) to the exercise or performance by such organization of its charitable, educational, or other purpose or function constituting the basis for the exemption under section 501 . . ." The crucial impact of this differential treatment is that the passive investment income of fraternal orders is not taxed. This exemption cannot be explained simply by the inappropriateness of taxing the organization as a separate entity in this situation. Here individuals are providing funds which are then invested for the purposes of benefiting the contributing members, and the exemption of this income is a "benefit" provided by the Government.
>
> We think this exclusion, provided only to particular organizations with particular purposes, rather than across the board, is sufficient government involvement to invoke the Fifth Amendment. By providing differential treatment to only selected organizations, the Government has indicated approval of the organizations and hence their discriminatory practice, and aided that discrimination by the provision of federal tax benefits.

The exemption was likewise considered to be financial assistance for purposes of the Civil Rights Act.

The approach of the court thus required it to undertake the initial inquiry into which tax provisions constitute tax expenditures as we have used this term and which do not. If the provision is a tax expenditure, then the benefits it confers constitute federal financial assistance and that assistance in turn is subject to further scrutiny: Is it assistance within the meaning of the Civil Rights Act? Here the court gave an affirmative answer.[16] Does the grant of assistance involve an unconstitutional act? Here the court, in keeping with nontax aid, indicated that the character of the tax assistance must be further examined to see if it involves Government with the private activity to the required extent. While this last test is not a clear one, the lack of clarity exists, under the current Supreme Court approach to cases involving private organizations, whether the assistance comes through the tax system or in other ways. If the provision is not a tax expenditure but part of the structure of an income tax, then the consequences described above do not follow.[17]

The Tax Expenditure Budget is thus an aid to courts seeking in this area of civil rights to probe the operation and effects of our tax system. The analysis that underlies the composition of that budget is the same as that chosen by these courts to decide the questions before them. That budget would assist the courts in classifying the charitable deduction, along with the previous exploration of the deduction by tax writers. But since the application of the Tax Expenditure Budget to tax-exempt organizations had not as yet been explored by those working with the concept, it was of no direct aid to the *McGlotten* court in that phase of the case. The court therefore had to undertake the analysis *de novo*.[18] Thus the issues raised by the case both indicate the guidance which the Tax Expenditure Budget offers to the solution of other legal issues — here the constitutional position of the discrimination practiced by a private organization and the meaning of the Civil Rights Act — and the necessity of applying tax expenditure analysis to areas of the tax system not yet fully covered by that analysis.

The Supreme Court in 1973 in a case involving the constitutionality, under the Establishment Clause of the First Amendment, of state financial assistance to parents of children attending religious schools, also applied the same consequences to tax assistance as to direct assistance. In *Committee For Public Education and Religious Liberty v. Nyquist*,[19] it held unconstitutional tuition grants given by New York to parents with incomes under $5,000 who had children attending nonpublic elementary or secondary schools. Since about 85 percent of the children in such schools attended church-affiliated schools (practically all Roman Catholic) the Court considered the tuition grants in the context of the First Amendment.[20] It then held equally unconstitutional companion New York legislation which granted state income tax deductions to parents of children in such nonpublic schools whose incomes ranged from $5,000 to $25,000. The effect of these tax deductions was to give the same dollar amount of assistance to parents with incomes just above $5,000 as the parents below that income level received through the direct tuition grants. The tax assistance gradually declined as the parents' income increased, and ended at the $25,000 level. Although the lower court had found a distinction between the direct tuition grant assistance and the tax deduction assistance and had upheld the tax assistance,[21] the Supreme Court found no constitutional difference and held both forms of assistance equally invalid:[22]

> These sections allow parents of children attending nonpublic elementary and secondary schools to subtract from adjusted gross income a specified amount if they do not receive a tuition reimbursement under §2, and if they have an adjusted gross income of less than $25,000. The amount of the deduction is unrelated to the amount of money actually expended by any parent on tuition, but is calculated on the basis of a formula contained in the statute. The formula is apparently the product of a legislative attempt to assure that each family would receive

a carefully estimated net benefit, and that the tax benefit would be comparable to, and compatible with, the tuition grant for lower income families. Thus, a parent who earns less than $5,000 is entitled to a tuition reimbursement of $50 if he has one child attending an elementary, nonpublic school, while a parent who earns more (but less than $9,000) is entitled to have a precisely equal amount taken off his tax bill. Additionally, a taxpayer's benefit under these sections is unrelated to, and not reduced by, any deductions to which he may be entitled for charitable contributions to religious institutions.[49]

In practical terms there would appear to be little difference, for purposes of determining whether such aid has the effect of advancing religion, between the tax benefit allowed here and the tuition grant allowed under §2. The qualifying parent under either program receives the same form of encouragement and reward for sending his children to nonpublic schools. The only difference is that one parent receives an actual cash payment while the other is allowed to reduce by an arbitrary amount the sum he would otherwise be obliged to pay over to the State. We see no answer to Judge Hays' dissenting statement below that "[i]n both instances the money involved represents a charge made upon the state for the purpose of religious education." 350 F. Supp., at 675.

(49.) Since the program here does not have the elements of a genuine tax deduction, such as for charitable contributions, we do not have before us, and do not decide, whether that form of tax benefit is constitutionally acceptable under the "neutrality" test in *Walz*.

While three Justices dissented from the Court's opinion, they equally drew no distinction between the direct tuition grant assistance and the tax assistance. They would have held both forms of assistance constitutional.[23] Their dissenting views serve to underscore the Court's unwillingness to develop a different line of constitutional result between Government aid cast in the form of a direct grant and Government aid cast in the form of tax assistance.[24] The *Nyquist* decision thus confirms the approach described above taken by the District of Columbia courts in the civil rights cases arising under the Federal income tax. The decision is further evidence of the usefulness of tax expenditure analysis to the resolution of constitutional issues growing out of Government assistance to individuals and activities.

The Effect on the Tax Process

A final thought may here be offered on discussions of tax structure, whether they are discussions around the concept of tax expenditures, or the economists' concept of a comprehensive tax base, or other such subjects. These discussions do have as their basic assumption the ability to instill some order into the process of structuring an income tax. There are some who, having watched the Congressional actions in the tax field over the years, feel that the assumption is unfounded and the quest for order futile. They appear to see the tax structure only as what is decided by the Congress, with no "image" of a proper structure against which to test those decisions. But this I believe is a view that is both too pessimistic and too anarchistic. It is interesting that policy makers, in the Executive Branch and also in the Congress, usually do seek to know the "right answer" to problems of structure. This is not to say that they will always urge the right answer, for many considerations impose their influence on the final answer. But there is generally — unfortunately not always — the desire at some point to know what is the right answer and how far from that answer is the final solution.

So criteria are needed. The principal criterion is generally found in the concept of "equity," a broad and often imprecise standard, but nevertheless a standard that legislators appreciate and feel. It is a standard that underlies much of the Treasury analysis for the Tax Expenditure Budget. An income tax seeks to tax fairly and equitably by placing the same income tax burden on those substantially in the same economic position, that is, with equal amounts of income determined in accordance with the tenets of that tax. The tax expenditure items represent departures from that standard, where the structure of the tax and tax equity are asked to yield ground to some non-tax objective.[25] Generally, legislators do realize when a measure they are asked to adopt is a departure from tax structure and tax equity and therefore must be defended on terms other than its rightful place in the tax structure — terms that in essence make it a "tax expenditure."

The task for the tax experts is to assist the legislators in developing the image of a proper tax structure and in analyzing the problems of structure and theory at the borderline. There is utility in describing how complex the tax structure really is, how incomplete are various theoretical concepts and approaches in explaining all the various parts of that structure, and how many points of decision there are in shaping the structure. But we must seek to do more than describe the difficulties and tangles. We must also strive constantly to develop the criteria that permit both order and rational criticism of disorder. To do otherwise is to turn the tax system over completely to those who thrive on disorder, for then their advantages are beyond judgment and control.

III

The Effects of Tax Expenditures on the Taxes

People and Corporations Pay

The presence of tax expenditures in the income tax system has wide ranging and significant effects on the tax liabilities of individuals and corporations. One aspect of the tax expenditure apparatus is the escape from tax liabilities that it permits. For some individuals, these tax expenditures mean that no income tax need be paid at all; for others, the tax paid will be nominal in comparison with the actual income received. The same consequences exist for corporations. Another aspect of the effects of tax expenditures on tax liabilities involves the differing ways individuals are affected. Thus, individuals are affected by the tax expenditure system as consumers, as wage or salary earners, as investors, or as recipients of benefits under income transfer programs. They are, however, affected in different ways, so that the resulting income tax liabilities may differ markedly from one status to the other. Still another aspect is the mechanics through which the tax expenditures operate to provide the escape from tax. These mechanics have created institutional investment and tax arrangements — "tax shelters" — that are entirely a function of the tax expenditures involved.

This chapter describes the varying effects on tax liabilities of the tax expenditure system, first in terms of individuals and then of corporations. The mechanics and their special effects are described in Chapter IV.

Tax Expenditures and the Tax Liabilities
of Individuals

Tax Expenditures and Tax Escape

The Tax Reform Studies of the Johnson Administration Treasury contain a description of the tax position of high-income individuals, starting as follows:

Effects of Tax Expenditures

Extreme variations in tax burdens exist among high-income taxpayers because of variations in the tax treatment of income according to its source. As a result, many high-income taxpayers are paying far less than their intended share of the income tax burden, and others are paying tax currently at very high rates.[1]

The Studies analyzed the tax payments of high-income individuals in terms of "effective rates of income tax" paid by those individuals. The effective rate of tax is the relationship between the actual tax paid and the individual's "real" or "actual income," the relationship being expressed in percentage terms. Real or actual income is essentially the income figure used on tax returns *increased* by the amounts of income excluded from the income tax and *increased* by the amount of taxable income offset by the personal deductions and personal exemptions. The effective rate of tax so determined measures the real bite of the income tax system.

Thus, suppose a married couple with two children has $100,000 of net salary income (after deducting any expenses incurred in earning that income), $50,000 of tax exempt interest, and $20,000 of personal expense deductions such as state and local taxes, mortgage interest, etc., and paid an income tax of $31,000, using round figures. Their "taxable" income — the figure to which the tax rates of the income tax are applied, would be $80,000, less four personal exemptions of $750, or $77,000. Their tax payment is thus 40 percent of their taxable income. But this relationship — actual tax to "taxable income" — does not express the real burden of the income tax on this family. Their actual income — the funds received that year and available for saving or consumption — is $150,000. The $31,000 actual tax is only 20.6 percent of this amount. This percentage — which is the actual effective rate of tax — measures the burden of the income tax on this family.

Thus, the concept of actual income is needed to compare the income tax burden placed on individuals at different economic levels or at the same economic level. The use of taxable income — the net figure arrived at after actual income is run through the tax laws with this or that provision pulling out various amounts of income and shielding the remaining amounts from tax — would simply hide what is happening under the tax laws. It would not reflect an individual's true economic position and his ability to pay income taxes. The tax expenditure analysis tells us that the difference between taxable income and actual income essentially represents the workings of the tax expenditure apparatus. The structure of the income tax proper would produce the actual net income figure — income actually received less the expenses of earning that income, and less the personal exemptions. This actual net income then goes through the second structure, that of the tax expenditure system, and comes out as the taxable income, which is the amount to which the rates of tax are applied to determine the tax to be paid.

Table 3.1 Percentage Distribution of Returns by Effective Tax Rate Classes: Present Law Tax as a Percent of Amended Taxable Income,[a] by AGI Classes, 1969 Levels

AGI (in thousands of dollars)	Effective tax rate classes													
	0 to 5	5 to 10	10 to 15	15 to 20	20 to 25	25 to 30	30 to 35	35 to 40	40 to 45	45 to 50	50 to 55	55 to 60	60 to 65	65 to 70
0 to 3	68.0[b]	0.5	1.5	6.0	(c)	(c)	(c)	(c)	(c)	(c)	(c)	(c)	(c)	(c)
3 to 5	14.2	2.5	11.0	63.0	(c)	(c)	(c)	(c)	(c)	(c)	(c)	(c)	(c)	(c)
5 to 7	3.6	2.1	22.5	71.5	(c)	(c)	(c)	(c)	(c)	(c)	(c)	(c)	(c)	(c)
7 to 10	.9	1.1	22.4	70.2	5.3	.4								
10 to 15	.5	.8	6.2	85.5	6.7									
15 to 20	.5	.7	4.2	72.2	20.1	2.3								
20 to 50	.4	.7	3.9	27.5	48.6	14.6	3.3	.7	.2					(d)
50 to 100	.3	.4	1.2	4.9	11.9	22.3	34.5	18.5	4.4	1.3	.3			(d)
100 to 500	1.0	.4	.5	1.6	14.1	15.5	11.2	15.3	19.4	12.2	5.6	2.6	.5	(d)
500 to 1,000	1.8	.6	.6	.6	24.6	30.0	4.7	5.0	3.5	2.6	4.9	7.9	12.7	.8
1,000 and over	4.0	.2	.2	.2	31.0	27.2	5.2	1.8	2.4	4.0	1.8	2.7	12.3	6.9
All classes	21.5	1.1	10.9	52.7	8.4	2.0	.9	.5	.3	.2	.1	.1	.1	1.0

[a]Amended taxable income is taxable income after deduction changes plus excluded capital gains, tax-exempt interest, and excess of percentage over cost depletion. Amended taxable income is used to maintain a common base for the effective rate computation under present law and under the reform program.

[b]Nontaxable are 67.6 percent.

[c]The percentages in these effective rate classes are not very meaningful because they reflect present law tax divided by a small amount of amended taxable income under the reform program. Amended taxable income for these taxpayers is much smaller than present law taxable income primarily because of the higher MSD under the reform program.

[d]Less than .05 percent.

The Treasury Studies provided tables[2] showing the effective rates of tax based on taxable income and then on actual income and the widening gulf between them as incomes increase. These tables are reprinted here, though they are based on the tax law prior to the 1969 Tax Reform Act. An interesting facet, discussed later, is the extent to which these tables still remain relevant despite that Act. These tables show a wide variation in effective rates of tax among individuals in the same economic class — ranging from zero to 65 percent for individuals in the million dollar and over class (Table 3.1). They also show that, as of 1969, the average effective rate of tax did not increase once incomes over $100,000 were reached and in fact actually declined for the still higher income groups (Table 3.2).

As the notes to the tables state, the effective rates on actual incomes are overstated, since lack of data prevented the full addition of all excluded items.

The Treasury Studies described the principal factors that operated to reduce income taxes for high-income taxpayers. One set of factors is that of the items

Table 3.2   Returns with Taxable Income, 1966: Marginal and Effective Tax Rates

Adjusted gross income class (thousands)	Average marginal rate[a]	Effective rate on taxable income[b]	Effective rate on adjusted gross income[c]	Effective rate on amended taxable income[d]	Effective rate on amended adjusted gross income[e]
0 to $5	16.0	15.3	7.5	15.0	7.4
$5 to $10	18.4	16.4	9.4	16.2	9.4
$10 to $20	21.5	18.1	12.3	17.8	12.2
$20 to $50	32.8	24.0	18.8	22.8	18.0
$50 to $100	51.1	35.8	29.5	32.6	27.3
$100 to $200	57.3 {	45.6	37.3	37.8	31.9
$200 to $500		52.3	41.7	37.9	32.0
$500 to $1,000	58.2	55.3	44.1	35.8	30.7
$1,000 and over	58.2	55.5	44.3	32.7	28.4

[a]Average rate applicable to top dollar of income taxable at normal and surtax rates.
[b]Statutory taxable income; adjusted gross income less exemptions and deductions.
[c]Statutory adjusted gross income.
[d]Statutory taxable income increased by items of excluded income. (Only excluded long-term capital gains, the largest single item of excluded income, are included in this computation; therefore the rates shown are slightly overstated as compared to table 3.1 where estimates are made as to other excluded items.)
[e]Statutory adjusted gross income increased by items of excluded income. (Only excluded long-term capital gains, the largest single item of excluded income, are included in this computation; therefore the rates shown are slightly overstated as compared to table 3.1. where estimates are made as to other excluded items.)

of excluded income, either income excluded directly or representing otherwise taxable income offset by special deductions, listed in their (1967) order of importance as: excluded half of capital gains; interest on state and local bonds; deductions for unlimited charitable contributions (largely representing the untaxed appreciation in the assets contributed); farm "tax losses"; percentage depletion in excess of basis; and deductions for intangible drilling expenses. Lack of data prevented ranking of several items: accelerated depreciation on buildings; interest on life insurance savings; and employee fringe benefits such as pension plans. Another factor of overall significance is the effect of the personal expense deductions — interest, taxes, charitable contributions, medical expenses, casualty losses, and child care.

These factors interact in ways that reinforce their tax reduction effect. Thus, the personal expense deductions can be fully offset against income that is taxable, with no part of the deductions being required to be allocated to excluded income. As a result, the combination of such deductions and excluded income can produce very low effective rates of tax despite the presence of large amounts of included gross income. Further, the deduction for interest on funds borrowed to invest in tax sheltered investments and capital gain items is available even though those investments produce no current taxable income and indeed may produce only "tax losses." Large interest deductions can thus be built up without the contemporaneous production of fully taxed income.

The Treasury Studies contained examples of individual cases[3] illustrating how these factors operated completely to eliminate tax liability for some high-income taxpayers:

— Taxpayer had $10,829,028 of amended gross income,[4] almost all in dividends, but paid no tax because of the unlimited deduction for charitable contributions; he had given $10,506,414 to charity, mostly in appreciated property which represented untaxed increase in wealth.

— Taxpayer had amended gross income of $1,313,811, mostly from oil and gas operations and capital gains, but paid no tax because of percentage depletion deduction (in excess of cost) of $865,644 and a farm "loss" of $828,571.

— Taxpayer had amended gross income of $1,284,718, mostly capital gains, but paid only $383 in tax because of the exclusion ($605,213) of one-half of the gains and an interest deduction of $587,693, which with other itemized deductions offset the included half of the gains and the remaining income.

54

— Taxpayer had income of $1,433,000, mostly from dividends and capital gains, but paid no tax because of real estate deductions of $804,000 (in excess of real estate income) and the exclusion ($575,000) of one-half of the capital gains.

— Taxpayer had income of $738,203, mostly from capital gains and interest, but paid no tax because of a "farm loss" of $450,084 and the exclusion ($249,182) of one-half of the capital gains.

A later analysis[5] by the House Ways and Means Committee of individual income tax returns for the year 1966, with adjusted gross income in excess of $200,000 but showing no income tax payments — a zero effective rate of tax — reinforced the above conclusions drawn in the Treasury Studies. Of the 154 returns examined, 21 of which had incomes over $1 million, one-third (49) were nontaxable because of the presence of the unlimited deduction for charitable contributions, by virtue of which the deduction offset all taxable income. It must be remembered that in most of these cases the charitable contribution was made with property that had greatly appreciated in value, but the appreciation was permitted to be excluded from income.[6] For another group of returns, about half of the cases (72), the deduction for interest was the principal factor making for absence of tax liability, in that the deduction offset the taxable income. But many of these cases involved additional factors, such as the presence of large amounts of capital gains and the consequent exclusion of one-half of the gains, or investment in one or more tax shelters which provided excluded income through percentage depletion and, more significantly, "tax losses" from oil, farm, or other shelter operations. The deductible interest presumably arose on loans to acquire the investments represented by the tax favored items, i.e., the appreciating securities and the shelter operations, so that it was the combination of factors that produced the total escape from tax liability. Another group (14 cases) involved the deduction of state income taxes as the ostensible factor, but here also the deduction in some cases combined with other items such as the excluded portion of capital gains, percentage depletion, and, in all likelihood, excluded interest on state or local securities.[7] Again, it was the combination of a deductible item and excluded income that produced the escape from tax.[8]

The above Treasury analysis, and the committee study based on it, did not present a comprehensive picture of all the factors involved or their quantitative influence because of the manner in which tax items are reported on individual tax returns, or are not reported. Thus, excluded interest on state or local bonds is not required to be reported. Tax losses obtained as a partner in a tax shelter syndicate, investing in oil, real estate, or cattle operations, for example, show up only as a partnership loss in overall dollar terms with no further breakdown on the investor's tax return, so that only by going to the partnership tax return can the underlying data be obtained. Accelerated depreciation taken on real estate investments is subtracted before adjusted gross income is obtained, and therefore does not appear as a separate item on the transcript sheets used in making the Treasury analysis. This is also the situation for intangible oil drilling expenses and percentage depletion, and for the farm deductions. As a consequence, the influence of tax sheltered investments is understated in that analysis.[9]

These reporting aspects also are responsible for other understatements of the tax reduction brought about by these factors. The committee analysis above referred to covered returns with reported adjusted gross income over $200,000. But a tax return showing only, say, $3,000 of adjusted gross income and a few dollars of tax, might have been filed by an individual with over a million dollars of actual income. If he had large accelerated depreciation or intangible drilling expense deductions, these would be applied against his gross income in determining adjusted gross income. Yet on the transcript cards used in compiling these statistics this millionaire would be indistinguishable from a wage earner receiving $3,000. Similarly, the millionaire's return could show zero adjusted gross income or a loss if these deductions were larger than the gross income. Also, as stated earlier, tax-exempt bond interest is not reported as gross income. Consequently, to the 154 returns in 1966 with adjusted gross income in excess of $200,000 on which no income tax was paid, there must be added an undetermined number of returns involving very large amounts of actual income and either no income tax liability or only a small tax payment, which are hidden away in the mass of tax returns showing small or negative amounts of adjusted gross income.

Finally, the Treasury Studies indicated that "high income taxpayers tend to show consistent income patterns, and thus consistent effective tax rates year after year."[10] Thus, high income taxpayers paying little or no tax in one year are likely to be found in other years in that period with the same escape from tax liabilities.

These effects of the tax expenditure system still remain after the 1969 Tax Reform Act. The principal change under that Act, as respects complete escape from tax, is that the unlimited charitable deduction is no longer available.[11] Thus, individuals who previously completely escaped tax by using that deduction, would now have to pay some tax, everything else remaining the same. The 1969 Act also introduced a minimum tax applicable to certain of the tax expenditures, such as the excluded portion of capital gains, accelerated depreciation, and percentage depletion, so that if these factors were responsible for complete escape from tax, then some tax would have to be paid. But the tax is weak; it does not exceed 10 percent of the preference amount (above a floor of $30,000 plus any regular income tax paid) and its coverage is limited — for example, the exclusion for state and local bond interest and the deduction for intangible oil drilling expenses are not affected.[12] In 1970, the minimum tax yielded only $115 million from individuals on tax preferences amounting to $4.5 billion, and $218 million from corporations. In 1971, the tax yielded $164 million from individuals on tax preferences of $4 billion. The "farm loss" deduction was largely undisturbed, although there is a recapture of some of the losses as ordinary income instead of capital gains when cattle or other products are sold.[13] The rates of percentage depletion were reduced somewhat — that on oil dropped from 27.5 to 22 percent — but the deduction for exploration costs and development was largely unaffected and not at all affected for oil. State and local bond interest was not affected. A limitation was adopted on the deduction for interest on loans incurred in connection with investment property, which can cut down the scope of this deduction in the case of sizeable loans.[14] All in all, there presumably are some wealthy individuals who will still completely escape tax. And those previously tax-free who find themselves paying some tax may also find the amount not large and therefore the effective rate low. For the entire group with incomes above $200,000, there will be a rise in the average effective rate due to an increase in the capital gain rate from 25 percent to 35 percent for those well-to-do individuals with significant amounts of capital gain.

Thus, despite some changes in 1969, the tax expenditure items still exert a powerful influence in permitting a very large escape from tax for wealthy individuals, and may for some still permit full escape. While complete post-1969 data are not yet available, the data so far published support the view that the wealthy still escape tax as a result of the tax expenditure system despite the 1969 changes. Effective tax rates on total income are still far below the statutory tax table rates for wealthy taxpayers. A study by Joseph A. Pechman and Benjamin A. Okner of the Brookings Institution for the Joint Economic Committee, based on 1972 incomes and current tax rules after the 1971 Act, shows an effective tax rate of 33 percent on actual income for those with incomes above $1 million (Table 3.3).[15] In judging these figures, we should remember that the effective tax rate under the present statutory tax rate tables for an individual whose actual net income (counting income from all sources less the expenses of earning that income) is $100,000, should be 45 percent; for $500,000, 64 percent; and for $1 million, 67 percent.

The actual income in Table 3.3, referred to as "expanded adjusted gross income" (Expanded AGI), includes the following (Table 3.4):[16]

The effect of the 1969 Act, through the increase of the top capital gain rate from 25 percent to 35 percent, has therefore kept the effective rate from actually declining in the very top brackets, as it did prior to 1969 (e.g., Table 3.2).[17]

Additional tables in the appendix to this chapter, also from the study by Pechman and Okner, show the distribution by income classes of the various tax expenditure items used in the text.[18] The appendix also contains tables

Table 3.3   Distribution of Expanded Adjusted Gross Income[a] and
Federal Individual Income Tax by Income Classes, 1972[b] (Income
classes in thousands; other dollar amounts in millions)

| Expanded AGI class | Expanded AGI | Federal individual income tax[c] | |
		Current law taxes	Percentage of expanded AGI
Under $3	$ 8,014	$ 34	.4
$3 to $5	27,611	468	2
$5 to $10	144,987	7,632	5
$10 to $15	216,272	18,788	9
$15 to $20	180,520	19,319	11
$20 to $25	109,880	13,287	12
$25 to $50	144,670	20,939	15
$50 to $100	39,511	9,104	23
$100 to $500	29,713	8,527	29
$500 to $1,000	4,227	1,273	30
$1,000 and over	6,906	2,244	33
All classes	$912,311	$101,614	11.1

[a]Expanded adjusted gross income is adjusted gross income as defined in the Internal Revenue Code modified to include the income items listed in table 3.4 below.
[b]Based on projections of individual income sources from 1966 levels. Assumes personal income of $925,000,000,000 in 1972.
[c]Revenue Act of 1971 applied to 1972 incomes. The tax liability figures differ from those published in the U.S. Budget because of different estimating procedures, particularly those related to capital gains.
Note: Details may not add to totals because of rounding.

included in the pamphlet on "Estimates of Federal Tax Expenditures" published by the House Committee on Ways and Means in June 1973 and referred to in Chapter I, which show the distribution of tax expenditure items by adjusted gross income classes. The estimates differ in a number of situations, the committee figures usually being lower.[18-1]

The Treasury statistics for 1970 indicate that about 106 individuals had adjusted gross income above $200,000 but paid no income tax.[19] Data for earlier years had indicated a rising trend considerably above this figure – 154 for 1966, 222 for 1968 and 301 for 1969.[20] The drop to around 100 indicates the effect of the 1969 Act, as described above — largely the elimination of the unlimited charitable contributions deduction and the adoption of the minimum tax. The figure of 106 may include some returns where the absence of tax can be explained on grounds other than the presence of tax expenditure items. Indeed, the Treasury has gone to great lengths in its attempts to explain away these 106 returns. The gap in its explanations, however, is that it does not give the actual income of these individuals, so that it is impossible to weigh

Table 3.4   Comparison Between Adjusted Gross Income, Taxable
Income, and Tax Liability Under Present Law and Under an
Expanded Adjusted Gross Income Base, 1972 Income Levels
(In millions)

Item	Adjusted gross income[a]	Taxable income	Tax liability
Present law[b]	$776,146	$478,230	$102,888
1/2 Realized capital gains	17,148	16,547	8,041
Constructive realization of gain on gifts and bequests	10,403	9,553	3,725
Tax-exempt state and local bond interest	1,916	1,892	1,086
Other preference income[c]	1,054	980	424
Dividend exclusion	1,969	1,751	476
Interest on life insurance policies	9,417	9,091	2,016
Homeowners' preferences[d]	15,545	28,686	7,278
Transfer payments	79,751	54,941	10,812
Personal exemptions and deductions[e]		42,075	10,897
Equals: Expanded AGI tax	$913,849	$643,746	$147,643

[a]The increase in taxable income is greater than the change in adjusted gross income
because the elimination of certain exemptions and deductions increases taxable income but
does not affect adjusted gross income.
[b]Revenue Act of 1971 applied to 1972 incomes. The tax liability figures differ from those
published in the U.S. Budget because of different estimating procedures, particularly those
related to capital gains.
[c]Excess of percentage over cost depletion and accelerated over straight-line depreciation.
[d]Includes effects of adding net imputed rent and disallowing itemized deductions for
mortgage interest and real estate taxes.
[e]Includes effect of eliminating the retirement income credit.
Note: Details may not add to totals because of rounding.

the explanations. The Treasury explanations carefully avoid giving the data
for each individual case, but instead lump various cases together and provide
only overall totals, so that it is impossible to obtain from such aggregate data
what is actually the situation in particular cases.[21]

The shift of a number of returns out of the "no tax" class into a minimum
tax payment tells us even more about the present escape from tax even after
the 1969 Act changes. Thus, Representative Henry S. Reuss has indicated that
394 individuals with adjusted gross incomes over $100,000 paid no tax in
1970.[22] Another group of 318 individuals at this income level did pay a
minimum tax. Representative Reuss stated that the minimum tax paid
averaged 3 percent for those individuals in the level of $100,000-$500,000

adjusted gross income; 4.42 percent for those in the $500,000-$1 million level; and 3.95 percent for those above $1 million.[23] These figures show that the "no tax" group is but the exposed segment of a larger group that is paying in tax only a very low percentage of their actual income.

A complete picture would require data on the actual income of: (1) those individuals with high adjusted gross incomes — and higher actual incomes — who pay no income tax; (2) those individuals with high adjusted gross incomes — and higher actual incomes — who pay a small amount of regular income tax and perhaps minimum tax and hence do not show up in the "no tax" list; and (3) those individuals who have low adjusted gross incomes or who have a tax "loss" on their returns and hence do not show up in the high adjusted gross income list, but who have high actual incomes and who may or may not pay a minimum tax.[24] The minimum tax, according to Representative Reuss's figures, does not place a significant burden on these individuals with high total income who pay no regular tax or only a small amount.[25]

The tax expenditure analysis can be rephrased in terms of the answer to the question: "Why don't wealthy persons pay income tax in the United States?" The factors described in the Treasury Studies and subsequent analyses as responsible for the complete escape from tax by some persons with large incomes and for low tax payments by others in this group are all tax expenditure provisions. They are all found in the Tax Expenditure Budget — capital gains; tax-exempt interest; excess depreciation on buildings and rental housing; charitable contributions; farm treatment; treatment of natural resources; personal deductions; and so on. While interest paid on loans to carry investment or business assets is not in that budget,[26] the deduction for that interest works its tax reduction in these tax escape situations by being combined with tax expenditure items. As a result of those items there can be no taxable income, or at least no current taxable income, earned through the use of the loans. Since there is no income produced by the loan to absorb the interest deduction, that deduction therefore can be used to offset other current income.

The cause of the escape from tax by wealthy individuals therefore is not to be found in the basic income tax structure but rather in the tax expenditure apparatus imposed upon that structure. If we are to restore fairness to the tax system and to end this intolerable escape by high-income individuals from a share of the tax obligations, our sights must be set on the Tax Expenditure Budget.

Tax Expenditures and Classes of Individuals

The tax expenditure items affect individuals in a great variety of ways but with varying impact, depending on the particular facet of an individual's earning or spending patterns that is involved. Some indication of the differing consequences may be obtained by examining several of these facets.

Individual as Consumer. The largest overall benefits from the tax expenditure items go to the individual in his capacity as a consumer. The overall amount is $20.7 billion.[27] Thus, we can include here tax expenditures for the following purposes:

Home ownership ($6.8 billion)
    deduction of interest on mortgages on owner-occupied homes
    deduction of property taxes on owner-occupied homes
State and local government services ($5.3 billion)
    deduction of nonbusiness state and local taxes (other than on owner-
        occupied homes)
Medical services ($1.9 billion)
    deduction of medical expenses
Credit purchases ($1.1 billion)
    deduction of interest on consumer credit
Education ($765 million)
    additional personal exemption for students
    exclusion of scholarships and fellowships
Casualty losses ($150 million)
    deduction for casualty losses
Child care and household expenses ($180 million)
    deduction for child care and household expenses

We can also here classify the support of philanthropy and of the election process as representing an individual's choice of how to spend his funds:

Support of philanthropy ($3.4 billion)
    deduction for charitable contributions
    deduction for contributions to educational institutions
Support of election process ($100 million)
    credit and deduction for political contributions

Finally, we would here include the overall standard deduction (in excess of the minimum standard deduction or low income allowance) allowed as an alternative to the itemization of personal expense deductions:

Standard deduction ($1 billion)

Several overall aspects may be considered. Most of the benefits to the consumer are provided through the deduction for personal expenses either as itemized, separate deductions or in the form of the standard deduction — indeed, all but the benefits for education (personal exemption for students and exclusion of scholarships and fellowships rather than a deduction) and the election process (can obtain either credit or deduction). Since benefits are in the form of deductions, exemptions or exclusions, they are of greater value to the individuals in the higher brackets. The amounts involved are subtracted from the top layer of income and hence are worth more, the higher the marginal rate of tax. Thus, the wealthier the individual who is spending the consumption dollar benefited by a tax expenditure, the greater is the assistance paid by the Government. Also, the higher the tax brackets of the individuals benefited, the greater is the amount spent in absolute terms for these items. Thus, itemized deductions as a percentage of adjusted gross income ran in 1969 from around 21 percent for the brackets $5,000-$10,000; 17 percent for the brackets $10,000-$20,000; 14 percent for the brackets $20,000-$100,000; and 19 percent for the brackets over $100,000.[28] The standard deduction after 1973 is 15 percent of adjusted gross income, for a maximum of $2,000. The open-endedness of some of these benefits — such as those for owner-occupied homes and philanthropy — also favors the better-off taxpayers. Only the deduction for child care and household expenses has a built-in factor that limits its benefit to individuals with incomes below $27,600.[29] The tax benefits from the treatment of these consumption expenditures are a considerable factor in reducing effective rates of tax for individuals from $10,000 to $50,000 or so, and the bulk of the amounts removed from the tax base is in these brackets.[30]

There is of course an erratic character to the total structure of consumer assistance provided by these tax expenditure items. Housing is assisted if home ownership is involved but not if rental quarters are utilized. Food and clothing purchases are not assisted. Medical services are assisted. Transportation by automobile is assisted where a credit purchase is involved and through deduction of the state and local taxes on gasoline, but direct expenses for other transportation are not assisted. The assistance for education is spotty. These consequences flow from the combination of planned and unplanned tax expenditures — the medical expense and charitable contribution items were planned, but the benefits represented by the deductions for interest and taxes have historical origins that do not present a similar degree of planning.[30-1]

Individual as Investor. The next largest set of benefits — over $13 billion — goes to the individual as an investor. One group of tax expenditure items in this category involves generalized investment activities of individuals which as a market or institutional matter can be readily pursued by them. These are:

General Investment Activities ($12 billion)
    Stock investments
        capital gain treatment in general
        exclusion of $100 of dividends
    Bond investments
        exclusion of interest on state and local obligations

Life insurance
    exclusion of interest on life insurance savings
Real estate generally
    capital gain treatment in general

A second group of tax expenditure items are of benefit only to sophisticated investors. These items essentially involve the tax shelter type of operation that produces large immediate deductions — "tax losses" — available to offset other income. These are:

Specialized Tax Shelter Investments ($1 billion plus)[31]
    Buildings — commercial, rental housing, and so on
        deduction of excess depreciation
        five-year amortization of housing rehabilitation expenditures
        deferral of capital gain on sale to occupants of certain low-income
            housing
        capital gain treatment in general
    Natural Resources
        expensing of exploration and development costs
        deduction of excess of percentage over cost depletion
        capital gain treatment of royalties on coal and iron ore
        capital gain treatment in general
    Agriculture — cattle, orchards, and so on
        expensing of raising and other costs
        capital gain treatment in general
    Leasing of equipment
        five-year amortization of railroad rolling stock
        deduction of excess depreciation: asset depreciation range
            approach, i.e., class lives for depreciation — 20 percent
            reduction
        capital gain treatment in general
    Timber
        capital gain treatment for certain timber income

As one would expect, we are here concerned with well-to-do individuals. This is certainly the case for the specialized tax shelter investments, where the general image is that of an investor in at least the 50 percent tax bracket. This is also largely the case for investments in state and local obligations. Moreover, while some moderate income individuals own stocks, the great bulk of investments in stocks are made by upper income individuals.[32] Capital gains are thus a predominant item of income for these individuals. Only the $100 exclusion of dividends can be said to be a tax expenditure designed with small investors in mind, though the bulk of its benefits in dollars goes to individuals with incomes above $15,000 simply because of the concentration of stock ownership and the fact that the exclusion comes off of the top layer of income. The tax expenditure item for life insurance is of greatest benefit for upper middle-income taxpayers for whom life insurance may be a significant form of investment.[33] In all of these cases the exclusions involved and the effects of the benefits are such as to reduce the top layer of income, and the extent of the benefits therefore turns on the marginal rate of tax. The wealthier the taxpayer who is making the investment, therefore, the greater the Government assistance to the investor per dollar of investment income benefited.

The tax benefits for capital gains overshadow all other items in their effect on the taxes paid by wealthy individuals. These benefits include both the exclusion of one-half of realized capital gain income and the exemption of the entire appreciation in value from decedents' income tax returns despite the allowance of a fair market value basis in the hands of the heirs. For individuals above the $100,000 income level, it is these benefits that cause the large reductions in effective tax rates on total income.[34] These individuals receive around 50 percent of the tax benefits of the capital gain exclusion. They number about 200,000 families out of 70 million taxpaying families. These benefits permit the accumulation of great personal wealth by these individuals. In turn, weak estate and gift taxes permit the transmission of much of that wealth to succeeding generations, to benefit anew from the capital gains provisions. All this is accomplished despite the progressivity of the tax rate schedules under these taxes, reaching into the 70 percent brackets, and despite the presence of a corporate income tax rate close to 50 percent. The difference between those printed rates and their actual effects on the accumulation of wealth lies in the tax expenditures for investors, and primarily in the benefits for capital gains.

Individual as Earner of Wages, Salaries, or Professional Income. A group of tax expenditure items is associated with the compensation of employees. Essentially, these items involve the "fringe benefits" provided by employers under present practices of industrial, commercial, and other private, and even public, employment. These benefits generally extend over the entire range of wages and salaries paid. They include:[35]

> *General Wage and Salary Employees* ($9.4 billion)
>> Fringe benefits provided by employers
>>> treatment of pension plans
>>> exclusion of medical insurance premiums and medical care programs
>>> exclusion of premiums on group term life insurance
>>> exclusion of meals and lodging
>>> exclusion of sick pay

exclusion of employee death and accident benefits
exclusion of privately financed supplementary unemployment
benefit plans
Government programs
exclusion of unemployment insurance benefits
exclusion of workmen's compensation benefits[36]
Government particular employment
exclusion of benefits and allowances to Armed Forces personnel

All of the above items, with the exception of the sick pay exclusion which is limited to a $100 weekly rate and, less significantly, of the group term life insurance exclusion which is limited to insurance under $50,000, extend to *executives* as well as wage and salary earners generally. Executives specially benefit from the treatment of pension plans in view of the large pensions they may receive, and from large group term insurance contracts. In addition, they benefit from two other tax expenditure items:

Executive Compensation
exclusion of certain income earned abroad and income earned in the
United States possessions[37]
treatment of stock options (included under capital gain treatment)

A *self-employed person* does not obtain the benefit of these tax expenditure items, with the exception of the exclusion for income earned abroad and the treatment of pension plans, though their benefits under the latter are considerably restricted by statutory limitations not applicable to the executive.[38]

All of these tax expenditure items operate by way of exclusion from gross income, so that the tax benefit from the amount excluded is determined by the employee's marginal tax rate. Here also, therefore, the more highly compensated the employee, the greater the Government assistance given to him per dollar of compensation benefited. For the highly compensated employee, the methods of compensation involved in these tax expenditure items interact with other available methods of compensation to form the ingredients of an "executive compensation package" which can be tailored to the executive's personal position and taste.[39] Essentially, the criteria turn on such factors as whether the executive prefers present benefits, in which event he will stress fringe benefits, group life insurance, and stock options if he has faith in the possibility of appreciation in the value of the stock; or whether he prefers future benefits, in which event he will stress pension arrangements and deferred compensation contracts.[40] Or he may stress the prestige factors, and stock options still carry this aspect.[41] In a publicly held company, he will presumably participate normally in the general fringe benefit arrangements in any event.[42] In closely held companies, the corporation and the shareholder-executive can almost freely plan the compensation package.

Top executives — and the top self-employed — also benefit, as respects their compensation, from the presence of investor tax expenditure items in our tax system as a result of an undesirable change introduced in 1969. This is the maximum tax on earned income, which sets a ceiling of a 50 percent marginal rate on earned income.[43] The reason stressed by Congress in adopting this approach was the belief that it would "reduce the pressure for the use of tax loopholes." The House Ways and Means Committee stated:

> The 50 percent limit on the tax rate applicable to earned income was adopted not as a tax relief measure but to reduce the pressure for the use of tax loopholes. Your committee concluded that one of the most effective ways to prevent the use of any remaining tax avoidance devices and to forestall the development of new methods of tax avoidance is to reduce the incentive for engaging in such activities by reducing the high tax rates on earned income.
>
> A major motivation for tax avoidance is to protect earned income from the top bracket rates by engaging in activities which create artificial losses or convert what would otherwise be earned income into capital gains.[44]

These "tax avoidance devices" referred to are the tax expenditure items applicable to investors and stock options in the case of executive compensation. Hence the tax system becomes involved in a circular process by which the tax expenditure apparatus first undercuts the effect of the regular rate structure for some forms of income and Congress then reacts not by dealing with the tax expenditure items themselves but by lowering the top rates on income not benefited by those items. The result, of course, is a weakening of the progressive character of the income tax system as a whole. It resembles the policies of less developed countries which, when faced with noncompliance by some sectors of the economy, react by reducing the income tax on other sectors rather than seeking to enforce compliance. It is not the path to effective taxation of incomes. Moreover, the reason advanced in the above Committee Report excerpt seems hardly credible. The executive in the 50 percent top marginal bracket is still attracted by the tax shelters, which are in general structured for that tax rate level. Moreover, his investment income is taxed at the marginal rates that would apply in the absence of the maximum rate — i.e., is still pushed into top brackets by the earned income — and the executive is interested in sheltering that investment income. While certain tax preferences — not all — offset the earned income eligible for the 50 percent maximum rate,[45] the effectiveness of tax shelters can outweigh that consequence. Consequently, one can expect that highly compensated executives and professional people will still be exploring the shelters provided by the tax expenditure items.[46] All in all, considering the complications it introduces, the limited benefits it supplies for all but a few highly compensated individuals, its ineffectiveness in reducing tax planning pursuits, and its inconsistency with a progressive tax structure, the maximum tax represents an unfortunate turn of the tax wheel.[47]

As to wage and salary employees generally, the tax expenditure items represent an aspect of the "wage package" that is tax-free and hence carries a special benefit per dollar of compensation compared with straight wages and salary.[48] Of course, some of the benefits are indirect in the sense that they save current expenses rather than constitute direct cash — as in the case of medical care, group term insurance, pension programs, and meals and lodging — and employees may prefer immediate spendable cash. But on the whole these fringe benefits are generally a part of the wage bargain in most unionized industries and concerns. Employees in smaller companies and not so well protected may not share in the benefits of these tax expenditure items. As a consequence, the governmental financial assistance represented by these items generally is skewed to employees in the unionized and better-paid industries.[49]

Individual as Recipient of Income Transfer Payments. The last set of tax expenditure items — $4 billion — is that involving or resembling income transfer payments to individuals. These payments are intended to provide assistance for those in need or otherwise to relieve hardships and can in general be styled welfare payments:

Income Transfer or Welfare Payments ($3.6 billion)
provisions relating to elderly: additional personal exemption, retirement income credit, and exclusion of social security and railroad retirement benefits
exclusion of public assistance benefits
additional personal exemption for blind

We can also here include the item relating to veterans:

Veterans Benefits ($480 million)
exclusion of certain benefits, such as pensions due to disability or paid by the Veterans Administration to veterans over age 65

While some of these items are limited to low-income individuals, such as public assistance payments, most cover individuals in all brackets. Since the mechanics of these items generally turn on an exclusion from income, the tax benefit is determined by the recipient's marginal tax rate. Here also, therefore, the better off the individual, the greater the Government financial assistance

67

given to him per dollar of transfer payment. Thus, about 57 percent of the transfer payments excluded from income are received by individuals with incomes above $10,000, and 68 percent of the tax benefits are obtained by this group. Over 40 percent of the tax benefits are received by individuals with incomes over $15,000.[50] This high allocation to these income groups is the result of the exclusion of social security retirement payments. While the exclusion of transfer payments is the most important tax expenditure for individuals in the $3,000-$10,000 range, it remains a dominant or significant item for individuals up to $50,000.[51]

An exception to the use of the mechanism of exclusion is the retirement income credit, the mechanics of which involve a credit against tax of 15 percent of retirement income up to a maximum retirement income of $1,524 for a single person, $2,286 for a married couple with one earner, and $3,048 for a married couple with two earners. The general purpose here is to provide the equivalent of an exclusion benefit measured by the average tax rate applicable to the first few tax brackets. But while the general impression is that the tax expenditures for the aged are to assist those elderly who are hard pressed, their effect is such that nearly half of the assistance in dollar terms goes to individuals with incomes above $10,000.[52] The additional exemptions and the retirement income credit for the aged are the dominant tax expenditure items for the under $3,000 income class, and are a significant item in the $3,000–5,000 class.[53] It must be noted, since we are here concerned with essentially welfare type assistance, that no assistance is given by these tax expenditures to individuals too poor to pay an income tax.

Overall Effects. The presence of tax expenditure items does favor low income individuals as well as wealthy individuals. This is shown in Table 3.5 from the study earlier mentioned for the Joint Economic Committee.[54]

The table indicates, for example, that elimination of the tax expenditures covered in the table would increase taxes in the first two brackets by 271 percent and 212 percent. The next highest percentage increase would come at the very top, about 97 percent for those over $500,000. But the large increases at the low-income levels are almost entirely limited to the aged.[55] The tax treatment of the aged is an upside-down method of assisting all the elderly, poor or wealthy, by in effect making grants to otherwise taxable individuals over age 65, but not to nontaxpayers. As a method of assisting the elderly, it has its own problems and it approaches the relief of their hardships very differently from the existing direct grant system also applicable to the elderly, which limits its assistance to low-income aged. If we were to separate this special group and confine our attention to the non-aged, then the distributive effect of the tax expenditure system for individuals is quite different from Table 3.5.

The consequences for the non-aged are essentially given in Table 3.6,[56] which shows that the tax expenditure system clearly affects the progressivity, and

Table 3.5   Comparison Between Tax Liabilities Under Present Law and Under Expanded AGI Base, by Income Classes, 1972 Income Levels (Income classes in thousands; other dollar amounts in millions)

Expanded AGI class[a]	Tax liability		Increase in tax liabilities	Percent distribution of tax increase	Percent increase in tax liabilties
	Expanded AGI base	Present law[b]			
Under $3	$ 126	$ 34	$ 92	.2	271
$3 to $5	1,460	468	992	2	212
$5 to $10	13,195	7,632	5,563	12	73
$10 to $15	26,063	18,788	7,275	16	39
$15 to $20	25,649	19,319	6,330	14	33
$20 to $25	17,614	13,287	4,327	9	33
$25 to $50	28,426	20,939	7,487	16	36
$50 to $100	13,352	9,104	4,248	9	47
$100 to $500	14,823	8,527	6,296	14	74
$500 to $1,000	2,527	1,273	1,254	3	99
$1,000 and over	4,407	2,244	2,163	5	96
All classes	$147,642	$101,614	$46,027	100	45

[a]Expanded adjusted gross income is adjusted gross income as defined in the Int. Rev. Code modified to include the income items listed in table 3.4.

[b]Revenue Act of 1971 applied to 1972 incomes. The tax liability figures differ from those published in the U.S. Budget because of different estimating procedures, particularly those related to capital gains.

Note: Details may not add to totals because of rounding.

hence vertical equity, of the income tax. The largest increases in tax that would come from elimination of tax expenditures would clearly fall on those over the $500,000 income level, and significantly so. The next largest would fall, still to an important extent, on the group above $100,000. Put the other way around, the presence of the tax expenditure system reduces taxes by 50 percent for those above the $500,000 income level and 43 percent for those between $100,000 and $500,000. However, it only reduces taxes by around 14 percent for those in the three lowest income brackets up to $10,000 and around 20 percent for the group from $10,000 to $20,000. Of course the tax expenditure system also has a marked effect on horizontal equity, as earlier discussions of the various items indicated. At any income level those individuals who receive income or spend their funds in ways benefited by that system obviously gain as against those who receive their income or use it in different ways. Whether one considers the effect on individuals at the same income level or the effect on individuals with different amounts of income, the tax expenditure system is the primary source of unfairness in our tax system.

Table 3.6 Comparison Between Tax Liabilities Under Present Law and Under Expanded Adjusted Gross Income Base, by Income Classes, Omitting Changes in Transfer Payments and Old Age Exemptions, 1972 Income Levels (Income classes in thousands; other dollar amounts in millions)

Expanded AGI class[a]	Tax liability		Increase in tax liabilities	Percent distribu- tion of increase	Percent increase in tax liabilities
	Expanded AGI base	Present law[b]			
Under $3	$ 40	$ 34	$ 6	.02	18
$3 to $5	543	468	75	.2	16
$5 to $10	8,893	7,632	1,261	4	17
$10 to $15	23,000	18,788	4,212	13	22
$15 to $20	23,802	19,319	4,483	14	23
$20 to $25	16,423	13,287	3,136	10	24
$25 to $50	26,767	20,939	5,828	18	28
$50 to $100	13,175	9,104	4,071	12	45
$100 to $500	14,778	8,527	6,251	19	73
$500 to $1,000	2,525	1,273	1,252	4	98
$1,000 and over	4,406	2,244	2,162	7	96
All classes	$134,352	$101,614	$32,737	100	32

[a]Expanded adjusted gross income is adjusted gross income as defined in the Int. Rev. Code modified to include the income items listed in table 3.4.

[b]Revenue Act of 1971 applied to 1972 incomes. The tax liability figures differ from those published in the U.S. Budget because of different estimating procedures, particularly those related to capital gains.

Note: Details may not add to totals because of rounding.

This unfairness can be demonstrated by looking at the tax expenditure system as one large composite grant to the individuals benefited. The amounts and distribution of these grants are shown in Table 3.7 for both aged and non-aged combined, taken from the Joint Economic Committee Study, and Table 3.8 for the non-aged.[57]

The latter table is the more pertinent. The upside-down effect of the tax expenditure system stands out. On the average, the individual with $3,000 is given an annual grant of a dollar. The millionaire is given an annual grant of $725,865. Whatever may be the defects of direct subsidies, they scarcely have this bizarre distributive effect. Others have addressed themselves to this peculiar system contained in the Internal Revenue Code, graphically describing it as "Uncle Sam's welfare program — for the rich" and elaborating on its upside-down character.[58]

Table 3.7   Average Tax Liability Under Expanded Adjusted Gross
Income and Under Present Law, by Income Classes, 1972 Income
Levels (Income classes and number of families in thousands)

Expanded AGI class[a]	Number of families	Average liability		Difference
		Expanded AGI base[b]	Present law[c]	
Under $3	5,923	$ 21	$ 6	$ -15
$3 to $5	6,874	212	69	143
$5 to $10	19,387	681	395	286
$10 to $15	17,535	1,486	1,075	411
$15 to $20	10,486	2,446	1,846	600
$20 to $25	4,954	3,556	2,685	871
$25 to $50	4,463	6,369	4,640	1,729
$50 to $100	625	21,363	15,467	5,896
$100 to $500	189	78,429	48,926	29,503
$500 to $1,000	6	421,167	204,416	216,751
$1,000 and over	3	1,469,000	742,802	726,198
All classes	70,445	$ 2,005	$ 1,461	$ 1,395

[a]Expanded adjusted gross income is adjusted gross income as defined in the Int. Rev.
Code modified to include the income items listed in table 3.4.
[b]Computed using tax rates of the Revenue Act of 1971 applied to the expanded AGI base.
[c]Revenue Act of 1971 applied to 1972 incomes. The tax liability figures differ from those
published in the U.S. Budget because of different estimating procedures, particularly those
related to capital gains.

This upside-down effect of the tax expenditure system can be expressed in
still another way. Table 3.9, covering aged and non-aged, shows the percentage
distribution of the tax benefits under the expenditure system by family groups.
Table 3.10 shows the distribution for the non-aged alone. The families at the
lower end of the income scale, covering brackets below $5,000, and including
18 percent of all families, receive 0.2 percent of the benefits of that system.
The average families, in the brackets $5,000 to $15,000 and including 53
percent of all families, receive 17 percent of the benefits. But at the upper end
of the income scale, those with incomes over $50,000 and comprising only 1.2
percent of all families, obtain 42 percent of the total benefits.

The income tax law is indeed a curious structure, harboring both a
progressive income tax system and tax expenditure grants for the well-to-do.
The grant system serves to undercut the progressive income tax system and
to leave us with a complicated mixture which is both a bad tax system and
a bad grant system.

Table 3.8 Average Tax Liability Under Expanded Adjusted Gross Income, Omitting Changes in Transfer Payments and Old Age Exemptions, and Under Present Law, by Income Classes, 1972 Income Levels (Income classes and number of families in thousands)

| Expanded AGI class[a] | Number of families | Average liability | | Difference |
		Expanded AGI base[b]	Present law[c]	
Under $3	5,923	$ 7	$ 6	$ 1
$3 to $5	6,874	79	69	10
$5 to $10	19,387	459	395	64
$10 to $15	17,535	1,312	1,075	237
$15 to $20	10,486	2,270	1,846	424
$20 to $25	4,954	3,315	2,685	630
$25 to $50	4,463	5,998	4,640	1,358
$50 to $100	625	21,080	15,467	5,613
$100 to $500	189	78,190	48,926	29,264
$500 to $1,000	6	420,833	204,416	216,417
$1,000 and over	3	1,468,667	742,802	725,865
All classes	70,445	$ 2,002	$ 1,461	$ 1,391

[a]Expanded adjusted gross income is adjusted gross income as defined in the Int. Rev. Code modified to include the income items listed in table 3.4.
[b]Computed using tax rates of the Revenue Act of 1971 applied to the expanded AGI base.
[c]Revenue Act of 1971 applied to 1972 incomes. The tax liability figures differ from those published in the U.S. Budget because of different estimating procedures, particularly those related to capital gains.

Tax Expenditures and the Tax Liabilities of Corporations

The items in the Tax Expenditure Budget have a material effect on the tax payments made by corporations. Just as in the case of individuals, we can here utilize the concept of effective rate of tax to describe the impact of the tax expenditures. The corporation tax is generally referred to as a 48 percent tax on corporate net income. If, then, taxable income for corporate income tax purposes and book income for corporate non-tax purposes, such as reporting to shareholders and creditors, were the same, the actual effective rate of corporate tax would correspond to the tax rate set forth in the Code. This is what would happen if there were no surtax exemption from that 48 percent rate, no special capital gains rate, no special deductions or exclusions, and so on. But these factors do exist, since a glance at the Tax Expenditure Budget shows a large number of items applicable to corporations. As a consequence, the taxable income of corporations is less than their book income, and the effective tax rate is not always 48 percent. Inevitably, the effective rate of actual tax in relation to total income will be less than 48 percent.

72

Table 3.9   Family Distribution of Expanded Gross Income and
Federal Income Tax Benefits, by Income Classes, 1972 Income Levels
(Income classes in thousands)

Expanded AGI class[a]	Percentage of families	Percentage of expanded AGI	Percentage of income tax benefits
Under $3	8	.9	.2
$3 to $5	10	3	2
$5 to $10	28	16	12
$10 to $15	25	24	16
$15 to $20	15	20	14
$20 to $25	7	12	9
$25 to $50	6	16	16
$50 to $100	.9	4	9
$100 to $500	.3	3	14
$500 to $1,000	.01	.5	3
$1,000 and over	.004	.8	5
All classes	100	100	100

[a]Expanded adjusted gross income is adjusted gross income as defined in the Int. Rev.
Code modified to include the income items listed in table 3.4.

Table 3.10   Family Distribution of Expanded Gross Income and
Federal Income Tax Benefits, Omitting changes in Old Age Exemp-
tions and Transfer Payments, by Income Classes, 1972 Income Levels
(Income classes in thousands)

Expanded AGI class[a]	Families	Percentage of expanded AGI	Percentage of income tax benefits
Under $3	8	.9	.02
$3 to $5	10	3	.2
$5 to $10	28	16	4
$10 to $15	25	24	13
$15 to $20	15	20	14
$20 to $25	7	12	10
$25 to $50	6	16	18
$50 to $100	.9	4	12
$100 to $500	.3	3	19
$500 to $1,000	.01	.5	4
$1,000 and over	.004	.8	7
All classes	100	100	100

[a]Expanded adjusted gross income is adjusted gross income as defined in the Int. Rev.
Code modified to include the income items listed in table 3.4.

The Treasury Tax Reform Studies, presented before the enactment of the 1969 Tax Reform Act, contained data on the actual effective corporate tax rate.[59] The data showed that this rate was 37.5 percent for all industries, which represents almost a one-quarter reduction from the theoretical 48 percent rate. This overall rate, however, submerged a series of quite different effective rates for different activities, the rates ranging from 5.3 percent for mutual savings banks to probably close to 47 percent for some services and trades. The Studies, therefore, also presented effective rates for a group of favored industries and some indication of the factors that brought the overall theoretical rate down from 48 percent to 37.5 percent. These are shown in the data of Tables 3.11 and 3.12.

All the factors listed in the Tax Reform Studies as reducing the effective corporate tax rate are found in the Tax Expenditure Budget. Some of the tax expenditure items contained in the data have, however, been affected by the 1969 Act. Thus, the special corporate capital gain rate is raised from 25 percent to 30 percent; multiple surtax exemptions are eliminated (fully in 1975); the excess bad debt deductions of commercial banks are largely removed, but only over a long transition period (ending in 1988), and those of other financial institutions (mutual savings banks and savings and loan associations) are somewhat reduced over a similar transition period;[60] financial institutions are required to treat both their net investment gains and losses as ordinary gains or losses, compared with prior treatment of the net gains as capital gains and the net losses as ordinary losses;[61] the rates of percentage depletion are somewhat reduced (from 27.5 percent to 22 percent for oil); and accelerated depreciation on new industrial and commercial buildings is reduced from 200 percent declining balance to 150 percent declining balance. The minimum tax added by the 1969 Act is also applicable to corporations, where it principally covers the items of depletion, excess bad debt reserves, and excess depreciation. But here also, because of the structure, its effect is not large in relation to the tax reduction afforded by these items.

These changes will have their effects. But a number of industries will still show far lower effective rates of tax than the overall effective rate, and the overall effective rate will still be less than 48 percent. Also, certain industries will be benefited by the new tax expenditure items added in 1969 and 1971, such as railroads and exporters. Moreover, the 1971 Act increased depreciation deductions, through reducing depreciable lives by 20 percent and removing the reserve ratio test, and also reinstated the 7 percent investment credit which had been dropped in 1969. The former change reduces the overall corporate effective rate to 35.7 percent from its previous level of 37.5 percent and the rate for manufacturing in general to around 41 percent, the difference being due to the specially benefited activities. Table 3.13 summarizes the effect of tax expenditures on the effective corporate tax rate.[62]

These tax expenditures — excessive depreciation and investment credits —

Table 3.11 Tax Rates on Corporate Taxable Income Compared with Actual Tax Rates on Total Net Income for Certain Classes of Corporations, 1965 Data (In percent)

	Tax without surtax exemption and without investment credit	Tax with surtax exemption and without investment credit	Tax with surtax exemption and with investment credit	Actual tax on taxable income	Actual tax on total net income
All industries	48	45.8	43.4	42.3	37.5
Petroleum	48	47.8	44.8	43.7	21.1
Other mineral industries	48	46.4	42.7	40.5	24.3
Lumber	48	45.1	41.2	29.6	29.5
Commercial banks	48	45.0	43.4	42.2	24.4
Mutual savings banks	48	43.8	42.4	34.1	5.3
Savings and loan associations	48	41.0	40.4	39.7	14.5
Other manufacturing	48	47.2	44.9	44.4	43.3

The reduction in the effective rate from 43.4 percent for all corporations to the actual rates in the fifth column is due to special provisions for computing taxable income which make taxable income less than total net income for the industries and activities benefited. The following are the principal special provisions involved, and their average effect on tax rates for all corporations combined:

	Percent
Effective tax rate on total net income allowing only the appropriate surtax exemption and investment credit	43.4
Reduction in effective rate due to—	
Excess percentage depletion	2.2
Excess exploration and development cost	.4
Tax-exempt interest	.9
Capital gain rate and definition	.8
Excess bad debt deduction of financial institutions	.6
Multiple surtax exemptions	.3
Excess depreciation on buildings	.5
Western Hemisphere Trade Corporation deduction	.2
Total reduction	5.9
Actual effective tax rate on total net income	37.5

Table 3.12 Factors Reducing the Tax Liabilities of Corporations, 1965 Data (Dollar amounts in millions)

	All industries	Selected industries						Other manufac-turing[a]
		Petroleum	Other mineral industries	Lumber	Commercial banks	Mutual banks	Savings and loan associations	
Total net income	$79,792	$6,861	$952	$542	$3,808	$155	$867	$37,531
Less:								
Excess percentage depletion deductions[b]	4,038	2,858	305		1			527
Tax-exempt interest	1,751	4	2	1	1,096	12	9	75
Excess bad debt deductions[c]	1,167				507	119	541	
Excess depreciation on buildings	950	10						190
Excess exploration and development costs[d]	700	540	20					25
Western Hemisphere trade deduction	346	141	54					116
Equals taxable income as reported	70,840	3,308	571	541	2,204	24	317	36,593
Tax that would be paid except for preferential treatment of capital gains and multiple surtax exemptions	30,745	1,481	244	223	957	10	128	16,445
Deduct:								
Benefits from taxation of capital gains at preferential rate	572	35	13	63	26	2	2	158
Benefit from multiple surtax exemptions	225					2		25
Equals actual tax paid to United States and foreign governments	29,948	1,446	231	160	931	8	126	16,262
Computed tax rates:								
As percent of taxable income as reported: Actual tax paid to United States and foreign governments	42.3	43.7	40.5	29.6	42.2	34.1	39.7	44.4
As percent of total net income: Actual tax paid to United States and foreign governments	37.5	21.1	24.3	29.5	24.4	5.3	14.5	43.3

[a]Total manufacturing excluding petroleum refining and lumber.
[b]90 percent of depletion deduction assumed to be in excess of cost-basis depletion. In the long run this could be less as owners of new mines and wells would have lower current deductions and thus more unrecovered cost for cost depletion.
[c]Excess estimated only commercial banks, mutual banks, and savings and loan associations.
[d]50 percent of exploration and development expenditures assumed to be in excess of depreciation.

Table 3.13   Factors Reducing the Effective Tax Rate of Corporations, 1965 and 1972 (in percent)

		1965		1972
Statutory Rate		48.0		48.0
Less surtax exemption	2.5		2.2	
investment credit	2.4		3.0	
excess depreciation on machinery and equipment-ADR class life system	___		1.4	
Reduction due to general tax expenditures	4.9		6.6	
General effective rate		43.1		41.4
Less exclusion of state and local bond interest	.9		1.8	
excess percentage depletion	2.2		1.8	
capital gains rate	.8		.6	
excess exploration and development costs	.4		.4	
excess bad debt reserves	.6		.4	
excess depreciation on buildings	.5		.4	
Western Hemisphere Trade Corporation rate	.2		.2	
DISC	___		.1	
Reduction due to specialized tax expenditures	5.6		5.7	
Overall effective rate, including specially benefited industries		37.5		35.7

plus a reduction in 1964 in tax rate from 52 percent to 48 percent, have significantly lessened the role of the corporation income tax. That tax in 1963 came to 4.3 percent of GNP, with all amounts calculated on full employment assumptions. Assuming, as economists believe, that corporate profits are relatively constant as a percentage of GNP on a full employment basis, the percentage of corporate tax should not change even though GNP increases, since the tax is not progressive. But the estimate for 1973 is 3.7 percent, a significant drop. The individual income tax, however, has remained about constant — 8.4 percent compared to around 8 percent. This percentage would, other things being equal, rise with an increasing GNP, since the individual income tax is progressive (the estimate for 1973 would have been 10.2 at 1963 tax rates). However, legislative changes in this period, reducing tax rates and increasing personal exemptions, the standard deduction and the low-income allowance, have kept the percentage from so rising.[63]

This decline in the significance of the corporate tax has another facet. Joseph A. Pechman has calculated the impact on individuals of both the individual income tax and the corporate income tax, assuming for this purpose that the corporate tax is borne one-half by the shareholders and one-half by owners of capital generally. He states that for 1966 the combined effective rate on family incomes (total income including accrued but unrealized appreciation on capital assets and imputed rent on owner-occupied homes) ranged from 5 percent at $5,000 to 42 percent for incomes over $1 million dollars. The corporate tax contributes most of the progression in tax payments, its contribution being well over half of the total. The relative contributions of the corporate tax and the individual tax are 29.5 percent and 12.7 percent at the $1 million family income level and 19.5 percent and 16.4 percent at the $100,000–150,000 level, while below the latter level the relative contribution switches. The effect of the corporation tax is also to redress the favoritism shown by the individual income tax to property income as against earned income, so that the combination of taxes is higher for property incomes, except at the bottom where it is the same, and at the top where it is higher on earned income. The combined effective rate at the top — 42 percent — contrasts, of course, with an individual rate schedule in the Code rising to 70 percent and a corporate tax rate of 48 percent. The difference between this effective rate and the Code rates is very largely the result of the Tax Expenditure Budget.[64]

The tax expenditures under the corporate tax can be divided between those items which affect corporations in general and those which are related to specific industries or activities. The following items apply to corporations in general:

> *Tax Expenditure Items Applicable to Corporations Generally* ($8.3 billion)
>> investment credit for purchases of machinery and equipment
>> deduction of excess depreciation — asset depreciation range: class lives for depreciation — 20 percent reduction
>> $25,000 surtax exemption (rate of 22 percent on first $25,000 of income)
>> expensing of research and development expenditures
>> capital gain treatment: 30 percent rate
>> deduction of excess depreciation on buildings (other than rental housing)
>> five-year amortization of pollution control facilities in pre-1969 plants
>> five-year amortization of employer child care and on-the-job training facilities

credit for employment of public assistance recipients under WIN program

Some of these items do have more meaning for some types of corporations. The investment credit and the class lives for depreciation help those concerns that make large investments in machinery and equipment, including special facilities. The special capital gain rate of 30 percent is useful only to the larger corporations with income subject to a 48 percent rate, since small corporations subject only to a normal 22 percent rate are not helped with respect to their capital gains by the special rate. The assistance given to research and development and to the purchase of pollution control facilities presumably is of most significance to particular types of manufacturing concerns. The excess depreciation allowed on buildings assists most those corporations with a need for considerable building space, which they own. And, of course, tax expenditure assistance gives aid only to taxpayers, so that those corporations that are losing money are not assisted, except to the extent that the loss is a reflection of the tax expenditure item and can be utilized against the positive income of other years through the three-year loss carryback and five-year loss carryover.

The *individual in business* obtains some of the tax expenditure benefits listed above, such as the investment credit, expensing of research and development expenditures, excess depreciation, and five-year amortization.

The other tax expenditure items affecting corporations, and individuals in business where relevant, are industry-specialized in their impact, and may be grouped as follows:

Tax Expenditure Items Applicable to Particular Industries ($6.7 billion)
    Natural Resources
        deduction of excess of percentage over cost depletion
        expensing of exploration and development costs
        Western Hemisphere Trade Corporations[65]
        five-year amortization of coal mine safety equipment
    Financial Institutions — Banks and Savings and Loan Associations
        exemption of interest on state and local obligations
        deduction of excess bad debt reserves
        exemption of credit unions
    Lumber Industry
        capital gain treatment for certain timber income
    Corporations with Foreign Interests
        exclusion of income of controlled foreign subsidiaries (deferral of tax)[66]
        items related to activities in less-developed countries:
            exclusion of gross-up on dividends of less developed country corporations

Western Hemisphere Trade Corporations
exclusion of income earned in U.S. possessions
deferral of export income (DISC)
Shipping
deferral of tax on shipping companies
Farming
expensing of raising and other costs, and capital gain treatment
Real Estate
deduction of excess depreciation on buildings
five-year amortization on housing rehabilitation expenditures
Railroads
five-year amortization of railroad rolling stock

The tax expenditure system thus means significant financial assistance to selected industries, with petroleum and other extractive industries, and the financial group of commercial banks, mutual savings banks, and savings and loan associations as the most favored groups. Looking back at the effective rates shown in the Treasury Tax Reform Studies for these industries and considering the changes in 1969 and 1971, we would expect the rate on the petroleum industry to stay about the same, with additional depreciation deductions offsetting the 1969 Act changes in percentage depletion and the minimum tax.[67] The effective rate on other mineral industries should also remain about the same. The effective rate on the lumber industry could rise to reflect the capital gain increase from 25 percent to 30 percent. But since for the average large company in this industry the income artificially treated as capital gain is close to 100 percent of total income, the effective rate will not be much over 30 percent. The tax savings are concentrated in these large companies.[68] The effective rates on the financial institutions will gradually rise over the slow transition to the new rules on bad debt reserves. But the commercial banks, which are the largest buyers of new state and local obligations, will still retain the exemption for interest on those obligations, and this expenditure item has been the one of greatest importance to these banks.[69] One estimate of effective tax rates for financial institutions, after taking account of the 1969 Act changes, is that of 28–29 percent for commercial banks, 26–28 percent for savings and loan associations, and 22–24 percent for mutual savings banks.[70]

As a consequence, apart from the overall effect of the investment credit, the class life — 20 percent reduction system of depreciation, and the surtax exemption providing a 22 percent tax rate for all corporations on the first $25,000 of their income, the significance of the Tax Expenditure Budget here lies in the very important financial assistance provided to a few industries. While attention has been called to the group of well-to-do individuals who pay no or little income tax because of tax expenditures, there has not been comparable attention focused on the large corporations that also escape tax or pay only a minimum tax. Many oil companies are in this category as far as United States income tax is concerned, though they do pay foreign income taxes, and the reason is traceable to percentage depletion and deduction of intangible drilling expenses. But in other industries, such as steel or petrochemicals, a zero tax may also occur although there are book profits. The reasons appear to be a combination of investment credits, excessive depreciation, and the benefits for natural resources, the latter obtained by subsidiaries engaged in that activity and included in a consolidated tax return so that their deductions are applied against income of the consolidated group. Also, a consolidated group containing a subsidiary engaged in the leasing of equipment, or a diversified company with a leasing division, would be able to use the large tax "losses" which leasing can generate because of excessive depreciation combined with a rising volume of leases. Clearly, more consideration should be given by the Treasury and Congress to corporate escapes from tax, so that knowledge of the various causes for the escapes can lead to reexamination of the tax expenditures involved.[71]

APPENDIX TABLES

Table A.1   Increase in the Tax Base Under Expanded Adjusted Gross Income, by Income Classes, 1972 Income Levels (Income classes in thousands; other dollar amounts in millions)

Expanded AGI class[a]	Taxable income		Increase in taxable income	Percent distribu-tion of increase	Percent increase in taxable income
	Expanded AGI base	Present law[b]			
Under $3	$ 882	$ 235	$ 647	.4	275
$3 to $5	9,556	3,159	6,397	4	203
$5 to $10	79,129	46,929	32,200	19	69
$10 to $15	144,981	108,694	36,287	22	33
$15 to $20	132,241	104,487	27,754	17	27
$20 to $25	84,875	67,686	17,189	10	25
$25 to $50	117,029	92,795	24,234	15	26
$50 to $100	36,512	29,108	7,404	5	25
$100 to $500	28,268	19,681	8,587	5	44
$500 to $1,000	3,890	2,148	1,742	1	81
$1,000 and over	6,434	3,309	3,125	2	94
All classes	$643,797	$478,231	$165,566	100	35

[a]Expanded adjusted gross income is adjusted gross income as defined in the Int. Rev. Code modified to include the income items listed in table 3.4.

[b]Revenue Act of 1971 applied to 1972 incomes. The tax liability figures differ from those published in the U.S. Budget because of different estimating procedures, particularly those related to capital gains.

Note: Details may not add to totals because of rounding.

Table A.2 Percent Distribution of Features Increasing the Tax Base Under Expanded Adjusted Gross Income, by Income Classes, 1972 Income Levels (Income class in thousands)

Expanded AGI class[b]	All features	Features affecting the tax base[a]							
		Capital gains[c]	Tax exempt interest, dividend exclusion, excess depletion, and other preference income	Life insurance interest	Home-owners' preferences[d]	Transfer payments	Other itemized deductions	Percentage standard deduction	Additional exemptions for age and blindness
Under $3	100.0	.9	.5	1	4	24	.5		69
$3 to $5	100.0	.9	.4	1	4	57	.5		36
$5 to $10	100.0	3	.7	4	10	62	3	1	15
$10 to $15	100.0	5	1	7	18	38	4	22	5
$15 to $20	100.0	7	2	8	24	27	5	23	3
$20 to $25	100.0	11	2	7	25	26	7	18	3
$25 to $50	100.0	22	4	6	24	21	10	11	3
$50 to $100	100.0	54	7	1	15	3	15	3	2
$100 to $500	100.0	69	14	.3	6		10	.4	.7
$500 to $1,000	100.0	81	11	.1	2	.05	5	.1	.1
$1,000 and over	100.0	90	6	.1	.8		2	.01	.03
All classes	100.0	16	3	5	17	33	6	13	7

[a]Beginning with the Revenue Act of 1971 as it applies to 1972 income and going to expanded AGI base.
[b]Expanded adjusted gross income is adjusted gross income as defined in the Int. Rev. Code modified to include the items listed in table 3.4.
[c]Includes effects of excluding 1/2 realized capital gains and taxation of gains transferred by gift or bequest.
[d]Includes effects of eliminating itemized deductions for mortgage interest and real estate taxes.
Note: Details may not add to totals because of rounding.

83

Table A.3 Influence of Various Provisions on Effective Rates of Federal Individual Income Tax, 1971 Act[a]
(Income classes in thousands; amounts in percentages)

Expanded AGI class[b]	Comprehensive tax rate	Deductions[c]	Exclusion of transfer payments	Homeowners' preferences[d]	Exclusion of life insurance interest	Other tax-exempt and preference income[e]	Capital gains	Actual tax rate
Under $3	2	1	.4	.1	.05	.04	.04	.05
$3 to $5	5	5	4	2	2	2	2	2
$5 to $10	9	9	8	6	6	5	5	5
$10 to $15	12	12	11	10	9	9	9	9
$15 to $20	14	14	13	12	11	11	11	11
$20 to $25	16	16	15	14	13	13	13	12
$25 to $50	20	20	19	18	16	16	16	15
$50 to $100	32	34	32	32	30	30	28	24
$100 to $500	48	48	46	46	45	45	43	30
$500 to $1,000	58	59		51	57	57	54	30
$1,000 and over	62	63		62	62	62	60	32
All classes	16	16	15	14	13	13	13	11

[a]Rates, exemptions and other provisions of the Revenue Act of 1971 scheduled to apply to calendar year 1972 incomes.
[b]Expanded adjusted gross income is adjusted gross income as defined in the Int. Rev. Code modified to include the income items listed in table 3.4.
[c]Includes effect of eliminating the percentage standard deduction; curtailing itemized deductions other than those for homeowners, eliminating age and blindness exemptions; and eliminating retirement income credit.
[d]Includes effect of disallowing personal deductions for mortgage interest and real estate taxes and taxing net imputed rent.
[e]Includes effect of taxing interest on state and local government bonds; disallowing excess of percentage over cost depletion; disallowing excess of accelerated over straight-line depreciation; and removing dividend exclusion.

Table A.4 Revenue Effect of Features Increasing the Tax Base Under Expanded Adjusted Gross Income Tax, by Income Classes, 1972 Income Levels (Income classes in thousands; amounts in millions)

Expanded AGI class[b]	All features	Capital gains[c]	Revenue tax exempt interest, dividend exclusion, excess depletion, and other preference income	Effect of features affecting the tax base[a]					Additional exemptions for age and blindness[e]
				Life insurance interest	Home-owners' preferences[d]	Transfer payments	Other itemized deductions	Percentage standard deduction	
Under $3	90	-.9	-.02	1	4	22	.4		64
$3 to $5	985	8	4	12	40	550	5		367
$5 to $10	5,539	156	39	218	564	3,365	174	86	937
$10 to $15	7,220	350	82	509	1,288	2,627	265	1,663	436
$15 to $20	6,295	441	110	515	1,489	1,653	329	1,565	194
$20 to $25	4,313	441	99	313	1,088	1,039	334	848	152
$25 to $50	7,719	1,692	321	394	1,868	1,450	894	892	209
$50 to $100	3,680	1,925	275	35	584	103	587	97	74
$100 to $500	5,582	3,862	784	18	313	2	540	21	43
$500 to $1,000	1,203	974	137	1	24		64	.40	2
$1,000 and over	2,128	1,918	135	1	18		52	.10	.80
All classes	44,754	11,765	1,986	2,016	7,278	10,812	3,247	5,172	2,478

[a]Beginning with the Revenue Act of 1971 as it applies to 1972 income and going to expanded AGI base.
[b]Expanded adjusted gross income is adjusted gross income as defined in the Int. Rev. Code modified to include the items listed in table 3.4.
[c]Includes effects of excluding 1/2 realized capital gains and taxation of gains transferred by gift or bequest.
[d]Includes effects of eliminating itemized deductions for mortgage interest and real estate taxes.
[e]Includes effect of eliminating retirement income credit.
Note: Details may not add to totals because of rounding.

85

Table A.5 Increase in the Tax Base Resulting from Various Features Under Expanded Adjusted Gross Income, by Income Classes, 1972 Income Levels (Income classes in thousands; amounts in millions)

Expanded AGI class[a]	All features	Increase in taxable income from							
		Capital gains[b]	Tax exempt interest, dividend exclusion, excess depletion, and other preference income	Life insurance interest	Home-owners' preferences[c]	Transfer payments	Other itemized deductions	Percentage standard deduction	Additional exemptions for age and blindness
Under $3	$ 648	$ 6	$ 3	$ 7	$ 28	$ 157	$ 3	$	$ 444
$3 to $5	6,397	56	24	80	268	3,651	34		2,284
$5 to $10	32,199	975	228	1,291	3,307	20,072	976	432	4,918
$10 to $15	36,239	1,827	419	2,636	6,633	13,737	1,307	7,829	1,851
$15 to $20	27,753	2,005	495	2,352	6,671	7,570	1,426	6,516	718
$20 to $25	17,188	1,811	397	1,284	4,346	4,414	1,278	3,148	510
$25 to $50	24,234	5,247	936	1,337	5,738	5,113	2,535	2,764	564
$50 to $100	7,403	3,987	527	72	1,147	221	1,118	204	127
$100 to $500	8,588	5,946	1,206	27	487	4	824	33	61
$500 to $1,000	1,743	1,416	197	2	34		91	1	2
$1,000 and over	3,124	2,824	194	2	26		77		1
All classes	$165,516	$26,100	$4,626	$9,091	$28,686	$54,941	$9,667	$20,926	$11,482

[a]Expanded adjusted gross income is adjusted gross income as defined in the Int. Rev. Code modified to include the income items listed in table 3.4.
[b]Includes effects of excluding 1/2 realized capital gains and taxation of gains transferred by gift or bequest.
[c]Includes effects of eliminating itemized deductions for mortgage interest and real estate taxes.
Note: Details may not add to totals because of rounding.

Table A.6 Revenue Effect of Selected Features Increasing the Tax Base Under Expanded Adjusted Gross Income, by Income Classes, 1972 Income Levels (Income classes in thousands; amounts in millions)

Expanded AGI class[a]	Excluded half	Capital gains		Tax-exempt interest	Dividend exclusion	Other preference income[b]
		Constructive realization	Total			
Under $3	$ −1	$ .5	$ .9		$ .3	$ −.3
$3 to $5	1	6	8		3	.8
$5 to $10	56	100	156	2	31	7
$10 to $15	126	225	350	12	61	9
$15 to $20	178	262	441	10	82	18
$20 to $25	207	233	441	13	68	19
$25 to $50	1,118	574	1,692	75	144	102
$50 to $100	1,255	670	1,925	118	61	95
$100 to $500	2,709	1,153	3,862	638	25	121
$500 to $1,000	757	217	974	111	1	25
$1,000 and over	1,634	284	1,918	108	.50	27
All classes	$8,041	$3,725	$11,765	$1,086	$476	$424

[a]Expanded adjusted gross income is adjusted gross income as defined in the Int. Rev. Code modified to include the income items listed in table 3.4.
[b]Includes the excess of percentage over cost depletion and accelerated over straight-line depreciation.
Note: Details may not add to totals because of rounding.

Table B.1 Estimated Distribution of Selected Items of Tax Preferences of Individuals by Adjusted Gross Income Class, Calendar Year 1972 (In millions of dollars)

Adjusted gross income class	Exclusion of benefits and allowances to Armed Forces personnel	Exemption for certain income earned abroad by U.S. citizens	Exclusion of income earned by individuals in U.S. possessions	Deferral of income of foreign controlled subsidiaries	Farming: Expensing and capital gain treatment	Timber: Capital gain treatment for certain income	Expensing of exploration and development costs	Excess of percentage over cost depletion	Investment credit	Depreciation on buildings (other than rental housing) in excess of straight-line	Asset depreciation range	Dividend exclusion
0 to $3,000	15	(1)	(1)	(1)	15	(1)	(1)	1	(1)	1	(1)	2
$3,000 to $5,000	150	1	(1)	(1)	50	2	1	5	45	3	(1)	10
$5,000 to $7,000	180	3	1	(1)	90	2	1	4	55	5	(1)	18
$7,000 to $10,000	130	5	1	(1)	130	3	2	11	95	10	1	27
$10,000 to $15,000	115	7	2	1	170	4	9	18	125	19	1	56
$15,000 to $20,000	55	16	3	1	100	3	7	20	90	17	1	55
$20,000 to $50,000	50	17	3	6	185	9	17	75	185	58	4	109
$50,000 to $100,000	4	1	(1)	6	60	8	11	61	80	36	2	20
$100,000 and over	1	(1)	(1)	11	50	19	22	105	75	21	1	3
Total	700	50	10	25	850	50	70	300	750	170	10	300

[1] Less than $500,000.

(Continued)

Estimated Distribution of Selected Items of Tax Preferences of Individuals by Adjusted Gross Income Class, Calendar Year 1972—Continued (In millions of dollars)

Adjusted gross income class	Deductibility of interest on consumer credit	Deductibility of interest on mortgages on owner-occupied homes	Deductibility of property taxes on owner occupied homes	Depreciation on rental housing in excess of straight-line	Housing rehabilitation	Disability insurance benefits	Provisions relating to aged, blind, and disabled					
							Combined cost for additional exemption, retirement income credit, and exclusion of OASDHI for aged	Additional exemption for blind	Sick pay exclusion	Exclusion of unemployment insurance benefits	Exclusion of workmen's compensation benefits	Exclusion of public assistance benefits
0 to $3,000	(1)	(1)	5	1	(1)	30	880	1	8	60	12	25
$3,000 to $5,000	10	15	25	4	(1)	45	820	2	16	95	26	20
$5,000 to $7,000	40	85	95	7	(1)	35	460	2	18	95	41	15
$7,000 to $10,000	145	310	240	14	(1)	35	640	2	34	160	66	5
$10,000 to $15,000	275	845	590	28	1	12	265	1	62	200	96	(1)
$15,000 to $20,000	235	835	640	25	1	7	135	1	55	60	63	(1)
$20,000 to $50,000	285	1,160	1,135	86	3	7	235	1	27	25	65	(1)
$50,000 to $100,000	60	195	340	53	8	3	75	(1)	4	5	5	(1)
$100,000 and over	50	55	180	32	12	1	40	(1)	1	(1)	1	(1)
Total	1,100	3,500	3,250	250	25	175	3,550	10	225	700	375	65

¹Less than $500,000.

(Continued)

89

Estimated Distribution of Selected Items of Tax Preferences of Individuals by Adjusted Gross Income Class, Calendar Year 1972–Continued (In millions of dollars)

| Adjusted gross income class | Net exclusion of pension contributions and earnings | | Premiums on term group life insurance | Exclusion of other employee benefits | | | | Exclusion of interest on life insurance savings | Deductibility of charitable contributions (other than education) | Deductibility of medical expenses | Deductibility of child and dependent care expense | Deductibility of casualty losses |
	Plans for employees	Plans for self-employed		Deductibility of accident and accidental death premiums	Medical insurance premiums of and medical care	Privately financed supplementary unemployment benefits	Meals, and lodging					
0 to $3,000	45	(1)	10	(1)	45	(1)	3	10	5	5	1	(1)
$3,000 to $5,000	150	(1)	40	2	180	(1)	13	35	20	60	12	5
$5,000 to $7,000	240	1	50	3	225	1	22	65	80	155	21	5
$7,000 to $10,000	580	2	95	6	430	1	33	105	195	300	36	10
$10,000 to $15,000	1,080	5	150	10	675	2	37	175	410	460	42	25
$15,000 to $20,000	740	9	90	5	400	1	27	160	380	320	43	30
$20,000 to $50,000	885	93	95	6	420	(1)	28	400	820	435	25	40
$50,000 to $100,000	195	76	15	2	85	(1)	5	130	450	115		15
$100,000 and over	85	14	5	1	40	(1)	2	120	740	50		20
Total	4,000	200	550	35	2,500	5	170	1,200	3,100	1,900	180	150

1 Less than $500,000.

(Continued)

90

Estimated Distribution of Selected Items of Tax Preferences of Individuals by Adjusted Gross Income Class, Calendar Year 1972—Continued (In millions of dollars)

Adjusted gross income class	Excess of percentage standard deduction over minimum standard deduction	Capital gains: individuals	Parental personal exemption for student age 19 or over	Deductibility of contributions to educational institutions	Exclusion of scholarships and fellowships	Exclusion of certain veterans' benefits	Tax credit or deduction for political contributions	Exemption of interest on State and local debt	Deductibility of nonbusiness State and local taxes (other than on owner occupied homes)
0 to $3,000	0	20	(¹)	(¹)	4	20	(¹)	5	(¹)
$3,000 to $5,000	1	70	8	3	26	45	1	(¹)	30
$5,000 to $7,000	12	120	39	7	32	50	2	(¹)	110
$7,000 to $10,000	63	190	102	20	26	110	7	5	335
$10,000 to $15,000	609	340	207	58	19	140	21	10	785
$15,000 to $20,000	254	340	122	70	12	60	17	25	835
$20,000 to $50,000	98	1,260	69	90	6	45	37	125	1,770
$50,000 to $100,000	2	1,080	72	20	(¹)	9	11	375	770
$100,000 and over	1	3,580	21	7	(¹)	1	4	455	665
Total	1,040	7,000	640	275	125	480	100	1,000	5,300

¹Less than $500,000.

IV

Operational Aspects of Tax Expenditures:

Tax Deferral and Tax Shelters

The special tax provisions through which the financial assistance represented by the Tax Expenditure Budget is made available exhibit a large variety of tax reduction techniques. Some tax expenditure items use the technique of exclusion from tax; others the device of a deduction; others the method of credit against tax, and so on. A description of these various techniques has several purposes:

— It is often hard to recognize a tax expenditure item when you see one in the Tax Code. The structure of the basic income tax also uses exclusions, deductions, credits, and the like. Hence, tax expenditure items have no special identification because of the method used. On the contrary, they have a protective coloration obtained through the resemblance of their operational aspects to the basic structural techniques utilized under any income tax system.

— An analysis of the devices utilized to achieve the tax reduction represented by these tax expenditure items may be of assistance in the exploration of remedies to reduce or eliminate those items not considered necessary or appropriate.

— The analysis of these devices also indicates that in some instances the techniques involved may be little understood by the Congress that votes these items and even less so by the public that accepts them. It may well be that Congress and the public are not aware that a certain technique really involves a tax reduction for the individual benefited, or while aware that a tax benefit is provided, are unaware of the full extent of that benefit and, as a consequence, greatly underestimate it. This, as later discussed, appears to be the situation for those items that involve the technique of "tax deferral."

Tax Deferral and Tax Shelters

Devices in General

The devices used are principally those of *exclusion* from gross income (the term "exemption" is often used) and of a *deduction* allowed as a subtraction from gross income in computing taxable income. Much less frequently utilized are the *credit against tax* and a *special tax rate.* Some of the exclusion items — only a few — involve amounts whose inclusion is deferred until a later period. Many of the deduction items represent deductions with no future tax consequences; others — a significant number — represent an acceleration of deductions that would otherwise be taken in later years and hence involve a *deferral of current tax liability.* These several devices are considered below in relation to the situations in which they are used. It will be seen that patterns emerge which perhaps have a bearing on the approaches or remedies useful to lessen the tax reduction benefits if that step is thought desirable.

Exclusion from Gross Income in the Computation of Gross Income

The first step in computing a taxpayer's taxable income is to find his gross income. The device of *exclusion from gross income* — the amount involved simply need not be counted as income of the taxpayer in the computation of his gross income — is used for all of the tax expenditure items benefiting the *individual as wage or salary earner.* The compensation represented by the item — for example, wages paid to an employee who is sick, or meals and lodging provided to an employee — is thus excluded from the taxable compensation received. The exclusion in all cases is off the top layer of income, so that its benefit is determined by the employee's marginal tax rate. The higher that tax rate, the more valuable is the exclusion — the greater is its worth measured in tax reduction dollars. In nearly every case the exclusion ends the matter and no further reflection of the item is involved. In the case of pension plans, the excluded item represents initially the employer contribution to a pension fund and subsequently the exemption for the earnings of the fund derived from the investment of the contributions. On retirement the pensions paid from that fund become gross income to the retired employee. The benefit overall is therefore that of a deferral of tax as respects the ultimate recipient. The employer, however, obtains an immediate deduction for the contribution. The employee on retirement will usually be in a considerably lower tax bracket than during his employment, especially when the tax benefits of the elderly are considered, so that deferral both produces a postponement of tax and the opportunity, usually realized, to have the ultimate inclusion at a lower marginal tax rate.[1] In the case of employee stock options, the excluded income — the value of the stock received on exercise of the option reduced by any

93

cost incurred by the employee — will be included in income on later sale of the stock, but only as capital gain income with the tax benefits accorded to that type of income. There is thus involved both deferral and some permanent exclusion.

These exclusions exist side by side — section by section — with the exclusions that form a part of the basic tax structure, such as exclusion of gifts and bequests[2] or the exclusion of amounts involved on the discharge of indebtedness. There is no identification of the tax expenditure items, and to the reader one exclusion therefore looks like any other exclusion. Each section describing an exclusion has the same statutory aura, both of tax terminology and place in the Code itself. But over half of the Code sections devoted to items specifically excluded from gross income involve tax expenditure items, and the majority of these relate to excluded compensation.

The exclusion device also characterizes most of the tax expenditure items benefiting the *individual as the recipient of income transfer payments,* such as social security retirement annuities and public assistance benefits. A number of these exclusions are not reflected in statutory sections explicitly covering the items, but rest upon administrative action; e.g., the exclusions of social security payments, public assistance payments, and unemployment benefits.[3] The device also figures importantly in the tax expenditure items assisting the *individual as an investor.* Thus, the exclusion characterizes most of the items classified under general investor activities; e.g., tax-exempt state and local bond interest, the first $100 of dividends, and the exclusion of interest on life insurance savings.[4] All of these exclusions are complete when they occur and have no offsetting effect in later years.[5]

The exclusion device does not figure as significantly in the tax expenditure items benefiting *corporations.* It is used in the tax-exempt state and local bond area for financial institutions; the non-grossing up of dividends received from less-developed country subsidiaries when a foreign tax credit is claimed (the failure to gross-up results in the exclusion of that part of the earnings of the foreign subsidiary which represents the foreign tax being credited); and the exclusion of income derived in the possessions of the United States.

In sum, individuals receiving financial assistance under the Tax Expenditure Budget in their activities as wage or salary earners, as investors in general investment pursuits, and as income transfer recipients do so under tax provisions excluding from their income the particular compensation, investment income, or transfer payments involved. The mechanism that thus characterizes these tax expenditure items, which represent about one-quarter to one-third of the total, is the device of the direct simple exclusion from income. But, put differently, this means that in considering the relationship of an individual's taxable income to his total, or economic income, a considerable part of the difference between the two is the result of the direct exclusion of some of his economic income because of the tax expenditure apparatus.

Tax Deferral and Tax Shelters

Deductions from Gross Income to
Compute Taxable Income

The next step in the computation of taxable income, after determining gross income, is to subtract the allowable deductions. The device of a deduction to be so subtracted from gross income is used for almost all of the tax expenditure items benefiting the *individual as a consumer.*[6] This is to be expected, since what is involved is assistance given to individuals on certain of their expenditures, thereby reducing the cost to them of that consumption. The operative way to make an expenditure of money beneficial in a tax sense is to treat the expenditure as a deduction. Thus, a considerable part of expenditures for personal living is made into current deductions from gross income. These deductions have no future relevance and hence represent direct tax reduction rather than tax deferral. They are not associated with any particular income item and hence are free to offset all types of taxable income up to the amount of the deduction. As in the case of exclusions, the deduction comes off the top layer of income, and hence its benefit is determined by the individual's marginal tax rate. The higher that rate, the more valuable is the deduction — the greater is its worth measured in tax reduction dollars.

These tax expenditure deductions, similar to the tax expenditure exclusions, exist in the Code alongside other deductions whose function is to allow for the expenses of earning gross income, such as general business expenses; specific business expenses such as depreciation, bad debts, losses; expenses incurred in the production of nonbusiness income (e.g., expenses of earning investment income such as investment advice). In other situations, the tax expenditure and the business expense are covered in the same section without any differentiation; for example, the deductions for interest and taxes. Again, like the exclusions, the tax expenditure deductions are outwardly indistinguishable from the basic deductions, though they involve about half of the sections devoted to deductions.

The deduction device figures very importantly in the assistance given to the *individual as investor.* For *investments in general,* it is the operative device used to assist capital gains, since one-half of the capital gain is deducted from gross income. But the use of the deduction device for this capital gain assistance is a draftsman's happenstance. We are not dealing with an actual expenditure, as in the consumer situation. An exclusion would be more appropriate since that is what essentially is happening — one-half of the gain itself is not being taxed.[7] At an earlier stage the draftsman did use the exclusion device. The present deduction — in effect an exclusion — has no future effect, and hence involves a present tax deduction with no deferral consequence.[8]

The deduction device is used in all of the assistance given to the individual as an investor in *specialized investments.* Here the use of the device most often has a special effect, that of accelerating deductions that would otherwise be taken in the future over the life of the investment. The tax expenditure

95

approach involves a telescoping of the future deductions into a special deduction, with immediate impact. This special deduction may cumulate all the future deductions on account of the investment into one year at the start of the investment, or into a few initial years with no deductions thereafter, or it may increase the pace of deduction over the earlier years of the investment and decrease that pace in the later years. Essentially, then, the tax expenditure approach here involves a capital expenditure which under normal tax rules would be spread over the life of an investment and provides instead a special deduction having far greater current impact than the normal treatment.

As examples:

— For *real estate,* the device is an acceleration of the deduction for depreciation, so that a far larger portion of the total deduction is made available in the earlier stages of the investment than would occur under proper financial accounting. The device also involves the current immediate deduction of interest cost during construction (such as interest on a construction loan) and taxes paid during construction (such as local real estate taxes), which taxes and interest would under customary financial accounting be part of the capital cost of the building to be depreciated over its useful life.

— For *oil,* the device is an immediate deduction for the intangible drilling costs of an oil well (these are the drilling costs — about 70 percent to 80 percent of the total cost of a productive well — not directly reflected in the cost of tangible items such as pipe), which costs would under proper financial accounting be a part of the capital cost to be deducted over the life of the productive well.

— For *cattle and orchards,* the device is an immediate deduction for the annual costs of raising or developing the animal or tree until it reaches a productive stage, costs which under proper financial accounting would be a part of the capital cost of the asset and be spread as deductions over its useful life.

— For *railroad cars,* the device is a five-year amortization deduction of the cost of the car, which cost would under proper financial accounting be depreciated over the life of the railroad car. This five-year amortization is also used for the costs of *rehabilitation of certain rental housing.*

The deduction device as here used achieves a deferral of tax rather than a once-for-all-time reduction of tax. But since the telescoping into one or a few years of deductions ordinarily spread over many years exerts a powerful cumulative effect on the amount thus pushed into the first or early years of an investment, a very large amount of income can be offset — "sheltered" — by this form of the device. Moreover, the income so sheltered is not limited to that generated by the property whose telescoped cost produces the deduction. Indeed, that income is usually so small in the current year in relation to the deduction that a "tax loss" is created by the investment. The operative tax effects of this "tax loss" are the core of the "tax shelter" investment process which we will later consider in detail. Sometimes the ordinary income deferred by reason of the special deduction is, when later taxed, treated as a capital gain, and thus obtains the benefit of that treatment, which adds to the shelter.

The deduction device is also used in the "percentage depletion" assistance to investors in oil and other natural resources. This deduction is based on an annual percentage of gross income from the resource property, and while it is a substitute for cost depletion (which, like depreciation, spreads the capital cost of a resource over its life), it is not limited at any time by the cost of the resource. It is therefore not a telescoping of future deductions but, instead, produces an offset against income without a future or deferral consequence. Since the deduction cannot exceed 50 percent of the net income from the property, it does not in itself create a "tax loss" effect.

In the case of *corporations*, the deduction device is used in the financial assistance given generally through excess depreciation on machinery and equipment under class lives and the 20 percent reduction in those lives. It is also used in the financial assistance provided to banks and savings and loan associations through increased allowances for bad debts, the deduction having no future effects. Corporations making the investments above described in the case of an individual investor also are given assistance through the deduction device. This device is also used, through five-year amortization, for investments in pollution control facilities in old plants, coal mining safety equipment, and employer child care and on-the-job training facilities.[9] A special deferral of tax approach is used for corporations engaged in export activities. An *individual in business* would, depending on the nature of the business, similarly obtain assistance through these tax expenditure deductions.

*Other Devices — Credits Against
Tax and Special Rates of Tax*

The exclusion and deduction devices characterize the operative form of nearly all of the tax expenditure items. A few additional devices occasionally are seen. The device of a *credit against tax* is used to assist the elderly, who receive such a credit for 15 percent of their retirement income up to an income of $1,524 for single persons, $2,286 for a married couple with one earner, and $3,048 for a married couple with two earners. Here the credit form is used deliberately, instead of a deduction, to eliminate the latter's effect of letting the tax benefit be determined by the taxpayer's marginal tax rate. The credit holds the initial assistance constant — a reduction in tax of 15 percent of retirement income — no matter what the taxpayer's marginal rate may be. The credit device, however, as customarily used, does not involve a refund of any credit amount in excess of the tax liability before application of the credit. Hence, such a credit helps in full only those with a tax liability at least as large as the credit — those with a lesser liability receive *pro tanto* less assistance, and those with no tax to be reduced by a credit receive no assistance.

The credit device is used in the assistance given to investments in machinery and equipment through the 7 percent investment credit. This credit was introduced in 1962, suspended in 1966–1967, supposedly finally withdrawn in 1969, but reintroduced in 1971. The novelty of this credit and the choice of this device as the form for this tax incentive had the effect of associating the credit device with tax incentives generally. Hence, a great many of the tax incentives subsequently suggested — and dreamed up — have the credit against tax as the operative device, e.g., a credit for manpower training, for educational expenses, for investment in depressed areas, and so on. The 1971 Act did add a credit for political contributions in addition to a deduction, the credit here being granted to provide more assistance to taxpayers with marginal rates less than 25 percent than would be afforded by the deduction; but non-taxpayers of course receive no assistance. That Act also added a credit for business employers who hire employees certified by the Secretary of Labor as trained under work incentive programs.

The income tax proper uses only a few credits — principally those for the tax withheld on wages and salaries (where the credit simply operates to recognize the prepayment of tax through such withholding) and the credit for foreign income taxes which, under our international accommodation to other income tax systems, treats a foreign tax as a prepayment of the United States tax. Consequently, a tax expenditure utilizing the credit device stands out with relative clarity and can be readily identified. It thus lacks the protective coloration possessed by those tax expenditures using the exclusion or, perhaps more so, the deduction device, especially where it is a special deduction within a deduction, such as accelerated depreciation for buildings or excess depreciation for machinery and equipment. The credit device also, as indicated above, does not involve the favoritism for the well-to-do individual or large-size corporation that is built into the exclusion or deduction device, since each taxpayer (with tax sufficient to absorb the credit) obtains the same rate of initial assistance per dollar of receipt or expenditure.

For these reasons, the credit against tax device is *a priori* more appropriate for the tax expenditure operation. A number of tax expenditure proposals are therefore framed as credits and supported on the ground that credits are fairer than deductions in these situations. This is so, but it does not sanctify tax expenditure proposals that use the credit device. Credits are better than deductions when the program involves a tax expenditure, but less fair and less appropriate than direct grants. As stated above, a credit against tax is useful only to a taxpayer with enough tax to absorb the credit. If his tax liability is less than the credit, then a part or all of the credit will be wasted. This would not be the result under a direct grant. This difficulty with a credit can be cured by making the credit "refundable," that is, to be paid as a tax refund to the extent the recipient's tax liability is insufficient to absorb the credit. A "refundable" credit against tax thus becomes similar in this respect to a direct grant of money from the Government.

There is still another aspect of the credit device that must be considered. As also stated above, the "initial assistance" provided by a credit is the same no matter what the taxpayer's marginal tax rate may be, as long as there is sufficient income tax liability to absorb the assistance (and even where the tax liability is insufficient if the credit is refundable). In this respect also, therefore, the credit is similar to a direct grant — an amount of money given by the Government to an individual or corporation — assuming the credit or direct grant is structured on the same terms, such as X percent of expenditures for a given purpose or Y percent of income. But here a crucial issue arises. Some direct grants are themselves includible in income, such as agricultural subsidies, mail-carrying subsidies, and other Government commercial subsidies. As a consequence, the amount of the grant becomes in the recipient's hands subject to the income tax just as are receipts from business sources or the like. Indeed, if the direct grant is *not* included in income, the very exclusion of the grant is itself a tax expenditure. For example, the tax expenditure items benefiting individuals as the recipients of income transfer payments — such as social security payments or unemployment compensation — are instances of direct grants excluded from income.

As a consequence, if Government assistance is structured as a credit against tax but the credit itself is excluded from income, the item would for that reason alone constitute a tax expenditure. While some of the proposals for credits against tax would make the credits refundable, none would include the credit itself in income. Government assistance in the form of credits against tax thus has a dual tax expenditure quality. First, since the credit is not a part of the normal income tax structure, but instead represents Government aid run through the tax system, it is a tax expenditure. Second, since that Government aid is not itself included in income, the exclusion of the credit is also a tax expenditure. This latter aspect, like any exclusion from income, of course is more beneficial to those recipients in the higher tax brackets. If the credit were changed into a direct grant, then the first tax expenditure aspect would be eliminated. But if the direct grant was not included in income, then the *exclusion* of the grant would itself be a tax expenditure, similar in this respect to the exclusion of the credit. If the grant were included in income, then there would be no tax expenditure aspect. However, if a credit against tax were itself includible in income, while the second aspect of the tax expenditure character

99

would disappear, the first aspect — that of using the tax system to provide Government assistance — would remain.

Advocates of credits against tax to replace tax expenditure deductions are thus on the right road, but have not as yet reached the proper end. Even if the credits were refundable — which is rarely proposed — and even if they were includible as income — which is not proposed — adding a whole series of credits for this and that would of course be shifting the complexities of the tax expenditure apparatus from one part of the tax return to another part. Further, the proliferation of the credit device would end its identification and instead provide these tax expenditures with protective coloration. Finally, as discussed in Chapter V, while a tax credit may be structured to resemble a direct grant by being made refundable and includible in income, the question remains: Why not resort to the use of the direct grant itself rather than seek only to resemble it through the credit?

The device of the *special rate of tax,* which is a recognizable identification of a tax expenditure, is also used only infrequently. It is the form of assistance provided to corporations on their capital gains, such gains paying only a 30 percent rate compared with the usual 48 percent rate. For individual capital gains, a special rate of 25 percent of the gain may be used where such assistance is greater than a deduction of one-half of the gain, which will be the case when the marginal rate of tax is over 50 percent. But this special 25 percent rate is now confined under the 1969 Act to $50,000 of gains. The special rate device is in effect used as a method of giving assistance to small corporations, through the 22 percent normal tax rate applicable to the first $25,000 of corporate taxable income. Technically, this is achieved by having a 22 percent rate apply to all income and a surtax rate of 26 percent apply to income above the surtax exemption of $25,000. The mechanism makes the exemption applicable to all corporations. But in the absence of a desire to assist small business there would not be a need for two corporate rates, and we would presumably have only a single rate — 48 percent under present rates — applicable to all corporate income. The special rate is in a sense also used to assist Western Hemisphere Trade Corporations, which are allowed a deduction determined by multiplying taxable income by the fraction 14/total statutory tax rate. This formula thus always produces a tax rate for Western Hemisphere Corporation 14 points less than the top rate of tax — at present 34 percent instead of 48 percent. The device was framed with this objective of a constant 14 point rate reduction.

Deferral of Tax — and Tax Shelters

Tax Shelters in General

The tax law requires that expenditures which are capital in character — such as the cost of a machine, building, or other asset — be reflected in computing taxable income by annual deductions over the life of the asset.[10] Each annual deduction represents the allocation of a part of the cost to the gross income from the asset for that year. This spacing, or apportionment, of the cost over the life of the asset is of course also characteristic of financial accounting in the determination of a yearly profit or loss. For machinery and equipment, the term "depreciation" describes the spacing of the cost; for mineral deposits, the term used is "depletion." While a capital expenditure must thus be apportioned through depreciation or depletion over the life of the asset, an expense that is current in character — such as the expense of a repair — is deductible immediately and reduces the gross income of the year in which the expense occurred. It is therefore important that an outlay be properly characterized as a *capital expenditure* or a *current expense,* since both the business and tax treatment of the two are quite different. Moreover, the form of the outlay is not always decisive. For example, wages paid on the construction of a building would be part of the capital cost of the building, but wages paid in the maintenance of the completed building are current expenses.

In determining annual profits from a business or other investment the income tax follows basic accounting principles. The tax expenditure system, however, in a variety of specialized investment situations, as described above, departs from this basic treatment and substitutes instead an acceleration of the deductions that normally would be spaced over the life of the investment. This acceleration may occur through regarding as a *current expense* for tax purposes an outlay which under the basic treatment would be a capital expenditure. Examples are:

> — the current expensing or write-off of the intangible drilling costs of an oil well (about 70 to 80 percent of the cost of the well);
> — the current expensing of the cost of raising livestock (feed, labor, pasturage, etc.) to be sold in later years or held for breeding;
> — the current expensing of the development costs of orchards, vineyards, etc. (irrigation, cultivation, pruning, spraying, etc.) until they reach a productive state (about 60 to 70 percent of total costs prior to productive state);
> — the current expensing of soil and water conservation expenditures, fertilizer costs, and land-clearing expenditures incurred to improve the condition of farm land;[11]
> — the current expensing of interest cost and local real estate taxes related to the construction of a new building.

The acceleration may occur, even though the cost is regarded as a capital expenditure and not a current expense, by altering the method of spreading the cost over the life of the asset so as to *allow a larger portion of the cost to be deducted in the earlier years* than would otherwise be deducted under the basic accounting treatment. Examples are:

> — the use of accelerated depreciation, such as 200 percent declining balance depreciation for real estate, which concentrates 40 percent of the cost of a building (with a 40-year life) in the first 10 years compared with 25 percent under straight-line depreciation;
> — the use of five-year amortization (spreading the cost over five years) of the cost of rehabilitating rental housing for low income persons, of railroad cars, or of pollution control equipment instead of depreciation over the entire useful life of the asset.

In addition to the acceleration provided by these various devices, the tax expenditure item of the 7 percent investment credit furnishes an added return of investment in the initial year. Moreover, the investment credit for computation purposes does not reduce the "cost" of the asset so that the accelerated depreciation deductions (but not the five-year amortization provisions) are still available for the full cost. The investment credit extends generally to machinery and equipment, livestock (but not horses), motion picture films, and some equipment in buildings, such as elevators and certain special facilities, but not to commercial buildings or residential housing.

Under these tax expenditures,[12] the acceleration of the reflection of the cost (and the investment credit where applicable) provide very large deductions in the first few years of an investment, or in the first year itself. One oil drilling fund announcement states 80 to 90 percent of the investment will be deductible in the year of investment. Other oil drilling funds (so-called functional allocation funds) are structured to produce deductions of 100 percent of the investment in the year of investment. Moreover, in other situations the investor's payment of his total investment can be spaced over several years, so that deductions match investments as made. Thus, a prospectus for a fruit plantation indicates that the investments will be spaced over five years, with between 80 and 90 percent of each investment share deductible in the year made. Also, as indicated later, since many investments are made with borrowed funds but with the deductions attributable to those funds available to the investor, his own investment will be offset very rapidly by the earlier deductions even where the total deductions occur over a period of time. Thus, a prospectus for a 15-year lease of locomotives shows all of the investors' own funds offset by deductions in the first three years. A prospectus for an investment in rental housing shows the investor's own funds, invested in three equal annual installments at the outset, returned (for a 50 percent bracket investor) in about one year for the first installment, 2.5 years for the second and four years for the third. A prospectus for the rehabilitation of low-income rental housing shows that the total "pay back" of an investment spaced over four years will occur in 3.5 years for a 50 percent bracket investor and in 2.5

years for a 70 percent bracket investor, i.e., even before the investment is completed. The interrelation of the particular tax expenditure involved with the other operative aspects of the tax shelter produces the variations in these "pay back" periods. But the common characteristic of all these different prospectuses is the very rapid return of the investor's own funds.

The annual income from the investment, however, will either be far lower in these years than the amount of the yearly tax deductions, or nonexistent. Thus, in the case of the oil well just drilled, or orchards and cattle before they reach a productive stage, or a building prior to completion, there will be no income at all from the asset, but the tax expenditure treatment will provide large deductions. Or, in the case of rental real estate, during the first ten years when gross income is reflecting the rents of that period, the tax expenditure deduction for accelerated depreciation will reflect (for a 40-year building) sixteen years of cost.[13]

As a consequence of this imbalance of income and deductions, these investments show a "loss" in their early years. The money invested of course is not "lost." Rather the "tax loss" is simply the reflection of the investment cost itself, showing up on the tax books either as a current expense before the asset is yielding any income at all, or as an accelerated write-off of cost while the asset is yielding its normal, unaccelerated income. An investor in oil does not say on drilling a successful well that he has "lost" his investment. An investor in cattle does not say he has "lost" his investment when he has raised a fine herd of cattle to be sold at a profit or used for breeding purposes. The investor in a fully occupied apartment house does not say he is "losing money" when his rents produce a cash flow that more than covers the cost of his maintenance and the amortization of his mortgage. Yet in these cases, and others like them under similar tax expenditures, the tax returns will show that all these investors have "lost" money on their investments.

What does the investor do with these "tax losses"? He offsets the "losses" against income which he has from other pursuits, as from dividends, capital gains, professional fees, executive compensation, and so on. In effect, he "shelters" that income from tax, since the offsetting "losses" simply eliminate dollar for dollar these items of income from taxable income. None of this is accidental of course. The investor enters the tax expenditure activity with the knowledge of its operation as a tax shelter and usually for the very objective of obtaining the tax shelter result. In fact, the term "tax shelter" is used in investment circles to describe these tax expenditure activities.

In many of these tax shelter activities the before-tax economic profit will be considerably lower than before-tax economic profits in other investment activities that are not associated with tax expenditures. This lower profit rate results from a variety of factors. In the case of low-income rental housing, HUD direct subsidy rules limit the before-tax return to 6 percent. In the leasing of machinery or equipment, the desire of the lessee to share in the tax shelter advantages may result in a very low before-tax return, the precise level turning on the bargain the lessee is able to strike — the lessee is "selling" a depreciation deduction and wants to be paid for it through lower rentals.[14] If the lessee is financially secure and enters into a net lease, so that little or no risk exists for the investor leasing the asset, there may be no before-tax profit at all during the lease, with any possible overall before-tax profit depending on the uncertain residual value remaining in the asset after the lease period is ended. In the case of orchards, the lure of the tax shelter itself may cause overproduction and result in a low before-tax return. Other investments may be too risky for the normal investor because of basic economic factors or characteristics of the investment, such as wildcat oil drilling or cattle raising at certain times. In these situations, however, the effect of the tax expenditure treatment is to produce a satisfactory, often very generous, sometimes extremely generous, after-tax profit. Thus, investments which would never be made for their before-tax economic profit, even if there were one, because that profit would be too low, standing by itself, in comparison with other investment opportunities, are made solely for the after-tax profit that is produced by the tax expenditure treatment.[15]

Put another way, a tax-exempt organization with funds to invest, such as a pension fund or college endowment, would not be found investing its funds in these tax shelters. The before-tax economic return is simply far too low or the investment is far too risky, and the tax shelter advantages are of no benefit to an organizational investor which is itself exempt from income tax. But for the high-bracket individual investor, who also would not invest except for the tax shelter treatment — using some typical examples — a before-tax return of 2 percent on a low-income rental housing rehabilitation project becomes for the 50 percent bracket investor a 24 percent after-tax return, for the 70 percent bracket investor a 66 percent return. The tax shelter for a low-income housing project turns a 4 percent before-tax return into a 23 percent after-tax return for the 50 percent bracket investor, a 40 percent return for the 70 percent bracket investor. The tax shelter on a practically riskless lease of locomotives to a railroad turns a negative before-tax return during the lease into a 21 percent after-tax return for a 70 percent bracket investor. It is for these reasons that the tax shelter investments are aimed at — often restricted to — investors who can expect to be in at least the 50 percent tax bracket over a period of years.[16] In short, these investments are "recommended only to those persons whose income is subject to federal income taxes at high effective rates and thus are in a position to benefit from the treatment presently given such investments under federal tax laws."

There are risks in some of these investments. The oil drilling may not yield any productive wells; the cattle may become diseased or suffer accidents or the prices paid for cattle may drop significantly; the orchard land may turn out not to be productive, or the trees may be affected by weather and disease, or prices may fluctuate; the operation may be badly managed; and so on.[17] But these risks are at least borne for the most part by the Government, since the investment if actually lost is fully deductible as a loss. And a number of situations, as equipment leases and some real estate ventures, present a minimum of risk.

These activities receiving the favorable tax expenditure treatment are specialized investment activities outside the investment situations generally available to individuals with funds to invest. Most of these individuals would normally think of the stock or bond markets or local real estate. The drilling of an oil well in Texas, the raising of cattle in Montana, the development of an orchard in Arizona or Mexico, the construction or rehabilitation of low-income housing in a distant city, the leasing of an airplane or a fleet of railroad locomotives, would not in themselves be regarded as investment opportunities for the doctor or executive or actor with money to invest. Indeed, presumably Congress, if it considered the character of the investor in these tax expenditure activities, had in mind a person really engaged in the business represented by the investment, on the scene and personally involved in the activities. For many individual operators in this situation, however, the tax shelter would not exert its full potential, since the individual might not have sufficient income apart from the activity to use the tax losses provided by the shelter. Also, his marginal tax bracket might not be high enough even for income from the activity itself, disregarding the tax loss, to produce a significant financial assistance effect from the tax expenditure. These tax expenditures thus became tax opportunities in search of investors in high brackets with incomes to be sheltered. A market mechanism was needed to bring the two together.

This market mechanism that emerged is the limited partnership, which joins the high-bracket investors having money as the limited partners with the individual or corporation having experience in the activity as the general partner. The partnership interests could thus be either privately placed or syndicated, and could be marketed by investment houses and others engaged in securing investment opportunities for clients. The tax treatment of the partnership form of enterprise permits the "tax losses" of the partnership to be utilized directly by the partners on their tax returns.[18] At the same time the partnership form insulates the limited partner from any further risk beyond his capital contribution. The investor takes on the "business" coloration of the partnership and obtains the tax expenditure benefits, but keeps his capital investment tightly controlled. The overall tax shelter of the activity operated by the partnership thus becomes a series of smaller shelters, proportionate in size to each partner's investment.

Once this partnership mechanism and private placement or syndication were developed, the tax shelters were no longer anchored to the insularity of the locations and business setting of the activities involved, but could be transported to any area where there was a high-bracket taxpayer with money to invest. The tax escape potential of tax shelters produced by the tax expenditure apparatus thus all at once became enormously enhanced and capable of use. The doctor became an oil driller, the athlete became a cattle rancher, the actor became an orchard grower, the lawyer owned part of a Boeing 707, the executive owned part of a fleet of locomotives, the investment banker became a real estate operator in an area far away — all without leaving their offices or in any way changing their regular activities.[19] The tax shelter business of the partnership became their business, but all neatly handled and packaged for them so that they need never see or participate in their new businesses.[20] The investment counseling houses and others specializing in these activities are thus operating a national supermarket in prepackaged tax shelters.

The syndicators are really not marketing businesses but selling tax expenditure deductions. The tax escape potential of these businesses derives, as we have seen, from the acceleration of the tax deductions for the investments made in the businesses. This is what the syndicators are selling and the limited partner investors are buying — be it in the form of accelerated depreciation in real estate and the expensing of interest and taxes during construction, five-year amortization for rehabilitated rental housing, current deduction of intangible drilling expenses in oil, current expensing of the development costs of orchards, accelerated depreciation and either five-year amortization or the investment credit in leasing.[21] The tax expenditure system makes these deductions marketable commodities in the hands of an oil-drilling company, a real estate developer, a cattle operator, or the entrepreneur with access to a company needing equipment which it is willing to lease.[22] The syndicates they form are merchandising these tax expenditure deductions in the form of "tax losses" generated by the syndicate's operations. These "tax losses" — which as we have seen are not real losses but only the return of the investor's investment through tax deductions — eliminate from tax not only the income from the syndicate's business but, more importantly, other income of the limited partners as well. The "tax losses" thus spill over to be used by the limited partners against their other income — a doctor's fees, an investment banker's commissions, an actor's earnings, an investor's dividends or capital gains, a top executive's salary.

The "selling" of tax benefits has been recognized as undesirable under an income tax. In the charitable area, Congress has acted to prevent charities from "selling" their tax-exempt status. Thus, it has removed from the scope of that exemption unrelated businesses operated by charitable organizations and investments entered into through borrowed funds. In both situations, Congress was concerned that the charity might be splitting its tax exemption benefits with outsiders, either through reducing the prices of goods produced by unrelated businesses which it owned and thereby unfairly competing, or by paying more for investment opportunities than could taxable investors.

106

Congress also has acted to prevent states and cities from "selling" the tax exemption on their bonds to businesses locating in their area. It thus made taxable the so-called industrial bond device under which the proceeds of state and local bonds were used to build plants or other facilities for those businesses. Congress has endeavored to prevent a loss enterprise from "selling" net loss carryovers to a profitable enterprise which sought to apply the purchased losses against its taxable profits.

In all these situations Congress saw a distortion of the purpose behind the tax benefits. It also saw that the "sale" brought undue advantages to the buyer, who usually paid a price far less than the tax reduction he was purchasing. The tax shelters are really but another variant of these activities. The tax advantages bestowed by Congress on certain industries and activities, which advantages are often wasteful in themselves, become even more wasteful where they can be sold to others. Such sales really make the buyers middlemen in passing on Government financial assistance to the sellers. Congress is thereby paying a commission to these middlemen investors so that they in turn will assist companies who desire to drill for oil, developers who wish to construct low-income rental housing, ranchers who want to use range lands or produce cattle, companies that desire to buy equipment. These commissions — the tax reductions obtained by the middlemen investors — are usually quite high, often outrageously so.

In these tax shelter situations, the key question to focus on is: Where does the Treasury money go? The Treasury is incurring revenue losses, and it is these losses — the tax expenditures — that produce the shelters. If we trace this Treasury money as it moves through the shelter device, we see that some of the money goes to those who put the shelter together — the managers of the syndicates, the investment bankers who market the syndicated interests, and the lawyers, accountants, and other advisers who participate in the process. A large part of the Treasury money, of course, goes to the investor who lives in the shelter. In the end only a part of the money goes to the activity which the tax expenditure is intended to assist. Assuming Government financial assistance is needed for the underlying activities involved, itself often an unfounded assumption, Congress could provide that assistance more efficiently by eliminating these expensive middlemen and paying the assistance directly to those engaged in the activities.[23]

One other aspect should be noted regarding these tax shelter investments, and that is the aspect of leverage. Several of these investment areas — perhaps the majority — typically involve highly leveraged investment under which the investor is using borrowed funds for a major part of his participation. Thus, nearly 100 percent debt financing may be obtained on low-income rental housing projects, with this debt-financing guaranteed by the Government. Equipment leasing and cattle operations are generally largely financed through borrowed funds, with the assets as the security.[24] In recent years, some oil-drilling funds have been structured to provide a large degree of leverage.[25]

Leverage is, of course, a traditional aspect of many an investment or business undertaking where the borrower expects to earn a higher rate of return on the use of the funds than he must pay for the borrowed money. He can thus add to the profit he expects to realize on the investment of his own funds the profits to be made on the borrowed funds. This assimilation to his investment of the profits on the borrowed funds produces a much higher rate of return per dollar of his own funds invested. The tax mechanics of these tax shelter investments, however, are such as to accentuate the traditional advantages of leverage, as will be discussed later.[26]

The Ingredients of the Tax Shelter

The tax shelters we are considering involve, in varying extent, three ingredients — the acceleration of deductions or, expressed in another way, the deferral of a tax otherwise presently payable; the use of leverage and the favorable tax consequences of the leverage; and capital gain consequences on the disposition of the asset. The first ingredient is always present; the second is generally present in most shelters with the possible exception of oil ventures, and even here it is now being introduced; the third ingredient is less prevalent — and also, even where present, is often less important in its impact than the other ingredients.

Ingredient of Deferral of Tax[27]

The investor in buying these tax shelter deductions is buying "deferral" of his tax liabilities on the income offset by the deductions. Through this offset he escapes current taxes on current income. He need only pay the deferred taxes when the investment is either closed out or in its later stages — unless before then his advisers may have worked out an arrangement that even escapes that consequence. In a number of instances, this postponement of tax and the nature of the shelter operate to switch the deferred tax liability from ordinary income to capital gain, which often improves the shelter considerably. The Congress, when it has thought about these shelters, unfortunately has usually focused only on the capital gain aspect and moved only to correct it, while letting the tax deferral stand. One has the feeling that "deferral" is not considered by legislators as much of an advantage — after all, the taxpayer is "only postponing" a tax payment that he will have to pay at some point.

Indeed, how could a legislator have cause to think otherwise when he hears a Treasury Department, pushing hard to legislate a tax escape for exporters

— DISC — tell him that only "deferral" is involved in the measure?[28] Or when a President and a Secretary of the Treasury in announcing increased acceleration of depreciation through the use of shortened tax lives unrelated to a taxpayer's replacement experience (Asset Depreciation Range System), state that the "liberalization of depreciation allowances is essentially a change in the *timing* of a tax liability. The policy permits business firms to reduce tax payments now . . . and to make up these payments in later years" (italics in original)?[29]

The syndicators of tax shelters know differently. They are using their computers and investment know-how to explain to their investors just how valuable this "only deferral" and "only timing" can be. They do so by relating the benefits of the deferral to investment yield after tax and thereby directly quantify the present value of the tax deferral. Essentially they are describing the present value to an individual of money in hand — money obtained through having to pay a tax only in the future and not right now. Even short-term deferrals for a year, which are the essence of the cattle feeding and rosebush shelters, are viable tax reduction devices.[30] But who tells this to the legislator? He understands "exemption" from tax liability and will often feel he should do something about that. But he views "deferral" as almost the opposite of exemption and hence not a cause for moral indignation. Indeed, how would one graphically and simply make it clear to a busy Congressman just how valuable is this "deferral" which he often so casually approves because at best he sees it as only a minor benefit? How would one make it clear that very often "deferral" may mean almost as much as "exemption" to the investor in a tax shelter?

I suspect the task of communication is not an easy one. Suppose an individual, A, in the 60 percent tax bracket, invests $100 in an asset. Assume that business accounting and normal tax rules would require the cost of the asset to be capitalized, but that a tax expenditure provision permits the cost to be expensed in the year of acquisition, thus deferring tax liability on the amount of income offset by the special deduction. Assume that the sale of the asset ten years later would produce ordinary income. How do you express or describe A's tax benefit?

Do you use the analogy of the interest-free, nonrecourse loan without collateral? Do you ask the Congressman if *he* would blithely let *his* debtors say they will pay their debts to him some time in the future and forget about interest or security in the meantime? Do you ask the Congressman if he would like to know a bank that would lend *him* money without an interest charge and without any collateral? Do you then say to the Congressman that some taxpayers are aware of such a bank — they call it the U.S. Treasury?

— The immediate deduction of $100 gives A an immediate tax saving of $60. The $60 tax will be postponed until the asset is sold. One way to describe the result is to say that the Government has made a loan of $60 to A without asking for interest, collateral, or a definite time for payment of the loan, since it will wait until A decides to sell the asset. The higher A's tax bracket, the larger the interest-free loan.[31]

— What is this loan worth to A? Assume that borrowing $60 from a bank would cost him 10 percent interest. A thus saves paying 10 percent a year on $60 — or $6 — less the benefit of the income tax deduction of $6 interest a year, or a net saving of $2.40 per year, for a total of $24 if he sells in ten years. The saving from deducting the cost of the asset in the first year instead of the tenth year, expressed in terms of the present value of money, would be worth $19.46 to A (using an after-tax discount rate of 4 percent if A can freely borrow at a 10 percent before-tax rate). Another way of looking at this benefit is to ask: "If A could earn 10 percent on his investment, what would he pay to get this interest-free loan?" The answer would be: "A would be willing to pay up to $19.46."

— A may be able to earn 15 percent on investments that he makes. If so, "A would be willing to pay up to $26.49" for an interest-free loan (using an after-tax discount rate of 6 percent).

Does it help to say that the *exclusion* from tax of a percentage of a given amount of income provides the same benefit as deferring the tax on that income? The particular percentage of exclusion depends on the taxpayer's marginal tax rate, what he can expect to earn on his investments, and the period of the deferral.

— Assume that A can earn 15 percent before tax on his investments. Instead of permitting A to defer tax on $100 of income (through the immediate deduction of the $100 cost of the asset) until a later sale of the asset, here assumed to occur in ten years, the Congress could provide the same benefit by excluding 43 percent of the $100 of income. In other words, A is indifferent between a proposal to exclude 43 percent of $100 of income and a proposal to defer the tax on that $100 income for ten years. Put differently, for a 60 percent taxpayer, the deferral of tax on income for ten years is almost the equivalent of excluding one-half of that income. A twenty-year deferral is equivalent to excluding 68 percent of the income.[32]

I ask these questions with the feeling that putting the matter in this way does not clearly get the point across to a busy legislator of the value of deferral.[33] But how to do it?

There is another aspect that must also be made clear, and that is how the value of deferral increases as the investor's tax bracket rises. This part of the task may be easier. Thus, one method of communication may be to compare the benefit of deferral with an equivalent subsidy made directly by the Government in the form of a grant or a loan. It can then be shown that, the *better off* the investor is and hence the *higher* his tax bracket, then the *more* he would receive as a grant and the *larger* the loan. In this way the lopsided or indeed upside-down character of tax deferral benefits presumably can be seen.

> — In our example involving A above, the higher A's bracket the greater is the "loan" or leverage obtained from the Government, and hence the less of A's money he has to risk to earn a profit. Thus, in any situation in which X dollars are needed to earn a certain rate of profit, if the cost of the investment is expensed, then the result is that the higher the taxpayer's bracket the less is *his* share of the investment and the greater the leverage accorded him by the Government — that is, the less is the amount of *his* money at risk.[34]

Some of the tax shelters, such as oil and cattle, essentially provide for immediate expensing of all or a major part of the investment, so that the example used above of a current deduction in the year of acquisition of an asset is applicable. Other tax shelters, such as real estate and leasing, while not giving immediate expensing, provide for an acceleration of the deduction of the investment cost and hence a very rapid write-off of the investment in its early years. The essentials of the situation are the same, however, with the extent of the tax deferral benefit depending on the degree of acceleration of the deduction.

This discussion of the benefits of tax deferral is amplified in the appendix to this chapter.

Ingredient of the Tax Consequences of Leverage

Any investor who can earn a profit on his investment will increase that profit if he borrows funds at an interest rate lower than the profit he expects to make. His cost for the borrowed funds is less than his return on the investment of those funds. In effect, the difference between profit and cost on the borrowed money gets added to the return made on the investment of his own funds, and the final return on that investment is a combination of the two returns. The result is a significant increase in the profitability of the basic investment.

The ingredient of a deferral of tax has the effect, as we have seen, of turning an investment that may be profitable before tax into a much more profitable investment after tax, or — more likely — of turning a before-tax low profit, or even an unprofitable investment, into a profitable investment on an after-tax basis. Essentially, looking at the dollars invested, deferral of tax considerably lowers the effective rate of tax on the income from the investment — and thus increases the after-tax rate of return. In a tax shelter, the higher return is thus obtained not from the market but through deferral of tax.

That same deferral mechanism can be applied to borrowed dollars, since the benefits of the tax shelter are equally operative for the investor whether the money invested is the investor's own funds or represents borrowed money. The acceleration of deductions that produces the deferral under the tax expenditure provision is also granted by that tax expenditure to borrowed money. The tax shelter investor can thus leverage his investment in the same basic manner as the traditional investor whose profitable rate of return comes through the operation of the market. As a consequence, the addition of the ingredient of leverage makes the tax shelter far more attractive. It permits the net benefits of tax deferral obtained on borrowed money (i.e., after the cost of the interest) to be added on to the tax deferral benefits obtained on his own funds. If the investor's own funds invested in the shelter are small in relation to the borrowed funds, the result is a very pronounced increase in the after-tax rate of return. Since most tax shelters are highly leveraged — 80 percent to almost 100 percent of the total invested — this focusing of the entire tax benefits of the shelter on the thin slice of the investor's own funds produces the very generous after-tax returns that these shelters provide.[35]

The operative mechanics of the tax effect of leverage in these shelters turn on the different manner in which the tax system views the investment of borrowed funds compared to the repayment of those funds. The tax system considers all the dollars involved in an investment in an asset or project, however those dollars are obtained, as making up the cost of that investment, to be deducted by the owner of the asset or project in determining taxable income. The dollars may be the investor's own dollars, or dollars borrowed on other collateral of the investor and with his personal liability, or dollars borrowed on the security of the asset involved and with no personal liability of the investor. The acceleration of deductions provided by the tax expenditures for these tax shelters thus applies to the borrowed dollars. If we consider the before-tax income from the investment as returning both capital — original cost — and profit on that capital, the tax expenditure provides a division that in the early stages of the operation considers all of the income as being a return of capital — in fact, more capital can be deducted than the total amount of income, i.e., the "tax loss" of the tax shelter.

During this period, the investor is also starting to repay the borrowed money. Typically, the money will be repaid under a schedule that amortizes the total repayment, interest and capital, on a level annual basis over the period of the loan. The parties will divide the level annual repayments between interest and capital by considering most of each earlier payment as interest and most of each later payment as capital. Interest paid is a deductible item for tax purposes. The investor in a tax shelter is thus securing large deductions for interest paid on the loan at the same time that he is obtaining under the tax expenditure large deductions to reflect the return of the cost of the overall investment.

The tax system thus views the moneys coming in from the investment as a return of capital, including the borrowed capital, but then views the moneys paid to the lender as a payment of interest, and not as a repayment of the borrowed money.[36] Since under the tax expenditures involved in these tax shelters both the return of capital invested and the payment of interest on borrowed money are deductible, the inconsistent treatment of the moneys coming in and going out produces the tax benefits from the leverage. If the tax system were consistent, so that the borrowed money were treated as an investment in the asset, on which investment the tax expenditure could work its acceleration of deduction effect, only to the extent that the loan was repaid, then the leverage effect of borrowing would not enhance the tax shelter. In effect, in any investment financed in part or entirely by borrowed funds in which the tax reflection of the cost of the investment is faster than the investor's repayment of borrowed funds, the effect of leverage on the after-tax rate of return will be greater than the traditional effect of leverage on the before-tax rate of return. Since the tax shelters are situations in which the tax reflection of the cost of an investment is greatly accelerated through tax expenditure deductions, the effect of leverage is in turn greatly enhanced.[37]

Ingredient of Capital Gain on Sale of Investment

In most of the tax shelter operations, if the asset that is obtained by those operations is sold, the sale transaction is treated as the sale of a capital asset. The gain is in turn treated as a capital gain and obtains the benefits accorded to such gains, principally the exclusion from income of one-half of the gain. "Gain" in the tax system is a technical concept, representing the difference between amount realized on the sale and the "adjusted basis" of the asset sold. "Adjusted basis" in turn is the cost of the asset reduced by any deductions previously taken that reflect a part of that cost.[38] Against this background, the third ingredient of a tax shelter operation — the capital gain effect — begins to emerge.

The acceleration of deductions reflecting cost that constitutes the first ingredient — tax deferral — has the result under the mechanics of computing gain of providing a low adjusted basis for the asset, since those deductions are subtracted from the initial cost. In fact, in many cases the adjusted basis may be zero or close to it. Hence, the sale will almost always produce a "gain" — even where the sale is only for a sum equal to or even lower than the amount

113

invested. In the case of an investment involving borrowed funds, those funds are considered a part of the original cost, and their "return" to the investor through accelerated deductions reduces the adjusted basis. On a sale, the acquisition of the asset by the buyer subject to the indebtedness for the remaining unpaid borrowed funds is considered a part of the amount realized by the seller, whether or not either he or the buyer is personally liable for the repayment. Thus, on an investment with borrowed funds, if the asset is sold before the loan is repaid, there will almost always be a "gain" on the sale since the remaining unpaid loan will automatically become part of the sales price for tax purposes. In the case of a partnership, the funds borrowed by the partnership are considered as part of the adjusted basis of the partners in the partnership, even though neither they nor the partnership may have personal liability.[39] Hence, the same results follow as in the situation of a single investor.

The "gain" in such situations is of course not a real or economic gain, but rather a "tax gain." It is a reflection of the previous acceleration of deductions. The "tax loss" produced by that acceleration is now balanced by a "tax gain." This is really — so far — the aspect of deferral of tax when the transaction is viewed as whole, since the income offset by the accelerated deductions emanating from the investment in an asset is now brought back into taxable income as a gain on the disposition of the asset. The income deferred is not only the income from the asset itself but typically also income of the investor from other sources, the tax shelter effect. But the total income so deferred reenters the tax accounts on the sale of the asset as "gain" from that asset, even though most of the income deferred had no relationship to the asset. The time involved between this balancing effect — the deferral of tax — provides the tax advantage of the ingredient of deferral since the investor has had the use of the deferred tax for this interval.

If the "tax gain," however, is treated as a capital gain, then this balancing effect is upset. For the acceleration of deductions offsets income dollar for dollar — each dollar of tax loss offsets a dollar of otherwise taxable income. But the "tax gain," if a capital gain, is included in income only at 50 cents on the dollar, since under capital gain treatment for individuals one-half of a capital gain is excluded. The tax swing between accelerated deduction at the marginal tax rate of the investor and inclusion of the balancing "gain" at one-half of that rate — the effect of the exclusion of one-half of the gain — is thus an automatic benefit produced by the tax expenditure.[40] The investor cannot fail to benefit. The tax expenditure approach is simply saying to the investor: "If you invest in this asset you can defer inclusion in income of an amount equal to the investment until you sell the asset. At that time, when tax must be paid on the deferred income, you need only pay one-half of the tax that would have been paid on that income if not deferred." Thus, a doctor who offsets, say, $30,000 of professional fees, otherwise taxable in the 50 percent bracket, by the "tax loss" from an investment in low income rental housing will later, on sale of the housing, in effect include the $30,000 of fees in income

— transformed, however, by the mechanics of the tax law into "gain" on the sale of housing — but at only a 25 percent rate of tax. He has both deferred a tax on the $30,000 of fees and cut the rate of tax on the fees by one-half.[41]

The tax swing could occur in another way. Where a nondepreciable asset is involved, such as farm land or cattle that are raised and not bought, the deductible expenditure does not affect the adjusted basis of the asset. But it does affect the other factor in the "gain" equation, that of "amount realized" on sale, since the expenditure will have enhanced the value of the asset. Hence, the "gain" *pro tanto* is a reflection of the accelerated deduction — farm land is more valuable because of the amount spent on land clearing; the cattle are more valuable because of the amount spent on feed and other costs of raising them.

The Congress in recent years has gained an understanding of this tax swing and has been whittling it away. In 1962 the "gain" reflecting previous depreciation deductions on *machinery and equipment* lost its "capital gain" classification — the deductions were thus said to be "recaptured" at rates applicable to ordinary income rather than capital gain. This also now covers five-year amortization on railroad rolling stock, pollution control equipment, and other facilities. In 1964 a limited recapture was applied to the sale of real estate. In 1969, there was a considerable extension of the recapture concept. In the *farm area:* The machinery and equipment recapture rule was extended to depreciation on sales of cattle, horses, and other livestock; the deductions for soil and water conservation and land clearing expenditures on farm land are recaptured on the sale of land (here the deductions did not reduce the adjusted basis of the asset but were reflected in the gain on sale through an increase in the value of the land and hence in the amount realized on the sale); farm "tax losses" are regarded as "excess deductions" and recaptured on capital gain sales of farm assets such as livestock or orchards — but in the case of individuals only as to annual farm tax losses in excess of $25,000 and only where the nonfarm income for the year is in excess of $50,000 (the recapture concept here is the same as that described above for farm land, since the value of the asset sold has been increased by the expenditures previously deducted).[42] In the *real estate* area: Deductions for post-1969 depreciation in excess of straight-line depreciation (e.g., 200 percent declining balance depreciation on rental housing and 150 percent declining balance depreciation on commercial buildings) are recaptured on the sale of the buildings; however, in the case of new rental housing (other than low-income housing) and rehabilitated rental housing, if the property has been held for 100 months, the recapture of excess depreciation is reduced 1 percent for each month thereafter so that no recapture exists after 16 years and 8 months; in the case of low-income federally or state assisted new rental housing constructed before 1975, if the property has been held for 20 months, the recapture is reduced 1 percent for each month thereafter, so that no recapture exists after 10 years.[43]

The remedy of recapture must be kept in perspective. It does not initially affect the ingredient of deferral. Rather, it reduces the ingredient of capital gain treatment and requires that the income originally deferred should, to the extent of recapture, be included at the time of sale at ordinary income tax rates rather than with capital gain benefits. If there is full recapture, so that all income deferred is fully included, then the benefit of deferral remains — i.e., the benefit from deferring tax due in one year to a later year. "Recapture," of course, occurs only if a sale is made. If no sale of the asset occurs but, instead, the investor holds the asset until its useful life ends, the income initially deferred will be restored to taxable income as the depreciation deductions decline in amount. In other words, the earlier acceleration of deductions is now reflected *pro tanto* in a level of depreciation deduction lower than would have existed in the absence of acceleration and with appropriate spacing. Here, there is no capital gain ingredient since the enlarged income from the investment is ordinary income taxable at the rates that, assuming no change in brackets, would have applied if there had been no deferral. (Parenthetically, an executive-investor or professional person-investor may have retired in the meantime, so that his tax bracket is now lower and he may have chosen the tax shelter with this planned retirement in mind.) The ingredient of deferral — made as usual more valuable by the ingredient of leverage — remains, however.

The investor-seller thus restores the deferred income earlier than the investor-holder, but the former may, to the extent recapture does not apply, pay only a capital gains tax and thus have the benefit of the capital gain ingredient. Whether, in the latter event, the investor-seller is better off than the investor-holder depends on whether the capital gains tax at sale is less or greater than the present value of the discounted ordinary income taxes to be paid later on by the investor-holder. In some cases, the investor-seller, even paying only a capital gains tax, can be worse off vis-a-vis the investor-holder, and *a fortiori* will be worse off if he pays an ordinary tax on sale because of recapture.[44] But these comparisons are still between investors both of whom benefit greatly from deferral. However the investors stand vis-a-vis each other, they both remain highly advantaged because of the tax shelter.

The value of the ingredient of capital gain, and hence the importance of the recapture remedy, depends on the time period between initial deferral and later sale. As that time period expands, the tax treatment of the sale becomes less and less significant. The value of deferral is a present value — the benefit of not paying a tax now. If the deferral is ended 10 or 15 years in the future, the present value of the detriment of the tax then to be paid will be quite small. Hence, whether that future tax is a capital gains tax or an ordinary income tax is not of great moment in such a situation. Thus, one computation shows that if the return on a real estate tax shelter is 20.9 percent after-tax for an investor in the 50 percent bracket, on a sale after ten years the 1969 recapture rule would lower the return to 20.1 percent; full recapture of excess depreciation over straight-line depreciation (the recapture rule for commercial buildings) would lower the return to 19.9 percent. Full recapture of all depreciation (the rule for machinery and equipment) would lower the rate of return to 17.9 percent. Conversely, a complete capital gain ingredient would have raised the rate of return from 17.9 percent to 20.9 percent.[45]

In only two situations in the 1969 Act did Congress focus directly on the ingredient of deferral in these tax shelters.[46] In the case of commercial buildings it reduced the rate of depreciation from 200 percent declining balance to 150 percent declining balance. This probably meant about a 15 percent reduction in the after-tax rate of return.[47] In the case of citrus groves it required that expenditures attributable to maintaining a grove must be capitalized, and not currently deducted, if the expenditures are incurred within the first three years after the grove is planted. The rule was extended to almond groves in 1970.[48] But otherwise in the farm area the Congress rejected proposals that would have eliminated the advantages of deferral and instead it focused on the lesser factor of the capital gain ingredient.[49] It did, however, apply the new minimum tax to some of the accelerated deductions — accelerated depreciation in excess of straight-line depreciation on machinery and equipment if subject to a net lease; accelerated depreciation in excess of straight-line depreciation on real property; five-year amortization of rehabilitation expenditures, railroad rolling stock and pollution control facilities. The tax also covers the excluded one-half of capital gains. But the minimum tax overall does not have an effective impact on these items.[50]

Congress in 1969 began to look at the ingredient of leverage and imposed a restriction on the deduction of interest incurred in connection with investments where there is no offsetting investment income currently included in gross income. Where the interest is in excess of $25,000 plus investment income and capital gains, only one-half of the interest is deductible.[51] The provision has its built-in limitations through a large exemption and disallowance of only one-half of the remaining excess interest. Moreover, rental property is considered a trade or business activity rather than investment unless the property is rented under a net lease arrangement, so that many real estate shelters are not affected. But this concern of Congress over the leverage ingredient, though only partly formed and not fully articulated, may be an important development.[52]

The Three Ingredients in Perspective

The tax shelters created by the tax expenditure provisions are composed in varying extent of the three ingredients of tax deferral, leverage, and capital gain treatment. The Government, through these shelters, thus says:

— If you invest your money in this sheltered activity, we will, through a fast write-off of your investment (acceleration of deductions), let you eliminate from income an amount of your salary – professional fees – dividends – other income – equal to your investment. You therefore need not pay now the tax on that income. We are thus lending you free of any interest charge the amount of that tax — it is yours to use as you see fit. This is the ingredient of deferral of tax.

— We will also do the same for any money you borrow for this purpose and invest in the sheltered activity. You will have as an expense of borrowing only the net interest cost that remains after the deduction of the interest on the loan; if you are in the 50 percent bracket, then the cost is only half of what the lender charges you. For that cost on what you can borrow, the Government will in turn lend you free of an interest charge a sum equal to the tax on the amount of the loan, i.e., your investment of the loan will result in an offset of your income. We do not care if you are not obliged to start repaying at this time the principal on the loan that you borrowed — our interest-free loan to you starts at once as soon as you invest. Nor are we concerned that you have no personal liability on the loan, and that the lender can look only to the security of the investment. This is the ingredient of leverage.

— You can repay these interest-free loans from the Government as you wish. You may prefer to repay the Government over the period of the shelter activity. If you prefer to repay sooner by selling your investment in the activity, we will in some situations — as where the sheltered activity involves oil, cattle, or orchards — let you forget about repaying half of our loan, and you can just keep that part. This is the ingredient of capital gain treatment.[53]

— If you invest in oil, we will also free you from tax on 22 percent of the income from the investment itself in addition to our loan of the tax on an amount equal to the investment. Here in effect you can forget about repaying all of the loan and may also exclude part of your profit on the investment itself.[54]

— Finally, if the activity involves a profit which you realize on the sale of the investment — as where you sell the oil wells, or where cattle or orchard prices rise significantly, or the land involved in your real estate venture or the building itself increases in value — you in addition can have the same privilege as any other investor of paying tax on only one-half of that profit.[55]

Clearly these tax shelters are a most generous gift by the Government to the high-bracket taxpayers with funds to invest and investment advice to steer them to the shelters. Just as clearly, all of these shelters, and the tax expenditures on which they depend, should be reexamined to see whether the nation is receiving any benefit in return for the generous gifts, whether any important social or economic policy is really being served by the perpetuation of the shelters. It is quite likely that the answer in many instances will be in the negative — indeed, there is no cost-benefit study which can be pointed to that supports solid affirmative benefits to the nation from the tax expenditures involved in these shelters.[56]

The studies that do exist show the contrary. A Treasury study of the oil tax expenditures showed minimal new reserves created — in no way commensurate with the large tax reductions involved.[57] A Department of Agriculture study shows that the production of cattle is not significantly aided by the tax expenditures for nonfarmers who invest in cattle shelters.[58] Housing studies are calling into question both the tax expenditures and the direct subsidies.[59]

But even the presence of benefits to the nation from the tax expenditure assistance underlying these tax shelters would not be enough to perpetuate the shelters. These tax shelters do no more than involve the use of middlemen to convey Treasury checks to the persons conducting the activities requiring Government financial assistance. In this process, the tax shelter middlemen pocket a significant part of the check for themselves, an amount far too large in relation to the economic role, if any, that they play. The tax shelter method of delivering Treasury assistance checks is thus extremely wasteful of Government funds. It also is far too generous to these middlemen, through the resulting tax favoritism they obtain.

The tax expenditure items in these tax shelter fields involve two aspects of inefficiency and wastage of Government funds. First, the assistance provided by the tax expenditure may not really be needed at all for the activity benefited, or may be larger than needed. Second, where the nature of the tax expenditure lends itself to tax shelter operation, the "commission" pocketed by the middlemen makes the delivery of the tax expenditure assistance itself an inefficient operation. Consequently, in those situations where financial assistance by the Government for the activities involved is required for justifiable public policy reasons, the task is still to explore methods of direct expenditure that do not permit the flagrant wastage of Government funds and flagrant abandonment of the principles of tax equity and fairness involved in tax shelters.[60] Surely the United States can find better ways to provide that assistance than having the tax landscape marred by these shelters.

119

APPENDIX

WAYS OF LOOKING AT THE BENEFITS

OF TAX DEFERRAL

This appendix amplifies the discussion in Chapter IV of possible ways in which the benefits of tax deferral can be explained. To make the appendix complete, and to follow the approach used in that chapter of communication with a busy Congressman, some of the earlier discussion is repeated.

Suppose an individual, A, in the 60 percent tax bracket, invests $100 in an asset. Assume that business accounting and normal tax rules would require the cost of the asset to be capitalized, but that a tax expenditure provision permits the cost to be expensed in the year of acquisition, thus deferring tax liability on the amount of income offset by the special deduction. Assume that the sale of the asset ten years later would produce ordinary income. How do you express or describe A's tax benefit?

Do you use the analogy of the interest-free, nonrecourse loan without collateral? Do you ask the Congressman if *he* would blithely let *his* debtors say they will pay their debts to him some time in the future and forget about interest or security in the meantime? Do you ask the Congressman if he would like to know a bank that would lend *him* money without an interest charge and without any collateral? Do you then say to the Congressman that some taxpayers are aware of such a bank — they call it the U.S. Treasury?

— The immediate deduction of $100 gives A an immediate tax saving of $60. The $60 tax will be postponed until the asset is sold. One way to describe the result is to say that the Government has made a loan of $60 to A without asking for interest, collateral, or a definite time for payment of the loan, since it will wait until A decides to sell the asset. The higher A's tax bracket, the larger the interest-free loan.

— What is this loan worth to A? Assume that borrowing $60 from a bank would cost him 10 percent interest. A thus saves paying 10 percent a year on $60 — or $6 — less the benefit of the income tax deduction of $6 interest a year, or a net saving of $2.40 per year, for a total of $24 if he sells in ten years. The saving from deducting the cost of the asset in the first year instead of the tenth year, expressed in terms of the present value of money, would be worth $19.46 to A (using an after-tax discount rate of 4 percent if A can freely borrow at a 10 percent before-tax rate). Another way of looking at this benefit is to ask: "If A could earn 10 percent on his investment, what would he pay to get this interest-free loan?" The answer would be: "A would be willing to pay up to $19.46."

— A may be able to earn 15 percent on investments that he makes. If so, "A would be willing to pay up to $26.49" for an interest-free loan (using an after-tax discount rate of 6 percent).

Does it help to say that the *exclusion* from tax of a percentage of a given amount of income provides the same benefit as deferring the tax on that income? The particular percentage of exclusion depends on the taxpayer's marginal tax rate, what he can expect to earn on his investments, and the period of the deferral.

— Assume that A can earn 15 percent before tax on his investments. Instead of permitting A to defer tax on $100 of income (through the immediate deduction of the $100 cost of the asset) until a later sale of the asset, here assumed to occur in ten years, the Congress could provide the same benefit by excluding 43 percent of the $100 of income. In other words, A is indifferent between a proposal to exclude 43 percent of $100 of income and a proposal to defer the tax on that $100 income for ten years. Put differently, for a 60 percent taxpayer, the deferral of tax on income for ten years is almost the equivalent of excluding one-half of that income. A twenty-year deferral is equivalent to excluding 68 percent of the income.[1]

Does it help to say that the *after-tax* rate of profit on what is *left at risk* under the tax expenditure of immediate deduction and deferral of tax is equal to the *before-tax* rate of profit *on the entire investment* as counted under financial accounting?

— Assume the asset in which A invested $100 will be sold for $250 in ten years, leaving A a profit of 150 percent before tax. If A had *capitalized* the cost of the asset, he would owe in tax 60 percent of $150 ($250 sales proceeds less $100 cost) or $90. A thus would have an after-tax gain of $60 on a $100 investment (sales proceeds of $250 less $90 tax less $100 investment), giving an after-tax profit of 60 percent. But if through immediate deduction A *expenses* the cost, his tax on sale is 60 percent of $250 ($250 sales proceeds less zero cost), or $150, leaving A with $100. A, however, in this situation has actually only invested $40, since $60 of the cost of the initial investment was repaid to him by the Government at the start through the deduction of $100. A has thus gained $60 ($250 sales proceeds less $150 tax less $40 initial investment) on a $40 investment, or a profit of 150 percent *after-tax*. In effect, his *after-tax* rate of profit on the $40 investment is equal to the *before-tax* rate of profit on the overall investment.

— A has ended up in the same situation as would a tax-exempt organization which had invested $40 and obtained a profit of $60, or 150 percent of its investment.

— In a progressive tax system, after-tax rates of profit should decline as the taxpayer's rate bracket increases. With expensing of cost substituted for capitalization, the rates of profit on the amount at risk are not affected by the tax system.[2]

Do you explain that the immediate expensing of an investment is the equivalent of allowing the investor a tax-free return of the income yield from what he has left at risk in the venture — his initial investment less the tax benefit of its write-off through the immediate deduction?

— In the example above, A has made a tax-free investment of his $40, since his *after-tax* rate of profit on $40 is equal to his *before-tax* rate of profit on the overall investment.[3]

— This is the form of explanation used by Professor Shoup in his book on Public Finance:[4]

> Thus, if a corporation is contemplating construction of a plant costing $1,000,000 it need supply only $600,000, if the tax rate is 40 percent. The remaining $400,000 will come from its savings of tax on profits from the remainder of its business. By deducting $1,000,000 instead of nothing, in the year of construction, it saves $400,000 in tax for that year. The cash flow from the $1,000,000 plant in future years will be taxed at 40 percent, since no further depreciation will be allowed. The corporation retains 60 percent of this cash flow. It contributed only 60 percent of the capital that made the cash flow possible. The corporation therefore obtains the same percentage rate of return on what it put in, of its own money, as if (1) there had been no income tax and (2) it had financed the entire $1,000,000 itself and had kept all the cash flow.[20]

(20.) The fact that completely accelerated depreciation, when coupled with complete loss offset, is equivalent to exemption of net return from the asset, under an income tax, was discovered by E. Cary Brown (see his "Business-Income Taxation and Investment Incentives," in *Income, Employment and Public Policy: Essays in Honor of Alvin H. Hansen* [New York, Norton, 1948], pp. 309–10), reprinted in Musgrave and Shoup, *Readings in the Economics of Taxation.* See also Musgrave, *Theory of Public Finance,* pp. 343–44.

The use by Professor Shoup of the term "discovered" in this context (see his footnote 20 above) is interesting. Perhaps a Congressman can be pardoned for not appreciating the benefit of deferral if its ramifications apparently eluded public finance specialists for 35 years of our income tax history.

Does it help to say that "permitting the capital cost of an asset to be expensed has the effect of exempting the income from ownership of the asset from taxation"?

— This is the way the Treasury Department, when it is being analytically objective, explains the tax benefits from an immediate write-off of an investment cost. The words above quoted are from the 1970 Treasury Department Study on Tax Depreciation Policy.[5] Footnote 4 of that Treasury Study amplifies the point:

> An intuitive explanation of this somewhat surprising result takes the following form: a $1,000 asset will generate some stream of revenue over its life; if the cost is expensed and the tax rate is 48 percent, the net cost of the asset to the owner (ignoring the slight discount of the deduction as above) is only $520, after tax. However, in the future, each $1 of revenue will be taxed fully, with no allowance for depreciation, leaving $0.52 of net return on the $520 investment, the same ratio as $1 to $1,000 as if there were no tax.
>
> Incidentally, in those cases, as in minerals taxation, where the total *present value* of expensing and depletion deductions may actually exceed the cost of the investment, the effective tax rate is negative. That is, in some instances the tax rate equivalent of an investment tax incentive is a tax rate less than zero.

Does it help to say that if a person reinvests the total tax savings from immediately deducting the cost of an asset, then this will be equivalent to *full exemption* of the entire income from the original investment?

— In the example used earlier of A investing $100 and having $60 of cost repaid to him through immediate deduction of the $100, it is said that A received a tax-free return on the $40 he had at risk equal to the before-tax rate of return. But the story can be continued. A may reinvest the $60 return of cost obtained through the initial deduction. If this investment is also expensed, it will generate an additional return of $36. On this second investment A thus has $24 at risk. Once again it can be shown that, on the $24 at risk, the after-tax rate of return is 150 percent. A third round is possible. A reinvests the $36 and receives back $21.60. The money at risk is $14.40. If A continues to reinvest the returns of the cost of the investments, the total investment will be $250 but the money at risk only $100. On this $100 at risk, A will earn 150 percent after taxes. A can thus be regarded as receiving back tax-free a profit of 150 percent of his $100 at risk. This is the return that an investor would receive on $100 at risk in a world without taxes, assuming he also earned 150 percent on his investment.

— In this sense, assuming A can reinvest his repayments of cost, with similar expensing of the reinvestments, A is indifferent to whether he is offered (1) *full exemption* from income tax on his initial investment or (2) a *deferral of tax* on a total sum invested (an immediate expensing of that sum) that would leave him with an amount of *his* money at risk equal to that initial investment. This is the way the above Treasury Study appears to view the situation.[6]

Does it help to illustrate the last two approaches, which indicate that an immediate deduction of the cost of an asset has the effect of exempting from taxation the income from ownership of the asset, by using the following example?

— Suppose A in the 60 percent tax bracket desires to receive $150 after-tax on a $1,000 plant. If A invests $2,500 in a plant that earns 15 percent and the investment can immediately be deducted, then he has *his* $1,000 plant and is also obtaining *his* $150 after-tax return. Essentially A is receiving $150 tax free on a $1,000 plant. The Government has *its* $1,500 plant and gets *its* return on that plant. In addition, A is managing the entire $2,500 plant, and is thus managing for the Government as well as himself. But this happens in a sense under any income tax system.[7]

Some of the tax shelters, such as oil and cattle, essentially provide for immediate expensing of all or a major part of the investment, so that the Treasury Department's description, and that of Professor Shoup which is along the same line, are fully applicable. Other tax shelters, such as real estate and leasing, while not giving immediate expensing, provide for an acceleration of the deduction of the investment cost and hence a very rapid write-off of the investment in its early years. The essentials of the analysis are the same, however, with the rate of tax on the money at risk being somewhere between the zero point of immediate expensing and the full tax rate, depending on the degree of acceleration of deduction. Thus, the Treasury Study indicates a variety of ways to show the benefits of accelerated depreciation — equivalence in asset price reduction, equivalence in investment credit percentages, lowered effective tax rate, increased rate of return. There is, however, no reference to these benefit descriptions and their upside-down effect dependent on the taxpayer's tax bracket, in the President's and Treasury Department's 1971 announcement of depreciation revision, providing an arbitrary 20 percent reduction in guideline depreciable lives and abandonment of any linkage with useful life.[8]

V

Tax Incentives as a Device for Implementing Government Policy: A Comparison with Direct Government Expenditures

Suggestions are constantly being made that many of our pressing social problems can be solved, or partially met, through the use of income tax incentives. Moreover, the present federal income tax is replete with tax incentive provisions. Some are intended to assist particular industries, business activities, or financial transactions. Others are intended to encourage nonbusiness activities considered socially useful, such as home ownership. This chapter considers the question whether tax incentives are as useful or efficient an implement of social policy as direct Government expenditures, such as grants, loans, interest subsidies, and guarantees of loans. The discussion will be in terms of the federal income tax, but it is intended to be helpful for other jurisdictions and other forms of taxation as well.[1]

The Nature and Extent of Existing Tax Incentives

If we take as our definition of tax incentive a tax expenditure which induces certain activities or behavior in response to the monetary benefit available, almost all of the tax expenditures included in the Tax Expenditure Budget, Table 1.1 in Chapter I, can be considered tax incentives. The Tax Expenditure Budget is thus essentially an enumeration of the present "tax incentives" contained in our income tax system. Many of the tax expenditures were expressly adopted to induce action which the Congress considered in the national interest. For example, the investment credit, adopted in 1962, suspended for a period in 1966–1967, repealed in 1969, and restored in 1971, was intended, along with greatly accelerated depreciation adopted in 1971, to encourage the purchase of machinery and equipment; the DISC exemption for exports was adopted to encourage exporting; excessive bad debt reserves for some financial institutions were allowed to encourage the growth of savings and loan associations and mutual savings banks; the charitable deduction was intended to foster philanthropy; the campaign contribution deduction and credit were intended to foster a wider participation in political contributions; the preferential tax treatment of qualified pension plans was intended to foster broad pension plan coverage; the corporate surtax exemption was intended to foster small business; and the five-year amortization of the cost of rehabilitated housing, employer-provided on-the-job training facilities and child care facilities, pollution control facilities, railroad rolling stock, and coal mine safety equipment, was intended to foster these activities and purchases of these items.[2]

Other tax expenditures whose origins are cloudy, because of their antiquity and absence of articulation of initial intentions, are now defended on incentive grounds, such as the incentive to home ownership in the case of the deduction for mortgage interest and property taxes, or the assistance to state and local governments in easing the way to the imposition of their taxes through the deduction for state and local taxes. Still other tax expenditure provisions were originally adopted as "relief provisions" to ease "tax hardships" or to "simplify tax computations." As their effects on the tax system have become clearer, some of these provisions have come to be defended on the basis of their incentive effects: for example, the oil intangible drilling expenses deduction, the percentage depletion allowance for oil and minerals, the Western Hemisphere Trade Corporation preferential rate, and the research and development expense deduction.[3] Moreover, to the extent that such "tax relief" — i.e., tax treatment that is special and not required by the concept and general standards of a net income tax — is granted for an activity that is voluntary, the relief is in effect an incentive to engage in that activity, even though the provisions may not be defended on incentive grounds. For example, if meals and lodging furnished an employee on the premises of an employer are not taxed, the effect is to make some employees more likely to choose such employment. If coal and iron royalties receive capital gains treatment and other royalties do not, investment preferences will be affected.[4]

The only tax expenditures that are not tax incentives, as the latter expression is here used, are expenditures related to involuntary activities of taxpayers. Most such provisions are designed to provide tax reduction in order to relieve misfortune or hardship — situations involving "personal hardships," as contrasted with the "tax hardships" that have brought about other special tax provisions, chiefly for business activities. The extra personal exemption for the blind is one example. The extra personal exemption for the aged is another

— we can't grow old any faster because of the exemption. Perhaps the other tax benefits for the aged — the retirement credit and the exclusion of social security retirement payments — also fall in this nonincentive category. This is not so clear, however, since the line between "tax incentive" and "relief for personal hardship" is fuzzy. The retirement credit provides some incentive to retire. Also, favoring retirement income may encourage saving for retirement. The employee sick pay exclusion may be in the nonincentive class, since sickness is presumably involuntary, yet the provision can have the incentive effect of inducing employers to provide such plans or unions to negotiate for such plans. The general medical expense deduction similarly has nonincentive characteristics; yet the presence of the deduction does tend to induce the purchase of health insurance and the greater use of medical services and equipment. The exclusion of unemployment insurance and public assistance benefits also has nonincentive characteristics, if we regard unemployment and need for public assistance as essentially involuntary conditions. Yet for some individuals the generality will not hold, and the tax result will add to the monetary inducement which makes the condition acceptable. The casualty loss deduction is also generally not an incentive, though in particular cases it may induce certain action that would otherwise be too risky, such as self-insurance, or ownership of a house in a hurricane area.

Special provisions designed to relieve personal hardships, as contrasted with tax incentive provisions, are relatively few in number. By and large, therefore, the classification guidelines underlying the Tax Expenditure Budget which separate tax expenditures from other tax provisions also serve to identify existing tax incentives and tax subsidies. The Tax Expenditure Budget may thus be used as an enumeration of those tax incentives.[5] Moreover, a classification between "tax incentive" financial assistance and "tax relief" financial assistance to alleviate the difficulties caused by personal hardships is not really essential for the purposes of this chapter. All of what is said as to the comparison of tax incentives with direct expenditures applies equally to the "tax relief" expenditures.

Recently adopted or proposed tax expenditures are nearly all in the tax incentive category. They include manpower employment or training tax credits, educational expense tax credits, tax benefits for business investment in central cities or rural areas, and tax credits or deductions for political campaign contributions.[6] In all these situations the direct purpose of the proposed tax change is to provide monetary assistance or benefit through the tax laws so as to make the desired course of action financially more palatable to the taxpayers involved, and thereby induce them to take that action. Whatever the aim of the economic benefit involved — be it to make an expensive activity less costly, to reduce its risk, or to increase the rate of after-tax profit — the incentive effect is the desired effect.

Tax Incentives

Comparison of Tax Incentives
with Direct Expenditures

The Tax Expenditure Budget thus serves to identify the tax incentives in our existing tax system and so to identify the areas in which Congress has given financial assistance through the tax system to induce desired action. But why through the tax system? Why not through a direct expenditure program? *Given* the Congressional decision to provide the assistance, when should it be furnished through a direct expenditure program and when through a special tax program?

This section of the discussion is concerned with criteria for evaluating the use of tax incentives as compared to the use of direct Government expenditures. This evaluation does not involve the issue whether we should seek to achieve the particular goals for which tax incentives are now used or suggested. We can assume it is understood that each incentive must serve purposes which the nation wants to achieve and is willing to finance, rather than let the marketplace determine the extent to which the result will obtain. This is not to say that every proposal for a tax incentive is presented or defended with a careful analysis along these lines. Far from it — many sponsors of tax incentives simply assume that if the benefit sought is helpful in their eyes in reaching a desired result, the incentive is in the public interest. But the present discussion assumes that these issues have been decided. Therefore, we are assessing the use of tax incentives as a technique to provide the Government assistance.[7] The discussion is applicable to those tax expenditures intended to alleviate personal hardships, although we have indicated that they might not be classified as tax incentives.

There are, of course, as stated earlier, a variety of ways to provide Government financial assistance — direct grants, loans, interest subsidies, guarantees of loan repayment or interest payments, insurance on investments, and so on.[8] These methods are here called budgetary or direct expenditures. Skilled tax technicians and budgetary experts can take any tax expenditure and devise a budgetary expenditure approach to serve the same goals as a direct expenditure.[9] For example, the British for some years used an approach under their tax law somewhat similar to our 7 percent investment credit to encourage the acquisition of machinery and equipment. The Labour Government subsequently dropped the tax technique and substituted direct cash payments.[10] The Conservative Government then dropped the direct grants and returned to tax provisions.[11] The existing tax incentive for charitable giving could also be structured as a direct expenditure program, under which the Government would match an individual's contribution to charity with a proportional contribution of its own to the same charity.[12] Tax credits to an employer for manpower training could be structured as grants

129

or contract payments to the employer. Tax benefits to the aged can be structured as cash to the aged. And so on.

It follows that a meaningful comparison between the tax incentive technique and the direct expenditure technique must involve *similar substantive programs.* There is no point to saying that in a particular situation a tax incentive is a more useful approach because it involves no Government supervision over the details of the action to be induced, whereas a direct expenditure involves detailed supervision. To say so is not to compare a tax incentive with a direct expenditure but simply to compare a loosely controlled method of paying out Government funds with a tightly controlled method. Direct expenditures can involve loose as well as tight supervision. Once we decide which substantive program we want, then we can go on to decide which technique — tax incentive or direct expenditure — is preferable for that program.

The matter of what type of substantive program is best calculated to achieve the desired goal lies in the fields of cost-benefit and cost-effectiveness analyses. These methods are being used more and more to devise and test direct expenditures, and they should *a priori* be equally applicable to programs using a tax incentive technique.[13] For present purposes I am assuming that the substantive analysis, as respects methodological approach, use of econometric techniques, and the like, should be of the same order whether a tax incentive or a direct expenditure is involved. This is not to say that this has been true with regard to tax incentives in the past. Far from it — and therein lie many of the problems with tax incentives. Nor can we say that it will be true as to future tax incentives. Nor can we say that all direct expenditure programs are carefully thought through.

A meaningful comparison between the two techniques must also be *realistic.* Thus, it must recognize that a tax incentive does involve the expenditure of Government funds. It is often said that a tax incentive is more useful than a direct expenditure because people do not like or will not respond to "subsidies." Such statements always assume that the direct expenditure is the "subsidy," whereas the tax benefit obtained in the tax incentive — the lower tax — is not so regarded. Perhaps we may find that this fiscal illusion has its usefulness, but we should at least be aware of what is the reality and what is the illusion.[14]

Some Asserted Virtues of Tax Incentives
— Falsely Claimed

Against this general background we can now consider some of the virtues and defects generally claimed for tax incentives and, on the other side of the coin, for direct expenditures. The first level of consideration relates to virtues claimed for tax incentives, but, in the light of the above background, falsely claimed.

Tax incentives encourage the private sector to participate in social programs. — Frequently a tax incentive is urged on the ground that the particular problem to be met is great and that the Government must assist in its solution by enlisting the participation of the private sector — generally business. The need for Government to participate can be fulfilled by a tax incentive, and this is asserted as a virtue of tax incentives — they provide Government assistance. Thus, a tax incentive for manpower training and employment proposed in the Senate was defended in these terms:[15]

> Tax incentives [are proposed] to encourage the fullest participation of the private sector in employment, upgrading, and training of less skilled people.
>
> . . . .
>
> . . . A tax incentive program should [make] . . . it economically possible for American business to play an important role in our manpower program. . . . I understand the objections that are at times put forward to the use of the tax system for social purposes. However, I think it is time we realized that in order to encourage business to participate in programs of this nature, Government must be willing to meet business half way. The most convenient form for subsidizing a businessman is through his income tax.
>
> . . . [This bill] enlists the job-creating potential of private enterprise by realistically recognizing the high initial costs involved in hiring, training, and providing supportive services for low-skilled individuals.

But all this is a non sequitur; it points not to the virtue of tax incentives but to the need for Government assistance. The existence of that need has no relevance to the question whether the need should be met by an incentive or by a direct expenditure.

Tax incentives are simple and involve far less governmental supervision and detail. — A whole swirl of virtues claimed for tax incentives is summed up in the general observation that they keep Government — that is, the Government bureaucracy — out of the picture: they involve less negotiation of the arrangements, less supervision, less red tape, no new bureaucracy, and so on. The manpower proposal referred to above was supported by this argument:[16]

> The advantages to a tax credit approach are numerous. The most important, however, is that the program can go into effect immediately upon enactment. Employment programs in the past have taken months and years to become operative. . . . Employers who participate in the

program will receive a tax credit of 75 percent of the wages paid to the employee for the first 4 months of employment, 50 percent for the next 4 months, and 25 percent for the balance of the individual's first year of employment. This is an uncomplicated program with the minimum of redtape. Any employer who hires a certified employee is eligible for the tax credit — it is as simple as that.

But this merely comes down to saying: "Let's have a manpower program under which the Government pays an employer, who hires a certified employee, an amount calculated as a percentage of the employee's wage." There is nothing so far that indicates whether the payment should be by way of a tax credit or a direct expenditure. Direct expenditure programs can also be structured to pay out Government money with few administrative controls. Thus, if an employer can obtain Government funds (i.e., a reduction in tax through the tax credit) for his employment activities by filling out a schedule on a tax return, a direct manpower program could be devised instead under which he would receive the same monetary assistance by filling out the exact same schedule on a piece of paper that had "Department of Labor" at the top in place of "Internal Revenue Service."

A Government that decides it is wise to pay out tax credit money via a simple tax schedule would be highly irrational if it also decided that it would be unwise to pay the same amount directly on the same basis. A dollar is a dollar — both for the person who receives it and the Government that pays it, whether the dollar comes with a tax credit label or a direct expenditure label. Nor is a new bureaucracy needed to pay out these amounts as a direct expenditure — a check-writing process is all that would be needed in keeping with the parallel to the tax credit. Nor, similarly, must there be long negotiations, complex contracts, and the like. It is not the tax route that makes the program simple — it is a substantive decision to have a simple program. In many cases, it is true, direct expenditure programs are probably overstructured and the urging of tax incentives is a reaction to, and a valid criticism of, badly designed expenditure programs. The cure lies of course in better designed expenditure programs.[17]

It should be added, parenthetically, that the alleged simplicity of tax incentives is likely to be illusory. Thus, the argument quoted above states that "[a]ny employer who hires a certified employee is eligible for the tax credit — it is as simple as that." But this is not really so, because the legislation actually proposed would have required the employer to be certified by the Secretary of Labor, and to be eligible for certification an employer would have had to prove that the employment program would not impair or depress the wages, working standards, or opportunities of present employees; that the business was not affected by strike, lockout, or similar conditions; that the employees in the program would be afforded an equal opportunity for full-time employment after the expiration of the credit period; that a formal on-the-job training program would be available; and that there would be no discrimination on account of race, color, religion, or national origin. Further complexities were involved in the proposed system for determining the creditable wage base, which was to be defined as the higher of the minimum wage or the wage customarily paid by the employer for such services.[18] The five-year amortization for pollution control facilities requires certification by state and federal authorities; the five-year amortization for coal mine safety equipment requires certification by the Secretary of the Interior.[19]

The tape is thus present in tax incentive programs and its color is red. This is not to criticize the particular programs, but rather to observe that those who design tax incentive programs, just as those who design direct expenditure programs, may find that complex requirements become desirable.

Tax incentives promote private decision-making rather than Government-centered decision-making. — It is said that better progress will be made toward the solution of many social problems if individual decision-making is promoted, and that since tax incentives promote this they should be preferred to approaches that underscore Government-centered decision-making. The view has been expressed that "[r]ecognition that tax incentives can account for real federal expenditures should not obscure the fact that such programs can eliminate the need for additional bureaucratic apparatus while promoting the use of private capital and initiative toward socially useful projects."[20]

We need not discuss the merits of private enterprise as a device for solving social problems, except to note in passing that many business groups who in urging tax incentives stress the virtues of private enterprise overlook the fact that they are really stressing private enterprise *plus* Government assistance. But wise or unwise, the contention that private enterprise should be allowed free play, without Government interference, tells us nothing as to the choice between tax incentives and direct expenditures, given the same substantive program. This contention is really a variant of the previous "red tape" argument. Just as we could design a direct expenditure program that provides for reduction of red tape, so we could design one that provides more flexibility for private decision-making and less scope for Government control. For example, the deduction for charitable contributions is sometimes cited as a method of Government assistance that promotes private decision-making — the taxpayer, and not the Government, selects the charity and determines how much to give. But a direct expenditure program under which the Government matched with its grants, on a no-questions-asked and no-second-thoughts basis, the gifts of private individuals to the charities they selected, would equally preserve private decision-making. Similarly, the freedom of choice that state and local governments have as to how to use the funds they borrow with the assistance of the tax exemption for the interest on their bonds can also be preserved by a direct expenditure program in which the Federal Government pays a part of the interest cost.[21]

It is true that many of the existing tax incentives are less structured than direct expenditure programs. But in part this reflects lack of scrutiny and foresight when the tax incentives were being planned or considered. If after a careful consideration it is decided that a simple structure is wise, then it would assume considerable irrationality to say that the simple structure will necessarily be kept if a tax incentive is used but scrapped in favor of a more complicated structure if a direct expenditure is used.

Some Asserted Defects of Tax Incentives

Tax incentives permit windfalls by paying taxpayers for doing what they would do anyway. — It is generally argued that tax incentives are wasteful because some of the tax benefits go to taxpayers for activities which they would have performed without the benefits. When this happens, the tax credit or other benefit is a pleasant windfall, and stimulates no additional activity. With respect to most, if not all, of the existing and proposed incentives this criticism is well taken, and indeed it is often difficult to structure a tax credit system which avoids this problem without increasing complexity and introducing arbitrariness.[22] But this also is a problem not unique to the tax incentive technique. A direct expenditure program similarly structured would be equally open to the charge. For example, grants or contract payments made to employers who hire unskilled employees as part of a manpower program may go to employers who for one reason or another would have hired those employees anyway.

It may be desirable in particular programs to tolerate this inefficiency or windfall. Or it may be desirable to attempt to eliminate it, perhaps by constructing a program under which taxpayers bid for the Government assistance needed and the assistance goes to the lowest bidders if otherwise qualified, just as in direct Government purchasing. It may be that such a substantive program is difficult to operate through the tax technique, but other ways of reaching only the marginal decision could be built into a tax incentive.[23] The significant question is what sort of substantive program is desired.

Tax incentives are inequitable: they are worth more to the high-income taxpayer than the low-income taxpayer; they do not benefit those who are outside the tax system because their incomes are low, they have losses, or they are exempt from tax. — This criticism of tax incentives in terms of their inequitable effects is properly levied against most of the existing tax incentives, and probably most of the proposed incentives. The existing incentives were never really carefully structured and in many instances just grew up, without serious thought ever having been given to the question whether they were fair in these terms. The entire process was molded by the fact that the positive tax structure was being affected, and within that structure tax benefits —

deductions and exclusions — had these effects as a matter of course. The deductions and exclusions of the tax incentive provisions and their inequitable effects took on the protective coloration of the deductions and exclusions that were a part of the basic tax structure.

The fact that tax benefits for the aged and the sick provide no benefits for those aged or ill who are too poor to pay income taxes was not even thought of as a difficulty, since the focus was, as in any positive tax system, on writing the rules for *taxpayers*.[24] The problem was sometimes thought about in the context of an individual who fell outside the tax system because of current losses, and at times a carry-forward of incentive benefits was provided. Thought was occasionally given to the fact that the deduction of mortgage interest or charitable contributions is worth more to the top-bracket taxpayer than the low-bracket taxpayer, but the disparity was generally dismissed on the grounds that all deductions had that effect. Sometimes this matter was regarded as worrisome, and a tax credit was used instead of a deduction, as in the case of the retirement income credit for the aged.

This unfairness persists even in recently proposed tax incentives. The tax credit for property taxes paid by the aged that passed the Senate in 1971 would not have helped poor families with incomes below the taxable level.[25] Manpower training credits do not help a new business experiencing initial losses and struggling to stay alive, or they would help only by deferring into the future, through a carry-forward provision, benefits needed at once.[26] No assistance is provided to a tax-exempt organization or local government incurring added expenses under its participation in manpower training or employment activities.[27] The $100 deduction (on a joint return) for political contributions, or alternative tax credit of one-half of the contribution up to a maximum credit of $25 (on a joint return), added in 1971, in effect bars individuals below the taxable levels from participating in the allocation of Government funds to their candidates. Thus, the credit approach in effect means that if a taxpayer sends $25 to a candidate, then the Government will also send $25 to the candidate — the effect of allowing a tax credit of $25 for a contribution of $50. But if individuals below these taxable levels — perhaps 25 percent to 30 percent of the electorate — contribute any money, the Government refuses to match those funds.[28]

Thus, the lesson is hard to learn. The 1969 tax reform legislation contained a tax incentive for the rehabilitation of low-income housing, using the device of five-year amortization of capital expenditures[29] which otherwise would be depreciated over a longer period. This device, which was proposed by the Treasury Department, has these interesting effects for individual taxpayers: for a taxpayer in the 70 percent bracket, the benefit is the equivalent of a 19 percent investment credit (assuming an expenditure with a 20-year life and a discount rate of 10 percent); for a taxpayer in the 20 percent bracket it is the equivalent of a 5 percent credit. In terms of interest costs on a loan made for rehabilitation purposes, the benefit of five-year amortization is equivalent for the 70 percent bracket taxpayer to reducing an 8 percent interest charge to 3 percent; for the 20 percent bracket taxpayer it is equivalent to reducing the 8 percent charge to 7 percent.[30] The inequitable effect of this tax incentive device is not mentioned either in the proposal or in the committee reports explaining it.[31]

It is clear, then, that most tax incentives have decidedly adverse effects on equity as between taxpayers at the same income level, and also, with respect to the individual income tax, between taxpayers at different income levels. As a consequence of these inequitable effects, many tax incentives look, and are, highly irrational when phrased as direct expenditure programs structured the same way. Indeed, it is doubtful that most of our existing tax incentives would ever have been introduced, let alone accepted, if so structured, and many would be laughed out of Congress. What HEW Secretary would propose a medical assistance program for the aged that cost $200 million, and under which $90 million would go to persons with incomes over $50,000, and only $8 million to persons with incomes under $5000? The tax proposal to remove the 3 percent floor under the medical expense deductions of persons over age 65 would have had just that effect.[32] What HEW Secretary would introduce a program under which social security benefits would be unaffected if the recipient's total income including the benefit were under $2,050, would be automatically increased by 14 percent if the recipient's income were between $2,050 and $2,550, by 15 percent if between $2,550 and $3,050, and so on up to 70 percent if over $100,000? That is the effect of the present exclusion from income of social security benefits paid to a single individual.[33] What HUD Secretary would suggest a subsidized loan program for housing rehabilitation under which a wealthy person could borrow the funds at 3 percent interest but a poor person would have to pay 7 percent or 8 percent? That is the effect as stated above of the five-year amortization of rehabilitation expenditures contained in the 1969 Tax Reform Act.

This criticism — that tax incentives produce inequitable effects and upside-down benefits — is valid as to the general run of tax incentives.[34] It demonstrates why tax incentives make high-income individuals still better off and result in the paradox that we achieve our social goals by increasing the number of tax millionaires. The marketplace does not work this way — the individual who earns his profits, even high profits, by meeting a need or desire of society, finds his rewards subject to the progressive income tax. The economic system is then functioning as it is intended it should, and the tax system, which acts as a control, is also functioning as intended. But when rewards are in the form of tax incentives, the latter control is eliminated and tax millionaires are produced.

This difference between the rewards of the marketplace and the rewards of the tax incentive also obtains for direct Government grants. Most direct

Government economic assistance for business activities is given on a *before-tax* basis and in one way or another enters as a plus in the income accounts of the person benefited. See for example: agricultural subsidies for domestic activities and exports; manpower subsidies; air carrier and maritime subsidies; land and forest conservation payments; credit subsidies (which reduce interest costs) for agriculture, exports, housing, small business, and other activities. But the tax incentives, as we have seen, do not work that way. The financial assistance afforded by the incentive, with the purpose of making *after-tax profits* high enough to induce the desired action by the taxpayer, is not itself included in income. The tax incentive thus produces both financial assistance and freedom from taxation. That freedom itself means much more to the well-to-do individual than to one in the lower brackets. The tax incentive is in fact a method of reward and assistance that is just upside-down from the way the country decided — when it adopted a progressive income tax — that the rewards of the marketplace should operate in combination with the income tax. The use that has been made — and is being made — of tax incentives is destructive of the equity of a tax system.

The irony of all this is illustrated by the Treasury Department's first proposing a housing rehabilitation tax incentive and then having to suggest that the incentive is a "tax preference" which must be guarded against by including it in the new minimum tax structure designed to prevent the wealthy from escaping all tax burdens.[35] This inclusion as a tax preference under the new minimum tax thus implicitly characterizes this tax incentive as a special tax benefit for high-bracket taxpayers.[36] The use of the direct expenditure route would have prevented this particular undermining of the tax system.

In some cases, however, the tax incentive could be fashioned to avoid this particular criticism, though the result would be a different program and one structured more closely along direct expenditure lines. For example, suppose in the case of the exclusion of social security benefits, that a uniform tax credit was used instead of the exclusion, the tax credit was included in taxable income, and any unused credit was paid to the taxpayer. This would be the equivalent of a direct expenditure program for all aged on a per capita basis, with positive taxpayers receiving a diminishing final share depending on their tax bracket, and those aged outside the tax system receiving their full share. The elements of inequity would be removed, and the tax incentive technique would be on the same footing as a direct expenditure under which each aged person received the same per capita amount. Indeed, this is how tax incentive programs *should* be structured if they are to be equitable and not involve the unfairnesses described. But this approach may only rarely be feasible given its novelty and the difficulties involved in convincing the business community and others who are the beneficiaries of tax incentives, let alone the policymakers in Government, of the appropriateness of making such changes as including the tax incentive amount itself in taxable income.[37] And though eliminating the aspect of inequity, this form of tax incentive would still raise the question of inefficiency compared with a like direct expenditure program, since some funds would be given under the tax incentive to many persons not in need of the assistance. In short, why not use a direct program and be done with it?

As an aside, we can here see the importance of distinguishing tax expenditures and tax incentives — so-called special tax provisions — from those provisions considered a proper and necessary part of the structure of an income tax. If an item is *properly* deductible in the latter sense, it does come off at the taxpayer's top tax rate, and its benefits are confined to those who are taxpayers. Given the decision to have an income tax at all, the result is equitable, within the concept of an income tax. An income tax is a tax on *net* income and not a tax on gross receipts; therefore the deductions from gross income required to produce the net income base must be allowed. Those deductions, generally speaking, are the expenses and costs incurred in the process of producing or earning the gross income received by the taxpayer.

Consider, for example, the deduction for moving expenses: it is a deduction and so benefits a taxpayer (reduces his tax) in accordance with his marginal tax rate. It also benefits only taxpayers; an employee who incurs moving expenses, but whose income is so low as not to leave him taxable, does not obtain any benefit or assistance. This is the correct result under a positive income tax system if the moving expense should properly be taken into account in the measurement of net income, as it should be if it is an expense in earning income rather than a personal expense. If it is the latter, the deduction is a subsidy or tax expenditure, inequitably cast, to induce labor mobility. Actually, the moving expense deduction is at the frontier of the positive income tax structure; a gradual shift is occurring, and such expenses are coming to be regarded as a factor proper and necessary to the measurement of net income.[38]

Tax incentives distort the choices of the marketplace and produce unneutralities in the allocation of resources. — This criticism is in one sense always valid, because that is what the tax incentive is designed to do. Generally, the critic is also saying or implying that the distortion introduced by the particular incentive is undesirable for various reasons. In large part this criticism is true of many existing incentives for reasons earlier described. The criticism has relevance because the distorting effects of tax incentives often pass unnoticed. But the criticism is of course equally applicable to direct expenditures, some of which certainly are unwise. Again, we are not here concerned with the overall role of Government or the extent to which and under what circumstances financial assistance is desirable to induce private action different from what the marketplace would provide. This criticism thus does not per se tell us when one or the other technique should be used.

It is interesting to note that, even within the area sought to be benefited by the tax incentive, the design of the incentive may push or pull in unneutral directions, which may or may not be desirable. Thus, a tax credit for pollution control facilities focuses on expenditures for machinery as the method of control to the exclusion of other methods, such as a different choice of materials involved in the manufacturing processes.[39] A tax credit for businesses located in urban slums may focus concentration on monetary assistance to the neglect of the provision of technical assistance.

Further, it is difficult if not impossible to keep tax incentives within proper bounds. Tax incentives for the oil industry or the cattle industry or low-income housing or whatever soon become syndicated tax shelters for doctors, executives, actors, and others far removed from the industry itself. Their only attachment to the industry involved is that of the "tax losses" which the ingenious minds can secure for them through bending the tax mechanics of the incentive to the tax shelter device. Tax incentive aid to an industry thus soon becomes a tax windfall to every doctor or other investor who is steered to that industry by tax shelter syndicators and advisers.

The defenders of tax incentives never really face this issue. They always point to the problems of the industry and find a "crisis" to require the continuance of the incentive. If the "national security crisis" begins to lose its weight as a defense for oil incentives, then the "energy crisis" will do. It is a "housing crisis" that is paraded by the real estate industry and a "food crisis" by the cattle and farming industries. However, as a lawyer describing the rosebush tax shelter said, "it is difficult to believe the United States is in the throes of a rosebush crisis."[40] The cry of "crisis" is always considered the complete answer, and further defense of the incentive is not needed. But the cry of "crisis" — assuming its validity — is only the first step in identifying the problem and in seeking the answer to whether Government assistance is needed. The presence of the "crisis" does not automatically tell us a tax incentive is better than a direct grant. It does not answer the tax unfairnesses and economic inefficiencies inherent in the tax shelters spawned by the tax incentive response to the "crisis." Indeed, the cry of "crisis" is really used to avoid those issues and to divert the legislators' minds from them. The hope is that the legislators will hear and see only the "crisis" and thereby either forget about the defects of the tax incentive solution or say that nothing should be done about them for fear of making the "crisis" worse.[41] There is indeed something almost awesome in the assertion that a tax incentive, which usually crept into the law long ago and often without any real relationship to an industry problem, suddenly becomes just the proper and only response to a current "crisis" never foreseen when the particular provision was adopted.

Tax incentives keep tax rates high by constricting the tax base and thereby reducing revenues. — This criticism of tax incentives states a fact that many overlook in their advocacy of tax incentives. The lack of an explicit accounting in the Federal Budget for the tax expenditures involved in tax incentives and the lack in most cases of an accounting in the tax statistical data combine to cause many to forget that dollars are being spent. As a consequence, the criticism that is made against direct expenditures — that they keep our tax rates high — is often lost sight of when tax incentives are involved. This criticism of tax incentives is thus a useful reminder that Government funds are being spent, and that therefore whatever degree of scrutiny and care should be applied to direct expenditures should also be applied to tax incentives.[42] Tax incentives are usually open-ended: they place no limit on how much tax benefit a taxpayer can earn. Hence it is difficult to foretell how much will be spent by the Government through a particular incentive. It is difficult in the nature of things to structure most tax incentives in order to provide a limit on their use. Thus, tax incentives are much like the uncontrollable direct expenditures in the budget.

In the end, the issue is whether, as to any particular area, we want direct Government provision of services or goods, Government financial assistance to encourage and assist private action to provide the services or goods, or reliance on private action unaided by the Government. If we choose Government provision or assistance, then public dollars must be spent, and whether they are dollars forgone through lost tax revenues or dollars spent directly through direct expenditures, the effect on tax rates will be the same. So also will the effect on the economy if the Government program succeeds, and the resultant effect on the revenue base and tax rates of the increased economic activity that such success may mean.

Summary of Asserted Virtues and Vices
of Tax Incentives

This description of the virtues and vices of tax incentives yields these conclusions: the *asserted disadvantages* — waste, inefficiency, and inequity — are true of most tax incentives existing or proposed because of the way they are structured or grew up. The whole approach to tax incentives — one of rather careless or loose analysis, failure to recognize that dollars are being spent, or to recognize the defects inherent in working within the constraints of the positive tax system — has produced very poor programs. But *if* the problems were recognized and *if* care were taken to design tax incentive programs that one would be willing to defend in substantive terms if the programs were cast as direct expenditure programs, then these disadvantages would not be involved, except to the extent that they are inherent in Government assistance itself. These are large conditions, and in most cases would be hard to bring about. For example, it would not be easy to give tax benefit assistance to groups outside the tax system but performing desired activities, such as local governments or tax-exempt organizations hiring the

140

disadvantaged — direct payments outside the tax system would be needed. And it would not be easy to design tax incentive programs which were not inequitable as between taxpayers in high and low brackets and between taxpayers and non-taxpayers. Indeed, there is no tax incentive in existence or proposed that meets the above standards. But for purposes of comparison we are here assuming that the standards could be met under some tax incentive programs.

Similarly, the *asserted advantages* of tax incentives — greater reliance on private decision-making and less detailed requirements — to the extent that they are true in fact (and they are often only illusory) are really criticisms of the complications and supervision built into direct expenditure programs, or else a reflection of the structural weaknesses of the tax incentive program, depending on the amount of detail and supervision appropriate to the particular program. In a rational world, one should assume that if after careful study it is considered that certain complexities and details are not needed and can be left out of a tax incentive program, then they should and can simply be dropped from the direct expenditure program. This may be a more difficult condition than the description suggests, but it is probably less difficult to bring about than the conditions for repairing tax incentives, or at least no more difficult. Again, for purposes of comparison, we are also here assuming this can be done in direct expenditure programs.

What Is Lost by Using a Tax Incentive
Rather than a Direct Expenditure

Given, under the assumptions just made, the same substantive program, under which Government assistance in the same amount is being given in ways and to persons that would be equally acceptable whether tax incentives or direct expenditures were used, what factors should determine the choice of framework for a particular program? We can approach this question by asking: What is lost if the tax incentive technique is used? There are several answers.

Tax incentives, by dividing the consideration and administration of Government programs, confuse and complicate that consideration in the Congress, in administration, and in the budget process. — Let us start with the Congressional consideration of tax incentive programs. By definition such programs are designed to induce action to meet a particular social goal — manpower training of the disadvantaged, education, housing, pollution control, or business location in desired areas, to use some recent examples — and would not be a part of the tax structure were they not deliberately cast as tax incentives. Such governmental programs would normally be considered by the appropriate Congressional committee charged with the legislative area involved: the House Education and Labor and Senate Labor and Public

141

Welfare Committees, the House and Senate Banking and Currency Committees, the House and Senate Interior and Insular Affairs Committees, the House Interstate and Foreign Commerce and Senate Commerce Committees, and so on. These committees are responsible for overseeing and developing legislation in their jurisdictional fields, and so are able to coordinate the Government's programs and policies. Tax legislation, however, goes to the House Ways and Means Committee and the Senate Finance Committee. These committees would normally not consider the substantive areas involved in most tax incentive programs. Tax incentives suddenly charge them with acting on substantive matters outside their fields of responsibility simply because the programs use the tax system. Although tax committees are highly competent in tax matters, they do not have as much insight into these programs or as much experience as the legislative committees normally handling the programs. This lack of familiarity with the programs extends also to the staffs of the tax committees. A similar situation as to both committee members and staffs would prevail if those legislative committees were suddenly to legislate on technical tax matters. Moreover, a tax incentive program considered by the tax committees would be isolated from the regular flow of legislation and activity in the field involved, and this isolation would make coordination and the consideration of priorities difficult.

The purpose of the Congressional committee system is to distribute expertise among the members of Congress. To cast solutions to social problems as tax measures and exchange expertise in those problems for unfamiliarity is, to say the least, both disruptive and unproductive.[43] Moreover, the jumbling of a number of different incentive programs in the tax committees would inevitably set in motion a "log-rolling" process in which careful consideration would be displaced by trading for support among members. Such a process is difficult to control once a committee is operating outside of its area of expertise and with no clear limits on subject matter to restrain it.

These difficulties could perhaps be overcome. Tax committees might refer incentive proposals to the appropriate legislative committees and accept their judgments, or both groups of committees could consider the matter jointly. Approaches like these are sometimes used in areas where a trust fund having earmarked taxes exists. But the system is awkward and leaves unanswered questions — for example, which committee would exert continuing oversight over the program? Given all the trouble and care that must be taken to patch up an arrangement basically at variance with the normal practice, what is gained by choosing that arrangement in the first instance and thereby dividing the governmental consideration of the program?

Much the same can be said about the parallel effect at the administrative level. Social programs are normally administered by executive departments such as Labor, HEW, HUD, and Interior. Taxes are administered by the Internal Revenue Service. A social program cast in tax terms must in the first instance be administered by the Internal Revenue Service, whose expertise does not extend to these other areas. Problems of lack of coordination with other substantive programs would also arise because of the isolation of tax incentive programs. Again, these difficulties could be patched up to some extent — and probably would have to be — by having the appropriate executive department provide some guidance to IRS. But why the divided arrangement in the first place?

At the budgetary level such a division of responsibility makes oversight and control more difficult. Budgetary problems exist even where several relevant executive departments have a hand in the same program or area. The difficulties are compounded when one of the agencies (IRS) really doesn't belong there in the first place, and when it distributes the funds by tax reduction rather than direct expenditure.[44] Our present budgetary process badly compounds these difficulties by giving no recognition or accounting to what is being spent on existing tax expenditures. Until 1968, when the Treasury Department published its analysis of tax expenditure programs and a Tax Expenditure Budget, there was no accounting for the existing tax incentives. The necessary data were not available to the public and were not comprehended within the Government. No one really knew what was being spent through the tax system or for what purposes.[45] In a real sense the $60 to $65 billion of tax expenditures is "lost" in our Government accounts. These expenditures are not in the Budget; they do not appear, for the most part, in Treasury Statistics of Income; they ended up in 1970 in an appendix to a statement by a Treasury official before a Subcommittee of the Joint Economic Committee of the Congress which was printed as an exhibit in the Annual Report of the Secretary of the Treasury.

The Statement of Managers in the Conference Report on the 1971 Revenue Act does require the Treasury Department to send annually to the tax committees a list of tax expenditure items, and presumably this submission would also be published annually in the Treasury Secretary's Annual Report along with other tax data regularly included. The material will also be made available to the Joint Economic Committee, presumably in time to be coordinated with its study of the Budget and Economic Report. The House Ways and Means Committee, pursuant to the 1971 Conference Report, did publish in October 1972 and June 1973 "Estimates of Federal Tax Expenditures."[46] But the identification of tax expenditures and the data are not to be found in the Budget itself.

An additional problem is the difficulty of coordinating the treatment of tax incentives with the overall handling of direct expenditures. For example, when overall expenditure limits are directed by the Congress or when the President decides to cut expenditures it is essentially impossible to apply the restrictions to tax incentives. So far, none of the various expenditure control devices, such as those voted in recent years by the Congress or adopted unilaterally by the

143

President, have in any way affected tax expenditures. Yet had these tax programs been structured as direct expenditures, they would have had no such immunity. In substantive terms they do not merit that immunity any more than the direct expenditures, yet their tax clothing shields them. For similar reasons, tax incentives are not covered by the annual budgetary review process; the Bureau of the Budget until recently did not even know about many of them or how much they cost, and as yet has not worked them into the Budget review process in the same manner as direct expenditures.[47] We do have "uncontrollable" areas in the Budget such as interest on the public debt, and since they can play havoc with a budget, an effort is made to keep them to a minimum, and at least to identify them and try to estimate their effect. But in the budget process this is not done for tax incentives.

Overall, therefore, a resort to tax incentives greatly decreases the ability of the Government to maintain control over the management of its priorities. This is true both as to the substantive programs to be introduced, modified, or dropped and as to the amounts to be spent in particular programs and areas. These consequences run counter to the whole thrust of our concerns with the ordering of national priorities and with the wise allocation of our resources, which we have come to see as limited and therefore in need of careful management.

Some of these difficulties could be met. Tax incentives could be identified, amounts estimated, and the data incorporated in the Budget. Unless this is done, comparisons of tax expenditures and direct expenditures must be comparisons of hidden programs with open ones. But even after such clarification, further difficulties would remain. Perhaps the President could be given authority to treat the tax incentive funds as direct expenditures for budgetary control purposes, and the incentives could be structured as far as possible to have them fall in the controllable rather than the uncontrollable expenditure pattern. Perhaps the tax incentive programs could be given yearly or biannual expiration dates, so that they could be reviewed in the same way as direct expenditures under the appropriation and budgetary procedures.

These present differences in the treatment of Budget expenditures and tax expenditures will become crucial if Congress really attempts to improve its control over the budgetary outlay and receipt totals. Many in Congress now recognize that as an institutional matter the Congress must adopt devices and procedures that will enable it to integrate its control over the spending process. This integrated control is necessary to permit Congress to obtain a rational view of budget outlays, the relationship of those outlays to revenue receipts, and in turn the effect of the totals and their interrelationships on the level and the direction of the economic position of the United States. Further, it is clear that obtaining this needed integrated control over the spending process will require changes in the handling of appropriations, in the relationships among the committees involved, and in the relationships between the Congress as a whole and the committee structure. Early in 1973 the Joint Study Committee on Budget Control in its Report[48] indicated the kinds of measures required if integrated control is to be maintained throughout the course of each Congressional budget and the decisions that must be faced if that control is to be both realistic and firm. Essentially, an initial Congressional resolution would fix the targeted figures for Budget outlays and receipts. As legislative and appropriations bills progressed, they would be compared with the targeted figures. Any increase in outlays in one area would have to be matched by decreases elsewhere or revenue increases. A resolution at the end of the session would provide the final reconciliation between outlays and receipts.

Our concern here is not with the details of this suggested integrated control over outlays and receipts or with the institutional steps required to permit committees or the Congress to resist pressures to depart from that control. Assuming that integrated control can be obtained over budget outlays, that control and its benefits would be defeated unless the control extends equally to tax expenditures. From a *quantitative* standpoint, these tax expenditures are so large that they cannot remain outside any rational system of Congressional control over Government spending. Also, *qualitatively* these tax expenditures cannot remain outside any procedures adopted by the Congress to integrate its control over Government spending. We know by now that a decision to provide Government financial assistance to a particular group or activity can be implemented either by a direct expenditure program or by a tax expenditure program. The direct budget or the tax expenditure budget are simply alternate ways of spending Government funds. There is thus no rationality in adopting controls and procedures for Government outlays that exclude tax expenditures from their coverage.

It is apparent that under the tax expenditure system the tax committees are simultaneously functioning as a legislative or authorizing committee and as an appropriations committee. The tax committees both *authorize* the substantive program — that is, decide to whom and for what purpose financial assistance will be given — and then *appropriate* the necessary funds through the reduction in revenue receipts. This being so, the proper course is to apply to the tax committees the rules ultimately adopted, as respects controls over budgetary outlays, for legislative committees and appropriations committees. Thus, rules governing increases in appropriations and the hurdles those increases must meet should also apply to new tax expenditures or increases in existing tax expenditures. Unless tax expenditures are thus included within any such new procedures and rules, the integration will be seriously incomplete and the control seriously impaired. Since there is no real difficulty in covering tax expenditures, the appropriate course is to include them under any new system of Congressional control over the budget.[49]

But this inclusion of tax expenditures within any new system of Congressional budget control, like the solutions available for other problems of Congressional consideration and for administrative operation, raises the questions: What is gained by turning what would normally be a direct expenditure program into a tax incentive program and then trying to structure the program so that it can nevertheless be handled as a direct expenditure program? Why detour through the tax system? Why inject the tax system into the program, when the program can be effectively structured without it?

Tax incentives will not improve the tax system and are likely to damage it significantly. — Certainly the tax system does not gain when expenditures are made through tax incentive programs. We have already seen that tax incentives are inimical to the equity of a tax system — indeed, in a sense that is necessary to their purpose and function. Moreover, the tax system is complex enough as it is, and to have a large number of tax incentives side by side with the provisions making up the structure of the tax itself can only cause confusion and a blurring of concepts and objectives.[50] Tax incentives make it more and more difficult to distinguish between what is subsidy and what is proper tax structure. This is especially so where the tax incentive is not identifiable as such but is merged into a provision that has a genuine relationship to the measurement of net income — as is, for example, the subsidy involved in accelerated depreciation for real estate, since some deduction for depreciation is appropriate.

Moreover, existing tax incentives breed new tax incentives. As activities emerge that compete with existing activities favored by tax incentives, the claim is put forth that the new activities must also have their own tax incentives to maintain balance in the marketplace. Thus, it is urged that recycled solid waste materials should receive the tax benefits accorded to the competing virgin materials.[51] Obviously, the progression of tax incentives under this approach can be endless — what about tax incentives for processes or materials not presently being utilized or even experimented with because they are not competitive with activities aided by existing incentives? A rational allocation of resources becomes very difficult once a tax incentive is introduced into the tent.

It is no answer to say, as do some cynics, that since the tax system today has so many special provisions there should be no objection, when worthwhile programs are involved, to adding still more to the heap. Rather, the effort should persist to contract those existing special provisions that are improper and wasteful. We know from long experience that provisions can be enshrined in tax laws far past their usefulness and long after their defects become clear. We should not, when alternatives are present, freeze in more special provisions, especially since programs in the complex areas of social policy to which many tax incentive proposals relate are essentially experimental in nature.

Tax Incentives

What Is Gained — Allegedly — by Using a Tax Incentive Rather than a Direct Expenditure

A great deal is lost when tax incentives are used. What is to be gained by that approach compared with the direct expenditure approach? Some have advanced answers which are essentially political in nature, and, I think, rooted in illusions or irrationalities. Professor Aaron has observed that the popularity of the tax device "derives from a peculiar alliance among conservatives, who find attractive the alleged reduction in the role of government that would follow from extensive use of tax credits, and liberals anxious to solve social and economic problems — by whatever means — before it is too late."[52] We have already discussed the illusion that tax credits for social purposes are simple and removed from the bureaucratic hand. The second illusion in the above answer is that the Congress will vote dollars through tax incentives that it refuses to appropriate through expenditure programs. Just why a Congress that focuses on the matter should be so inconsistent is not explained. Certainly many members of tax committees, such as Chairman Mills, have recognized that tax incentives do involve expenditures — "back-door spending" in his words — and that a legislator concerned with expenditure levels and expenditure control should not, while holding the front door shut, let hidden expenditures in through the back door.[53] But perhaps irrationality will govern; administrators and legislators will devise and accept programs structured as tax provisions which they would reject as direct expenditures, or will refuse to improve direct expenditure programs, or will spend money through tax incentives that they would not appropriate as direct expenditures. In that event, rational considerations will not change matters.[54]

There is another answer, which also appears to be irrational or illusory. This is the claim that businessmen respond to tax credits but not to other forms of Government assistance; that there is a glamor and magic possessed by dollars of tax reduction that will attract the businessman who would pass up dollars offered through direct expenditures. To the extent that this answer rests on the belief that tax incentives are really simpler, or that complexities can be sheared away only if tax incentives are used, it rests on beliefs already discussed and found either unrealistic or true only if the underlying Government policies are themselves irrational. To the extent that the answer rests on the claim that business regards tax incentive dollars as "clean dollars" — just part of a tax computation — but sees direct expenditure dollars as somehow unclean because they are a subsidy, one can only answer that business probably does not respond this way, or that if it does, it is behaving irrationally. Experience with direct subsidies — the SST program or the guaranteed loans to the Lockheed company, for example — suggests that business firms are willing to and do calculate profit prospects in the light of Government subsidies.[55] Similarly, the argument that business is familiar with tax credits — though until the investment credit there were no credits widely used in the corporate tax system — but not with other forms of Government assistance is certainly not always true. Lack of business familiarity could be overcome by publicizing direct subsidies. The manpower training credit proposal quoted earlier suggested the "the Department of Labor . . . be required to make [the proposal's] provisions known to the unemployed and potential employers in the business community."[56] Such a duty could equally well be placed on that department if it were administering a direct expenditure program.[57]

There may be an aspect of this asserted preference for tax incentive programs that is not illusion or irrationality, but more serious. It may be that legislators and the beneficiaries of tax incentive programs — businesses receiving accelerated depreciation or percentage depletion, state and local governments receiving tax exemption on their bonds — fear that once the public is fully aware of the amounts involved and can weigh expenditure costs against benefits received by the nation, the tax incentives will be found wanting in many respects. In this view, the deeper the incentive is buried in tax technicalities and tax terminology, the more it looks like any other technical tax provision, the more it partakes of the protective coloration of the tax law that can be obtained by such outward similarity to ordinary tax provisions, then the more desirable the tax incentive becomes. The public must dig hard and deep to find the subsidy and evaluate it. But such an approach to Government expenditures — the preference for the hidden subsidy over the open subsidy — is contrary to all experience with budgets, and to efforts to achieve a rational use of resources. If this is the argument for tax incentives, it should not be accepted.

Conclusion

What, then, is the balance sheet regarding these two methods of Government assistance, direct expenditures and tax incentives? I conclude from the above observations that, as a generalization, the burden of proof should rest heavily on those proposing the use of the tax incentive method. In any particular situation — certainly any new situation — the first approach should be to explore the various direct expenditure alternatives. Once the most desirable of these alternatives is determined, if one still wishes to consider the tax incentive method for the same substantive program, the question must be what clear advantages can be obtained by using the tax method. Again, as a generalization, I think it unlikely that clear advantages in the tax incentive method will be found. Moreover, I stress strongly that the advantages must be clear and compelling to overcome the losses that accompany the use of the tax incentive, even the well-structured incentive. The problems of achieving a well-structured incentive are in themselves formidable. Even assuming that such problems as unfairness and windfalls are overcome, there are still the losses and drawbacks I have described: confusion and divided authority in the legislative and administrative processes, difficulties in maintaining budgetary control, confusion in perceiving and setting national priorities, and dangers to the tax structure itself.[58]

It could be that a program of Government assistance that is broadly based, relatively simple, and properly structured can be more readily administered if joined to the tax system. Some have defended the deductions for charitable contributions and personal interest and taxes on this ground, though pointing to the need to correct abuses and recognizing that the corrections would make the tax incentive more like a direct expenditure program.[59] Others have defended the investment credit for the same reasons, again with a recognition that improvements can be made.[60] But none of these incentives has had to meet the test of comparison with a carefully structured direct expenditure program. Only after that is done can we reach the point of well-informed choice.

These are the general guidelines. There may be particular cases to which they do not apply because special considerations are involved. Even so, care must be taken to look hard at special considerations advanced as reasons for an exception to be made "in this particular case." The legislative halls are crowded with advocates skilled in tying their problems to the last exception and in devising techniques to make each step from the last precedent appear to be only short, logical, and harmless. Our gaze can thus be averted from the constantly widening gap between proper tax structure and each additional special provision.[61]

One question raised by this discussion especially merits more research and thought. Just why is it that in many cases legislators appear willing, with hardly any thought, to accept an expensive tax incentive program when they would just as quickly reject a similar direct expenditure program, even a much smaller one? Why do they require lengthy study and analysis of direct expenditure programs before legislative and appropriation committees while they are ready to enact tax incentives on no more than generalizations and hunches? Is it that they do not realize, or stop to think, that dollars are spent by tax incentives? Is it that tax bills are so complicated that hardly any of the legislators study them unless prodded by an industry or taxpayer that is hurt, in his tax pocketbook, by a tax bill, and that therefore tax incentive provisions dispensing largesse slide by — although this would be a case of the proper concession of tax expertise to the tax committees papering over their lack of expertise in the areas involved in tax incentives. Is it that the legislators know full well what is involved, despite the complexity of tax bills, but believe the public will not perceive what is being done because of the complexity of tax bills and because tax expenditures do not show up in the budget? To claim this would almost be a claim that any expenditure of funds is acceptable to a legislator — the more money to constituents the better — but most legislators do not appear to follow this principle. Is it that the legislators familiar with the direct programs in the areas involved do not want to antagonize the tax committees by voting against tax incentives and thereby foster opposition to their own direct programs?[62]

Another puzzling question is why the insights and analyses developed through academic research seem to be reflected reasonably rapidly in much of Congressional legislation on direct expenditure programs and other matters but show so long a time lag before they have an influence on tax legislation. This is especially noticeable in the tax incentive provisions that become part of the tax system.

We could ask similar questions about administrative agencies. Just why do administrators of direct expenditure programs allow tax incentive proposals to be pushed when the funds involved in such programs could be used, and probably much better used, as coordinated parts of the direct expenditure programs? Is it that their policy is to accept gratefully contributions from any source? Is it that they will not face up to the need either to improve the direct expenditure program or squarely demonstrate the erratic and wasteful character of the tax incentive proposal? Is it that they are sometimes negligent in their legislative intelligence and are simply left at the legislative starting gate when the tax incentive is adopted? And why should a Treasury Department which is charged with preserving the integrity of the tax system ever willingly propose or accept a tax incentive solution except in the unusual and rare situation when a tax credit may possibly be properly tailored, and better suited to the purpose — conditions which do not appear to exist as to any of the new incentives that have been pushed by the Treasury in the present Administration except perhaps for the investment credit?

With *new* situations — that is, new or expanded Government programs — we are in a position to follow a rational course in choosing between these methods, though the experiences with the incentives added in the 1969 and 1971 tax legislation indicate the lessons must be relearned by the Treasury Department and the Congress. During the 1960's, as attention turned increasingly to Government financial assistance to meet urgent social problems, almost every problem brought proposals of a tax incentive as the solution; often the tax incentive was the first solution to be advanced. The Treasury Department responded by pressing the White House staff and other agencies to devise, with the Treasury, nontax alternatives for comparison on a cost-effectiveness basis. For example, the Treasury, with HEW, developed the federal guaranteed student loan program and expanded scholarship and work programs, so that they could be pushed in opposition to a tax credit for college tuition. In the manpower field, the Treasury urged strong and expanding federally supported training programs which could be advanced instead of a tax incentive. The skepticism with which specialized tax incentives for social problems were regarded by the Treasury, together with a realization that a negative answer to proposals of tax incentives did not solve the social problems, led the Treasury to be a strong force within the Government in developing and pushing direct expenditure programs, both to counter tax incentive proposals and to move forward to meet the social problems in other ways.

Indeed, after the adoption in 1962 of the investment credit, which was proposed by the Treasury, and a deduction for contributions by the self-employed to their own pension plans[63] which was opposed by the Treasury, no other tax incentive was enacted by the Congress. The attitude of the Treasury Department in the 1960's was reflected in this statement of Treasury Secretary Henry Fowler, accompanying the submission of a tax reform program developed in the Treasury of the Johnson period:

> In working on the structure of our tax system, one is confronted with the suggestions for tax incentives to enlist private initiative to meet our social and economic problems. We have given careful consideration in this proposed revision of our tax system to such possible solutions to these problems. We believe that our social and economic needs can better be served through direct measures outside the tax system, rather than by tax credits and other forms of tax incentives. Consistent with this conclusion, we have also attempted to minimize distortions caused by existing special tax provisions.
>
> Indeed, it has been our experience that when the proposed tax incentives are viewed as alternatives to budget expenditures, there are direct nontax methods available which are feasible and helpful, and which give greater benefits for the budgetary costs involved than do the tax incentives. Examples of effective nontax methods of achieving objectives that had been sought through the tax system include guaranteed loans, equal opportunity grants, and other programs to assist students and their families with the costs of higher education; direct grants for water pollution control projects; rent supplements and interest subsidies to increase the supply of low- and middle-income housing; and Government contracts with private employers to train hard-core unemployed for jobs. These methods achieve the important objectives in a manner consistent both with an equitable tax system and with careful and responsible budgetary control by the executive and the Congress.[64]

But Administrations change and the Treasury changes with them! The stance of the Treasury in the early 1970's is favorable to the use of tax incentives. Consider, for example, this expression of attitude by Assistant Secretary of the Treasury Edwin Cohen in 1969:

> Tax incentives, if carefully designed and explicitly described and circumscribed in the statute, have advantages in some areas in their simplicity of operation, in the reduction of bureaucracy and in the enlistment of private capital toward the attainment of national goals. They must be approached with caution, bathed in the floodlight of public attention and scrutiny and weighed in the balance with the obvious need of maintaining the equity of our tax system.[65]

This attitude, though sounding more cautious than that prevailing in years prior to the 1960's, is nevertheless more receptive to tax incentives than that developed in the previous Treasury administration.

This receptivity is reflected in the legislation enacted in 1969 and in subsequent developments. The Tax Reform Act of that year brought in four new tax incentives, using the technique of five-year amortization of costs, for rehabilitation of low-income rental housing, pollution-control facilities, railroad cars, and mine safety equipment. The first was suggested by the Treasury and the second apparently in part acquiesced in by it. In 1970 the Treasury recommended a costly tax incentive for exports,[66] reversing a position previously taken, and in 1971 it radically revised by regulations the tax rules governing the depreciation of machinery and equipment to introduce a tax incentive for investment in those assets.[67] The 1971 Revenue Act reintroduced the investment credit, incorporated the 1971 Treasury incentive regulations on depreciation (except for the revised first-year convention which it rejected), and adopted a tax incentive for exporters (DISC), all pressed upon the Congress by the Treasury. The Congress on its own, with varying intensity of objection from the Treasury, adopted five-year amortization for the construction of facilities for employer-provided on-the-job training programs and child care facilities; a tax credit for employers who employ persons registered in Labor Department work incentive programs; a large increase in the child care deduction, including household expenses; and a tax credit and deduction for political contributions. The Treasury is still pursuing the tax incentive route and in April 1973 recommended a tax credit to provide for property tax relief for the elderly, a tax credit for tuition paid to private elementary and secondary schools, and a tax credit for exploratory oil drilling. This unfortunate Treasury receptivity to tax incentives can only lead others also to press this technique and thereby both weaken the tax structure and militate against the revision of existing tax incentives.[68]

With *existing* tax incentives, the task is one that falls in the category of "tax reform," where progress is difficult and slow. The tax reform proposals developed in the Johnson Treasury,[69] related, in the case of the income tax, almost entirely to tax incentives and involved varying degrees of scaling down and restructuring existing incentives. Only a few of the proposals related to defects in the fitting together of the tax structure proper (for example, multiple corporation provisions and mineral production payment provisions) or changes in the application of that structure, such as elimination or reduction of tax for those below or around poverty income levels. This helps place in perspective the whole matter of tax reform. The 1969 Tax Reform Act also follows this pattern, and most of its major reforms consist of reducing the scope of existing tax incentives, such as those relating to real estate, financial institutions, capital gains investment, natural resources, and farm activities.

We do learn some things as the tax years pass by; the newer additions both in tax structure and special provision are in general more carefully tailored with an eye to many of these problems than their predecessors. For example, compare the moving expense and medical expense deductions with those for personal interest and taxes as originally adopted early in our tax history. Or compare the structure of the 7 percent investment credit with the provision for accelerated depreciation for real estate as it appeared in 1954.[70] The 1971 investment credit improves over the 1962 credit by restricting its potential to create tax shelters for individuals leasing equipment.[71] Unfortunately, and most discouragingly, we also can forget almost overnight what we so painfully learned over a long period, as the earlier discussion of the upside-down structure of the new five-year amortization for housing rehabilitation expenditures indicates.

It seems likely that "tax reform" for many existing incentives will be in the direction of contracting the area of incentives by reducing the number of those eligible for benefits, reducing the extent of the benefits, and removing the undue advantages granted upper-income groups. The degree of change will presumably vary with the breadth of the incentive: those that involve specific areas and provide tax benefits for a restricted group — for example, accelerated depreciation for real estate and the natural resource provisions — will, or at least should, be subject to examination regarding cutbacks in scope and benefit, whereas incentives with broad reach — for example, the charitable, interest and tax deductions — will probably be scrutinized for particular abuses. This, in general, was the tenor of the Tax Reform Act of 1969.

Once we begin to recognize that the existing tax incentives represent expenditures of funds that in many cases should be dispersed directly, we must develop legislative and administrative techniques to move the funds involved — to the extent that Government financial assistance is still considered desirable — from the Tax Expenditure Budget to the regular budget. The tax committees or the Office of Management and Budget could indicate to the Congress and the administrative agencies concerned the amounts involved in particular tax incentive programs.[72] A period of time would then be allowed for the appropriate legislative committees and administrative agencies to develop direct expenditure programs, and a time limit could be put on the duration of the tax incentive programs. At the end of this period the tax incentive would be ended and the new direct expenditure program funded with the dollars returned to the revenue side of the budget.[73] Certainly, new tax incentive programs, if any are to be adopted, should have a time limit set on their operation, to permit such a shift to a direct expenditure program, or at least to permit evaluation of the effectiveness and operation of the tax incentive.[74]

The varied approaches necessary to replace tax expenditures with direct governmental assistance and the nature of "tax reform" in these areas are discussed further in Chapters VI and VII.

For the present, a de-escalation of existing particular incentives would be progress, though it would leave a set of tax incentives that probably would not be used at all if we were able to treat the problems fully as new problems. But this is the path of tax history and indeed all legislative history. Knowing all this, let us at least attempt not to repeat past mistakes in future solutions.

APPENDIX*

A NOTE ON REGULATORY TAXES

Chapter V compares the use of tax incentives with direct expenditure programs to achieve desired policy goals. The emphasis is on incentives under the income tax, but the discussion would have general application to other taxes, such as the estate and gift taxes, intended to be all-inclusive in their application to a particular measure of ability to pay, e.g., income, or wealth transmitted to the succeeding generation. Tax incentives operate to induce desired action through subsidizing that action and thereby providing governmental financial assistance to the person undertaking the action. The comparison favors resort to the direct programs in nearly all cases as the method of providing the encouragement of governmental financial assistance.

There are in the federal tax system a number of tax provisions designed to function as regulatory devices. These regulatory tax provisions operate by making more expensive either the continuance of present conduct where that conduct is contrary to a desired policy goal or a change to conduct inconsistent with the policy goal. The regulatory tax provisions do not provide financial assistance comparable to direct expenditure programs, and have not been classified as tax expenditures. Also their specialized function, when compared with the broad-based income tax, for example, does not call for the techniques of tax expenditure analysis as applied to the income tax.[1] But these regulatory taxes do involve a resort to the tax system as a solution to particular national problems. Tax incentives also involve resort to the tax system for the solution of problems, the solution being that of subsidy and financial assistance. Although our analysis indicates, as stated above, that the use of the income tax system for subsidy purposes is an undesirable method of solution, it does not follow from this that use of the tax system in other ways is also undesirable as compared with non-tax approaches. That comparison requires its own criteria and analysis.

The regulatory taxes are usually in the form of special excise taxes, such as the older taxes relating to narcotic drugs, white phosphorous matches, adulterated butter, filled cheese, cotton futures, and wagering, and more recent taxes relating to the purchase of foreign securities (interest equalization tax) and the activities of private foundations. The older measures were often prohibitory, e.g., the taxes on matches or adulterated butter, and were adopted when there were doubts under earlier judicial precedents as to the constitutional legality of direct regulation by the Congress. The newer measures mentioned above were in one sense chosen as preferable to direct measures, but the choice was in large part influenced by the fact that the

155

committee involved — the House Ways and Means Committee — in these areas could assert jurisdiction over the problem only by using a tax solution.[2]

Chapter V discusses the criteria applicable to choosing between a tax incentive approach and a direct expenditure approach, where the preferred solution to a particular problem is that of Government financial assistance to induce a change from socially undesirable conduct or inactivity to desirable conduct. But suppose the preferred solution is not that of assistance in making the change, but rather a method of directly stopping or curtailing the undesirable conduct. Among possible methods for this path of solution, Government can consider a direct regulatory approach controlling the conduct or a tax regulatory approach that makes continuation of the conduct too expensive. What criteria are applicable to the choice between these methods? There is at present considerable interest in using the tax regulatory approach to achieve the goal of improving the quality of the environment. An example is the suggested federal tax on sulfur dioxide emissions into the air by power plants and other users of fuels with a high sulfur content.[3] In view of the interest in these pollution taxes and their novelty, the following discussion of the use of regulatory taxes and the criteria applicable to their choice as against other approaches, especially a direct regulatory approach, is in terms of a pollution tax.

The Pollution Tax in Theory

A pollution tax is a charge imposed for every unit of pollutant discharged into the environment. An example would be a 15 cent charge on every pound of sulfur dioxide emitted into the atmosphere. Pollution taxes have drawn the support of economists and environmentalists primarily for the following reason: pollution taxes in theory, according to their supporters, provide a mechanism by which any particular level of abatement of pollution can be attained at the least cost possible.

As an illustration of what is meant by "least-cost abatement," suppose two polluters, A and B, each emit 100 pounds of pollutants. It costs A 50 cents to eliminate one pound of pollution, but it costs B $1 a pound. If each eliminates 50 pounds of pollutants, then total pollution is reduced by 100 pounds. The total cost of abatement is $75. Clearly a cheaper way to eliminate 100 pounds of pollutants would be to have A stop polluting entirely, while B does not abate at all. Then 100 pounds of total abatement costs only $50.

The notion of "least-cost abatement" may be viewed as an unnecessary concept to introduce into a discussion of pollution control. If the desired solution to the pollution problem is to eliminate all emissions of pollutants, then a least-cost abatement — and a pollution tax — approach is not the appropriate path. Clearly, regulation of a prohibitory character is the necessary technique. Current legislative policy, established in 1972, regarding water pollution does favor the regulatory approach and carries that approach to its full conclusion by adopting the goal of *elimination* by 1985 of the discharge of pollutants into navigable waters. This final stage would be reached after passing through the stages of, first, required adoption of "the best practicable control technology currently available" and, next, cessation of pollution unless the polluter can demonstrate that cessation is "not attainable at reasonable cost," in which event the limit is that consistent with "the best available technology, taking into account the cost of such controls." The legislation thus first uses regulation with elements of discretion in interpreting the legislative standards, and then moves to absolute prohibition.[4] But many economists consider such an approach likely in the end to prove unfeasible except in rather special situations. They believe the costs of total elimination may be out of proportion to the benefits attained, and hence larger than the nation will desire to pay.[5]

If total elimination is not the goal — and this statement is not intended to pass judgment on the current solution for water pollution but rather to continue the theoretical analysis — it becomes necessary to decide what level of pollution is tolerable, and then attempt to obtain the abatement that is desired from existing levels at the least possible cost in terms of the nation's resources. Large sums of money could be wasted if attention is not paid to the question of least-cost solutions. Returning to the example above, the abatement goal for A and B was a 50 percent reduction in total emissions. But reaching that goal by asking A and B to each cut emissions by 50 percent — the approach of uniform reduction by each — increases the cost of attaining the goal by $25, or 50 percent, above the least-cost solution.

Pollution taxes lead to least-cost abatement in the following manner: Assume the pollution tax is set at 50 cents a pound. If a polluter can eliminate a pound of pollutants from his emissions for less than 50 cents, he will save money by doing so rather than paying the tax. Therefore, a polluter will eliminate as many pounds of pollutants from his emissions as he can, so long as the cost of abatement is less than 50 cents a pound. Once the cost exceeds 50 cents, it is in his economic interest to pay the tax rather than to further abate the pollution. If it costs him 30 cents a pound to eliminate up to 75 percent of his emissions, but costs 70 cents a pound thereafter, he will only eliminate 75 percent of his emissions. Thus, after the 50 cents a pound tax is adopted, all abatement that can be achieved at less than 50 cents a pound will be undertaken, but there will be no abatement that costs more than 50 cents a pound. The abatement so achieved has been obtained at the least possible cost. There would be a cheaper way to attain the same total abatement only if some polluter could reduce his emissions further at a lower cost than is being incurred by someone who is presently abating.[6]

How does the pollution tax compare *in theory* with other possible approaches to pollution abatement? The obvious alternative approach is that of *direct regulation.* As stated above, if total elimination is the goal, then the regulatory approach is the necessary technique. If, however, the goal is something less than total elimination, then regulation becomes only an alternative technique rather than the sole path. It is generally argued by many economists that the regulatory approach could not as effectively result in least-cost abatement as does the tax approach. Indeed, they feel that any practicable regulatory plan is likely to result in something far from least-cost abatement. Studies have shown that a regulation imposing *uniform abatement* — in which each polluter must abate by 90 percent or some such figure — can in certain situations result in abatement costs of two or three times the least-cost figure.[7] Further, a regulation requiring each polluter to *install particular equipment,* such as emission control equipment at a final stage, will also fall short of least-cost abatement since in many cases abatement would be attainable at less expense through other equipment, changes in fuels or plant processes, or even changes in the product produced — such as a shift from dyed to undyed products.[8] Theoretically, direct regulation could impose least-cost abatement by telling every polluter to do precisely what he would do if a pollution tax were introduced. But such a regulation would appear unworkable. Government administrators would probably be overwhelmed by the necessity of computing cost figures for every polluter,[9] a burden that the pollution tax places on the individual polluter himself, so that each plant in an industry is itself encouraged to seek the most economic way to reduce *its* pollution.

If the antipollution goal were the "maximum abatement technologically feasible," regulation presumably could require each polluter to abate as much as possible — the only way of reaching the goal. But such a goal is not as straightforward as one might think initially. Any amount of abatement is feasible — if we are willing to use very expensive processes, or shut down industries, and the like. Clearly, regulators in applying the standard "maximum technologically feasible" would have to make judgments as to whether certain techniques that are available are nevertheless too expensive to be "feasible." They would also have to decide whether abatement should be achieved by forcing a reduction in production or a shift in production from one product to another. Thus, wholly apart from whether it would achieve the aggregate result desired, "maximum feasible" is not as well-defined a term as might be imagined. There are many paths that could and would be followed in achieving a "feasible" application of a "maximum feasible" standard. It is thus highly unlikely that regulation utilizing a "maximum feasible" standard will lead to achievement of the desired level at the least possible cost.

Positive financial inducements such as *tax incentives* and *direct subsidies* likewise do not lead to least-cost abatement. Such tax incentives — credits against tax or deductions, for example — are usually granted for pollution-control capital expenditures, regardless of the effectiveness of the equipment purchased or the superiority of abatement through methods not involving capital expenditures.[10] Nor are tax incentives which fall short of complete cost reimbursement for the changes involved, both capital cost and operating costs, likely to induce those changes unless they are compelled by other measures, and in that situation the tax incentive becomes a gratuity for doing what would be done in any event. It is likely that direct subsidies would be similarly misdirected. The only form of subsidy that could lead to least-cost abatement would be the mirror-image of a pollution tax; that is, a subsidy that pays a polluter in proportion to the abatement achieved — for example, 15 cents for every pound of pollutant eliminated from the polluter's emissions. A polluter would be induced to abate if and only if the cost of abatement were less than 15 cents per pound. But such a subsidy scheme appears administratively unworkable. It seems impossible to establish a subsidy system that neither provides windfall gains to some polluters (for "reduction" in pollution that they would have undertaken even without the subsidy) nor denies proper subsidies to others. Consider how the subsidizing agency is to determine the base level of pollution for each polluter, the abatement from which level is to be subsidized. What about firms that have cut pollution before the subsidy was introduced? Expansion of production and new firms present special difficulties. Could a nonpolluter claim that, but for the subsidy, he would have polluted a great deal?

The stress in the above discussion has been in terms of the theory of least-cost abatement to explain the theoretical support for a pollution tax, and the comparison between a pollution tax and other approaches has used that criterion. As indicated earlier, the criterion is not applicable if society determines its objective to be the total elimination of a pollutant. There may also be other situations, as discussed later, when other factors will outweigh the least-cost criterion and govern the choice. But the least-cost criterion will usually be a relevant factor. A pollution tax appears in theory more likely, because of its essential structure, to satisfy that criterion than do other approaches.[11]

As discussed later, however, the pollution tax approach and the regulatory approach may not be mutually inconsistent, and in some instances may well be complementary.

With this background, indicating the theoretical support for the pollution tax compared with other approaches, we may turn to a consideration of the structure of such a tax. The obviously important question is that of the tax level. The level at which the pollution tax should be set depends primarily upon the environmental goal sought for the particular pollutant. What is the quality of environment desired, or put another way, how much pollution abatement is desired? The question obviously is not easy to answer. It depends on the costs of abatement and on an estimate of the benefits to be gained by reducing pollution. Abatement is desirable until the point when benefits no longer exceed the costs. Precise estimates of costs would require knowledge of all available technology and the operations of every polluter. Estimates of the benefits from abatement would be even more difficult to ascertain. Injury to health and other physical damage caused by pollution are not known with any certainty. Moreover, there are likely to be wide differences of opinion on what price tag to put on damage from pollution, particularly scenic damage and injury to recreational areas. Thus, there will be no scientific certainty in the political process' judgment as to what level of abatement is worth the costs involved. But this judgment must be made whatever technique is used — whether regulation, subsidies, or taxes, to improve the environment.

After the desired quality of environment is determined, the level of the pollution tax should be set so that the tax will induce the amount of abatement necessary for the attainment of the desired quality. Setting the tax will be an imprecise process, just as was setting the desired environmental quality. Those urging the pollution tax approach say it should be possible to set the tax at about the right starting level. Some knowledge, although far from complete, of the costs of abatement should already be available from the studies necessary to establish the environmental quality desired. Then, with this knowledge of the approximate costs of reducing emissions, the tax can be set at the level which will make the desired abatement cheaper than paying the tax. Fifty percent abatement, for example, would be attained if the tax were set at a level such that abatement of half of the emissions could be achieved at a cost per pound less than the tax rate. Of course, information regarding costs may not be altogether accurate; but supporters of the tax approach assert that it is possible to learn about the costs of abatement by observing what effects the tax has. If there is less abatement than anticipated, then the costs must have been underestimated. The information the tax thus provides regarding costs can be used to recalculate the proper tax rate or to redefine the environmental quality desired.

Thus, whether we are interested in a regulation approach or in a pollution tax we must first determine the desired environmental quality, and this in turn will determine the degree of abatement needed. If it is a regulation approach we will use to achieve the abatement, we must set a standard that embodies the desired environmental quality and mandates the required abatement. If it is a tax approach, we must set a rate that will achieve the desired quality level through the interplay of cost of abatement and tax payment. Both approaches require a good deal of knowledge regarding overall data and the characteristics of particular firms. But it is argued that an advantage of the tax over a regulatory approach is that the tax can operate effectively without the Government's need to know the cost of abatement for each individual polluter. To set the tax rate it is only necessary to know in general the costs of abatement. Once the rate is set, the tax is essentially operative, since each firm will determine the effect for it of the interplay between the costs of abatement and the tax it will pay for nonabatement. The regulatory approach, however, appears to require a greater degree of knowledge as to each firm, as administrators decide how the chosen standard is applicable to the particular firm, since generally the standard is phrased in terms that have some generality, e.g., "best practicable" or "best available" technology.[12] If regulation takes the approach of a set environmental standard, then some authority has to determine which industry, and which firms in an industry, are responsible for meeting the standard. In other words, if the standard is not met, who is to be held responsible for the failure? In the end, here also information as to each firm would seem a necessary ingredient.

Under each approach, tax or regulatory, there can be error in aiming at the target — either the regulatory standard or the tax rate may be wide of the target. The real danger, as stated later, presumably comes if the error sets up irreversible conditions. Otherwise, the course under either approach lies in correction of the standard or tax rate in the light of experience.

At this point in the theoretical comparison between the tax approach and the regulatory approach we do come to a crucial difference. This difference is generally discussed in terms of the tax approach involving a "license to pollute," and those using the phrase intend it as derogatory to the tax approach. It is obvious that if the goal is to be short of total elimination, then either a regulation approach or a tax approach will leave some pollution to continue, and one can, if one wants to, call the result a "license to pollute." But the regulation approach permits the continuing pollution to be a free item to the polluter. In contrast, the tax approach levies a tax — a user charge — on the polluter so that he must pay society for the damage he is inflicting through the remaining pollution. The "licensed pollution," if one does want to use that term, is thus a free ride under the regulation approach but a paid-for result under the tax approach — both of course achieving the desired abatement. This difference — between a free ride and a charge for the continuing pollution — would seem a basic difference between the two approaches.

The important point is that a pollution tax set at the proper rate would not allow — or "license" — any pollution that should be stopped. This follows because, if the tax rate is set properly, it should be approximately equal to the damage that would be caused by adding one more pound of emission beyond the level set by the desired environmental quality. The initial assumption in our earlier example was that a 50 cent tax would induce every polluter to reduce his emissions until the cost of further abatement exceeds 50 cents per pound. If the pollution tax has been set at the proper rate, then the desired environmental quality will be achieved; that is, all further reduction will not be worth the cost of abatement.

Thus, if 50 cents is the proper tax rate, abatement that costs *less* than 50 cents a pound — the abatement that will occur under the tax — is worth the cost of abatement, whereas abatement that costs *more* than 50 cents a pound is not worth the cost. This implies that the benefit of reducing emissions by one pound is 50 cents. In other words, one pound of pollutant beyond the optimal level causes 50 cents worth of damage. Of course, because the lower the level of pollution the less the marginal damage caused by adding one more pound of pollutant emission, any further reduction in pollution beyond the desired environmental quality will lead to a decrease in damage — an improvement in the environment — that is worth less than 50 cents for each pound of abatement.

But the tax induces all abatement that can be achieved at less than 50 cents a pound. For all the remaining pollution, the cost of abatement — which exceeds 50 cents a pound — is greater than the benefit — 50 cents a pound or less. Abatement whose cost exceeds its benefit should, under the initial assumption, not be undertaken. The remaining pollution represents that element of pollution which society has determined must be tolerated. Hence, the continuance of that pollution cannot be regarded as licensed pollution in a perjorative sense. Only if society determines that all pollution should be eliminated can it be really said that the pollution continuing after the tax is "licensed."[13]

This discussion of the "license to pollute" issue and the comparison between a free ride under the regulatory approach in contrast to continued payment under the tax approach, lead to an advantage that is asserted for the tax approach. Unless the standard used in a regulation is altered, a firm or an industry can rest on its efforts once it meets that standard, so that the amount of pollution conceded to continue when the standard was set will so continue. Any subsequent improvement in the environment can come only if a new standard is set. A regulatory approach could perhaps involve a "prod," such as setting the standard quite high, then giving variances that reflected a reasonable view of existing technology, and then gradually tightening the regulatory effect through withdrawal of the variances. Another "prod" could be Government-provided technology when it is felt individual firms could not afford the necessary research. But such prods rest on Government knowledge and action. In contrast, under the tax approach, there is a built-in incentive — the constant payment of the tax or user charge — goading a firm or an industry to see if a new technology or a new production method will shift the originally assumed balance between cost and tax to a higher degree of abatement. This will occur if the change in abatement cost calculations now makes the tax more expensive, so that the further abatement becomes desirable as a matter of net profits for the firm. There is therefore an inherent safety factor for society in the tax approach.[14] The advantage under the tax approach of the prod effect of the continuing tax payment cannot, however, be pushed too far. Since many will see an aspect of unfairness in requiring continuing payments when the standards overall are met, the "price" still to be paid cannot be made too large. If it is, society will consider that the tax charge has been pitched at the wrong level. Hence, there is a tension between society's tolerance of the continuing tax payment as being a fair one and the efficacy of the continuing payment to spur further improvement.

An argument advanced against the pollution tax is that, conceding its efficacy in achieving least-cost pollution, it might be the wrong approach because the tax would lead to higher prices. Of course, a regulation approach also raises prices because the resort to antipollution measures by a polluter in response to the regulation will increase his costs of production. While under both approaches the costs of abatement will thus have an effect on prices, the efficiency of the tax approach in achieving the least-cost abatement should in theory make its overall cost lower than under a regulation approach, and hence involve a lesser initial impact on prices. But the pollution tax will cause a further price effect, since the tax must, as indicated above, be paid even after the desired abatement has been achieved.

This effect of the pollution tax on prices would, in the viewpoint of those proposing the tax, be nothing remarkable in our economic system. On the contrary, the price rise caused by the continued tax payment would result in our environmental resources being treated precisely the same way as other scarce resources. A manufacturer now pays for his raw materials, equipment, land, and labor. With the pollution tax, he would also pay for his use of the environment, i.e., the damage he causes to the environment. If two identical products cost the same to produce, but one production process creates pollution while the other does not, then resources are best utilized when the nonpolluting product has a price advantage. Resources would thereby move from production processes causing pollution to nonpolluting processes. Moreover, the tax would induce the amount of reallocation of resources that economic theory dictates, assuming the tax is set at the correct rate. This is because, as pointed out earlier, the proper tax rate is the damage caused by one more pound of pollutant emission beyond that allowed by the environmental quality desired. This is the "marginal cost" of pollution beyond the amount desired, and the proper price for such a product is just that "marginal cost."

Some polluters may have to go out of business because the tax forces their prices too high. But there is nothing new about firms going out of business because consumers are unwilling to pay for the costs of production. Perhaps governmental assistance will be needed to ameliorate problems arising from the transition to a pollution tax. But in the long run any reallocation of resources resulting from the imposition of a properly set tax is desirable. And, even in the short run, estimates of the President's Council on Environmental Quality indicate that few firms would have to close down because of antipollution efforts.

It is often argued that if a regulation approach is used, then in this setting a tax approach is redundant or even punitive.[15] This argument, of course, overlooks the basic differences between the two approaches in the "free ride" aspect of regulation compared with the "user charge" aspect of the tax. In the light of this difference, however, and the consequences that flow from it, the combination of approaches is certainly not punitive, and need not be redundant, but instead could be complementary. Thus, the Clean Air Amendments of 1970, using a regulatory approach, authorized national air quality standards to be set by the Environmental Protection Agency and called for state plans to meet those standards. In addition, President Nixon proposed in February 1972 a pollution tax on the sulfur content of fuel as a method of moving to the desired abatement of the sulfur pollution in air. The tax was thus viewed by the Administration, and also its many proponents among environmental groups, as a beneficial complement to the basic regulatory approach.[16] The House Ways and Means Committee, to whom the proposal was referred, did not consider it.

If all else were equal, it is probably doubtful that society would prefer the tax approach just because it provides a user charge for the pollution which society considers tolerable. Under this "all else being equal" condition, we might be satisfied not to impose such a charge and permit the free ride that the regulation approach affords. The latter seems more in keeping with our traditional views on allocation of risks and damages. But on the other hand, if all else is not equal — if the prod aspect of the tax approach is important, if the tax approach accommodates better than the regulatory approach to the large imperfections in our knowledge and data, if the continuing user charge is not regarded as unfair in magnitude, and so on — then the user charge aspect of the tax approach is not a basis for faulting that approach or preventing us from turning to it.

The Pollution Tax in Practice

The above discussion sketches the theoretical setting for the pollution tax approach and the advantages asserted for it by its supporters in comparison to other approaches, principally the regulatory approach with which it primarily must be compared. We may now move on to the factors that can in particular situations affect this general theoretical comparison.

When the Tax Is Unnecessary

At the outset several situations should be noted in which a pollution tax does not even have theoretical advantages:

A total prohibition is called for: As earlier indicated, in some cases, such as mercury pollution, the damage caused by the pollutant is so great and the cost of abatement so low that there is no reason to allow any pollution. Hence, a prohibitory regulation approach is required.

No prohibition is necessary: At the opposite extreme, it may be that economic forces make emission of a particular pollutant beyond desired levels to be unprofitable in itself, so that the pollutant will not be discharged in excessive amounts even without a tax being imposed or a regulation required.

Uniform abatement is least-cost abatement: It is conceivable, though unlikely, that every emitter of a particular pollutant will have to pay about the same to achieve the same level of abatement. In that case, there is no inefficiency in simply requiring through regulation that all the polluters abate to the same extent.

When Measures in Addition to the Tax Are Necessary

In other situations, a pollution tax may have to be accompanied by other measures to obtain the desired end result:

The possibility of the tax being too low is too grave a risk: There always will be some guesswork in deciding what tax rate is necessary to achieve the desired environmental quality. The tax may be set too low. It is possible that too low a rate will lead to intolerable or irreversible damage to the environment. This may well be the case for certain geographical areas if a nationwide tax rate is used. To prevent such consequences, a regulation could be imposed setting maximum permissible emission levels, regardless of the tax. It must be recognized, however, that any such regulation could lead to significant increases over the cost of abatement attainable when the tax is used alone. And there must be data available that permit the regulation itself to be pitched at a safe precautionary level.

Collective facilities may be necessary: Although the tax may induce each individual polluter to seek the least-cost abatement he can achieve alone, it may not sufficiently encourage joint ventures among polluters to build collective facilities — such as waste disposal plants — that will lead to even cheaper abatement. The Government may need to build such facilities, charging polluters for their use.

The tax may not eliminate intolerable local or temporary conditions: Even if the tax leads to the desired environmental quality in the country at large or in a particular region, pollution levels in the immediate vicinity of a particular polluter may be intolerable. The Government may therefore have to compel the polluter to reduce emissions below the level induced by the tax or to purchase all property in the area where pollution is intolerable. Similarly, exceptional circumstances, such as temporary peak periods of pollution caused by unusual atmospheric conditions or other events, could cause dangerous levels of pollution even though polluters are emitting no more pollutants than would be acceptable under normal circumstances. In these cases, temporary regulations, such as the prohibition of any polluting for a short period, may be necessary in addition to the pollution tax.

Problems Relating to Administrative Feasibility of the Tax

There may be situations in which the feasibility of a pollution tax is affected by special problems:

Problems with measurement: The cost, or even the feasibility, of measurement of pollution emissions cannot be ignored. There may be no instrumentation available to measure emissions. Or the cost of the measuring equipment and its use may be so great that abatement of pollution ends up costing more through use of a pollution tax than through a regulatory approach not involving such measurement if the latter approach is available. The remedy, however, need not always be abandonment of the pollution tax, but may lie in the substitution of a surrogate tax. Thus, instead of a tax on sulfur dioxide emissions there can be a tax on the sulfur content of the fuel used. Or, rather than measuring lead emissions from every automobile, the lead in the gasoline, which is all emitted later by the automobile, could be taxed.[17] Or instead of measuring every pollutant dumped into a stream, it may be satisfactory to measure only what is known as the biological oxygen demand (BOD) created by the pollutants as an indication of how much damage has been caused to the water.

Care, however, must be used in choosing the surrogate tax. For example, a tax on electricity itself would not be a suitable substitute for a tax on sulfur dioxide emissions by power plants; the tax may "punish" the power companies, but it induces a reduction in emissions only by the very indirect route of causing reductions in power production. It is thus no effective inducement to the power companies to switch to less polluting technologies. Moreover, the tax would hit all producers of electricity and not just those producers responsible for the sulfur dioxide emissions. In general, a surrogate tax must be viewed with skepticism, since it may offer a less efficient solution than non-tax approaches.

Problems arising from periodic changes in tax rates: Because of inflation, technological innovation, and increases in the number of polluters — as well as faulty initial information — the tax level may have to be changed from time to time in order to achieve the desired environmental quality. If the changes are too frequent and unpredictable, polluters cannot continue to adjust to them without there being inefficiencies arising from lack of planning. A capital expenditure undertaken after a rise in the tax rate may make unnecessary a prior expenditure for another abatement technique — one that seemed the proper response to the lower tax earlier imposed. Nevertheless, if policymakers show some restraint in shifting tax levels, the problems created should not be significantly greater than those that would be caused by a change in a regulation, required for similar reasons.

When the Tax May Be Objectionable as Regressive

Polls have shown that one's desire for a cleaner environment increases with one's wealth. Yet the burden of cleaning up the environment may be borne disproportionally by the low-income groups, as prices for goods and services increase. This regressive burden of the cost of abatement will also be characteristic of a regulation approach, since the cost of changing fuels, adding new equipment, and so on, will be borne by the consumer. For this reason, in some circumstances a subsidy approach may be preferable to either a pollution tax or a regulation. For example, rather than taxing municipalities for dumping sewage into streams and rivers, it might be better to grant subsidies for construction (and proper use) of sewage treatment facilities. The cost of treatment facilities would then be borne in part by the progressive federal tax system rather than entirely by a local tax structure that is likely to be regressive.

Since, as stated earlier, a pollution tax requires a user charge for the remaining pollution compared with the free ride of regulation, overall it could, all else being equal, increase prices more and hence operate with greater regressive effect. All else may not of course be equal, and the theoretical advantage of the pollution tax in least-cost abatement may more than offset the user charge effect. But, aside from the special subsidy case considered above, any general price effect on low-income households of pollution taxes, or regulatory approaches, should not be a cause for faulting these solutions if otherwise desirable. Any adverse distributional consequences should, as is true with user charges for Government services or living costs generally, be offset by appropriate modification in income tax rates and exemptions or in welfare or income maintenance payments. In other words, this aspect is but one of many bearing on the distribution of income in our society.[18]

The Differing Income Tax Treatment of the Tax Approach and the Regulatory Approach

Under traditional income tax rules a fine paid to a government for the violation of a regulation is not deductible in computing the net income of a business subject to the tax.[19] Hence, where a regulatory approach is used to control pollution, the entire cost of violation is in the first instance borne by the company. The monetary aspects of the calculation whether to spend deductible dollars to achieve compliance with the regulation or to incur a nondeductible fine involve a "before-tax" consideration as to the cost of violation. On the other hand, a regulatory tax levied on business, including a user charge, is deductible for income tax purposes. Hence, the calculation of the company as to the costs of equipment or other steps to control pollution compared with the costs of paying the pollution tax is all on an after-tax basis. There is thus a difference between the regulatory approach and the tax approach. A company that chooses to pollute and pay a pollution tax can come out better than a company that chooses to pollute and pay a fine, all else being equal. Economists in setting the levels of the pollution tax must keep in mind that the tax paid will be deductible.

Two Aspects of the Structure of the Tax

Geographical uniformity: The costs of abatement, the benefits of abatement, and the desired environmental quality are likely to vary from region to region within the country, and even within a region or state. It would therefore seem that the tax rate should vary from area to area just as should a regulatory approach. This may be the desirable result, but several considerations should be kept in mind. First, nonuniformity in tax rates may induce relocation of polluting industries, with the result that the desired air quality in some areas will deteriorate, causing the need for a tax rise, perhaps a substantial one. To prevent such deterioration, maximum tolerable emission levels for newly located firms could be set by regulation. But such regulation is unlikely to lead to least-cost abatement within the region affected. Second, if nonuniformity is permitted, discretion is likely to be introduced into the pollution tax system. Instead of one tax applied to all, the tax will depend on how the country is divided into areas and what standards are used to determine the rate in each area. If there is too much discretion, there is opportunity for political maneuvering to the unjust benefit of some polluters, and there is opportunity for polluters to delay the exercise of discretionary judgment through appeals within the agency and to the courts. Third, nonuniformity may, as stated above, cause relocation of polluting industries and, apart from the effect on air quality, there can be adverse effects on labor and communities from the consequent industrial changes. Presumably, no general rule as to the superiority or inferiority of nonuniform tax rates can be stated.[20]

Disposition of tax proceeds: If the proceeds of a pollution tax are dedicated to an antipollution agency, there is a danger that the agency will have an incentive to seek higher tax rates than desirable or even to encourage polluters to pay the tax rather than abate (perhaps by the agency's not providing sufficient technical guidance to polluters). Thus, it would seem preferable to put the proceeds into general revenues. However, the proceeds could be used to cushion any special regressive impact of the tax. For example, all cities might be required to pay a pollution tax on sewage disposal, but a rebate made to those which build treatment plants.

Enforceability of the Pollution Tax

It is often claimed that a pollution tax is superior to a regulation because the tax is easier to enforce. This claim does not follow as a matter of logic. But there are two reasons why it is asserted that such superiority in practice may perhaps be expected. First, there is likely to be less discretion built into the mechanics of imposition of the pollution tax. Once the tax level is set by the legislature, or even by an authorized agency, the basic discretion is likely to be in drawing boundary lines for areas having different rates. With a regulation there are likely to be questions regarding what abatement is "reasonable," "feasible," "technically available," or the like. Such questions could give rise to frequent litigation, and courts may have to devote substantial amounts of time resolving them.

A pollution tax is also more likely to be enforced because it is not an all-or-nothing imposition, leading to showdowns in enforcement, as can be the case with a regulation. Once a polluter appeals a decision against it, the reviewing agency or court is much more likely to stay the imposition of a regulation — such as one to add certain equipment — than to stop collection of a tax, which can be refunded (although the tax may induce changes by the polluter that cannot be reversed). More important, an agency is more likely to seek enforcement of the tax than of an all-or-nothing regulation.

But it must be recognized that these supposed enforcement advantages of the tax approach over the regulatory approach could turn out in practice not really to exist. The tax approach may itself require flexibility to be workable, and with flexibility comes discretion and hence problems similar to discretionary regulation. Also, the economic consequences of enforcing a tax before an industry has adjusted itself, psychologically as well as technically, to the necessary pollution reduction, could well lead to problems similar to those in enforcing a regulatory approach.

An Overall Consideration

Much of the above discussion has been cast in theoretical terms so as to present the essential argumentation made by the proponents of a pollution tax approach. Even in these terms, the choice between a tax or a regulatory approach is not of one or the other across the board, and often is a case of "it all depends." But the problem of choice is much more difficult than the discussion so far discloses. Skeptical economists have observed that "we are at the beginning, not the end, of the era of applied economics of environmental protection."[21] Our knowledge, sadly, is scanty in comparison with the problems to be solved. It may be comfortable to say that in theory a pollution tax should bring about least-cost abatement. But in practice will firms respond in accordance with theory, or will so many other factors intrude — imperfect operating procedures, other pulls on management, inadequate analysis of the situation, and so forth — that rational response is not forthcoming? Under these circumstances, "license to pollute" under the tax approach may have a sharper meaning, just as in other circumstances the "free ride" of regulation may be longer than we anticipated. Lack of knowledge may plague us in setting a tax rate, just as it can frustrate regulators in setting a standard. The least-cost approach may be counter-intuitive to normal ideas of fairness — why should the worst polluter remain still able to pollute because his costs of correction are high? The caution of legislators who choose the more traditional approach of standards and regulation may be understandable in this setting, and they may well feel justified in placing the burden of proof for the tax approach on the economists.

Professor Marc Roberts has offered some general observations, alongside much skepticism:[22]

> The apparent decentralization that fee schemes offer seems most attractive when achieving a very specific level of ambient quality is not really crucial — when marginal damages are low. The case is stronger when technical options are complex and rapidly changing, and when the marginal costs of abatement vary significantly for different abatement rates and among waste sources. It is stronger still when the prices of resources used in abatement reflect their marginal social opportunity costs. When there are many discharges, the errors made in forecasting the response to fees of various sources are more likely to cancel out.
>
> In contrast, when the technology of waste control is simple and well known, and when the marginal costs of control are quite similar for different sources and removal rates, standards may be easier to implement. Standards also have advantages when waste sources are not obviously cost minimizers. They become even more attractive when the marginal benefits of varying ambient conditions are high, when we have a clear target in mind. This is particularly so when we opt for a corner solution such as eliminating water-borne discharges of mercury or ending the use of apartment house incinerators.
>
> A similar point can be made about the limits of fees when the environmental problem is not one of residual flows, e.g., when the issue

is the location and character of a capital facility. Charges seem a poor device for trying to optimize power plant siting or highway location or for influencing the safety precautions taken in reactor design. Are we even willing to trust fees for such residuals as high level radioactive wastes? If not, is it because the necessary fees are too complex, or because when the risks are great, even economists aren't willing to depend upon the efficacy of the price system!

A conference held in 1971 by the Council on Law-Related Studies, which surveyed a wide range of effluent charge proposals on air and water pollution, concluded with a cautious position:[23]

With respect to all charge schemes considered, the conference raised questions of administrative feasibility or cost. The number of pollutants to which different charges might be applied, the number of substandard conditions for which different groups of co-polluters might be jointly responsible, and the number of variations in a receiving medium's capacity to assimilate wastes, all suggested the need for flexible and elaborate systems of charges. Simple ones could not bring about efficient solutions. But how complicated could a charge system become before the costs of complexity began to outweigh the added benefits? Answers could not be pieced together in sufficient detail from anecdotes and generalizations set before the conference on this point.

The deeper question of feasibility was whether charges alone could be relied upon to induce an efficient pattern of responses by polluters. Setting charges was recognized as a risky enterprise in the absence of detailed knowledge of polluters' abatement costs and other factors influencing their investment decisions. And the more flexible the responses desired, the harder it seemed to elaborate a charge system that would work without serious friction. The correct charge level was not likely to be chosen on the first try, but a small error in setting it could have disproportionate consequences. Reactions to any charge would, unavoidably, be delayed. Faced with a certain charge, a polluter might commit himself to a course of action which became inappropriate in the face of a subsequently higher or lower charge. Nor could it be assumed that polluters would freely collaborate among themselves on efficient collective measures for controlling or treating their wastes. While some conferees remained of the view that a well-conceived charge strategy would minimize these difficulties, others were persuaded that a mixed strategy, combining direct regulations or controls with economic incentives, had a better chance of succeeding. A third view was articulated by participants from industry, who made clear their preference for direct regulation over the greater costs and uncertainties

171

they feared industry would have to bear under any effluent charge scheme.

Legislative Consideration and
the Administration of the Pollution Tax

For our present purposes we do not need more definite conclusions. Suffice it to say that the economists presumably will be able — for some situations — to offer a case for the pollution tax approach that is sufficiently persuasive to cause policymakers seriously to weigh the use of that approach. Perhaps the tax approach in a particular case may be superior to the technique of regulation; perhaps it may be a useful complement to that technique.

The pollution tax approach thus appears to be a suitable device in the arsenal of techniques to be used by Government to achieve the desired quality of the environment. Hence we can conclude that, in a proper setting, resort to the tax system can be appropriate for this purpose. Since the "charge" to be made would presumably be structured as a "tax" and administration and enforcement would follow "tax patterns," the tax system becomes involved.

We might here pause to ask why we earlier said the use of income tax subsidies or incentives is generally undesirable compared with direct grants, but here are saying that the use of a tax for regulatory purposes may be desirable in some situations compared with a direct regulatory approach. One count against the income tax subsidy was its varying after-tax benefits depending on the income tax status of the person benefited — the wealthier the individual or the larger the company, the higher the subsidy, with no subsidy to tax-exempt nonprofit and governmental units. A pollution tax borne to avoid the higher cost of equipment or operational procedures to reduce pollution also has a similar consequence — the wealthier the individual or the larger the company, the less the cost of continued pollution, with full cost to the nonprofit and governmental units. This result also obtains, however, as to the cost of the equipment and procedures themselves, a proper business expense, so that both those costs and a pollution tax involve after-tax consequences. Where the pollution tax is really a user charge, the result is proper. In the range where the pollution tax is intended to operate with coercive effects, then the similarity to the defects of the tax subsidy may be initially troublesome. However, even in that range the coercive force of the pollution tax lies in its cost comparison with the equipment or operational measures utilized to reduce the pollution and, as stated above, the deductibility of the pollution tax leaves this comparison on an after-tax basis. It is the comparison itself that is important, and the amount of the pollution tax must therefore be set at a level that induces the desired end result. What is then relevant in the deductibility of the pollution tax is that those setting the amount of that tax must remember its deductible character and realize that the comparison is on an after-tax basis for the tax as well as the alternatives. The upside-down defect associated with financial assistance under tax subsidies would thus not appear to be applicable to the coercive aspect of a pollution tax.

The tax subsidy has also been faulted for its inefficiencies, because it can rarely be on target. This would be true in the pollution field, since the financial assistance of a tax subsidy by itself would not, as we have seen earlier, be likely to cause conduct different from that without the subsidy. This is equally true as to a direct grant, since it also cannot be aimed at the target. How much should be paid under the grant to cover both costs of equipment and operations, remembering that if not enough is paid, perhaps unless all is paid, the desired change in pollution emissions would not be achieved? The grant, moreover, would have to vary from company to company. There would be no, or perhaps little incentive, for a company to minimize costs. But the pollution tax approach cannot be faulted for not aiming at the target, since in theory its aim is better than any other approach and that is why economists urge its use. In this respect, then, the use of the tax system for a regulatory purpose does not suffer from the serious defect involved in resort to the tax system for subsidies to provide financial assistance.

At this point, however, we do run into a different set of problems. We saw in the consideration of tax incentives that resort to the tax system rather than to direct expenditures had the distinct drawback of involving the Tax Committees — and the Internal Revenue Service — in fields quite foreign to their customary jurisdiction.[24] A pollution tax has the same disadvantage. Other committees — primarily the Public Works Committees and also the Commerce Committees — have been charting legislative policy in the environmental area. They were responsible, for example, for the Clean Air Amendments of 1970 and the Water Pollution Control Act amendments of 1972, the basic statutes regarding abatement of air and water pollution. These statutes follow a regulatory approach. But when, as in 1972, a tax on sulfur emissions is recommended as a complement to the Clean Air amendments,[25] jurisdiction shifts to the Tax Committees.[26]

The Tax Committees simply do not have the background or experience of the Public Works or Commerce Committees. Nor do they have staffs that are informed and competent with regard to the problems of environmental control. It seems seriously wrong on the one hand to ask the Tax Committees and their staffs to learn *de novo* this complex field, and on the other hand to keep the Public Works and Commerce Committees and their staffs from playing a role first in assessing the desirability of a pollution tax approach and then in structuring such a tax and relating it to the regulatory approach. It would also be a poor way to determine substantive policy to place the latter committees in the role of opposing a tax approach because adoption of that approach would cause them to lose "jurisdiction" to the Tax Committees. But our legislative mores are such that the temptation to opposition on this ground can certainly arise.

Clearly, some appropriate accommodation between these two sets of committees is required. The primary role should be maintained by the Public Works and Commerce Committees in view of their prior activities. After they determine the desirability and, if the decision is affirmative, develop the basic structure of a tax, then they should be able to obtain the judgment of the Tax Committees on any aspects that require tax expertise. Thereafter, oversight of the administration of the tax should remain with the Public Works or Commerce Committees. It must be recognized that this approach is contrary to the normal scheme of things, since taxes, and user charges cast as taxes, belong to the Tax Committees. Yet it is obvious that where use of the tax system is made for regulatory purposes, the focus is really on the regulatory goal and not the tax apparatus. Hence, unless there is no prior regulatory history and no prior committee experience elsewhere — an unlikely situation — or unless the tax aspects outweigh the regulatory aspects — which may sometimes be possible — the Tax Committees should not be made the primary forum for the legislative consideration. Where it is appropriate that the Tax Committees do become the primary forum, then the coordination equally should flow between those committees and the committees that have customary jurisdiction over the area. These views are applicable whether a pollution tax is involved or whether it is a "regulatory tax" in some other area that is under consideration.

Similar factors apply to the administration of a pollution tax. It would seem appropriate to place as much of the administration of a pollution tax as is possible in the Environmental Protection Agency. This is certainly so as to any discretionary or other aspects requiring coordination with whatever direct regulatory approaches may exist. It would be undesirable to have one set of policies determined by the Internal Revenue Service and another set by the EPA, especially where the pollution tax is complementary to a regulatory approach. Concentration of responsibility in the administrative agency having cognizance over the substantive area affected by a regulatory tax would seem a generally desirable pattern of administration of such a tax.

VI

The Varied Approaches Necessary to

Replace Tax Expenditures with

Direct Governmental Assistance

Federal tax reform occupies an important position in the agenda of tasks that the decade of the 1970's must face. This can be said even though the previous decade was a period of almost continual legislative change directed at the task of improving the federal tax system. The Revenue Acts of 1962 and 1964, the Excise Tax Reduction Act of 1965, the Tax Adjustment Act of 1966, the Foreign Investors Tax Act of 1966, and finally the Tax Reform Act of 1969, were the major events in that decade, and they were accompanied by many measures of lesser significance. But while much was accomplished, the need for reform was indeed so vast that much remains to be done.

Moreover, the three years since 1969 were, unfortunately, all downhill years for tax reform. The Treasury did not propose a single legislative change that would have tightened the tax laws. Instead, it successfully pushed new tax expenditures and accepted others proposed by the Congress. It thereby created the climate that produced the Revenue Act of 1971, the worst measure in many a decade from the standpoint of the integrity and fairness of the tax system. This period after 1969 was thus a betrayal of tax reform.[1] The task is to restore the momentum achieved in the decade of the 1960's and then move on to further accomplishments.

One aspect of this struggle for reform, an aspect both heartening and discouraging, is the realization of how much we have to learn about the problems and goals of tax reform. Fiscal experts have been writing about tax reform for a long period. Yet, when Congress does allot legislative concern and time to the matter and considers tax reform legislation, it is evident that on a number of matters the experts are unprepared and thus fail the legislators. Of course, the legislators far more often fail the experts and either reject changes that are carefully prepared or muddle them up. That is the way of the political process, and such failures can be expected no matter how unwelcome they may be. But the failures of experts should not be a way of life, for those failures often make it impossible for legislators having the will for reform to achieve meaningful change.

This lesson must not go completely unlearned. Hopefully, we have realized that there should always be a stockpile of recommendations, researched and analyzed as carefully as possible, to be placed before the Congress in an attempt to stimulate concern or to be available when that concern suddenly becomes manifest because of a particular turn of the political wheel. The Treasury Tax Reform Studies and Proposals, prepared under President Johnson, placed before the Congress early in 1969,[2] and forming the backbone of the 1969 legislation, are an example. But our stockpile is now low in the income tax field, though somewhat better off in the estate and gift tax area.[3] Moreover, academic research in these tax policy and fiscal matters, vitally necessary both to maintaining the stockpile and improving its content, is undermanned and underfinanced.

Tax Expenditure Analysis and Tax Reform

A lesson that we are just commencing to comprehend concerns the overall nature of reform of the federal income tax.[4] Much of this lesson emerged in the 1969 legislation, but its beginnings in one sense arose with the tax expenditure study made by the Treasury Department in 1967–68 and published late in 1968. This study led, as we have seen in Chapter I, to the development of the Tax Expenditure Budget. This budget lists those expenditures that are presently made through special provisions in the income tax system to achieve various social and economic objectives. The tax expenditure programs are written in tax language and utilize a variety of tax techniques for their accomplishment, such as special exclusions or exemptions from income, deductions, credits against tax, deferrals of tax, or special rates of tax. Since they utilize tax language and tax techniques, these expenditure programs are in these respects indistinguishable from the provisions whose function it is to develop the income tax itself. In the past, efforts to reform the income tax tended to look at that tax as representing a single structure — an "income tax." The reformers talked in terms of base broadening, elimination of preferences, elimination of loopholes, and the like, and picked their reform targets wherever they found any departures in their lights from tax equity or tax fairness. But the Tax Expenditure Budget serves to show us that the income tax is composed of two structures. One structure consists of the inherent provisions necessary to construct an income tax, and represents the United States understanding of a normative income tax. The second structure consists of the special provisions constituting the programs of financial assistance set forth in that budget. It is this latter structure that represents the "tax incentive" programs and the measures providing relief from personal hardships that have been built up over time within the income tax.

The Tax Reform Act of 1969 in one respect resembled previous efforts at reform, in that the matters considered in the framing of that Act and in the final legislation were drawn from both of the structures described above without any conscious effort to distinguish the two structures. But an analysis of that Act and its legislative journey indicates that the legislation for the most part involved efforts to eliminate or reduce the scope of certain tax expenditures. Thus the main changes in that legislation, apart from rates and levels of exemptions, were concerned with: increases in the capital gains rates, changes in the definition of capital gains and the disallowance of certain interest expense related to capital gain income and other tax expenditure items; reduction in the depreciation benefits accorded real estate; reduction in the percentage depletion allowances accorded natural resources, especially oil; repeal of the investment credit; reduction in the bad debt reserve and other tax benefits accorded to financial institutions; revision of the charitable contributions deduction to strip away most of the tax gimmicks and to eliminate abuses in the use of foundations; revision of the tax-exempt organization area to tighten the taxation of unrelated business income; modest reduction in the various tax benefits accorded farming, especially cattle and citrus groves; introduction of a mild minimum tax to counteract selected tax expenditures; increase in the standard deduction to lessen the use of the itemized personal expense deductions and thus mitigate the lack of horizontal equity inherent in the tax expenditures involved in those deductions. Areas in which struggle took place but no change resulted involved the tax benefits granted to state and local bond interest and the consequent monetary aid to state and local governments, and the allocation of the personal expense deductions between taxable income and income exempted from tax under certain tax expenditures. Finally, a number of new tax expenditures adopted in the Senate failed of approval in the final Act: a tax credit for college education expenses; elimination in the case of the aged of the 3 percent floor under the deduction for medical expenses; a deduction for transportation expenses of disabled persons. Also, a number of additional tax expenditures were adopted, involving five-year amortization of the costs of pollution control facilities, rehabilitation of low-income rental housing, railroad cars, and mine safety equipment.

To be sure, the 1969 Act did involve structural changes unrelated to tax expenditures by which mistakes and defects in the basic tax structure were corrected. Examples are: the elimination of the abuses of multiple corporations; the elimination of abuses involved in the treatment of mineral production payments; the ending of tax-free dividends paid from depreciation reserves; the treatment of restricted stock transferred as compensation to employees; the treatment of stock dividends; and the partial elimination of abuses involved in multiple family trusts and trusts to accumulate income. In all these cases time had shown that the experts had not properly constructed these parts of the technical tax structure. The beneficiaries of the technical malfunctioning did not press social and economic objectives in defense of their existing benefits.[5] There were also tax policy changes in the overall application of the income tax, all involving tax reductions and grouped together by the tax committees under the heading of "tax relief." These tax relief provisions involved: the use of the poverty income levels as a base to start the income tax, thus exempting individuals and families with incomes below those levels; increases in the minimum standard deduction (low-income allowance) and the personal exemptions as methods of eliminating or reducing the tax for those below or around poverty income levels; personal exemption increase, together with the standard deduction increase, to reduce tax liabilities for middle-income groups; the use of a new rate schedule for single persons to reduce the difference between their tax liabilities and the lower tax liabilities of married couples with the same incomes; and the application of a maximum tax to earned income.

The major part of the legislative material in the Tax Reform Act of 1969 thus related to the tax expenditure structure of the income tax, with the balance relating to the basic income tax structure and to the level of rates and exemptions. While the revenue loss involved in the "tax relief" provisions was large, $9 billion in the long run, the amount of revenue involved in the tax expenditure area was also very significant, totaling almost $7 billion, counting revenue gains and losses together. Less than $1 billion in revenue was involved in corrective provisions relating to the basic structure.[6]

The Revenue Act of 1971 concentrated almost entirely on tax expenditures. This time, however, the effort was solely in the direction of adding new tax expenditures, with both the Treasury and the Congress pushing their favorites. No tax expenditures were dropped, and there were no significant changes in the basic income tax structure other than raising the low-income allowance to bring the starting point of the income tax up to the current poverty levels. Tax reform was a forgotten goal.[7]

The struggles underlying the legislation of 1969 and 1971, when analyzed in this fashion, are seen as predominantly involving the tax expenditure provisions of the income tax. Moreover, progress or setback in tax reform can be measured in terms of these provisions. But it is only recently, with the construction of the Tax Expenditure Budget, that we have come to analyze tax legislation in this manner. The separation of the income tax into two structures and the consequent use of the Tax Expenditure Budget to divide legislative tax issues between those issues concerned with the basic or inherent income tax structure and those relating to the tax expenditure apparatus is one facet of the relationship between that budget and tax reform. The other facet is the recognition that the tax provisions reflected in that budget do represent Government expenditures and involve financial assistance to particular groups. This being so, "tax reform" for these items is really "expenditure reform." The recognition that we are here involved with expenditures and not inherent income tax provisions provides an entirely new dimension and approach for tax reform.

In the discussion of the tax incentives in the Tax Expenditure Budget we saw that the incentives could have been and can be structured as direct expenditures, and thus can be tested in direct expenditure terms. We also observed that when so tested many tax incentives will be seen as either inequitable, often to the point of being so grossly unfair as to be ludicrous, or ineffective. To here repeat a few examples:

— the deduction of mortgage interest on a residence: if cast as a direct expenditure this would be the equivalent of the Department of Housing and Urban Development paying to a bank 70 percent of the interest on a mortgage loan entered into by a wealthy family, whether the loan be for its town home, a summer residence, or a winter residence, but only paying 19 percent of the interest on a home mortgage of a $10,000 family, and paying no part of the mortgage interest of a family with so little income that it did not pay an income tax;

— the extra personal exemption for the elderly, enlarged to an additional $750 in the 1969 Act: this is the equivalent of the Department of Health, Education and Welfare assisting the aged through the payment of cash allowances under which the largest benefits, $87.50 per month, would be paid to those aged couples whose incomes exceed $200,000, and the smallest benefits, around $21 per month, would go to couples with incomes between $2,800 and $3,800 — the poorest couples would of course receive no cash allowance;

— the five-year amortization allowed for expenditures of rehabilitating low-income rental housing, adopted in the 1969 Act: if cast as a direct expenditure this would mean the Department of Housing and Urban Development loaning money for rehabilitation purposes at a 3 percent interest rate to wealthy persons but at 7 percent and 8 percent interest rates to low tax bracket persons;

— a proposal adopted in the Senate in 1969 but rejected in Conference, to eliminate for the aged the 3 percent floor on medical expenses so as to provide for the elderly relief from the expenses of medical care: if cast as a direct expenditure this would be the equivalent of the Department of Health, Education and Welfare making direct grants for medical payments totaling $210 million, of which $93 million would go to those elderly having incomes above $50,000 and only $8 million to those with incomes below $5000.[8]

179

Although these examples represent no more than a translation of tax language into direct expenditure language, that translation is often sufficient in a particular case to highlight the inadequacy of the tax expenditure route. The examples underscore the point that whatever are the cost-benefit analyses or other analytic techniques available for examining direct expenditure proposals, those techniques are equally pertinent to tax expenditure proposals.

The fact that a tax expenditure program can be recast as a direct expenditure program really takes us to the heart of tax reform, for it opens up a new way to consider the entire subject. We can regard a major aspect of income tax reform as involving the reexamination of all of the tax expenditure provisions now contained in the income tax. We should start by examining the list of tax expenditures in the Tax Expenditure Budget and seeking to decide which should go and which should remain. In a sense, that of course is what tax reformers have always done, whether they talked in terms of base broadening, elimination of preferences, or needed elimination of loopholes. For their targets, their lists of preferences and loopholes, usually included many of the items in the Tax Expenditure Budget.

The tax expenditure analysis, however, tells us why that traditional approach is not enough. The analysis helps us to understand why that approach can deal with some problems of tax reform but why it fails to reach others, as indeed it did as recently as 1969. For tax expenditure analysis conceives of the special provisions — the preferences and loopholes of the tax reformers — as Government financial assistance comparable to that contained directly in the budget. So viewed, this aspect of tax reform becomes a review of budgetary programs. Tax reform, as stated earlier, is here really "expenditure reform."

The questions of this aspect of tax reform then become:

— Which tax programs — which tax expenditures — which tax incentives — which special tax provisions — can simply be dropped without substituting another form of Government financial assistance, because on review it is seen that Government policies and priorities do not require the expenditure of federal funds for the purposes involved in these items?

— Which tax programs cannot be simply dropped — because Government policies and priorities do require the expenditure of federal funds for the purposes involved — but can be readily changed from tax expenditures to direct expenditures, in a way that achieves an improvement in equity and efficiency?

— Which tax programs, in the group which cannot simply be dropped, would have to meet special criteria regarding the structure of a substituted direct expenditure program, so that a change must await the development of the latter program?

— Finally, which tax programs function much more efficiently and effectively as tax expenditure programs than as direct expenditures so that any consequent loss in tax equity or strain on the tax structure must yield to the need for the use of the tax system in this special case to carry out a particular Government policy?

The approach involved in these questions indicates why in many cases strong pressures for tax reform will not lead to change despite the validity of the case for reform when stated in tax terms. The demonstration of tax preference is not enough *if* the tax preference is providing monetary assistance for a purpose deemed important by the Congress and no acceptable substitute program supplying the needed financial assistance is presented to the Congress. Urging "tax reform" in these circumstances is clearly not enough, and has not succeeded up to now. Those urging reform must go on to say: The financial assistance will be continued efficiently and effectively by a direct expenditure program, the specifics of which are described, which can be substituted for the tax program and therefore the tax expenditure can be dropped — i.e., a tax reform can be accomplished.[9]

This is not to say that in cases where financial assistance is not needed, so that no alternative direct program is required and the special tax provision should simply be dropped, the push for tax reform will succeed. It may also fail, but for a different reason. The failure may be due to political and lobbying pressures led by the group profiting from the special tax benefits, and to the ability of that group to muster the votes and manage the legislative maneuvers required to fend off attack. In the struggle for tax reform it is important to analyze failures as well as applaud successes. A failure on such political grounds may require a different legislative approach when the effort is renewed. Or the effort may have to await the neutralization of a particular Representative or Senator whose views and position in the legislative structure can combine to defeat the reform. But these aspects go to legislative strategies and tactics, and to the counting of votes in our political process. A failure, however, because of the absence of an alternative effective program of providing financial assistance — because of the absence of a method of converting the required assistance from a tax expenditure program to a direct expenditure program — can be repaired only by the experts through the formulation of the direct expenditure program. This done, the case for tax reform and for the change to a direct expenditure program moves on to the political level. The vacuum that would have been left by a tax change dropping the tax expenditure alone, and the resulting absence of financial assistance, would be filled by the alternative direct program so that the case for tax reform cannot be faulted on that score. The matter must then become one of counting votes.

An overall view of much of the future task of tax reform, under this analysis, can therefore be obtained by examining the list of tax expenditures in the light of the questions posed earlier. A word of caution is in order, however, before we examine the list. This approach clearly does not encompass all there is of the task of tax reform. For one thing, the tax expenditure list may be — some would say it is — incomplete. But this factor goes to the list and not the nature of the approach. For another, there are tax structure defects that lie outside the tax expenditure analysis, places where the experts or Congress have not put the basic or inherent income structure together in proper technical fashion: for example, income accumulated in trusts;[10] problems turning on the present tax separateness of corporation and shareholders, such as the treatment of corporate distributions in kind.[11] Here tax reform — tax revision may be a better term — consists of patient technical analysis and legislative persuasion. These are areas in which interested and objective research bodies, such as the American Law Institute, can play a significant role.[12] Then there are the larger questions of tax policy relating to the application of the important parts of the structure, such as the level of personal exemptions and the low-income allowance and whether these aspects should be structured as deductions or credits against tax, the rate progression, and the relative distribution of the burden among households,[13] to draw on recent examples. Another illustration is the nature of the corporate tax and whether the United States should have a tax system that integrates corporate income with shareholder income, or one that, as at present, taxes corporations separately from their shareholders.[14] Another subject that combines both technical detail and broad tax policy issues is the proper interrelationship of an income maintenance plan (or negative income tax) to the positive income tax, and the structural problems in reflecting the relationship agreed upon.

But even taking into account these two fields of technical structure and tax policy, I believe that a very large part, probably the largest part, of legislative controversy regarding income tax reform lies in the area of tax expenditure analysis. We can therefore turn to the tax expenditure list and to a reclassification of that list among the categories that parallel the questions posed earlier.

Classification of Tax Expenditure Items by Reference to the Need for Government Financial Assistance

Tax Expenditure Items that Do Not Require Substitute Governmental Financial Assistance

A considerable number of items on the tax expenditure list might be dropped without substituting any alternative program of financial assistance from the

Government. The additional revenue so obtained could be used for rate reduction or other tax reduction purposes, or for budgetary purposes. In most of these instances, tax history has resulted in a tax expenditure for a group or activity that has no present claim for such governmental assistance. Current budgetary priorities and policies would simply leave the matter to the judgment of the private sector. For these items the pace of tax reform progress is largely measured in political terms. There being no need under the above assumptions for a substitute direct program, the issue comes down to whether the legislators desire to retain or drop the provision. In other words, who has the votes — those who would benefit from the existing provision or those seeking to have the benefits withdrawn?

The past failure to study carefully the tax expenditure items from this approach has in many cases left us with inadequate information. There are, however, a number of items as to which it would seem appropriate that the proponents for retention of tax expenditures should be called upon to make the case for their continuance. They should be required to demonstrate that, as a matter of national priorities and policies, they should continue to receive financial assistance for the activities involved, and, if so, assistance of the magnitude and in the manner now being obtained. The Treasury and other Government agencies affected should, where appropriate, prepare cost-benefit studies to indicate just what, if anything, the United States is obtaining in return for the benefits presently being granted to individuals and businesses under these tax expenditures. What policies and objectives of the United States are being advanced by these tax programs, and how efficiently and effectively do the programs operate? A searching look should be taken, with the same skeptical scrutiny that a hard-pressed Budget Director urged to keep his expenditures down would apply to items in the regular budget. In this process of analysis and scrutiny the burden of proof, and it should be a rigorous burden, should be placed quite clearly on those contending to keep the tax programs.[15] The entire process of examination requires a tough-minded objectivity. As I have said elsewhere: "There is no one so pessimistic about the future of his country or his industry as a taxpayer who is about to lose a tax preference."

The following items listed in the Tax Expenditure Budget could be explored from this standpoint to see if they fall in this first category:

The items under *International Affairs.* These items cover:

> — exemption for certain income earned abroad by United States citizens
> — This exemption, which is $20,000 a year for a person residing abroad for at least a year ($25,000 for a three-year resident) or, if not a "resident" abroad, who has been "present" abroad for seventeen months during an eighteen month period, is a remnant of earlier broader exemptions to encourage individuals in business abroad to meet foreign

competition. The exemption, be it for executives, scholars, or missionaries, presumably serves in a general way to reduce the costs to employers since they can offer United States tax savings as an inducement to employment abroad. In some cases an individual who is subject to a foreign tax on his earnings can parlay the exemption and the foreign tax credit into a larger benefit, since the tax credit flowing from the foreign tax on the $20,000 or $25,000 can be used to offset United States tax on foreign earnings above the exemption or on investment income from foreign sources.[16] The exemption, incidentally, does not apply to employees of the United States Government. Its continued limited presence in the Code, despite attempts to eliminate it entirely, is the result of pressure from international business concerns and American Chamber of Commerce groups abroad.

— special rate of tax for Western Hemisphere Trade Corporations — This rate, 34 percent instead of 48 percent, was introduced in 1942 as a special measure for a few corporations engaged in activities in Latin America who lobbied to avoid the impact of increased World War II tax rates. It came to be used largely by corporations exporting to the Western Hemisphere who simply set up special domestic subsidiaries to "handle" their exports.[17] The Treasury has never found proof that the special rate increased exports, and moreover, the exporters are unintended beneficiaries. As the discussion below regarding DISC indicates, the United States should cease using the tax system to subsidize exports. While exporters represent numerically the largest number of Western Hemisphere Trade Corporations, the principal dollar benefits of the special rate flow to corporations engaged in natural resources activities in the Western Hemisphere, and there is no national need to subsidize those activities.

— exclusion for parent corporations of "gross-up" on dividends paid by less developed country subsidiary corporations — This exclusion is a remnant of the earlier technical treatment under the foreign tax credit of dividends paid by foreign subsidiary corporations to United States parent corporations. The earlier treatment, by a technical defect, gave both a credit and a deduction for the foreign tax applicable to the subsidiary's earnings represented in the dividend. In 1962 this defect was corrected by including the foreign tax on those earnings as part of the dividend — "grossing-up" the dividend. But a number of corporations engaged in activities in Latin America fought a successful rearguard action to preserve the benefits of the defect for those activities, using the semantic lever of "assisting less-developed countries." There appears to be no evidence that this technical windfall has anything to do with encouraging investment in those countries, and its continued presence is unjustified.[18]

— exclusion for parent corporations of income of controlled foreign subsidiary corporations — Until 1962, as a result of the way the Code grew up, the profits of foreign subsidiary corporations were not taxable by the United States until repatriated as dividends. In 1961 the Treasury urged the end of this tax preference for foreign investment and proposed that those profits be taxed currently as earned, similar to profits earned in the domestic market. The multinational corporations fought this proposal, and a complicated compromise in the 1962 Act applied current taxation by the United States to so-called "tax haven" activities involving utilization of those foreign countries having a low rate income tax or no income tax.[19] The controversy has continued. Labor unions have been in the forefront urging full current taxation of all foreign subsidiary activities; representatives of international business have defended the status quo and in some cases urged elimination of the 1962 changes. The efforts of the international business groups are directed to showing how foreign direct investment benefits the United States, through increased jobs and activities by the concerns investing abroad.[20] Essentially, these arguments and any supporting data are presented through the eyes of these multinational companies, to show that, in *their* particular business posture, investment abroad was a rational use of *their* capital funds, technology, management, and so on. But this approach does not negate the beneficial domestic use by others in the United States of the funds involved; thus, capital not needed for domestic activities by a multinational company can be utilized domestically by other companies. Nor does the approach give hard evidence of why the foreign activity requires a tax preference over domestic investment, which is the result of the deferral of United States tax granted by the present Code for the earnings of the foreign investment when the foreign tax rate is below the United States rate.[21] The more persuasive arguments are advanced by those economists who urge tax neutrality between investment abroad and at home as distinctly preferable to tax favoritism to investment abroad.[22]

— exclusion of income earned by corporations or individuals in United States possessions — This exclusion applies to United States corporations having branches in our possessions, principally Puerto Rico, and to our citizens earning income there. It was originally intended only to defer tax until the income was brought to the United States, but has been applied to provide complete exclusion.[23] The discussion above regarding exemption for the earned income of individuals and deferral for foreign direct investment is here also applicable. However, consideration would have to be given to how changes in these provisions would affect Puerto Rico and a study made of the appropriate United States tax relationship to activities of United States taxpayers in Puerto Rico.

— partial exemption of export income (DISC) — DISC was pushed into the Code in 1971 by the Treasury seeking a tax incentive for exporters. A reluctant Congress, skeptical about the whole idea, adopted deferral of tax for only half of the DISC earnings instead of the full deferral urged by the Treasury. The deferral can be so extended in time as to be close to initial exemption in its value to the exporter. The Treasury then actively marketed the DISC concept, urging through speeches and literature that businesses organize DISCs. Business probably sees the DISC concept as a windfall handed to it by the Treasury, especially since the use of a DISC involves a minimum of interference with existing corporate operations and structures for exporting. The use of a DISC really involves not much more than hoisting a flag at company headquarters emblazoned with the letters DISC — but this symbolic act means a significant dollar reduction in tax liabilities. Labor opposes the DISC provision on the same ground. The devaluation of the dollar and the developing international monetary reforms are the basic answers to our overall trade posture. It is such large factors as these, together with comparative rates of growth and inflation here and abroad, worldwide grain shortages, changes in our foreign policy, and the like, that basically determine the levels of our exports and imports. When these major factors operate to produce an increase in exports, the effect is essentially a windfall to exporters, often accompanied by increased costs to others because of increases in import prices resulting from devaluation or increases in food prices. Consumers must thus pay for these windfall profits of exporters. It is a ludicrous tax policy that then hands the exporters through DISC a tax windfall through elimination of the tax on the windfall profits and asks consumers to pay for this loss in tax revenues. The exporters involved are not small folk, but the major companies in the United States. On top of this, DISC is one of the most complicated statutory mechanisms in the Code, partly because it negates so many otherwise applicable rules. The United States should be leading the way to ending tax subsidies for exports instead of devising new subsidies for other countries to emulate.[24]

Farming (expensing of capital costs and the capital gain treatment on sale of products) under *Agriculture:*

— The Treasury Tax Reform Studies sought to eliminate the farm tax shelter by essentially disallowing current deductions for "loss farming."[25] But the 1969 Act, in large part at the then Treasury's urging, adopted a far weaker approach based on the denial of capital gains on the sale of cattle and other assets to the extent loss deductions were previously taken. As a consequence, the farm tax shelter still exists.[26] A recent study by the Department of Agriculture[27] shows that the shelter is beneficial only for the wealthiest of "loss farmers," those investors in the very top brackets. It also implies that the basic beneficiaries are the management companies who operate the shelters and the ranchers whose lands are leased for the shelter cattle. The basic cattle activity is really not aided — indeed, it seems almost ridiculous to assert that the survival of the cattle industry depends on luring 70 percent bracket investors into dubious ventures.

The items under *Natural Resources.* These items cover:

— expensing of exploration and development capital costs

— deduction of the excess of percentage depletion over cost depletion
— These tax expenditures for the natural resources activities, primarily oil from the revenue standpoint, are in the forefront of all discussions of tax reform. The debating points by proponents of the expenditures generally center around national security and the pressure on energy sources.[28] But these debates rarely focus on the comparative efficiency of the tax expenditure approach and the alternatives of direct programs applicable to the various energy sources, including some sources not presently utilized perhaps because of the artificial price favoritism shown oil by the tax expenditures. The study made for the Treasury Department in 1968 indicates that the tax expenditure approach is highly inefficient, in that the resulting new oil reserves are almost miniscule in relation to the tax revenues involved.[29] Probably the central issue is that of the price for gasoline. The oil companies would presumably urge that the earnings now represented by lower taxes under these tax expenditures would have to be replaced by higher prices of gasoline to the consumer. But this is certainly not a reason for continuance of the tax expenditures, since it is not a national priority to maintain a lower price for gasoline through tax subsidies. Moreover, the question of the price level is obviously linked to our oil import policy and our environmental policies.[30]

— capital gains treatment of royalties on coal and iron ore production

— This treatment represents a special concession to lessors who had entered into contracts at fixed royalties, which contracts became disadvantageous as prices rose. There is no justification in using the tax system — giving capital gain rates instead of ordinary income rates — to bail out these lessors.

— five-year amortization for coal mine safety equipment — This tax expenditure, added in 1969 as a token gesture of aid — it involves about $1 million in revenue — to small operators when the Coal Mine Health and Safety Act raising the level of health and safety standards was adopted, is due to expire in 1974. It also is an elective alternative to the 1971 investment credit, and hence could also be dropped.

The items under *Commerce and Transportation,* except the investment credit and perhaps shipping companies. These items cover:

— excess depreciation on buildings (other than rental housing) — The 1969 Act reduced the benefits of accelerated depreciation for commercial and industrial buildings, cutting the declining balance rate from 200 percent to 150 percent and providing recapture of depreciation taken over straight line depreciation. But even the remaining benefits are unjustified, judging from the priorities reflected in our direct programs. The Congress has not seen any national need for direct programs to subsidize office buildings, motels, shopping centers, factories, and the like, and the tax expenditure assistance for commercial and industrial buildings is thus at odds with our priorities in the building area. This subject will be further considered in the discussion on housing.[31]

— asset depreciation range — class lives for depreciation, 20 percent reduction — In 1962 the Treasury adopted class lives, by industrial classifications, for depreciation purposes in place of lives for particular assets. This approach was essentially designed for administrative simplification. The class lives were set at around the thirtieth percentile of lives in use in the various industries, and this liberality was intended as an incentive to modernization that would both counteract any claims that previous Internal Revenue Service practices were so restrictive as to impede even future modernization and any claims that the class lives themselves were out of line with expected actual experience and obsolescence. At the same time, to eliminate tax preferences for those concerns choosing to retire their assets at a slower rate than the class lives, a reserve ratio test was adopted which mechanically measured tax depreciation against actual retirements and would operate to lengthen lives for particular companies if their actual retirements showed a slower rate. This test was coupled with a generous transition period, again to counter possible assertions of restrictive attitudes and to give business time to adjust to the admittedly generous class lives. Any company retiring its assets more rapidly than its class life could use the reserve ratio test at once to justify a faster life.[32]

In 1971 the Treasury, by administrative action, eliminated the need to comply with the reserve ratio test as respects companies with slower rates of retirement, and also reduced the class lives by 20 percent. However, it offered no empirical data on actual retirements to justify these steps. When legal action by public interest groups against these steps was commenced,[33] the Treasury countered by pressuring Congress to legislate the changes into the Code, and Congress reluctantly agreed.[34] The result is a major tax expenditure item that uses depreciation not as a measure of net income, which is its proper function under an income tax and under financial accounting, but as an incentive for investment in machinery and equipment. The 1971 Act also reinstated the 7 percent investment credit, an admitted tax incentive for the same purpose of encouraging such investment. It is clearly wrong to use two approaches to the same end, and of the two the rapid depreciation device is ill-suited compared with the investment credit.[35]

Steps should be taken to restore the depreciation deduction to its proper place as a factor in measuring net income and to end its incentive function. Thus, the 20 percent reduction in class lives should be scrapped, a survey made of actual retirement practices, and class lives altered to reasonably correspond to those practices, taking account of reasonably expected obsolescence. The reserve ratio test can be used as a mechanism to test the claims of particular concerns to more rapid lives than the class lives. An alternative is to set class lives distinctly on the liberal side and use the reserve ratio test to extend class lives for companies with slower retirements as well as to allow still shorter lives for companies with faster retirements. Any use of the tax system to subsidize investment in machinery and equipment should be confined to the investment credit, an aspect which is discussed later.[36]

— exclusion by individuals of $100 of dividends — This exclusion is the remnant of the move in the 1954 Act to reduce the income tax on shareholders. That move in large part was made to achieve indirectly the tax reduction for top-bracket individuals, in whom holdings of stocks are concentrated, which it was thought could not be achieved directly. The principal device then adopted was a credit against tax of 4 percent of the dividends, and a $50 dividend exclusion was a balancing device for small shareholders. The 1964 Act eliminated the credit, but the political price paid was an increase of the exclusion to $100. There is no national interest in using Government funds to subsidize corporate shareholding, and the choice of this form of private investment, as against other forms such as savings accounts, bonds, and so on, had best be left to the marketplace.

— capital gain treatment generally for corporations — While this item may perhaps be viewed in the overall context of capital gains, there is a special aspect that many consider relevant when corporations are involved. Corporations are essentially engaged in business activities, and hence, even where the business is that of investment, it can be said that business income does not require any special governmental assistance. Thus, even if capital gains of individuals are in the end to be given special treatment, that preference need not extend to corporate investment except in the case of mutual funds.

— deduction of excess bad debt reserves of financial institutions — The 1969 Act in principle removed this deduction for commercial banks and in part for savings and loan associations and mutual savings banks. But the complete transition to the new approach, which is designed to limit deductions to actual bad debt experience as in the case of other businesses, will take considerable time, until 1988. This delay was part of the compromise in the 1969 dispute.[37] There is no essential justification for the long delay or for the residual favoritism shown savings and loan associations and mutual savings banks.

— exemption from tax of credit unions — This exemption is a remnant from the period when mutual enterprises were considered as non-taxable because of their mutuality, despite their being engaged in business activities. The 1962 Act largely ended this attitude, and the exemption for credit unions stands out as unfinished business. Their worthiness is not per se a passport to governmental financial assistance and certainly a tax subsidy is not warranted.

— deductibility by individuals of interest on consumer credit — A Government that does not extend financial assistance to individuals buying an automobile, or a refrigerator, or furniture, or any other consumer good, should not be called upon to extend that assistance to those who decide to buy on credit and pay interest. The present tax deduction for that interest is of course a grant of financial assistance, and benefits those who are better-off and able to purchase more expensive items. While economists would in theory include in income

190

the rental value of consumer durables, along with the rental value of owner-occupied homes, and under this approach deduction of the interest would be appropriate, no tax system adopts this approach. This being so, the deduction for interest on consumer credit is a tax expenditure that requires defense on expenditure grounds, a defense that is hard to support.[38]

— expensing of research and development expenditures — In principle these expenditures should be capitalized. Expensing perhaps might be justified as a simplification device, but the present Code pushes beyond financial accounting. The question remains whether financial assistance is generally desirable for the type of research and development undertaken by business, which is often product development and, if so, whether the tax route should be used.

— exemption of the first $25,000 of income from corporate surtax — This exemption, and the 22 percent rate applied to the first $25,000 of corporate income, are defended as an aid to small business. There are of course direct programs to assist small business, and the ever-increasing scope of the Small Business Administration is an illustration. If, in addition, broad-scale, automatic financial assistance is desired, then the surtax exemption may be appropriate. But there is no reason to extend the assistance to larger corporations as is the present result, under which the exemption is granted to every corporation, large or small. Whatever dividing line is used, $25,000 or some other figure, the exemption should be phased out so that it would eventually disappear as a corporation's income increased.

— five-year amortization for railroad rolling stock — This tax expenditure was added in 1969 in a bargain with the railroads over the 1969 repeal of the investment credit and is due to expire in 1974. Under the 1971 reinstatement of the investment credit, a railroad company must elect between the credit and the five-year amortization. The credit is usually more advantageous, and hence the amortization could be dropped. The requirement of the election would seem to indicate that direct assistance to the railroads would not be a priority item.[39]

The exclusion for individuals of sick pay, the exclusion of certain other employee benefits, the exemption for individuals of interest on life insurance savings, the deduction by individuals of personal casualty losses, five-year amortization for certain pollution control equipment for plants in existence prior to 1969, and five-year amortization of employer-provided child care and on-the-job training facilities, under *Health, Labor, and Welfare:*

— the exclusion for individuals of sick pay, i.e., compensation paid by an employer to an employee absent from work on account of injuries or sickness — This exclusion finds its continued presence in the Code attributable to organized labor's efforts to retain *"its* loophole." In the 1964 Act labor unions were successful in compromising a Treasury and House effort to eliminate the exclusion, and the present complex provision is the end result. While the exclusion is limited to amounts not in excess of $100 a week and for the first thirty days of illness generally to amounts not in excess of 75 percent of the weekly wage rate and to an absolute limit of $75 a week, still the exclusion has an upside-down effect. It provides a Government cash benefit to sick employees in proportion to their marginal rate, and the higher that rate the higher the grant, while the worst-off employees not subject to an income tax do not receive any grant. The unions lobbying for the continuance of the exclusion were seeking to retain the tax benefits of their negotiated wage continuation plans, but they were perpetuating an unfair method of Government assistance.

— the exclusion of certain employee benefits, covering disability insurance benefits, group term life insurance under $50,000, meals and lodging supplied by the employer on his premises, employer-financed supplementary unemployment benefits, employer-provided medical insurance premiums and medical care, and employer-provided death benefits up to $5,000 and accident benefits — In these situations the employer is paying compensation to his employees in forms other than direct wages, and the costs involved are deductible by the employer. The exclusion from the employee's income of these forms of compensation benefits those employees whose negotiating power enables them to command these benefits, e.g., group term life insurance or medical care, or who work in activities where tradition or circumstance occasion the benefit, e.g., employer-provided meals and lodging. These tax expenditures, moreover, being structured as exclusions, favor those with the highest marginal tax rates. While in some employment situations there may be a problem in classifying a benefit as compensation or as merely a part of the employment environment, e.g., lower cost meals in an employer cafeteria, the above enumerated benefits would presumably result in taxable compensation except for the specific exclusions. There is no special reason to favor these forms of compensation, and their inclusion in income would seem appropriate. Any required adjustments in the employer-employee relationship could be reflected in changes in the wage base. The exclusion of employer-provided medical insurance premiums and medical care should be reexamined against the background of comprehensive national medical care programs. The item of employer-provided disability insurance benefits also belongs in this category or with the treatment of sick pay.

— the exemption for annual interest on life insurance savings, i.e., the interest on premium payments accumulating for the benefit of the insured and contributing to the cash value of the insurance — This exemption is one of the silent exclusions of the Code. The exclusion is not expressly enumerated and occurs through long-standing administrative interpretation.[40] Its effect is to make insurance a tax preferred investment over other forms of investment available to middle-income families, though not over owner-occupied residences whose annual rental value is also excluded. While there is some kinship between the two exclusions to the extent that the income element may not be so obvious at first glance, the taxation of the life insurance interest appears more manageable administratively — though this factor requires study — and closer to taxation of other investment income, for example, interest accumulating in savings accounts. The questions are thus whether national priorities require governmental assistance for life insurance purchases and, if so, why the upside-down tax expenditure route should be chosen.[41]

— the deduction by individuals of personal casualty losses — Under the present Code the Government is a co-insurer with an individual against casualty losses to his nonbusiness property. The Government's share of the co-insurance increases with the individual's marginal tax rate, which is again an upside-down method of reimbursement for such losses. If financial assistance is to be given by the Government for these losses to nonbusiness assets, as a home, an automobile, a boat, and the like, it would seem that the assistance should be limited to severe, above average losses, and the assistance should be a direct grant to avoid the upside-down unfairness of the tax expenditure assistance.[42]

— five-year amortization for certain pollution control equipment for plants in existence prior to 1969 — This item was added in 1969 in the wake of the repeal of the investment credit and is due to expire in 1974. "Pollution control" has been a magic talisman for the tax committees, and tax expenditure programs to assist private companies in buying pollution control equipment have been adopted by the tax committees without any real scrutiny. An example, in addition to the five-year amortization, is the exception under industrial development bonds permitting the use of those bonds by states or cities to finance the purchase of such equipment by private companies. In contrast, direct programs in this area generally do not involve assistance to private companies but focus on aid to states and localities.[43] The 1971 reinstatement of the investment credit requires a taxpayer to elect between the credit and the five-year amortization. The credit is usually more advantageous, and hence the amortization could be dropped.

— five-year amortization of employer-provided child care and on-the-job training facilities — This tax expenditure item tumbled into the tax law in 1971 without any supporting data, any estimate as to revenue cost, any study on the need or desirability of Government financial assistance. It would seem fitting to remove the item with the same amount of research.

The deduction by individuals of gasoline taxes (not related to business activities) under *Aid to State and Local Financing:*

— an automobile owner using his car for nonbusiness activities cannot deduct the cost of his gasoline, the federal tax on the gasoline, or his road tolls, but he can deduct his state gasoline tax. Since gasoline tax revenues are used almost entirely for road construction, like the tolls they are a charge for use of the highways. The House in the 1964 Act legislation recognized the incongruity of this deduction alongside nondeduction for the federal taxes used for the Highway Construction Trust Fund, but state governors and the American Automobile Association defeated the proposed change. There would seem to be no need either for this federal financial assistance to automobile owners or for such an indirect way of aiding states in imposing charges for their roads.[44]

The listing of all of the above items, as stated earlier, is on the premise that Government financial assistance is not needed. This is always the key question, and a judgment on each of these items must be made by asking whether as a nation we would desire to pay money directly for the activities involved. Thus, in the international area, if it is tax deferral for foreign investment that Congress is considering, it should ask if it would vote to pay directly to large multinational companies, and others, significant amounts to locate productive facilities abroad, amounts which become larger the greater the size of their foreign operation. If it is the exemption for $25,000 of income earned abroad that is under scrutiny, Congress should ask if it would undertake to pay directly part of the salaries of the executives sent abroad by these companies. If it is the DISC deferral, it should ask if it would directly pay large multinational companies, and others, significant amounts every time we devalue our currency (or other countries revalue their currencies) or negotiate new trade arrangements with the Russians or Chinese. We can certainly doubt that there would be affirmative answers to these questions.

The selection of the particular items is based generally on their previous legislative consideration and the relevant 1969 tax reform debates or 1971 debates, which largely appear to indicate that other factors, and not a considered Congressional judgment that financial assistance is needed, are responsible for their continued presence. Most of the above items have been involved in varying degrees in the tax reform activities of the past decade. The principal exceptions are the basic corporate surtax exemption (though its multiple corporation aspects were at long last removed in 1969), the exclusion of the interest element on life insurance savings, and the expensing of research and development expenditures.

The important point as to the items listed, however, is that *if* financial assistance is considered necessary, the items would then generally seem to fall in the next category, encompassing programs where direct financial assistance can readily be structured. For example, if it is decided that elimination of tax expenditures for natural resources should be accompanied by Government assistance to oil and mineral exploration, the direct programs can readily be devised. The same can be said, as another example, for tax expenditures for farming. Nevertheless, in the 1969 debates on these items the degree of tax change appeared to turn on vote counting and not on the aspect of whether an alternative assistance program was needed or available.

Changes in the treatment of these items would require appropriate consideration of transitional mechanisms in those situations in which an abrupt ending of the tax assistance could have too severe or too destabilizing an impact. The necessary transitional mechanisms can readily be devised where needed, so that the consequences of abrupt change are not valid arguments against change itself.

The treatment of *individual capital gains* under *Commerce and Transportation* may also belong in this first category, judging from the 1969 history when the maximum rate on capital gains was in effect raised from 25 percent to 35 percent without any discussion of alternative direct assistance to private investment. Moreover, changes in the present system of exempting from income tax the appreciation in value of property passing at death, perhaps the largest defect in the capital gain area, seem related to reform of the estate and gift taxes and not to provision of direct budgetary programs of assistance.[45] The preferential treatment of individual capital gains has a number of elements:

(1) Only one-half of the gain is subject to tax, so that the rate of tax on capital gains is only one-half of that applicable to other forms of income. Thus, an individual in the top bracket paying tax at 70 percent on dividends pays only 35 percent on his capital gains. This is about the rate applicable (36 percent)

195

to the incomes of families in the $25,000 range. Those families in turn — if they have capital gains — are taxed at half of their rates on those gains.[46]

(2) On the first $50,000 of capital gains of a married couple ($25,000 for an individual), the maximum rate is 25 percent of the total gain. This limitation benefits those recipients whose marginal rate is above 50 percent, reached at $44,000 of income for a married couple. This 25 percent rate is the vestigial remnant of the pre-1969 Act treatment when this rate applied to unlimited amounts of gain. In effect, the 1969 Act raised the maximum rate from 25 percent to 35 percent for those in the top brackets, except for the first $50,000 of gain. It appears generally agreed that the complexity resulting from this remnant warrants a complete demise of the 25 percent rate.

(3) Exemption of gain on assets transferred at death, with the decedent not being taxed under the income tax on the appreciation in value of assets left in his estate and with the heirs taking a tax cost equal to the value of the assets, so that the gain forever escapes income tax.[47] This exemption — a zero rate of tax on the gain on such assets — obviously presents an impediment to increasing the tax rate on gains realized during life, since the attraction of a zero rate at death would cause owners to hesitate selling appreciated assets. Thus it is important in thinking about the treatment of capital gains to focus on this complete escape from tax at death.

Study after study has shown the impact of the capital gains tax preferences on limiting the progressivity of the individual income tax. Thus, the Treasury Tax Reform Studies stated that these preferences were by far the most important factor in enabling the wealthy to escape their fair share of the income tax.[48] Pechman and Okner, in their 1972 statistical analysis of income tax preferences, present a similar conclusion, indicating that 80–90 percent of the tax preferences enjoyed by individuals with over $500,000 of income are capital gain preferences, and 68 percent for those in the $100,000 to $500,000 bracket.[49] Indeed, not taxing capital gains as income under an income tax is very much like not taxing expenditures on luxury goods under a consumption tax.

The writings of tax economists are increasingly presenting the conclusion that these preferences cannot be supported. The earlier supporting arguments are by now discredited, e.g., that capital gains somehow are not "income" or that the rate preference is needed as an averaging device to prevent the unfairness of taxing in the year of sale an appreciation that may have developed over many years — we have developed an averaging system that includes capital gains.[50] The remaining support for these preferences lies in doubts concerning the effect of full taxation of capital gains on the rate and character of investment in an economy in which private investment, initiative, and risk-taking are highly important.[51] My reading of the economists is that they recognize these doubts as serious but insufficient to cause us to drop the goal of full taxation of capital gains on a sale during life or at death. This view has

196

been stated this way: Once society decides on its objectives regarding the growth rate in our economy, we should then turn to the tax system and see if those objectives require any sacrifice of tax equity. If so, the choice of preferential treatment of capital gains is hardly the efficient method of utilizing the tax system to serve growth objectives, let alone its distinct unfairness. Because we desire a certain rate of growth, we should not as a first choice of method say we will pretty much give up on taxing the actual income of the wealthy. There are other ways in which the tax structure can be modeled to preserve whatever rate of private investment is considered necessary to meet those growth objectives. Principal among these is a reduction in the top rates of the income tax, perhaps to 50 percent and perhaps in the form of a maximum effective rate of 50 percent on total income. Other methods are the allowance of capital losses in full which would complement taxation of the gains in full, so that Government bears a greater share of the cost of investments that go wrong[52] and, if necessary, increased reliance on an investment credit technique. Indeed, the thrust of this emerging consensus is the full taxation of capital gains as the primary goal of tax reform.[53]

An argument sometimes advanced for preferential treatment of capital gains is that the gain often is a reflection of price inflation, and hence, since the higher value does not command any larger amount in terms of real goods, the gain is not a real gain. But our income tax throughout is based on current dollars and not dollars adjusted because of price level changes. Thus, bondholders and holders of other fixed claims who suffer real losses, when the price level rises contrary to the expectations on which the interest rates on these claims were based, do not obtain tax losses. Any change in present rules would have to consider the net effect of inflation on the individual. For example, holders of capital assets who obtain inflationary gains may also have debts which they incurred to obtain those assets, and those debts are now lighter since they can be paid in inflated dollars. In addition, the rise in asset values, such as for securities, has over the years been greater than the increase in the price level, and the relationship is such that an exclusion to reflect the effect of inflation would be less than the present 50 percent exclusion. It would be closer to a 30–40 percent exclusion. Further, since the gain is not currently taxed when it accrues but only on "realization" through a sale or similar disposition, the investor has had the benefit of a deferral of tax liability. If account were taken of this deferral benefit, then for most asset holdings the deferral benefit would clearly outweigh the effect of price level changes, the relationship between the two depending on the length of time the asset was held. Hence an adjustment for both tax deferral benefit and price level change would require for many gains not a percentage exclusion but rather an inclusion of more than 100 percent of the gain. In this view the present 50 percent exclusion is certainly on the generous side.[54]

Pathways to Tax Reform

Tax Expenditure Items that Require Substitute
Governmental Financial Assistance — Which
Assistance Can Readily Be Programmed

A number of tax expenditure items now provide financial assistance for activities where the groups assisted could probably justify the appropriateness of some financial assistance from the Government. However, analysis of the special tax provisions involved has demonstrated in a number of these situations that serious inequities, inefficiencies, and waste result from using the tax system to supply that assistance. Both tax policy and direct budgetary policy would thus appear to dictate a conversion of some or all of the funds involved from the Tax Expenditure Budget to the regular budget. This could be accomplished by the concurrent removal of the special tax provision and the adoption of a direct expenditure program structured to provide whatever financial assistance is appropriate and in the form desired. Any amounts not so converted would simply remain part of general revenue receipts.

Tax reform would in this category encompass a double-sided approach: removal of the special tax provision and simultaneous adoption of a direct expenditure program, using funds made available by the tax change. In the past, tax reform proposals in this area have generally dealt only with the first aspect, that of removal of the special tax provision. For this reason they have been vulnerable to objections by those benefited by the special tax provision that its continuance was vitally needed, as an incentive, subsidy, benefit, assistance, or whatever. But we should now realize that these objections, if valid, go only to the *need* for Government financial assistance and not to the *form* of that assistance. Those now benefited by the special tax provision should also be required to prove that the *form* of assistance must be through the tax system and must sustain the burden of showing the efficiency and fairness of tax assistance as against direct assistance.

Nearly all of the remaining items in the tax expenditure list appear to fall in this category, with the exception of a few matters discussed later. We are here considering items in which the formulation of the direct expenditure program would in general not appear to be a difficult matter. Presumably straightforward grant or loan expenditure programs would usually be involved. In some cases, somewhat comparable direct expenditure programs presently exist, though often involving smaller amounts than are involved in the tax expenditure program. The important task is to interest the administrative agency having cognizance of the particular field to concern itself with working out the direct expenditure program. It is really unfortunate that up to now these administrative agencies have largely left unexamined the tax expenditure items in their areas, allowing the tax funds to be spent without coordination with their own objectives and programs. In other cases, also unfortunately, they have uncritically joined the benefited groups in defense of the tax programs. These agencies do not seem to ask themselves the critical question: If there were made available to us in our regular budgets the amounts represented by the tax expenditure programs in our areas, would our priorities lead us to spend this money in the same way and for the same persons as under those tax programs?

Congress would also have to accommodate its procedures to permit coordinated consideration of these items by the tax committees and the committees having jurisdiction over legislation involving direct assistance. That coordination may require the development of new committee procedures and techniques. But the need for such coordination should not be viewed either as an obstacle or as a reason why tax expenditure assistance in this category should be perpetuated. The Congress has by now realized that if it is to play a positive role in the processes and policies relating to control over direct budgetary outlays, it must work out new legislative procedures to enable that role to be fulfilled.[55] Tax expenditure assistance is in this regard essentially no different from direct outlays. Such tax expenditure assistance likewise must be kept under proper control and surveillance if full control over Government outlays is to be maintained and proper economy in Government realized. Hence any coordination and new techniques worked out for direct outlays should be accompanied by parallel efforts regarding tax expenditure assistance.

The following items would appear to fall in this category:

— Exclusion of military benefits and allowances, under *National Defense*. Presumably, to the extent appropriate, the financial benefits now resulting from the tax exclusion could be provided through direct compensation. Since the tax exclusion benefit is determined by the taxpayer's marginal rate, the present use of the tax system to supplement direct compensation works inequitably in favor of better paid military personnel.

— Capital gains treatment for certain timber income, under *Agriculture*. The present tax treatment of timber makes income from growing timber eligible for taxation at capital gains rates. A lumber company can treat the value of the timber it grows and cuts as a capital gain at the time the timber is cut. This preferential treatment was adopted in 1943 as an aid to timber-growing. Its ramifications extend beyond this artificial capital gain treatment and permit large integrated companies with logging and later manufacturing operations, through the handling of deductions and the adroit valuation of the cut timber, to have almost 100 percent of their total income taxed at the preferential corporate capital gain rate of 30 percent instead of the customary 48 percent rate.[56] The present tax benefits, the bulk of which go to a few large companies in a discriminatory fashion, are defended on the ground that they afford funds for the timber companies to carry out desirable conservation practices, and this defense helped defeat a Treasury proposal in the 1964 Act to end the preferential treatment. The evidence, however, points more to an industry defensive rationalization than to recognized conservation gains directly produced by the tax benefits. Thus, the benefits are in no way conditioned on the practicing of good forestry programs.[57] But, in any event, *if* the conservation link of the present tax benefits is supportable, and *if* federal financial assistance is considered appropriate, then it seems clear that conservation programs financed with direct grants could readily be substituted. The Federal Government and the states already have a number of direct programs and the requisite experience is present.[58]

— Deferral of tax on shipping companies, under *Commerce and Transportation.* The Merchant Marine Act allows certain shipping companies to obtain an indefinite deferral of income tax on amounts deposited in construction funds used to replace merchant vessels.[59] Direct subsidies are also provided. The present tax assistance could thus readily be restructured as direct assistance.

— Tax benefits for the aged (additional personal exemption, retirement income credit, and exclusion of social security retirement payments) and the blind (additional personal exemption), under *Health, Labor, and Welfare.* There seems to be general agreement that the benefits accorded to the aged under the tax system are a most discriminatory and complicated set of provisions that simply cannot be defended on any rational terms. Recommendations have been made to preserve these benefits for lower and middle-income aged but under a fairer and simpler tax structure,[60] and this is at least a first step. But a large amount of federal money is involved, about $3.5 billion, and HEW and the Treasury should be studying whether financial assistance of this magnitude should more appropriately be structured either through a direct grant system or incorporated into social security assistance. This would then mean, for the tax system, that age would not be a factor in the determination of tax liability, so that persons with the same amount of income would be taxed the same in this respect, whether aged 25, 64, or over 65. Since the present tax system for the aged is the product of ad hoc accretions far removed from any thoughtful planning, such a reexamination is needed. There has been no published empirical study providing comparisons of consumption needs and other relevant factors between the aged and those under age 65 at the same levels of income, or analysis to indicate that age should be a factor in income tax liabilities. As a group, more of the elderly are poor than those at other age levels, but of course many of the nonaged are also poor. Undoubtedly, adoption of an income maintenance plan providing cash income for the poor, including the working poor, would provide a new background against which to consider these tax expenditures for the aged. Federal tax assistance to the blind, involving only $10 million, could also be structured as a direct program. This step would have the added virtue of ending the persistent efforts to provide tax benefits for other disabled individuals. Those benefits would here also turn on a taxpayer's marginal rate and thus be of no assistance to the disabled poor.[61]

— Exclusion of unemployment insurance, workmen's compensation, and public assistance benefits, under *Health, Labor, and Welfare.* These exclusions are not an appropriate part of the definition of net income, but rather simply constitute an addition to the direct monetary amount paid under the benefits, again in an unfair way because the tax benefit (and hence the addition) is determined by the taxpayer's marginal rate. The direct programs are, however, associated with the relief of misfortune or hardship. This being so, any tax change would seem to depend on the development of an income maintenance program under which persons are given financial assistance without regard to the cause of their economic need. The Family Assistance Plan before the Congress in 1971–72 did treat these particular benefit payments as offsets against a money allowance, in that the benefits were included in measuring the family's "income" to see what amount of family assistance, if any, is to be paid. These benefits would thus be "income" for the purpose of a *negative income tax system,* which the Family Assistance Plan essentially represented. Once this concept takes hold, it may be considered appropriate also to include such benefits in "income" under the *positive income tax system.*[62]

— Deduction of child and dependent care expenses, and household expenses, under *Health, Labor, and Welfare.* The primary inquiry here should be directed to whether the child and dependent care aspects of this tax expenditure item could be absorbed by various direct programs. Its presence in the tax system reflects the earlier absence of direct child care programs available to a family where both spouses were employed, just as the adoption of the medical expense deduction, discussed next, reflected the absence of comprehensive medical care programs. Tax expenditure items of this character evidence the sensitivity of the tax system to concern over the lack of federal assistance in social areas. Relief through the tax system is thus the point where social advance wedges into the federal budget and is often the forerunner of larger and more adequate direct programs in later years. Unfortunately, the tax expenditure item usually remains as an inequitable and vestigial program.

The child care deduction, prior to the change in 1971 increasing its scope, was estimated to be used by about 260,000 families, at a revenue cost of $30 million.[63] The increase in 1971 is expected to add over a million families and involve a total revenue cost of around $180 million. But direct expenditure programs for child care under consideration by the Congress total far more, about $2 billion over three years, and would benefit far more families.[64] These programs are structured to assist low-income families, with the assistance declining as income increases, so that better-off families using the facilities provided by these funds can do so by paying a fee. This method of direct program assistance contrasts directly with the tax expenditure assistance, which provides no aid to the poor but then aid increasing as income and marginal tax rates rise, until the $18,000 income level is reached; the assistance is then phased out for incomes above $18,000 and disappears at $27,600. Seventy percent of the $145 million 1971 additional child care tax expenditure assistance went to families with incomes of $10,000 to $50,000, with almost one-half going to families between $15,000 and $50,000. Also, the direct programs stress their "developmental" character, centered on the needs of the children and the family, and not "custodial" care, which is what is in effect made available under the tax provision. There is thus a conflict between the divergent ways in which the two approaches are developing.[65] The question to be explored is whether the tax expenditure program should be dropped and its funds used instead as part of the direct programs.[66]

The Senate Finance Committee in 1971 injected the deduction for household expenses — amounts paid for the services of a maid, cook, or other domestic help — unrelated to child care, though the deduction for these expenses is dependent on the presence of a child in the family. Thus, the household services need not relate to the child but the child becomes the passport to the household services deduction. This Committee is reaching out on all sides for programs to take people off welfare and is pushing tax incentive programs for this purpose, thereby using its jurisdictional lever.[67] The 1971 household services deduction is one result of this policy, and the desire of the Committee, especially the Chairman, for that deduction in turn led to the increase in the child care deduction.[68] But there is a strange irony in giving tax benefits to upper middle class families to aid them in employing servants to help solve welfare problems. It is clear that no direct program of this character — Government grants to better-off families to subsidize their obtaining domestic help — could stand the light of public scrutiny. But here it is, buried in the child care tax expenditure. This is another illustration of how one tax expenditure program, itself dubious, expands to encompass additional programs that are even more ill-advised.

— Deductibility of medical expenses under *Health, Labor, and Welfare.* The present tax system, through the tax deduction for medical expenses, provides federal financial assistance to meet medical expenses above the level of 3 percent of income. But here also the extent of the assistance is determined by the taxpayer's marginal rate, so that the poor receive nothing and the wealthy receive the most assistance. Change here, however, presumably depends on the adoption of a federally financed plan for universal and comprehensive medical care. When that is done, this deduction should then be reexamined (and also that for one-half of medical insurance premiums up to a total of $150), just as the absence of the 3 percent floor in the medical deduction for the aged was reexamined and the floor instituted when Medicare and Medicaid were adopted in 1965.[69]

— Additional personal exemption for students and exclusion of scholarships and fellowships, under *Education.* These items are intended to provide assistance to families with children in college. But the tax expenditure assistance is again upside-down, favoring better-off families and providing no aid to the poor.[70] The exclusion of scholarships and fellowships favors this type of income as against the earnings of students who must work to have the funds needed for college tuition. It contrasts with the direct federal programs for student assistance, which are aimed at those students who are in need of assistance.

— Exclusion of certain veterans' benefits, under *Veterans Benefits and Services.* A change in this item could be linked to an increase in the direct benefits themselves, and perhaps also, as with workmen's compensation benefits, to the development of an income maintenance program.

Most of the items in this second category have figured in tax reform activities of the past decade. The principal exceptions are veterans' benefits; the unemployment, workmen's compensation, and public assistance benefits; the additional personal exemption for students; and the exclusion of scholarships and fellowships.[71]

Developments in the 1969 legislation seem to support the tax reform approach described here for items in this category, involving the substitution of direct expenditure programs for the tax expenditure items. There was retrogression under that legislation when tax expenditure programs were adopted, in the form of five-year amortization, for assistance in the acquisition of railroad cars, pollution control equipment, and mine safety equipment, and in the rehabilitation of low-income housing. No one of these tax programs had received much or any previous research or analysis, and some, notably for pollution control equipment, were opposed strongly by the agencies concerned with these fields. But there was advance in that all the provisions were structured to expire in five years, so that the agencies concerned and the Congress could review their effect. It remains to be seen whether the Treasury and the appropriate agencies will use the interval to prepare and execute research programs designed to measure the efficiency of the programs and, equally important, to measure the efficacy of alternative direct expenditure programs.

Pathways to Tax Reform

Tax Expenditure Items that Require Substitute
Governmental Financial Assistance — Which Assistance
Necessitates Specially Structured Programs

The *first two categories* considered above cover most of the items in the Tax Expenditure Budget. The few that remain appear to impose special requirements that must be incorporated into any alternative program of direct assistance, and thus to lift such programs out of the more usual run of federal assistance programs. In other words, the use of the tax system in these cases provides financial assistance under criteria or circumstances which, if they must be duplicated in a direct program replacing the tax expenditure, will necessitate some special structuring of that program.

We can here include in this *third category* the following:

— Exemption of interest on state and local obligations and deductibility of various state and local taxes, under *Aid to State and Local Financing.* Here the task, as to the first item, is to devise a direct subsidy that state and local governments will consider to possess sufficient automaticity and freedom from federal control. The use of a taxable bond on which a significant portion of the interest cost is automatically paid by the Federal Government should be a suitable approach.

— Deduction of charitable and educational contributions, under *Health, Labor, and Welfare* and *Education.* Here the task is to devise a direct subsidy that continues private designation of the charitable donee and freedom from federal control. The thinking here is still in the initial stages, with some researchers exploring a system of direct matching grants.

— The tax assistance accorded to owner-occupied homes and rental housing, under *Housing and Community Development.* As to *owner-occupied housing,* the task is to devise a direct subsidy that can replace, for those homeowners for whom assistance is proper, the present tax incentives of the deduction for mortgage interest and property taxes. As to *rental housing,* the task is to devise a direct subsidy for *low-income housing* to replace the present inefficient and over-generous tax shelter that now exists through the deduction of accelerated depreciation for new housing, five-year amortization in the case of rehabilitated housing, and other real estate tax benefits. The research here seems to be gathering momentum, and the problem could be solved if HUD and the Treasury would recognize their joint responsibilities for the solution.

— Deduction and credit for political contributions, under *General Government,* added in 1971. Here the task is to devise either a direct subsidy that continues private designation of the political candidates to be benefited, such as a matching system outside the tax law, or a system of direct

Government financing of political campaigns without reliance on private funds. The research will have to draw on the experience in 1972 under the new tax expenditures.

— Treatment of pension plans, under *Health, Labor and Welfare.* Under the present tax system, employer-financed pension plans provide a deduction to the employer when it makes a contribution to the plan but deferral of taxation on the employee until he retires and a pension is paid. The income earned on the amounts held by the plan is also exempt from income tax. The net result is beneficial to those employees who are members of these pension plans — and who in the end are fortunate enough to receive pensions. But this private pension system creates many perplexing problems. For example:

(1) The employer, as long as it does not discriminate in favor of highly-paid or supervisory employees, can establish the basic requirements and pension levels. If, for example, the employer chooses a plan that has delayed vesting of the employee's right to a pension or no vesting, employees who leave their employment may receive no pension at all despite long years of service for the employer. A similar loss can occur, even under a vested plan, if the employer becomes bankrupt and there are insufficient funds in the plan to meet the expected pension benefits. These defects of the private pension system are the subject of current legislative consideration.[72]

(2) The pension levels in many plans, especially in closely-held companies, provide large pensions for highly-paid executives and shareholder-executives. It is questionable whether present tax benefits should be available for these large pensions.

(3) The availability of tax benefits for large pensions paid to highly-paid executives and shareholder-executives contrasts with the much lower levels qualified for favorable tax treatment in the case of self-employed professionals and sole proprietors. These lower levels, for so-called H.R. 10 plans, are the result of doubts in some quarters on the wisdom of tax subsidies for the retirement savings of these groups. The picture, however, has been considerably confused by the present Treasury's decision in the 1969 tax reform debates to support "professional corporations" utilized by doctors, lawyers, and other professional groups to secure the tax benefits accorded to corporate pension plans.[73] By utilizing these professional corporations, which are established under specially enacted state laws, professional people can have the pension benefits accorded to executives and still in large part continue the conduct of their activities according to the mores of their professions. But resort to such corporations obviously involves instabilities, since without the lure of the pension benefits the corporate form would not be used by these groups.

(4) The above aspects relate to individuals covered by pension plans. But about half the employee population works for employers which do not have

pension plans. The uncovered employees are typically those who work for smaller companies and they are generally nonunionized and not as well paid as covered employees. The tax expenditure for pension plans provides about $4 billion of tax benefits, but the decision on which employees will obtain these tax benefits is left to the employers. If an employer decides not to establish a pension plan, then its employees will not share in the tax expenditure benefits. The resulting unfairness is beginning to be reflected in policy discussions. Thus, there is growing awareness of the imbalance that would result from legislation strengthening employees' rights when a pension plan does exist, as by mandating more rapid vesting, but doing nothing about those situations where the employer chooses not to establish any plan, weak or strong. The policy recommendations of the Nixon Administration to remedy this imbalance favor tax exemption for amounts set aside by an individual in a special retirement fund. But obviously such an approach favors the better-off employee who is in a position, first, to save something and, second, not to have to use the savings later for the education of his children, a larger house, an emergency, and so on.[74] Much the same favoritism exists under the H.R. 10 mechanism for professional persons, which for the same reason favors the better-off professional. As a consequence, some have suggested that employers be required to establish plans for their employees which will provide legislatively-established minimum retirement benefits. Since the private pension plan is a tax-favored supplement to the social security system, which is the basic national program to meet retirement needs, then to provide such a supplement for all employees it seems necessary either to directly supplement social security or to require all employers to participate in supplementation through private pension plans.[75] It is obvious that considerable thought and policy discussion are required to determine the national priorities in this area and the extent to which tax expenditures are at all appropriate. The present tax expenditure apparatus is clearly unfair and inadequate.

The first three matters in this category mentioned above will be discussed separately in Chapter VII. If the difficulties of developing adequate alternative direct programs for an item in these areas are such as to cause continued use of a tax expenditure program, then the particular item would be classified in the *fourth category,* involving areas where the use of the tax system is necessary to carry out a governmental policy.

Finally, we could probably place in such a *fourth category* the 7 percent investment credit for machinery and equipment, under *Commerce and Transportation.* This is a tax subsidy of broad scope and high visibility, so that its purpose as an incentive is readily apparent. The important task here is to develop the credit so that it can become a flexible macroeconomic tool to be used counter-cyclically to dampen business demand for credit and funds in a tight money period and to spur investment demand in a slack period.[76] That development should also involve consideration of applying the credit only to net additional investment, the base recommended when the credit was first advanced in 1961. At the same time, care needs to be taken that the existence of this special credit does not become the continuing wedge for those urging the adoption of a whole flock of tax subsidies in other fields where the direct approach is clearly preferable. This has been its history in the past, and while the necessary care was taken in the 1960's, this so far has not been the case starting in 1969. Also, the United Kingdom experience, which covers both the use of the tax system and of direct grants to stimulate investment in machinery, equipment, and buildings, should be studied to develop the considerations involved in choosing in the United States between the tax system and direct programs for such purposes.[77]

Conclusion

Looking back over this classification of items in the Tax Expenditure Budget, we see that we must concentrate on three categories:

— *first,* those items whose proponents carry a burden of proof to demonstrate the need for continued Government financial assistance, as to which it is expected a number will not be able to sustain the burden so that the tax expenditure can be dropped, while any items for which the burden *is* sustained will then be in the second category;

— *second,* those items as to which it can quite probably be expected that the burden of showing the need for continued Government financial assistance will be sustained and as to which alternative direct programs can most likely readily be constructed to provide that assistance;

— *third,* those items as to which continued Government financial assistance will be considered necessary and which require the development of alternative direct programs that must meet special criteria to provide that assistance.

It appears that most of the items in the Tax Expenditure Budget relating to the regular budget functions of International Affairs, Agriculture, Natural Resources, and Commerce and Transportation would fall initially in the *first category.* These budget functions essentially cover the tax incentive programs providing financial assistance to investment and business operations. The thrust of regular budget trends has not been in the direction of particularized aids to business and investment, as contrasted with broad programs of highway construction, transportation, and the like. Hence the particularized tax programs should be reexamined.

Most of the tax expenditure items relating to the regular budget functions of National Defense, Health, Labor and Welfare, Education, and Veterans Benefits and Services would initially probably fall in the *second category*. These budget functions essentially cover the tax programs designed to give financial assistance to ameliorate special hardships (e.g., the expenses of the aged and the ill) and some tax incentive programs in the social area (e.g., scholarships, interest on life insurance savings) and the environment (e.g., forest conservation, pollution control). Many of these tax programs essentially derive from earlier periods when the Federal Government was not involved in large scale direct programs in these areas. But with federal outlays for income maintenance and for investment in human resources now exceeding defense expenditures as the main part of our regular budget outlays, the expenditure setting has obviously changed. It is thus appropriate to reexamine the role of these tax programs in the new setting.

The items relating to the regular budget function of Housing and Community Development, the special category of Aid to State and Local Financing, the functions of Health, Labor and Welfare and of Education as they concern the support of philanthropy, and General Government as respects political contributions would fall initially in the *third category*. In these areas the role of the Federal Government has steadily increased in the scope of direct programs and funds involved, so that a reexamination of the role of the tax programs is likewise in order.

The overall amounts involved in each of the three categories are roughly the same, assuming the tax treatment of pension plans is in the second category.

The pathways to reform of the present tax expenditure apparatus are reasonably clear. They are: research in some areas, the exercise of responsibility by the administrative agencies involved, leadership toward reform by the Office of Budget and Management and the Treasury Department, improved Congressional coordination between the tax committees and the committees with jurisdiction over direct expenditures, and a political will to reform on the part of legislators. Clearly, after a reexamination involving these elements, some tax programs would be shifted into a category different from the initial classification made above. But it is likely that the shifting would largely relate to the first and second categories, depending on the importance of the need for continued financial assistance. It seems less probable that an objective reexamination involving careful expenditure scrutiny would place many tax programs in the third or fourth category. If this is so, then a rigorous scrutiny of the Tax Expenditure Budget in the light of present priorities and direct expenditure programs would signal a very marked reduction in the Tax Expenditure Budget. Both tax policy and expenditure policy would be improved by this development.

VII

Three Special Tax Expenditure Items:

Support to State and Local Governments,

to Philanthropy, and to Housing

Most of the tax expenditure programs should either be scrapped because the federal financial assistance they provide is not warranted by the nation's priorities or be replaced by direct assistance measures that can readily be devised. But a few of the tax expenditure programs require further analysis. These few appear in their tax format to involve special requirements that must be incorporated into any alternative arrangement of direct assistance. These requirements thereby lift these programs out of the more usual run of federal assistance measures. In other words, the use of the tax system in these cases presently provides monetary assistance under criteria or circumstances which, if they must be duplicated in any direct program that replaces the tax expenditure, will necessitate some special structuring of that program.

We can here include the following:

— Exemption of interest on state and local obligations and deductibility of various state and local taxes, under *Aid to State and Local Financing.*

— Deduction of charitable and educational contributions, under *Health, Labor, and Welfare* and *Education.*

— The tax assistance accorded to owner-occupied homes and rental housing, under *Housing and Community Development.*

These three matters will now be discussed separately.

Assistance to State and Local Governments

The tax expenditure system provides assistance to state and local governments through the exemption of interest on state and local obligations and through the deductibility of nonbusiness state and local taxes.[1] The exemption will be considered first, with the deduction of taxes then considered in connection with revenue sharing.[2]

State and Local Obligations

Events of 1969. The exemption from income tax of the interest on state and local obligations remains a feature of our income tax despite persistent publicizing of its tax inequities.[3] The two main legislative efforts to alter the situation were in 1942 and 1969, and both failed. But the difference in approach developed in the quarter-century separating these efforts is highly instructive. In 1942 the effort was a frontal one, simply to eliminate the exemption. In 1969 the focus of the effort was to find an alternative method of aiding state and local governments that would materially lessen the use of tax-exempt securities.

We have come to recognize the tax expenditure character of this exemption in its provision of federal financial assistance through the tax system to state and local governments. The reliance of those governments on that assistance and their need for it is accepted. Any effective effort to alter the exemption to improve the equity of the tax system must therefore include finding a replacement for the tax assistance. The events of 1969 illuminate the difficulties.

The House Ways and Means Committee, which initiated the 1969 effort to change the situation, recognized the exemption's inequitable effects on the tax system and its inefficiency in furnishing financial assistance:

> Capital outlays of State and local governments for such projects as schools and other public buildings, highways, water and sewage systems, and antipollution facilities have doubled during the past decade. In order to market an increasing volume of securities to finance these public projects in competition with a growing volume of private borrowings, State and local governments have been offering higher yields, and the differential between tax-exempt and taxable securities of comparable quality has been narrowing. Historically, the ratio of yields on tax-exempt issues to taxable issues has been as low as 60 percent, but in recent years it has been close to 75 percent.
>
> The ratio of yields has varied in response to the general availability of credit, the demand for credit and the proportionate demand by State and local governments to the total market demand for credit. As a result, high income individuals and institutions otherwise subject to high tax rates who constitute a major portion of the market for tax-exempt State and local securities have been receiving significantly larger tax benefits

than needed to bring them into the market. Recent estimates place the annual saving in interest charges to State and local governments at $1.3 billion, but the annual revenue loss to the Federal Government has been estimated at $1.8 billion.[4]

On the tax equity side, the exemption permits upper-bracket individuals and commercial banks to escape their share of the tax burden. While in a sense the bondholders pay a "tax" to the state and local governments in the form of lower interest rates, that "tax" allows them to avoid a far higher federal tax. The bondholders therefore willingly enter into the exchange. On the efficiency side, the exemption gives less in aid to those governments in the form of lower interest rates than it costs the Federal Government in revenue — perhaps a 30 percent wastage. Moreover, as the need of those governments for capital funds inevitably becomes ever greater, the method of assistance, i.e., whatever lowering of interest rates the exemption could achieve, is inevitably painting those governments into a corner. They are forced to sell more and more bonds to buyers who really are not the obvious buyers of those bonds but who are only tempted to do so because of the exemption. High-bracket individuals should normally be buying equities, and banks should be making business loans. To tempt them away from those natural pursuits into buying more and more tax-exempt bonds, and to draw individuals in lower-brackets and other financial institutions in the same direction, will require higher interest rates on the bonds to make the exemption worth more. The interest savings to the state and local governments will thereby decrease, while tax inequity increases as the higher-bracket individuals and banks obtain the benefit of interest rates higher than is needed to tempt *them* into the exempt market. At the same time, natural buyers of bonds, such as private pension trusts, state and local retirement funds, and educational and charitable institutions, are not attracted by the tax exemption, since their income is already exempted.[5]

While the exemption's negative aspects steadily become more apparent, state and local governments in the 1969 debate underscored two of the exemption's affirmative aspects from their viewpoint:

— The assistance provided by the exemption is freely available to them, for any project they choose, without the Federal Government exercising any control.

— The assistance is open-ended because the amount of assistance depends solely on the amount of obligations issued by the governmental unit.

Thus, whatever limitations financial markets or bond ratings and the like may impose, the exemption vis-a-vis the Federal Government has the effect of a blanket, automatic, no-strings-attached, open-ended, federal grant-in-aid to the issuing governments. Obviously, the governors and mayors relish these aspects of the exemption approach and want to preserve them.

The House Ways and Means Committee in 1969 recognized this and sought to duplicate these attributes in its alternative to the exemption. It provided, in its version of the Tax Reform Act legislation, that if a state or local government *elected* to issue a *taxable* bond, the Treasury Department would be required to pay periodically to the issuing government, as bond interest payments fell due, from 30 percent to 40 percent of the interest payment (from 25 percent to 40 percent for bonds issued after 1974).[6] The Secretary of the Treasury was to proclaim the figure for each quarter, and the percentage effective when a bond was issued would apply throughout its life. It was understood when the bill passed the House that the percentage would be changed to a flat 40 percent. A permanent legislative appropriation would cover the cost of the subsidy, similar to the appropriation for interest on federal bonds. The cost to the Treasury of the interest subsidy would be met by revenues from income taxes on taxable bonds or other investments that taxpayers would hold instead of exempt bonds. The payment of the interest subsidy was to be automatic, with no federal review of a bond — no inquiry as to the advisability of the project for which it was issued or the issuer's ability to pay.

In its essentials this alternative duplicated the affirmative attributes of the tax exemption route. But the alternative was never discussed on its merits. A variety of pressures — the chaotic monetary situation in mid-1969; the influence of investment houses seeking to preserve their present business in tax-exempts and the dependence of some state officials on political contributions from some of these sources; a lack of understanding of the House proposal in responsible state and local quarters; the attitude of the Administration, ranging from opposition to hands-off but not encompassing support or even full explanation of the proposal and the issues; the coverage under the minimum tax and the "allocation of deductions" proposals of interest on any future tax-exempt bond that might be issued, and of outstanding interest under the minimum tax — all combined to prompt a mass lobbying effort by state and local officials concentrated on the Senate Finance Committee. The lobbying campaign was operated jointly by representatives of state and local governments organized as the Conference for Intergovernmental Fiscal Relations and by the Investment Bankers Association, though the latter was not named as a member of that conference. They coordinated the direct testimony of state and local officials before the Committee and the barrage of letters, visits, and calls to the legislators. The arguments and debating points were erroneous or specious, but that quality did not detract from the effect of the massed character of the effort.[7] The alternative simply disappeared under the attack.[8] But the problem remained.

Events Since 1969. The state and local governments, the governors and mayors, all congratulated themselves that they had won a major battle. But almost immediately, as the emotional pitch of the lobbying campaign waned, some began to have doubts and second thoughts. After all, they had turned down a generous offer of assistance that involved no strings. And the problems which that offer was designed to meet still existed unsolved. The battle did not solve them.

The difficulties state and local governments face in meeting their capital needs and the increasing limitations of the tax expenditure type of assistance furnished by the exemption are still evident. Studies indicate both the dependency of the tax-exempt market on purchases by commercial banks and the likelihood that in the decade ahead the economic environment will be one in which commercial banks will not be massive buyers of state and local bonds.[9] The adverse effect of the exemption on tax equity — the indefensible escape from tax liability that it permits — still persists. Moreover, these factors work perversely: the more inefficient the tax exemption mechanism becomes as a method of assistance as the interest rates rise on the exempt bonds, the more inequitable the exemption becomes as a part of the income tax.

Frank Morris, President of the Federal Reserve Bank of Boston, summarized the situation in these terms:

> For years students of the municipal bond market have been discussing five important structural defects in the market. First is the fact that tax exemption on state and local government bonds is a rather glaring source of inequity in our income tax structure. Second is the potential for the misallocation of capital which stems from the fact that the tax-exempt bond market creates a special incentive for very wealthy people, who can afford to be risk takers, to channel funds into securities in which the risk of default is little or none. Third is the fact that, from the standpoint of the U.S. Treasury, the subsidy given to state and local governments through tax exemption is an extremely inefficient one; since only a part of the subsidy is actually received by the intended beneficiaries. Fourth is the marked cyclical sensitivity of the municipal bond market which stems from its excessive dependence on the commercial banking system. Fifth is the fact that the secondary market for municipal bonds is, generally speaking, not as good as the secondary market for corporate or U.S. Government bonds; and municipal bonds must, accordingly, be viewed as less liquid than other bonds.[10]

All of these points suddenly became much clearer to those involved in the 1969 campaign, and the points underscored the need to broaden the financing options available to state and local governments. The volume of future issues of state and local obligations was seen as both large in itself and as part of a large aggregate demand that would be placed on savings.[11] Agencies such as the Urban Development Corporation of New York recognized that their huge demand for debt capital could not readily be met by the tax-exempt market in view of its inherent limitations. That market automatically excludes as buyers the tax-exempt institutions — pension funds, colleges, and the like. It has built-in geographical limitations, since many residents of a state desire to buy only bonds that are issued within that state and hence exempt from the state income tax as well, but not bonds from other areas which have no such exemption for them. It relies, as stated above, on the commercial banks as buyers, since tax-exempt institutions, and also low-tax buyers such as life insurance companies, mutual savings banks, and savings and loan associations, are excluded, while other institutional buyers taxable at full corporate rates, such as fire and casualty insurance companies, do not have the available profits. This dependence on commercial banks produces great swings in buying demand, since in times of full employment and monetary tightness the commercial banks turn off as buyers and instead lend all available funds to business customers. State and local governments find themselves the low man on the financial totem pole. In such a period their interest costs rise as they raise rates in efforts to attract individual buyers,[12] but clearly those buyers cannot sustain the need of these governments for capital.

Efforts to attract commercial banks and individuals make the tax exemption a highly inefficient subsidy. The Boston Federal Reserve Bank study shows that for individual taxpayers in the highest tax brackets, tax exemption has an efficiency rating of 50 percent or less over the last ten years.[13] Considering all buyers and not only those in the highest brackets, various studies have shown ranges of efficiency that center around 70 percent. The lower level of efficiency for the top-bracket taxpayers indicates the extreme tax unfairness of the exemption, for its greatest rewards obviously go to such brackets. In their case, half of the cost of the subsidy to the Federal Government goes to them and not to state and local governments.[14] For a taxpayer in the 70 percent bracket, the inefficiency is even more marked. Using 1970 average figures, as against taxable bonds at interest rates of 9.11 percent, on a purchase of tax-exempt bonds paying a 6.75 percent rate, he would net $4.02. The state or city would save $2.36.[15] In other words, the Treasury pays the 70 percent individual $4.02 so that a state or city can save $2.36.

When those involved in the 1969 battle focused on these facts, they saw that their response in 1969 had been far too rigid. In that year they had concentrated on the "threat" to tax exemption that they saw in the House proposals for "allocation of deductions" and a minimum tax, which had included tax-exempt interest as a tax preference. In so doing, they had lost sight of the significant assistance offered by the taxable bond subsidy of the House bill. The former had triggered the traditional knee-jerk responses of "don't tamper with tax exemption" and "preserve the status quo." The customary emotions triggered by those responses — responses and emotions which the lobbying efforts were directed to bringing forth and on which the efforts relied — prevented any rational assessment of the situation. The House subsidy was caught in the attack, and no attempt was made to separate it from the tax preference proposals directly affecting tax exemption. But once the reassessment set in, events swiftly changed. Two aspects became quite clear: first, there was a need to broaden the financing options of state and local governments; second, the necessary broadening required federal financial assistance. The question then became: In what way should the federal assistance be obtained?

In facing this post-1969 question, the representatives of state and local governments saw several avenues. One was the taxable bond subsidy approach of 1969. The Congress was already beginning to use taxable state and local bonds in several program areas. Thus, the Medical Facilities Modernization Act of 1970 provided that obligations evidencing loans to public bodies for hospital facilities could be purchased by the Federal Government and resold in the private market as taxable obligations with part of the interest paid by the Federal Government.[16] A similar provision was adopted, also in 1970, for the rural water and sewer loans of the Farmers Home Administration.[17] Further, the Housing and Urban Development Act of 1970 authorized public bodies to issue directly "new community" obligations on a taxable basis, with part of the interest to be paid by the Federal Government.[18] In all these cases, the issues were also guaranteed by the Federal Government.[19]

A second approach was that represented by the various "development bank" proposals. The first of these had been made in 1968 and 1969 in the form of an Urban Development Bank, which would issue its own taxable bonds and in turn lend its funds to state and local governments at subsidized interest rates.[20] The Administration had made a proposal along this line in 1971 in the proposed Environmental Financing Authority, which would purchase waste treatment bonds of state and local governments, where those governments could not themselves borrow directly on reasonable terms, with the EFA financing these purchases by issuing its own taxable obligations. In the EFA situation there would be federal control over the issuance of the state and local obligations, since purchases could be made only if the obligations were guaranteed by the Environmental Protection Agency under the authority of the basic substantive programs in this area.[21] The 1970 situations of taxable bonds earlier described were similar in this regard, since federal control was present inasmuch as the projects for which the state and local obligations were issued themselves had to obtain federal approval in order to receive project aid.[22] The year 1971 also saw a variety of development bank proposals, initiated by various legislators, to finance rural or urban programs. These proposals had a common theme — a federal agency would be established that would lend amounts to various public bodies to finance specific or broadly framed substantive programs, with the federal agency obtaining its funds through the marketing of its own taxable obligations.[23]

As legislation and proposals of the "development bank" character grew in volume and variety, the contrast between it and the taxable subsidy of 1969 also grew clearer. The state and local representatives saw in the "development bank" approach the clear presence of Federal Government control. Federal agencies were involved, with programs and bureaucracies and red tape of their own to which the state and local units seeking funds would have to conform. The assistance would be there, in the form of loans at subsidized interest rates, but the conditions and the projects assisted would be of federal devising. In contrast, the House 1969 taxable bond subsidy suddenly appeared in the light that its advocates had always proclaimed for it. For the subsidy was granted on an automatic basis, with no bureaucracy or federal control. Its operative character thus paralleled the automaticity of the subsidy of tax exemption. The essentials were the same, but the taxable nature of the subsidized obligations would open up the entire bond market for state and local governments, and this would give them, on *their* terms, the additional financing option they desired.

The events since 1969 therefore moved with increasing momentum toward the taxable bond subsidy as the solution. Its own virtues were now fully perceived, and stood in marked contrast to the specter of federal control that loomed in the development bank proposals. The Boston Federal Reserve Bank held a conference on this matter in 1970, and its president there urged a 50 percent subsidy for taxable bonds.[24] This proposal, and its accompanying argumentation, coming from such an expert and respected source, jarred some of the state and local officials present into looking seriously for the first time at this approach. Policy positions announced by the National League of Cities in 1969 and 1971 moved cautiously toward a taxable bond approach.[25]

The dramatic breakthrough came in August 1971 at a Seminar on State and Local Finance sponsored by the Federal Reserve Bank of Boston. The members included staff officials of all the state and local government organizations — e.g., the National League of Cities, the National Governors' Conference, the National Association of Counties, the Municipal Finance Officers Association, the U.S. Conference of Mayors; members of the investment banking community, including the Investment Bankers Association of America and commercial banks; and academic people. The Seminar after two days of discussion agreed on the following consensus:[26]

> The Federal Government should provide state and local governments with an additional method for obtaining access to the credit markets. Specifically, the group agrees that state and local governments should have the option of issuing fully-taxable obligations (of the character presently tax exempt under the Internal Revenue Code) with the Federal Government obligated to pay to the issuer, without any restrictions, a fixed percentage of the interest cost. This percentage should be set at a level sufficient to encourage widespread use of this option.

Since this Boston Seminar, the National Governors' Conference has adopted a policy statement that is supportive of a taxable bond subsidy.[27] The Investment Bankers Association, seeing this change of position on the part of state and local governments, who after all are its customers and clients, also swung over to support that approach.[28] As 1971 closed, the stage thus seemed set for efforts by the state and local governments to obtain legislation authorizing the taxable bond subsidy, on the elective basis proposed in 1969.

In 1972 the Senate Committee on Banking, Housing and Urban Affairs held hearings on S. 3215, which proposed an elective taxable bond alternative with a subsidy rate of 33.3 percent.[29] Reflecting the consensus reached in Boston in 1971, the taxable bond approach was supported by the Securities Industry Association, representing bond dealers and commercial banks, the National League of Cities and National Conference of Mayors, the Municipal Finance Officers Association, and the National Association of Cities. No group testified against the approach — except the Treasury, which asked for time to study the matter. The Committee reported favorably on the proposal and referred it to the Senate Finance Committee.

The Treasury in April 1973 then joined the growing consensus and proposed the elective taxable bond approach at a 30% subsidy level. The emphasis in the proposal was on broadening the market for state and local government obligations, and the tax equity aspect was given only minor significance. The proposal was described as follows:

> The proposal will provide a more stable market for state and local government obligations by enabling these governments to compete more effectively with corporations, especially when market rates are high. It will also make municipal obligations attractive to pension trusts and other exempt organizations, which presently do not typically invest in tax-exempt obligations. The subsidy program will also tend to reduce the supply of tax-exempt obligations and slightly depress interest rates on those remaining, thereby reducing both municipal borrowing costs and the availability and attractiveness of exempt obligations to high bracket taxpayers.
>
> The Treasury estimates subsidy costs for the first year of $180 million, with an offsetting amount of increased tax receipts, depending on the amount of new municipal borrowing stimulated by the subsidy and the average marginal tax bracket of investors in tax-exempt obligations. A reasonable estimate is that there would be little net gain or loss to Treasury at the 30 percent subsidy level. . . .
>
> Public borrowing by state and local governments has increased substantially over the past decade and is expected to continue at high levels. As more exempt issues are offered, their interest rates have increased. At the same time banks are beginning to reduce their holdings in exempt obligations. By making a broader market available to state

and local governments through the offering of obligations carrying taxable interest at rates competitive with corporate obligations, these governments will be better able to meet their growing responsibilities. Just as it was and is felt to be good federal tax policy to allow state and local governments to issue exempt obligations at a saving to these governments, it is felt that the taxable, subsidized municipal bond proposal is based on sound federal-state tax policy. In this way, while the exempt bond market will be preserved, a genuine option will be afforded municipal borrowers.[30]

In this setting the central question is the amount of the subsidy to be paid by the Federal Government.[31] The "Boston consensus" sought a percentage level of subsidy "sufficient to encourage widespread use of the [taxable] option." Studies have indicated that a 33.3 percent subsidy — i.e., the Federal Government paying one-third of the interest on a taxable state and local bond — would supplant only about 10 to 15 percent of new issues, and the remaining issues would still be going out as tax-exempt. A 40 percent subsidy would give a higher degree of substitution but still leave a quite large volume of tax-exempt securities to be issued. A 50 percent subsidy would probably result in taxable bonds almost entirely displacing tax-exempt issues, especially if, as would seem likely, commercial banks withdrew from seeking tax-exempt bonds. The savings in net interest costs to the state and local governments reflect these consequences at the different subsidy levels. As an example, in a period comparable to the three-year period 1968–1970, the savings would have risen from a total of $50 million per year on new issues for a 33.3 percent subsidy, to $170 million for a 40 percent subsidy, and to $350 million for a 50 percent subsidy. The net cost to the Treasury of the substitution of the taxable bond subsidy for the subsidy of tax exemption would have been around zero for a 33.3 percent subsidy, $50 million per year for a 40 percent subsidy, and $70 million for a 50 percent subsidy, if the banks were to cease seeking tax-exempt securities. The introduction of the taxable bond subsidy approach would have little effect on the yields of other taxable securities and therefore would neither disrupt the market for taxable securities nor affect the cost of long-term credit to private borrowers.[32]

The Senate Banking Committee, in reporting favorably in 1972 on a 33.3 percent subsidy,[33] seemed influenced in using such a low rate by worries over the "cost to the Treasury" of a higher rate. It thought that the Treasury's then generally negative attitude could be influenced favorably if no additional cost were involved.[34] But studies made subsequent to the 1972 Hearings of that Committee indicate that the cost figures provided at those Hearings were on the high side for the 50 percent subsidy.[35] Moreover, and really much more to the point, this factor of net cost to the Treasury should not be regarded as a criticism of the proposal or an obstacle. Federal grants to state and local governments totaled about $35 billion in 1972, which dwarfs any added cost from the bond subsidy proposal. In addition, the Congress in 1972 decided that further federal assistance to these governments was needed. The general revenue sharing bill enacted in 1972 thus provides for around $6 billion annually through 1976. Any loss to the Treasury under the bond subsidy at least would go directly to the state and local governments, and not be wasted in tax windfalls to high-bracket taxpayers as is the case today under exemption.[36] There would be no wasteful "commission" paid to those taxpayers on the taxable bonds, in contrast to the present situation under which a wealthy individual is paid $4.02 so that a state or city can save $2.36.

A 50 percent subsidy could displace new issues of tax-exempt bonds entirely, so that only taxable bonds would be marketed.[37] But even if some tax-exempt bonds were to be issued, the interest rates on those bonds would be less than paid today, since they would be forced to a level around 50 percent of the taxable bonds as compared to around 75 percent at present. Hence, the benefits of tax exemption on those issues would be materially reduced. Using data for 1970 adjusted to reflect the effect of the subsidy, a 70 percent bracket purchaser of a tax-exempt bond paying 4.55 percent would net $1.82 as against the purchase of a 9.11 percent taxable bond.[38] This $1.82 benefit compares with that of $4.02 at present. Only taxpayers in brackets between 60 and 70 percent would probably find the purchase attractive, and even for many in these brackets the game would presumably seem not worth playing any more. The benefit that would be received by those investors who would still buy tax-exempt bonds would be sheer wastage, since state and local governments would not save any interest cost on the issuance of those tax-exempt bonds. Those bonds would have been issued simply to use whatever market remained among the high-bracket individual buyers.

It thus appears that a 50 percent subsidy level for the taxable bonds optionally issued by state and local governments is the level best suited to accomplish the objectives of this solution to the tax-exempt bond problem.[39] If a flat 50 percent subsidy level is for some reason not chosen, the next approach could be 40 percent for maturities over five years, which should cause an almost complete switch to taxable bonds in this range. There also should be discretion in the Treasury Secretary to fix the percentage between 40 percent and 50 percent for shorter maturities, when such a step is necessary to increase the efficiency of the federal subsidy in that range.[40]

The adoption of an elective taxable bond subsidy approach would in turn focus attention on remaining problems. Presumably the present industrial development bond classifications would essentially carry over, and only those industrial development bonds now tax-exempt would be eligible for the direct subsidy.[41] Special assistance could be given to those local governments that are at the weak end and would have financing problems under any approach, such as some small cities and certain large urban cities. Thus, assistance could be furnished through a state bank marketing bonds on a state-wide basis and buying the obligations of localities, as in Vermont today. Moreover, federal "development banks," where they were thought useful as adjuncts to federal programs, could still be explored, and presumably would be supported by state and local governments, for they would then be additional financing alternatives and not exclusive assistance routes. Additional matters for resolution could well appear in the wake of a taxable bond approach.[42]

In sum, the solution for the present tax expenditure item of tax-exempt state and local bond interest will have to provide federal assistance on terms that resemble the affirmative attributes of the assistance available through the tax exemption. The solution therefore must permit freedom of choice by state and local governments as to both the use to which the aid money will be put and the quantity of aid available. The solution also will have to permit those governments the legal alternative to resume the issuance of tax-exempt bonds as a fallback if the subsidy solution turns out to be less useful than the exemption device. This is not to say there is inherent logic in these requirements for a solution. Over 90 percent of the annual federal assistance to state and local governments, through grants and other mechanisms, does not involve these attributes. Similarly, financing assistance to state and local governments to raise capital funds should not necessarily be on a different basis. The answer instead lies in history and the attitude currently taken by these governments. Even though, through inefficiency, tax exemption assistance involves waste and federal revenue loss, it does produce some assistance to these governments compared to the alternative of simple repeal of the exemption.[43] And, apparently, these governments do not regard the harmful effect of the tax exemption's inequity as their worry or a reason to forgo the assistance they now obtain. Given their political power, these governments can place requirements on alternative methods of assistance. Those seeking alternative methods accept the realities of the situation, as the House Ways and Means Committee proposal for an elective taxable bond subsidy and subsequent developments indicate.

The taxable bond subsidy differs in one important respect from the present tax expenditure approach. Under that approach, neither the cost — the revenue lost by the exemption — nor the amount of assistance given — the interest savings — appears in the regular budget. Under the proposed alternative, the financial assistance would appear in the budget as a direct expenditure. Naturally this would eventually become a sizable figure.[44] Some state and local government representatives have observed this and have wondered if the Federal Government would tolerate the growing cost of the subsidy for long:

> [It] would not be unreasonable for a Congressman or a budget director to question the rationale for continuing a very costly subsidy program.

220

It is also interesting to note that the present $1.86 billion savings from tax exemption is an amount substantially in excess of most congressional appropriations for urgently needed individual urban programs. From the hard cold logic of experience, city officials doubt that they would continue to receive from Congress a direct automatic unrestricted subsidy of the necessary magnitude for state and local bond issues. This is further borne out by the unhappy experience of local governments abroad whose capital projects depend upon the permission of the central government.[45]

Of course, the present tax expenditure assistance through the tax exemption is just as costly, perhaps even more so because of the wastage, but the cost is effectively hidden.

The crucial question may well be whether those involved in the problem and the search for a solution place a large value on the hidden character of the present method of financial assistance, a value which offsets that method's inherent limitations. Unfortunately, this could block exploration of more effective, though open, alternative methods outside the tax system. It would also in the final analysis be unrealistic. For if the Constitution does not guarantee the tax exemption — and I believe most lawyers think that it does not — then that exemption and method of aid are also subject to federal control.[46]

Indeed, even apart from this aspect, since direct federal grants are now far in excess of the assistance obtained from tax exemption — a ratio of over $40 billion with general revenue sharing to $2 billion annually — the states and localities must already place their faith in the rationality of the Congress for over 90 percent of the annual aggregate federal assistance they now obtain. It would be wrong to base solutions in the area of financial assistance to state and local governments with respect to the issuance of their obligations on the assumption that the Congress, made up of elected representatives from the states, will act in bad faith to injure those states and their cities and localities. Unless more effective methods of financial assistance for those obligations are found, not only will the inequitable effects of the present exemption persist, but also the present scheme will prove itself increasingly incapable of supplying state and local governments with the assistance they need. Fortunately, therefore, it now appears from the post-1969 developments earlier described that alternative methods will not be discarded because of their openness.

In summary, the potential of the exemption device to provide greater financial assistance to state and local governments has been exhausted. At this juncture, therefore, the task is to broaden the financial options open to state and local governments for raising capital funds. Such a broadening of financial options can only be helpful to those governments. It would also improve the equity of the federal tax system. Whether one approaches the situation from the aspect of federal tax reform or from the aspect of improving the financial position of state and local governments, the end result would be of benefit to all governments.

Relationship to Revenue Sharing
— and State and Local Taxes

The issue of revenue sharing — a grant of funds directly to state and local governments without being categorized as part of any particular substantive program — has been before the Congress since 1969 as a result of a Presidential recommendation.[47] The consideration of this issue culminated in a general revenue sharing measure enacted in 1972.[48] This approach to assisting state and local governments is not directly a tax policy issue since no tax expenditure item is involved. The legislation essentially involves only a direct expenditure approach and does not alter the Internal Revenue Code.[49] Consequently, I will not discuss the wisdom of revenue sharing.

I would like to raise a different question. We have seen that the assistance now given to state and local governments through the tax expenditure item of exemption of interest on their obligations is in need of reform. This being so, should not the Congress, if it decides to continue the revenue sharing approach and to maintain the policy of large annual grants to those governments, then use that approach to achieve a rational direct expenditure solution of the tax-exempt bond interest problem through resort to the taxable bond subsidy alternative described above? Further, in those areas where no alternative is really needed, we should also be able to achieve the necessary tax reform by merely eliminating the tax expenditure. Thus, there is no reason for the income tax to give consumers financial assistance on the purchase of gasoline through a deduction for state gasoline taxes. The Treasury has several times recommended that this deduction be ended,[50] and the House did so in 1963. But the combined opposition of state governors and automobile associations keeps the deduction alive. The continued deduction of personal property taxes, primarily on automobiles, is another undesirable feature of the tax system.

There may be other tax expenditure facets involving assistance to state and local governments to be explored in this connection.[51] The central point is that the very large expenditure involved in revenue sharing made for the purpose of assisting state and local governments should at least be a vehicle to bring more rationality into the federal-state and federal–local relationships through the modification or elimination of existing inefficient and inequitable tax provisions whose sole defense is that they presently provide some degree of assistance to those state and local governments. This *quid pro quo* is entirely in keeping with the purposes and policies of revenue sharing and with needed tax reform.

Three Tax Expenditure Items

Support of Private Philanthropy:
the Deduction for Charitable Contributions

The charitable contributions deduction, a feature of the income tax since 1917, occasioned more discussion during the 1969 legislation than at any other time in the intervening period and certainly far more than on its adoption. Three aspects were examined: the general contours of the deduction itself; its interrelationship with the treatment of any appreciation in value that may be present when noncash assets, usually securities but sometimes land or works of art, memoirs, correspondence, and the like, are given to charities; and other various mechanisms — some said "gimmicks" — through which the basic deduction could be enhanced. The terms "charities" and "charitable contributions" cover all types of recipients to whom deductible gifts may be made, including educational institutions such as colleges and universities, foundations, religious organizations, community charities, and other charitable activities falling within the more restricted use of the term.

The 1969 Tax Reform Act's final passage saw Congress cutting back the mechanisms by which tax advantages could be obtained from charitable contributions. It thereby indicated that the remaining tax advantages, especially for gifts of appreciated property, are exceptions to regular tax rules. This underscores the tax expenditure character of those advantages. At the same time, charitable organizations, especially colleges and universities, successfully pleaded the importance of the financial assistance involved in these tax expenditures. There thus began to appear the first serious consideration of the consequences of the tax expenditure approach to financial assistance for private philanthropy. In the end there was an emerging, though incomplete, awareness of the nature of the alternatives that would have to be made available if essential changes in the tax expenditure approach — and tax reform in this area — are to occur. In brief, tax reform here also requires for its realization a satisfactory alternative solution to the social problem of how to support philanthropy.

The 1969 Act made the following changes in this area:[52]

— It revised the limits on the amount of the charitable deduction, setting the general limit at 50 percent of adjusted gross income in place of the previous 30 percent. Twenty percent remains the limit for contributions to private foundations.

— It ended existing escapes from the general limit, such as the special unlimited charitable deduction and two-year charitable trusts.[53]

— It fully recognized, with respect to appreciated property, the inconsistency of allowing a deduction for the full value of the property but then not including the appreciation in income. Consequently, that appreciation must now be taken into account to reduce the deduction in the gifts of all property where the appreciation would be ordinary income if the property were sold;[54] in the gifts of letters, correspondence, memoirs, files, and so on;[55] in the gifts of tangible personal property if its use is unrelated to the exempt purposes of the recipient, such as works of art to an organization where possession and use of art are not in keeping with the functions of the recipient; and in the gifts of securities to private foundations.[56] This last item is the most significant recognition of the inconsistency.[57] Moreover, where the appreciation in value is not taken into account to reduce the deduction for the gift, as in the case of gifts of securities to colleges, the limit is to be 30 percent of adjusted gross income, not 50 percent. Finally, the Act stopped the tax planner's device of pushing the exemption of the appreciation even one step further through a "bargain sale" of the appreciated asset to the charitable donee.

In essence, the traditional deduction of cash gifts remains, but with the expanded 50 percent limit, and also the traditional deduction of gifts of appreciated securities — and works of art for museums. But now there is an explicit recognition that the exemption of the appreciation is understood as a departure from normal tax treatment and therefore as a special tax benefit for educational and other operating philanthropic institutions. This recognition is seen in the use of a special 30 percent limit for such gifts of appreciated property and, perhaps even more to the point, in the elimination of the exemption for the appreciation in the case of gifts to private foundations. Congress rejected the arguments of the colleges[58] that somehow the exemption of the appreciation was consistent with tax logic. On the other hand, the retention of the appreciation exemption for the colleges is a recognition of their contention that the gift of appreciated securities is an essential part of the financial support they obtain by the tax mechanism. Moreover, their claim of necessary reliance on such support is generally recognized through the retention of the basic charitable deduction essentially unchanged. The Congress underscored this attitude by rejecting the "allocation of deductions" proposal which the House had adopted, under which the charitable deduction, and other personal expense deductions, would have been allocated pro rata between taxable income and exempt income, with the portion allocated to exempt income then disallowed as a deduction.[59]

Against the 1969 background, let us consider, as we did in the case of tax-exempt bonds, the essential characteristics of the tax expenditure approach as a method of providing federal financial assistance to private philanthropy. First, it clearly is a method of federal assistance. While the end result is often described as "private support," and the relevant tax provisions as inducements or incentives to such support, the tax expenditure aspect is clear. The provisions involve federal assistance in that the contributors are allowed to reduce their tax liabilities through deduction of contributions made to their charitable donees. The amounts involved in the tax liabilities forgone are shifted away from the Federal Government to the charities through the mechanism of the charitable gift and the allowance of that personal gift as a deduction from gross income. The charitable contribution deduction is a special tax provision not required by, and contrary to, widely accepted definitions of income applicable to the determination of the structure of an income tax.[60] It is, in short, a tax expenditure as the term is used in the Treasury Tax Expenditure Budget, and the charitable contribution deduction is included therein.[61]

The important attributes of this form of federal assistance are similar to those of tax-exempt obligations. For while the assistance to philanthropy comes from the Federal Government, its allocation is privately directed — the Government funds are paid to particular institutions at the direction of private persons. Moreover, the assistance is blanket, automatic, no-strings attached, open-ended aid. The terms are those used earlier to describe the exemption for state and local bond interest, where the direction of the aid comes not from private persons but from governors and mayors. In the case of the tax-exempt bonds, private persons purchasing the bonds are the third-party beneficiaries of that mechanism — it was *their* benefits that gave rise to the tax inequities — and they only participate indirectly in the allocation of the aid in that as bondholders they form the marketplace which determines at what price the bonds are sold. In the case of the deduction for private philanthropy, private persons direct the flow of the funds, and the act of direction affects *their* tax liabilities.

This delegation to private persons of the expenditure of public funds on philanthropy has some interesting aspects. The amount of public funds which a private person can allocate depends on his marginal tax bracket and hence his income position and wealth generally.[62] Put in other words, a gift of $100 cash and a consequent deduction of $100 is worth $70 to the person in the 70 percent bracket — he saves a $70 tax and thus allocates $70 of public funds — and only $14 to a person in the first bracket. As a consequence of this effect of the tax expenditure, taxpayers in the brackets over $20,000 – who constitute only 5 percent of all taxpayers – allocate almost two-thirds of the Government's financial assistance granted through the charitable deduction, although their gifts total only about 25 percent of all itemized charitable contributions.[63]

Moreover, the amount of public funds involved depends on whether the gift is of cash or appreciated property, such as securities. If the gift is of appreciated securities, for a person in the 70 percent bracket a gift of $100 of stock that had cost the donor nothing (to simplify the arithmetic — generally very low basis stock is involved in these gifts) rather than being worth $70 in tax saving is worth at least $105. For if he had to sell that stock, e.g., to obtain funds to pay a tax bill of $70 on $100 of income — which tax bill he in effect pays by giving the $100 stock to charity and offsetting the $100 income by the $100 deduction — he would have a capital gain of $100 (again assuming a zero basis) and a tax of $35 (if above the limit on the 25 percent rate). This would leave him $65 after the sale, or $5 short, so that payment of the tax bill would cost him $105. Paying the tax bill through the charitable deduction thus is worth $105 to him.[64] The treatment of gifts of appreciated property compared with cash can be expressed in other terms. A person who gives $100 in cash obtains a deduction of $100, but a person who gives $100 in fully appreciated property obtains a total benefit equivalent to a deduction of $150. These illustrations do not depend on the taxpayer's selling stock to pay his tax bill. The illustration of payment of a tax bill is chosen to contrast two ways of paying that bill — one by a sale of the stock and the other by a gift of the stock. The illustrations equally hold for any situation in which the taxpayer desires or expects to sell the stock to realize cash; in the example above more cash can be realized by giving the stock away to charity since he will save what otherwise would have been paid in tax on the sale.[64-1]

There are other idiosyncracies. Suppose a person receives $100 of taxable income and $100 of exempt income and is in the 70 percent bracket. He pays a tax of $70 on these two items, so he has an effective rate of 35 percent on the $200. But if he contributes $100 to charity he need not pay the $70 tax. If a person who is actually in the 35 percent bracket, paying a 35 percent marginal rate with all income being taxable, contributes $100, he saves only $35 in tax payments. It is this inequality which would have been corrected by the 1969 House "allocation of deductions" proposal.[65] Put differently, if all economic income were taxed, and the top rate lowered to 35 percent, the first taxpayer would have secured a 35 percent benefit from his contribution, i.e., reduced his tax from 35 percent on $200, or $70, to $35, a benefit of $35. Under the present rates, but with "allocation of deductions," he would have reduced his tax from 70 percent of $100 to 70 percent of $50 (since one half of the $100 gift would be allocated to the $100 exempt income) or from $70 to $35, also a benefit of $35.

The tax inequities in the charitable deduction and the companion treatment of the appreciation element in contributions of property are evident from this description. Why should a gift of property reduce tax liability more than a gift of cash? Why is the charitable deduction allocated entirely to taxable income and not at least prorated between taxable and exempt income? Why should a contribution be less costly to upper-bracket persons? These are the questions people have in mind when they speak of tax reform in this area.

The tax expenditure involved can now be expressed in direct expenditure terms:

— If a person below the personal exemption levels — a non-taxpayer — contributes $100 to a philanthropy, he contributes the entire sum and the Government contributes nothing.

— If a person in the first bracket contributes $86 to a philanthropy, the Government contributes $14 to that same philanthropy (i.e., he makes a gift of $100 and obtains a deduction worth $14).

— If a person in the 70 percent top bracket contributes $30 in cash to a philanthropy, the Government contributes $70 to that same philanthropy.

— If a person in the 70 percent top bracket informs the Government he is selling fully appreciated stock to pay his tax bill or to obtain cash for other reasons and would like $100 paid to a philanthropy, the Government pays the $100 to that philanthropy and also pays the person $5 — or perhaps $6.50 or even $15.50.[66]

So expressed, the tax expenditure approach appears irrational if judged by criteria customarily applicable to direct expenditure programs.[67]

The charitable organizations, and private colleges and universities in particular, in 1969 chose to rely on and defend this method of financial assistance. They stressed the importance of private gifts to their operating budgets and, in the case of the educational institutions, to their capital funds. The latter institutions also stressed the special role played by gifts of appreciated securities in the case of certain of the institutions. The American Council on Education testified that only 1 percent of donors gave 75 percent of the gifts to higher education in 1962–63.[68] Moreover, in the case of some colleges, gifts of appreciated securities run as high as 50 to 70 percent, or even higher, of total gifts from individuals.[69] It is clear, then, that our colleges, insofar as such support through "gifts" is concerned, are really receiving nearly all of the support from the Government with the "donors" providing very little of their own funds and instead "voting" through the deduction these appropriations of Government funds to the colleges.[70] This reliance of the colleges on "contributions," and their financial problems in general, carried the day for them and other charities in 1969, though similar arguments failed the foundations when it came to appreciated property.

But 1969 is past, and the question remains whether this reliance on the tax expenditure approach for providing financial assistance is a wise course in the future for these institutions. Are the foundations of the present approach too shaky to endure? That approach is contrary to tax logic, as the 1969 debate and Act underscored, especially with respect both to the exemption of appreciated property and the allocation of the charitable deduction entirely to taxable income. The tax unfairness of the deduction method in its favoritism for the upper-bracket taxpayers is also evident. Moreover, for many charitable organizations the trend toward expansion of the standard deduction in an effort to restore it to its earlier role, when it was used by nearly 90 percent of the taxpayers instead of itemization of their personal expense deductions, means the elimination of the explicit recognition of the charitable deduction.[71]

When "philanthropic logic" as seen by the colleges and others is so contrary to "tax logic," a tension and instability exist. The tax reformers will attempt to chip away at the tax inequities in order to remove the tax illogic. The philanthropic institutions, having a vested interest in preserving an unfair and inequitable tax system, must defend the existing abuses and inequities and oppose their correction — they must defend the exemption of the appreciation element in the gifts, must oppose allocation of deductions, must keep a watchful eye on the unlimited deduction for charitable contributions under the estate and gift taxes, and so on. College presidents must appear before Congressional committees and sit in Senators' anterooms as lobbyists alongside the oil company executives, the oil investors, the hobby farmers, and the real estate operators — all pressing their claims that the special provisions of the tax system applicable to *their* activities should not be changed and contending that the national interest will be adversely affected by any change. One wonders whether college presidents relish the role or comprehend that many legislators and Government officials believe that some of the presidents are not even aware of the role itself.

In the case of tax-exempt bonds, the understanding had clearly emerged that tax reform could not be achieved until an acceptable alternative form of financial assistance outside the tax system was made available. The tax reformers understood this and offered an alternative at the outset. The debate in 1969, confused as it was, was in essence over the acceptability of the House alternative. But there was no similar understanding at the outset of the 1969 debate over the charitable deduction, and the tax reformers proceeded without offering an alternative. Rather, they disputed the financial effects of the changes on the charitable organizations and asserted that the charitable organizations and the colleges had greatly exaggerated the effects of the House changes. But the debate indicated that the financial concerns of the organizations, especially the educational institutions, are strongly felt by the Congress, and the risks involved in making tax changes on the basis of thereafter seeing what the actual effects would be are too serious to permit that course to be followed. Tax reform must here also turn into the search for an alternative solution.

We can therefore ask, as we did in the case of tax-exempt bonds, what should be the attributes of that alternative. We felt that for tax-exempt bonds the alternative would have to approximate the present tax expenditure, in that the financial assistance to state and local governments would have to be on terms that resemble closely those that characterize the effect of the tax expenditure. But is this the situation for the support of private philanthropy? One wonders whether an HEW Secretary would make the following proposal to the Congress:

We propose to establish a Division of Charitable and Educational Assistance which will distribute its funds as follows:

— Suppose a person calls and says: "I am too poor to pay an income

228

tax but I am contributing $20 to my favorite charity. Will the Government also help it?" The answer here will be: "We appreciate your sacrifice but we cannot use our funds in this situation."

— Suppose a person calls and says: "I am quite well-off and want to send a check for $3,000 to one of my favorite charities. Will the Government also aid it?" The answer here will be: "We are delighted to be of assistance and are at once sending a Government check for $7,000 to that charity."

— Suppose a person calls and says: "I am really very wealthy with a considerable fortune in various stocks that originally cost me or my family very little. In fact, I will be selling about $2 million of stock to pay my income tax this year and to raise cash for other purposes as well. I think that a particular charitable institution deserves support and while I have decided not to contribute anything myself, I am calling to inquire whether the Government will contribute to it." The answer here will be: "We understand the situation and will be delighted to contribute $2 million to that institution. We will of course say it is in your name. And, in appreciation of your suggesting this to us, we are sending you a check for $100,000, tax-exempt of course."

— Finally, if a person makes application to the Office for Private Foundations and says he is establishing a foundation which he will direct and manage, with the advice of his wife and one or two friends, and is contributing, say, $1 million in cash to it, then the Government will send him funds in the amount of $2.3 million to be placed in the foundation, also under his control. (We have discontinued the system under which if the person paid his income tax, or obtained cash for other purposes, by selling appreciated stock, we would ourselves fully fund the foundation for him and then give him a payment, itself tax-exempt, for thinking of the idea.)

While this direct expenditure mechanism would mirror the present tax expenditure approach,[72] the latter was never consciously designed to operate in the manner that has emerged. Rather it grew up that way without the Government or philanthropy really thinking through its implications. In 1969, Congress began to see what was involved, but chose to stay with it in the absence of an alternative.

It is evident that the Government assistance provided under the present tax expenditure approach has two characteristics:

— the aspect of private choice, in that Government funds are allocated, without any questions being asked, to the institution designated by the taxpayers involved.

— the aspect that the wealthier the contributor, the smaller his own gift and the larger the Government's matching gift, ending in the situation where the Government gives everything plus a payment to the "contributor."

The charitable organizations, we can assume, would like to see the first aspect retained, that of private choice. It is hard to see an insistence on the second aspect, or its acceptance by the public if stated in direct terms.[73] Is there any system of Government matching to be devised that embodies the aspect of private choice but is better than the bizarre upside-down character of the tax approach in the weighting given to the choices of different private selectors?

In answering this question, we must remember that when philanthropy worries about the effect on "private giving" if the present deduction is tampered with, it is not the truly "private" share of such giving that philanthropy is concerned about but the retention of the Government's contribution represented by the deduction and triggered by the activities of donors.[74] This concern, however, requires as earlier stated that an alternative must at least maintain the equivalent amount of Government support, and also not reduce the aggregate of "private giving" below the net after-tax cost to donors today.

In the search for an alternative, some writers have suggested the elimination of the charitable deduction from the tax system and the substitution of a direct Government matching contribution, using a formula that would turn on the proportion of a person's total economic income that was given to charity. Thus, under a proposal made by Professor Paul McDaniel, if a person gave under 2 percent of his total income to a charity or group of charities, then the Government would *automatically* match 5 percent of his gifts, with no questions being asked. If he gave 2–3 percent of his income, the gifts would be matched on a 10 percent basis. And so on, with an added 5 percent of matching for each additional percentage point of income until a maximum of 50 percent matching where the gifts are over 10 percent of income. The percentages specified for the federal matching share are set at levels that would have equaled the $3.8 billion revenue lost — i.e., the Government financial assistance given to charities — under the charitable deduction in 1971. As contributions increase, the total federal share under matching will also automatically increase, just as the revenue loss under the charitable deduction now increases. Appropriations for the matching funds could be on a ten year basis. The provisions of the tax law regarding the deduction for charitable contributions would be dropped, and the appreciation in gifts of securities and other property would be taxable.[75]

Professor McDaniel's estimates indicate that while philanthropy under his matching schedule would receive as much federal assistance as under the present deduction, the total going to philanthropy would increase. This estimate is based on the assumption that *private giving* — the amount actually borne by the donor — would increase, since donors would reduce their gifts by only 50 percent of the increased taxes resulting from repeal of the charitable deduction.[76] Today a donor's gift in effect consists of two checks — his own and the Government's, the latter being the tax reduction brought about by the charitable deduction. The donor is both making a gift of his own funds and acting as a paying agent for the Government. The aggregate of the second set of checks will be the same under Professor McDaniel's matching schedule, with the Government becoming its own paying agent when triggered into action by the private gift. But he believes the aggregate of the first set of checks will be larger, and philanthropy will be the gainer. Even if donors reduce the amount in the first set of checks — their own — to the net cost to them under the present deduction, the total going to charity will be the same as at present, since the overall amount contributed by the Government can be structured to be the same under both approaches. There presumably would be some shift in the relative amounts that particular segments of philanthropy would receive, but Professor McDaniel believes that these shifts should not be significantly large.[77] And obviously, this matching schedule, unlike the upside-down "matching" under the present deduction, is an effort to inject widespread pluralism into the allocation of Government funds going to philanthropy in contrast to the restricted character of the present "tax pluralism."[78]

This direct matching approach would not involve the consequence of the present tax system that A's private choice to support a charity makes B's tax burden higher than A's, for under the approach A and B would bear the same tax liability given the same income. But B would still see some of his tax money being spent by the Government as A directed — the element of private choice. Moreover, the wealthier A was, the more of the Government's funds he could command, though the actual amount at his command would depend on the proportion of his income that he gave to charity. Would the public and the Congress, if faced with this proposal or some other matching variant, accept for the support of philanthropy such a system of private choice and private command openly expressed, especially if information were public on the Government's contributions and also on the private gifts that triggered them? Would the private foundation system as we know it today remain acceptable under this approach?[79]

If private choice and public expenditure at private command cannot survive openness, or if a workable matching system cannot be devised, and an alternative solution is still sought, then it must lie in other ways by which direct governmental assistance is given. We do have direct Federal Government assistance today for higher education, totaling $6.1 billion in fiscal year 1971 and $7 billion in 1972. The total in 1971 was made up essentially of student support, including grants, loans, and veterans' education benefits, about 50 percent; research aid, 30 percent; institutional aid, 20 percent.[80] Private gift support was estimated at $1.86 billion in 1971,[81] or somewhat under one-third of the Government aid. Government funds are also contributed to the arts and to public educational broadcasting.[82] It seems clear that if higher education, the arts, and some other philanthropic activities are to continue to play the role we desire for them, there must be a considerable enlargement of Government aid.[83] Congress in 1972 recognized this and authorized increased aid to higher education in very large amounts, both for the institutions and their students. Actual appropriations, however, are still far short of the authorizations.

If we can work out the ways to accomplish this aid and still maintain the requisite degree of independence for the institutions involved,[84] then we could of course let these methods of far larger support absorb the portion of support that currently depends on tax deduction. But could we through direct expenditure programs duplicate the present tax expenditure system under which any type of charity, whatever its function and size, can get some federal assistance as long as some persons choose to make contributions to it?[85] Should we want to duplicate it?

At this point we can only raise questions, and only a few questions. Serious thinking about an alternative solution has barely started. One question is whether the charities themselves, and especially the colleges and universities, should join in the effort. The seriousness of their present and future needs for funds should compel them to think about alternatives. The tax expenditure approach, even if retained, will not produce the necessary funds; other avenues of governmental assistance must be explored. In this light, they could join with those who recognize the instability and unfairness of the tax expenditure approach and seek to devise more lasting and productive alternatives.[86]

Support for Owner-occupied Homes and Rental Housing

The tax expenditure system provides extensive financial support for private housing, primarily for owner-occupied homes but also for rental housing. The tax expenditure items involved may be considered under those two headings.

Owner-occupied Homes

The Treasury Tax Expenditure Budget lists under Housing and Community Development tax expenditures for owner-occupied homes in the form of deductions to individuals for interest on mortgages and for property taxes on residences.[87] The description of the Tax Expenditure Budget also states that:

> Some items were excluded where the case for their inclusion in the income base stands on relatively technical or theoretical tax arguments.

232

This is the case, for example, with the imputed rent on owner-occupied homes, which involves not only a conceptual problem but difficult practical problems such as those of measurement.[88]

Economists have considered these provisions as serious inequities in the tax system.[89] They stress the discrimination that results from the tax laws markedly favoring homeowners over renters at the same levels of income. Professor Henry J. Aaron in a recent study considered that housing consumption is consequently about 20 percent larger in the aggregate, through more individuals owning homes than otherwise would and through some individuals owning more expensive homes than they would in the absence of these tax subsidies.[90] Economists have also pointed to the fact that since deductions are involved (and an exclusion in the case of imputed rent), the tax expenditure items provide greater financial assistance to the wealthier homeowners. The amount of tax assistance is measured by the marginal tax rate of the taxpayer and thus increases as income increases. Data to this effect are also included in Professor Aaron's study.[91] Regarding the different treatment accorded homeowners and renters, the standard deduction and the 1969 increase in that deduction move in the opposite direction from the tax expenditure items of mortgage interest and property taxes. Under that increase, from 10 to 15 percent of adjusted gross income and from a $1,000 to a $2,000 maximum, about 62 percent of taxpayers are expected to utilize the standard deduction, so that a large number of renters in effect will be securing deductions approaching, but not equaling, those of homeowners.[92]

Others besides economists have noted these aspects of the tax system. Former Secretary of HUD Romney was reported as expressing the view that:

> "[The] most fundamental aspect of housing and urban problems" is that the housing and tax policies of the past had helped most Americans to move into decent homes but that the same Americans were denying the support needed in establishing policies and laws that would do the same for low-income citizens who "live under deplorable conditions in our core cities."
>
> "The people who benefit usually are not aware that they are being helped" . . . referring to both the tax write-offs for interest paid on home mortgages and housing loans guaranteed by the Government.[93]

This financial assistance through the tax system to home-ownership is also commented upon — perhaps for the first time in such a setting — in the Fourth Annual Report on National Housing Goals, transmitted by the President to the Congress in 1972:[94]

Federal tax law permits homeowners to deduct mortgage loan

interest and property tax payments from their taxable income. It is estimated that in 1971, the allowance of these deductions decreased Federal revenues by $4.7 billion. No comparable tax benefits exist for occupants of rental housing, although they may benefit from lower rentals if the property owners shift forward some of their tax savings.

. . . [S]uch subsidies through the tax system are worth relatively more to higher income homeowners, since such families generally live in more expensive homes that carry larger mortgage loan and property tax payments. Moreover, the tax savings afforded by the deduction of mortgage interest and property taxes varies directly with the tax bracket of the homeowner.

As can be seen, the tax savings from the deductions for mortgage interest and real estate taxes saved the average homeowner $175 in taxes. However, only 3.2 percent of taxpayers with adjusted gross income (AGI) of under $3000 benefited from the deductions for mortgage interest and real estate taxes and their average tax savings was only $30 per return. At the other extreme, 87 percent of taxpayers with AGI of $100,000 or more benefited from the deductions, and the average tax savings was $1892.

The Congress has shown a marked determination to stay away from consideration of these tax expenditure items. The Treasury proposal in 1963 to limit itemized deductions to the amount above a 5 percent of gross income floor found real estate associations joining with the charities and state and local governments in quickly establishing strong Congressional opposition to the proposal.[95] The minimum tax and the limitation on the interest deduction of individuals, adopted in 1969, both exclude from coverage the interest paid on mortgages on owner-occupied homes.[96] The Congress appears decidedly to favor assisting home ownership, and apparently it is not about to consider the question whether this should be done under the tax system or through direct expenditure policies. Still, it may be worthwhile to reflect briefly on possible direct expenditure alternatives.

Here also it seems clear that no HUD Secretary would attempt to mirror in direct financial assistance the effect of the present tax expenditure approach. If cast in direct expenditure language, the present assistance under the itemized deductions for interest and taxes would look as follows:

— For a married couple with more than $200,000 in income, HUD would for each $100 of mortgage interest on the couple's home, pay $70 to the bank holding the mortgage, leaving the couple to pay $30. It would also pay a similar portion of the couple's property tax to the state or city levying the tax.

— For a married couple with income of $10,000, HUD would pay the bank

234

on the couple's mortgage $19 per each $100 interest unit, with the couple paying $81. It would also pay a similar portion of the couple's property tax to the state or city levying the tax.

— For a married couple too poor to pay an income tax, HUD would pay nothing to the bank, leaving the couple to pay the entire interest cost. The couple would also have to pay the entire property tax.

While this upside-down result mirrors the tax assistance now provided,[97] it would presumably not be followed in a direct approach to federal assistance. Would the other aspects of the tax expenditure approach be retained? For example, the tax expenditure assistance to home ownership is open-ended, with no limit on the amount of assistance that a particular taxpayer may obtain since *all* mortgage interest and *all* property taxes are deductible. There is therefore no limit on the size or value of the homes to be assisted and indeed no limit on the number of residences for which a taxpayer may receive assistance — his primary residence, a summer home, a winter home, and so on. There is no control exercised over the location of the homes to be assisted. Presumably, direct federal assistance would maintain free choice of location but would limit the amount or scope of the assistance. Existing FHA insurance for mortgages extends to homes with a value not over $20,000 to $30,000. The home ownership program adopted in 1968 and providing for a subsidy that at its maximum reduces the interest cost on a mortgage to 1 percent, is limited to families with incomes under about $5,000 to $10,000.[98] The Senate proposal, adopted in the Emergency Home Finance Act of 1970, to assist homeowners through an interest subsidy on FHA mortgages that would permit loans to them at 7 percent, is limited to homes costing less than $20,000 in low-cost areas and $30,000 in higher-cost areas, and also limited to owners whose income is not more than the median income for the relevant area.[99] The experiment conducted by HUD in 1972 of the effect of direct cash grants to be spent on housing is in terms of providing such "housing allowances" only to "needy families."[100]

The tax expenditure items for housing — deductions for mortgage interest and property taxes — constitute the largest items in the Government program to assist private housing, far in excess of direct expenditure programs in the housing area. Thus, for 1970, these tax expenditures came to $5.4 billion, and the direct expenditures came to $2.7 billion.[101] The latter programs, largely for public housing and subsidized low-income rental housing, appear in the budget. The tax expenditures for housing do not. Indeed, the Office of Management and Budget seems to be oblivious of this tax expenditure assistance, for it is not even mentioned in the Special Analysis describing the federal housing programs.[102] Hence, the budget gives the appearance of our federal housing programs being designed to help only the needy and low-income groups. Yet the opposite is clearly the case, since about 40 to 50 percent of the tax expenditure programs go to benefit those in income groups above $20,000.[103] Our largest housing program is kept pretty much out of sight and out of mind when Government assistance for housing is discussed.

Little thought has been given to structuring methods of enlarged direct financial assistance to home ownership as a substitute for the tax expenditure assistance. Tax reformers have thought only about eliminating or cutting back the tax assistance, without providing a substitute.[104] Given Congressional attitudes toward home ownership, the latter course does not seem likely. Moreover, will the increase in the standard deduction result in renters also entering a claim for direct assistance if the tax approach, including the standard deduction, is ever to be discarded?[105] Perhaps after further expansion of the standard deduction, Congress might some day recognize that with almost all taxpayers using it, the standard deduction could be eliminated, a floor put under itemized deductions as a group if itemization is to be retained, and individual tax rates reduced, with the rate reduction taking the place of the alternative of direct assistance. Or would such a move still have to be accompanied by positive, earmarked direct assistance to homeowners?[106]

The ramifications of the tax expenditure approach for private housing are wide indeed. State and local governments presumably find support for their property taxes in the deduction granted for those taxes, though little is known as to the effect of that deduction on the levels of those taxes. Savings institutions, such as savings and loan associations compelled to invest in homes, and others with considerable investments in this sector, find their market supported by the tax deductions. Those interested in tax reform in this area will presumably have to concentrate on these factors and on the structuring of alternatives before Congress pays attention.[107]

Rental Housing

The tax system blundered into its present tax expenditure assistance for rental housing, primarily multiple-unit housing. Accelerated depreciation was adopted in 1954 for machinery and equipment and, automatically without any focused attention to the point, was also extended to newly constructed buildings. A lesser degree of accelerated depreciation was available for used buildings under administrative rules. Taxes and interest costs incurred by a builder during construction were always permitted to be expensed currently instead of capitalized as part of the building's cost, the latter being in accordance with financial accounting. Court decisions and administrative interpretation solidified the rule that depreciation should be based on the full cost of a building, even though the building was largely or indeed entirely financed by loans secured only by the building itself.[108] Hence the very high leverage possessed by equity in real estate ownership did not prevent the owner from taking depreciation on the full cost of the building. Finally, on any sale of the building the gain in tax terms, resulting from over-depreciation and the expensing of construction taxes and interest, was taxable at capital gain preference rates without any allocation between ordinary income and capital gain (i.e., recapture) to reflect the prior expensing of those items.

This interlocking combination of tax benefits, which extended to commercial and industrial real estate as well as rental housing, became the "real estate tax shelter" of the late 1950's and 1960's.[109] With no conscious intent on the part of the Congress to grant financial assistance to real estate, the situation suddenly became one in which these tax provisions, when attacked for their inequities, were strongly defended as vitally necessary to provide an adequate supply of commercial buildings and rental housing units. Much of the financing for real estate, and investor attention and policies in this area, were designed around the tax assistance. As a consequence, a system of governmental assistance which no one had planned and which had never been rationally structured to perform that function, became a key factor in real estate investment. It has also become a key tax inequity, permitting well-to-do individual investors to escape all or a considerable part of their income tax liabilities.

The 1969 legislation was very much concerned with the "real estate tax shelter." Its adverse effects on tax fairness had been described in the Treasury Studies submitted early in 1969.[110] The Congress in 1969 clearly indicated it did not see a national commitment to use federal funds to support *industrial and commercial buildings.* As a consequence, it reduced the accelerated depreciation on new buildings of this character from 200 to 150 percent declining balance, and strengthened the recapture rule, first adopted in 1964, to classify as ordinary income the portion of the tax gain on a sale reflecting depreciation in excess of straight-line depreciation. Depreciation on used industrial and commercial buildings was restricted to the straight-line method.[111] Some computations indicate that these changes may have reduced the after-tax present value return on investment in commercial office buildings by about 15 percent, with most of this effect resulting from the reduction in accelerated depreciation.[112]

This is considerable progress, but some tax expenditures remain for industrial and commercial buildings. One study indicates that the combination of lives used and the accelerated depreciation remaining after 1969 will still result in tax depreciation for office buildings considerably in excess of the actual rate of depreciation, and in excess of the rate of decline used in financial accounting.[113] Indeed, the study indicates that straight-line depreciation would be too rapid. Mortgage financing requiring little equity money and using, over a term substantially equivalent to the life of the property, a level annual payment with a gradually increasing return of principal would seem to substantiate that conclusion. The immediate expensing of interest and taxes on unimproved land and during any construction period, instead of their capitalization, is also an important tax expenditure that remains.[114] Finally, the recapture rule is more lenient than that for machinery and equipment, since the latter rule recaptures as ordinary income all return of cost reflected in the sales price, while the real estate recapture is limited to return of cost less straight-line depreciation.[115] There would appear no reason, judging from the debate in 1969, why these tax expenditures should remain in the tax system.[116] The regular budget does not provide direct Government assistance to these buildings, and no national priority would require their being assisted through the tax system. Removal of the tax expenditures for commercial buildings might affect the rent patterns for office buildings, shopping centers and the like, but there is no national need to subsidize those rents. If, on the other hand, it were to be decided that federal financial assistance should be given, the means should be that of direct expenditures and not the tax system.[117]

Rental housing is another matter. In contrast to the commercial building aspect, HUD here joined private interests, mostly builders and developers, in pressing to retain the tax benefits for rental housing. Consequently, concern over housing caused Congress in 1969 to leave the tax rules for rental housing virtually unchanged. Even so, the 1969 changes have left a very muddled situation. Accelerated depreciation on new rental housing remains at 200 percent declining balance, though depreciation is reduced to the straight-line method on used buildings except for 125 percent declining balance if the remaining life is more than twenty years. Here also a study shows that even straight-line depreciation for apartment buildings is more rapid than true depreciation.[118] The recapture rule is tightened for luxury housing (though not to the same extent as in commercial real estate) with a phase-out starting after ten years of holding and any recapture ending after sixteen and two-thirds years.[119] Recapture on publicly-assisted housing for those with low and moderate incomes is phased out more rapidly, ending at ten years as under prior law.[120] Also, responding to a HUD proposal, any gain on the sale of lower-income housing can be deferred if the sale is to the occupants of the building and the proceeds are reinvested in similar housing — in other words, by not taxing the gain on the sale, the Government relieves the buyers of having the seller's capital gains tax passed along to them in the sales price.[121] And the Congress added a Treasury recommendation providing five-year amortization for rehabilitation expenditures on low- and moderate-income rental housing buildings — and then recognized it had to include the resulting tax benefit as a "tax preference" under the minimum tax.[122] Indeed, this new tax shelter is one of the more incredible legislative changes in recent years, when its tax benefits for the wealthy are placed alongside its inefficiency as an incentive. The minimum tax also includes as a preference the excess depreciation over the straight-line method on all buildings.[123]

Three Tax Expenditure Items

Under the 1969 legislation, tax expenditures are still used to assist all rental housing — luxury housing as well as low-income housing, rehabilitated housing as well as new housing. The real estate tax shelter still flourishes.[124] The tax assistance is not really planned directionally within the housing area. Yet housing assistance through direct expenditures in the budget is largely directional; by and large, it does not assist luxury housing and favors new units over rehabilitation of existing units.[125] If scarce housing appropriations are husbanded for new, low-income housing, why should tax expenditures use funds for other forms of housing? Indeed, the tax committees' reports in 1969 underscore the concern for low-income housing and imply no national priority to assist luxury housing.[126] There is no reason why tax assistance should be continued for *luxury or middle-income rental housing.*

Low- and moderate-income rental housing is another matter. The Federal Government does spend large sums to assist that housing in a variety of ways — principally through payment of the interest above 1 percent on loan capital, through rent supplements, and by financing the construction of low-rent public housing.[127] An increase in the supply of low- and moderate-income housing is clearly high on our national agenda, and this goal will require considerable federal assistance. But the crucial question is why that federal assistance should in the end be shaped around a tax expenditure policy never planned for that purpose and which as a consequence is thoroughly inequitable from a tax standpoint and inefficient from a housing standpoint. The tax inequity is clear: the tax provisions create the shameful "real estate shelter" and permit upper-bracket individuals to shield from the income tax income derived from regular sources — executive salaries, investment banking fees, professional fees, dividends, and the like — and for corporations, regular business profits, because these persons and corporations invest in housing. We have the paradox of cutting a tax escape path through our income tax system, through which the tax millionaire and others well-off may pass, in the hope of building more rental housing. We should do better.

The tax expenditure assistance is also inefficient. It can only really be useful to individuals and corporations with income sources in addition to whatever flows from the rental units — it is a tax shelter for nonrental income — and thus excludes from its scope both tax-exempt institutions seeking to invest their funds and investors concerned only with housing (as to the latter, however, only after the shelter has eliminated their housing income from tax). Also, since deductions are involved whose benefits are determined at the marginal tax rate, the assistance is more generous the wealthier the investor. In this upside-down tax expenditure world for rental housing, the investor in the 70 percent tax bracket has a better *after-tax* rate of return than an investor in the 50 percent bracket — the complete negation of a progressive tax system.[128]

This pattern of Government tax assistance to low-income housing is as complex as it is bizarre. Under HUD subsidy programs — "Section 236" programs — a developer of a low-income housing project can obtain a mortgage loan guaranteed by the Government and subsidized for the difference between the required amortization payments at the actual interest rate on the loan and what the payments would be at 1 percent interest rate. This loan can actually cover nearly the entire projected cost. While the loan is made for 90 percent of the total cost, 10 percent of cost (exclusive of land cost) is considered as a "Builder's and Sponsor's Profit and Risk Allowance" in lieu of any direct builder's profit. The loan thus provides the developer with the funds needed to build the project. But he now must obtain the funds that provide him with his actual profit, since the 10 percent BSPRA above is a paper figure. So the developer "sells" to "investors" the tax deductions to be generated by housing — accelerated depreciation on the full cost though that cost is met by borrowed funds, and deduction of interest and taxes during the construction period. These investors are individuals in the 50 to 70 percent brackets or corporations searching for these tax deductions — "tax losses" — to offset taxable income from other sources. Both the developer and the investors are seeking their profits from these tax losses. Whatever the investors "invest" in the project — i.e., whatever they pay for the tax losses — becomes the amount the developer will take out of the project. The more they pay, the greater is his "profit." But by the same token, the return on their "investment" — the dollars of taxes currently saved in relation to dollars "invested" — is reduced.

A *modus vivendi* is reached between seller and buyer of tax deductions under which both gain. Generally, the developer on new rental housing can obtain amounts from the investors equal to about 15 percent of the mortgage. Out of this the developer then pays the syndication fees — the legal, accounting, underwriting, and sales costs of finding the investors and placing them as limited partners in a limited partnership with the developer as general partner[129] — and a working capital requirement of 2 percent of the mortgage. The balance is the developer's profit or fee, about 65 to 70 percent of what the investors put in. Developers consider this an adequate recompense for their efforts in developing the project — getting the land assembled, the zoning approved, the community satisfied, the building built, and so on, and the risks of site problems, cost overruns, delays, and so on.[130]

Investors in the 50 percent bracket in turn obtain around a 15–20 percent annual after-tax return on the funds they invest, which is a handsome return. If the investors are in the 70 percent bracket, they can in effect do more with the tax losses. While the developer might charge them a higher sales price for those losses, generally the developer's sales price is based on 50 percent bracket investors so that the 70 percent investor gets a bonus. And the middlemen in the syndication process, the lawyers, investment houses, and accountants, also benefit from the transaction. All these groups are significantly benefiting from the tax deductions, which is an indication of the generosity inherent in the tax benefits. But the housing has been built with the subsidized loan itself, and not the tax deductions. Those deductions are simply an elaborate, wasteful, and inefficient method of providing the developer with a profit — a method that makes "tax millionaires" out of the investors who purchase the tax shelter. Obviously they are not true investors in housing, but are rather purchasers of tax deductions in a nationwide market built up through syndication of those deductions.

HUD has trapped itself into this inequitable and irrational situation we have been describing. It limits the return to the investor in federally assisted low-income rental housing to a 6 percent *before-tax return* on the amount invested in the project above the mortgage. This return is clearly inadequate as an investment matter — it comes to about 4 percent of the investor's actual investment.[131] Indeed, prospectuses in this field inform investors that they should not invest for the cash distributions from the project. But HUD uses this 6 percent limit in the knowledge that the tax laws will provide a much higher *after-tax return.* The prospectuses here also are clear — they state that the primary benefits to the investor-limited partner will be in the use against taxable income from other sources of the tax deductions obtained through the investment.[132] As stated above, we must keep in mind that these limited partners are not really investors but buyers of "tax losses."[133]

The 1969 rehabilitation tax expenditure functions with the same mechanics, except that the tax benefits are much greater. The developer can sell the enhanced benefits — which are deductions of the total investment, including the amount of the mortgage loan, over five years rather than "only" accelerated depreciation (the use of "only" is itself an indication of the largesse in this approach, in view of the significant tax benefits of accelerated depreciation) — for about 20–25 percent or even 30 percent of the mortgage. The investors, in turn, despite the higher sales price for these rehabilitation tax benefits, can obtain an after-tax return of around 40 percent.[134] And yet these greatly enhanced profit returns are presumably all really wasted, since it is still the HUD subsidized mortgage that must produce the rehabilitation. Studies indicate that the rehabilitation tax benefits will not in themselves produce nonsubsidized projects, for such projects financially could not usually provide the necessary low-priced rentals that are required.[135] Hence, the 1969 rehabilitation tax expenditure is just a super-grade shelter added to the real estate tax shelter area. All in all, this rehabilitation tax incentive ranks as one of the worst proposals made by the Treasury, an outcome not entirely unexpected since no real thought was given to its design or coordination with HUD housing programs. It is — unfortunately — a splendid example of all that is wrong in using a tax expenditure to meet a social problem.

HUD apparently has not considered just what rate of return is required to achieve the necessary equity investment in low- and moderate-income housing — assuming that equity investment is necessary — and how the returns presently being obtained through the tax system relate to the requisite rate of return.[136] Does the developer-sponsor of low-income housing need for his efforts the high level of compensation he now receives under the tax system through the "sale" to investors of accelerated depreciation and other deductions? Does the individual investor in the 70 percent bracket require an after-tax return of over 20 percent, or the individual in the 50 percent bracket and a corporation require an after-tax return of over 15 percent on new low-income housing?[137]

Perhaps after all the parties to a proposed low-income housing venture have come together and put in their contributions — the insurance company with its loan, the investor with his equity, the developer with his packaging, HUD with its subsidy check for the interest on the loan and maybe its check for rent supplements — the venture still will not move until the Treasury appears to put in its tax benefit check. But no one has really inquired just how large that Treasury check must be to make the venture feasible. The Treasury check simply arrives without any realistic financial relationship to the venture.

Of course, the real inquiry is why there should be any Treasury tax benefit check at all. For this is an area where we know direct Government assistance is required and is present — the HUD check — and this Government direct assistance really dwarfs the tax expenditure assistance — the Treasury check. In a $4.2 million new low-income housing project, typical of the projects of this nature, given a 7 percent, $3.7 million, forty-year mortgage and a sale for $1 after twenty years, HUD would put in over the first twenty year period about $3.6 million, which subsidy has a present value of about $2 million. The present value of the tax benefits of accelerated depreciation and expensing of interest and taxes during construction during that period would come to about $600,000 to a 60 percent bracket taxpayer.[138] This relationship between "HUD checks" and "Treasury checks" is reflected in the overall amounts of the HUD subsidies and the Treasury tax expenditures for low-income housing.[139] The study that is sorely required is how necessary is that Treasury check and, to the extent it is necessary, how can the assistance it represents be shifted to direct federal assistance.[140]

One of the questions to be answered in such a study is whether the private investor is needed in this subsidized low-income housing area. The financing mechanics earlier described involved a private developer obtaining his profit, for his time and risk, by selling tax benefits to private investors, thereby building the "tax shelter" as well as the housing project. But increasingly a variety of "community developers" are entering the scene. Such a developer may, for example, be a local community development corporation, or a tenants' association representing the prospective tenants.[141] These groups formerly cooperated, and in some cases still continue to cooperate, with the private developer by assisting him in obtaining the necessary zoning approvals, building permits, and the like, and in acting as the bridge between the developer and the community in which the project was located. But these community groups are now learning how the tax shelter game is played, and as a result they want to be a principal in that game. So they are themselves becoming the developers, and they are selling the tax benefits to the investors. These community developers can actually perform in the same way as a private developer, being the general partner in a limited partnership with the private investors. Or they may act as nonprofit sponsor-developers, in which case there would not be any private investors, and the mortgage loan amount is somewhat greater. In effect, the direct assistance of the Government is somewhat greater if the nonprofit sponsor route is followed, but the actual dollar benefits to the community developer may be greater if it acts as a private developer and builds the tax shelter to obtain funds from private investors by selling them tax benefits.[142]

But what is the role of the private investor at this point? There is indeed something ludicrous in a tenants' association in Boston selling the tax benefits of a rehabilitation project in Boston to a Florida high-bracket investor who may never set foot, or eye, on the project. Clearly, that investor is really adding nothing unique to the project itself, and may well be hindering its success. For the "investor" — remember he is only a purchaser of tax losses — may be a source of discontent. If, for example, rents must be raised to meet higher operating expenses, the tenants may well see the added rental cost as simply going to line the pockets of wealthy investors. And in truth the process of making wealthy people wealthier and subsidizing the rich in our society as a method of providing housing for low-income groups is an inherently contradictory approach that is bound to cause tension.[143]

The "investor" in this contradictory approach is there only to provide, in a bizarre, roundabout way, the dollars that mean to the private developer a profit above "his costs." But to provide that profit, the Treasury pays the investor $1 so that he in turn will pay the developer 70 to 75 cents. The obvious question is why perpetuate the middleman "investor" if the approach is so inefficient, wasteful, and inequitable? These consequences are inevitable under that approach. The developer is selling the tax benefits to the investor. Since the investor desires to earn a handsome return on *his* investment in purchasing those benefits, he will pay the developer an amount considerably less than the benefits themselves, i.e., considerably less than the cost to the Treasury. Hence part of that Treasury cost is automatically siphoned off to the investor and away from the developer. In addition, part of the remaining amount — the 70 to 75 cents that goes to the developer in the form of the payment by the investor — must in turn be paid by the developer to the syndicator who brought the developer and investor together and to the lawyers and accountants who did the paper work. This is indeed a real irony, for these payments are but an added wasteful expense on top of the wasteful expense of having the investor present at all. The developer thus receives a net amount of around 65 to 70 cents. The Treasury is paying out $1 in tax benefits so that the developer can end up with 65 or 70 cents. Clearly, the virtues of private capital are obviously not here present. This is underscored when the developer is a community group not one whit aided by private investors in the picture except as a source of dollars for that group to meet their costs and provide funds in hand — dollars that could be given to the group at far less expense directly by the Government. In this light the situation is in no essential respect different from the tax-exempt bond area where the Treasury pays top-bracket middlemen purchasers of tax exempt bonds $1 in order to provide 58 cents in assistance to state and local governments through lower interest rates on the bonds.[144] But these exorbitant commissions to the wealthy are the result of a tax expenditure approach to provide the ultimate financial assistance. Yet HUD has never explained to the Congress or the public this wasteful and inequitable middleman role of the private investor in Government-subsidized rental housing. And also far from explaining this role, the Treasury made it more wasteful and inequitable in 1969 in the case of rehabilitated housing.

If private developers require an amount in the range of 15 percent of the mortgage to perform their role in providing low-income housing, then the question arises why should HUD not pay them the necessary amount directly? The entire 15 percent would not even be needed, since the portion presently paid over by the developer in syndication fees, about 3 percentage points of the 15 percent, would no longer be required. The direct approach would involve a lower cost to the Government compared to the present tax expenditure approach, since the amounts now siphoned off by the investors and syndicators would be saved.[145] And if community groups are to be given financial assistance for such housing, above the present HUD direct assistance, when they act as developers, then why should HUD not also pay them directly whatever additional amounts are appropriate?[146] If these are not the routes that should be followed, a study should then explore other ways of structuring whatever assistance is considered necessary, in addition to the HUD direct subsidy, to obtain this low-income housing.[147]

In seeking the best method of direct assistance we do not face the difficult question of private choice present in the financing of philanthropy or the freedom of choice present in the assistance to state and local governments. For HUD financial assistance is directional, in that HUD can determine what housing it wants to assist — as to cost, kind, and location.[148] There is no problem of preserving freedom of choice for the investor, assuming that an investor is needed at all. It is in the nature of tax expenditure assistance not to be directional.[149] Indeed, that is why the investment credit is a useful macroeconomic tool, since it operates, and designedly so, over the broad area of all machinery and equipment. But assistance for housing must be directional, and directional aid is the essence of a well-constructed direct program.

The question is how the dollar amount of the present tax assistance that

244

turns out after study to be really needed can be shifted to HUD's budget and structured into its policies. We might well find that a shift of $150 million to $200 million (at 1972 levels) — after all, the portion of the tax expenditure devoted to low- and moderate-income housing is really not large compared to that going to other rental housing[150] — to the HUD budget would adequately cover the governmental assistance required for presently HUD subsidized rental housing. There would no longer be any need for tax assistance to low- and moderate-income rental housing.

Once the need for tax expenditures for low- and moderate-income housing is removed, the question could be asked whether there is any need for tax assistance to all the rest of rental housing, such as middle-income, semi-luxury and luxury apartments. This housing does not presently receive any direct Government assistance. There is, moreover, a crucial difference in the function of present tax expenditures between HUD-subsidized and nonsubsidized rental housing. Without the present tax benefits, roundabout and wasteful though their assistance to the developer may be, the *subsidized* housing would not be built. The HUD 6 percent limit on the return to the developer is obviously inadequate. Since the rents cannot be increased, the developer has nowhere else to turn for his profit except to sell the tax benefits through the tax shelter syndication process. Parenthetically, this present *sine qua non* aspect of tax benefits for subsidized housing is of course no evidence of any inherent virtue in tax incentives, but rather a result of the HUD direct subsidy system and the national priority of setting rental ceilings for this housing. But when we turn to *nonsubsidized* housing the picture is completely different. Here the Government may be getting little or nothing in return from the financial assistance given through the tax benefits, be the assistance in any particular case roundabout through the tax shelter syndication or through direct use of the tax benefits by the developer.[151] Indeed, the net result of such financial assistance may be harmful to the housing field.

A study presented to the Joint Economic Committee indicated that the tax assistance to nonsubsidized housing may have somewhat increased the quantity of buildings, especially expensive buildings, and the surface luxuriousness of the buildings. But partly because of market adjustments to the subsidies and partly because of their effect to induce rapid turnover and consequent shoddiness in maintenance, the useful life and true quality of the buildings are probably reduced. Further, because the tax assistance is given to all such housing, including that which would have been built anyway, the assistance expressed in terms of total cost applied to the actual induced increase in the supply of new buildings rates quite low against a cost effectiveness criterion.[152]

Given these effects of the present tax assistance, the proper question is simply why not eliminate that assistance and let the marketplace govern rental housing for middle and upper income groups. There would be no HUD subsidy, as there is none today, and no tax benefits. Most of the trade associations in the housing field have expressed institutional dismay over any proposed elimination of tax assistance for rental housing. They have voiced the customary pessimism about the future that immediately descends on any industry faced with the loss of its tax benefits.[153] Most of these associations indicated that the basic result of a loss of tax assistance would be a rise in rents. But this contention by no means is as conclusive against such a change as the associations seem to consider. First, it is not at all clear that rents in nonsubsidized housing would rise or rise by much. One builder, in taking a contrary view and directly attacking the present tax benefits, stated that many builders today do not even use accelerated depreciation and hence its elimination should not affect rents.[154] Second, if rents for such housing did rise, why should this be a national concern requiring Government action? Certainly we do not have a national priority to support a low-rent structure for luxury or semi-luxury housing. The burden of proof, therefore, both for retaining Government financial assistance for non-HUD-subsidized rental housing and for providing that assistance through the tax system must be placed on those who urge the continuance of the present tax benefits. Moreover, given the strong case against the present system, any proof made for its continuance must be solid indeed and not just unsupported pessimism.

At any event, if HUD became concerned about rent increases (or lessened housing starts because of rent problems) for units renting at the lower end of the present nonsubsidized housing rent scale, direct rental subsidies could be paid to the developers. Or perhaps a direct subsidy to the lenders of mortgage money for the rental units involved could be utilized, since that subsidy would by lowering interest costs permit a lower rent structure. Certainly, such direct assistance would be less costly and less wasteful than the present tax assistance to non-HUD-subsidized rental housing.

Looking at the overall situation, a shift of a relatively small amount to the HUD budget to replace the present tax assistance for *subsidized* rental housing would permit the elimination of the entire tax expenditure apparatus for all residential rental real estate.

This therefore is the course of research that tax reformers — and housing reformers — must pursue if progress is to be made in this area.[155] The responsibility does not rest on reformers alone. The Congressional committees involved, such as Ways and Means and Banking and Currency in the House, and the executive departments, Treasury and HUD, should also be directly engaged in the search for a direct assistance approach. The 1969 legislation squarely invites this course. The five-year amortization for rehabilitation, the deferral of tax on sale to tenants of lower-income housing, and the special recapture rule for low- and moderate-income housing all have a five-year termination date; they will end in 1974 unless renewed. This appears to be an indication that the tax expenditure policies for housing must be reexamined and compared with alternatives outside the tax system.

VIII

Corrective Reform Measures to Moderate Tax Expenditure Abuses: Alternatives to Substitution of Direct Programs for Tax Expenditures

Federal tax reform must cope with the tax expenditure structure that has grown up within the income tax system. One course, as described earlier, is to survey the entire list of tax expenditures to see which can be dropped without any substitute federal financial assistance, which can be replaced by direct programs of financial assistance and what are the contours of those direct programs, and which should be retained as representing the best available vehicles for providing desired financial assistance. This course involves a direct approach to the situation and in that sense is to be preferred. But direct approaches often incur head-on opposition, and past experience in the tax field indicates that this would be so for a number of the existing tax expenditures. Even so, the direct approach should be followed as far as possible, although some of the attempts end in defeat, since current defeats in tax reform often precede future victories. At the same time, it is desirable and probably necessary to consider other courses of reform. For the most part these courses are indirect approaches in the sense that they assume the continuance of some tax expenditures but seek to modify the tax benefits produced by the expenditures and thus reduce the tax abuses and inequities generated by those expenditures. These indirect approaches will be grouped in two classes: those involving restraints on the operation of the tax expenditures, especially the tax shelters, and those involving restraints on the taxpayer's overall use of the tax expenditures.

Pathways to Tax Reform

Restraints on the Operation of Tax Expenditures:
Curbing the Tax Shelters

The indirect restraints that have been proposed on the operation of tax expenditures relate essentially to those expenditures that have produced the tax shelters for the well-to-do. These restraints in turn are suggested both by the effects of the tax shelters themselves — the sheltering of income — and by the shelter ingredients of deferral, leverage, and capital gain treatment.

Reduction of the Scope of the Shelters

The purpose of a tax shelter is to shelter income — income from the particular investment, be it a rental building, an oil well, a farm — and income from other and unconnected sources such as dividends, professional fees, executive salaries, and the like. The driving force behind the use of tax shelters is the second effect, that of the sheltering of unrelated income from tax liability. The large accelerated deductions generated by the sheltered investment swamp any current income from that investment and spill over — flood over is more descriptive — against other unrelated income. Consequently, one approach to reducing the effect of tax shelters is to confine these accelerated deductions to income from the particular investment. In the case of real estate, for example, the deductions generated by construction interest and taxes, by depreciation, and by mortgage interest — the principal shelter deductions — under this approach could only be applied against income generated by the particular real estate. Any excess of deductions could be carried forward to offset income from the building in future years or any gain on sale. A similar rule could be applied to the other tax shelters.[1]

The Treasury Department Tax Reform Studies and Proposals had suggested that the farm tax abuses be curbed by limiting the deductions of farm losses to farm income and $15,000 of nonfarm income, unless the taxpayer computed his farm loss under accounting methods requiring the capitalization of development costs and thereby reduced the amount of current deductions.[2] This last aspect of the Treasury Proposals sought to confine the anti-spillover effect of the restraint to "tax losses," that is, artificial losses created by the tax shelter operation, and thereby still permit the offsetting of true economic losses on an investment against unrelated income. Thus, one consequence of an income tax is that the Government shares in losses as well as gains, so that if an individual or corporation suffers a loss in one venture the Government absorbs part of the loss through the reduction in taxable income from other ventures. This aspect of the income tax encourages risk-taking and venture capital. Efforts to curb tax shelter abuses should not dampen this sharing in real losses. Hence, proposals to restrict the use of excess deductions against

248

unrelated income should be limited to deductions computed under tax expenditure provisions and not extended to those arising under proper income tax concepts. Essentially this demarcation would be spelled out for each shelter, as in the farm proposal above.[3]

The proposal to limit the tax expenditure deductions involved in tax shelter activities to income arising from the asset producing the deductions, so that the "tax losses" could not be used against unrelated income, should be applied both to individuals and corporations. Application of the proposal only to individuals would simply prompt banks and other corporations to enter into tax shelter operations or increase their already existing shelter activities. Thus, the denial in 1971 of the investment credit to individual lessors of machinery and equipment has been a factor in inducing commercial banks to expand their tax shelter leasing activities. There is no reason to look askance at tax shelters conducted by individuals but then to favor their use by corporations, for the tax abuses are basically the same. This coverage of both corporations and individuals would require that the proposal be applied asset by asset, rather than by industry activity. An individual or corporation owning several buildings, or oil wells, or equipment leases, should not be able to use the tax expenditure deductions from one building against the income from another building, and similarly as to wells or leases. Any contrary approach, such as permitting an industry-wide use of the deductions so that the "losses" from one building can be applied against rental or sales income from other buildings, simply favors corporations in that industry and wealthy individuals with a significant number of tax shelter projects. It would also lead to very fancy tax shelter packaging that would combine various projects the timing of whose tax losses and income payouts would be appropriately matched. There is no sound reason to deny the tax shelter route to the passive investor with one or two such ventures but permit the more active wealthy individual or a corporation with a larger number of ventures still to play the tax shelter game.[4] Of course, a proposal to limit tax expenditure deductions to the income from the asset that produced the deductions, while curbing tax shelter activities, would still leave the income from the asset itself sheltered in the initial years of operation. While later on the income would become taxable in increasing amounts as the shelter deductions ran out, the value of the tax deferral would be significant.

The above avenue to reducing the use of shelters would confine the benefits of the tax expenditure provisions to the income obtained directly from the benefited activity. Another approach is to restrict the use of the tax expenditure provision where that use lends itself to tax shelter operation. Thus, the 1971 Act denied the investment credit to individual lessors engaged in tax shelter leasing of equipment rather than in the regular business of leasing equipment. A like rule could be applied to similar tax expenditure provisions, such as five-year amortization for railroad cars or pollution control equipment or accelerated depreciation. The problem with this approach, however, is that while restricting wealthy individuals from using a tax shelter, it does not restrict corporations. As stated above, the denial of the investment credit to individual lessors appears in part to be responsible for the rapidly growing use by commercial banks of tax shelter equipment leasing to reduce their taxable income.[5] A broader solution is needed, if this approach is to be followed. One suggestion is to confine the use of the investment credit and other relevant tax expenditure provisions to the actual user of the equipment, so that it would not be in a position to "sell" these tax benefits to a lessor engaged in tax shelter leasing. But such a limitation on these tax expenditures would confine their benefits to users of equipment that were making profits and hence could utilize the tax reduction potential of the benefits. Companies needing equipment but in an operating loss or low tax posture, or in other special tax situations, would be deprived of the tax expenditure assistance, and this would be an unfair denial of such assistance. Today such companies — such as railroads, airlines, oil companies, utilities where required to flow-through the investment credit, and companies with large foreign tax credits — are the lessees of the commercial banks' tax shelter leases. Of course, this problem is really an illustration of the lack of wisdom in ever turning to the tax expenditure route in the first place to grant assistance rather than to a direct subsidy. Suggestions to overcome this defect of tax expenditure assistance, such as to make the investment credit refundable to a company not having enough tax liability to absorb the credit, are really suggestions to transform the tax expenditure assistance into a parallel to direct assistance.[6]

Limitations on the Ingredient of Leverage

One of the principal ingredients in tax shelter operations is that of the tax consequences of leverage, under which the deferral effect of the acceleration of deductions can be obtained on borrowed dollars used in the investment as well as on the taxpayer's own funds. The tax law permits the taxpayer to obtain these accelerated deductions derived from the borrowed funds on a timing basis that does not reflect the repayment of those funds. As we saw earlier, the tax system views the moneys coming in from the tax shelter investment as a return of capital, including the borrowed capital, but then views the moneys paid out to the lender as a payment of interest, and not as a repayment of the borrowed money. If the tax system were consistent so that the borrowed money were not treated as an investment in the asset, on which investment the tax expenditure could work its acceleration of deduction effect, except at the rate that the loan was being repaid, then the leverage effect of borrowing would not enhance the tax shelter.

The needed restraint is thus indicated by the ingredient of leverage itself.

The tax reflection of the cost of the investment insofar as that investment is based on borrowed dollars should not be faster than the investor's repayment of the borrowed funds. Hence, the tax shelter benefits of acceleration of deductions should be confined to the taxpayer's equity investment, i.e., the initial investment, if any, of his own funds and the subsequent increase in his own investment as he repays the principal of the borrowed funds. This restraint, as in the suggestion of confining deductions to income from the investment, would be limited to the acceleration of deductions produced by the tax expenditures and not to deductions under the income tax proper.[7] The two suggested restraints are not alternatives and are compatible with each other.

The description of this proposed restraint is in terms of borrowed funds that can be directly related to the sheltered investment, such as a borrowing secured by the investment itself. This is the typical situation in these investments. But suppose the investor, to defeat the restraint, borrows funds under a general obligation or secured by other property not involved in sheltered activity, such as diversified stocks or securities. Are the dollars so borrowed now the taxpayer's "own funds" when invested in the tax shelter and thus an equity investment in that shelter, entitled in full to the accelerated deductions it produces, or are the dollars still borrowed funds? The question itself, and the problems it raises, are not enough to negate the proposal since in most cases the borrowing is related directly to the sheltered investment. Presumably any borrowing not so related would qualify as an equity investment so as to avoid the need for too detailed a tracing of dollars. The problem would then be confined to the appropriate technical treatment of the receipt of borrowed money under the income tax proper. Thus, if a taxpayer with appreciated securities needs money but instead of selling the securities and realizing a taxable gain, borrows on the securities, the present law does not find a gain. This rule could be reexamined, and if the gain were taxed, then the borrowing would properly be treated as the taxpayer's own funds — just as would funds obtained on a sale of the securities.[8]

Payment for the Ingredient of Deferral

A prime ingredient of tax shelters is the deferral of tax on current income, achieved through the acceleration of deductions provided by the shelter. This deferral, as described earlier, is an interest-free loan from the Government in the amount of the tax deferred. Here, also, the ingredient suggests an appropriate restraint — eliminate the interest-free character of the deferral loan by charging interest on the deferred tax.

Some economists have suggested, as a fundamental change in the income tax, a "cumulative averaging" or "cumulative assessment" system that would

251

make the timing of tax liabilities essentially an unimportant matter.[9] Under this approach taxpayers would in effect earn interest on taxes paid and owe interest on taxes deferred. Assuming that the interest rate used reflects market rates, the deferral of taxes simply introduces another source of borrowed funds and enhances general liquidity. Early payment of taxes becomes a method of investment. This cumulative averaging would, according to its proponents, permit a taxpayer to choose any rate of depreciation or other timing of deductions and any rate of realization of income.[10] Under this approach, the present tax shelters would simply be absorbed by such optional arrangements. Cumulative averaging is of course aimed at broader goals, such as major simplification of the income tax by removing the present stress on accurate yearly timing and the provisions supporting that stress, and also achieving greater equity among taxpayers through its averaging effects. But a by-product of its adoption would be the essential elimination of the tax shelter problem, as its proponents observe,[11] since the deferral offered only to a few today at no cost would become, in effect, available to all, but at an interest cost.

We are unlikely in the immediate future to see the tax shelter problem solved this way. Cumulative averaging is a major change that still requires discussion and experimentation. Some economists dislike the use of a lifetime to average income; others are concerned about its counter-cyclical effects; others see many complexities in its operation.[12]

In the absence of such a change, the question reverts to whether the interest-free loan of specific tax shelters can be altered through charging interest in those situations on the deferral of tax obtained. The Senate version of the Tax Reform Act of 1969 sought to meet the tax benefits obtained by the use of family trusts to accumulate income for later payment to beneficiaries — which achieves a deferral of tax if the rate of tax on the trust is less than that on the beneficiary — by charging, in effect, 6 percent interest on the deferred tax.[13] The provision was not carefully prepared, and this, plus opposition by trust companies and the tax bar, led to its deletion in Conference. But the suggestion has basic validity, both for the shelter of accumulation trusts and for the tax shelters we are considering. It remains to be seen whether the idea can technically be translated into a workable arrangement that, as in the other restraints earlier discussed, would apply the interest charge to the deferral obtained by the acceleration of deductions under the tax shelter. We will return to this matter in the later discussion of the minimum tax.[14]

Removal of Ingredient of Capital Gain on Sale of Investment

The third tax shelter ingredient is that of the application of capital gain treatment on the sale of the investment to the "gain" created by the acceleration of deductions. The tax cost of the investment is reduced by those deductions, and this reduction produces *pro tanto* a "gain" on the sale of the investment. This "gain" is simply a reflection of the earlier offsetting of ordinary income by the accelerated deductions. However, in some tax shelters it is given the same preferred treatment as is accorded to capital gain resulting from a real economic appreciation in value. Thus, if an oil well is drilled at a cost of $100,000, and $70,000 of the cost is deducted at once through the deduction of intangible drilling expenses, offsetting $70,000 of unrelated dividend income of the investor, a sale of the well for $150,000 produces a $120,000 capital gain. ($150,000 received less $30,000 cost, the latter being the $100,000 original cost reduced by the $70,000 return of cost through the deduction.) $50,000 of the gain is the result of an economic profit on the transaction and $70,000 of the gain is a reflection of the earlier deduction. The entire $120,000 receives capital gain treatment, generally exclusion of one-half of the gain from income. Hence, $35,000 of the deferred dividend income is simply not taxed at all.

In the last decade the tax law has been moving slowly to change this aspect of tax shelters, by treating the gain reflecting the earlier deduction as representing ordinary income and not capital gain. This treatment is styled "recapture of income" — the ordinary income deferred by the acceleration of deductions is "recaptured" on the sale and does not become transformed into capital gain. This "recapture" approach was applied in 1962 for machinery and equipment; in 1964 in a limited way to real estate, but rejected in that year for oil wells; in 1969 to a greater extent than in 1964 for commercial buildings, though not as far as in the case of machinery and equipment, and for rental real estate other than low-income rental housing (though not as far as commercial buildings); also in 1969 for depreciation on livestock and certain farm land expenses; and also in 1969 in a very limited way for other farm losses.[15]

The proper approach here is to extend the principle of full recapture to all of these tax shelter situations. As a consequence, any gain that arose as a reflection of the earlier deferral of ordinary income would yield ordinary income instead of capital gain. The ingredient of capital gain treatment — the transformation of deferred ordinary income into capital gain — would no longer be a benefit provided by these shelters. The principal areas remaining to be so covered are oil, rental housing, commercial buildings and farm activities. There are no technical difficulties in this extension of recapture — it is simply a matter of political will.

Where the recapture approach is applied today, it does not extend to the disposition of an asset at death. This cutoff of recapture at death is a reflection of the general treatment of appreciation in property transferred at death. Under that treatment the appreciation escapes income tax entirely, since the decedent is not taxed and the heir takes as his tax cost the value of the property at death. While a case can certainly be presented to except recapture from this liberal treatment of gain at death, it is unlikely that the differentiation would be made. Instead, therefore, the recapture aspect is more likely to be merged into the general question of how to treat appreciation in property transferred at death. The proper approach is of course to tax the appreciation to the decedent, and such a result is the most important reform to be made in the area of capital gains.[16]

In summary, there are a number of indirect approaches which can be pursued to reduce the tax inequities produced by tax shelters. These approaches relate to the operational aspects of shelters and if pursued would significantly restrict their effects. The approaches are indirect in that the tax expenditure treatment in these situations would remain in the tax law but the benefits would be reduced. In effect, the suggestion to restrict the scope of the shelters by preventing spillover to unrelated income is equivalent to saying that the financial assistance of the tax expenditure is to be sharply confined — and thus reduced — to the particular investment. The suggestions affecting the ingredients of the shelters are equivalent to saying that the present full tax expenditure financial assistance is really not needed but rather than go to the mat on this point through an effort to substitute a lesser direct program, or no program at all, the cutback can be achieved in these indirect ways.

Restraints on the Use by Individuals of Tax Expenditure Assistance

The previous discussion and suggestions for reform related to the operational aspects of certain tax expenditures, those that create tax shelters. We may now shift the focus of reform to look at an individual taxpayer's overall use of tax expenditure assistance, including the tax shelter area. Here we assume that the direct approach of substitution of direct expenditure programs and the indirect approach of restraints on the operation of the tax shelters have achieved some results — or perhaps failed entirely — but that a significant number of tax expenditures remain so that major escapes from tax still exist for the well-to-do. In such a situation we can turn to approaches that deal in a collective way with the aggregate escape from tax produced by the tax expenditures, without any particular regard for which tax expenditure produces the escape for a particular individual.[17]

Allocation of Personal Deductions

We earlier saw that the technical methods used to provide tax expenditure assistance involve in some situations exclusions from gross income and then

254

in others deductions from the remaining gross income, which together serve to reduce the income subject to the tax.[18] These methods cover most of the tax expenditures benefiting the individual as a wage and salary earner, as an investor, and as a recipient of transfer payments. In addition, deductions from gross income are used to carry out the tax expenditures benefiting the individual as a consumer. These "consumer deductions" in effect can be seen as further reducing the taxable income previously circumscribed by the other tax expenditures. Further, one important deduction in the earning of income is that of interest on money borrowed for the purposes of making investments in securities, real estate, and so on. While this type of interest is not a tax expenditure, it has its own tax avoidance consequences, since the deduction is available without regard to whether or not the investment currently produces taxable income. For this reason the interest deduction figures prominently in the tax shelter area. The Code combines in one provision both the deduction of such interest and interest on money borrowed for consumer items, and considers the totality of interest payments as one of the itemized deductions standing as an alternative to the use of the standard deduction.[19]

The combined operative effect of the various tax expenditures has a powerful impact on the tax liabilities of those individuals with large amounts of tax expenditures. For some well-to-do individuals the impact has been to eliminate tax liability entirely. These individuals would first reduce their gross income by the tax expenditure exclusions or deductions relating to investment activity — the exclusion of tax-exempt interest; the deduction (in effect an exclusion) of one-half of capital gains; the deduction (in effect an exclusion) for percentage depletion on natural resources, primarily oil; one or more tax shelter accelerated deductions such as real estate accelerated depreciation, oil intangible drilling expenses, or farm "losses." Most individuals would not have all of these items, since each would probably confine his investment activity to only a few areas as his personal inclinations dictated. But the consequence would be a taxable amount (adjusted gross income) far lower than economic income. Then the individual would proceed to take his itemized personal deductions, primarily the consumer deductions for interest, state and local taxes, charitable contributions, and in some cases medical expenses or casualty losses. He would also, along with interest on a mortgage on his residence or summer home and perhaps other major consumer items, deduct interest on money borrowed for investment purposes. These itemized deductions would be applied exclusively to offset whatever taxable income remained after the previous tax expenditure exclusions and deductions. The result would be little or no taxable income left to be taxed — and some individuals with economic income in the high hundred thousands or millions would escape tax entirely, while others had only to pay a tax that was negligible in relation to their total economic income. Thus, the Johnson Treasury Department Tax Reform Studies and Proposals describe one case in these terms:

The unfairness of the present system is illustrated by the following case:

An individual had a total income of $1,284,718 of which $1,210,426 was in capital gains, the remaining $74,292 from wages, dividends, and interest. He excluded one-half of his capital gains, which he is allowed to do under present law, thereby reducing his present law (adjusted gross) income to $679,405 (after allowing for the $100 dividend exclusion). From this income he subtracted all his personal deductions, which amounted to $676,419 and which included $587,693 for interest on funds borrowed presumably for the purpose of purchasing the securities on which the capital gains were earned. As a result, after allowing $1,200 of personal exemptions his taxable income was reduced to $1,786 and he paid a tax of $274. His overall tax rate, therefore, was about two-hundredths of one percent.[20]

The data further showed that in the case of 1,100 tax returns in 1964 with adjusted gross income over $200,000, but with an effective tax rate of 22 percent or less, 40 percent ($256 million) of the total actual income apparent from the returns ($658 million) was excluded from tax because it represented the excluded one-half of capital gains, excess percentage depletion, or farm losses. There was $220 million of ordinary income, but this was offset by itemized deductions of $182 million. In effect this left taxable only the included portion of capital gains. Since the capital gains tax in 1964 could not exceed 25 percent of total capital gains, the effective tax rate on the total economic income of this group was bound to be less than 25 percent. As a result a very large portion (about 40 percent — more, if data were available on tax-exempt interest for example) was taxed at a zero rate — that part consisting of excluded items other than capital gains and that part offset by itemized deductions — and the remainder (about 60 percent) was capital gain taxable at a 25 percent rate.[21]

The Johnson Treasury Department in its Tax Reform Proposals recommended the "allocation of deductions" proposal as one method of reducing this excape from tax. It said:

Deductions which reduce taxable income are justified only to the extent that they are properly assignable to that income. When an individual receives income in forms that are excluded from taxation — such as the items discussed above in connection with the minimum tax [e.g., tax exempt interest, excluded one-half of capital gains, percentage depletion, appreciation on charitable gifts of appreciated property] — it is not consistent or proper to permit him to subtract all of his eligible deduction items from that part of his income which is subject to tax and ignore the excluded part.

Corrective Reform Measures

The Treasury recommends that an individual's itemized deductions be allocated between his taxable income and his excluded income, with only the part allocable to the taxable income to be permitted as deductions in computing tax . . . . An exemption would be provided to insure that taxpayers with less than $5,000 of excluded income need not make this allocation.[22]

This recommendation was joined in by the Nixon Treasury Department and was accepted by the House Ways and Means Committee in the Tax Reform Act of 1969. The Committee urged the same reasons for the change:

The fact that an individual who receives tax-free income can charge the entire amount of his personal deductions to his taxable income gives him a double tax benefit. He not only excludes these tax preference amounts from his tax base but he also, by allocating his personal deductions only against his adjusted gross income, may reduce his tax payments on this taxable income. As a result, taxpayers with substantial tax preference amounts and personal deductions can wipe out much or all of their tax liability on substantial amounts of otherwise taxable income.

. . .

Your committee does not believe that individuals with untaxed income should be allowed to reduce their taxable income by charging all their personal deductions to their taxable income. These personal expenses are not a part of cost of earning the taxable income and may be paid just as well out of tax-exempt income as out of taxable income.[23]

But in the Senate the proponents of tax expenditures strongly attacked the proposal, with state and local governments, colleges, and oil interests in the forefront. The proposal fell under the attack and was not contained in the final legislation.[24]

The allocation of deductions proposal merits consideration as a method to curb the tax escape that is involved in the cumulative use of tax expenditures by an individual. Its aim is to temper that cumulative use so as to prevent the use from eliminating tax liability entirely or leaving it negligible. The premise of the proposal assumes the existence of a number of tax expenditures for the policy reasons related to those expenditures, but then asserts a counter-policy that the income tax should not be completely undermined by the cumulative use of expenditures. The device to prevent this is to treat the payments involved in certain tax expenditures, those represented in the itemized deductions, as coming in ratable amounts from excluded income and remaining taxable income. This would confine the effect of those deductions to an allowance only for the portion so allocable to taxable income. The present system also allocates these itemized deductions, but allocates them entirely to taxable income. But that is no more justifiable than allocating them entirely to excluded income. Since the consumer activities they represent — i.e., interest on a residence mortgage, a charitable contribution — are not in fact allocable to any particular income receipt, it is appropriate to use the ratable allocation approach inherent in the allocation of deductions proposal.[25]

The important questions are the items to be allocated and the excluded income to which ratable allocation is made. While in principle most tax expenditures would be eligible for one or the other aspect of this allocation, it is useful to avoid as much complexity as possible by limiting the approach to the important areas of excluded income allowing serious tax escapes for the well-to-do, which would be left after other approaches to tax expenditures have been considered. The House Bill in 1969, for example, included, in the items to which itemized deductions would be allocable: tax-exempt interest; the excluded one-half of capital gains; appreciation in the value of property donated to charity; intangible drilling expenses and percentage depletion; accelerated real estate depreciation; and farm tax losses.[26] The itemized deductions to be allocated were those enumerated in the Code as alternatives to the standard deduction, i.e., principally interest, taxes (to the extent both are not trade or business expenses), charitable contributions, medical expenses, and casualty losses. The House Bill had an overall exemption of $10,000 of excluded income, which is high enough; the initial Treasury proposal used a $5,000 exemption, and was estimated to apply to 400,000 taxpayers, nearly all with over $50,000 of adjusted gross income.[27] Thus the complexities in the proposal are limited to the taxpayers enjoying the largest escape from tax, who can scarcely complain that a complex device is used to counter their complex tax planning.[28]

Limitation on Interest Deduction

The above discussion of the allocation of deductions proposal has mentioned the deduction for interest and indicated that it was one of the itemized deductions to be included under that proposal. But the large scope of the interest deduction, its important effects in the tax expenditure system, and its consequences for escape from tax liability by well-to-do individuals warrant special attention to the deduction.

Code section 163 allows a deduction for "all interest paid or accrued within the taxable year on indebtedness." Prior to 1969, "all interest" pretty much meant all interest. The section covered:

— interest incurred in trade or business operations — which without the section would generally be deductible (under section 162) as an expense of carrying on trade or business;

— interest incurred in connection with investment activities — which without the section would generally be deductible (under section 212) as an expense involved in the production of income or the maintenance of property held for the production of income;
> — interest on residential mortgages;
> — interest on other consumer activities, whatever their nature, such as purchases of automobiles, clothing, and so forth, on credit, student loans, and so on.

The deduction allowed for interest involved in residential mortgages and other consumer activities is a tax expenditure item, and we have discussed it elsewhere, especially in connection with housing. It would also be one of the personal expenses to be allocated under the allocation of deductions proposal as an indirect limit on its present effect. Interest arising in trade or business is presumptively a proper expense to arrive at net income, is therefore not a tax expenditure, and is not usually a source of tax abuse or escape — though we can come back to this aspect later. Interest arising in connection with investment activities is also presumptively a proper expense to arrive at net income and is therefore not a tax expenditure — but is a potent source of tax escape when combined with investment activity receiving tax expenditure assistance. For example, in the analysis of the returns of the 154 individuals with adjusted gross income in excess of $200,000 who paid no income tax in 1966, 72 — or almost 50 percent — of the returns benefited primarily from the deduction for interest related to investment activity.[29] But the interest deduction by itself is not the operative factor in the tax escape — it is the interest deduction linked with the concurrent presence of tax expenditure assistance that is the reason for the escape. Consider a simple situation: an individual borrows $100,000 at 8 percent interest and purchases $100,000 worth of 6 percent state and local bonds. If there is a deduction for the $8,000 interest paid, the escape from tax lies in that deduction *combined* with the absence of income from the investment because of the tax exemption granted by tax expenditure assistance to the interest on state and local bonds. This would obviously be an abuse of the interest deduction — or a far too generous application of the tax expenditure assistance. The premise on which deduction is granted under an income tax for interest (or any other expense) related to investment activities is that the amount is spent in an effort to earn income that is taxable, and hence the deduction is proper to arrive at net income. If the income is not taxed, the premise for the deduction disappears. The remedy then would be to deny the interest deduction. The Code has long done this — section 265(2) denies a deduction for "interest on indebtedness incurred or continued to purchase or carry obligations . . . the interest on which is wholly exempt from [tax]."[30]

But this illustration indicates only one obvious linkage of interest and tax expenditure assistance. There are many other linkages developed by taxpayers which build mainly on the techniques used to provide that assistance. The linkages of primary importance relate to tax expenditures involving deferral of income and those involving capital gain treatment. For example:

— as to *capital gain treatment,* if an individual borrows $100,000 at 8 percent interest to invest in securities or real estate or other assets which appreciate in value to $250,000, only one-half of the capital gain is included in income. If the interest is deductible in full, there is an obvious tax abuse. The situation is no different from the tax-exempt bond case, except that here only one-half of the income from the investment is excluded.

— as to *deferral,* if an individual borrows in 1970 $100,000 at 8 percent interest to buy cattle to be fed in 1970 and sold in 1971, a deduction in 1970 of the costs of the investment, both the interest and the cost of feed, will serve to defer otherwise taxable income (executive salary, professional fees, and so on) into 1971 — this is the purpose of the tax shelter. The disparity in the timing of deduction and income that results from treating the expenses as currently deductible and not a capital expenditure (or a part of inventory cost) produces the abuse. The deferral is the equivalent, in benefit to the taxpayer, of a permanent, partial exclusion of the income deferred. The situation is therefore also no different from the tax-exempt bond case, except that there is only a partial exclusion of income (the tax benefit effect of the deferral). In the bond and capital gain situations, the linkage is between the interest and the investment obtained with the interest. In a deferral situation, in addition to any income from the investment, there is also a linkage with other income (salary, fees, and so on) whose inclusion is deferred because of the investment. But the tax escape is the same.

— the other aspects of the farm shelter and the other tax shelters turning on deferral of income — real estate, oil, leasing, etc. — all involve the same abuse of the interest deduction where borrowed money and the consequent leverage are an ingredient of the shelter along with the ingredient of deferral. The deferral is equivalent in monetary benefit to a permanent, partial exclusion of income, the degree of exclusion depending on the length of the deferral and the appropriate rate of discount for the individual.

— the capital gain area also involves the aspect of deferral. If an individual in 1970 borrows $100,000 at 8 percent interest to buy $100,000 worth of securities or land and the asset appreciates in 1970 to $150,000 but is not sold, then the present tax system does not currently tax the appreciation but postpones the tax until the asset is sold. However, the $8,000 annual interest is currently deductible. The operative effect is the same as in the tax shelters, for the interest deduction offsets otherwise taxable income (executive salary, professional fees, and so on) and thus defers taxation of that income until the future. The situation for the current year is no different from the tax-exempt bond case, for in effect we here have currently "tax-exempt stock" as respects the accrued appreciation in value of the securities. The ultimate result is equivalent to a partial exclusion, in addition to the exclusion of one-half of the gain ultimately realized, the extent of the partial exclusion depending as in other deferral situations on the length of the deferral and the appropriate rate of discount.

These are the escapes from tax in which the deduction for interest on money borrowed for investment purposes is one of the operative factors.[31] What are the possible remedies? The allocation of deductions proposal is not of full assistance here, since it presupposes the coexistence of itemized deductions and income currently realized but affirmatively excludible under some item of tax expenditure assistance. It would be applicable if an interest deduction and a realized capital gain, of which one-half would be excluded, occurred in the same year, since part of the interest would be allocated to the excluded portion of the capital gain and deduction disallowed for that part. But if there is only the interest deduction and appreciation in value of an asset not yet realized, then there is no excluded item under the allocation of deductions mechanism to which to allocate some of the interest deduction. In the case of the deferral achieved through tax shelters, if the item causing the deferral is treated as one of the "excluded" income items to which allocation is made, such as accelerated depreciation for real estate or intangible drilling expenses, then the allocation mechanism operates. But, if not, then the interest deduction would stand.

One remedy is to require direct capitalization of the interest in these situations. This would be appropriate where the borrowing is clearly related to an asset that is not yet productive of current income — for example, interest on a loan used to finance the construction of a building or the acquisition of unimproved land.[32] In a number of tax shelter situations, this required capitalization would end the tax escape provided by the interest deduction, since it would end the deferral obtained by the deduction of interest prior to the time the asset is intended to be productive. But assuming this were to be done — and those favoring the tax shelters would oppose the requirement — there would still be left situations in which the borrowing could not be so traced to any particular asset, such as a loan to carry diversified securities. There would also be situations in which the asset could be currently productive, such as stock with a dividend rate lower than the interest cost, but the goal of the investment and borrowing is appreciation in value of the asset.[33]

The House Bill under the 1969 Act achieved an indirect capitalization approach by limiting to current investment income (including capital gain) an individual's deduction for interest, in excess of $25,000, incurred on borrowing for investment purposes. Any interest not offset by investment income could not be deducted but could be carried forward to offset future investment income. Any capital gain offset by the deduction of interest would be treated as ordinary income. Thus, if an individual had a $30,000 interest deduction (disregarding the $25,000 floor) and a $30,000 capital gain, while ordinarily only $15,000 of the gain would be included, under this provision the entire $30,000 gain would be included. This would use up the entire interest deduction, in contrast to the Code rule which would leave $15,000 of the interest deduction to offset other income. The House Ways and Means Committee gave the following reasons for the provision:

> The itemized deduction presently allowed individuals for interest, makes it possible for taxpayers to voluntarily incur substantial interest expenses on funds borrowed to acquire or carry investment assets. Where the interest expense exceeds the taxpayer's investment income, it, in effect, is used to insulate other income from taxation. For example, a taxpayer may borrow substantial amounts to purchase stocks which have growth potential but which return small dividends currently. Despite the fact that the receipt of the income from the investment may be postponed (and may be capital gains), the taxpayer will receive a current deduction for the interest expense even though it is substantially in excess of the income from the investment.
>
> Your committee believes that a taxpayer who borrows substantial amounts in order to make investments and who is motivated by investment considerations rather than tax considerations generally is interested in investments which will produce a profit after taking the interest expense into account. Where the taxpayer's investment, however, produces little current income, the effect of allowing a current deduction for the interest is to produce a mismatching of the investment income and related expenses of earning that income. In addition, the excess interest, in effect, is used by the taxpayer to offset other income, such as his salary, from taxation.
>
> . . .
>
> Your committee does not believe it is appropriate to allow an individual taxpayer to currently deduct interest expense on funds borrowed for investment purposes where the interest expense is substantially in excess of the taxpayer's investment income. Since the amount of funds borrowed by a taxpayer for investment purposes generally is within the taxpayer's control, it would appear that a taxpayer who incurs interest expense for this purpose, which is substantially in excess of his investment income, is primarily interested

in obtaining the resulting mismatching of income and the expense of earning that income, so as to be able to insulate other income from taxation. During the course of your committee's analysis of a number of nontaxable, high-income tax returns for 1966, it was found that a significant number of these taxpayers claimed a deduction for "other interest" (that is, interest other than home mortgage and interest incurred in connection with a business) substantially in excess of their investment income. In these cases, the excess interest was used to insulate other types of income received by the taxpayer from taxation.[34]

The required "capitalization" under this approach is indirect, in that the interest is not allocated to any particular asset but rather to all investment assets taken together. Hence, the interest would be deducted only as those assets collectively produced income — intended to correct the deferral aspect — and any income so absorbing the interest deduction could not be available for capital gain benefits — intended to correct the capital gain aspect. While the "collective capitalization" eliminates tracing among investment assets, it introduces another problem to be discussed below.

The provision was dropped by the Senate[35] but a different version was included in the final legislation, as Code section 163(d) applicable to individuals.[36]

Under this Code section, only one-half of any interest in excess of investment income (and the $25,000 floor) is disallowed in the current year, and the remaining one-half is deductible by the individual. The disallowed one-half can be carried forward to offset future investment income.[37] Any capital gain offset in the current year by investment interest is not allowed the benefit, otherwise accorded to capital gains, of exclusion of one-half of the gain. The reduction of the interest disallowance to one-half is a compromise result, but the compromise itself produced a different theoretical basis for the provision. The provision is now explained as follows:

> An unlimited deduction for interest allows taxpayers to voluntarily incur a substantial interest expense on funds borrowed to purchase growth stocks (or other investments initially producing low income) and to then use the interest deduction to shelter other income from taxation. Where a taxpayer's investment produces little or no current income, the effect of allowing a current deduction for interest on funds used to make the investment is to allow the interest deduction to offset other ordinary income even though the gains finally obtained from the investments might result in capital gains.[38]

The stress here is on the capital gain relationship, and this in turn can explain the disallowance of only one-half the excess interest. Assuming all investment gain, other than current return, to be capital gain, then the limitation operates in the same fashion as the exclusion of interest incurred to carry tax-exempt securities. Since tax-exempt bond interest is fully excludible, the interest expense linked with the bond interest is fully disallowed (under section 265). Since only one-half of capital gain income is excludible, only half of the interest expense linked with the capital gain is disallowed (under section 163(d)). This has been described as a "capital deduction" approach,[39] since it eliminates the realized capital gain advantage and hence the abuse of interest expense linked to a capital gain transaction. As to the *capital gain effect,* it is collective capitalization where the interest does not exceed the capital gain.[40] The provision reduces the *deferral effect,* however, only by one-half, since it is collective capitalization only as to one-half the excess interest. The House provision requiring full collective capitalization was accordingly a preferable provision. The present provision is to be faulted not for what it achieves but for its more limited objective.[41]

There are problems of structure and operation with the new provision.[42] For example, it applies only to "investment interest," that is, interest on indebtedness in connection with property held for investment, so that trade, or business-incurred, interest and consumer interest are not covered.[43] Interest on a residential mortgage is fully deductible, even though in actual sequence the mortgage may have been placed to provide funds to purchase the investment asset. But these tracing problems and defects are marginal.[44] In determining the net investment income against which the interest is offset, the calculation uses straight-line depreciation and cost depletion, though actual taxable income is determined by accelerated depreciation and percentage depletion, which seems too generous as the calculation produces a higher net investment income than the tax return indicates. The $25,000 floor is too high on equity grounds and seems too high even in terms of administrative feasibility. Corporations are not covered.

Is the provision likely to be effective, and if so, in what cases? In asking these questions we here are disregarding both the high $25,000 floor and the disallowance of only one-half of the excess interest, since both are defects in the provision. The questions go rather to the concept itself without these drawbacks. The crucial question here is whether a taxpayer who borrows to engage in a tax shelter investment or to carry appreciating stock or realty which is currently unproductive will have enough current investment income of a non-capital gain nature, from other sources, to absorb the interest expense sought to be deducted. If so, the "collective capitalization" would defeat the effectiveness of the provision. In these situations, the remedy would lie in moving on to direct capitalization. If the current investment income is in the form of realized gain, then the provision operates effectively.

The answers to these questions lie in an analysis of the nontaxable and low effective rate returns of well-to-do taxpayers where the interest deduction is a large item. In all likelihood a considerable number of these cases would be affected — and perhaps even some despite the present disallowance of only one-half the excess interest. Thus a return with a $1.2 million of capital gains, and about $75,000 of current investment income, but an interest deduction of $587,000 would be affected.[45] There appear to be a number of returns where a large interest deduction exists, in the hundreds of thousands of dollars, but very little current dividends, interest, or other investment income or capital gains. In other cases, the current investment income is not sufficient to absorb the interest deduction and it is offset against capital gains. One suspects that the provision would have sufficient bite to justify its presence, and that the effort should be to strengthen it.[46]

Is the provision unfairly effective? The Treasury Department argued in the Senate as follows, in opposing the House provision in 1969:

> [The] bill in fact fails to correct many of the problems in this area. By permitting the interest deduction to the extent of investment income, it discriminates against the taxpayer who has only earned income out of which to pay his interest expense. The abuse is the same in either case, though under the bill the individual with earned income, but not a person receiving dividends or other investment income, might lose his interest deduction.
>
> We have been studying many alternatives to the approach of the bill. The only truly equitable solution would require tracing the interest expense to the particular investment for which the funds were borrowed. We are inclined to believe, however, that an attempt to trace investment interest to the related investment would be administratively unworkable. Other alternatives do not appear to correct any substantial number of the actual abuses and uniformly add extraordinary complexity.
>
> In light of these considerations, the Administration recommends that the interest provision of the bill be deleted, although we shall continue to explore the problem in an effort to develop a workable solution. The Allocation of Deductions provision (referred to below) will prevent individuals from offsetting all of their interest deductions against ordinary income when they have tax preferences, such as capital gains, in the current year, and will serve as a major limitation on the use of interest expense as a tax shelter.[47]

This objection is echoed in the reasons given by the Senate Finance Committee in dropping the House provision:

> The House was concerned that the present deduction for interest allows taxpayers to voluntarily incur a substantial interest expense on funds borrowed to purchase growth stocks (or other investments initially

producing low income) and to then use the interest deduction to shelter other income from taxation. Where a taxpayer's investment produces little or no current income, the effect of allowing a current deduction for interest on funds used to make the investment is to allow the interest deduction to offset other ordinary income while the income finally obtained from the investments results in capital gains.

. . .

The Treasury Department, however, recommended to the committee that the interest limitation be deleted pending further study. It noted that there is an abuse in this area which results from the possibility of acquiring growth property with borrowed funds, deducting the interest expense against ordinary income, and then treating the ultimate gain on the property as a capital gain. It believes, however, that the House provision did not correct many of the problems in this area. Particularly it expressed concern that the provision would affect the taxpayer who has only earned income more severely than an individual who also has investment income.

In view of this, the committee believes this provision of the House bill should be deleted pending further study of this problem. However, investment interest expense in excess of investment income is an item included in the base for the minimum tax on preference income which is provided in the committee amendments.[48]

The objection, however, is not strong enough to warrant dropping this remedy of a limitation on the interest deduction. We are concerned with taxpayers who should not be entitled to a current deduction for investment interest since the investments they have made, almost always by design, are not producing current taxable income. The fact that some taxpayers will escape the scope of this particular remedy because their other investment activities, not supported by borrowed funds, do produce enough income to absorb the interest deduction, should not be the lever to permit them to continue their escape from tax as well as to allow all others to escape. The chances are that most of the well-to-do utilizing the interest deduction as a tax escape are in the category where they have no cause to complain if their escape path is blocked. If others are still able to escape tax, the proper effort is to seek further refinement of remedies to reach those still escaping. These efforts may well be in the direction of increased direct capitalization. But the argument, "Don't stop to catch me since the other fellow is escaping," simply means everyone continues to escape. Tax reform lies not in postponing efforts to block some escape until all exits are sealed, but in systematically sealing off one exit after another. As this is done, attention becomes focused on the exits still open, the unfairness they present becomes more glaring, and, as a consequence, greater imagination, ingenuity, and effort are brought to bear on those exits.

A limitation on the deduction for investment interest is an appropriate indirect restraint to reduce the abuses and tax escapes resulting from the use by individuals of tax expenditure assistance.[49] It is a proper companion device to an allocation of deductions.[50]

Minimum Tax

The above discussion of indirect restraints has focused on individuals who, in connection with or as part of, their use of tax expenditure assistance have large annual deductions for personal expenses (charitable contributions, state and local taxes, consumer interest, and so on) and investment interest. The allocation of deductions proposal and the limitation on the deduction of investment interest have been described as useful indirect restraints on the abuses and tax escapes involved in tax expenditure assistance. But suppose a well-to-do individual benefiting from that assistance does not have either large personal expense deductions or investment interest expense, or, if he has the latter, it is absorbed by investment income. Here, clearly, these two indirect measures would not produce any restraint. The individual still would have his escape from tax: he could be enjoying deferral of income or exclusion of income through tax shelter activity — real estate, farm operations, leasing, natural resources — in which he had invested his own funds, as is often, for example, the situation in the natural resources area, where the percentage depletion and the intangible drilling expense deduction operate, or had invested funds not traceable to a borrowing for the tax shelter investment and hence not covered by the interest limitation. Or he could be benefiting from the preference accorded to capital gains or to tax-exempt state and local bond interest. Consequently, he would have a larger economic income than the taxable income on his tax return and hence a low effective tax rate on his total income, or even no income tax at all. The Treasury Department Tax Reform Studies showed such cases as:[51]

> — an individual with economic income of over $1 million from dividends, personal deductions of $41,000, but a tax of only $397 because of percentage depletion and intangible drilling expense deductions;
> — an individual with $1.3 million of economic income from capital gains and oil and gas operations, personal deductions of $178,000, but no tax because of percentage depletion and farm losses;
> — an individual with $1.4 million of economic income from capital gains and dividends, personal deductions of $41,400, but no tax because of real estate deductions;
> — an individual with economic income of $738,000 from interest and capital gains, personal deductions of $3,000, but no tax because of a farm loss.

To meet these situations, the Johnson Treasury Department recommended a "minimum individual income tax:"

Tax reform must come to grips with the fact that under present law it is possible for some individuals with very large incomes to pay little or no tax, while other individuals with far less income are required to pay a higher percentage of their income in tax and persons with low and modest incomes are required to pay a significant share of their income in tax. This situation is indefensible. It arises because certain types of income enjoy a favored tax status under the Internal Revenue Code. Whatever may be the merits of each of these tax preferences, of overriding importance is the principle that every individual with substantial income should pay a minimum tax toward the cost of Government that in itself bears a relationship to the income involved.

The preferential provisions and the resulting exclusions from income that contribute most significantly to this disparity in treatment among individuals are:

The exclusion of one-half of the taxpayer's net long-term capital gains, with the alternative of taxation of the entire gain at a maximum rate of 25 percent.

The exclusion of interest received on State and local government bonds.

The exclusion resulting from percentage depletion in excess of the capital invested in the ownership of minerals or other natural resources.

The exclusion of the appreciation on charitable gifts of appreciated property, such as stocks, to the extent that this appreciation is taken as a deduction.

The Treasury recommends a minimum tax to be applied to an income base broadened to include the amounts now omitted because of the exclusions referred to above. The schedule of rates for the minimum tax would be graduated from 7 to 35 percent. The tax is designed so that when applied to the expanded income base it yields a tax equal in amount to the tax payable under the regular rates on half as much income. Thus the minimum tax would have the effect of placing a 50 percent ceiling on the amount of an individual's total income which may be excluded from tax. The individual would be required to pay this minimum tax whenever it exceeded his liability under present law definition.

An individual would ordinarily not be subject to the minimum tax (that is, he would not find the minimum tax to be larger than his regular tax) unless the sum of his excluded items exceeds the amount of his regular taxable income. In no event, however, would an individual need to be concerned at all with the minimum tax computation if his total income — computed on the expanded basis — is less than $10,000 (or $5,000 for a married individual filing a separate return).

. . .

Relationship of Minimum Tax and Allocation of Deductions Proposals. — The allocation of deductions proposal included in the program would, in general, require an individual to allocate his nonbusiness expense deductions only to the extent allocable to taxable income. This is a basic reform of the deduction provisions and is justified no matter how large or small the individual's exempt income is in relation to his taxable income. However, it would not adequately correct the tax situation of an individual whose total income significantly exceeds his nonbusiness deductions and consists of a disproportionate amount of exempt income in relation to taxable income. This situation would be corrected by the proposed minimum tax, which as indicated above, generally applies if an individual's exempt income exceeds his taxable income. In determining whether the minimum tax is larger than the regular tax and therefore is to be paid for a year, the allocation of deductions proposal will apply in computing the regular tax, but not the minimum tax where the exempt items themselves are included in the expanded income base. Thus, the allocation of deductions proposal will have its impact in cases where an individual has less exempt income than taxable income.

Corporations Not Affected. — Like the allocation of deductions proposal, the minimum tax would not apply to corporations. The corporations whose income would include the four tax-exempt items to any significant degree are found mainly in only a few industries. The question of whether the tax structure for these specific industries should be altered depends upon an analysis of their particular economic and competitive positions. On the other hand, with respect to individuals, the impact of the minimum tax is not so localized. Moreover, the minimum tax is directly associated with the progressive nature of the individual income tax.

Effects of the Proposal. — The minimum tax would affect approximately 40,000 tax returns, and, based on 1969 income levels, would result in an estimated annual revenue increase of $420 million. The bulk of this revenue increase—60 percent—would be paid by taxpayers with $500,000 or more of exempt income each year. Another 25 percent would come from individuals with between $100,000 and $500,000 of exempt income.[52]

The proposal had a tortured legislative history.[53] The Nixon Treasury, seeing the problem but casting about for an alternative approach, devised a Limit on Tax Preferences proposal under which enumerated tax preferences were aggregated and, if they exceeded 50 percent of the total of the individual's gross income plus the preferences, the excess in preferences was disallowed and included in income to be taxed. The preferences differed from those in the proposed minimum tax: capital gains and tax-exempt interest were not included but intangible drilling expenses, accelerated real estate depreciation, and farm losses were included.[54] A five year carryover of unused preferences was provided.[55] The House adopted this proposal, adding capital gains and tax-exempt interest (on a transitional basis) but dropping percentage depletion and intangible drilling expenses. The House Ways and Means Committee stated:

> *Present law.* — Under present law, there is no limit on how large a part of his income an individual may exclude from tax as a result of the receipt of various kinds of tax exempt income. Individuals whose income is secured mainly from tax-exempt State and local bond interest, for example, may exclude practically all their income from tax. Similarly, individuals may pay tax on only a fraction of their economic income, if such income is derived primarily from long-term capital gains (only one-half of which are included in income) or if they enjoy the benefits of accelerated depreciation on real estate. Individuals may also escape tax on a large part of their economic income if they can take advantage of the present special farm accounting rules or can deduct charitable contributions which include appreciation in value which has not been subject to tax.
>
> *General reasons for change.* — The present treatment which imposes no limit on the portion of his income that an individual may exclude from tax results in an unfair distribution of the tax burden. This treatment results in large variations in the tax burdens placed on individuals who receive different kinds of income. In general, high-income taxpayers, who get the bulk of their income from personal services, are taxed at high rates. On the other hand, those who get the bulk of their income from such sources as tax-exempt interest and capital gains or who can benefit from accelerated depreciation on real estate, pay relatively low rates of tax. In fact, individuals with high incomes who can benefit from these provisions may pay lower average rates of tax than many individuals with modest incomes. In extreme cases, individuals may enjoy large economic incomes without paying any tax at all.
>
> For example, in 1964, 1,100 returns with adjusted gross incomes over $200,000 paid an average tax of 22 percent of income (adjusted to include amounts such as 100 percent of capital gains, and farm losses exceeding actual losses). These 1,100 returns paid tax on about 32 percent of such income after various exclusions and personal deductions.

And they paid tax on even less than 32 percent of income if the latter is broadened to include tax-exempt interest from State and local bonds. Moreover, in recent years there have been a significant number of cases where taxpayers with economic incomes of $1 million or more paid an effective tax amounting to less than 5 percent of their income.

This is obviously an unfair situation. In view of the level of the tax burden on our citizens, at this time, it is particularly essential that our taxes be distributed in a fair manner. Your committee believes that no one should be permitted to avoid his fair share of the tax burden—to shift his tax load to the backs of other taxpayers.

Explanation of provision. — Your committee's bill contains a number of provisions which are designed to reduce drastically the ability of individuals to escape payment of tax on economic income. To this end, it contains provisions designed to reduce the specific tax advantages that may be received from such items as tax-exempt securities, percentage depletion, farm losses, accelerated depreciation of real estate and deductions for charitable contributions of appreciated property.

In addition, for the reasons discussed above, your committee's bill provides a "limit on tax preferences" to assure that those individuals who are financially able to pay tax will include in taxable income at least one-half of their economic income. The objective of this provision, which is designed to work hand in hand with the allocation of deductions provision contained in the bill, is to insure that the minority of high-income individuals who pay little or no tax under present law will generally no longer be able to do this.

Under the limit on tax preferences provided by the bill, in the case of individuals, estates, and trusts, a 50-percent ceiling is to be imposed on the amount of a taxpayer's total income (adjusted gross income plus the tax preference items) which can be excluded from tax. In other words, an individual is to be allowed to claim the exclusions and deductions comprising tax preference income only to the extent that the aggregate amount of these preferences does not exceed one-half of his total income. In order to confine the operation of the provision to individuals with substantial amounts of tax preference income, the limit on tax preferences is not to apply if an individual's total tax preferences for the year do not exceed $10,000 ($5,000 for a married person filing a separate return).[56]

The concept of a minimum tax then underwent a drastic change in the Senate. It turned from a proposal to apply a minimum alternative tax to individuals at progressive rates into a flat rate supplementary tax at 5 percent on individuals and corporations, with a $30,000 exemption. The Senate Finance Committee gave these reasons for the change:

271

The committee has adopted many provisions that are specifically designed to reduce the scope of existing tax preferences. However, the committee believes that an overall minimum tax on tax preferences is also needed to reduce the advantages derived from these preferences and to make sure that those receiving such preferences also pay a share of the tax burden. As indicated below, the committee has amended the House bill to substitute an overall minimum tax for the limit on tax preferences and the allocation of deductions provisions in the House bill. Under the committee provision, individuals and corporations are to total their tax preference items, subtract an exemption of $30,000, and apply a 5 percent rate to the remainder. This will be their minimum tax.

The committee believes that this minimum tax will be a more effective and considerably simpler method of imposing tax on preference items than the House provisions. The House provisions would place a limit on certain tax preference items of individuals (amounting to one-half the sum of these tax preferences and income subject to tax) and would also require personal deductions to be allocated between taxable income and tax preference income. The House bill incorporates both these provisions because neither provision alone would impose significant taxes on those with substantial amounts of nontaxable income. For example, if the limit on tax preferences were used alone, then an individual could have tax preference income amounting to as much as one-half his total economic income and yet not pay any tax on such preferences. Accordingly, an additional provision, such as allocation of deductions, was required.

However, the House approach for the combined use of the limit on tax preferences and the allocation of deductions has important drawbacks. While these provisions together would impose significant taxes on those with substantial amounts of tax preference income, they produce different tax burdens on preference income for two individuals with the same amounts of tax preference income but with different amounts of taxable income. Moreover, these provisions would greatly complicate the preparation of tax returns for those to whom they apply. Much of this complexity arises from the inclusion of regular taxable income and tax preferences in the same tax base. This presents difficulties wherever there is a limitation on a particular deduction based on income under the regular tax computation since the limit on tax preferences affects the amount of taxable income and the amount of taxable income in turn affects the particular deduction and the limit on tax preferences.

Moreover, the House provisions for a limit on tax preferences and allocation of deductions would apply only to individuals and not to corporations. In large measure, this is because these provisions do not lend themselves to the taxation of preferences enjoyed by corporations. For example, a corporation with sufficient tax preferences to be affected by these provisions could arrange to escape from their impact by merging with other corporations with relatively small amounts of tax preference income.

The minimum tax provided by the committee avoids these problems since it merely involves applying the 5 percent rate to tax preference income in excess of the specified exemption. It also differs from the House provisions in that it does not treat differently two individuals with the same amounts of tax preference income merely because they have different amounts of taxable income. In addition, the minimum tax is readily applicable to corporation tax preferences since, unlike the House provisions, it is not feasible for corporations to avoid this tax through mergers.[57]

These reasons will not pass muster. Since the individual income tax is itself progressive, a minimum tax should also be progressive, and further, therefore, individuals with the same amount of preference income but differing taxable incomes should be treated differently; the complications stressed by the Finance Committee apply to the House and Nixon Treasury version of a limit on tax preferences but not to the separate minimum tax proposal; the treatment of corporations really involves separate issues, as the initial Treasury proposal indicated; moreover, the inclusion of corporations presumably pushes toward a flat rate tax whereas for individuals a progressive approach to a minimum tax is essential.

On the floor of the Senate the tax rate was raised to 10 percent but the base was decreased by subtraction of the amount of the regular tax. As finally enacted, the minimum tax took the Senate form. The tax, sections 56–58 of the Code:

> — applies to individuals and corporations;
> — is at a 10 percent rate;
> — extends to enumerated preferences less $30,000 and less the amount of the regular tax, and also, under a 1970 amendment, less a carryover for seven years of the excess in a prior year of the regular tax of that year over the preferences of that year in excess of $30,000[58] — this last change reduced its impact by $100 million, or about 18 percent;
> — covers as enumerated preferences:
> *as to individuals*
> > — the excluded one-half of capital gains;

273

— accelerated depreciation on real estate, and on personal property if the latter is subject to a net lease, in excess of straight-line depreciation;

— percentage depletion in excess of the basis of the property;

— amortization of pollution control facilities and of railroad rolling stock in excess of accelerated depreciation;

— excess of fair market value of stock received on exercise of a stock option over option price;

— excess investment interest (until 1972);

as to corporations

— the above (in the case of capital gains, the excluded part is 37.5 percent) except accelerated depreciation on personal property and excess investment interest (and stock options are not relevant);

— excess reserves for bad debts in the case of banks and other financial institutions.

The combined revenue yield was given as $635 million, of which $285 million was derived from individuals.[59] The $635 figure was reduced by $100 million by the 1970 amendment allowing a seven-year carryover of "unused regular tax." The actual collections in 1970 under the minimum tax on individuals came to only $117 million, considerably lower than the estimate. This represented an effective rate of 4 percent on the total preferences subject to the tax.[60] The actual collections for the minimum tax on corporations came to only $218 million, also considerably below the estimate.

Clearly, the new minimum tax has many weaknesses. It is not progressive but at a flat 10 percent rate. As a consequence, for an individual in the 70 percent bracket, his preferences if taxed become subject to an effective rate of 10 percent — quite a difference from 70 percent, and equal to the effective rate on a single person with around $5000 of total income. The maximum rate of capital gains would rise from 35 percent for an individual in the 70 percent bracket to 36.5 percent (given a $100 gain, there is a regular tax of $35 – 70 percent of $50 – and a minimum tax of $1.50 – 10 percent of $50 excluded gain less $35 regular tax). The $30,000 floor is too high. The carryover of unused regular tax is too generous.[61]

The question remains whether the minimum tax — or rather the concept of a minimum tax — can be built into a significant indirect restraint on the tax expenditure escapes. As discussed above, there is a role to be played by such a tax since the two other indirect restraints — the allocation of deductions and the limitation on investment interest — leave a gap in their coverage. An appropriate minimum tax would involve the following factors:[62]

(a) *floor* — a reasonably low floor, just enough to restrict worries about the scope and complexities of the tax to those relatively few individuals enjoying serious tax escapes — here, around $10,000 seems appropriate as a first threshold.[63]

(b) *coverage* — an adequate coverage of the important tax preferences gauged in relation to the items which permit serious tax escapes for the well-to-do. We have considered this aspect before in connection with the allocation of deductions proposal and in many respects the issues are the same. The principal problem — apart from the obvious in-fighting of the various pressure groups to protect their tax expenditures — is that some preferences produce exclusions of income, as to which no difficulty in application of the tax would arise, but others involve deferrals of income where the impact would be different, a point to be discussed below.

(c) *relation of preference income to taxable income* — both the initial Treasury proposal and the limit on tax preference approach were designed to reach only those taxpayers whose use of these tax preferences in totality was significant. Significance was here measured by the relationship of that total to the individual's taxable income. Thus, if an individual had taxable income of $200,000 and tax preferences of $25,000, the minimum tax would not apply since the preferences did not sufficiently reduce the overall tax burden. In this light, the greater the taxable income, and hence the regular tax burden, the larger could be the absolute amount of tax preferences to be tolerated. The Treasury — and House — approaches in effect used a 50–50 threshold, in that total preferences equal to total taxable income would, in general, be tolerated. In other words, $50 of taxable income would shelter $50 of preferential income. The present Code substitutes, in this comparison, the regular income tax on taxable income for the taxable income itself, and tolerates total preferences up to that level — plus $30,000 and the carryover. In effect, for a top-bracket taxpayer the threshold is 70 percent of his taxable income; in other words, out of a total of $100 income, $59 of taxable income will shelter $41 (70 percent of $59) of preference income.[64] The choice between the two levels of comparison initially is not one of theory[65] but one of the bite of the minimum income tax — the level of preferences to be tolerated. Some such relationship is appropriate to confine the "engine" of the minimum tax to the proper target area, under this view of the tax.

Put differently, a minimum tax without a relationship of tax preferences to taxable income, such as the present minimum tax would be if the regular tax were not subtracted, becomes a *supplementary* tax on tax preferences, to be added to the regular tax. On the other hand, an approach which involves the relationship of the tax preferences to the taxable income, such as the initial Treasury approach (and essentially the House approach) makes the minimum tax an *alternative* to the regular tax, this alternative to be paid if it is the higher figure. The alternative approach focuses on the overall tax being paid, so that if that figure becomes "too low" — however that level is set — because of "too much" indulgence in tax preference benefits, then the alternative minimum tax takes over and counteracts the cumulative effect of such use of tax preferences. The supplementary tax focuses on the effect of tax preferences in reducing the effective rate of tax, especially as to the progressive rates for individuals, and seeks directly to counteract that effect by adding another tax to the regular income tax as so reduced. The supplementary tax is thus closer to a direct attack on the preferences, albeit the approach is still indirect in the sense that it involves resort to the use of another tax, i.e., the minimum tax rather than direct removal or limitation of the preferences under the regular tax. The alternative tax is further removed from such directness since its target is elimination of "undue advantage" — again, however that be measured — from the use of preferences. For any particular individual, given the *same* rates, the supplementary tax will have the greater bite when tax preference exclusions from income are involved, except in a situation where the only income items are preference income. If the rates of the alternative tax were set higher than for the supplementary tax, as the following discussion on rates indicates might be the case, then the difference in the bite would narrow, the final result depending on the relationship of preference income to regular income. Where tax preference items in the nature of deductions are involved, no general comparison can be made since the results depend on the structure of the alternative tax. I lean to the view that the more appropriate concept of a minimum tax is that of the alternative tax approach, as in the original Treasury design of that concept.[66] The present Code, with its subtraction of the regular tax, but using a flat rate, is an in-between position, though the subtraction of the regular tax moves it toward the alternative classification.

(d) *rate of tax* — the initial Treasury proposal and the limit on tax preference approach, both structured as an alternative tax, utilized a progressive rate; the initial Treasury approach did so directly with a rate scale from 7 percent to 35 percent on the expanded base (taxable income plus enumerated preferences); the limit on tax preference approach did so by subjecting the excess preferences (the amount over 50 percent of the total of regular income plus preferences) to the regular progressive rates. The structural differences did not give rise to different substantive consequences, except for capital gains. The separate rate scale approach has its advantages and is probably less complex. The principal question is how high the minimum tax rate should reach.[67]

Here, the limiting factor is probably the treatment of capital gains, since by far the most significant preference covered by the minimum tax is the excluded one-half of capital gains.

The effect of the initial Treasury minimum tax, reaching to 35 percent, was to raise the top rate on capital gains from 25 percent to 35 percent, and this in large part accounted for its revenue effect. (The technique of the limit on tax preferences was such as to keep the rate at 25 percent, even with capital gains included, though the House bill, but not the Nixon Treasury approach, accomplished the 35 percent result directly by eliminating the 25 percent alternative rate.) But now, for most well-to-do individuals, the top rate on capital gains is 35 percent (70 percent top rate applied to one-half of the capital gain). Hence, if a minimum tax structured upon the initial Treasury concept of an *alternative tax* is to have an effect on the capital gain preference, the top rate must exceed 35 percent.

The initial Treasury approach was designed to provide a rate scale that, when applied to the base of regular income plus enumerated preferences, yielded a tax equal to that payable under the regular tax on half of the total income. If the one-half level were increased to 60 percent, then the minimum tax rate scale would run from 8.4 percent to 42 percent. Also, ipso facto, only total preferences not in excess of 40 percent, rather than 50 percent, of regular income, would be tolerated — $60 of taxable income would shelter $40 of preference income. This approximates the relationship under the present minimum tax, since out of $100 of total income, a 70 percent taxpayer will escape that tax if his preference income is $41 and his regular income $59 — i.e., $59 of taxable income shelters $41 of preference income (disregarding the $30,000 floor and assuming all income is subject to the 70 percent marginal rate). Again, the numbers in the rate scale of a minimum tax based on the alternative tax approach, and the consequent relationship of taxable and preference income, depend upon the desired effectiveness of the minimum tax. If one desired a top rate of 50 percent, then the minimum scale would run from 10 percent to 50 percent, which in effect increases the one-half level to a little over 70 percent.[68]

(e) *treatment of deferred income* — if a preference item of a top-bracket taxpayer subject to the minimum tax involves direct exclusion of the item (e.g., the usual effect of percentage depletion), then the minimum tax approach works properly to limit the effect of the exclusion by applying the minimum rate instead of a zero rate. But what if the preference item subject to the minimum tax instead of an exclusion involves a deferral of income — say, $100 of dividends deferred because of a $100 deduction for accelerated depreciation of an asset? The $100 of dividends in effect will be subject to a minimum tax, let us say, of $42 under an 8.4 percent to 42 percent rate scale. Several years later, $100 will be included in regular income when the deferral is ended, as on sale of the depreciable asset and recapture of income. At that time, the $100 will be subject to the regular 70 percent tax, so that the $100 item has in effect paid a tax of $112. Is this too high; is it $42 too much?

Suppose there were no minimum tax and instead an annual interest charge of 10 percent were made for the ability to defer $70 of tax, which would be the effect of the deferral of the $100 of dividends. Since the "interest" would be deductible, the taxpayer would be out-of-pocket a net of $2.10 a year ($7 interest on $70 deferred tax less $4.90 worth of interest deduction, 70 percent of $7). If the minimum tax in the case of deferral items is regarded as an interest charge, then about 29 years' deferral would have to exist before the $40 minimum tax equaled the present cost of the future net interest charges (using a discount rate of 2.10 percent if the taxpayer can borrow freely at that after-tax rate). If the taxpayer could earn 15 percent on his money, then he presumably would be willing to pay up to a $40 present minimum tax to defer the $70 payment for 19 years, using an after-tax discount rate of 4.5 percent. If a 50 percent taxpayer were involved, the minimum tax would be $30, the net interest charge $2.50, and 19 years of deferral would be needed before the $30 equaled the present cost of the future net interest charges (using a discount rate of 5 percent after-tax); or the taxpayer would be willing to pay up to $30 for 13 years of deferral if he could earn 15 percent before tax on his money.[69] As a consequence, whether the minimum tax plus the later regular tax is too much depends on the extent of the deferral and the consequent relationship of the minimum tax to an interest charge for that deferral. The fact that the minimum tax is in addition to the later regular tax, or even that both together exceed 100 percent, does not in itself mean the approach is wrong. Put another way, if the rate of minimum tax is considered "proper" where the tax preference produces a 100 percent exclusion of income, then it is too high where the exclusion is less than 100 percent. A deferral of income is the equivalent of a partial exclusion of income, the degree of exclusion depending on the length of the deferral.[70]

Hence, if the rate of minimum tax reaches up to 40 percent or so, and if deferral-type preferences are included in the base, it would be proper to devise an adjustment factor that would recognize the partial character of the exclusion produced by such deferral preferences.[71] This adjustment factor could perhaps be some form of credit against the later regular tax when the deferral is ended and the consequent degree of exclusion is known. Exactness is not required, but rather a reasonable approximation of an appropriate charge. Thus, a credit could be given for the minimum tax, reduced by a fixed percentage for each year of deferral, with the percentage calculated in relation to, say, a 50 percent tax rate and an average rate of discount.[72]

(f) *application to corporations* — the initial Treasury approach (and the House Bill) did not apply the minimum tax to corporations, the reasons given being that the preferences involved affected only a few industries and that the progressive nature of the suggested minimum tax was related more to the individual tax than to the corporate tax. The present Code minimum tax, using a flat rate, does apply to corporations — and perhaps because of that application does use a flat rate. Hence, since in the case of *individuals* a progressive minimum tax is clearly desirable, if inclusion of corporations under a minimum tax would cause rejection of a progressive rate, then the strategic course is not to cover corporations. Leaving this factor aside, however, a minimum tax in theory is equally applicable to corporations. While its effect may be limited to a few industries, principally oil and financial institutions, still this consequence does not conclusively argue against the application of the tax. Once a progressive minimum rate structure is set for individuals, then its counterpart could be devised for corporations. For example, if a 60 percent factor were used to set an individual rate scale of 8.4 percent to 42 percent, the minimum rate for corporations could be 28.8 percent (60 percent of 48 percent corporate rate), applied as an alternative tax.[73]

A properly structured minimum tax is appropriate as an additional indirect restraint on the use of tax expenditure assistance.[74] Given the appropriateness of these three indirect restraints — allocation of deductions, investment interest limitation, and minimum tax — care would have to be taken to work out their interrelationships.[75] The combination would involve some complexities, but their impact would be confined to a small group of well-to-do taxpayers, presumably possessing adequate professional advice — which advice also, presumably, they needed in order to get involved in the tax shelter or other preference activity in the first place. It seems clear that the factor of tax complexity should not be used as a shield by well-to-do taxpayers engaged in tax escapes which in themselves present a considerable degree of business and financial complexity.

The use of these restraints would also have an effect on the degree of assistance offered by the tax expenditures, and that effect would have to be weighed in the consideration of the particular preference items. That weighing, presumably, would involve some of the considerations, discussed earlier, that are relevant to a direct approach to the items. But in that weighing there is here the additional factor of balancing the importance of preserving and enhancing the fairness of the income tax against the importance of the need for the assistance offered by the tax expenditure system. Even if the merits of such assistance are recognized and no direct alternatives are available (or for other reasons the tax expenditure assistance will continue) still those merits must yield some ground to the competing policy of maintaining the fairness of the income tax. In that competition of policy goals, some middle ground must be found, and the use of these indirect restraints is a device designed to achieve that resolution. Moreover, these indirect restraints by their very presence call attention to the existence of the preferences they cover — and label them as preferences — so that the preferred status is underlined and no longer debatable. Further, a minimum tax, by stressing the trade-off mentioned above between the merits of tax assistance through these preferences and the fairness of the income tax, is by its nature geared to continued examination of that trade-off. If the yield of the tax is too low, if the amount of the preferences used grows too large, if some individuals escape its scope, these consequences point to defects in the tax and call for correction. Those seeking greater fairness are in a position to assert that the minimum tax is not working, and something more must be done.

Pathways to Tax Reform

The Aspect of the Maximum Tax on Earned Income

The 1969 Act introduced a maximum tax on earned income. Under this tax a marginal rate of 50 percent is fixed on the taxation of earned income, so that if an individual had only earned income his maximum tax rate applicable to that income under the income tax rate scale could not be over 50 percent. The provision was present in the House Bill,[76] urged by the Nixon Treasury,[77] rejected in the Senate,[78] and approved in Conference.[79]

The Johnson Treasury, which also recommended a maximum tax, though structured differently, had recognized the relationship of the benefit of such a maximum tax to a taxpayer's use of tax preferences resulting from the tax expenditure system. Accordingly, its base for the maximum tax was the taxpayer's total economic income, that is, his taxable income plus the major sources of excluded income.[80] If a taxpayer is paying up to 70 percent on his earned income and zero on other income excluded or deferred through tax preferences, so that his effective rate of tax on this total income is quite low, say 15 to 20 percent, it is the height of generosity to lower the tax rate on his earned income because *it* exceeds 50 percent and to completely overlook the zero rate on the other income. But this aspect was apparently not accepted by the Nixon Treasury, and in any event its recognition came only belatedly to the Congress. As a consequence, the Code maximum rate on earned income does take some account of the use of preferences by a taxpayer who also has earned income, in that the amount of the earned income favored by the maximum rate is reduced by the excess of preference income over $30,000. The items of preference income are those used for the base of the minimum tax.[81] But, as we have seen, those items are quite limited in coverage, as the result of pressure groups seeking to avoid the impact on their tax expenditures. Clearly, the offset for preference items required under a maximum tax concept should not be circumscribed by parallelism with the base of a minimum tax if that base gets narrowed too much by pressures favoring the tax expenditures. There indeed is misplaced concern in worrying about an executive or professional person paying over 50 percent on salary or fees when at the same time he has significant amounts of tax-exempt bond interest or natural resource income excluded through percentage depletion, or is already deferring the inclusion of some of his earned income by a deduction for intangible drilling expenses.

Moreover, the Johnson Treasury had used the concept of a maximum tax only in the form of a maximum *effective rate* — a taxpayer should not pay over in tax more than half of his total income — and not in the form of a *marginal rate* of tax as in the Code provision. Also, the Johnson Treasury had emphasized the relationship of the maximum tax concept to the treatment of appreciated assets transferred at death:

It is necessary to emphasize that the establishment of such a maximum tax is feasible only in conjunction with the recommended treatment for the taxation of appreciated assets transferred at death or by gift. A high proportion of those who would benefit from the maximum tax proposal are also large holders of appreciated assets. They, therefore, now benefit from the permanent exclusion from income taxation of the appreciation on these assets, which is possible under present law. Unless this special tax benefit is removed, it would be unfair to provide additional benefits through any reduction in the tax rate applicable to annual dividends, interest, and other income mainly derived from those assets. Indeed, such treatment would be inconsistent with the concept of the maximum tax as setting a limit on total tax paid in relationship to total income including capital gains.[82]

Indeed, even with this aspect properly dealt with, a maximum tax may well be too generous in the case of taxpayers with large dividend income, on which the 70 percent top rate would be tempered by a maximum tax, but who also have large accrued appreciation on capital assets on which a tax is in effect being deferred since the gain is not being realized. This aspect is equally present in the case of a taxpayer with a sizeable earned income.

The defects and consequent undue generosity of the present maximum tax are so apparent that the proper course would be to remove the tax.[83] It is time to think about taxpayers paying too much in income taxes when we find significant numbers of well-to-do individuals paying at effective rates above 50 percent on their total economic income. At that point, consideration should be given to a maximum effective rate of 50 percent on economic income, as an alternative perhaps to reducing the top marginal rates. Such consideration, for example, would be appropriate if capital gains are to be included in full.[84]

Information on Use of Tax Expenditures

The income tax return was devised to inform the Internal Revenue Service of a taxpayer's taxable income. It has never really been looked at from the standpoint of advising the Service, and the Government, of the extent to which an individual or corporation is using the tax expenditure system. As a consequence, solid data on the effects of many of the tax expenditures are lacking. Tax expenditures have been made a part of our income tax, but we remain in considerable ignorance about what is happening under them — who is using what expenditures and the extent of that use.

One cause of the lack of data on the use of tax expenditures by individuals is that the information is not really sought by the Government. For example the tax return does not in any way indicate the amount of tax-exempt bond interest that is excluded by an individual. A proposal to include the reporting of this interest was adopted by the Senate in 1969 but dropped in Conference because of the sensitivity in that year of state and local governments to any change in this area. Clearly, the return form should be restructured so as to obtain information on the use of tax expenditures by individuals. Appropriate questions should be devised to ascertain the economic income of well-to-do taxpayers. Perhaps this could be accomplished by requiring an annual balance sheet to be filed by these individuals. Such a requirement exists now for corporations, under which they must reconcile their book profits with their taxable income. Similar data on tax expenditures should also be required for partnerships.

If this balance sheet requirement, or other appropriate technique, were restricted to well-to-do taxpayers, the added paper work would not be a significant burden. The Government would thereby become informed on the use being made of the tax expenditure system and the benefits it generated for particular classes of taxpayers. Information would then replace the conjecture and rough estimates that at present mark much of the Treasury's and the Government's knowledge about the operation of the tax expenditure system.[85]

Notes

CHAPTER I: THE TAX EXPENDITURE BUDGET

1. See, for excerpts from that speech, Annual Report of the Secretary of the Treasury on the State of the Finances for Fiscal Year 1968, 322. See also, for earlier discussion of the subject, Stanley S. Surrey, "Federal Tax Policy in the 1960's," 15 Buffalo Law Review 477, 488 (1966).

2. See pages 326–340 of Report, note 1 above.

3. Statement of Joseph W. Barr, Secretary of the Treasury, in Hearings on the 1969 Economic Report of the President before the Joint Economic Committee, 91st Cong., 1st Sess. (1969). See also statement by Stanley S. Surrey on the Tax Expenditure Budget, in Hearings on Economic Analysis and Efficiency in Government before the Subcommittee on Economy in Government of the Joint Economic Committee, 91st Cong., 1st Sess. 82 (1969).

4. Annual Report of the Secretary of the Treasury on the State of the Finances for Fiscal Year 1970, 306–308.

5. A Senate floor amendment, §323, H.R. 10947, Revenue Act of 1971, as passed by the Senate, required publication in the budget of tax expenditure items. See 117 Cong. Rec. S18,763–18,768 (daily ed. Nov. 16, 1971). The present Treasury opposed this amendment. The Treasury in the previous administration would have favored the approach. The Conference Committee deleted the amendment, with the following explanation, H.R. Rep. No. 708, 92d Cong., 1st Sess. 49 (1971):

Budget Information With Respect to Revenue Losses and Indirect Expenditures

Amendment No. 74: The Senate amendment amends the budget and accounting act to require the budget submitted by the President (or special analyses presented with the budget) to contain estimates of losses in revenue from provisions of the Federal income tax laws and also estimates of indirect expenditures through the operation of Federal tax laws.

The conferees concluded that it would be more appropriate to have such estimates of tax expenditures made by the Treasury Department and to have the estimates submitted annually to the Committee on Ways and Means of the House, the Committee on Finance of the Senate and the Joint Committee on Internal Revenue Taxation. It is expected that these tax expenditure reports to the tax committees will initially be modeled after similar reports previously made and included in the Annual Reports of the Secretary of the Treasury in 1968 and 1970. Modifications may, of course, be made from time to time in consultation with the tax committees. In addition to making these reports to the tax committees on an annual basis, the Treasury Department may desire to include these data on tax expenditures in the annual report of the Secretary of the Treasury. The Treasury Department has indicated its willingness to submit information to the tax committees in the manner indicated above and as a result the amendment no longer appears necessary. The Senate recedes.

6. Statements of Senators Javits and Long, 117 Cong. Rec. S21,098–21,099 (daily ed. Dec. 9, 1971).

7. Subcommittee on Economy in Government of the Joint Economic Committee, Report on Economic Analysis and the Efficiency of Government, 91st Cong., 2d Sess., 20–21, 23 (1970).

In the summer of 1973 I came across two items on the relationship of tax expenditures to the regular budget. The first is an article by Joseph P. McKenna, "Tax Loopholes: A Procedural Proposal," 16 National Tax Journal 63 (1963), in which he stated that "tax exemptions" should be recorded in the budget as revenue received and also as an expenditure, as I am recommending. The second is the requirement under the budget laws of West Germany that financial aids and "tax aids" be listed, amounts given, and effects summarized. This requirement was introduced in 1967 as a part of budget stabilization policies, and is contained in the Law for the Furthering of Stability and Economic Growth (Stabilization Law), June 8, 1967. "Tax aids" under this requirement are similar to tax expenditures as I use the latter term.

8. The Joint Economic Committee has said:

> Recent estimates of the budgetary costs of major Federal tax subsidies show that out of 36 comparable items, eight declined, eight remained unchanged, and *twenty* increased from 1971 to 1972. . . . Once they become law, the amounts of these tax expenditures are not subject to control by either Congress or the Executive.

Joint Economic Committee, Report on the 1972 Midyear Review of the Economy, 92d Cong., 2d Sess. 16 (1972).

9. Statement of Treasury Secretary George P. Shultz, in Hearings on General Tax Reform before the House Ways and Means Committee, 93d Cong., 1st Sess. (April 30, 1973).

10. See Stanley S. Surrey, "Tax Subsidies as a Device for Implementing Government Policy: A Comparison with Direct Government Expenditures," in The Economics of Federal Subsidy Programs, Part 1 – General Study Papers, Joint Economic Committee, 92d Cong., 2d Sess. 745 (1972); Hearings on The Economics of Federal Subsidies before the Subcommittee on Priorities and Economy in Government of the Joint Economic Committee, 92d Cong., 1st Sess. 43–59 (1972).

11. House Committee on Ways and Means, Estimates of Federal Tax Expenditures, June 1, 1973. The tax expenditure estimates are for the calendar years 1967–1972. This pamphlet also includes a table containing the estimated distributions of these tax expenditures by income classes, for the calendar year 1972. This table appears as Appendix Table B.1, in Chapter III.

12. See Staff Study, The Economics of Federal Subsidy Programs, Joint Economic Committee, 92d Cong., 2d Sess. 4 (1972). The text comparison of magnitudes is incomplete. If some of the tax expenditure items were converted to direct subsidy programs and the subsidies included in taxable income, Congress presumably would want in some situations to increase the subsidy levels to take account of the taxable

status. As a result, the tax subsidies — now converted to direct programs — would then show up in the regular budget in much larger amounts than are now listed in the Tax Expenditure Budget.

13. Joint Economic Committee, 1972 Joint Economic Report, S.Rep. No. 708, 92d Cong., 2d Sess. 43 (1972).

14. See Annual Report, note 1 above, at 327, 329–330.

15. Henry C. Simons, *Personal Income Taxation* (Chicago, University of Chicago Press, 1938) 50.

APPENDIX TO CHAPTER I

1. The text discussion here in part follows that in Stanley S. Surrey and William F. Hellmuth, "The Tax Expenditure Budget — Response to Professor Bittker," 22 National Tax Journal 528 (1969), replying to Boris I. Bittker, "Accounting for Federal 'Tax Subsidies' in the National Budget," 22 National Tax Journal 244 (1969).

2. Annual Report of the Secretary of the Treasury on the State of the Finances for Fiscal Year 1968, 327, 329–330.

The budget laws of West Germany require the listing of "tax aids;" see Chapter I, note 7. The definition used in the Reports issued by the Finance Ministry is much the same as in the Treasury Department analysis: "Tax aids are special exceptional rules which deviate from general tax norms and result in the reduction of public revenues."

3. [Footnote not in quotation] The reference in the quotation is to the depreciation system as it stood in 1968, namely, the accelerated tax methods of double-declining balance and sum-of-the-years-digits when applied to machinery and equipment as compared with the straight-line method. The 1971 statutory change, adding the asset depreciation range approach and dropping the reserve ratio test, is recognized in Table 1.1 as a tax expenditure.

4. This measurement traces back to the definition of income used by Henry C. Simons in *Personal Income Taxation* (Chicago, University of Chicago Press, 1938), 50:

> Personal income may be defined as the algebraic sum of (1) the market value of rights exercised in consumption and (2) the change in the value of the store of property rights between the beginning and end of the period in question.

This approach is often referred to as the Haig-Simons approach to the measurement of net income. See also Boris I. Bittker, Charles O. Galvin, Richard A. Musgrave, and Joseph A. Pechman, "A Comprehensive Income Tax Base?" (Branford, Conn., Federal Tax Press, Inc., 1968), which reprints articles by these authors in 80 Harvard Law Review 925 (1967) and 81 Harvard Law Review 44, 63,1016 and 1032 (1968) along with additional remarks. See also John D. Bossons, "Income Tax Reform in Canada: A Reply to Professor Bittker," Working Paper Series No. 6821, Institute for the Quantitative Analysis of Social and Economic Policy (Toronto, University of Toronto, 1968). See Commission to Revise the Tax Structure, *Reforming the Federal Tax Structure* (Washington, D.C., Fund for Public Policy Research, 1973), containing recommendations based upon the Haig-Simons concept.

5. The income tax has its problems of application, and perhaps theory, in areas not represented directly in a market economy, such as those referred to in the text associated with imputed income. Imputed income from leisure activities and from bank checking account services could be added to the examples of such income from asset

ownership and the household services of a nonemployed spouse. For one, the problems of measurement are difficult, though the range of difficulty varies; thus, it could be met for home ownership but probably not for leisure. And the outer dimensions of such imputed income merge into the effects and unneutralities of the income tax, as with any tax, when injected into the habits of a society. Thus, the choice of an occupation, often involving a balance of personal enjoyment as against monetary reward, will to some extent be affected by the presence of the income tax. Second, in addition to the problem of measurement, there is also the matter of public understanding, which would, presumably, on the whole find the inclusion of such imputed income to be an unfamiliar approach difficult for people to relate to an income tax.

The decision to exclude imputed income from income tax coverage, one made by nearly all countries using an income tax, brings in turn other questions which must, because of this exclusion and this initial departure from the economists' norm for measuring net income, be decided against the background of the initial departure from that norm. Essentially, in this context, those questions cannot always be answered on the basis of the proper theoretical approach, since that was discarded in the initial departure, but take on the context of second best choices. Examples here are the treatment of the second working spouse in a family and child care expenses, which issues often lead to the consideration of a general earned income credit. These borderline problems of imputed income, however, do not negate the essentials of tax expenditure analysis but rather serve to indicate the definitional difficulties — at the borderline.

6. There are other problems with including gifts and bequests in the measurement of net income. Probably our society would not be content to leave the taxation of inherited wealth solely to the application of the income tax. Studies indicate that, given the marginal income tax brackets of the recipients after an averaging technique was applied to the receipt of a gift or bequest, the rates of tax applied to that receipt could well be considerably less than many would like applied to the receipt of inherited wealth. Thus, those marginal income tax rates would probably cluster between the $10,000 and the $20,000 brackets, about 22 to 32 percent. See discussion in Boris I. Bittker, "Federal Estate Tax Reform: Exemptions and Rates," 57 American Bar Association Journal 236 (1971). This is especially so for those desiring to limit severely the inequalities which the receipt of inherited wealth involves, a view which is likely to gain increasing acceptance. This being so, that view can be met only by a strengthened estate and gift tax applicable to the donor of the wealth or a cumulative accessions tax applicable to the recipient, or perhaps both. But these are taxes separate from the income tax. If some form of such a separate tax is needed properly to reach inherited wealth, then coverage of that wealth under the income tax is not needed, and indeed would make the problem more complex. For a consideration of some structural estate tax issues, see Jerome Kurtz and Stanley S. Surrey, "Reform of Death and Gift Taxes: The 1969 Treasury Proposals, the Criticisms and a Rebuttal," 70 Columbia Law Review 1635 (1970).

The income tax treatment of gifts and bequests is also related to the treatment of the family unit, earlier discussed in the text. The economist is likely to coordinate the two aspects, by disregarding donative transfers within the unit which he has chosen for the measurement of the tax. If, for example, the incomes of husband, wife and minor children are aggregated, then gifts from one member of this unit to another are disregarded. But gifts to persons outside the unit are income to the recipient and not deductible by the unit. Income tax systems in actual operation, however, invariably exclude all gifts from income, whether within or outside the family unit. While this exclusion can cause many interpretative difficulties, especially if the basis for the exclusion is not articulated, the approach of the economists would also carry its own load of operative problems. Moreover, if the general exclusion is viewed as in effect extending to a broader group the exclusion the economist would make for intra-unit gifts, then the application in actual practice of the broader exclusion presumably could be channeled within rational structural and interpretative borders. For contrasting views of economists, see Richard Goode, *The Individual Income Tax* (Washington, D.C., Brookings Institution, 1964) 100–102, and Report of the Royal Commission on Taxation [Canada] (Ottawa, Canada, Queen's Printer) Vol. 3, Ch. 17.

7. For a discussion, see Kurtz and Surrey, note 6 above, at 1381–1389.

8. No major income tax system has yet explored the current taxation of accrued appreciation in value, and hence its benefits, problems, borderlines, and administration remain largely unsketched. For some references, and a consideration of the effect on tax structure of *not* currently taxing accrued appreciation in value, see Stanley S. Surrey, William C. Warren, Paul R. McDaniel, Hugh J. Ault, *Federal Income Taxation, Cases and Materials* (Mineola, N.Y., The Foundation Press, Inc., 1972) vol. I, 923–936.

9. Shifts in the applicable dividing lines between the allowable expenses incurred in earning business or investment income and the nondeductible personal expenses occur through the interplay between the efforts of Congress, the administrators, and the courts in searching for the proper location in the various substantive areas involving problems of line-drawing. Thus, the courts, opposing the administrators, took an overgenerous approach to the "travel and entertainment" expense deduction which by stressing the business component resulted in the deduction of considerable personal consumption under the guise of business entertaining. The pendulum swung the other way when Congress recognized the presence of this large element of personal consumption and through statutory change in 1962 (section 274) stressed that presence by setting limits to the deduction, though not going as far as the Executive had desired. In the moving expense area the courts, following a somewhat inconsistent course set by the administrators, were less generous to deductibility and stressed the personal element in moving from one job to another. The Congress, by changes in 1964 and 1969 (section 217), stressed the business element and expanded the deduction. In other areas, such as travel away from home, clothing, legal expenses, and education, the Congress has allowed the courts and administrators to establish the dividing lines, through their interpretations of the opposing strengths of sections 162 and 212 vis a vis section 262.

10. See the discussion in Chapter I of the origins of the Tax Expenditure Budget. Professor Bittker would disagree. He does not find sufficient basis in the Haig-Simons definition or in the tax expenditure approach to construct a normative income tax, and instead sees in our present tax only "an assemblage of value judgments on scores of issues that could plausibly have been decided differently. To bestow the label 'correct' on any of these human creations is to misuse the term." Boris I. Bittker, "The Tax Expenditure Budget — A Reply to Professors Surrey and Hellmuth," 22 National Tax Journal 538, 542 (1969); see also note 1 above.

11. William D. Andrews, "Personal Deductions In An Ideal Income Tax," 86 Harvard Law Review 309 (1972).

12. As to medical expenses, Professor Andrews states (note 11 above, at 314):

> Thus, in evaluating the medical expense deduction the underlying question is whether medical services should be included or excluded in the refined concept of personal consumption for tax purposes. For many purposes, of course, medical services are properly classed as personal consumption. But for purposes of

interpersonal comparisons of taxable capacity there are persuasive reasons for excluding medical services. As between two people with otherwise similar patterns of personal consumption and accumulation, a greater utilization of medical services by one is likely not to reflect any greater material well-being or taxable capacity, but rather only greater medical need.

As to charitable contributions, he states (note 11 above, at 346):

As in the case of the medical expense deduction, there are substantial grounds for excluding from our definition of taxable personal consumption whatever satisfactions a taxpayer may get from making a charitable contribution. The charitable contribution deduction is quite different from the medical expense deduction since there is no reason to view the charitable contribution as offsetting some particular personal hardship like disease or injury. But there are other good reasons why a charitable contribution may rationally be excluded from the concept of taxable personal consumption. In the case of alms for the poor, for instance, the charitable contribution results in the distribution of real goods and services to persons presumably poorer and in lower marginal tax brackets than the donor. These goods and services, therefore, should not be taxed at the higher rates intended to apply to personal consumption by the donor. In the case of philanthropy more broadly defined — the support of religion, education, and the arts — benefits often do not flow exclusively or even principally to very low bracket taxpayers. But the goods and services produced do have something of the character of common goods whose enjoyment is not confined to contributors nor apportioned among contributors according to the amounts of their contributions. There are a number of reasons for defining taxable personal consumption not to include the benefit of such common goods and services. The personal consumption at which progressive personal taxation with high graduated rates should aim may well be thought to encompass only the private consumption of divisible goods and services whose consumption by one household precludes their direct enjoyment by others.

13. Most states in their sales taxes do not reach medical services, apparently on the policy ground of the undesirability of burdening those services with a tax, though some states do tax medicines and a few may reach medical services. Legal services also are not usually placed under these taxes, in large part because they are rendered to business entities and the taxes in theory are intended to apply only to personal consumption. See in general John F. Due, *State and Local Sales Taxation* (Chicago, Public Administration Service, 1971) 69, 86–93, 98–100. The European value-added taxes seem often to exclude medical services, but to cover legal services and often medicines.

14. "Should the United States Adopt The Value-Added Tax?," A Report of a Subcommittee of the Special Committee on Value Added Tax, Section of Taxation, American Bar Association, 26 Tax Lawyer 45 (1972).

15. Professor Andrews recognizes that in his stress on the "uses" of funds he is departing from the traditional approach in defining the nature of an income tax. He gets to his focus on "consumption" and "uses" of funds by reading literally Henry Simons' definition, quoted in note 4 above, which contains the term "consumption." Professor Andrews also recognizes that in his making "consumption" into a term of art having a substantive content presumably identical with the base of a tax aimed directly at consumption, he is making an "unintended" application of the term as used in the Simons definition. The use of consumption as part of an algebraic total under

the Simons definition, as Professor Andrews recognizes, is not the consumption which his article is all about; e.g., note 11 above, at 315, 375.

16. Professor Andrews appears to sense this, for as indicated above, while he starts on the "income" tax side of the river, he soon moves on to a bridge that combines "consumption" tested by a consumption tax standard and "accumulation" by an income tax standard, with both being taxed. However, he appears to be seeking rapidly to reach the other bank, which contains only a "consumption" tax with accumulation discarded.

Professor Andrews' approach takes him to the recognition of the value of tax expenditure analysis as respects the sources of income, since he finds distinctions as to source and hence income exclusions not appropriate to an income tax. On this he is of course correct under the traditional Simons approach, although his source analysis is soon turned into the inappropriateness of source distinctions for a consumption tax — where he is also correct, though the point is a different one. Moreover, the fact that source distinctions have no place either in an income tax or a consumption tax does not mean we should substitute a consumption tax for an income tax. But Professor Andrews seems to doubt the utility of tax expenditure analysis when it comes to deductions from income in contrast to exclusions from income, or at least he questions the appropriateness of that analysis as to personal deductions. However, the analysis is equally applicable to deductions, personal or otherwise, as to exclusions. What Professor Andrews appears to be questioning is the definitional concepts used in constructing the Tax Expenditure Budget, since where he would find that a deduction is allowed for a purpose extraneous to the concept of the tax involved, he also would appear ready to classify the item as a tax expenditure. However, in determining this crucial question of whether the deduction is extraneous, he is engaged as the text discussion states, not in testing the item under the concepts of an income tax, but under the concepts of a consumption tax — a tax not presently used at the national level in the United States.

17. See, for example, discussion in C. Harry Kahn, *Personal Deductions in the Federal Income Tax* (Princeton, Princeton University Press, 1960) 12–16, 88–89, 127–128. This aspect of the classification appears to be recognized by Andrews. For further discussion of the medical expense as a tax expenditure, see Chapter VI, and for the charitable contributions deduction see Chapter VII.

18. Joseph A. Pechman, *Federal Tax Policy* (New York, W.W. Norton, rev. ed., 1971) 81–86. There are also elements of this approach in Professor Andrews' discussion of the medical expense deduction (note 11 above, at 335–337).

19. See Chapters II and V.

20. For the same reasons, I find Professor Andrews' use of horizontal equality to justify the medical deduction equally unsatisfactory (note 11 above, at 337–339). While he, and presumably Pechman, would say the resulting difference in treatment between 70% families and 14% families can be taken care of by the tax rate structure, I do not see how changes in the rate structure can compensate for the upside-down effect of the deduction and ever approximate the results of a direct expenditure program with no tax deduction.

21. The text discussion on the treatment of medical expenses is also applicable in large part to the treatment of property casualty losses incurred by individuals, as through fire, theft, or accident.

22. See Chapter VI.

23. While a Treasury study in this area is presumably under way, IRS News Release No. 1125, 717 CCH 1971 Stand. Fed. Tax Rep. ¶6608, and has caused accounting firms to consider and comment upon the problem, the area is still largely unexplored. For

background, and a point of view, see John S. Nolan, "The Merit in Conformity of Tax to Financial Accounting," 50 Taxes 761 (1972).

Present tax accounting provisions that depart from the financial rules appropriate to an income tax in a manner *adverse* to the taxpayer also require study. These departures, such as the treatment of reserves for anticipated expenses, have their history in concerns over tax administration problems, and are not basically intended to penalize taxpayers. If continued after careful study, the departures would resemble the decisions, relatively few, in other areas consciously to differ from a normative tax; see the discussion in Chapter V.

24. Presumably, any "unrelated business income" of tax-exempt organizations that is not made subject to the income tax on unrelated business income would produce a tax expenditure under the Treasury guidelines. Also, the exemption of investment income of such organizations, the more typical situation, would presumptively indicate a tax expenditure.

For some discussion of these questions under the corporate tax, but a discussion not in tax expenditure terms, see William A. Klein, "Income Taxation and Legal Entities," 20 UCLA Law Review 13, 43–51 (1972).

25. See, for example, the estimates in Joseph A. Pechman and Benjamin A. Okner, "Individual Income Tax Erosion by Income Classes," in The Economics of Federal Subsidy Programs, Part I – General Study Papers, Joint Economic Committee, 92d Cong., 2d Sess. 13 (1972), considered in Chapter III. Those estimates are "cumulative," while those in the Tax Expenditure Budget are not; see text below. Hence, items in the Pechman and Okner study which are included toward the last in their calculations will show a considerable increase over the amounts in the Tax Expenditure Budget.

26. Matters of this nature are mentioned in the House Ways and Means Committee pamphlet on tax expenditures, note 11 in Chapter I, as "limitations" affecting the estimates there given. The pamphlet goes on to state: "It is believed, however, that despite these limitations, the order of magnitude of the amounts involved may be helpful to the tax committees" (p.2).

Another point may be mentioned. Some tax expenditures are the result of excluding direct budget expenditures from the income tax, for example, unemployment compensation. If the direct expenditure were to be included in tax, the Congress of course might desire to increase the amount of the direct expenditure to take account of its taxable status. Other tax expenditures are the result of omitting an item from income, for example, scholarships, or allowing five year amortization for rehabilitation of rental housing. Here if Congress desired to substitute a direct grant for the tax expenditure, but with the same quantitative effect, since the grant itself should be includible in income the amount of the grant would have to be higher than the revenue loss from the tax expenditure.

27. Thus, the tax expenditure estimate for the present tax exemption of the interest on state and local bonds was originally given as $1.8 billion for 1969. (The revised figure for that year in the House Ways and Means Committee pamphlet, note 11 in Chapter I, is between $2 and $2.2 billion.) This figure represented the revenue that would be obtained in fiscal 1969 on the $124 billion of then outstanding bonds having an average interest rate of 3.22% if that interest were taxed. Of course, if the interest were taxed, then the interest rate would change, along with shifts in holdings. It has been estimated, for 1969, that without tax exemption those bonds would have carried an average interest rate of 4.72%, and at an average tax rate of about 45% on taxable bonds, the revenue yield would be $2.63 billion. See Chapter VII.

28. Emil M. Sunley, Jr., "Tax Incentive for the Rehabilitation of Housing," The Appraisal Journal (July 1971), 393–394.

29. See Chapter IV.

30. The text discussion here in part follows that in Stanley S. Surrey, "Tax Incentives – Conceptual Criteria For Identification and Comparison with Direct Government Expenditures," in Tax Incentives Symposium conducted in November 1969 by Tax Institute of America (Lexington, Mass., Heath Lexington Books, 1971).

Under recent legislation the Department of Finance of the State of California is required to study and publish every two years the tax expenditures contained in each of the taxes in the state tax system, certainly an innovative and desirable approach to state taxation. The 1972 preliminary report overshoots the mark, however, for it tends to treat every exemption, exclusion, or deduction as a tax expenditure without regard to what provisions would be required under a normative model of the particular state tax under consideration.

31. Indeed, as to broad-based taxes on consumption, it would be interesting to see whether the structure of the particular tax chosen to reach personal consumption — e.g., a retail stage sales tax, a value-added tax, a graduated tax on personal expenditures — would lead to a difference in the tax base involved, i.e., a difference in the concept of "consumption" that forms the base of each tax. Thus, as to items considered by Professor Andrews in the context of consumption, there would not seem to be any difference in structure among these taxes that would lead to a difference in definition as respects medical expenses. Each form of tax would seem to be able to cover or exclude such expenses in the same manner. But this is not so clear as to charitable contributions, which could directly be reached by a personal expenditure tax on the donor but presumably not by a retail sales tax or value-added tax. However, if one chose to say that a charitable contribution is a "purchase" of the satisfaction that one obtains through making the gift, then the transaction can be regarded as a taxable "sale" and reached by these taxes. The taxes could of course reach the goods purchased by the charitable organizations and perhaps some of the services provided by them. But I am content to leave such questions and the definitional contours of "consumption" to those more interested than I am in having the United States adopt a national tax on personal consumption. I would rather see our energies concentrated on improving our present national taxes — income, estate and gift, and payroll — rather than diverted to the structuring of a new tax on personal consumption, even if the latter took the form of a progressive tax on personal expenditures.

32. See Appendix to Chapter V.

33. For a general discussion of revision of the estate and gift taxes, see Kurtz and Surrey, note 6 above.

CHAPTER II: SOME USES OF THE
TAX EXPENDITURE BUDGET

1. For example, income tax subjects listed by the House Ways and Means Committee for its 1973 Panel Discussions on General Tax Reform, 93d Cong., 1st Sess. (1973) are all to be found in the Tax Expenditure Budget. The items listed for Congressional review in the Mills-Mansfield "Tax Policy Review Act of 1972," H.R. 15230 and S. 3657, 92d Cong., 2d Sess. (1972) are with one exception also all found in the Tax Expenditure Budget.

Tax expenditure items predominate in S. 3378, a comprehensive tax reform bill introduced in the 92d Congress, 2d Sess., by Senator Gaylord Nelson and other senators, 118 Cong. Rec. S4287 (daily ed. March 21, 1972) and H.R. 1040, introduced by Rep. James C. Corman in the 93d Congress, 1st Sess., 119 Cong. Rec. H44 (daily ed. Jan. 6, 1973). These bills, which do include structural changes, are an interesting catalog of reform proposals. The structural changes, as expected, largely consist of matters that only expert tax technicians would discover and debate. The income tax reform proposals of Senator Edmund S. Muskie all relate to tax expenditure items, 119 Cong. Rec. S1050 (daily ed. Jan. 23, 1973).

The pamphlet on Estimates of Federal Tax Expenditures, House Ways and Means Committee, June 1, 1973 (see note 11, Chapter I) states:

> The purpose of these tax expenditure data is to provide information as to the economic benefits provided by the tax laws to the various sectors of the economy. To aid in the analysis, the cost and beneficiaries (in terms of areas of activity) are shown by the same functional categories as outlays in the Federal budget. The listing of any of these provisions involves no direct, or indirect, presumption about the desirability of any of them in terms of public policy. These tables, however, are intended as a tool which may be helpful to the tax committees of Congress in reviewing various provisions of the tax laws.

2. See also discussion in Stanley S. Surrey, "Complexity and the Internal Revenue Code: The Problem of the Management of Tax Detail," 34 Law and Contemp. Problems 673 (1969); Sidney I. Roberts and others, "A Report on Complexity and the Income Tax," 27 Tax Law Review 325 (1972). In the article first cited, I urged that the responsibility for the management of tax detail be delegated to the Treasury Department, to be exercised through authoritative regulations. But this assumed the Treasury would always be ready to recognize its responsibilities to the general public and not seek by regulation to benefit a particular group. The experience, however, with the Treasury's efforts in 1971 to greatly enhance the worth of the depreciation deduction by a regulation requires a caveat to the earlier suggestion. That 1971 development serves to indicate that protection is needed against Treasury action wrongly favoring particular persons. It is not enough to say that those considering the action erroneous can take their case to the Congress. In the legislative arena, it is all important who has the burden of persuading the Congress to take action. It would be unfair to deny access to the courts to taxpayers whose tax liabilities were *increased* by Treasury action and to say *their* only remedy lay in attempting to secure a legislative reversal. It is equally wrong to close the courts to those asserting that Treasury action wrongly favors particular taxpayers. This being said, however, the task of determining who should have standing to sue to contest such Treasury action and in what situations still remains. Perhaps the courts will work this out satisfactorily. If not, then Congressional action will be required to furnish the appropriate guidelines.

3. Appendix Table B-1, Chapter III.

4. The latest episode was in 1969, when the proposal passed the Senate — see 115 Cong. Rec. 37,066–37,070 (1969) — but was not accepted in Conference. The text quotation from Senator Murphy's statement proposing the amendment is at 37,066; the allocation of revenue loss is in a 1967 letter to Senator Long included at 37,068.

5. E.g., *Coffey v. State Educ. Fin. Commn.,* 296 F. Supp. 1389 (S.D. Miss. 1969).

6. 309 F. Supp. 1127 (D.D.C. 1970), appeal dismissed *sub nom. Coit v. Green,* 400 U.S. 986 (1971).

7. 309 F. Supp. at 1134.

8. *Green v. Connally,* 330 F. Supp. 1150 (D.D.C. 1971), affirmed *mem. sub nom. Coit v. Green,* 404 U.S. 997 (1971).

9. 330 F. Supp. at 1164.

10. Ibid at 1164. Since the initial *Green* decision, and in many respects because of it, and in part in order to place litigation of the issue in a traditional setting, the Internal Revenue Service has swung from a Ruling allowing the deduction to some segregated schools, IRS News Release Aug. 2, 1967, 677 CCH Stand. Fed. Tax Rep. ¶6734 (1967), to a Ruling denying it but not stating the legal grounds on which denial rests, IRS News Release, July 10, 1970, 707 CCH Stand. Fed. Tax Rep. ¶6790 (1970), and finally to a Ruling stating that racially segregated schools are not "charitable" within the common law rules and hence not "charitable" under the Code provisions. Rev. Rul. 71–447, 1971–2 Cum.Bull. 230. The final decision in *Green v. Connally* stated that a strong case could be made for this approach but preferred to rest on a direct interpretation of the Code rather than first interpreting the common law of charities.

11. 338 F. Supp. 448 (D.D.C. 1972). For a criticism of the decision, see Boris I. Bittker and Kenneth M. Kaufman, "Taxes and Civil Rights: 'Constitutionalizing' the Internal Revenue Code," 82 Yale Law Journal 51 (1972).

McCoy v. Shultz, —F. Supp.— (D.D.C. 1973), refused to consider as unconstitutional income tax deductions for contributions to, and income tax exemption for, an organization that excluded women members. The court found the tax provisions did not constitute sufficient governmental involvement, but did not refer to the constitutional status of direct aid to such an organization. The decision left open the question whether as a matter of statutory interpretation the Code does grant these tax benefits to organizations practicing sex discrimination.

12. 338 F. Supp. at 445.

13. Ibid at 462.

14. Ibid at 458.

15. Ibid at 459.

16. The issue here is one of statutory interpretation: does "Federal financial assistance" as used in the Civil Rights Act cover tax assistance. The article by Bittker and Kaufman, disagreeing with the *McGlotten* decision, note 11 above, marshals legislative history and other arguments to support the view that the *McGlotten* court wrongly interpreted the Civil Rights Act. This may be so, especially since Congress and others were not accustomed to thinking of special tax provisions in tax expenditure terms and hence in terms of Governmental assistance. But a decision that, as presently used, "Federal financial assistance" in the Civil Rights Act does not cover tax assistance does not militate against the validity of tax expenditure analysis. Rather, such a decision would raise the question as to whether now, as a *de novo* legislative policy, a Congressional distinction should so be made with respect to the scope of the Civil Rights Act. On this policy question, the burden of proof should be on those who desire to draw that distinction. Of course, if such a distinction is to be made, then in any particular situation where direct federal assistance would violate constitutional standards, the question would remain as to the constitutional validity of tax expenditure assistance.

17. The Bittker and Kaufman article, note 11 above, criticizing the *McGlotten* decision, raises a number of questions regarding the propriety and utility of the standards and classifications used under tax expenditure analysis. This criticism follows Bittker's previous objections to tax expenditure analysis and to the comprehensive tax base concept of economists (see his articles cited in notes 37 and 39 of the Bittker and Kaufman article). Here, parenthetically, he continues to equate tax expenditure analysis exclusively with the Haig-Simons definition of income, despite the nonexclusivity of that definition as the base for such analysis, as pointed out in the Appendix to Chapter I. But the Bittker and Kaufman article, as did the prior criticism, stirs up so many problems at the borderline, as well as nonexistent problems in view

of the nonexclusive use of the Haig-Simons definition, that it loses sight of the main issues in areas far removed from the borderline.

Thus the article does not squarely face the main question: in a situation in which direct aid may not be given by the federal Government, for constitutional or even statutory reasons, what should be the treatment of assistance under the tax system? Presumably, this question in a rational governmental system should turn on the correspondence of the tax assistance to the direct aid. There may be degrees of correspondence, just as there may be degrees of correspondence between direct grants and forms of non-tax indirect aid. But where the correspondence is close, as in the segregated school situation of *Green v. Connally,* notes 6 and 8 above, or in assistance to parents of children in parochial schools, discussed later in the text, the burden must be upon those who would strike down the direct aid but sustain the tax assistance. However, in talking about the problems of differentiating among the myriad tax provisions and their effects, the article does not deal with the problem of the tax assistance that is so close to direct assistance that a decision to strike the latter but sustain the former would to many seem irrational, as it did to the courts in *Green v. Connally* and *McGlotten.* Finally, in part the criticism in the article seems to reflect the view that in *McGlotten* direct aid should itself be held constitutional, and of course this view can color how one sees tax assistance. All of the above is not to be taken as agreement with many of the article's minor points, which seem to disregard the insurance businesses of fraternal organizations and their exemption, the exemption of their investment income, their role as "organizations" in the community so that assistance to them has a stamp different from assistance to businesses generally, and so on.

18. The court clearly reached the proper answer as to the income tax exemption for fraternal organizations. The exemption of their investment income, and also of their insurance businesses, are important aids. The social club is a harder question. The present tax structure does confer some benefits, an aspect perhaps not realized by the court: an exemption of $1000 for nonexempt function income; nonrecognition of gain on sale of club property used for exempt purposes if proceeds are reinvested in assets involved in the performance of its exempt function; and an exemption for investment income set aside for charitable purposes. (Query: To what extent does this collective charitable deduction differ from or add to the charitable deduction the members possess as individuals?) Also the court stressed the phrase "and other nonprofitable purposes" in the §501(c)(7) exemption of social clubs to show the exemption had a broad sweep and hence there was no mark of Government approval in the designation of an exempt social club. However, the cases indicate that the quoted phrase is limited by the preceding descriptive words, "operated for pleasure, recreation," so that all nonprofit organizations are not covered, e.g., a club with a commercial and not a social orientation is not exempt under this provision. The subject thus requires further exploration.

19. 93 S.Ct. 2955 (June 25, 1973).

20. The Court also held invalid in *Sloan v. Lemon,* 93 S.Ct. 2982 (1973), tuition grants paid by Pennsylvania to parents of children attending nonpublic elementary and secondary schools. Chief Justice Burger and Justices White and Rehnquist dissented. In *Nyquist* the Court also invalidated "maintenance and repair" grants made directly to nonpublic schools.

21. *Committee for Public Education and Religious Liberty v. Nyquist,* 350 F. Supp. 655 (S.D.N.Y. 1972). A three-judge Federal Court in Ohio, after first holding direct aid granted by Ohio to parents to be unconstitutional, in a subsequent case held an income tax credit granted by Ohio to be equally unconstitutional, *Kosydar v. Wolman,* 353 F. Supp. 744 (S.D. Ohio 1972).

22. 93 S.Ct. at 2974 (some footnotes omitted). The Court had to deal with a prior decision, *Walz v. Tax Commission,* 397 U.S. 664 (1970), holding that exemption of churches from the New York property tax, granted as part of a broad exemption for religious, charitable, literary, and other such organizations did not violate the First Amendment Establishment of Religion clause. The Court in *Walz* had distinguished the grant of exemption from a direct money grant, as did the concurring opinion of Justice Brennan. Justice Douglas, dissenting, equated the subsidy of grant and the subsidy of tax exemption, while Justice Harlan, concurring, stood somewhat in between. In *Nyquist,* the Court had this to say about *Walz* (93 S.Ct. at 2975):

> Tax exemptions for church property enjoyed an apparently universal approval in this country both before and after the adoption of the First Amendment. The Court in *Walz* surveyed the history of tax exemptions and found that each of the 50 States has long provided for tax exemptions for places of worship, that Congress has exempted religious organizations from taxation for over three-quarters of a century, and that congressional enactments in 1802, 1813, and 1870 specifically exempted church property from taxation. In sum, the Court concluded that "[f]ew concepts are more deeply embedded in the fabric of our national life, beginning with pre-Revolutionary colonial times, than for the government to exercise at the very least this kind of benevolent neutrality toward churches and religious exercise generally." *Id.,* at 676–677. We know of no historical precedent for New York's recently promulgated tax relief program. Indeed, it seems clear that tax benefits for parents whose children attend parochial schools are a recent innovation, occasioned by the growing financial plight of such nonpublic institutions and designed, albeit unsuccessfully, to tailor state aid in a manner not incompatible with the recent decisions of this Court. See *Kosydar v. Wolman,* —F. Supp.— (SD Ohio 1972), *aff'd,* —U.S.— (1973).
>
> But historical acceptance without more would not alone have sufficed, as "no one acquires a vested or protected right in violation of the Constitution by long use." 397 U.S., at 678. It was the reason underlying that long history of tolerance of tax exemptions for religion that proved controlling. A proper respect for both the Free Exercise and the Establishment Clauses compels the State to pursue a course of "neutrality" toward religion. Yet governments have not always pursued such a course, and oppression has taken many forms, one of which has been taxation of religion. Thus, if taxation was regarded as a form of "hostility" toward religion, "exemption constitute[d] a reasonable and balanced attempt to guard against those dangers." *Id.,* at 673. Special tax benefits, however, cannot be squared with the principle of neutrality established by the decisions of this Court. To the contrary, insofar as such benefits render assistance to parents who send their children to sectarian schools, their purpose and inevitable effect are to aid and advance those religious institutions.
>
> Apart from its historical foundations, *Walz* is a product of the same dilemma and inherent tension found in most government-aid-to-religion controversies. To be sure, the exemption of church property from taxation conferred a benefit, albeit an indirect and incidental one. Yet that "aid" was a product not of any purpose to support or to subsidize, but of a fiscal relationship designed to minimize involvement and entanglement between Church and State. "The exemption," the Court emphasized, "tends to complement and reinforce the desired separation insulating each from the other." *Id.,* at 676. Furthermore, "[e]limination of the exemption would tend to expand the involvement of government by giving rise to tax valuation of church property, tax liens, tax foreclosures, and the direct confrontations and conclicts that follow in the train

of those legal processes." *Id.,* at 674. The granting of the tax benefits under the New York statute, unlike the extension of an exemption, would tend to increase rather than limit the involvement between Church and State.

One further difference between tax exemptions for church property and tax benefits for parents should be noted. The exemption challenged in *Walz* was not restricted to a class composed exclusively or even predominantly of religious institutions. Instead the exemption covered all property devoted to religious, educational or charitable purposes. As the parties here must concede, tax reductions authorized by this law flow primarily to the parents of children attending sectarian, nonpublic schools. Without intimating whether this factor alone might have controlling significance in another context in some future case, it should be apparent that in terms of the potential divisiveness of any legislative measure the narrowness of the benefited class would be an important factor.

In conclusion, we find the *Walz* analogy unpersuasive, and in light of the practical similarity between New York's tax and tuition reimbursement programs, we hold that neither form of aid is sufficiently restricted to assure that it will not have the impermissible effect of advancing the sectarian activities of religious schools. (footnotes omitted)

The pointed observation in the last quoted paragraph on the setting of the *Walz* religious exemption in the context of a broad charitable exemption is also reflected in part of an earlier footnote, note 38, in *Nyquist* (93 S.Ct. at 2970):

Because of the manner in which we have resolved the tuition-grant issue, we need not decide whether the significantly religious character of the statute's beneficiaries might differentiate the present case from a case involving some form of public assistance (*e.g.,* scholarships) made available generally without regard to the sectarian-nonsectarian, or public-nonpublic nature of the institution benefitted. See *Wolman v. Eseex,* 342 F. Supp. 399, 412–413 (SD Ohio 1972), aff'd, 409 U.S. 808 (1972). Thus, our decision today does not compel, as appellees have contended, the conclusion that the educational assistance provisions of the "G. I. Bill," 38 U. S. C. §1651, impermissibly advance religion in violation of the Establishment Clause. . . .

The court in *McGlotten v. Connally* distinguished *Walz* in these terms (338 F. Supp. at 459 n.58):

Defendant's reliance on *Walz v. Tax Commission,* 397 U.S. 664 (1970) for the proposition that tax exemptions provide insufficient Government involvement to violate the Constitution is misplaced. The holding in *Walz* was that exemption of church property from state property tax did not violate the First Amendment Establishment Clause. As such, it was premised on historical considerations peculiar to the First Amendment:

Few concepts are more deeply imbedded in the fabric of our national life, beginning with pre-Revolutionary colonial times, than for the government to exercise at the very least this kind of benevolent neutrality toward churches and religious exercise generally . . . .

397 U.S. at 676. The history of the Fourteenth Amendment leads in exactly the opposite direction. It was designed explicitly to deal with the cancer of racial discrimination and a *strict* rather than *benevolent* neutrality is required on the part of Government. *See Green v. Connally,* . . . .

See also the discussion of *Nyquist* and *Walz* in Chapter VII in connection with the charitable deduction under the federal income tax.

23. Chief Justice Burger and Justices White and Rehnquist dissented. Chief Justice Burger stressed that (93 S.Ct. at 2990):

> ... government aid to individuals generally stands on an entirely different footing from direct aid to religious institutions. . . .
>
> This fundamental principle which I see running through our prior decisions in this difficult and sensitive field of law, and which I believe governs the present cases, is premised more on experience and history than on logic. It is admittedly difficult to articulate the reasons why a State should be permitted to reimburse parents of private-school children — partially at least — to take into account the State's enormous savings in not having to provide schools for those children, when a State is not allowed to pay the same benefit directly to sectarian schools on a per-pupil basis. In either case, the private individual makes the ultimate decision that may indirectly benefit church sponsored schools; to that extent the state involvement with religion is substantially attenuated. The answer, I believe, lies in the experienced judgment of various members of this Court over the years that the balance between the policies of free exercise and establishment of religion tips in favor of the former when the legislation moves away from direct aid to religious institutions and takes on the character of general aid to individual families. This judgment reflects the caution with which we scrutinize any effort to give official support to religion and the tolerance with which we treat general welfare legislation.

Justice White stressed more traditional First Amendment criteria, as he viewed them in this case (93 S.Ct. at 2997):

> But whatever may be the weight and contours of entanglement as a separate constitutional criterion, it is of remote relevance in the case before us with respect to the validity of tuition grants or tax credits involving or requiring no relationships whatsoever between the State and any church or any church school. So also the Court concedes the State's genuine secular purpose underlying these statutes. It therefore necessarily arrives at the remaining consideration in the three-fold test which is apparently accepted from prior cases: Whether the law in question has "a primary effect that neither advances nor inhibits religion." *Abington School District v. Schempp, supra.* While purporting to accept the standard stated in this manner, the Court strikes down the New York maintenance law, and for the same reason invalidates the tuition grants, because its "effect, inevitably, is to subsidize and advance the religious mission of sectarian schools." See *ante,* p. —. But the test is one of "primary" effect not *any* effect. The Court makes no attempt at that ultimate judgment necessarily entailed by the standard heretofore fashioned in our cases. Indeed, the Court merely invokes the statement in *Everson v. Board of Education,* 330 U.S. 1, 16 (1947), that no tax can be levied "to support any religious activities . . . ." But admittedly there was no tax levied here for the *purpose* of supporting religious activities; and the Court appears to accept those cases, including *Tilton,* that inevitably involved aid of some sort or in some amount to the religious activities of parochial schools. In those cases the judgment was that as long as the aid to the school could fairly be characterized as supporting the secular educational functions of the school, whatever support to religion resulted from this direct,

Tilton v. Richardson, supra, or indirect, *Everson v. School District, supra; Hunt v. McNair,* —U.S.—, contribution to the school's overall budget was not violative of the primary effect test nor of the Establishment Clause.

There is no doubt here that Pennsylvania and New York have sought in the challenged laws to keep their parochial schools system alive and capable of providing adequate secular education to substantial numbers of students. This purpose satisfies the Court, even though to rescue schools that would otherwise fail will inevitably enable those schools to continue whatever religious functions they perform. By the same token, it seems to me, preserving the secular functions of these schools is the overriding consequence of these laws and the resulting, but incidental, benefit to religion should not invalidate them.

Justice Rehnquist thought that the *Walz* decision validated the New York tax deductions and considered those deductions no different from the personal exemptions or the standard deduction in the federal income tax — a line of reasoning that certainly overlooks the very specific target of the tax deduction in *Nyquist.* But he also would hold both the tuition grants and the tax deduction valid under general First Amendment criteria.

24. The House Ways and Means Committee in 1972 considered a proposal for a federal income tax credit to parents for tuition paid to private elementary and secondary schools. This credit was suggested as a means of aiding church-affiliated schools, whose students constitute 91 percent of the private school attendance. Direct Government financial aid to these parochial schools was recognized as being unconstitutional. The proponents of the tax credit hoped that the aid granted through the tax system would be accepted as constitutional by the courts. The push behind the credit had major political overtones. For background, see Hearings on Tax Credits For Non-Public Education, before the House Ways and Means Committee, 92d Cong., 2d Sess. (1972); article by Eileen Shanahan, *N.Y. Times,* Aug. 7, 1972, at 19; H.R. 17072, 92d Cong., 2d Sess., Oct. 11, 1972 and Staff Analysis of that bill, Bur. of Nat. Affairs, Taxation and Finance, Oct. 25, 1972.

In April 1973 the Treasury recommended a similar tax credit, equal to 50% of the tuition paid subject to a maximum of $200 for each child. The credit would be refundable to the extent it exceeded any tax due, and would diminish by $1 for each $20 of income over $18,000. See Statement of Secretary George P. Shultz, in Hearings on General Tax Reform before the House Ways and Means Committee, 93d Cong., 1st Sess. (April 30, 1973). It is clear that such a tax credit would be a tax expenditure. It would also appear to be clearly unconstitutional under the *Nyquist* decision, which was subsequent to the proposal. Indeed, it would have seemed unconstitutional even under the prior state of the law. See, for example, the opinion of Professor Paul Freund, Harvard Law School, in the 1972 Hearings above, at 449–460.

25. For a discussion of the analysis underlying the Tax Expenditure Budget and the relationship of tax equity to that analysis, see Appendix to Chapter I.

CHAPTER III: THE EFFECTS OF TAX EXPENDITURES
ON THE TAXES PEOPLE AND CORPORATIONS PAY

1. House Committee on Ways and Means and Senate Committee on Finance, 91st Cong., 1st Sess., U.S. Treasury Department, Tax Reform Studies and Proposals (Comm. Print, 1969), 79 (hereinafter cited as Treasury Tax Reform Studies).

2. Ibid., 80–81.

3. Ibid., 89–94.

4. "Amended gross income" used in these examples is "adjusted gross income" (a statutory term, covering items of included income less most of the expenses of earning the income; it excludes the personal deductions) plus the excluded part of long-term capital gains. It understates actual income since it does not include all excluded income items because of lack of data.

5. House Committee on Ways and Means, Tax Reform Act of 1969 [H.R. 13270], H.R. Rep. No. 413, 91st Cong., 1st Sess. 9 (1969).

6. The Treasury Tax Reform Studies, note 1 above, at 20, described the unlimited charitable deduction as follows:

> The unlimited charitable deduction requirements ostensibly require that the donor give most if not all of his income to charity. Thus, it is often assumed that persons using the unlimited deduction are turning over their entire annual incomes to charity. In fact their contributions typically consist of greatly appreciated property for which deductions based on fair market values are claimed. In this way they retain their annual incomes untaxed, since the appreciation in value of the property contributed is not subject to tax.

This unlimited charitable deduction was repealed in the 1969 Act, but individuals may still deduct contributions of appreciated property up to 30% (instead of the 50% available for cash contributions) of income and the appreciation need not be included in income. For a further description of the effect of charitable contributions of appreciated property, see Chapter VII.

7. The federally tax-exempt interest and perhaps some of the other excluded items may have been taxable under the state income tax and thus increased the amount of that deduction. A number of these cases presumably involve situations in which the high state tax reflects a large income in the prior year. The state tax on that income would be taken as a deduction in the subsequent year when paid, so that it would offset the income of that year rather than the higher income of the prior year. However, a full understanding of what is happening here would require data on the total income of both years, including all excluded income.

8. The remaining cases principally involved fifteen instances of large investment or business deductions not explained by the data and four instances in which the credit for income tax paid to foreign governments offset the United States tax.

9. Mortimer M. Caplin, "Minimum Tax for Tax Preferences and Related Reforms Affecting High Income Individuals," 4 Indiana Legal Forum 71, 104–107 (1970).

10. Treasury Tax Reform Studies, note 1 above, at 87.

11. The deduction is eliminated under a transitional sliding scale which brings the upper limit in 1975 to 50% of income, the general figure for cash contributions to publicly-supported organizations; Internal Revenue Code of 1954 §170(f)(6) (Internal Revenue Code of 1954 hereinafter referred to as Code). Taxpayers are permitted to deduct charitable contributions up to 50% of income; where appreciated property is given, the limit is 30%. This deduction is taken against taxable income and does not absorb any nontaxable income.

12. The minimum tax is discussed in Chapter VIII.

13. In general, see Charles Davenport, "Farm Losses Under the Tax Reform Act of 1969: Keepin' 'Em Happy Down on the Farm," 12 Boston College Industrial and Commercial Law Review 319 (1971).

14. This limitation is discussed in Chapter VIII.

Notes to Chapter III

15. Joseph A. Pechman and Benjamin A. Okner, "Individual Income Tax Erosion by Income Classes," in The Economics of Federal Subsidy Programs, Part 1 – General Study Papers, Joint Economic Committee, 92d Cong., 2d Sess. 13, 22 (May 8, 1972). This informative paper is the source for much of the post-1969 data. See also Hearings on The Economics of Federal Subsidy Programs before the Subcommittee on Priorities and Economy in Government of the Joint Economic Committee, 92d Cong., 2d Sess. 41–113 (Jan. 14, 1972).

The enlarged income resulting in the table from the various changes made by Pechman and Okner in present law adjusted gross income is called by them "expanded adjusted gross income." It is closer to actual income, as the term is used in the text discussion of this chapter, than the "amended gross income" in the Treasury Studies, since the Pechman and Okner adjustments include more of the tax expenditure items than do those Studies. The differences in content do not represent substantive differences in viewpoint but rather differences in availability of data, except that Pechman and Okner include imputed rent, the exclusion of which under the Code is not listed as a tax expenditure; see note 16 below.

16. Adapted from a table in Economics of Federal Subsidy Programs, note 15 above, at 23. (The change eliminates the item of income-splitting; see note 18 below.) All of the items in this table are in the Tax Expenditure Budget, except that of imputed rent. The inclusion in the table of this item enlarges homeowners' preferences by somewhat over 100% over those in that Budget (deduction of mortgage interest and property taxes). See Henry J. Aaron, *Shelter and Subsidies* (Washington, D.C., The Brookings Institution, 1972), 55.

The transfer payments included are social security and railroad retirement, public assistance, workmen's compensation, unemployment insurance, and veterans' disability compensation. The itemized deductions included are the present list *except:* state income taxes, medical expenses in excess of 5% of income, charitable contributions in excess of 3% of income, interest up to the amount of property income, child-care, casualty losses, miscellaneous items such as alimony and unreimbursed expenses of employees, and a standard deduction of $1,300.

17. The effective rates in Table 3.3 are generally lower than in Table 3.2, since, as explained in note 15 above, the former table contains a larger actual income base through inclusion of tax expenditures not covered in Table 3.2, the inclusion resulting from data available under Brookings Institution research programs; see Economics of Federal Subsidy Programs, note 15 above, for a description of those programs.

18. Economics of Federal Subsidy Programs, note 15 above, 23–24, 34–37. The tables have been altered to omit the aspect of tax reduction due to the "income-splitting" rate schedule for married couples, viewed by the authors of the study as an erroneous treatment of family income but not considered by the Treasury as a tax expenditure item, as noted in the Appendix to Chapter I. Mr. Pechman supplied the data needed to make this alteration.

For another source of such quantitative data, see Commission to Revise the Tax Structure, *Reforming the Federal Tax Structure* (Washington, D.C., Fund for Public Policy Research, 1973).

18–1. See note 11 in Chapter I. See Appendix to Chapter I, note 25, for some causes of the differences.

The distribution among *adjusted gross income* classes must be handled with caution. As the text above after note 9 and below at note 23 indicates, individuals with high actual incomes may show up in the statistics as having little or no adjusted gross income. Thus, the distributions of excess depreciation on rental housing and rehabilitation housing showing significant amounts of these tax expenditures in all adjusted gross income classes are suspect for this reason.

19. Statement of the Hon. Edwin S. Cohen, Undersecretary of the Treasury, in Hearings on Tax Subsidies and Tax Reform before the Joint Economic Committee, 92d Cong., 2d Sess. 148 (1972). Preliminary data for 1971 indicate there were 72 individuals with over $200,000 adjusted gross income, of which two were over $1 million, who paid no tax; April 1, 1973 News Release by Senator Walter Mondale.

20. Joseph A. Pechman, "Distribution of Federal and State Income Taxes by Income Classes," 27 Journal of Finance 179, 180 (1972).

21. Statement of Undersecretary Cohen, note 19 above. He states seven returns showed no tax because of foreign tax credits averaging 62% of *adjusted gross income*, but does not give the actual income of these individuals. Another group of 12 returns involves high state taxes paid in year 1970 on high incomes for 1969, so that the state taxes deducted against lower 1970 incomes offset the latter. While these individuals did pay high federal taxes in 1969, the complete picture requires actual incomes for both years. Another set, 12 cases, involves the offsetting of large charitable contributions against taxable income — an example of using a tax expenditure item to offset taxable income and leaving exempt income unaffected. The largest group, 55 cases, involves interest deductions offsetting taxable income; here also presumably there was large untaxed income either in capital gain, appreciated property, or tax shelters — no explanation can be adequate without an indication of actual income. The final group (20 cases) consists of miscellaneous deductions for losses on securities pledged to secure loans, investment counsel fees, and so on; here also we need to know actual incomes.

Undersecretary Cohen buttresses his explanation by saying that 15,211 individuals above $200,000 *adjusted gross income* paid tax at an effective rate of 44.1% of adjusted gross income and 59.5% of taxable income. But this figure must be placed alongside the 32% effective rate on *actual income* shown in the Joint Economic Committee data referred to in the text, for only the latter provides the real story. The Treasury reference to *adjusted gross income* thus cloaks the essential matter at issue, as Representative Reuss observed in relation to Undersecretary Cohen's figures in the Hearings; see Hearings, note 19 above, at 169:

> Well, that sounds reassuring to somebody who doesn't know what adjusted gross income is. But is it not a fact that adjusted gross income is one of those lovely Treasury terms which deliberately excludes the very loophole income we are talking about — capital gain, oil depletion, tax exempt bonds, interest on life insurance savings, and so on? So that these people did make millions, taken together, on which they paid no tax whatever, and this 44% figure merely relates to that portion of their income which wasn't loophole income, isn't that so?

The glossing over by the Treasury of these important differences obviously spreads confusion and misunderstanding; e.g., 118 Cong. Rec. E7765 (daily ed. Sept. 7, 1972), containing a *Chicago Tribune* editorial relying on these Treasury figures to state that the rich are not escaping tax. Roger A. Freeman, *Tax Loopholes, The legend and the reality* (Washington, D.C. and Stanford, Calif., American Enterprise Institute for Public Policy Research and Hoover Institution on War, Revolution and Peace, 1973) also utilizes this material. Indeed, the pamphlet achieves its subtitle by a general disregard of the inefficiencies of tax expenditures.

22. Statement of Representative Henry S. Reuss, 118 Cong. Rec. H2258 (daily ed. March 20, 1972).

23. Statement of Representative Henry S. Reuss, 118 Cong. Rec. H4238 (daily ed. May 8, 1972). The total number of minimum-tax payers was 18,646, and the total tax $116,875,000. Statement of Representative Henry S. Reuss, 118 Cong. Rec. H2569,

2570 (daily ed. March 27, 1972). Preliminary data for 1971 are along the same lines; April 15, 1973 News Release by Senator Walter F. Mondale.

24. 1,302 individuals who showed no adjusted gross income paid some minimum tax, showing that they had actual incomes. Representative Reuss stated the incomes presumably averaged $86,600 ($30,000 exemption under minimum tax plus 10 times average minimum tax of $5,660 — the tax is 10%). Statement of March 27, 1972, note 23 above, at 2570.

25. See also Caplin, note 9 above, at 110, applying the 1969 Act changes, including the minimum tax, to examples in the Treasury Studies and similarly showing low effective rates on actual incomes.

26. The deduction for interest paid on loans involved in acquiring investment or business assets is considered as an appropriate expense in determining net income for an income tax. Interest on loans involved in consumer credit or mortgages on residences is considered a tax expenditure.

27. See Table 1.1 in Chapter 1 for the data. These estimates, largely from Treasury sources, are in a number of cases lower than those provided in the study presented to the Joint Economic Committee, note 15 above.

28. House Report, note 5 above, at 202.

29. The maximum deduction of $4,800 for child care phases out, 50 cents for each $1 of income over $18,000. The deduction for political contributions is limited to $100 for a joint return, with the alternative of a $25 credit for a contribution of $50.

30. See Appendix Tables for the distributive effect of homeowners' preferences and certain other itemized deductions. While the A set of tables includes imputed rental income of homes in homeowners' preferences, the effect should not differ appreciably when compared to that of mortgage interest and taxes, although the amounts would be reduced by about half; see note 16 above.

30–1. The present variation in horizontal equity among middle income groups is in large part traceable to these tax expenditure items. A counter-effect is the expansion of the standard deduction, an expansion made in part for simplicity and in part to produce greater horizontal equity. See the following from the Treasury Tax Reform Studies, note 1 above, at 76–79 (the "itemized personal deductions" there referred to are the consumer tax expenditure items described in the text):

> [For] taxpayers above the poverty levels up to the middle-high brackets, there is now a considerable range of effective tax rates due to variations in the ratio of itemized deductions to adjusted gross income (AGI). In the income ranges around $10,000 to $20,000, the bulk of taxpayers are distributed over a range in which the effective rate on the most favored is half the effective rate on the least favored.
>
> . . .
>
> These variations in rates arise due to itemized personal deductions. These deductions are also a source of complication on the tax return. Whether any taxpayer computes his correct tax depends upon his accuracy in recordkeeping and reporting, as well as upon his sophistication in knowing what is deductible. Further, the itemized deductions reflect at least some problems of tax policy. The homeowner gets the advantage of deducting the interest on his housing investment and his property tax, while the same expenses are borne by the tenant in his rent without their being deductible. Without arguing that particular itemized deductions should or should not be allowed, they should not make so much difference in tax liabilities for people at the same income level as the present variations in effective tax rates reflect.

. . .

Because the standard deduction no longer properly serves its intended purpose — to simplify the tax system for most taxpayers who have average levels of deductions — and because this failure creates unwarranted tax inequities between taxpayers who are able to itemize their personal deductions and those who are not able to separately itemize their deductions, it is proposed to expand the standard deduction and thereby restore it to its former relative position.

31. The text total is just a guess since the data do not permit an accurate assessment. The Treasury has stated that out of the aggregate of $5.9 billion (calendar year 1971) of tax expenditures allocable to individuals with over $100,000 of adjusted gross income, only $250 million represented tax shelter items with the bulk of the $5.9 billion derived from capital gains. Remarks of Undersecretary Edwin S. Cohen to the Tax Forum of the U.S. Chamber of Commerce, Nov. 29, 1972. The difficulty with this $250 million figure is that it relates to the $100,000 *adjusted gross income* class. But individuals with very low or negative adjusted gross incomes include tax shelter participants — that is the very cause of such low income. Hence more data are needed to obtain a reliable estimate. See text at note 9, and note 21 above.

32. A Federal Reserve Board study in 1966 showed that individuals in wealth units above $200,000 owned 65% of the publicly traded stock held by individuals, and 83% of marketable securities other than stock. They held 54% of all investment assets owned by individuals; Basic Facts: Distribution of Personal Income and Wealth in the United States, The Cambridge Institute (1972).

33. See Appendix Tables for the distributive effects of these tax expenditures. As to life insurance, see also Richard B. Goode, *The Individual Income Tax* (Washington, D.C., The Brookings Institution, 1964), 134–135.

34. See, e.g., Appendix Tables A-3 and A-4 and Table B-1. They obtain about 45% of the tax exempt interest benefits received by individuals.

35. These items are found under Health, Labor, and Welfare in the Tax Expenditure Budget.

36. Workmen's compensation benefits are for the most part paid to replace earnings lost due to a work-related injury or sickness, though a small part is compensation for physical loss and to that extent is not a tax expenditure.

37. While the exclusion of income earned abroad is limited to a maximum of $25,000, this amount comes off of the top layer of compensation. Moreover, the interaction of this exclusion with the mechanics of the credit for foreign taxes paid by the citizen residing abroad magnifies the effect of the exclusion in the case of higher-paid employees. See B. Hughel Wilkins, "A Note on the 'Gore Amendment'," 18 National Tax Journal 321 (1965).

38. The self-employed professional may be tempted to incorporate under special state professional corporation laws passed for this purpose, by which step he becomes a highly compensated executive and obtains all the assistance offered to that group.

39. See generally, George W. Hettenhouse, "Cost/Benefit Analysis of Executive Compensation," Harvard Business Review (July-August 1970) 114; John P. Kelsey and Joseph M. Buckheit, "The Impact of the Tax Reform Act of 1969 on Executive Compensation," 4 Indiana Legal Forum 246 (1970).

40. Deferred compensation arrangements — such as individual contracts to pay the executive at a later date money earned in the present — are not listed as tax expenditure items. But their present favorable treatment is considered by some as an improper application of the tax rules, and the area represents a situation in which the experts must do some more technical work.

41. The 1969 Act considerably reduced the tax benefits of the stock option arrangement.

42. The treatment of fringe benefits in general represents a zone of uncertainty under an income tax law, since a technical classification is required between items that represent compensation and items that represent only the character of working conditions in the industry or business. Included in the latter are arrangements where the measurement of benefit for a particular employee is either difficult or produces a *de minimis* amount not worth the administrative effort to value and tax. Thus, items such as ordinary employee merchandise discounts or low-cost company restaurants do not produce taxable compensation. Executives may receive special valuable fringe benefits; e.g., low interest rate loans, loan guarantees by the employer.

43. Code §1348. On the maximum tax in general, see Kelsey and Buckheit, note 39 above; Richard Reichler, "The Impact of the Maximum Tax on Earned Income on Compensation Planning," 29 New York University Tax Institute 1321 (1971); M. Gordon Ehrlich, "Tax Planning as Affected by the Maximum Tax on Earned Income," ibid. at 1471; David E. Watts, "The Maximum Tax on Earned Income: Section 1348," 26 Tax Law Review 1 (1970); Daniel I. Halperin, "Maximum Tax Not for Those Indulging in Deferred Compensation and Tax Preferences," 22 Southern California Tax Institute 619 (1972).

44. House Report, note 5 above, at 208.

45. The tax preferences are those covered by the minimum tax (see Chapter VIII), to the extent they exceed $30,000. Interestingly, "deferred compensation" — a term not readily definable — is not considered earned income for the purpose of the maximum tax.

46. The maximum tax may cause some executives to switch from stock options, deferred compensation arrangements, and the like, to additional current cash payments as the vehicle for increased compensation.

47. The Treasury Tax Reform Studies, note 1 above, at 17, recommended a maximum individual income tax, but of a far different order. This recommendation was that an individual not be required to pay more than one-half of his total income in income tax. The concept of "total income" was stressed. It was further stated that the establishment of such a maximum tax — which represented an effective 50% rate and not a marginal 50% rate — was feasible only in conjunction with the recommended income taxation of appreciated assets transferred at death, since a high proportion of those who would benefit from the maximum tax proposal would also be large holders of such assets. They thus now benefit from the present permanent exclusion of that appreciation in assets so transferred, and such result would be inconsistent with the concept of total income to be used for the maximum tax.

48. The items excluded are either paid by employers directly to employees (e.g., sick pay, death benefits) or are financed by employer payments made to plans, trust funds, and the like (e.g., pension payments, group term life insurance), to the state (e.g., workmen's compensation benefits), or as tax payments (e.g., payroll tax to finance unemployment insurance benefits). All of the payments are deductible by the employer from his income for his income tax purposes.

49. For a general summary of employee wage and benefit payments, see Chamber of Commerce of the United States, Employee Benefits, published biannually. Note also the following quoted from Jerome Rosow, Assistant Secretary for Policy Evaluation and Research in Department of Labor, *N.Y. Times,* Dec. 11, 1970 at 47, col.2:

> We get some very important insights from a pioneering survey of workingmen by the University of Michigan Survey Research Center. This study found that American workers generally expect that working entitles them to more than a

paycheck; that the lack of these extras is a source of worker concern, and that millions of workers — primarily in lower income categories — are *not* in jobs where employers provide such benefits as medical, surgical or hospital insurance; life insurance, retirement, or, for women workers, maternity leave.

It is generally thought that about one-half of nonagricultural workers are not covered by employee pension plans, and this one-half is to be found largely in small company employment. Many of the other one-half who are normally covered will never, because of vesting requirements, actually qualify for benefits or will receive an inadequate amount.

50. See Appendix Tables A-4 and A-5. "Transfer payments" in these tables include the exclusion of social security retirement payments, public assistance, workmen's compensation, unemployment insurance, and veterans disability payments. However, the social security retirement payments are by far the largest component. The total for these transfer payments is greatly in excess of the estimates in the Tax Expenditure Budget. These Appendix Tables A are constructed on a cumulative basis, so that the marginal rates applicable to the items included toward the last become much higher than for the first items. As Appendix Table A-3 indicates, the item of transfer payments is next to the last item covered. The tax benefit percentages under the Treasury and Joint Committee Staff estimates, Appendix Table B-1, are 20% for taxpayers over $10,000 income level and 12% for groups over $15,000.

51. See Appendix Table A-3.

52. See Appendix Table A-4.

53. See Appendix Table A-3.

54. See Economics of Federal Subsidy Programs, note 15 above, at 26; the changes indicated in that footnote are also made here. This table covers the same items as the previous tables from that study.

55. See Appendix Table A-4.

56. This table is derived by omitting from Table 3.5 the amounts, shown in Appendix Table A-4, for transfer payments and additional exemptions for aged and blindness (the latter is here negligible). While "transfer payments" in that table include more than exempt social security payments of the aged, see note 16 above, this component is by far the largest. Since the tax consequences of the items in Table A-4 are calculated on a cumulative basis, the total in text Table 3.6 for the remaining amounts is on the high side, since no adjustment was made in constructing that table for the effect on the cumulation of dropping the two items. Also, the aged themselves are included in the expanded AGI class and in present tax payments. But their numbers are so small that the table essentially represents the effects on the non-aged of removing their tax expenditure benefits.

57. Text Table 3.7 is from Appendix Table A-5 in Economics of Federal Subsidy Programs, note 15 above, at 36. See note 56 above for the derivation of text Table 3.8. For another table showing the same general effect as text Table 3.7, see Martin Pfaff and Anita B. Pfaff, "The Grants Economy as Regulator of the Exchange Economy," in The Economics of Federal Subsidy Programs, note 15 above, at 120, 151.

58. See Statement of Philip M. Stern, in Hearings on the Economics of Federal Subsidy Programs before the Subcommittee on Priorities and Economy in Government, note 15 above, at 73; Philip M. Stern, *The Rape of the Taxpayer* (New York, Random House, 1973) chapter 1. The numbers in this material are based on the Pechman and Okner study, note 15 above, and unlike the text tables include the effects of income-splitting for married couples. Those effects are not, however, really important for the top brackets.

59. Treasury Tax Reform Studies, note 1 above, at 99–100.

60. Commercial banks had been allowed by administrative ruling a reserve for bad debts (to reflect possibly uncollectible loans) determined for each bank on the basis of an industry-wide 2.4% figure, which was applied by a bank to its noninsured loans outstanding. On the basis of *actual* bank loss experience — the rule applied to other corporations — the reserve rate would be around 0.2% of loans. The 1969 Act requires a change to the figure of 1.8% until 1976; 1.2% until 1982; 0.6% until 1988; and thereafter actual experience. Code §585. Under the transitional rules, commercial banks presently over their reserve limits will in effect be limited to a deduction of actual losses.

Mutual savings banks and savings and loan associations by law had been allowed reserves equal to 60% of taxable income or 3% of qualifying real property loans. The 1969 Act eliminated the 3% method (used by mutual savings banks mostly) and reduced the 60% figure to 40% by 1979. This will still leave a reserve far more generous than actual loss experience would permit, and means 40% of economic income goes untaxed. Code §§593, 596. The Act also straightened out technical defects in the prior formula which had made it even more generous. The Act, however, still leaves some technical defects operative, such as the mechanics of the intercorporate dividend deduction, which can reduce the taxes of mutual savings banks investing in corporate stocks.

For the effect of the prior rules, see the material on Tax Treatment of Financial Institutions, in Treasury Tax Reform Studies, note 1 above, at 458–475. For a discussion of the 1969 changes, as well as the prior rules, see Daniel I. Halperin, "Federal Income Taxation of Banks," 64 National Tax Association Proceedings 307 (1971).

61. For the prior effect, see references note 60 above.

62. The data are from a talk by Emil M. Sunley, Jr., Office of the Secretary of the Treasury, before the Cornell Executive Development Program, June 1972; the material is arranged differently. Since the revenue effect of the excess depreciation will about double over the next few years, this could reduce the text figures to around 34.3% and 40%.

63. Charles L. Schultze et al., *Setting National Priorities, The 1973 Budget* (Washington, D.C., Brookings Institution, 1972), 402–405. See also Nancy H. Teeters, "Built-in Flexibility of Federal Expenditures," 3 Brookings Papers on Economic Activity 615, 616 (1971).
The Joint Economic Committee has stated:

> One indication of the unfairness of the tax burden can be seen in the shifting composition of the Federal tax system away from the relatively progressive individual and corporate income taxes. . . . Individual income taxes drop as a share of the total tax burden from about 46 percent in fiscal 1969 to an estimated 43 percent in fiscal 1973. At the same time, corporate income taxes, which in 1960 provided 23 percent of total revenue, drop from 20 percent in 1969 to an estimated 16 percent in 1973. Taken together, this represents about a 7 percent decrease in the most progressive Federal taxes in only 4 years. During the same time social insurance taxes rose from almost 21 to an estimated 29 percent, or approximately 8 percent. Thus, the effect of the revenue changes from fiscal 1969 to fiscal 1973 has been to shift the tax burden away from the relatively progressive income taxes to the more regressive payroll taxes.

Joint Economic Committee, 1972 Joint Economic Report, S.Rep. No. 708, 92d Cong., 2d Sess. 34 (1972).

64. Pechman, note 20 above, at 188. Part of the difference is due to the inclusion in family income of accrued but unrealized appreciation on capital assets and imputed rent on owner-occupied houses, items not in the Tax Expenditure Budget.

65. The natural resources industries receive the major portion of the Western Hemisphere Trade Corporation benefit. This benefit essentially provides a 34% instead of a 48% rate for income from operating activities in the Western Hemisphere outside the United States. It thus covers the branch operations in Latin America of natural resources companies, which operations are in branch form to obtain the benefits of percentage depletion and the intangible drilling expense deduction.

66. The Tax Expenditure Budget estimate of $325 million is apparently based on the assumption that, if deferral of tax for foreign subsidiaries were eliminated, those subsidiaries would repatriate half their earnings through dividend distributions and the foreign withholding taxes would offset United States tax remaining after tax credit for the foreign taxes on the subsidiary profits. But this assumption as to repatriation may be too high, and if it is, the estimate should be much higher — perhaps double. See Peggy B. Musgrave, "Tax Preferences to Foreign Investment," in The Economics of Federal Subsidy Programs, Part 2 – International Subsidies, Joint Economic Committee, 92d Cong., 2d Sess. 176, 192 (June 11, 1972).

67. This appears to be the result for the total of the United States income tax and creditable foreign income taxes in relation to worldwide income, the figure comparable to the earlier Treasury Study. However, the U.S. oil companies appear to have large excess foreign tax credits for payments to foreign countries in which their oil is located, and these excess credits were not counted in the Treasury Study. If these unused credits are added, the effective rate on worldwide income may be around 40%. See data prepared by Price Waterhouse & Co. for 1970, made available by the American Petroleum Institute, and referred to in James C. Cox and Arthur W. Wright, "The Economics of the Oil Industry's Tax Burden," in *The Petroleum Industry's Tax Burden* (Arlington, Va., 1973, Taxation With Representation). The critical question here is whether these very large foreign payments are really "taxes," as the Treasury technically so classifies them, or either "royalty payments" or "excise taxes," in which event they would be deductible expenses but not available to be offset as credits against U.S. taxes on foreign income. Prof. Adelman points out that since the payments are essentially computed on the basis of "fictional" receipts derived from artificial prices, the tax per barrel is completely independent of actual receipts and only slightly affected by costs. The tax base is thus not related to net profits, and in this light the taxes are excise taxes. The industry price structure reflects this view. See M. A. Adelman, "Is the Oil Shortage Real?," Foreign Policy (Winter 1972–73) 85.

68. See the material on Tax Treatment of Timber, in Treasury Tax Reform Studies, note 1 above, at 434–438.

69. See material referred to in note 60 above. This material, however, does not take account of the recent entrance of commercial banks into tax-sheltered leasing (see Chapter IV), and for some banks this new tax expenditure activity may outweigh in tax reduction importance the tax-exempt interest benefit. Joseph W. Barr, a banker himself, states in "A Revised Regulatory Framework," in *Policies for a More Competitive Financial System* (Boston, Mass., Federal Reserve Bank of Boston, 1972) 205: "[The] *largest* commercial banks are heading pell mell towards or have reached a zero U.S. income tax rate because of their use of accelerated depreciation and the investment credit in their leasing companies and the application of the foreign tax credit to their foreign income." (207). For a discussion of bank lessors, see Vincent John McGugan, "Competition and Adjustment in the Equipment Leasing Industry," Research Report No. 51, Federal Reserve Bank of Boston (November 1972); C. Rogers

Childs, Jr. and William G. Gridley, Jr., "Leveraged Leasing and the Reinvestment Rate Fallacy," 156 The Bankers Magazine 53 (1973).

70. See Halperin, note 60 above, at 330. The text estimate for the commercial banks may be on the high side. It does not take account of the entrance of these banks into tax shelter leasing; see note 69 above. Those mutual savings banks that invest in corporate stocks are significantly tax-assisted by the imperfections in the mechanics of the intercorporate dividends received deduction; see Halperin, ibid, at 322–323. See also D. Kenneth Biederman, *Federal Income Taxation of Savings and Loan and Commerical Banking Industries* (Washington, D.C., National League of Insured Savings Associations, 1973), giving an estimate of 17.5% for commerical banks (1972) and 20.6% for savings and loan associations (1971); the latter figure would be 27% if the 1969 Act changes were fully in effect.

71. Representative Charles Vanik, in a statement before the Joint Economic Committee, has compiled data on the tax situation of the largest industrial corporations; see Hearings, note 19 above, at 3. The information was based on reports filed with the SEC, annual corporate reports, and other public information, and not on income tax returns. These data show that some major corporations paid zero tax and some tax at low effective rates, though all had book profits. Unfortunately, the data do not provide information on foreign taxes paid or on net operating loss carryover situations. Nor do the data indicate which tax factors contributed to the low or zero tax payments. This is the result of limitations inherent in the material on which the data were based. But the results strongly point to serious escapes from taxation by many large corporations. There is clearly a responsibility on the Treasury Department to probe further, using its income tax return sources.

CHAPTER IV: OPERATIONAL ASPECTS OF
TAX EXPENDITURES: TAX DEFERRAL AND
TAX SHELTERS

1. Where the employee's benefits in the pension plan are not vested, an immediate inclusion of the employer contribution in his income would not be appropriate. Lump-sum pension distributions on retirement are in some situations given capital gain treatment as well, so that deferral here means some permanent exclusion.

2. Some economists might call the exclusion of gifts and bequests a tax expenditure since they would regard the receipt of a gift or bequest as income. But, as discussed in the Appendix to Chapter I, the basic concept of an income tax has not so evolved.

3. The statutory basis for the administrative rulings providing these exclusions is left either unstated or unclear in the rulings. The earlier rulings, as on social security benefits, simply stated the end results, I.T. 3447, 1941–1 Cum. Bull. 191, restated in Rev. Rul. 70–217, 1970–1 Cum. Bull. 12 (social security benefits); I.T. 3230, 1938–2 Cum. Bull. 136 (unemployment benefits). Later rulings, as on public assistance training allowances, refer to exclusion of payments made in the interest of the general welfare or for promotion of the general welfare, Rev. Rul. 63–136, 1963–2 Cum. Bull. 19 (payments to jobs service corpsmen to assist school dropouts and others).

4. The exclusion of this interest is not reflected in a statutory provision or indeed in administrative ruling. It just exists.

5. As described later, the present capital gain benefit is by way of deduction, though previously it was by exclusion. And some aspects of the capital gain benefit, such as

the nontaxation at death of appreciation in value of assets transferred, although the fair market value of the asset becomes the tax basis for the heir or other recipient, is essentially an exclusion from income. Also, sections providing for nonrecognition of gain in transactions involving corporate mergers or other reorganizations, or the exchange of one building for another, essentially operate by way of current exclusion, with possible offsetting effect in later years depending on whether the asset is sold or held until death.

Imputed rent from the ownership of a home is excluded by administrative action never considering such rent to be a form of income. It is not listed as a tax expenditure, as explained in the Appendix to Chapter I.

6. The exclusion device is used for scholarships and fellowships, here treated as a consumption item since the items essentially pay for tuition. Also, when appreciated property is contributed as a charitable contribution, the nontaxation of the appreciation as income is essentially an exclusion. Political contributions are benefited by a credit against tax as well as a deduction, depending on which route is more beneficial.

7. See also note 5, above.

8. The sections providing for nonrecognition of gain on certain transactions, see note 5, above, do operate as a deferral of tax since the excluded appreciation is preserved for possible future taxation through holding down the tax basis of the new asset received on the exchange of the appreciated asset.

9. The assistance given to shipping operations combines a number of devices. Under the Merchant Marine Act (see Pub. L. No. 91–469 [H.R. 15424] (Oct. 21, 1970)), shipowners are allowed to reduce taxable income by deposits into a construction fund, and gain from the sale or other disposition of a ship is excluded from income if deposited into such a fund. The earnings of the fund are also excluded. Vessels constructed with the proceeds of the fund have their basis for depreciation reduced below actual cost to reflect the earlier tax benefits. Under the Tax Code, shipping operations conducted through tax haven foreign corporations are excepted from the provisions currently taxing tax haven corporations and instead receive the deferral of tax given to foreign subsidiaries not involving tax haven operations (Code §954(b)(2)). Shipping operations conducted by foreign corporations with ships registered in a less developed country receive the benefits accorded to less developed country corporations (Code §955(c)(2)).

10. In general, see Code §263; Treas. Reg., §1.263(a)-1, 2.

11. The Senate Finance Committee, Tax Reform Act of 1969, S. Rep. No. 552, 91st Cong., 1st Sess. 95 (1969) describes these various farm rules as follows:

Under present law, income or losses from farming may be computed under more liberal accounting rules than those generally applicable in the case of other types of business activities. In general, where a significant factor in a business is the production or sale of merchandise, the taxpayer must use an accrual method of accounting and inventories. The effect of these accounting rules is to postpone the deduction of the costs of the merchandise until the accounting period in which the income from its sale is realized. These rules need not be followed, however, with respect to income or deductions from farming. In other words, a cash accounting method may be used for this purpose under which costs are deducted as incurred. A taxpayer in the business of farming is also allowed to deduct expenditures for developing a business asset which other taxpayers would have to capitalize.

For instance, the expenses of raising a breeding herd of livestock may be currently deducted. The same thing is true of expenditures to develop a fruit orchard. There also are certain other capital expenditures in connection with farming operations which a taxpayer may elect to currently deduct from ordinary income. The capital expenditures which qualify for this treatment are soil and water conservation expenditures (sec. 175), fertilizer costs (sec. 180), and land-clearing expenditures (sec. 182). Under normal business accounting rules, these expenditures would be added to the basis of the farm property and, thus, would reduce the amount of capital gain realized when the property is sold. However, by allowing these expenses to be currently deducted, they reduce ordinary income rather than capital gain income.

12. The builders of shelters seek to utilize every possible acceleration device. Thus, in addition to those described, there is also the use of first-year additional depreciation, over any amount otherwise available in that year, equal to 20% of the cost of an asset but limited to a maximum of $4,000 deduction on a joint return (section 179); while intended for "small business," it can be one more piece added to a shelter. Also, there are possibilities in the prepayment of interest expense, despite the sharp limitation imposed in 1968 on that device, Rev. Rul. 68–643, 1968–2 Cum. Bull. 76.

13. The Senate Finance Committee Report for the 1969 Act, note 11 above at 212, describes the real estate shelter in these terms:

Accelerated depreciation will frequently allow deductions in excess of the amount required to service the mortgage during the early life of the property, thus producing in many cases a tax loss deductible against other income even though there is a positive cash flow. In addition, accelerated depreciation usually produces a deduction far in excess of the actual decline in the usefulness of the property. In addition, by holding the property for 10 years, the taxpayer can arrange to have all the gain resulting from excess depreciation (which was offset against ordinary income) taxed as a section 1231 gain, at capital gain rates. The tax advantage increases as the taxpayer's income moves into higher tax brackets.

As a result of the fast depreciation and the ability to deduct amounts in excess of the taxpayer's equity, economically profitable real estate operations normally produce substantial tax losses, sheltering from income tax the economic profit of the operation and permitting avoidance of income tax on the owner's other ordinary income, such as salary and dividends. Later, the property can be sold and the excess of the sale price over the remaining basis is treated as capital gain except for the limitations in section 1250.

Because of the present tax situation, when investment is solicited in a real estate venture it has become the practice to promise a prospective investor substantial tax losses which can be used to diminish the tax on his income from other sources. Thus, there is, in effect, substantial dealing in "tax losses" produced by depreciable real property.

14. That is, a company needing equipment has the alternative of itself buying the equipment and depreciating the cost in its tax return. Presumably, in this case it would finance the purchase with a bank loan or other borrowing. But the company may not be in a position to secure adequate financing. Or the company may not desire more borrowing to show up on its balance sheet. Or it may have operating losses, so that the depreciation deduction is not useful. Hence, if it turns to leasing as an alternative, it in effect is letting the lessor-owner take the depreciation deduction. Indeed, a corporation to whom a depreciation deduction only offsets income taxable at a 48% rate may simply prefer to lease from individuals in the 70% bracket, since the

depreciation deduction is thus "worth more" to those individuals and they will "divide" the additional benefit (difference between 70% and 48%) with the lessee.

Some equipment leasing companies with a large volume of leases do make a before-tax profit because of that volume and the differential between the interest rate at which they can obtain large amounts of borrowed funds and the rate implicit in their arrangements with their lessees. Presumably this profit would result without the investment credit or accelerated depreciation. The large amounts of accelerated depreciation that are built up produce considerable tax net operating losses for the lessors. Hence, these companies are usually found as subsidiaries or divisions of concerns with other enterprises showing tax profits, to be offset by the leasing tax losses. Bank holding companies with leasing subsidiaries or banks with a leasing department are another example. However, since the typical bank lease relies on the tax advantages for its profitability, the volume of leasing for a particular bank is set by the level of the bank's otherwise taxable income; without other taxable income to be offset, the bank's leasing operations would be unprofitable. Provident National Bank and Lease Financing Corporation, "What Every Banker Should Know About Leveraged Leasing" (1972). For a detailed discussion of equipment leasing, see Vincent John McGugan, "Competition and Adjustment in the Equipment Leasing Industry," Research Report No. 51, Federal Reserve Bank of Boston (Nov. 1972).

There is an underlying legal question whether these equipment leases are really "leases" or are "sales" with the financing provided by the purported "lessor." If they are sales, then the "lessee" and not the lessor obtains the accelerated depreciation and other tax expenditure benefits and the tax magic disappears. The tax borderline between sale and lease requires more attention, as the following from Stanley S. Surrey, "Tax Reform and the Treatment of Capital Expenditures," 115 Cong. Rec. 11,952 (1969) indicates:

> It would seem possible to reach this [leasing] abuse through administrative action, by a more careful delineation between genuine lease transactions and transactions which are essentially financing arrangements for acquisitions of equipment by the purported "lessee." The delineation can be in terms of the portion of the asset retained by the lessor at the end of the lease, taken at its present value and compared to the cost of the asset. If that present value is significant in relation to that cost and is used as the expected salvage value which cannot be currently depreciated, a lease is involved. The depreciation deduction and the credit would then be properly available to the lessors. But if that value is not significant, a sale and not a lease is present and the depreciation deduction and credit properly belong to the user of the property and not to the purported lessor. His role in this situation is that of financing the acquisition by the user, just as in the case of a loan used by the borrower to acquire property. The determination of what is a significant value could be based on a formula which would remove the tax motivations from these arrangements and thereby separate out the transactions that are not based on a pre-tax profit that is economically rational.

The emphasis here is on the present value of the future residual, discounted, of course, for time. The Internal Revenue Service previously did not pay attention to the discount aspect, so that residuals far in the future qualified the transaction as a lease regardless of present value. It seems now to be shifting to the present value approach. TMM 72–18, Sept. 4, 1972, at 9 (Tax Management, Bureau of National Affairs).

There are some lawyers who contend a lease need not have a residual value to be a true lease. While this contention seems difficult to sustain, if it is valid a possible approach to the needed delineation in this situation would be that of testing a lease that does not have a residual value as if it were a financial transaction and seeing if the implicit interest rate is a reflection of market rates. If it is not, then the transaction depends for its market efficacy on its tax advantages and should not be regarded as a "lease" but rather a dealing in those advantages.

15. This facet of the tax shelter raises the interesting question of what Code §183, added in 1969, is referring to when it speaks of "an activity not engaged in for profit." This section, whose history relates to the problem of individuals seeking to deduct the costs of "hobbies" or other nonprofitable ventures, disallows deductions attributable to the activities referred to in the quotation. Clearly the investors in tax shelters are not investing in the before-tax profit yielded in these transactions, but only in the after-tax result. As the text indicates, they are investing in a tax deduction. Does the real thrust of §183 lie in requiring an expectation of a realistic before-tax profit, one commensurate with the investor's normal investment outlook? Should the existence of a small before-tax profit, a paltry plus, in some of these shelters be enough to provide safe conduct to an investor who in his other, not tax-sheltered, investments seeks a far greater before-tax return? For a discussion of the case law prior to §183, see George E. Zeitlin, "Tax Planning in Equipment-Leasing Shelters," 21 Southern California Tax Institute 621 (1969). Also on leasing, see William M. Goldstein, "Equipment Leasing After the 1969 Act," 29 New York University Tax Institute 1589 (1971).

16. For example, as to real estate shelters, see the Report of the Real Estate Advisory Committee, Securities and Exchange Commission (Oct. 12, 1972), 68, stressing that this aspect should be spelled out in prospectuses of real estate limited partnerships.

Corporations, in the 48% bracket, are also investors in shelters, such as rental housing or equipment leases. For a discussion of equipment leasing, see McGugan, note 14, above.

17. A major cattle tax shelter program, Black Watch Farms, Inc., did fail in 1970 — and, as the *Wall Street Journal* reported: "That left the herd owners, who included such as doctors, stock brokers and other affluent investors who knew little about the care of cattle, stuck with the responsibility for thousands of animals scattered on ranges across the country." *Wall Street Journal,* April 6, 1971, at 36, col.1; see also Sept. 1, 1971, at 1, col.5. For another article on the company and its bankruptcy, see *Farm Journal* (November 1970), 18, implying rapid growth and management problems as the sources of the trouble.

18. A partnership itself does not pay an income tax under the Code. Instead, the partnership computes its income and deductions, following the rules generally applicable to individuals. Then each partner picks up his share of income and deductions according to the partnership agreement, and uses those items directly on his return. A partnership may have a few partners or hundreds — an oil drilling partnership may have eight hundred partners. A general partner may form a number of partnerships; thus, an oil drilling program may involve a dozen or so different limited partnerships for a year's operations.

In many respects the tax rules regarding partnerships and even the nontax rules are in large part being developed around the use of the limited partnership to further tax shelters, and are being molded by skillful lawyers for just this purpose.

19. Or the Governor becomes a cattle rancher; see "Reagan May Have Found a Tax Shelter in Cattle Breeding Herds," *N.Y. Times,* June 13, 1971, at 71, col.1; Dec. 5, 1971, at 69, col.3.

The following is from an article by Peter Barnes in the *San Francisco Bay Guardian,* August 3, 1972, as printed in 118 Cong. Rec. H7618 (daily ed. Aug. 14, 1972):

The talk wasn't only of ophthalmology and orthopedics at the recent convention of the American Medical Association. On one day the announcement board at the Fairmont Hotel listed, among others, the following meetings: Tax Sheltered Investment Financial in the Bali Room, Mountain Shadows Ranch Tax Shelter Investments in the Garden Room and Gemini Financial Tax Counsel in the Crocker Room.

The following is from an article describing the new fringe benefit of free investment counseling services provided by some companies for their key executives, *Wall Street Journal,* Aug. 3, 1972, at 1, col.6:

> Many recipients of the new fringe benefit are almost pathetically grateful for the advice they get. Consider the case of Mr. Smith (not his real name), who is the chief financial executive of a huge Midwestern company. Mr. Smith may have known his way around the world of debentures and corporate tax dodges, but he admits his own affairs were untidy, to say the least. He estimates he will save $40,000 to $60,000 this year on tax shelters alone, brought to him by the financial adviser hired by the company. "I'd never used shelters before," the executive says. "I guess I spent too much time working."

The following is from The Talk of the Town, in the *New Yorker,* (Oct. 17, 1970), 33:*

> Now that the passengers hijacked by Arab guerrillas have been released unharmed, our attention has returned to a tantalizing sentence in one *Times* account of the guerrillas' destruction of the Pan American 747 jet in Cairo. "The jet, which is owned by the First National City Bank and another bank, not identified, is leased to Pan Am with the Bankers Trust Company as trustee," the *Times* said. Naive enough to have believed that a Pan American jet would be owned by Pan American, we were amazed to have the *Times* inform us — in one sentence, as if reporting a routine business arrangement familiar to all — that the plane was owned by a jumble of banks, one of them anonymous. (Could it be, we wondered, that in the world of high finance there are not only numbered bank accounts but numbered banks?) We were curious enough to approach a financially astute friend of ours, a man we'll call Martin G. Cashflow, and ask him to explain who owns what.
> "No big corporation owns what it appears to own," Cashflow said. "It wouldn't make sense taxwise."
> "But why would a group of banks own a 747?" we asked.
> "The banks don't actually own the 747," Cashflow said. "No bank owns what it appears to own."
> We were more puzzled than ever. "You mean even the banks that aren't anonymous are not really the banks that own the 747?" we asked.
> "That's not the point," Cashflow replied. "The banks probably represent a bunch of trust-account customers who have grouped together to buy a 747."
> "But why would a bunch of trust-account customers want a 747?" we asked. "Would they all be going to the same place at the same time? Three hundred and sixty-two of them?"
> "They don't want a 747," Cashflow said, in the manner of someone explaining the milk-producing property of cows to a well-behaved but slow-witted child. "They want the depreciation."

"Depreciation?"

"Depreciation," Cashflow said. "For tax purposes, depreciation cancels out income, and airplanes happen to have a very good depreciation picture. In five or six years, they can be totally depreciated, and then they can be sold."

"But who would want to buy a totally depreciated airplane?" we protested. "If it's totally depreciated, it doesn't exist."

"Of course it exists," Cashflow said, trying to keep a condescending smile from surfacing. "It's only for tax purposes that it's totally depreciated. It would still fly, and show movies, and all that. Also, it would be very valuable for the next owner, because he could totally depreciate it all over again."

We considered the hijacking for a while in the light of the new information provided by Cashflow. "Aha!" we said, at last. "Then the Arab guerrillas made a mistake. They're supposed to be against the American government. But by blowing up the 747 they destroyed twenty-four million dollars' worth of depreciation, and that means that the trust-account customers will now have to pay the American government taxes on the income from twenty-four million dollars that was going to be cancelled out by the depreciation, and the government can use the money to put armed guards on 747s and send Phantom jets to Israel and replace burned-out U.S.I.A. libraries."

"Don't be silly," Cashflow said. "The plane was fully insured, and nine and half million dollars of the insurance was carried by the government, which will now have nine and a half million dollars less to spend on guards and jets and libraries. For people without professional tax advice, those guerrillas aren't so stupid."

"Except that they have one big problem left," we said. "They're Marxist revolutionaries, and what's the use of being Marxist revolutionaries if no one owns what he appears to own? If they took everything away from the big corporations and the banks, they still wouldn't have anything."

"Are you kidding?" Cashflow said. "They'd have some fantastically valuable depreciation."

*Reprinted by permission;©1970 The New Yorker Magazine, Inc.

20. A sponsor of cattle shelters announced "nationwide special public meetings for highly-taxed individuals and corporations" in sixteen cities to present its year-end 1970 cattle feeding program; "the General Partner estimates 80–85% of an investment is tax deductible in 1970."

The use of tax shelters is not restricted to syndicated partnerships. Corporations with income from other sources can operate tax shelter activities, with the shelter tax losses offsetting the other income. See the following from a statement made by Senator Robert P. Griffin in introducing a bill regarding farm tax shelters used by corporations, 118 Cong. Rec. S15,216 (daily ed. Sept. 19, 1972):

Mr. Griffin. Mr. President, today I am introducing a bill (S. 4008) to close a tax loophole that now gives some large corporations an unfair advantage over small family farmers.

At present, most business losses are deductible for Federal income tax purposes. Some of the corporate conglomerates capitalize on this by operating agricultural businesses at a loss in order to offset income from other profitable nonagricultural activities. This "tax-loss farming" by some corporations means unfair competition for the family farmer and it means a loss of revenue for our Government.

Farming activity represents the sole source of income for most small farmers. It is their very means of survival. The risks are great. Adverse weather conditions, crop disease, and market conditions are just a few of many factors that can spell financial disaster for the small family farmer.

Losses from farming activities do not, however, necessarily have a serious impact on conglomerates. These large corporations can use farm losses to reduce their Federal income tax liability by offsetting them against profits from other profitmaking activities.

Use of the consolidated return makes this possible. Profits and losses from various operations are combined on a single balance sheet.

. . . .

Under the legislation I am introducing, a corporation would not be allowed to offset a farming loss except to the extent that income is actually derived from farming activity.

In recent years, a number of family-operated farms have elected the corporate form for their business operations. Family farms would still have that option under my legislation. The bill would simply preclude corporations from using farming activities as a tax dodge to reduce Federal taxes due on the profits from other nonfarming activities. Farm corporations that do not have nonfarm income would not be affected by the legislation.

According to the most recent Internal Revenue Service figures, 8,696 of the 20,468 corporations engaged in farming in 1969 reported deficits on their farming operations. These corporations claimed losses of $221,987,000 for 1969.

We must close this glaring tax loophole and eliminate the unfair competition resulting from tax-loss farming by large corporations.

21. Whenever tax depreciation is faster than actual depreciation, there is the potential for substantial tax benefit, and tax architects will strive to erect a tax shelter on the foundation so offered. Thus, motion pictures and their tax treatment have recently been used by some as the foundation of a new variant of tax shelter, though here the rating by the courts may be a low one unless the shelter is very carefully constructed; see *Carnegie Productions, Inc. v. Commissioner,* 59 T.C.— (No. 63) (1973). The contracts of professional athletes offer rapid depreciation possibilities for the owners of teams in the various sport leagues.

22. The reason many of those promoting these syndications, such as real estate developers, have tax expenditure deductions to sell is because they already have sheltered all of their own income.

23. See Chapters VI and VII. See also Paul R. McDaniel, "Tax Shelters and Tax Policy," National Tax Association – Tax Institute of America Symposium on Tax Reform (1973).

24. An announcement of a 1970 cattle feeding tax shelter program states:

Cattle feeding attracts investors because it offers the right combination of tax economics:

(1) Cattle represent strong asset values — almost all of the capital costs can be borrowed.

(2) Investor's money is used mostly for tax-deductible items paid and deducted near the start of the Program in 1970.

(3) No income is reportable until the fat cattle are sold.

25. Under these tax shelter funds, large oil companies would provide leases to the

fund for cash and a 71% nonrecourse note. If the drilling is unsuccessful, the partnership can in effect default and the note need not be paid. If the drilling is successful, the oil company has an option to acquire an interest in the well through cancellation of the note. The limited partners in the drilling fund are thus drilling largely with borrowed money and in effect securing three additional dollars of deductions via borrowed money for each dollar of deduction resulting from their own funds — hence, so-called "3 for 1" deals. In addition, the funds expect to receive capital gain treatment on the sale of the successful wells, in exchange for the cancellation of the note. Such a fund has received (in 1970) an opinion of counsel supporting the planned tax consequences, but stating "As in any sophisticated planning program, a degree of risk is involved which we understand will be spelled out to the limited partners" and that, as to the capital gain feature, "the risk of ordinary income treatment is well within acceptable tolerances for the knowledgeable investor."

The Internal Revenue Service, however, is beginning to question these funds; e.g., see Rev. Rul. 72–135, 1972–1 Cum.Bull. 200, stating that such a "loan" made by the general partner was in reality a capital contribution and not a loan, so that the limited partners could not utilize the leverage for tax purposes. In Rev. Rul. 72–350, 1972–2 Cum.Bull. 394, the Service further stated that a loan to such a fund by a non-partner was not really a loan but capital placed at risk, and hence the partners here also could not use the leverage for tax purposes. The Service would have been inherently skeptical of a loan by a non-partner with no security except the partners' funds to be used in drilling. To overcome that skepticism, these funds had given the lender a right to convert its creditor position into an interest in the venture itself if the well proved successful. But the Service recognized that under this arrangement the "creditor" position would be short-lived: if the well were unsuccessful that would be the end of the matter; if it were successful, the "creditor" would convert to an equity position; which scenario would develop would be soon determined.

See Robert T. Johnson, "What CPAs Should Know About Oil and Gas Tax Shelters," Journal of Accountancy 56 (Oct. 1972).

26. For further discussions of some of these tax shelters, see Chapter V. See also the descriptions of the real estate shelter in Statements by Adrian W. DeWind and Jerome Kurtz in Panel No. 4, Panel Discussions on General Tax Reform, before the House Ways and Means Committee, 93d Cong., 1st Sess. 520 and 553 (1973) and its defense in Statements by Alan J. B. Aronsohn and Wallace R. Woodbury, at 507 and 526; the descriptions of the cattle, orchard, and farm shelters in Statements by Charles Davenport and Roland L. Hjorth in Panel No. 5, at 615 and 646 and their defense in Statements by Herrick K. Lidstone and Claude M. Maer, Jr. at 635 and 654; also the discussion of shelters in Statements by Paul R. McDaniel (real estate, leasing, and oil), Martin D. Ginsburg (in general) and Kenneth A. Goldman (motion pictures and in general) in Panel No. 6, at 697, 879, and 855, and their defense in Statements by J. Waddy Bullion (oil), Wayne E. Chapman (real estate), and Milton A. Dauber (oil), at 868, 890, and 719. See also, as to equipment leasing, McDaniel, note 23 above.

For an overall description, see Hugh Calkins and Kenneth E. Updegraft, Jr., "Tax Shelters," 28 The Tax Lawyer 493 (1973). Philip M. Stern, *The Rape of the Taxpayer* (Random House, New York, 1973) also contains descriptions, though in a different style, of these tax shelters.

27. The text at this point is partially based on Stanley S. Surrey, "The Tax Reform Act of 1969 — Tax Deferral and Tax Shelters," 12 Boston College Industrial and Commercial Law Review 307 (1971).

28. See generally Hearings on Tariff and Trade Proposals before the House Ways and Means Committee, 91st Cong., 2d Sess. 499 et seq. (1970); Hearings on

Amendments 925 and 1009 to H.R. 17550 before the Senate Committee on Finance, 91st Cong., 2d Sess. 9 et seq. (1970). This proposal, to establish a tax vehicle called a "Domestic International Sales Corporation" to handle exports, was adopted in the Revenue Act of 1971, but Congress limited the deferral to 50% of export income. See Code §§991–997.

29. Statements by President Nixon and Treasury Secretary David M. Kennedy on Asset Depreciation Range, January 11, 1971, CCH Stand. 1971 Fed. Tax Rep. ¶6366.

This explanation of deferral does influence legislators. See the following statement of Senator Robert Taft, Jr., Cong. Rec. S6213 (daily ed. May 5, 1971):

> One democratic hopeful has said that the proposed ADR system is, "nothing more than a shallow attempt to permit businessmen to avoid paying tax." Accelerated depreciation is not a tax avoidance device at all. It simply defers the time when taxes are paid. By taking the depreciation now, instead of in later years, the businessman simply generates cash flow which can be used to modernize his plant and equipment. By taking depreciation now there will be less depreciation to take later and taxes will be accelerated in later years when capital equipment has been modernized and the plant is more efficient and productive.

There are two errors in this view. The first is in failing to see the present value to a taxpayer of money retained through having to pay a tax only in later years rather than now, or, put differently, the lesser money cost of paying $1 some years from now rather than now. This is discussed in the subsequent text. The second error comes from looking only at a particular asset rather than the taxpayer and all his assets. In a stable business, as each asset is replaced, the deferral of tax on that asset offsets increased taxes on other assets as their deferral is ended, so that the original deferral in effect is never made up. In a growing business, the additional assets contribute still more deferral. See the following from Rudolph J. Englert, "How to Minimize Corporate Taxable Income," in Peter C. Reid, *Corporate and Executive Tax Sheltered Investments* (New York, Presidents Publishing House, Inc., 1972), 42–45:

> Equally helpful are timing differences that accelerate deductions for tax purposes. Consider depreciation, for example. Many companies now use accelerated depreciation for tax reporting purposes. This is one basis for a tax-sheltered investment: the income taxes are minimized with no unfavorable effect on reported earnings.
>
> . . . .
>
> A slightly more complex example of this accounting principle is illustrated by the [following] financial balance sheet. . . . Income before depreciation and taxes each year is assumed to be $1 million. During the first year, the company purchased machinery for $1,100,000, with an estimated life of ten years, after which it would have no salvage value. For financial reporting purposes, the company uses straight-line depreciation of $110,000 a year. But for tax purposes the company turns to the accelerated sum-of-the-years digits method, providing depreciation of 10/55 of the total cost for the first year, 9/55 the second year, 8/55 the third year, and so on.
>
> A look at the timing differences in the tax accounting and the financial accounting reveals how tax benefits can be achieved without hurting reported earnings. For both tax and accounting purposes, income before depreciation and tax comes to $1 million. For financial reporting purposes, depreciation is

$110,000, but for tax purposes it is $200,000, almost twice as much. Income before tax is thus $890,000 for financial purposes, $800,000 for tax purposes.

Assuming a tax rate of 50 percent, the favorable effect on reported earnings is $45,000. This happy situation lasts only until the sixth year, however. The figures then are less favorable. Income before taxes and depreciation is still $1 million, and depreciation for financial reporting purposes remains at $110,000. But depreciation for tax purposes is now only $100,000. Thus, while income before tax for financial reporting purposes continues to be $890,000, income for tax purposes is $900,000. The initial tax advantage of accelerated depreciation has become a disadvantage, because the tax liability now exceeds the amount which would have been payable had the company used straight-line depreciation for both tax and financial purposes.

This illustration, however, does not take into account any possible acquisitions of fixed assets after the first year. Normally, there is a constant cycle of replacements, providing new accelerated depreciation that again minimizes taxes without adversely affecting earnings. Theoretically, such continuous postponement of the so-called turn-around period can go on as long as the company keeps acquiring new fixed assets.

Accountants require companies to show the deferred taxes in a special account. Consequently, a company receiving the benefits of tax deferral will show very large amounts of deferred tax liability which will never actually be paid, i.e., when a particular deferred tax is paid, the account will have been replenished by a new deferral on new assets.

See also Richard L. Pollock, Tax Depreciation and the Need for the Reserve Ratio Test (U.S. Treasury Department, 1968), 15: "As long as these taxpayers continue to replace, that tax-free loan [from accelerated depreciation] is continually renewed."

30. The entire cattle feeding tax shelter is aimed initially at a deferral of tax for *one year* — the investor makes his investment (usually with funds borrowed on the cattle as security), say, in 1970, and obtains deductions for nearly the entire amount invested, so as to offset and make nontaxable income from other sources in 1970. The cattle are purchased in the fall and fed, and after fattening are sold the next year, with the profit on sale being ordinary income in 1971, and the balance a return of his investment. This is deferral for only *one year* — yet a packager of such a program announced in 1970 the offering of subscriptions for $5 million in a limited partnership; the minimum subscription is $20,000. See note 24 above.

The "rosebush shelter" also is essentially predicated on the value of short-term deferral. Here a high-income taxpayer leases land adjacent to a professional nursery and purchases a large quantity of immature rosebushes that will grow to a saleable condition over more than one year. The cost of the rosebushes, which is financed largely by a bank loan, is immediately deductible — hence the deferral. The lawyer who described this shelter said:

> Defenders of intangible drilling expenses and percentage depletion deductions are heard to speak of the energy crisis. Whatever the validity of that defense of the mineral tax laws may be, it is difficult to believe the United States is in the throes of a rosebush crisis.

See Ginsburg, note 26 above, at 887.

31. Bankers do not make interest-free loans — time and the present value of money are what their business is pitched upon. But when bankers become Secretaries of the

Treasury they refer to deferral of tax as essentially a matter of "timing," text at note 29 above, as if nothing of importance were involved in the deferral.

32. Given the same rate of discount, there are two variables that determine the relationship between deferral and exclusion: (1) The longer the period of deferral, the higher is the comparable percentage of exclusion; (2) the lower the taxpayer's marginal tax rate, the higher is the comparable percentage. Thus, for a 70% taxpayer, deferral for 10 years is equivalent to 36% exclusion, and deferral for 20 years is equivalent to 59% exclusion. For a 50% taxpayer, the percentages are 52% and 76%. For a 20% taxpayer, the percentages are 70% and 90%.

These figures do not mean that deferral of tax helps the low-income taxpayer more than the high-income taxpayer. Just the contrary. Deferral of tax on $100 of income for a 70% taxpayer provides him with $70 to invest. At his high marginal rate, it is only necessary to exclude 36% of his income to obtain the equivalent of the present value of ten-year deferral. But at a 20% marginal rate, it is necessary to exclude 70%. This can be put another way: If Congress desired to give $20 to everyone through the tax system, it could do so by excluding $100 for the 20% taxpayer, but it need exclude only $28.60 for the 70% taxpayer.

33. This problem is also present in making clear the cost to the Government. See the discussion in the Appendix to Chapter I on the use of "cash grant equivalents" to state the present value of the Government's commitment where deferral of tax for several years is involved. The "cash grant equivalent" will be higher than the immediate revenue cost.

There are difficulties also in quantifying the benefits of deferral to the investor. For example, see C. Roger Childs, Jr. and William G. Gridley, Jr., "Leveraged Leasing and the Reinvestment Rate Fallacy," 156 The Bankers Magazine 53 (1973), discussing the computations appropriate for a bank engaged in tax shelter leasing of equipment and stressing that the arrangement should be regarded as a source of funds through "an interest free (and, in the case of banks, a reserve free) loan from the United States government in the form of deferred tax liabilities" (60).

There are difficulties also for publicly-held corporations in expressing the benefits of tax deferral in such a way that their earnings per share figures will reflect those benefits. In other words, how show to maximum advantage on a profits statement a tax shelter investment that currently produces low earnings but whose advantages are buried in reduced current tax liabilities. The accounting profession is struggling with this problem, which involves on the one hand corporate executives keeping shareholders happy with a high earnings per share outlook and on the other hand, leaving accountants satisfied they are reflecting proper accounting standards and properly recognizing the deferred tax liabilities.

34. See Paul R. McDaniel and Alan S. Kaplinsky, "The Use of the Federal Income Tax System to Combat Air and Water Pollution: A Case Study in Tax Expenditures," 12 Boston College Industrial and Commercial Law Review 351, 360–364 (1971), giving alternative methods of viewing the deferral advantage of the tax expenditure of five-year amortization allowed for pollution control equipment. The alternative methods posit other equivalent assistance programs:

> — viewed as an investment credit, the deferral is the equivalent of a 7.97% investment credit for a large (48% tax) corporation and a 3.65% credit for a small (22% tax) corporation;
> — viewed as a direct grant, the deferral is the equivalent of a grant of $11,952 on the purchase of $150,000 of equipment by a large corporation and a grant of $5,479 for a small corporation;

— viewed as an interest-free loan, the deferral is the equivalent of an interest saving of $24,038.70 by the large corporation and $11,029.10 by the small corporation;

— viewed as a reduction in interest rates on traditional financing, the deferral is the equivalent of a reduction from 10% to 7.99% for a large corporation and to 9.38% for a small corporation.

35. See, for example, the description of the effect of leverage in the real estate shelter in Kurtz, note 26 above.

36. Investors have sought to magnify the discrepancy by prepaying interest, but a Treasury ruling in 1968 materially limited this gambit by denying immediate deduction and requiring allocation over future years for a prepayment of interest that materially distorts income, and considering prepayments in excess of twelve months as a material distortion, Rev. Rul. 68–643, 1968–2 Cum. Bull. 76. The ruling was referred to with approval in House Ways and Means Committee, Tax Reform Act of 1969 [H.R. 13270], H.R. Rep. No. 413, 91st Cong., 1st Sess. 73 (1969). An investor may be able to arrange for delayed repayment of capital, so that initial payments are entirely interest.

37. Tax shelter ingenuity seems limitless. For a "double shelter" which combines the tax shelter of leasing pollution control equipment with the leverage financing obtained at a lower cost through the use of pollution control state or local industrial development bonds (which still may be issued on a tax-exempt basis under Code §103(c)(4)), see Darsey M. Lynch, "The Developing Role of Leveraged Tax-Shelter Leasing in Pollution Control Financing," Investment Dealers' Digest 24 (Sept. 12, 1972).

38. See generally Code §§1001(a) and (b), 1011, 1012.

39. Treas. Reg. §1.752–1(e).

40. The benefit is even greater in some cases. Under the capital gain treatment of individuals, the first $50,000 of capital gains is subject to a maximum rate of 25% on those gains. Hence, if an investor is in a bracket above 50%, the 25% maximum rate is more beneficial treatment than exclusion of one-half of the gain. There may be a slight increase because of minimum tax; see Chapter VIII.

For corporations with taxable income above $25,000, a 30% capital gain rate is substituted for the regular marginal rate of 48%.

41. The text is discussing a situation in which the sale is in effect at a price (including any unpaid debt) equal to the investor's original total cost. If the sale is above that figure, then the additional gain is capital gain per se and not a reflection of the deferred income. If the sale is below original cost, then some of the investment is not recovered on sale and an equivalent amount of income deferred is not brought into account, but instead the earlier deduction now reflects *pro tanto* the final recovery of the investment, though earlier in time than would normally be the case in the absence of the tax expenditure.

42. For a description of the changes, see Charles Davenport, "Farm Losses under the Tax Reform Act of 1969: Keepin' 'Em Happy Down on the Farm," 12 Boston College Industrial and Commercial Law Review 319 (1971); Daniel I. Halperin, "Capital Gains and Ordinary Deductions: Negative Income Tax for the Wealthy," 12 Boston College Industrial and Commerical Law Review 387 (1971). The $25,000 and $50,000 limitations do not apply when a corporation is involved.

The Senate Finance Committee, Tax Reform Act of 1969, S. Rep. No. 552, 91st Cong., 1st Sess. 95–97 (1969), provides this background:

The special farm accounting rules were adopted as a means of relieving the ordinary farmer of the bookkeeping chores associated with inventories and an accrual method of accounting. These rules, however, by combining the current deduction of expenses which are capital in nature with capital gains treatment on the sale of livestock or orchards have resulted in a tax abuse which the committee agrees with the House should not be allowed to continue. These rules have allowed some high-income taxpayers who carry on limited farming activities as a sideline to obtain a substantial tax loss (which does not represent an economic loss) which is then deducted from their high-bracket, nonfarm income. These tax losses often arise because of the deduction of capital costs which usually would reduce capital gains on the sale of farm property, but which instead are used to offset ordinary income when incurred.

. . . .

Thus, the combination of a current deduction against ordinary income for various farm expenditures which are capital in nature and the capital gains treatment granted on the sale of the asset to which the expenditures relate produce a significant tax advantage and tax saving for the taxpayer whose ordinary income is taxed in a high bracket.

The utilization of these tax advantages by high-income taxpayers is not merely a theoretical possibility. In recent years, a growing body of investment advisers have advertised that they would arrange a farm investment for wealthy persons. Emphasis is placed on the fact that after-tax dollars may be saved by the use of "tax losses" from farming operations. In addition, numerous partnerships and syndicates have been established for the purpose of allowing wealthy investors to make farm investments so as to obtain these tax advantages.

. . . .

The basic problem which arises in connection with farm losses is that the deductions with respect to property, which gives rise to capital gain income when sold at a subsequent date, are currently deducted from ordinary income. In most cases, the effect of this is to give the deductions twice the value for tax purposes of the income to which they relate.

43. For a description of the changes, see C. Willis Ritter and Emil M. Sunley, Jr., "Real Estate and Tax Reform: An Analysis and Evaluation of the Real Estate Provisions of the Tax Reform Act of 1969," 30 Maryland Law Review 5 (1970).

It should be noted that for machinery and equipment, all depreciation is recaptured on sale, to the extent there is a gain on the sale. But, for real estate, only depreciation in excess of straight-line depreciation is recaptured,* a result quite favorable to real estate. Even straight-line depreciation is presumably too rapid for real estate. See Paul Taubman and Robert H. Rasche, "Economic and Tax Depreciation of Office Buildings," 22 National Tax Journal 334 (1969).

44. Draft Manuscript of Gerard M. Brannon and Emil M. Sunley, Jr., "Should We 'Recapture' Depreciation" (1970).

45. See Ritter and Sunley, Jr., note 43 above, at 26.

46. Congress before this, in one special area, did look at the benefits of deferral and adopt a mechanism that eliminated those benefits. It permitted mortgage insurance companies to deduct special reserves required under state law to meet possible adverse economic cycles that would require large payments under the mortgage guarantees. The reserves were excessive in relation to normal loss possibilities since they were established to meet catastrophic losses from depression conditions. The allowance of these reserves, ordinarily not permitted for tax purposes, would operate to defer tax on significant amounts of income. To remove the benefits of the consequent deferral,

Congress then required the companies to invest the tax savings in special non-interest-bearing bonds issued by the Treasury Department. The absence of interest on this required investment of the deferral tax savings thus removed the tax deferral benefit on that part of the reserve required to meet the possibility of those catastrophic losses. See Code §832(e), added by Pub. L. No. 90–240, §5(e) (Jan. 2, 1967).

47. See Ritter and Sunley, Jr., note 43 above. The 1969 Act also reduced depreciation on old buildings from 150% declining balance to straight-line depreciation, except that used residential rental property with a useful life of twenty years or more when acquired may be depreciated at a 125% declining balance rate.

48. Code §278. But this change has not prevented the offering of limited partnerships in some tax shelter citrus grove operations.

It is said that the change in the citrus grove shelter was pushed by Florida orange grove owners who were concerned that increasing exploitation of the shelter was causing overproduction and lower prices. See Halperin, note 42 above, at 390, n.12.

49. See Davenport, note 42 above.

50. See Chapter VIII.

51. To the extent capital gain is offset by an allowable interest deduction, the gain is to be included in full without the benefit of the exclusion of one-half of the gain. See also Halperin, note 42 above, at 402–407.

52. See Chapter VIII.

53. The text would also apply to real estate to the extent that the recapture of depreciation is incomplete. The text would not apply to cattle or orchards in the limited situations where the recapture of farm tax losses representing excess deductions applies.

54. This is the effect of percentage depletion on successful oil wells, which excludes 22% of the gross income from the well, or 50% of the net income if the latter is the lesser amount, regardless of the amount of the investment in the well. Hence, to the extent the cumulative amount of the percentage depletion exclusion reflects the initial deduction of the investment, the loan created by that deduction need not be repaid. Thereafter, the percentage depletion exclusion is eliminating part of the income from the well from tax.

55. This is simply a reference to the basic capital gain treatment for any real gain on an investment, i.e., excess of amount realized over original cost, so that the recapture factor is not present.

56. See Joint Economic Committee, 1972 Joint Economic Report, S.Rep. No. 709, 92d Cong., 2d Sess. 38 (1972) stating: "In fact, there is no body of significant evidence showing that these special tax provisions achieve their special objectives, let alone evidence that they achieve their objectives efficiently."

57. CONSAD Research Corp., "The Economic Factors Affecting the Level of Domestic Petroleum Reserves," House Ways and Means Committee and Senate Committee on Finance, 91st Cong., 1st Sess. (Comm. Print, 1969); House Ways and Means Committee and Senate Committee on Finance, 91st Cong., 1st Sess., U.S. Treasury Department, Tax Reform Studies and Proposals, (Comm. Print, 1969), 413. See also David G. Gadda, "Taxation as a Tool of Natural Resource Management: Oil as a Case Study," 1 Ecology Law Quarterly 749 (1971); and other references in Chapter V.

58. Virden L. Harrison and W. Fred Woods, Farm and Nonfarm Investments in Commercial Beef Breeding Herds: Incentives and Consequences of the Tax Law, U.S. Department of Agriculture, ERS-497 (April 1972).

59. See Chapter VII.

60. This aspect is discussed in Chapters VI, VII and VIII.

APPENDIX TO CHAPTER IV

1. Given the same rate of discount, there are two variables that determine the relationship between deferral and exclusion: (1) The longer the period of deferral, the higher is the comparable percentage of exclusion; (2) the lower the taxpayer's marginal tax rate, the higher is the comparable percentage. Thus, for a 70% taxpayer, deferral for 10 years is equivalent to 36% exclusion, and deferral for 20 years is equivalent to 59% exclusion. For a 50% taxpayer, the percentages are 52% and 76%. For a 20% taxpayer, the percentages are 70% and 90%.

These figures do not mean that deferral of tax helps the low-income taxpayer more than the high-income taxpayer. Just the contrary. Deferral of tax on $100 of income for a 70% taxpayer provides him with $70 to invest. At his high marginal rate, it is only necessary to exclude 36% of his income to obtain the equivalent of the present value of ten year deferral. But at a 20% marginal rate, it is necessary to exclude 70%. This can be put another way: If Congress desired to give $20 to everyone through the tax system, it could do so by excluding $100 for the 20% taxpayer, but it need exclude only $28.60 for the 70% taxpayer.

2. If the profit on the transaction is treated as capital gain (but not subject to the 25% alternative rate), then the tax on the sale where the item is capitalized is only $45 instead of $90. A, therefore, would have an after-tax gain of $105 on an investment of $100 if the item had been capitalized, or an after-tax profit of 105%. Where the item is expensed, he has an after-tax gain of $135 on an investment of $40, or an after-tax profit of 337.5%. The combined advantage of accelerated deduction and the capital gain benefit give him an *after-tax* rate of profit greater than his *before-tax* rate of profit. This is discussed further below. See also William D. Andrews, *Federal Income Taxation* (Boston, Little, Brown, 1969), Appendix A.

3. The matter can be expressed in still another way. A can be considered as investing $40 and receiving back his original investment plus $60. The Government has "invested" $60 and also received back that investment plus $90. A's gain on the investment he made is 150%, free of tax. Looking back at the interest-free loan analogy, it will be seen that if A had borrowed $60 from a bank and then capitalized the $100 cost, A would have ended up with a $36 profit on his original $40 investment, or an after-tax profit of 90% (proceeds of $250 less tax of $90 less $60 loan repayment less $24 net interest cost less $40 investment) compared with that of 60% if he had used $100 of his own capital. The leverage of the loan has increased A's after-tax profit from 60% to 90%. When A "borrows" interest-free from the Government, he ends up with $60 profit ($24 more than in the bank loan case because of the absence of interest cost), or an after-tax profit of 150%. A is obtaining the advantage of leverage without paying the cost of leverage, i.e., interest. The leverage of the loan plus the absence of interest cost enable A to achieve after tax the same rate of return on his investment as he would expect to make before tax, i.e., his investment is tax-free.

4. Carl S. Shoup, *Public Finance* (Chicago, Aldine Publishing Co., 1969), 302.

5. 116 Cong. Rec. 25,684–25,695 (1970).

6. This is the way the matter is described in Richard A. Musgrave, *The Theory of Public Finance* (New York, McGraw-Hill, 1959), 343–344. Note also that when Professor Shoup, in his footnote 20 quoted above in the text, uses the term "asset," as does the Treasury Department, the term presumably does not refer to the overall amount of the investment.

While A may be indifferent to the choice of exemption or deferral posited in the text, there is a difference to the economy, since the deferral route, to provide indifference to A, does involve a larger amount of investment.

7. Under a tax system that did not provide the benefit of the current write-off of the cost of an investment but instead used proper accounting, if A invested $1,000 in a plant, he would obtain $60 after a tax payment of $90 on the $150 before-tax profit. Since A desires $150 after-tax, he needs a $2,500 plant, which will provide a before-tax return of $375 and after a tax of $225 will give A a $150 return after-tax. If, however, the investment cost can be immediately expensed, A can invest the $2,500, obtain the $1,500 tax benefit of the $2,500 deduction, leaving his net investment cost at $1,000. The plant still earns $375, which after a tax of $225 leaves A with $150. But now this $150 after-tax is earned on his $1,000 investment, and thus A has his $150 after-tax profit on that investment. He is managing a $2,500 plant, which also yields a return of $225 to the Government on its $1,500 portion of the plant. But where A had invested $1,000 in a plant without any immediate write-off of the investment, as first described, A is managing a $1,000 plant which in a sense also consists of two parts, one a $600 part which is A's and on which he earns $60 after-tax, and a $900 part which earns $90 (the tax) for the Government. In return for the benefit of the immediate deduction, A has in effect agreed to manage a $2,500 plant so as to obtain his $150 after-tax return on *his* $1,000 part.

8. See discussion in text of Chapter IV, at note 29.

CHAPTER V: TAX INCENTIVES AS A DEVICE FOR IMPLEMENTING GOVERNMENT POLICY

1. The text discussion is partially based on Stanley S. Surrey, "Tax Incentives as a Device for Implementing Government Policy: A Comparison with Direct Government Expenditures," 83 Harvard Law Review 705 (1970) and a version of that article written earlier but published later, "Tax Incentives — Conceptual Criteria for Identification and Comparison with Direct Government Expenditures," in *Tax Incentives,* a Symposium conducted by the Tax Institute of America (Lexington, Mass., Heath Lexington Books, 1971), 3–38. See also, Stanley S. Surrey, "Tax Subsidies as a Device for Implementing Government Policy: A Comparison with Direct Government Expenditures," in The Economics of Federal Subsidy Programs, Part 1 – General Study Papers, Joint Economic Committee, 92d Cong., 2d Sess. 74 (1972).

2. Other tax expenditures in this class of special tax provisions adopted with the express intention of inducing desired action include the treatment under the foreign tax credit of dividends paid by the corporations of less developed countries, capital gains treatment in general, the exemption of credit unions, the special treatment of timber capital gains, the hundred dollar dividend exclusion, the deduction for one-half of medical insurance premiums, the exclusion for certain employee group term life insurance, the exclusion of certain income earned abroad, and the deferral of tax on shipping companies with tax haven incorporation. Accelerated depreciation on real estate is another example, although it was originally adopted largely as a happenstance along with accelerated depreciation provisions for investment in personal property.

3. Additional examples include the bad debt reserves for banks, the cash method of accounting for farmers, and the special personal exemption for students.

4. Incentive effects are also produced by the exemption of military pay earned in combat zones.

5. Professor Henry Aaron has compiled another inventory of existing tax incentives, arranged according to the types of economic decisions which the tax provision influences. Henry J. Aaron, "Inventory of Existing Tax Incentives — Federal," in *Tax Incentives,* note 1 above, at 39. He uses the term tax incentive to denote any tax

provision which is "defended or advocated primarily because it so alters resource allocation as to improve economic efficiency." He excludes "tax provisions defended primarily because they are alleged to have favorable effects on the distribution of income by income class, family status, age groups or other socio-economic categories." Thus, he would exclude tax expenditures for the aged and the blind. His tax incentives fall into three main categories: those influencing *household behavior* — spending patterns (for example, the charitable contributions deduction), place of employment (for example, the exemption of certain income earned abroad), portfolio choice (for example, capital gains), or occupational choice (for example, exclusion of certain military benefits and allowances); *business behavior* — investment in capital (for example, the investment credit), composition of the wage offer (for example, the exclusion of employer contributions to pension plans), industrial composition (for example, the tax benefits to agriculture and natural resources), business location (for example, the Western Hemisphere Trade Corporation provision), or legal form of business (for example, the exemption of credit unions); and *state and local government behavior* — sources of finance (for example, deductibility of state and local taxes).

For a discussion of incentives in state and local taxes, see Lloyd E. Slater, "Tax Incentives in State and Local Governments," in *Tax Incentives,* note 1 above, at 51. See also Preliminary Report of the Department of Finance, California (1972), listing tax expenditures in the California tax system.

6. See the discussion on the 1971 Revenue Act and the April 1973 Treasury proposals in Chapter I.

7. In recent years the hearings before the Senate Finance Committee on the proposal of Senator Robert Kennedy to promote more urban housing for low-income groups through extensive use of tax incentives provide the most extensive Congressional discussion of this subject, a discussion that as far as I know is not elsewhere duplicated. The hearings involved Senator Kennedy as a proponent of tax incentives for this purpose and the Secretary of HEW and the Undersecretary of the Treasury as opponents, all three favoring the goal of more urban housing for low-income groups. See Hearings on S. 2100 before the Senate Committee on Finance, 90th Cong., 1st Sess. (1967). The task of supervising the preparation of the Treasury's position and supporting arguments made this author realize how little material was available on the criteria to assess the use of tax incentives. The dearth existed in the Treasury, in the agencies involved with direct expenditures, and in the general literature. The testimony of Treasury Undersecretary Barr thus represents the beginning of the efforts of some to work systematically on this aspect.

8. On direct subsidies in general, see the innovative study by the Staff of the Joint Economic Committee, The Economics of Federal Subsidy Programs, 92d Cong., 2d Sess. (1972), and the subsequent papers and hearings on this subject.

9. See Laurence Stone, "Tax Incentives as a Solution to Urban Problems," 10 William and Mary Law Review 647, 651–53 (1969) (describing possible assistance devices for urban housing). See also Richard E. Slitor, "Tax Incentives and Urban Blight," in *Tax Incentives,* note 1 above, at 257 (generally defending tax incentives). For other discussions of tax incentives, see Walter J. Blum, "Federal Income Tax Reform — Twenty Questions," 41 Taxes 672 (1963); Jerome Kurtz, "Tax Incentives: Their Use and Misuse," 20 Southern California Tax Institute 1 (1968); Paul R. McDaniel, "Alternatives to Utilization of the Federal Tax System to Meet Social Problems," 11 Boston College Industrial and Commercial Law Review 867 (1970).

10. The tax provision was the Finance Act of 1954, 2 & 3 Eliz. 2, c. 44, §16, repealed by the Finance Act of 1966, c. 18, §35. Direct grants were instituted by the Industrial Development Act of 1966, c. 34, §1.

11. Investment Incentives, Cmnd. No. 4516 (1970); Industrial and Regional

Development, Cmnd. No. 4942 (1972). Cash grants are to be used as regional incentives.

12. See Chapter VII. Where the charity is a religious institution, a direct Government contribution could raise questions under the establishment of religion clause of the First Amendment. But such a direct subsidy as part of a subsidy plan for contributions generally should be considered constitutional if the present tax provision is, since there is no practical difference between the two.

13. For recent examples of such studies applied to tax incentives relating to *natural resources,* see CONSAD Research Corp., "The Economic Factors Affecting the Level of Domestic Petroleum Reserves," in House Ways and Means Committee and Senate Committee on Finance, 91st Cong., 1st Sess., U.S. Treasury Department, Tax Reform Studies and Proposals (Comm. Print, 1969); Mid-Continent Oil and Gas Association, Analysis and Comment Relating to the CONSAD Report on the Influence of U.S. Petroleum Taxation on the Level of Reserves, April 25, 1969; CONSAD Research Corp., "Comments on Mid-Continent (MC) Oil and Gas Association Critique," 115 Cong. Rec. 34,015, 34,016 (1969). The CONSAD Report is commented on in articles by Robert F. Byrne and Wilbur A. Steger, "Assessment of the Effectiveness of Federal Tax Incentives for Natural Resources" and Leslie Cookenboo, "Economic Significance of Petroleum Tax Provisions" in *Tax Incentives,* note 1 above, at 85 and 105 respectively. See also Edward W. Erickson and Stephen W. Millsaps, "Taxes, Goals, and Efficiency: Petroleum and Defense," in The Economics of Federal Subsidy Programs, Part 3 – Tax Subsidies, Joint Economic Committee, 92d Cong., 2d Sess. 286 (1972). As to *buildings,* see Paul Taubman and Robert H. Rasche, "The Income Tax and Real Estate Investment," in *Tax Incentives,* note 1 above, at 113; Paul Taubman and Robert H. Rasche, "Economic and Tax Depreciation of Office Buildings," 22 National Tax Journal 334 (1969); Richard E. Slitor, "Tax Incentives and Urban Blight," in *Tax Incentives,* note 1 above, at 257 (a paper sympathetic to the use of tax incentives); Paul Taubman and Robert H. Rasche, "Subsidies, Tax Law, and Real Estate Investment," in Economics of Federal Subsidy Programs, above, at 343. As to *environmental pollution,* see Douglas B. Wilson, "Tax Assistance and Environmental Pollution," in *Tax Incentives,* note 1 above, at 247; Paul R. McDaniel and Alan S. Kaplinsky, "The Use of the Federal Income Tax System to Combat Air and Water Pollution: A Case Study in Tax Expenditures," 12 Boston College Industrial and Commercial Law Review 351 (1971), and materials cited therein. As to the *investment credit,* see Gerard M. Brannon, "A Requiem for the Investment Tax Credit," in *Tax Incentives,* note 1 above, at 175 (describing existing studies on the credit); Gerard M. Brannon, "The Effects of Tax Incentives for Business Investment: A Survey of the Economic Evidence," in Economics of Federal Subsidy Programs, above, at 245; Paul Taubman, "The Investment Tax Credit, Once More," 14 Boston College Industrial-and Commercial Law Review 871 (1973). As to *cattle,* see Virden L. Harrison and W. Fred Woods, "Farm and Nonfarm Investment in Commercial Beef Breeding Herds: Incentives and Consequences of the Tax Law," U.S. Dept. of Agriculture, ERS-497 (1972). As to *timber,* see Emil M. Sunley, Jr., "The Federal Tax Subsidy of the Timber Industry," in Economics of Federal Subsidy Programs, above, at 317.

The 1973 Panel Discussions on General Tax Reform, held before the House Ways and Means Committee, 93d Cong., 1st Sess. (1973), cover a number of these incentive areas, such as real estate, natural resources, international activities, investment credit and accelerated depreciation, farm operations, and other tax shelter areas.

14. Joseph T. Sneed, "The Criteria of Federal Income Tax Policy," 17 Stanford Law Review 567, 602–603 (1965).

15. 115 Cong. Rec. 12,875, 12,876 (1969) (statement of Senator Charles Percy). The bill is S. 2192, 91st Cong., 1st Sess. (1969). This bill and statement are generally illustrative of the various proposals for a tax incentive for manpower training and employment and their supporting argumentation. As another illustration, see the proposal of Senator Herman Talmadge, adopted in 1970 in the Senate Finance Committee version of social security and welfare revisions, which bill was not finally acted upon by the Congress. 116 Cong. Rec. 25,013 (1970); H.R. 17550, §612 as reported by the Senate Finance Committee; H.R. 17550, §411, as passed by the Senate. A limited job credit was finally adopted in the Revenue Act of 1971 (Code §50A).

16. 115 Cong. Rec. 12,875, 12,876 (1969) (statement of Senator Charles Percy).

17. The discussion of manpower tax credits in Kenneth R. Biederman, "Alternative Tax Subsidies for the Training and Employment of the Unemployed," in The Economics of Federal Subsidy Programs, Part 4 – Higher Education and Manpower Subsidies, Joint Economic Committee, 92d Cong., 2d Sess. 541 (1972), glosses over this aspect. The paper in general analyzes the possible levels of effectiveness of various employer tax credits for training and employment. There appear such statements as:

> Whether a tax incentive program would prove a more efficient means of administering an employment-training program for the hard-core unemployed than a direct subsidy program depends upon the controls built into such a program. [561] . . .
>
> . . .
>
> The results showed that these tax incentives could be used to accomplish at least the shortrun employment and training of the hard core, and that from a strict economic standpoint the degree of effectiveness and the program cost could be controlled. It was not possible to ascertain from the results whether the tax credit would prove more cost effective than direct subsidy methods; this would be contingent upon many things, such as program design and administrative complications. But because of these, a stronger argument can be made for the generalized use of tax credits rather than attempt to construct complicated tax subsidy programs with the intent of attaining highly specialized program impact. Such complications undoubtedly would increase per unit administrative costs and thereby decrease the attractiveness of the credit approach. [567]

But clearly, the inquiry to be made is, if we are satisfied with the structure and implementation of a tax credit in this manpower area, why these cannot be duplicated in a direct subsidy program, and then a comparison made? Moreover, if they cannot be so duplicated, then why not, and does this inability throw light on the appropriateness of the tax credit program?

18. The limited job credit adopted in 1971 (Code §50A) requires certification by the Secretary of Labor that the employee is placed in employment under a work incentive program; the employee cannot have certain familial relationships to the employer; the credit must be repaid if the employee is let go. There is a carryover and carryback of unused credit.

19. Code §§169 and 187. The low-income housing incentive legislation discussed in 1967 and 1968, see note 7 above, was studded with requirements of "approval by the Secretary of Housing and Urban Development."

20. Joint Economic Committee, 1969 Joint Economic Report, H.R. Rep. No. 142, 91st Cong., 1st Sess. 20 (asterisk footnote by Senator Abraham Ribicoff). See also idem at 80 (views of Senator Herman Talmadge).

21. See Chapter VII.

22. See the discussion on "wastage" in manpower tax credits in Biederman, note 17 above, at 563–565.

23. There may of course be areas in which incentives aimed at the margin are not helpful or feasible and only a macroeconomic policy is appropriate.

24. If we had a *negative* income tax as well as a *positive* income tax, then the direct expenditures involved in the negative income tax payments to those whose incomes were below the level of positive tax would, to that extent, provide some assistance to balance the assistance given to taxpayers through the tax expenditures contained in the positive tax system. And also, of course, direct programs in many fields presently provide assistance to nontaxpayers as well as taxpayers. But the existence of such direct programs and a negative income tax would not make the tax incentives or special tax relief equitable. The jumble of financial assistance these varied methods would provide would only by extreme happenstance provide an equitable continuum of assistance structured to provide funds to those most in need of the assistance.

25. Tax Act of 1971, H.R. 10947, 92nd Cong., 1st Sess. §319, as passed in the Senate. The provision was not retained in the final legislation.

A similar unfairness exists in most versions of a proposed tax credit for educational expenses. See, e.g., Tax Reform Bill of 1969, H.R. 13270, 91st Cong., 1st Sess. §917 (1969) as passed by the Senate; the provision was not retained in the final legislation. A similar unfairness also existed in the proposed deduction for transportation expenses of handicapped persons. See Tax Reform Bill of 1969, idem, §915 (1969) as passed by the Senate; this provision also was not retained in the final legislation.

26. Canada at one period appeared to be shifting from tax incentives to direct expenditures in providing government assistance to regional economic expansion. Regional Development Incentives Act of 1968–69, c. 56. One reason given was the ineffectiveness of tax incentives when new ventures are involved.

27. The limited job tax credit adopted in 1971 (Code §50A) has these same defects. Since the basic Labor Department program does provide direct assistance to public employment, that program could just as well have been extended to private employment, and hence use of the tax credit route was unnecessary. See also the criticism of this tax credit in Biederman, note 17 above, at 549, on the ground of duplication of existing direct programs.

28. The new Code sections are 41 (credit) and 218 (deduction), effective for 1972.

The "check-off" system (Code §6096(a), as amended), also added in 1971 (and amended in 1973), but effective for the 1976 election, under which taxpayers paying income tax may designate that $1 be paid to a non-partisan presidential election campaign fund with the amounts then distributed among the political parties if appropriation legislation is enacted, is a tax expenditure in the sense that a system of Government assistance to presidential candidates is triggered initially by the "votes" of individuals who pay income taxes. There is, however, no direct reduction in tax liability as in the case of other tax incentives. Here also, only *taxpayers* have votes as to the use of Government funds and nontaxpayers are excluded.

29. Tax Reform Act of 1969, Pub. L. No. 91–172, §521(a), adding Code §167(k).

30. See Hearings on H.R. 13270 before the Senate Committee on Finance, 91st Cong., 1st Sess., 4903–4908 (1969) (statement of Charles Davenport).

31. Nor is it explained that the operative effect of the provision would be to give investors in these rehabilitation projects an after-tax return of 40% for an individual in the 70% bracket. Not having made a careful study of the proposal, the Treasury probably had no real understanding of its effects.

See also Emil M. Sunley, Jr., "Tax Incentive for the Rehabilitation of Housing," The Appraisal Journal (July 1971), 381.

32. Tax Reform Bill of 1969, H.R. 13270, 91st Cong., 1st Sess. §914 (1969), as passed by the Senate. The provision was not retained in the final legislation.

33. The text figures refer to the tax year 1972 when the $750 personal exemption became effective and, with the $1,300 low-income allowance, leaves single individuals whose income is less than $2,050 free of income tax.

Professor Henry J. Aaron uses this example:

> Yesterday on the floor of Congress, Senator Blimp introduced legislation to provide cash allowances for most of the aged. Senator Blimp's plan is unique, however, in that it excludes the poor. The largest benefits, $70 per month, are payable to aged couples whose real income exceeds $200,000 per year. The smallest benefits, $14 per month, would be payable to couples with income between $1,600 and $2,600. Widows, widowers, and unmarried aged persons would receive half as much as couples. No benefits would be payable to those with very low incomes.

Professor Aaron states this is a way of describing the (then) additional $600 personal exemption for the aged (now $750). Henry J. Aaron, "Tax Exemptions — The Artful Dodge," Transaction (March 1969), 4. The figures for 1972 would be, respectively, $88 a month for the $200,000 couple and $18 a month for the couple whose income was between $2,800 and $3,800.

34. For corporations, most tax incentives will favor a large corporation over a small corporation, since a special tax deduction or similar benefit taken at a 48% rate by a large corporation is worth more than twice the assistance provided when the deduction is taken at the 22% rate applicable to small corporations. Corporations incurring losses may receive no benefit. The use of a tax credit rather than a deduction would eliminate the first aspect, but would probably leave the loss corporation without assistance (except for a carry-forward of unused credit), since tax incentive credits in excess of tax liability typically are not paid out.

35. See article by Eileen Shanahan in *N.Y. Times,* Dec. 22, 1969, at 25, col. 4: "There are four other new tax preferences in the bill: tax incentives (which is what preferences always are at their birth) aimed at stimulating . . . the rehabilitation of old residential housing. . . ."

36. Code §57(a)(2).

37. See the discussion in Chapter IV on the use of credits against tax. The credits against tax proposed in 1973 by the Treasury for property taxes of the aged and for tuition amounts paid by parents to private elementary and secondary schools are refundable when the tax liability is not large enough to absorb the credit, but are not includible in income. See Statement of Treasury Secretary George P. Shultz in Hearings on General Tax Reform before the House Ways and Means Committee, 93d Cong., 1st Sess. (April 30, 1973).

Where the tax incentive amount is similar to a contribution to capital, it would not be included in income but would reduce the basis of property related to the contribution. This is the treatment accorded under present tax law to direct grants designed as contributions to capital rather than as operating subsidies. See Code §§118, 362(c).

There are other ways to structure a special tax provision to eliminate inequities. For example, the system of special bad debt reserves for financial institutions could be handled by allowing the deduction of the special reserve but then requiring the tax savings to be invested in special federal bonds that do not carry interest. This approach, which eliminates the advantages of deferral of tax, is now used in the tax treatment of special reserves for mortgage insurance companies. See House Ways and Means Committee and Senate Committee on Finance, 91st Cong., 1st Sess., U.S. Treasury Department, Tax Reform Studies and Proposals, 467 (Comm. Print, 1969); note 46 in Chapter IV.

38. See Tax Reform Act of 1969, Pub. L. No. 91–172, §231 (expanding the deduction of Code §217 and extending it to include self-employed individuals). There is often a hazy line between business expenses properly deducted from gross income for the purpose of an income tax, and personal expenses, which should not be deducted. Thus, commuting expenses are personal, but the expenses of providing comfortable working conditions in an office are business; wearing nice clothes at work is a personal expense, but wearing uniforms is a business expense. The borderlines that evolve are a part of the "generally accepted structure of an income tax" that is used as a standard to identify tax expenditures. We sometimes speak of tax changes designed to provide incentives for taxpayers when what is really involved is the removal of imperfections in the design of a proper tax structure that inhibit their activities. See, e.g., the discussion of the Foreign Investors Tax Act of 1966, in Stone, note 9 above, at 648.

If one disagrees with the classification of an item as a tax expenditure and believes instead that the item is a necessary part of a proper income tax structure, then the "upside-down" character of the financial assistance is acceptable or rather disappears, since the deduction of the item is a step in reaching net income. For further discussion of this aspect, with particular reference to medical expenses and charitable contributions, see the Appendix to Chapter I. See also Chapter VI.

39. See Wilson, note 13 above, at 251–253; McDaniel and Kaplinsky, note 13 above, at 364–370.

40. See Statement by Martin D. Ginsburg, in Panel No. 6, Panel Discussions on General Tax Reform, House Ways and Means Committee, 93d Cong., 1st Sess. 881, 887 (1973).

41. Much of this use of "crisis" and avoidance of the underlying issues is evident in the statements defending tax incentives in the various Panel Discussions on General Tax Reform before the House Ways and Means Committee, note 40 above.

42. Senator Charles Percy's statement on the manpower training bill included, in the section claiming that the proposed program was uncomplicated, the sentence: "This bill would require no Federal appropriations." 115 Cong. Rec. 12,876 (1969). If this is intended to convey the idea that Government funds are not being used, it is subject to the criticism on this page of the text. If it is intended to convey the thought that such legislation can be passed more quickly than direct expenditure legislation because no appropriation bill is needed, it is really an attack on the whole process of appropriation bills. If it is intended to convey the thought that the Congress will spend tax expenditure dollars but not direct expenditure dollars, it appears to charge the Congress with being irrational, as to which see the later text discussion on this aspect.

43. The 1969 Tax Reform Act is an example of the hasty judgments that may result from this system. Without any study at all, the House Ways and Means Committee, in dealing with that measure, committed the Government to an expenditure of nearly half a billion dollars for pollution control facilities installed by industry. Without any study at all, the Treasury induced the Committee to commit the Government to an expenditure of over $300 million for the rehabilitation of low-income rental housing. Neither action was taken with any regard to the overall priorities in the pollution control and housing areas. These comments also apply to the five-year amortization provided in the 1971 Act for employer on-the-job training facilities and child care facilities, first raised in the House Ways and Means Committee by a member. No one asked how much the provision would cost and no one knew. If the question had been

asked, no one could have answered it, since the proposal had not been studied and no one had any factual data to form the basis of a cost estimate.

The irrationality of the tax incentive approach is illustrated, unconsciously to be sure, in the following argument advanced by the National Realty Committee in a statement in 1973 before the House Ways and Means Committee defending existing tax subsidies to housing:

> [The] relative tax advantage afforded to low and moderate income housing in 1969 did result in a flood of capital into these fields and did produce all-time records of housing production and rehabilitation. *Whether or not the specific housing programs involved were well designed — or well administered — is a matter for other committees of this Congress. . . .* (italics added)

Statement of Albert A. Walsh, President, National Realty Committee, in Hearings on General Tax Reform before the House Ways and Means Committee, 93d Cong., 1st Sess. (March 26, 1973).

44. One defect in the administration of tax incentives by the IRS is that the IRS agents are "income-oriented" and tend to look askance at deductions and credits having no relation to the measurement of income. This attitude could result in an uneven administration of incentive programs. The agents, not seeing the purpose behind the deductions and credits, since they are not tax purposes and so are outside the general expertise and background of the agents, are likely to view the benefits as too generous and to raise audit problems for claimants. This is less likely to occur in the administration of a direct expenditure program, since it would be in the hands of an agency interested in the success of the program. Thus the existence of an IRS audit system is not necessarily, contrary to the claim sometimes made, an argument for using tax incentives. Moreover, other agencies, such as the Department of Labor, have inspection or audit systems, and still others could develop them.

Another problem in the use of the tax system to provide financial assistance lies in the ability of recipients to fathom that system compared with their relating to the receipt of a direct grant. This is especially important for tax incentives essentially involving transfer payments or like assistance. As an example, assuming Congress desires to give assistance to the elderly on their property taxes or assistance to parents for the education of their children, the intended beneficiaries can probably understand far better what they are receiving and go about getting it far more easily if the money comes as a direct grant check rather than as a deduction or credit against tax on a complicated tax return. This is even more the case if the tax incentive credit is made refundable and available to people who might not otherwise even file a tax return. See John K. McNulty, "Tax Policy and Tuition Credit Legislation: Federal Income Tax Allowances for Personal Costs of Higher Education," 61 California Law Review 1, 72–3 (1973).

45. See Statement of Stanley S. Surrey on the Tax Expenditure Budget in Hearings on Economic Analysis and Efficiency in Government before the Subcommittee on Economy in Government of the Joint Economic Committee, 91st Cong., 1st Sess. (1969).

It is sometimes said that a tax incentive has the advantage of "permanency" since tax provisions generally are only infrequently reexamined, whereas direct expenditures are usually reviewed annually, and that some programs to be effective require such permanency. However, if as a general matter periodic review of Government expenditures is considered desirable, no program should be removed from that scrutiny except for compelling reasons. If in a particular case such reasons are determined to exist, then devices to postpone review are available under the direct expenditure route: for example, longer appropriations and trust funds. Resort to the tax system is thus not necessary to accomplish the prevention of periodic review, if that is a desirable goal.

46. See Chapter I.

47. The Special Analyses in the 1973 Budget demonstrate the lack of information, analysis, and coordination of tax expenditures in contrast to direct expenditures:

> Special Analysis P, as to "Federal Aid to State and Local Governments" merely mentions, at 244, the tax expenditures (tax exempt bonds and deduction for state and local taxes) and provides amounts.
>
> Special Analysis L, as to "Income Security," does mention, at 179, for the first time the tax expenditures in this area, such as those for the aged, veterans, welfare recipients, disabled, and unemployed:
>
>> In addition to benefit outlays in the form of cash or services, there is a third type of income security benefit provided by the Federal Government, the "tax transfers" included in this analysis for the first time this year. Specific provisions of the personal income tax law reduce tax liabilities for particular groups of persons. These constitute Federal outlays just as fully as if the taxes had been collected, and a check then sent to the beneficiaries of these tax transfers. Most of these benefits accrue to the elderly, and constitute a $4.3 billion income supplement to the Nation's senior citizens.
>
> The analysis, while providing amounts, does not, however, analyze the effects of these tax expenditures or their relationship to direct programs.
>
> Special Analysis J, at 136, 145, on "Manpower Programs," mentions the support for day care to "middle income families" under the tax laws, with no further data or analysis, in contrast to the material provided for direct expenditures in this area.
>
> Special Analysis I, at 117, on "Education," K, at 153, on "Health," M, at 202, on "Housing," R, at 279, on "Research and Development," and S, at 296, on "Environmental Programs" make no mention of the tax expenditures in these areas and never include the Treasury in the list of agencies administering programs.

The Special Analyses in the 1974 Budget continue this pattern of general disregard for tax expenditures. Special Analysis N, "Federal Aid to State and Local Governments," has language similar to 1973 (211); Special Analysis K, "Income Security," refers to "tax transfers" to cover the tax expenditure benefits, lists the amounts in various tables, and describes those for the aged (168), but drops the 1973 language quoted above; Special Analysis I, "Manpower," does not contain the 1973 reference to day care tax benefits; and the other Special Analyses do not mention the tax expenditures in their areas.

48. Recommendations for Improving Congressional Control over Budgetary Outlay and Receipt Totals, Report of the Joint Study Committee on Budget Control, 93d Cong., 1st Sess. (April 18, 1973).

49. Statement of Stanley S. Surrey on Tax Expenditures in Relation to Congressional Control over Budgetary Outlay and Receipt Totals, in Hearings on the Budgetary Process before the House Select Committee on Committees, 93d Cong., 1st Sess. (June 20, 1973).

50. It has been pointed out that phrasing the assistance in terms of tax benefits may in some cases make it so difficult for potential beneficiaries to determine their rewards

that they will fail to take advantage of them. See Stone, note 9 above, at 654; Ralph S. Rice, "Tax Reform and Tax Incentives," 34 Law and Contemporary Problems 782, 796 (1969).

51. 118 Cong. Rec. E6629–6630 (daily ed. June 30, 1972). See, however, the criticism of this proposal in Report of the Tax Policy Advisory Committee to the Council on Environmental Quality (Feb. 1973), 29, though this Report elsewhere seeks to use tax subsidies and does not consider direct grants, as in the case of proposed tax relief for existing plants respecting their antipollution costs, page 15.

52. Aaron, note 33 above, at 5.

53. For a comprehensive discussion by Chairman Mills on the "back-door spending" character of tax incentives, see 113 Cong. Rec. 36,404 (1967).

Indeed, in very rare moments the Congress does discuss a proposed tax incentive in terms of its subsidy and expenditure effect. In the Senate consideration of the 1971 Revenue Act, Senator Robert Taft, Jr., proposed a tax credit for "historic barns," under which 10% of the yearly cost of maintenance could be credited against income tax. The Secretary of the Interior would be required to certify which barns, at least forty years old, were of "historic, architectural, or artistic significance because of [their] location, construction, or exterior appearance." Senator Taft said:

> Mr. President, since the turn of this century our conservation efforts have largely been directed toward the preservation of the wilderness. As important as these efforts are I think that we must recognize the need to preserve some of the artistic, historic and architecturally beautiful buildings which have graced our Nation's landscape. They have become so much a part of the great heritage of this country. This is particularly true with some of our Nation's barns.

Senator Wallace F. Bennett, speaking in opposition and using material supplied by the Treasury, was in a position to achieve a statesmanlike position and to offer the obvious fiscal arguments against the proposal:

> Mr. President, while the Senator from Ohio was talking, I have been sitting here thinking about an old historic barn that used to be in the backyard in which I played as a child. If I had known that there would be some kind of program to preserve it, I am sure that my father would not have torn it down.
>
> Mr. President, this amendment represents a partial solution to one limited aspect of the broad problems affecting our environment. The amendment provides a cash subsidy — in the form of a tax credit — equal to 10 percent of the cost of maintaining the exterior appearance and structural soundness of historic barns. I emphasize that this is a cash subsidy, and not a tax provision, because the program would be entirely within the discretion of the Secretary of the Interior. The Secretary of the Interior would have the sole discretion to determine who would receive the benefits of the provision.
>
> If a cash subsidy of this type is to be provided at the discretion of the Secretary of the Interior, it should be provided through an appropriate bill to appropriate funds to the Secretary for that purpose. There is simply no reason or justification to utilize back-door financing through a tax credit.
>
> . . .
>
> Mr. President, I believe the problem is too complex and too important to be dealt with on such a basis as we would be dealing with it here at this time of night. No Senate committee has studied it properly. I suppose it would be the

Senate Committee on Interior and Insular Affairs that should study the question
of these historic barns and other historic structures.

Therefore, much as I hate to do it, I respectfully suggest to the Senator from
Ohio that this amendment does not belong on the tax bill.

The proposal was defeated. Of course, the Treasury in recent years has forgotten these
arguments when it decided to propose a number of its own tax incentives. Then there
has been no mention of "back-door financing."

The reference for the historic barns proposal is 117 Cong. Rec. S19342–19344 (daily
ed. Nov. 22, 1971).

54. See the following from "Improving Federal Program Performance," Committee
for Economic Development (Sept. 1971), 38:

> Subsidies are often politically attractive since they benefit those directly
> affected, while their costs are diffused among all taxpayers. Tax relief incentives
> or credit guarantees, whose costs are not explicit and do not appear in the budget,
> are even more politically attractive than direct subsidies. Consequently, while
> they, like other subsidies, can be useful, they are likely to be even less vulnerable
> to scrutiny and criticism. This political advantage sometimes promotes their use
> in cases where economic efficiency calls for a tax, rather than a subsidy, and even
> in cases where they represent relatively inefficient types of subsidies.
>
> When tax relief incentives, loan guarantees, or other indirect subsidies are
> used, their costs, including foregone tax revenues, should be estimated and
> published both at the inception of the program and on a continuing basis
> thereafter.

55. Some segments of business recognize both the utility of Federal direct subsidy
programs to assist business in carrying out certain social goals and the disadvantages
of tax incentives; see the following from "Social Responsibilities of Business
Corporations," Committee for Economic Development (June 1971), 55–57:

> The evidence clearly indicates that many of the goals of American society
> can best be realized by developing a system of incentives for private firms to do
> those social jobs which business can perform better and more economically than
> other institutions. Indeed, the entrepreneurial thrust of business — if encouraged,
> guided, and carefully audited by government at all levels — may well be
> indispensable in achieving a permanent solution to the urban and other
> socioeconomic problems that have badly overtaxed the capacity of public
> agencies.
>
> A more extensive system of incentives should be developed quite carefully
> to ensure that the most appropriate measures are used to produce the desired
> action by business enterprise, that these are tailored precisely to each situation,
> and that the results are evaluated by competent agencies and accounted for to
> the public.

The discussion then describes important specific incentives, such as government
contracts for services and supplies, cash subsidies, loans, credit guarantees, and
insurance. It then considers tax incentives:

> Tax incentives in the form of timing advantages include such provisions as
> accelerated depreciation, current deductions for what might otherwise be capital
> items (as in the case of research and development expenditures), and soil and

water conservation expenses. Other measures which provide incentives through differential tax treatment include such items as percentage depletion, capital gains, and the investment credit. . . . The benefits of the resulting increase in investment and in economic activity tend to be widely dispersed.

On the other hand, where the focus on desirable social goals is much narrower, there may be some question as to the value of tax incentives. Under these conditions, it may be difficult to use tax incentives effectively because they cannot be applied specifically to individual company and job requirements, administered with the degree of assurance required, or easily altered to meet changing conditions. Accordingly, where these considerations are important it may be preferable to utilize contractual incentives or direct subsidies to afford a greater degree of control as to the application and results.

In developing a much more extensive system of economic incentives so that business can and will undertake more of the nation's social improvement tasks, two guiding principles will be of special importance:

1. Greater business involvement should be induced only in those areas of activity in which private enterprise is qualified to do a better job than other institutions. In areas such as education, professionals are certainly better qualified than businessmen to teach students. But business can and should be encouraged to contribute its managerial and organizational skills to strengthen the performance of educational and other institutions when necessary, although not in any sense to displace them.

2. The specific incentives provided to business should be primarily contractual in nature, or in the form of subsidies reflected in the expenditure side of the federal budget rather than in the form of special tax incentives. The budgetary process is the best means for allocating public funds among the full spectrum of competing public requirements, since the allocation is subject to legislative and public scrutiny and review. The process is increasingly being accompanied by performance evaluation to determine how well the intended objectives are met. Its integrity should be respected and it should be utilized to the fullest.

56. 115 Cong. Rec. 12,875, 12,876 (1969).

57. Professor Holland has observed, using employment and training of the disadvantaged as an example, that business accounting and organizational structure militate generally against tax incentives compared with direct expenditures. Tax incentives operate at an overall company level by reducing the final tax. But the problem that occasioned the tax incentive is often focused at the plant level, where a plant manager is faced with additional expenses that make a particular program unprofitable without the tax incentive. As a consequence, unless somehow the tax saving at the overall level is allocated within the company to the particular plant, that plant manager is saddled in the company's books with a poor performance. A direct expenditure approach would not have this result. Daniel M. Holland, "An Evaluation of Tax Incentives For On-the-Job Training of the Disadvantaged," 2 Bell Journal of Economics and Management Science 293 (1970).

58. After a very careful examination, Professor Holland has concluded that a direct approach is to be preferred in the area of training and employment of the disadvantaged; note 57 above. He believes a direct program can be better structured at the margin to induce the desired employer activity.

See also the preference for direct subsidies expressed by the Committee for Economic Development, note 55 above.

The Joint Economic Committee has stated:

Despite the distorted distribution of tax benefits the erosion of the income tax system might be acceptable if the special provisions efficiently achieved the specific social or economic goal toward which they are aimed. A somewhat distorted distribution of benefits might be the price that must be paid for an oil depletion allowance to stimulate oil exploration or for an excess depreciation provision to stimulate the production of rental housing. In fact, there is no body of significant evidence showing that these special tax provisions achieve their specific objectives, let alone evidence showing that they achieve their objectives efficiently.

Joint Economic Committee, 1972 Joint Economic Report, S. Rep. No. 708, 92d Cong., 2d Sess., 37–38 (1972).

59. This is further discussed in Chapter VII.

60. Indeed, the relative simplicity of the investment credit, which can generally be applied with very little supervision, may have misled businessmen into thinking all tax credits are simple in structure. Yet, as stated earlier, the tax credit proposals in social areas have far more details and complexities. On the investment credit generally, see Brannon, note 13 above; also Chapter VI.

61. Perhaps a word should be said about tax disincentives. When should the tax system be used as a disincentive to specific conduct? In the case of the sumptuary excise taxes — the taxes on alcohol and tobacco — the disincentive effect is presumably generally regarded as appropriate, assuming the need for the revenue involved. But as a general proposition specific excise taxes, other than user charges, for revenue purposes at the federal level are not highly regarded. The elimination in 1965 of most of the federal excise taxes of this nature reflected this attitude.

Where revenue is not involved, then a specific excise can be useful, given the substantive problem and the general acceptance of the specific solution. The interest equalization tax, adopted in 1965 as a balance of payments measure, to make the purchase of foreign securities more expensive is an example. But this approach has its dangers and presumably should be kept to a minimum. Thus, the use of specific excise taxes as regulatory devices to control pollution or to channel the control in certain directions has the disadvantage found with tax incentives, since it involves the tax committees and their staffs in very complex matters normally the province of the legislative committees having substantive jurisdiction of the problems and also diffuses subsequent oversight of the administration and effectiveness of the excises. Indeed, the criteria which should govern the choice between direct regulatory devices and tax measures for the improvement of the environment have yet to be clearly articulated. For example, the House Ways and Means Committee has apparently not been given, by its staff or the Treasury, a discussion of such criteria as a background against which to consider specific proposals for tax measures, such as a tax on sulfur dioxide emissions. See the Appendix to this Chapter for a discussion of the choice between the direct regulatory approach and a regulatory tax, in the context of pollution taxes.

User charges can also present difficulties similar to specific regulatory excise taxes, though generally the user charges have been in large part developed by or in conjunction with the legislative committees.

The use of the tax system as a regulatory device is certainly much less clear when the purpose is to shore up other substantive measures, usually of a criminal and prohibitory nature, e.g., the federal excise and occupation taxes related to gambling.

While the federal income tax has many tax incentives, it has only a few provisions that can be viewed as tax disincentives. Examples are the nondeduction of business expenses associated with grass roots lobbying and political contributions (Code

§162(e)(2) and Regulations §1.162–20), the violation of federal and state laws governing private bribes and kickbacks (Code §162(c)(2)), the violation of the antitrust laws (Code §162(g)), the payment of illegal bribes and kickbacks to Government officials (Code §162(c)(1)), the payment of rebates or kickbacks by physicians or other suppliers of services under Medicare and Medicaid (Code §162(c)(3)), and the payment of fines and penalties generally (Code §162(f)); the nondeduction by an individual of net wagering losses (Code §165(d)). Congress in 1969 indicated it desired the nondeduction on "public policy" grounds of business expenses to be restricted to the above categories, where presumably allowance of a deduction either goes too much against the grain (bribes, kickbacks, and the like), would permit an undue advantage arising from the leverage of money (lobbying and political contributions), or would unfairly lighten the punishment (fines and penalties).

It is interesting to note that while tax incentives have been widely used, the use of disincentives under the income tax is minimal. Congress — and tax lawyers — have been quite willing to mix tax incentives into the tax structure but are very wary of mixing morals and enforcement against nontax pursuits into that structure. In the latter situation they stress the desirability of keeping a proper measure of net income for an income tax, and see the danger of tampering with that measure for nontax goals. There have occasionally been proposals for a disincentive use of the income tax to solve urban problems, such as the disallowance of a depreciation deduction to slum landlords who fail to maintain their properties and who are in violation of local building codes. Here also the use of the tax system for enforcement purposes, as in the excise taxes on gambling, has pronounced weaknesses.

Treasury Undersecretary Edwin S. Cohen, in a Statement in the Hearings on Tax Subsidies and Tax Reform before the Joint Economic Committee, 92d Cong., 2d Sess. 147, 156 (1972), providing data on tax subsidies pursuant to its request, went on to mention "shortcomings" or "difficulties" with tax subsidy analysis. Among these he listed the "penalties" arising from provisions that increase the tax burden and affect its distribution. However, his choice of illustrations indicate a degree of confusion in the current Treasury analysis of "tax subsidies." Thus, he lists the tax on corporations and its differential impact depending on who bears its burden; the estate and gift taxes which have an effect on the distribution of the tax burden; and the income tax rate structure itself which may involve a "penalty" to one group or another depending on how the treatment of single persons, married couples, etc. is viewed. But all of this really has nothing to do with the analysis of tax incentives or subsidies but rather concerns itself with the general level of the tax burden in the United States and its distribution.

62. Thus, Professor Paul R. McDaniel, then Legislative Assistant to Senator Albert Gore, has pointed out that in the debate and vote on Senator Gore's amendment under the 1969 Tax Reform Act to strike out the five-year amortization provisions, including that for pollution control facilities, Senator Edmund S. Muskie, who had jurisdiction over direct programs in those pollution control areas, spoke against the amendment. 115 Cong. Rec. 37,885–37,886 (1969).

In the vote on the expansion of the child care deduction in 1971, Senator Walter F. Mondale voted for the expansion though its policies seemed in direct contradiction with those he was espousing in guiding a major direct child care program through the Senate; see Chapter VI.

63. Code §401 (c) and (e).

64. House Committee on Ways and Means and Senate Committee on Finance, 91st Cong., 1st Sess., U.S. Treasury Department Tax Reform Studies and Proposals (Comm. Print, 1969), 7–8.

65. Remarks of the Honorable Edwin S. Cohen, Assistant Secretary of the Treasury for Tax Policy, before the Twenty-Eighth Annual New York University Institute on Federal Taxation, New York, Nov. 11, 1969 (Treasury Department Release K-266), 15–16.

66. The so-called DISC proposal, adopted in the House but not approved by the Senate. See, in general, Hearings on Amendments 925 and 1009 to H.R. 17550 [Trade Act of 1970] before the Senate Committee on Finance, 91st Cong., 2d Sess., 9–45 (1970).

67. Treasury Department News Release, Jan. 11, 1971, CCH 1971 Stand. Fed. Tax Rep. ¶6366; Treasury Department News Release, June 22, 1971, CCH 1971 Stand. Fed. Tax Rep. ¶6736.

68. See Chapter I.

69. Tax Reform Studies and Proposals, note 64 above.

70. The investment credit structure itself pointed to problems, such as the precedent effect of a credit of this nature.

71. The problem regarding leasing under the investment credit was caused by confining the credit to taxpayers and placing a limit on the credit in terms of tax liabilities, thereby inducing concerns which could not use their credits to "barter" them to others and thus enlarge the tax abuses in leasing syndicates and similar arrangements. While the "bartering" may have widened the use of the credit by avoiding the limitation based on tax liability and thus corrected what may have been the undesirability of the limitation, the detour too generously compensated the middleman lessor. The 1971 version greatly restricts the use of the credit in this fashion by individual lessors.

72. The proposed Mills-Mansfield Tax Policy Review Act of 1972, H.R. 15230, 92nd Cong., 2d Sess. (1972) listed 54 tax preference items (all but one taken from the Tax Expenditure Budget) to automatically be eliminated from the Code over a three-year period unless Congress voted to retain a particular item.

The Joint Economic Committee has stated in 1972:

> We urge the Administration to provide to the Congress by this summer detailed evaluations of at least one-third of the special provisions in the individual and corporate income tax laws, so that Congress can decide whether the provisions fairly distribute their benefits and efficiently achieve their specific objectives.
>
> . . .
>
> In the future, the Department of the Treasury should provide the Congress with detailed analytical studies of proposed special provisions in the tax law prior to enactment. In addition, the Department of the Treasury should provide analytical evaluations of the same provisions periodically thereafter, beginning no later than three years after enactment.

Joint Economic Committee, 1972 Joint Economic Report, S. Rep. No. 708, 92d Cong., 2d Sess. 39 (1972).

73. This is the rational — and optimistic — approach. But suppose the tax committees desire to retain jurisdiction over the amounts involved in the tax expenditure areas, even when recast as direct programs. Could they then devise direct grant or loan programs to be administered by the Treasury Department and so preserve their jurisdiction? The result of course would be the continuation of the present undesirable situation, even confounded. Clearly, a focus on the alternative of direct expenditures must be made forceful enough to obtain both the direct programs

themselves *and* their location within the proper operational executive departments and Congressional committees, rather than within the Treasury and the tax committees.

74. The 1969 Tax Reform Act puts five-year termination dates on the new five-year amortization incentives for pollution control facilities, rehabilitation of low-income housing, railroad cars, and mine-safety equipment. The more generous provision for recapture of depreciation on federally assisted housing projects also has a five-year amortization provision.

But these time limits will not have served their purpose if no one in Government is collecting the needed data and attempting to ascertain the effectiveness of these tax incentives. See, as to pollution control facilities, a discussion of this aspect in McDaniel and Kaplinsky, note 13 above. One suspects that, because of the very nature of the tax incentive technique, the responsibility for such study in most cases will not be found.

The 1971 Act placed a five-year limit on the new five-year amortization provisions for employer on-the-job training facilities and child care facilities. The other new tax expenditure items added by that Act do not contain a termination date; a five-year limit placed by the Senate on DISC was opposed by the Treasury and rejected in Conference.

APPENDIX TO CHAPTER V

* Harris L. Hartz, J.D., Harvard, 1972, and now a member of the New Mexico Bar, participated in developing this Appendix.

1. See the discussion on tax expenditures and excise taxes in Appendix to Chapter 1.

2. See also the tax disincentives found in the income tax, discussed in note 61 to Chapter V.

For a discussion of the New York City tax on cigarettes according to their tar and nicotine content, see William Drayton, Jr., "The Tar and Nicotine Tax: Pursuing Public Health through Tax Incentives," 81 Yale Law Journal 1487 (1972); see also the proposal of Senator Frank E. Moss for a similar federal tax, 119 Cong. Rec. S907 (daily ed., Jan. 18, 1973).

3. 2 BNA Environment Reporter 1226, 1250, 1333 (1972); 118 Cong. Rec. S.1427 (daily ed., Feb. 8, 1972).

4. Federal Water Pollution Control Act Amendments of 1972, P.L. 92–500 [S.2770] Oct. 18, 1972. See discussion in Charles L. Schultze et al., *Setting National Priorities: The 1973 Budget* (Washington, D.C., The Brookings Institution, 1972) 381–385. See also *Effluent Charges on Air and Water Pollution* (Washington, D.C., Environmental Law Institute, 1973).

5. Schultze, note 4 above, at 382.
6. Schultze, note 4 above, at 370.
7. Schultze, note 4 above, at 370:

> Cost differences between the uniform reduction and least-cost approaches to pollution cleanup are very large. According to one estimate, achieving current targets for controlling sulfur emissions into the atmosphere would cost two to three times as much under the former as under the latter.[3] A study of water pollution in the Delaware River basin estimated that current water quality standards would be roughly 50 to 100 percent more costly to achieve with uniform reductions than with a least-cost approach. A similar estimate of the

costs of controlling BOD discharges in the Great Lakes region comes to the same conclusion.

(3.) U.S. Department of the Treasury, Press Release, "Pure Air Tax Act of 1972: Background and Detailed Explanation" (Feb. 8, 1972), p.5.

8. Schultze, note 4 above, at 371:

> To require a uniform percentage reduction of all firms would be inappropriate for other reasons. It would come to grips only imperfectly with the complexities of pollution control. Requiring a smelter that uses virgin ore to reduce the pollutants it generates by 85 percent might leave far more pollution in the environment than would a 50 percent cutback applied to a smelter using scrap as raw materials. Inducing consumers to switch from bleached to unbleached household paper products would reduce water pollution much more than would requiring producers of bleached paper to eliminate 80 percent of the pollutants from their bleaching process.

9. Schultze, note 4 above, at 371:

> In theory, a regulatory agency could establish for each firm rules and pollution limits that meet these criteria. The limits would have to be different for each firm and would have to be based on a consideration of the cost and effectiveness of all of the available alternatives for reducing pollution, including the possibilities of changing raw materials and switching product varieties. In practice, however, this is an impossible task. There are some 40,000 individual industrial sources of water pollution alone. A regulatory agency cannot know the costs, the technological opportunities, the alternative raw materials, and the kinds of products available for every firm in every industry. Even if it could determine the appropriate reduction standards for each firm, it would have to revise them frequently to accommodate changing costs and markets, new technologies, and economic growth.

10. Paul R. McDaniel and Alan S. Kaplinsky, "The Use of the Federal Income Tax System to Combat Air and Water Pollution: A Case Study in Tax Expenditures," 12 Boston College Industrial and Commercial Law Review 351 (1971); Marc J. Roberts, "River Basin Authorities: A National Solution to Water Pollution," 83 Harvard Law Review 1527 (1970); Arnold W. Reitze and Glenn Reitze, "Tax Incentives Don't Stop Pollution," 57 American Bar Association Journal 127 (1971). See also the discussion in Chapter V on tax incentives.

11. Schultze, note 4 above, at 371–372:

> [A] tax could be levied on each unit of each kind of pollutant discharged into the air or water. Faced with these taxes or "effluent charges," each firm would find it in its own interest to reduce pollution by an amount related to the cost of reduction and through the use of the least-cost means of doing so. It would compare the cost of paying the effluent charge with the cost of cleaning up pollution, and would choose to remove pollution up to the point where the additional cost of removal was greater than the effluent charge. The larger the effluent charge, the greater the percentage of pollutants a firm would find it advantageous to remove. Firms with low costs of control would remove a larger percentage than would firms with high costs — precisely the situation needed

to achieve a least-cost approach to reducing pollution for the economy as a whole. The kinds of products whose manufacture generated a lot of pollution would become more expensive and would carry higher prices than those that generated less, and consumers would be induced to buy more of the latter.

12. Schultze, note 4 above, at 386:

> If effluent charges were imposed on each of the major water pollutants, economic factors would begin to work for, rather than against, a reduction of pollution. As was pointed out above, unbleached household paper products cause 85 to 90 percent less pollution (in the form of dissolved solids) than do bleached products. If an effluent charge were imposed, the price of bleached products would have to be raised relative to that of unbleached products, promoting a shift in consumer purchases toward the less-polluting good. Similarly, choices of raw materials and manufacturing methods would shift in favor of those that cause less pollution. A central regulatory authority would not have to undertake the exceedingly complex job of trying to decide, industry by industry and process by process, what pollution limits were consistent with the use of "best practicable" and "best available" technologies. Nor would primary reliance have to be placed on the government's ability (which is notoriously weak) to enforce complex regulations against industry.

13. See Report of the Tax Policy Advisory Committee to the Council on Environmental Quality (Feb. 1973) 19.

14. Schultze, note 4 above, at 372:

> This continuing incentive is important. The quantity of air and water available to the nation is fixed, roughly speaking. But as economic activity grows over time, the volume of pollution discharged into the air and water will rise unless an ever-increasing percentage of pollutants is removed.

15. John F. Burby, "Environment Report/White House Plans Push for Sulfur Tax Despite Strong Industry Opposition," 4 National Journal, 1663–1665 (Oct. 28, 1972).

16. Schultze, note 4 above, at 388–393. The difference between the Administration view and that of the environmental groups toward the tax lay in the structure of the tax — its rate and the application to regions which were clean-air regions under the EPA standards. See John F. Burby, "Environment Report/White House, Activists Debate Form of Sulfur Tax; Industry Shuns Both," 4 National Journal 1643–1650 (Oct. 21, 1972); National Journal, note 15 above, at 1664–1671 (Oct. 28, 1972). See also *Effluent Charges on Air and Water Pollution,* note 4 above, at 78.

17. There may, of course, be problems with a tax on leaded gasoline. Such a tax was the first pollution tax recommended to the Congress, in 1970. Unfortunately, it had the appearance of a revenue-raising measure even more than of a pollution tax, and this aspect made it initially suspect — and properly so. Further, the very novelty of such a tax in comparison with a regulatory approach increased that suspicion for the House Ways and Means Committee. The tax never received Committee approval. See Hearings on the Tax Recommendations of the President, before the House Ways and Means Committee, 91st Cong., 2d Sess. (1970); National Journal, note 16 above, at 1647 (Oct. 21, 1972).

18. See Report, note 13 above, at 26; *Effluent Charges on Air and Water Pollution,* note 4 above, at 77–78.

19. Code §162(f); Regulations, §1.162–21.

20. See the discussions as to whether a tax on the sulfur content of fuel should apply to clean-air regions, Schultze, note 4 above, at 392; National Journal, note 16 above. Also see *Effluent Charges on Air and Water Pollution,* note 4 above, at 58, 89.

21. Marc J. Roberts, "Environmental Externalities: Policy Options and Prospects," Seminar on the Institutional Arrangements Associated with Planning and Implementing Water Quality Management Decisions, Victoria, British Columbia, March 30–31, 1973.

22. Roberts, note 21 above. For further consideration of the pollution tax approach, see the following references: John H. Dales, *Pollution, Property and Prices* (Toronto, University of Toronto Press, 1968); J. Clarence Davies III, *The Politics of Pollution* (New York, Pegasus, 1970); Annual Report of the Council of Economic Advisors (1971); Annual Report of the Council on Environmental Quality (1971); A. Myrick Freeman, III and Robert H. Haveman, "Economic Incentives and Environmental Quality," 64 National Tax Association Proceedings 90 (1971); A. Myrick Freeman, III, and Robert H. Haveman, "Water Pollution Control, River Basin Authorities, and Economic Incentives: Some Current Policy Issues," 19 Public Policy 53 (1971); Larry E. Ruff, "The Economic Common Sense of Pollution," The Public Interest (No. 19, Spring 1970) 69; Donald N. Dewees, *Automobile Air Pollution: An Economic Analysis* (Cambridge, Mass., Harvard University, 1971); Orlando E. Delogu, "Effluent Charges: A Method of Enforcing Stream Standards, 19 Maine Law Review 29 (1967); Marc J. Roberts, "Organizing Water Pollution Control: The Scope and Structure of River Basin Authorities," 19 Public Policy 75 (1971); Hearings on Economic Analysis and the Efficiency of Government, before the Subcommittee on Priorities and Economy of the Joint Economic Committee, 92d Cong., 1st Sess. Part 6 (1971); Hearings before the Subcommittee on Air and Water Pollution of the Senate Committee on Public Works, 91st Cong., 2d Sess. (1970); Hearings on Implementation of the Clean Air Act Amendments of 1970 before the Subcommittee on Air and Water Pollution of the Senate Committee on Public Works, 92d Cong., 2d Sess. (1972).

23. *Effluent Charges on Air and Water Pollution,* note 4 above, at 92.

24. See Chapter V.

25. Clean Air Amendments Act of 1970, P.L. 91–604 (Dec. 31, 1970).

26. The House Ways and Means Committee also had jurisdiction over the proposed tax on leaded gasoline and, presumably much to the distaste of that committee, was thereby plunged into an extremely complex environmental issue for which it had no preparation, background, or staff experience. See note 17 above.

CHAPTER VI: REPLACING TAX EXPENDITURES
WITH DIRECT GOVERNMENTAL ASSISTANCE

1. The impetus and credit for the 1969 reforms belong not to the Treasury then in office but to the Congress and the studies of the previous Treasury. Indeed, the new Administration first dragged its feet on tax reform, then belatedly joined the parade when it realized the Congressional mood for reform, but in important areas worked hard to defeat or dull reform proposals. Rowland Evans, Jr. and Robert D. Novak, *Nixon in the White House* (New York, Random House, 1971), 194–201, 211–223.

2. House Committee on Ways and Means and Senate Committee on Finance, 91st Cong., 1st Sess., U.S. Treasury Department Tax Reform Studies and Proposals (Comm. Print, 1969) (hereinafter cited as Treasury Tax Reform Studies).

3. Treasury Tax Reform Studies, note 2 above, at 331; see also Jerome Kurtz and

Stanley S. Surrey, "Reform of Death and Gift Taxes: The 1969 Treasury Proposals, The Criticisms, and a Rebuttal," 70 Columbia Law Review 1365 (1970).

4. The text discussion is partially based on Stanley S. Surrey, "Tax Incentives As a Device for Implementing Government Policy: A Comparison with Direct Government Expenditures," 83 Harvard Law Review 705 (1970). See also Stanley S. Surrey, "Tax Subsidies as a Device for Implementing Government Policy: A Comparison with Direct Government Expenditures," in The Economics of Federal Subsidy Programs, Part 1 – General Study Papers, Joint Economic Committee, 92d Cong., 2d Sess. 74 (1972).

5. In a sense, multiple corporate surtax exemptions and other multiple corporation abuses could be considered a structural defect within the tax expenditure benefit of the lower corporate rate and other benefits accorded to small business, since through the use of multiple corporations a large business would divide into a series of "small businesses" under common control.

6. For a list of the major items in the 1969 Act, and the revenue gains and losses involved, see Staff of the Joint Committee on Internal Revenue Taxation, General Explanation of the Tax Reform Act of 1969 (1970), 20–21.

7. See Chapter I for an enumeration of the tax expenditures added by the 1971 Act, and also those considered but not enacted, as well as new tax expenditures recommended by the Treasury in 1973.

8. 115 Cong. Rec. 37,067–37,069 (1969) (letter to Senator Russell Long).

9. See Statement by Stanley S. Surrey, in Panel No. 1, "Objectives and Approaches to Tax Reform and Simplification," in Panel Discussions on General Tax Reform, House Ways and Means Committee, 93d Cong., 1st Sess. 9 (1973).

10. The present technical structure of the tax treatment of trusts favors the family that adds a trustee to the family dinner table: (1) The trust can accumulate income taxable at a rate lower than the rate of the beneficiaries to whom the income is ultimately distributed; while a mechanism requires the distributed income to be "thrown back" over the years of accumulation and thus added to the beneficiaries' income, so that the proper rate is achieved (assuming the mechanism works properly), the intervening deferral of tax liability at the higher rate is quite advantageous to the family; the deferral can be heightened through the use of foreign trusts in tax haven countries; (2) the grantor of the trust can, by appointing himself, a family member, or a bank or friend as trustee and through the use of reserved powers, maintain considerable control over the disposition of the trust income and yet have the income currently taxed at rates lower than those applicable to the grantor. It is doubtful that the Congress intends a social policy of preferring families with trusts over those without trusts or is desirous of granting tax incentives for the creation of trusts. The present defects seem attributable, rather, to the failure of Congress to comprehend the benefits of tax deferral and to the complexities of the technical issues involved in trust legislation — plus, of course, the opposition of trust companies and the organized tax bar to the curing of these defects.

11. Thus, some issues involve: to what extent should distributions by a corporation of appreciated assets involve a corporate tax on that appreciation; the treatment of corporate liquidations; the distinctions between corporate dividend distributions and corporate capital distributions; and the like. These issues concern matters of considerable complexity and technical sophistication.

12. The aspects of reform in this area are considered in Stanley S. Surrey, "Complexity and the Internal Revenue Code: The Problem of the Management of Tax Detail," 34 Law and Contemporary Problems 673, 688 (1969).

13. This subject encompasses the proper treatment of single persons compared with

married couples; married couples where one spouse works compared with couples where both work; large families compared with families with fewer children; heads of households, e.g., an adult with one or more dependents, compared with single persons and married couples; and the like. The issues involve much more than traditional tax policy and extend to attitudes toward sex equality, marriage, women in the labor force, and population growth. There is no "right tax answer," and countries differ in their responses. For a current discussion in the United States, see Hearings on Treatment of Single Persons and Married Persons where Both Spouses Are Working, before the House Ways and Means Committee, 92nd Cong., 2d Sess. (1972); for an international comparison, see The Income, Fortune and Estate Tax Treatment of Households, 57a Cahiers de Droit Fiscal International (Rotterdam, International Fiscal Association, 1972).

14. While this treatment of the corporation tax has been a subject of considerable discussion — and change — in Europe and Canada in recent years, it has not been a serious issue in the United States. Many public finance economists tend to push toward integration of the corporate and individual income taxes, while other economists and tax lawyers generally do not find this a question of immediate priority. I am in the latter group. For a general discussion, see Joseph A. Pechman, *Federal Tax Policy,* (Washington, D.C., The Brookings Institution, revised ed. 1971), 140–148.

15. Professor Henry J. Aaron states:

> [T]ax policy makers *should* confront proposed "reforms" in the tax system in the same way budget makers *should* confront proposed expenditures. In both cases, a desire to examine the proposal apart from its effect on aggregate demand requires that the proposal be paired with some offsetting change which cancels out the impact of the tax change on aggregate demand — for example, a new expenditure may be paired with an expenditure cut or a tax increase; a new tax proposal may be paired with another tax change with offsetting revenue effects. The resulting package of proposals will generate benefits and costs — changes in real goods and services . . . available to households, and these changes should be evaluated on the basis of weights assigned to different households. In short, tax changes, like expenditure changes, should be subject to benefit-cost analysis. In any case, the decision to modify or to retain given tax provisions, like the decision to continue or modify expenditures, expresses results of a frequently implicit calculation in which benefits and costs are compared.
>
> Tax reformers should not be unduly discouraged because they are unable legitimately to appeal to such simple litmus tests of tax proposals as whether or not the proposal causes taxable income to conform more closely to the Haig-Simons income definition. It seems extremely likely, to this writer at least, that most of the tax provisions now on the agenda for tax reform will fare just as badly under such empirical scrutiny as they fare when judged for conformity with some academic income definition.

Henry J. Aaron, "What Is a Comprehensive Tax Base Anyway?," 22 National Tax Journal 543, 547 (1969).

I do not see why this rigorous test is to be applied to items that may fall in the category just described in the text, i.e., those items that can be dropped without substitute programs. The items were not subject to cost-benefit analysis when they came into the tax law. The burden of "Henry Aaron-type" proof should be on those seeking to maintain these tax expenditures, not on those seeking to eliminate them. The Henry Aaron proof burden may have to be borne by the proponents of change in certain situations, such as the items described in the third category below, but these should be the exceptional situations.

16. B. Hughel Wilkins, "A Note on the 'Gore Amendment,'" 18 National Tax Journal 321 (1965). See also Statements in Panel No. 11, Taxation of Foreign Income, Panel Discussions on General Tax Reform, House Ways and Means Committee, 93d Cong., 1st Sess. 1671 (1973).

17. Stanley S. Surrey, "Current Issues in the Taxation of Corporate Foreign Investment," 56 Columbia Law Review 815, 830–838 (1956). See also Statements in Panel No. 11, note 16 above.

18. For a description of the operative aspects, see United States Income Taxation of Private Investments in Developing Countries, United Nations ST/ECA/126 (1970), 60–64. Those on both sides of the general question of the treatment of foreign income appear to agree on the elimination of this particular windfall; see Panel No. 11, note 16 above.

19. For a general description, see United States Income Taxation of Private Investments in Developing Countries, note 18 above, at 27–45.

20. For example, Economic Implications of Proposed Changes in the Taxation of U.S. Investments Abroad, National Foreign Trade Council, Inc. (1972); see also, The Multinational Corporation, Studies on U.S. Foreign Investment, Vol. 1, U.S. Department of Commerce (1972).

21. Much of the argument of the multinational companies rests on the contention that they do not invest abroad because of tax reduction. This is presumably true for most large companies, though they, as well as many smaller enterprises, benefit from tax planning involving international arrangements. But in the end the tax issue does not turn on the factor of tax-induced motivation for the foreign investments but rather whether the investment, be it tax motivated or not, should enjoy a tax preference compared with investment in the United States. In this respect the matter is similar to the multiple corporation problem. Prior to 1969 some businesses organized their operations with 500 or 1,000 subsidiaries, thereby obtaining the tax advantages of 500 or 1,000 corporate surtax exemptions. Many of these enterprises claimed genuine business reasons for this form of operation. But Congress in 1969 recognized that, whatever the motivation for this organizational form, there was no reason to give it tax advantages or prefer it over a business of similar size operating entirely within only one corporate structure. The Congress therefore limited a multiple corporate enterprise to a single surtax exemption.

22. Peggy B. Musgrave, "Tax Preferences to Foreign Investment," in Economics of Federal Subsidy Programs, Part 2 – International Subsidies, Joint Economic Committee, 92d Cong., 2d Sess. 176 (1972) and discussion in Hearings on Tax Subsidies and Tax Reform, before the Joint Economic Committee, 92d Cong., 2d Sess. 192–196, 200–202 (1972); Peggy B. Musgrave, *United States Taxation of Foreign Investment Income* (Cambridge, Mass., Harvard Law School, 1969).

For the range of viewpoints and arguments, see Statements in Panel No. 11, note 16 above. The defenders of deferral are engaged in the tactics of strategic retreat and rear-guard action, such as suggesting elimination of deferral for "runaway corporations" manufacturing goods abroad for import into the United States, eliminating deferral for foreign shipping subsidiaries, or eliminating the escape hatch of minimum distributions. The Treasury in April 1973 took an intermediate position, recommending elimination of deferral where the foreign subsidiary enjoyed substantial tax incentives or manufactured abroad for import into the United States; see Statement of Treasury Secretary George P. Shultz in Hearings on General Tax Reform before the House Ways and Means Committee, 93d Cong., 1st Sess. (April 30, 1973), and the further explanation of those recommendations in a Treasury Department Release of June 11, 1973.

There are, of course, many technical issues involved in working out the tax mechanics of eliminating deferral, which issues are discussed in the above Statements and which are all surmountable. (For example, what form of limitation on the foreign tax credit is appropriate under a nondeferral approach?) Also, financial accounting requires that in reports to shareholders the profits of controlled foreign subsidiary corporations must be consolidated with the accounts of the United States parent corporation, so that the elimination of tax deferral is consonant with the requirements of financial accounting. Moreover, many corporations are using the minimum distribution approach to avoid the details of the anti-tax haven rules, and that approach if applied at the regular United States tax rate (rather than 43% as at present) is close to a nondeferral concept.

23. See Surrey, note 17 above.

24. For pros and cons regarding DISC, see Hearings on H.R.10947 [Revenue Act of 1971], before the Senate Finance Committee, 92d Cong., 1st Sess. (1971) and the floor debate in the Senate. See also the Statements in Panel No. 11, note 16 above. Most economists who look at DISC see it pretty much in the image of an airplane whose design is such as to make it impossible to leave the ground. Any possible payoff in increased exports is utterly inefficient in terms of revenue loss compared with balance of payments gains, in view of the price elasticity of exports; e.g., with an elasticity of 1.5%, a benefit which reduces the price of an export from $100 to $99, would raise sales to $100.50, which means a balance of payments gain of 50 cents for $1 of revenue loss. See Gerard M. Brannon, "The Revenue Act of 1971 — Do Tax Incentives Have New Life?," 14 Boston College Industrial and Commercial Law Review 891, 899 (1973).

The credit for foreign taxes is not listed as a tax expenditure. This nonlisting may require more analysis. Looked at only as a national matter, the foreign tax credit is not needed to measure net income, and a deduction would suffice. But the question remains to what extent the structuring of a normative income tax is to be affected by the requirements of proper international tax relationships. At present, judging from international tax treaties and conferences, those relationships require that recognition be taken by one country of the coexistence of income taxes in other countries. Although the foreign tax credit device per se has its set of problems as a method for that recognition, as does any other method, it presumably remains the most appropriate device. While economists, formerly generally favorable to that credit on tax neutrality grounds, are now raising more questions based on the aspects of national productivity and benefits to the United States, e.g. Statements by Peggy B. Musgrave, note 22 above, and in Panel No. 11, note 16 above, these questions do not seem to weigh the factor of international relationships and the effect for the United States, with respect to investment from abroad, if other nations should also withdraw from use of a foreign tax credit.

While this reexamination of the role of the foreign tax credit is useful, it seems likely the credit will remain in a basic form in our tax law as a reflection of appropriate international relationships. There are, however, a number of operating aspects of that credit that appear to invite tax abuse and hence require reexamination. For example, the use of the "overall limitation" in addition to the "per country limitation" permits an averaging of taxes paid in foreign countries, and thus is an incentive for corporations doing business in high-rate countries to invest in countries with low rates (with the total averaged taxes offset fully against the U.S. tax on the total foreign income) rather than in the United States. If deferral is not eliminated, consideration should be given to applying both limitations, but then confining the credit to the lower amount. Also, if deferral is to remain, consideration must be given to restrictions on the use of foreign losses to reduce the U.S. tax. See also the Statements in Panel Discussion No. 11, note 9 above, especially that of Stanford G. Ross at 1716.

The subject of the United States income tax treatment of nonresidents receiving income from United States sources has not been considered from the standpoint of tax expenditure analysis. This subject is also infused with the interplay between appropriate international relationships and national tax structures. Moreover, since the nonresident is not fully subject to U.S. tax jurisdiction, any U.S. income tax on the nonresident cannot in the end be based fully on the totality of his income, so that the basic tax expenditure analysis as applied to our citizens is not fully applicable. Nonetheless, this is a field in which more thought should be given to the consideration of a normative tax structure as qualified by the requirements of proper international tax relationships.

25. Treasury Tax Reform Studies, note 2 above, at 152–163.

26. See Chapter IV. For a range of viewpoints on the farm tax shelter, see the Statements in Panel No. 5, Farm Operations, in Panel Discussions on General Tax Reform, note 9 above, at 615.

27. Virden L. Harrison and W. Fred Woods, "Farm and Nonfarm Investment in Commercial Beef Breeding Herds: Incentives and Consequences of the Tax Law," U.S. Dept. of Agriculture, ERS-497 (1972). See also Virden L. Harrison, "Accounting Methods Allowed Farmers: Tax Incentives and Consequences," U.S. Dept. of Agriculture, ERS-505 (1973), discussing the artificial tax losses permitted under the present tax shelters and indicating that the wealthier the individual otherwise is, the greater are his "losses" in farm operations. One only has to translate "losses" into tax reduction rather than actual reverses to make this seeming paradox understandable.

28. See, e.g., House Ways and Means Committee, Tax Reform Act of 1969 [H.R. 13270], H.R.Rep. No. 413, 91st Cong., 1st Sess. (1969); Senate Finance Committee, Tax Reform Act of 1969, S.Rep. No. 552, 91st Cong., 1st Sess. (1969).

29. Treasury Tax Reform Studies, note 2 above, at 413–433; see also references in Chapter V. For a range of viewpoints, see the Statements in Panel No. 9, Natural Resources, in Panel Discussions on General Tax Reform, note 9 above, at 1243. The Treasury in April 1973 proposed an investment tax credit for exploratory oil drilling; see Statement of Treasury Secretary Shultz, note 22 above.

30. See in general M. A. Adelman, "Is The Oil Shortage Real?" Foreign Policy (Winter 1972–73) 76.

31. See Chapter VII.

32. See in general Richard L. Pollock, *Tax Depreciation and the Need For The Reserve Ratio Test* (Washington, D.C., U.S. Treasury Department, Tax Policy Research Study, No. 2., 1968).

33. *Common Cause v. Connally,* U.S. District Court for the District of Columbia, Civil Action No. 1337-71. See also Note, "The Controversy over Treasury Implementation of the Asset Depreciation Range System as an Attempt at Meaningful Depreciation Reform: A Give-Away or a Vital Step?" 41 University of Cincinnati Law Review 171 (1972). For a substantive evaluation of the administrative changes, see Emil M. Sunley, Jr., "The 1971 Depreciation Revision: Measures of Effectiveness," 24 National Tax Journal 19 (1971).

34. The Congress was disturbed by the Treasury's insistence on providing both the investment credit and the 20% reduction in class lives, the combination being viewed as just too much tax benefit to the business sector. It did reject the Treasury's change in the first year convention, which would have permitted a company to obtain depreciation for three-quarters of the year of installation as against the existing rule

of thumb of six months depreciation; the existing convention assumed all assets to be installed on July 1, whereas the Treasury sought to use the arbitrary date of April 1. The revenue loss involved in the proposed convention change was about half of the total loss for the entire Treasury proposal. The move in the Senate to defeat the 20% reduction in class lives lost by one vote. For legislative consideration of this matter, see the House Ways and Means Committee and Senate Finance Committee Hearings and Reports on the 1971 Revenue Act and the floor debates, especially in the Senate. See also 118 Cong. Rec. S14506-S14517 (daily ed. Sept. 11, 1972).

35. Discussions on rapid depreciation rarely separate the issues. The initial inquiry would seem to be whether the use of tax depreciation for the purpose of measuring net profits as accurately as possible should be altered to use tax depreciation for the incentive purpose of inducing increased investment in machinery and equipment as a means of encouraging economic growth. This inquiry in turn divides into the desirability and need of the latter encouragement, which is an overall economic and social question, and the suitability and effectiveness of rapid depreciation as an incentive to be used for the purpose. Most proponents of rapid depreciation seem to gloss over the second aspect. They also tend to disregard efforts to balance the interference with tax equity in using rapid depreciation against the effectiveness of such depreciation as an incentive tool. Further, the discussion is often confused by reference to the liberal capital recovery allowances used in other countries, without any examination of the relevance of such comparison or any attempt to determine whether other countries themselves are simply following an erroneous path which has for them all the problems and defects many in this country see in the use of rapid depreciation as an incentive. Moreover, those who resort to the argument based on international comparisons do not inform us that the cost of capital is only a minor part of the total production cost of assets, that transportation and other costs are also part of the comparative costs of exporting, or that there is little correlation between the relative rapidity with which the cost of capital is recovered under the tax systems of various countries and the relative standing of those countries with respect to the production of goods as a percentage of gross national product. Nor do they indicate that, as a consequence of recent devaluations of the dollar, the comparative capital cost figures have changed favorably to the United States, or that, essentially, in a world of flexible exchange rates changes in the competitive potential of a country would be offset by changes in exchange rates. See, for example, the discussion by advocates of the present system, John S. Nolan, C. Lowell Harriss, and Pierre A. Rinfret, in Panel No. 3, Tax Treatment of Capital Recovery, in Panel Discussions on General Tax Reform, note 9 above, at 345. Opponents of rapid depreciation, such as Martin David and Robert Eisner in the above Panel Discussion, concentrate on the aspect of balance between equity and effectiveness and find it adverse to the use of rapid depreciation. See also Gerard M. Brannon, "The Revenue Act of 1971 — Do Tax Incentives Have New Life?" 14 Boston College Industrial and Commercial Law Review 891 (1973); Paul Taubman, "The Investment Tax Credit, Once More," idem, at 871. Opponents also indicate that an incentive used to promote growth must be a flexible device that can be adjusted to reflect short-run anticipated economic conditions and can be turned off when that is the proper step under the economic forecast. Rapid depreciation is ill-suited to such flexibility, especially since some depreciation deduction is required to measure net profits, and confusion can only result in combining a flexible incentive with an instrument needed to measure net profits. Opponents of rapid depreciation find some form of an investment credit much to be preferred over rapid depreciation. See also the references in Chapter V.

Discussion can properly be had on the steps needed to permit effective administration of the depreciation deduction, as a measure of net income, so as to minimize controversy between taxpayers and revenue agents. But here proponents of rapid depreciation have not been helpful contributors, for in their zeal to defend rapid depreciation they rarely stop to balance the need to solve administrative problems against undue generosity to taxpayers or serious inequity among taxpayers. They defend both use of the 30th percentile to set class lives and the 20% permitted reduction from those lives, and then trample over any consideration of the merits of the reserve ratio test. One suspects many proponents of rapid depreciation recognize that any careful consideration of the utility of that test would defeat their efforts to hold on to the very large tax benefits that rapid depreciation allows. Accordingly, they have steadily mounted a cliche campaign against the reserve ratio test — "complex," "unworkable," and so on — and defeated all efforts to engage in a rational examination of that test and the techniques required for the Internal Revenue Service to apply it; e.g., Joel Barlow, "The Tax Bias Against Investment in Production Facilities," National Tax Association – Tax Institute of America Symposium on Tax Reform (1973). The Nixon Administration apparently never sought to explore these points, but instead dropped the test in order to accomplish its desire of achieving business tax reduction through rapid depreciation.

On the error of using the depreciation deduction both as a measure of net income and as an incentive, see the 1961 Tax Message of President Kennedy, in Hearings on President's 1961 Tax Recommendations before the House Ways and Means Committee, 87th Cong., 1st Sess. 25 (1961).

The Tax Expenditure Budget does not include methods of accelerated depreciation for machinery and equipment, such as the double declining balance method. See Appendix to Chapter I. It is interesting, however, to observe that for their financial accounting many companies use straight-line depreciation, although using accelerated methods for tax purposes. Also, Congress in seeking in several provisions for a benchmark for normal depreciation has used straight-line depreciation; e.g., §§163(d)(3)(C) and 312(m).

36. The 1971 Act also ratified a Treasury-proposed change to permit current deduction as "repairs" of amounts falling within industry repair guidelines, so as to avoid administrative disputes whether the amounts are deductible "repairs" or "capital expenditures." Empirical data on the validity of these guideline allowances are required to judge their appropriateness, and to determine whether this is an additional tax expenditure incentive. The Treasury has not published the needed data.

37. For a description of the 1969 Act changes, see Staff of the Joint Committee on Internal Revenue Taxation, General Explanation of the Tax Reform Act of 1969 (1970), 137–145. For a discussion of this tax expenditure, see Treasury Tax Reform Studies, note 2 above, at 458; Daniel I. Halperin, "Federal Income Taxation of Banks," 64 National Tax Association Proceedings 307 (1971).

One irony of this 1969 reform is that just as the commercial banks are beginning to lose the benefits of the tax expenditure for bad debts, they are discovering the tax reduction wonders of the equipment-leasing tax shelter and using that shelter to more than offset any tax increases from the bad debt change. See Chapter IV.

38. The tax expenditure deduction for interest on home mortgages is considered in Chapter VII. The deduction for interest on funds borrowed for business use or investment purposes is an appropriate deduction, as a cost of earning income. There are problems with that deduction, however, growing out of its interaction with tax shelters and other tax expenditures. Also, drawing the proper distinctions and

classifications in the area of interest payments may involve technical problems. See Chapter VII, note 107.

39. Individual lessors generally do not obtain the investment credit and hence would use the five-year amortization provision. This provision has permitted a generous tax shelter for individuals leasing to railroads and should be dropped for this reason. See Chapter V. The Senate in 1972 passed a bill for a $2 billion Government guarantee of the financing of railroad rolling stock, along with other provisions to ensure better utilization of equipment. S. 1729, 118 Cong. Rec. S12693-S12727 (daily ed. Aug. 4, 1972). This measure indicates that if the provision of additional railroad rolling stock is a national priority requiring Government assistance, then direct measures are available and a tax expenditure is not required.

40. The insured is not currently taxed on the interest being earned on the portion of his premiums allocated to the cash value reserve of his life insurance policy. This is the administrative understanding referred to in the text. If he surrenders the policy during his life, only the excess of cash surrender value over total premiums paid is considered income, so that much of the accumulated interest is not taxed in this situation. There is no income tax on life insurance proceeds paid by reason of the insured's death. Code §101(a).

41. For a discussion of this tax expenditure, see Charles E. McLure, Jr., "The Income Tax Treatment of Interest Earned on Savings in Life Insurance," in Economics of Federal Subsidy Programs, Part 3 – Tax Subsidies, Joint Economic Committee, 92d Cong., 2d Sess. 370 (1972). This paper states that the bulk of this tax expenditure assistance goes to families in the income range $5,000 to $25,000. See also Chapter III.

42. This item is, however, in a sense related in its effect on individuals to the item of medical expenses. See the later discussion of medical expenses in this chapter and also the discussion of these items in the Appendix to Chapter I.

43. Water pollution legislation enacted in 1972 does provide for federal loans to small business for buying effluent-control equipment. This demonstrates that if financial assistance is to be granted to private businesses, then direct programs can be readily structured for that purpose.

44. Treasury Tax Reform Studies, note 2 above, at 206–209. The Treasury in 1969 renewed the 1964 proposal for nondeduction, but the Congress again refused. See Hearings on H.R. 13270 [Tax Reform Act of 1969] before the Senate Finance Committee, 91st Cong., 1st Sess. 561 (1969).

45. See Kurtz and Surrey, note 3 above, at 1381. For a different approach to this problem, see Richard B. Covey, "Possible Changes in the Basis Rule for Property Transferred by Gift or at Death," 50 Taxes 831 (1972).

46. The minimum tax, where applicable, increases the top capital gains rate to 36.5%.

47. In lifetime transfers of assets by gift, the donor's tax cost carries over to the donee, so that at this stage deferral of tax and not complete exemption occurs. Exemption is also accorded to sales of residences by taxpayers over the age of 65 if the sales price is under $20,000, with the exemption scaled down if the price exceeds $20,000.

48. Treasury Tax Reform Studies, note 2 above, at 82–89.

49. Joseph A. Pechman and Benjamin A. Okner, "Individual Income Tax Erosion by Income Classes," in Economics of Federal Subsidy Programs, note 4 above, at 25.

50. See, e.g., Pechman, note 14 above at 96–99; Richard B. Goode, *The Individual Income Tax* (Washington, D.C., The Brookings Institution, 1964), 184–221; Martin David, *Alternative Approaches to Capital Gains Taxation* (Washington, D.C., The Brookings Institution, 1968); Martin David and Roger Miller, "The Lifetime

Distribution of Realized Capital Gains," in Economics of Federal Subsidy Programs, note 41 above, at 269.

51. Probably reflecting these doubts (or is it reflecting the power structure in the country?), no industrialized country taxes capital gains in full as ordinary income.

52. If capital gains are to be taxed, albeit as ordinary income, only when sales take place (or also on transfers by gift or at death), then full deduction for capital losses poses a problem, since the taxpayer can take his losses currently but postpone his gains by not realizing them. It would therefore presumably be necessary to allow capital losses to be applied only against capital gains, somewhat as today, but perhaps with a loss carryback as well as a carryforward, and perhaps as against ordinary income up to say $5,000 with an unlimited carryover until the loss is used up in this way or against capital gains. If the allowance is so limited, search should be made for a less complex definition of capital gains and losses than we have today, so that the hope of the reduced complexity to result from treating capital gains as ordinary income is borne out in actual structure.

53. See Statements of Richard A. Musgrave and Harvey E. Brazer in Panel No. 2 on "Capital Gains and Losses," in Panel Discussions on General Tax Reform, note 9 above, at 284 and 257.

There are dissenters, including those who seek to turn the income tax into a tax on consumption, and those who really do not regard capital gains as income, e.g., Statements of Norman B. Ture and Dan Throop Smith, in Panel No. 1 on "Objectives and Approaches to Tax Reform and Simplification," in Panel Discussions on General Tax Reform, note 9 above, at 153 and 35, and those who stress what they see as harmful effects on the economy, e.g., Statements of Henry C. Wallich and B. Kenneth Sanden, in Panel No. 2, above, at 270 and 245.

For Statements on the treatment of capital gains at death, see Panel No. 10, Estate and Gift Tax Revision, Panel Discussions on General Tax Reform, note 9 above, at 1487. Here some who would formerly have defended the present absence of taxation are conducting a strategic retreat and recommending substitutes for taxation at death, such as a carryover of the decedent's basis or a special estate tax on the gain, e.g., see Statements by Bart A. Brown, Jr. and Richard B. Covey in Panel No. 10 above, at 1504 and 1541. See also Richard B. Covey, Stanley S. Surrey, and David Westfall, "Perspectives on Suggested Revisions in Federal Estate and Gift Taxation," 28 Record of Assoc. of Bar of City of New York 42 (1973); also in 112 Trusts and Estates 102 (1973).

Even with capital gains taxed in full as ordinary income, the economist would recognize a preference if the gain is to be taxed only on sale (including transfer by gift or at death), since the consequent deferral of tax on the appreciation in value is a distinct benefit to the taxpayer. See, e.g., Carl S. Shoup, *Public Finance* (Chicago, Aldine Publishing Co., 1969), 323. The economist sees the continued holding of the asset as in effect a combined decision to sell and reinvest in the same asset, and hence the reinvestment does not in this regard differ from any other decision to invest income. Also, the accrued gain can be utilized effectively, as by a borrowing based on the security of the asset. The amounts involved are large; one estimate states that for the period 1948–1964, $682 billion in appreciation in value of assets accrued but only $147 billion was realized on sale, Kul B. Bhatia, "Accrued Capital Gains, Personal Income and Saving in the United States, 1948–1964," Review of Income and Wealth, Series 16, No. 4 (December 1970), 374 (Brookings Institution Reprint 200). See also a paper by James W. Wetzler, "The Effective Rate of the Capital Gains Tax," included in the Statement by Musgrave, note 53 above; Martin J. Bailey, "Capital Gains and Income

Taxation," in Arnold C. Harberger and Martin J. Bailey, *The Taxation of Income from Capital* (Washington, D.C., The Brookings Institution, 1969), 11. But "realization" of gain is a concept well ingrained in every modern tax structure, and no country applies the income tax to accrued but unrealized appreciation in value. Canada, for example, in recent years debated a step toward such taxation but declined the experiment. However, the effort should be made to reexamine the treatment of borrowing on the security of appreciated assets; see Chapter VIII.

Even when realization occurs, modern income tax structures still defer the tax on certain exchanges by not recognizing the gain where it is thought immediate tax would inhibit appropriate business transactions, such as corporate mergers, the incorporation of a proprietorship, and the like. Here the deferral approach requires that the new asset obtained on the exchange take the cost basis of the asset given up. Some of these tax postponement exchanges could well be reexamined, such as that covering real estate exchanged for real estate.

If a complete shift to taxing realized capital gains (and gains on gift or at death) as ordinary income is not obtainable, then the course should be to tax gains on gift and death; to increase as much as possible above the present 50% the percentage of inclusion of a gain; eliminate the special 25% rate; lengthen to a year the present six months dividing line between short-term gains included at 100% of the gain and long-term gains included at a lower percentage; contract as much as possible the coverage of assets and transactions given capital gain treatment.

54. See Musgrave, note 53 above, presenting data on these points, including a paper by Roger Brinner, "The Appropriate Tax Treatment of Nominal Capital Gains" (1973). Mr. Brinner's paper indicates that using data for the period 1947–1972, a person in the 50% bracket holding stock for 10 years should include 90% of the gain; for 20 years, 116%; and 25 years, 129%. For a 70% bracket person, the respective percentages are 84%, 101%, and 109%. The use of data for the period 1947–1959 would increase the percentages since the inflation rate change was not marked in those years; in contrast, the percentages would be lower under data for the period 1960–1972. See also a paper by P. A. Diamond, "Inflation and the Comprehensive Tax Base" (M.I.T., 1973), finding similar results.

It would thus be unwise to go to an approach that would start with a high percentage of inclusion and then reduce that percentage gradually as the holding of the asset increases, since the end result will be a low percentage of inclusion for assets held a long time, assets which have received the benefit of a long deferral of tax on the accrued gain. Moreover, such an approach would be clearly inconsistent with taxation at death. Also, even if we were to ignore the benefit of deferral, an adjustment of the percentage of inclusion to reflect inflation would call for an *increasing* percentage of inclusion of gain as the holding period lengthened rather than a decreasing percentage. If the asset is increasing in value at a greater rate than the rate of inflation, then the ratio of real gain to inflationary gain will increase rather than decrease the longer the asset is held. Thus, if the rate of asset value growth is 8% and the rate of inflation is 4%, the percentage of inclusion fractions required to remove the effect of inflation would be 50%, 54%, 59%, 67% and 87% for periods of 1, 5, 10, 20, and 50 years respectively. See Diamond, above.

Another argument sometimes advanced against full taxation of capital gains is that gains on sales of corporate stock reflect the retained earnings of the corporations involved and those retained earnings have already been taxed to the corporation under the corporate tax. This argument, of course, neglects to say why this should protect other capital gains, such as gains on real estate. But even those who dislike the use by the United States of a separate corporate tax and who prefer instead to see the corporation's income integrated with the income of the shareholder and taxed at the individual level and there only, do not see that such a result is approximated by combining a corporation tax with the present preferential treatment of capital gains on stock. The additional tax burden they see as imposed by the corporation tax is larger, measured in percentage of income per dollar of corporate profits, for the low-bracket shareholder than for the high-bracket shareholder. In contrast, the preferential exclusion of one-half of the capital gain results in a larger tax reduction, measured in percentage terms, for the high-bracket shareholder. As a consequence, "relief" for the presence of the corporation tax is granted by the capital gain preference where that relief is least justified. In actual numbers, looked at in terms of such "relief," the percentage of inclusion of a gain (that reflected corporate retained earnings) would be zero at a 48% individual rate bracket (around $40,000) and 60% at the top bracket, and minus 467% below the first bracket. Moreover, this aspect aside, gains on corporate stock often reflect more than previously taxed corporate earnings. Further, some would simply see the corporation tax as a separate tax and not try in any way to adjust the individual tax to the existence of the corporation tax; they are equally not concerned by the treatment of dividends as fully taxable income.

55. Improving Congressional Control Over Budgetary Outlay and Receipt Totals, Interim Report of the Joint Study Committee on Budget Control (Feb. 6, 1973). See also the discussion in Chapter V.

56. See Treasury Tax Reform Studies, note 2 above, at 434–438; Emil M. Sunley, Jr., "The Federal Tax Subsidy of the Timber Industry," in Economics of Federal Subsidy Programs, note 41 above, at 317.

57. Sunley, note 56 above at 326, notes that a 1968 Department of Agriculture publication outlining the significant milestones in the history of forest conservation does not mention the 1943 tax legislation.

58. Sunley, note 56 above, at 334; see Senate Committee on Agriculture and Forestry, Forestry Incentives Act of 1972, S. Rep. No. 856, 92d Cong., 2d Sess. (1972), also 118 Cong. Rec. S9421–9424 (daily ed. June 15, 1972).

59. Pub.L. No. 91–469, 91st Cong., 2d Sess. (Oct. 21, 1970).

The special treatment of controlled foreign subsidiaries engaged in shipping operations, an exception to the 1962 legislation governing the use of tax havens, is included in the general item of income of controlled foreign subsidiaries under *International Affairs.* This exception was the result of Defense Department statements that the United States-owned foreign flag fleet could be of assistance to the United States in time of war. If so, then a direct subsidy is appropriate rather than use of the tax system, which operates to provide substantial current benefits to individuals and companies engaged in shipping.

60. Treasury Tax Reform Studies, note 2 above, at 231–236. The recommendations essentially involved a flat basic additional exemption which declined and then vanished as income rose, together with inclusion of social security retirement payments in income. See Note, "Aid to the Elderly: What Role for the Income Tax?" 41 University of Cincinnati Law Review 93 (1972). The Congress, however, has not warmed to these recommendations and instead is moving to enlarge the tax benefits through a considerable increase in the retirement income credit — a step which would involve a revenue loss of $375 million (1972 data). Under the proposal, an individual could receive $5,142 of retirement income and pay no tax and a married couple could receive $7,962; the comparable figures for earned income under the House version would be $4,300 and $6,820. See House Ways and Means Committee, Social Security

Amendments of 1971 [H.R.1], H.R. Rep. No. 231, 92d Cong., 1st Sess. 237–247 (1971), and Senate Finance Committee, S. Rep. No. 1230, 92d Cong., 2d Sess. 587–596 (1972). The proposal was not adopted by the Conference Committee.

61. A proposal for a special deduction of up to $600 for disabled persons who cannot use public transportation was adopted in the Senate in connection with the 1969 Tax Reform Act, 115 Cong. Rec. 37,077–37,079 (1969), but rejected in Conference.

62. Stanley S. Surrey, "Income Maintenance Programs," 24 Tax Law Review 305, 330 and n.9 (1969). The definition of "income" used in the Family Assistance Plan (FAP) had a wider coverage than gross income under the current income tax. This is because it is obviously necessary to reach as realistic a determination as possible of the actual funds available for a family's support and consumption to insure the family is eligible for assistance based on need as measured by lack of resources. The items included under FAP but excluded under the income tax emphasize the tax expenditure character of the latter. FAP, of course, can have its own policy reasons for an exclusion, e.g., training allowances, so that exclusion from FAP does not mean the item, if also excluded under the income tax, is not a tax expenditure. The development of "income" for FAP purposes is bound to have an effect on the positive income tax, for over time the differences between the two approaches will increasingly require defensible justifications.

The proper coordination between the FAP benefit payment itself and the positive income tax is not yet developed. FAP payments would not have been part of gross income for the positive income tax, and where a family benefited by FAP would be subject to that income tax (i.e., the two systems overlap), the regular income tax liability would not be a factor in computing income for FAP purposes. It would seem that one possible path of coordination lies in having the FAP family subject to both systems pay only the lower of the "tax amounts," i.e., the regular income tax or the "tax" generated by applying the negative tax rate of the FAP system, in effect thus permitting the family to choose the route under which its disposable income after tax is higher. Another path lies in making the regular income tax a deduction in computing the resources available to the FAP family. With these approaches, it would not be appropriate to include the FAP benefit payment itself as an item of gross income for the regular tax, so that its exclusion would not be a tax expenditure. The exclusion in this view is a proper aspect of the coordination between negative and positive income tax structures.

Another approach is to treat the income tax personal exemptions and the low-income allowance as a credit against income tax, but then make the credit refundable where an individual's or family's income tax liability is less than the credit. The amount of excess credit so paid directly becomes in effect a negative income tax. There are of course policy and technical problems in this approach, such as the amount of the credit, the relationship of family composition and size to that amount, and the level of the positive income tax for the first bracket. The solutions to these problems determine the amount of tax liability change and income redistribution which the approach involves. The British are moving to a credit approach as respects employed persons and retired persons. Proposals for a Tax-Credit System, Cmnd. 5116 (1972). But their approach is narrower than that of a full-fledged income-maintenance credit and also their high initial starting rate for the income tax eliminates some problems the United States would face. Nevertheless, the British experience should be closely followed to see what guidance it offers for us.

63. The estimate is at 1970 income levels but assumes the 1973 tax law regarding personal exemptions, low-income allowances, and standard deduction levels.

64. Senate Committee on Labor and Public Welfare, Comprehensive Headstart,

Child Development, and Family Services Act of 1972 [S. 3617], S. Rep. No. 793, 92d Cong., 2d Sess. (1972). This measure passed the Senate.

65. The following quotations from the Senate Report, note 64 above, on direct child care programs, reveal the nature of some of the differences:

> We found, moreover, that the recently adopted child care deductions in the Revenue Act of 1971 will provide no assistance to families living in poverty and very little if any assistance to families with incomes between $4,000 and $8,000.
>
> Treasury Department statistics reveal, for example, that a family of four with an income of $5,000, spending $500 on child care, would realize no tax savings under this Act; and a family of four, with an income of $7,000, which spends $700 on day care would realize a savings of only $77 [at 4].
>
> . . .
>
> First, child development programs under our bill are totally voluntary. This differs sharply from some other day care proposals before the Congress, including some of the provisions in H.R. 1 as passed by the House of Representatives. Under our bill, no family is required to place their child in a day care program, a Head Start program, a part-day program or a nutrition program. These programs are offered solely and exclusively to families who chose to benefit from them. The bill specifically states in its first paragraph, that "child development programs must build upon the role of the family as the primary and most fundamental influence on children and must be provided only to children whose parents or legal guardian request them (Section 2(a)(1)).
>
> Second, the bill offers a whole series of services to children and families. It is not restricted to day care generally, or programs in day care centers specifically. Indeed, it doesn't even place a priority on day care. Instead, it assures that parents will have the opportunity to choose among the greatest possible variety of family supporting services — including part-day programs like Head Start, after school or full day developmental day care for children of working mothers, prenatal services, in-the-home tutoring and child development classes for parents and prospective parents.
>
> Third, the bill has increased and clarified the priority on strengthening family life by making full day, day care available only to children whose parents are out of the home all day. Services for children whose mothers are at home are limited generally to part-day programs or in-the-home-tutoring that builds on the mother-child relationship [at 9].
>
> . . .
>
> Moreover, the sliding scale fee basis in the program provides little or no financial incentives for families with incomes in excess of $10,000 to purchase day care for their children. In contrast, the increased child care income tax deductions signed into law last year provide considerable financial incentives to families in these income ranges to purchase day care, if both parents work [at 13].
>
> . . .
>
> The central requirement is that child development programs must, in fact, be developmental — centered on the needs of the children and the family — and not custodial in nature.
>
> The Committee intends that meeting the needs of the children and families served must be the overriding concern of those administering the bill at the departmental, prime sponsor and project level.
>
> Programs which meet the standards of this Act will require significant

expenditures per child. The Office for Child Development has estimated that desirable programs of group day care for 3– to 5-year-old children would cost an average of $2,372 per child, and that programs for children in school would cost an average of $635 per child. The same OCD study found that purely custodial services for children age 3 to 5 would cost an average of $1,425, and $310 for children in school.

The committee finds, on the basis of extensive testimony, that programs which do not provide developmental services may, in fact, have a stunting effect on the intellectual and emotional growth of the child, while programs that do provide such services may stimulate such growth. The bill therefore requires the additional expenditure per child necessary to provide developmental services [at 16–17].

. . .

The bill provides that children from all income levels are eligible to participate. Priority is placed on the provision of free services to children from families with incomes below the Department of Labor's lower living standard, adjusted for regional, and metropolitan, urban and rural differences. The committee expects the Bureau of Labor Statistics to develop this more sophisticated and detailed, three-way breakdown of metropolitan, urban and rural differences in the cost-of-living during the FY 1973 planning year. After the reservation of funds for poor children served under Headstart, two-thirds of the funds under this bill are reserved to provide services to children from families with incomes below the BLS lower living standard, and up to one-third of the funds are available to serve children from families with incomes above this lower living standard on a sliding scale fee basis established by the Secretary of HEW [at 17–18].

. . .

The bill provides that no charges be made to families with an annual income equal to or less than $4,320, with adjustments in the case of families with more than two children. Charges for other families may be made in accordance with a fee schedule established by the Secretary based on ability to pay. However, such fees may not exceed 10 percent of the difference between the free services level and 85 percent of the lower living standard budget, and then 15 percent of any income between that level of 85 percent of the lower living standard budget and 100 percent of the lower living standard budget [at 45].

See also the fee scale prescribed in the Economic Opportunity Amendments of 1972, H.R. 12350, Conference Committee Action reported at 118 Cong. Rec. S14,074 (daily ed. Sept. 5, 1972) for Project Headstart. No charge is made for the child of a family with an annual income less than $4,320. A graduated fee schedule is prescribed up to the level of the lower living standard budget determined by the Bureau of Labor Statistics. Beyond this level the HEW Secretary is given discretion to fix the fees.

See the extended discussion of child care in Charles L. Schultze et al, *Setting National Priorities: The 1973 Budget* (Washington, D.C., The Brookings Institution, 1972), 252–290.

The Tax Committees handle both the child care deduction and the proposed direct programs of child day care considered in connection with family assistance programs. The House Committee Report on the family assistance bill in 1971, note 60 above, did not address itself to the relationship between the two programs, although both programs were increased in the bill. The Committees on Labor and Welfare and Education and Labor handle the major child care programs.

66. In the 1971 legislative consideration of the child care deduction there was an unsuccessful effort to convert it into a deduction that determined adjusted gross income rather than an itemized deduction in the deduction group alternative to the standard deduction. Proponents of the change argued that child care expenses were really expenses directly incurred in the earning of the family income and hence just as much deductible as other business expenses. The courts have taken the other view and turned down taxpayers asserting this position. *Nammack v. Comm'r,* 56 T.C. 1379 (1971), *aff'd mem.,* 459 F.2d 1045 (2d Cir. 1972). Much of the force behind the position that child care is a real business expense derives from the view of womens' groups that the expense of child care is generally offset against the working wife's probable earnings to see how much *net* income *she* would add to the family by working. Under these mores, the child care deduction assists her in obtaining a freedom of decision on a parity with the husband. See, e.g., comment on *Nammack* decision in 41 University of Cincinnati Law Review 264 (1972). In this view, it would seem that if decisions as to who works outside the home were made regardless of sex, there would be no basis for the child care deduction. If so, as a matter of tax structure it is hard to see why the expense is really a business expense and not a personal expense. What steps Congress should take to assist in altering current mores regarding women and career occupations is a matter for direct expenditure programs, such as those for child care and development assistance, and not tax programs. Of course, if the imputed income of a family member staying home and providing child care and household services were taxed, then tax differences in this respect between that member working or staying at home would not exist; also there should be no deduction for amounts paid to others for child care and household services. This view then shifts the argument to whether a child care deduction is appropriate to offset the nontaxation of such imputed income. But tax measures having this function would seem to be properly classed as tax expenditures, and to be judged accordingly.

For discussions of the 1971 changes, see Alan A. Feld, "Deductibility of Expenses for Child Care and Household Services," 27 Tax Law Review 415 (1972); Roland L. Hjorth, "A Tax Subsidy For Child Care: Sec. 210 of the Revenue Act of 1971," 50 Taxes 133 (1972); William A. Klein, "Tax Deductions For Family Care Expenses," 14 Boston College Industrial and Commercial Law Review 917 (1973).

67. Another example is the tax credit adopted in 1971 for employers who hire individuals trained under the Labor Department WIN program for welfare recipients, a measure originating in the Senate Finance Committee.

68. In 1972 the Senate Finance Committee proposed, and the Senate adopted, a provision extending the employer tax credit for hiring welfare recipients (WIN) to cover nonbusiness employers. This would give individuals a tax credit for employing household help and is the logical extension of the household services part of the 1971 child care change. See Senate Report, note 60 above, at 596–599. The proposal was dropped by the Conference Committee, along with all other income maintenance provisions.

69. See the discussion of the medical expense deduction in the Appendix to Chapter I. For the distribution among income classes of direct medical program benefits and of tax expenditure benefits, see Statement of Karen Davis on Financing Medical Care Services: The Federal Role, in Hearings on the Costs of Medical Care before the Subcommittee on Consumer Economics, Joint Economic Committee, 93d Cong., 1st Sess. (May 15, 1973). The benefits under Medicaid are, for those under age 65, distributed 67% to families under $5,000 income, 15.3% to families between $5,000 and $9,999, 10.6% to families between $10,000 and $14,999, and 6.9% to families with $15,000 and over. The tax expenditure benefits under the medical deduction are

distributed among those income classes as follows: 10.6%, 25.8%, 28.3%, and 35.4%. The tax expenditure benefits provided through employer medical assistance are distributed among those income classes as follows: 14%, 35.3%, 27.4% and 23.3% (data from above Statement and Karen Davis).

70. About 45% of the benefits of the additional personal exemption for students goes to families with incomes over $15,000; 75% goes to families with incomes over $10,000. On the other hand, reflecting the distribution of scholarships and fellowships, about 70% of the benefits of this exclusion goes to families under $10,000 (Appendix tables in Chapter III). The additional personal exemption for a student is available if the parents contribute more than half of the student's "support." Since students from higher income families generally attend more expensive schools and live at a higher cost level, they have higher total "support" costs. Hence, these students can have higher incomes and still qualify for the additional exemption. The structure of this tax expenditure thus inherently favors the better-off families. Further, funds not spent on "support" are not counted, so that if a student saves his income or uses it for a non-support item, such as a car, he has enhanced his ability to qualify as a dependent. See David S. Mundel, "Federal Aid to Higher Education: An Analysis of Federal Subsidies to Undergraduate Education," in The Economics of Federal Subsidy Programs, Part 4 – Higher Education and Manpower, Joint Economic Committee, 92d Cong., 2d Sess. 407, 445–446 (1972).

71. It may be that some of the items in the second category will after examination of alternative programs be found to belong in the third category, i.e., where the alternative programs necessitate really special requirements.

The text discussion does not specifically cover the standard deduction. That deduction is a residual item, whose treatment depends on what happens to the itemized personal expense deductions — interest, taxes, charitable contributions, medical expenses, casualty losses, child care — to which the standard deduction is an alternative.

72. See, e.g., Hearings on Tax Proposals Affecting Private Pension Plans before the House Committee on Ways and Means, 92d Cong., 2d Sess. (1972); Hearings on S. 3598 [Retirement Income Security For Employees Act, 1972], before the Subcommittee on Labor of the Senate Committee on Labor and Public Welfare, 92d Cong., 2d Sess. (1972), and the bill reported by this Committee. This consideration has been renewed in the Congress in 1973. See, e.g., developments regarding S.4, 93d Cong., 1st Sess. (1973).

73. The courts had invalidated Treasury Regulations which did not grant recognition to these professional corporations. In the 1969 legislation the Treasury threw its weight against an amendment that would have sustained those Regulations for a period of time to permit the issue to be studied. With the consequent defeat of the amendment, the professional corporation became imbedded in the tax scene.

74. Statement of Daniel I. Halperin, in House Hearings, note 72 above, at 306.

75. Idem.

76. See, e.g., Statement of Arthur F. Burns, Chairman, Board of Governors of the Federal Reserve System, before the Subcommittee on Priorities and Economy in Government, Joint Economic Committee, 92d Cong., 2d Sess. 9 (Dec. 7, 1972):

> For the immediate future, the best hope for greater stability in housing lies in continued progress in controlling inflation, and particularly in better management of our fiscal affairs so that less reliance would need to be placed on credit policy to stabilize the overall economy. By making greater use of fiscal tools, sectors of the economy that are relatively immune to monetary policies could be made to bear their share of restraint during periods of excess demand.

Specifically, the Board recommends flexible use of the investment tax credit as a means of achieving greater stability in outlays by business firms for machinery and equipment. These expenditures are large, cyclically volatile, and relatively insensitive to monetary policy. During periods of credit restraint, expenditures for machinery and equipment have repeatedly drawn on resources that otherwise would have been available for housing.

If the investment tax credit were lowered in boom times and raised in slack periods, we would experience more stability in business demand for external financing, and therefore also in market interest rates and in the flow of funds for housing. This tax flexibility could be achieved by authorizing the President to vary the investment tax credit within prescribed limits, perhaps from zero to ten or fifteen per cent. Before a change in rate could become effective, a sixty-day waiting period should be allowed for disapproval by either House of Congress, analogous to the procedure for reorganization plans.

In a speech in June 1973 at the American Bankers Association International Monetary Conference, Chairman Burns used "perhaps 3 or 4 percent" rather than zero as the lower range for a flexible credit. See also the discussion of Robert Eisner, in Panel No. 3, note 35 above.

77. The investment credit does have different results from a direct subsidy: (1) The credit does not reduce the basis for depreciation, whereas a direct subsidy would, under present law, be treated as a contribution to capital and reduce that basis (Code §362(c)). The nonreduction of basis under the credit produces distortions as among taxpayers, favoring those in higher brackets since the extra depreciation is worth more to such taxpayers; see Emil M. Sunley, Jr., "Towards a More Neutral Investment Tax Credit," 26 National Tax Journal 209 (1973). See also the discussion of credits against tax in Chapter IV. (2) The credit is not available to nontaxpayers, such as state and local governments, colleges, and others; see Robert Eisner, in Panel Discussion No. 3, note 35 above. There are also structural aspects of the credit that produce variances from an across-the-board reduction in the price of new machinery and equipment and hence variances in benefits among industries and taxpayers. (3) The limitation of the credit to $25,000 of tax liability plus 50% of the excess of tax liability over $25,000 induces companies with losses or low effective tax rates to "sell" their credits by leasing rather than buying equipment, thus helping to create tax shelters in equipment leasing. The denial in 1969 of the investment credit to individual lessors in tax shelter leasing syndicates has had the effect of shifting this tax shelter activity to the commercial banks. A direct subsidy would be available to such loss companies; similarly, a removal of the limitation turning on tax liability and making the credit refundable to a loss company would have the same effect. These variances require further consideration; see article by Sunley, Jr., above, and also Paul R. McDaniel, "Tax Reform and the Revenue Act of 1971: Lesions, Lagniappes and Lessons," 14 Boston College Industrial and Commercial Law Review 813 (1973), recommending that the credit be allowed only to the "user" of the equipment so as to end tax shelter activity and also that the credit be refundable and includible in income, thereby turning the credit into a close parallel of a direct subsidy.

CHAPTER VII: THREE SPECIAL TAX EXPENDITURE ITEMS

1. The following description appears in Special Analysis P, "Federal Aid to State and Local Governments," Budget of the United States, Fiscal Year 1973, at 244–245 — it is one of the few references in the budget to tax expenditure assistance:

Apart from direct Federal aid, many other Federal activities that are not included in this analysis affect the finances of State and local governments. For example, the exemption of interest on State and local bonds from Federal income taxes reduced interest costs to State and local governments by $2.0 billion in 1971. This exemption results in about $3.0 billion in "lost" revenues to the U.S. Treasury. Similarly, since taxpayers may deduct State and local taxes from Federal taxable income, a portion of State and local taxes is offset by a reduction in the taxpayers' Federal liability. In 1971, the value of this deduction in terms of tax savings to individuals was approximately $8.5 billion.

2. The text discussion is partially based on Stanley S. Surrey, "Federal Income Tax Reforms: The Varied Approaches Necessary to Replace Tax Expenditures with Direct Governmental Assistance," 84 Harvard Law Review 352 (1970).

3. See, e.g., Lyle C. Fitch, *Taxing Municipal Bond Income* (Berkeley, Calif., University of California Press, 1950); David J. Ott and Allan H. Meltzer, *Federal Tax Treatment of State and Local Securities* (Washington, D.C., Brookings Institution, 1963).

4. House Committee on Ways and Means, Tax Reform Act of 1969 [H.R. 13270], H.R. Rep. No. 413, 91st Cong., 1st Sess. 172–173 (1969). The Committee used estimates of the tax effects that would occur if outstanding bonds, at their present interest rates, were made taxable. A more appropriate measure would be the effects of the present system compared to the consequences under taxable bonds and the interest changes that such taxation would involve. Clearly the latter involves some guess work. Under Treasury data, as of 1969, the revenue loss under the latter approach was estimated at $2.63 billion and the interest savings for state and local governments at $1.86 billion. Harvey Galper of the Urban Institute used estimates for 1970 of $3.3 billion and $2.5 billion in Hearings on S. 1015, S. 1699, S. 3001, and S. 3215 [Federal Financing Authority], Senate Committee on Banking, Housing and Urban Affairs, 92d Cong., 2d Sess. 277 (1972).

5. See generally Stanley S. Surrey, "Federal Income Taxation of State and Local Government Obligations," Tax Policy (May-June 1969), 3. But see Patrick Healy, "The Assault on Tax Exempt Bonds," Tax Policy (July-Aug. 1969), 2. While state and local governments sought in 1969 in debate and maneuver to deny or downgrade these problems, they also at times gave evidence of recognizing the difficulties that lay ahead. Idem, at 5–6.

6. H.R. 13270, 91st Cong., 1st Sess. §§601, 602, as passed by House, 115 Cong. Rec. 22,808 (1969). For an earlier recommendation of this approach, see Remarks of Honorable Stanley S. Surrey, Assistant Secretary of the Treasury, on "Tax Trends and Bond Financing," before the Municipal Forum of New York, June 13, 1968, and on "The Financing of New Social Programs — and Tax Exemption," before the Fifth Municipal Conference, Investment Bankers Association, Sept. 27, 1968.

7. See generally Stanley S. Surrey, "The Tax Treatment of State and Local Government Obligations — Some Further Observations," Tax Policy (Sept.-Oct. 1969), 3, 8–15. But see Patrick Healy, "Further Comments on Proposed Capital Financing Alternatives," Tax Policy, (Jan.-Feb. 1970), 1.

The campaign itself is illustrative of the way such lobbying efforts are conducted. It also illustrates how little attention is often paid by key figures to crucial events in the tax scene. There is every indication that top level names are signed to statements and letters without any real thought to the stakes involved. Thus, Mayor Lindsay of New York City, despite the financial woes of the city, almost casually, it seems, invoked the usual rhetoric and turned down the subsidy. Hearings on H.R. 13270 [Tax Reform

Act of 1969] before the Senate Committee on Finance, 91st Cong., 1st Sess. 3628–3629 (1969); see in general idem, at 2989–3371, 3599–3894.

8. The Senate Finance Committee said:

> While there may be a problem here, the committee, because of its concern that any action with respect to State and municipal bonds could have a deleterious effect on the market for these bonds, and because of the high interest costs which are now being paid on new issues of such bonds, concluded that any action possibly having an impact on State and local government bond prices would be particularly unfortunate.

Senate Committee on Finance, Tax Reform Act of 1969, S. Rep. No. 552, 91st Cong., 1st Sess. 218 (1969). Chairman Russell B. Long had put it more directly during the Hearings:

> If you have to be elected from a State and you find that every elected official down there is against what you are asked to vote for, you would be inclined to recognize the facts of life, and not only do they make a logical argument, they have the power to take you out of office if you cannot appreciate it.

Hearings on H.R. 13270 [Tax Reform Act of 1969], note 7 above, at 3372 (1969). See also 115 Cong. Rec. 40,868 (1969) (statement of Chairman Wilbur Mills regretting that final version of 1969 Act did not contain the House provision).

9. Thus, Frank E. Morris, President, Federal Reserve Bank of Boston, has concluded:

> [State] and local governments are likely to be facing in the 1970's capital requirements of a magnitude which their traditional financing vehicle, the tax-exempt bond market, is not likely to be able to handle in any reasonably efficient manner.

Frank E. Morris and Stanley S. Surrey, "The Case for Broadening the Financial Options Open to State and Local Governments," in Financing State and Local Governments, Federal Reserve Bank of Boston, June 1970. The paper provides an "efficiency index" to measure the effectiveness of the tax-exempt market from 1945–1970 and also an index of the "indifference rate for commercial banks," which largely determines the efficiency of the market. See also Kent Sims, "Municipal Bonds and Public Needs," Federal Reserve Bank of San Francisco Monthly Review, July 1970, reprinted in 116 Cong. Rec. 31,661 (1970); David J. Ott and Attiat F. Ott, "The Tax Subsidy through Exemption of State and Local Bond Interest," in the Economics of Federal Subsidy Programs, Part 3 – Tax Subsidies, Joint Economic Committee, 92d Cong., 2d Sess. 305 (1972).

10. Frank E. Morris, "Restructuring the Municipal Bond Market," New England Economic Review (Jan.-Feb. 1971), 47.

In 1972 Mr. Morris provided the following data to support his view that commercial banks cannot absorb the quantity of new state and local issues required to meet the needs of those governments, in an address before the First Public Finance Conference, Security Industries Association, Sept. 15, 1972:

> The history of the municipal bond market is that it has tended to perform relatively well whenever the economy had a substantial amount of slack and

commercial banks had both the resources and the inclination to absorb 70% to 80% or more of the new offerings. When these conditions did not prevail, it has tended to perform relatively poorly. In tighter money markets, interest rates on municipal bonds had to rise high enough to induce individuals to absorb that part of the market which the commercial banks were forced to vacate in order to meet the borrowing needs of their business customers, large and small.

The decade of the 1960's was the golden age for the tax-exempt bond market, primarily because of the greatly increased participation of commercial banks as investors in the market. During the decade of the 50's, commercial banks absorbed less than 21% of the net new issues of municipal bonds; during the 60's they absorbed almost 70% of the new issue volume. As you all know, however, their support of the municipal market had considerable cyclical volatility. In the tight money years of 1966 and 1969, commercial bank participation in the market declined to only 33% and 5% of the new issue volume, respectively.

At the end of 1960 commercial banks owned about 25% of the total of municipal bonds outstanding; by the end of 1970 they owned almost 50% of the total outstanding. At the end of 1960 municipal bonds constituted less than 9% of commercial bank portfolios; by the end of 1970 this percentage had risen to more than 15%. Commercial banks found room in their portfolios for this great increase in municipal bonds by reducing the percentage of their assets held in United States Government obligations from almost 31% at the end of 1960 to a little over 13% by the end of 1970.

I believe that there was a one-shot quality in the level of support of the municipal bond market by commercial banks in the 60's. In my judgment, the commercial banks will not be in a position to support the municipal market on a similar scale in the 70's. This is the principal reason why I think we must be planning now for the establishment of an alternative, taxable market for municipal bonds.

One element in the problem is the sheer volume of projected state and local issues. Net new issues of municipal bonds rose from $5.2 billion in 1960 to $11.8 billion in 1970 and a whopping $20.2 billion last year. We are projecting a "normal level" of net new issues of $31.1 billion in 1980.

What would be required of the commercial banks, given this projected volume, if they were to lend the same degree of support to the municipal bond market in the 70's that they did during the decade of the 60's? We estimate that if the banks were to absorb, on the average, 70% of the net new issue volume through 1980, commercial bank holdings of municipal bonds would have to rise from the end of 1971 level of $82.9 billion to about $225 billion by 1980. This would mean that commercial banks would own more than 61% of the total outstanding volume of the state and local issues and that municipal bonds would constitute 21% of commercial bank portfolios. This, in my judgment, is not likely to happen for the following reasons:

1. Many banks, large and small, are already finding that there are both limits to the amount of tax-exempt income that they can effectively utilize and limits to the amounts that they can invest in tax-exempt securities if they are to be prepared to meet the needs of their commercial and industrial customers.

2. The bank holding company vehicle is providing commercial banks with new ways of employing their funds which will compete powerfully in profitability with investments in municipal bonds and some of these alternative investment opportunities, such as leasing companies, generate large depreciation throw-offs which may substantially reduce the need for tax-exempt income.

3. The larger banks in the country which have mature foreign branches are now generating large foreign tax credits which also reduce the need for tax-exempt income. This is one reason why municipal bonds are currently a declining proportion of the portfolios of the weekly reporting member banks of the Federal Reserve System.

4. Commercial banks, both large and small, have reduced their portfolios of United States Government bonds close to a practical minimum. Their ability to make further shifts in portfolio composition in favor of municipal bond holdings at the expense of U.S. Government bond holdings is going to be much more limited in the 70's than it was in the 60's.

For these reasons I firmly believe that commercial banks will not be able to play in the future the dominant role which they have played in the past in supporting the municipal bond market. Questions of tax equity aside, there are simply not going to be enough high-bracket individual investors to support at reasonable interest rates the $31 billion net new issues of tax-exempt municipal bonds in 1980. These are the reasons why I feel that state and local governments must have available to them an alternative, taxable bond market instrument if they are to meet their capital needs in a reasonably adequate manner during the decade ahead.

11. Harvey Galper, Remarks before the Seminar on State and Local Finance, Federal Reserve Bank of Boston, Aug. 30, 1971. In later testimony, note 4 above at 278, Mr. Galper stated:

The second problem is a probable longer run insufficiency of capital funds to finance the needed facilities of State and local governments over the next decade. Studies have indicated that the long-term borrowing demands of these governments will be in the area of $30 billion by 1975 and $50 billion by 1980.

Furthermore, commercial banks may be unable to attract the financial resources over the coming decade to absorb as large a proportion of total municipal offerings as they have in the sixties when they purchased over 71 percent of net new issues. Thus, the ability of the municipal bond market, as it is presently constituted, to provide for the growing financial demands of the State and local sector is subject to question.

12. Galper, note 11 above.

13. Morris and Surrey, note 9 above, at 125.

Under the "efficiency index" of the Boston Federal Reserve Bank, 100% efficiency occurs when all of the benefits of tax exemption flow to the issuing governments — which would require an interest rate of 2.25% under present tax rates and corporate bond yields. Zero efficiency would occur when all of the benefits of tax exemption flow to the investor, i.e., when interest rates on tax-exempt bonds made them comparable to corporate bonds to a tax-exempt buyer.

14. Susan Ackerman and David Ott, "An Analysis of the Revenue Effects of Proposed Substitutes for Tax Exemption of State and Local Bonds," 23 National Tax Journal 397, 398 (1970); see also Robert P. Huefner, "Municipal Bonds: The Costs and Benefits of an Alternative," 23 National Tax Journal 407 (1970).

15. The individual would on the taxable bond pay in tax 70% of $9.11, or $6.38, leaving a net of $2.73. Purchase of the tax-exempt bond provides $6.75 interest, or a net gain of $4.02. The issuing authority saves $2.36, the difference between $9.11 and $6.75.

16. The subsidy would be sufficient to bring the net interest cost to the public issuer down to the level of the interest costs paid by private nonprofit hospital borrowers subsidized under the federal legislation.

17. H.R. 15979, 91st Cong., 2d Sess. (1970) enacted as Pub. L. No. 91–617 (Dec. 31, 1970); see 116 Cong. Rec. 22,740–22,744 (1970), for House enactment. The House Ways and Means Committee, Tax Treatment of Interest on Farmers Home Administration Insured Loans, H.R. Rep. No. 1112, 91st Cong., 2d Sess. 2–3 (1970) states:

> Studies by the Treasury Department and the Bureau of the Budget have indicated that it is costly to the Federal Government to use federally insured tax-exempt obligations to finance loans to local governmental units. The studies indicate that while the tax exemption makes it possible to resell the insured loans at a lower interest rate than would otherwise be possible, the loss of tax revenue resulting from the exemption more than offsets the benefits of the lower interest payments.
>
> Additionally, it was concluded that the sale of bonds which are both tax exempt and insured by the Federal Government would give these bonds a competitive advantage over both State and local securities which are subject to Federal income tax. As a result, the sale of such bonds could well have increased interest rates on other bonds, particularly those issued by States and localities and hampered their ability to finance other vital public needs.
>
> . . .
>
> The proposed legislation will not increase interest rates to the local communities involved in the federally insured loans since these communities can continue to obtain loans at present low interest rates of not over 5 percent, which are below the current market rates on good quality, long-term, tax-exempt bonds. Moreover, the bill does not in any way interfere with the right of local governments to issue tax-exempt obligations.

18. Pub. L. No. 91–609 (Dec. 31, 1970).

19. See, in general, Statement of Murray L. Weidenbaum, Assistant Secretary of the Treasury, in Hearings on S. 582, S. 632, S. 638, and S. 992 [Coastal Zone Management] before the Subcommittee on Oceans and Atmosphere of the Senate Committee on Commerce, 92d Cong., 1st Sess. 225–234 (1971).

A fourth illustration, similar to those in the text is the use of taxable bonds by the District of Columbia to finance the construction of its new subway, the bonds obtaining a 25% interest subsidy and a guarantee from the Federal Government.

20. See Surrey, Remarks before Fifth Municipal Conference, Investment Bankers Association, note 6 above; 115 Cong. Rec. 1316–1317 (1969) (remarks of Senator John Sparkman); Charles M. Haar and Peter A. Lewis, "Where Shall the Money Come From?," The Public Interest (Winter 1970), 101; Peter A. Lewis, "The Case for the Urban Development Bank," in Federal Reserve Bank of Boston Compendium, note 9 above, at 159.

21. Budget Message of the President, Fiscal Year 1971, at 31, reprinted in 116 Cong. Rec. 2077, 2084 (1970). See also Statement of Paul A. Volker, Undersecretary of the Treasury for Monetary Affairs, in Hearings on H.R. 5790, before the House Public Works Committee, 92d Cong., 1st Sess. (1971); Statement of Murray L. Weidenbaum, note 19 above.

22. While the obligations purchased by the public were not issued directly by the Federal Government, they were guaranteed by it. The 1970 legislation in effect provided separate "development banks" for the programs involved; the hospital

legislation was described in the Senate as "a sort of public hospital urbank." 116 Cong. Rec. 10,557 (1970) (remarks of Senator Edward M. Kennedy).

23. See, e.g., 92d Cong., 1st Sess., H.R. 9688, Title 8, Housing and Urban Development Act; S. 2223, Rural Development Bank; S. 580, H.R. 3550, National Development Bank; S. 1958, National Domestic Development Bank; S. 2058, Small Community Development Agency; H. R. 7594, State and Metropolitan Development Agency.

24. Morris and Surrey, note 9 above, at 132.

25. The 1971 statement of the League recommended as the first choice a subsidy for state and local bonds purchased by state and local pension funds. But this is clearly recognized as a halfway house, and inferior to a subsidized taxable bond approach. Frank E. Morris, President of the Boston Federal Reserve Bank, has pointed out the limitations of the pension fund proposal, note 10 above, at 51; essentially it adds only a limited group of new buyers whereas the pertinent question is why there should be any such restriction on the available buyers.

26. Federal Reserve Bank of Boston, Release R792, Sept. 2, 1971, noted in American Banker, Sept. 3, 1971, at 1, col.2; *Washington Post,* Sept. 3, 1971, p.D8.

27. Policy Positions of the National Governors' Conference, Sept. 1971, p.12. The statement is cautiously worded, but is regarded as authorizing the representatives of the Conference to pursue the taxable bond route rather than the development bank route.

28. See *Wall St. Journal,* Dec. 1, 1971; *N.Y. Times,* Dec. 1, 1971.

29. Senate Hearings, note 4 above.

30. Statement of Treasury Secretary George P. Shultz, in Hearings on General Tax Reform before the House Ways and Means Committee, 93d Cong., 1st Sess. (April 30, 1973). The proposal contained the following exceptions:

> An otherwise eligible issue will not qualify if--
> A. the Secretary determines that the net interest expense is unrealistically high based on fair market value.
> B. the maturity of the obligation is less than one year.
> C. it is held by a congressionally established entity owned in whole or in part by the United States, or by a unit which is an issuer of obligations to which section 103(a)(1) applies.
> The limitation in subdivision C is necessary to avoid further federal interest subsidy payments on loans made by HUD, HEW, Commerce, and other federal agencies at interest rates which are already heavily subsidized. It will also prevent one state from purchasing subsidized, taxable obligations of another state with proceeds from its own issuance of subsidized obligations.

The reason for the first exception is not clear, since the Treasury now subsidizes, through tax exemption and would continue to do so, a state or local bond, whatever the interest rate. However, under the Treasury proposal the 30% subsidy is applied to the "net interest expense," which, in addition to interest paid to the bondholder, also includes the amounts paid to intermediaries in the course of issuing the bonds and in day-to-day servicing of the issue. The first exception does permit a control over those costs.

31. Indicative of the attitudes on this subsidy approach is the decision of the House Ways and Means Committee in its 1973 Panel Discussions on General Tax Reform, 93d Cong., 1st Sess., to limit the discussion on tax-exempt bonds to a consideration of that approach. All the panelists, including a mayor apparently representing the

viewpoint of state and local officials, favored the approach; Panel No. 8, An Alternative to Tax-Exempt State and Local Bonds, in Panel Discussions above, at 1171. The discussion took place on February 23, 1973, before the Treasury proposal had been made.

32. See Statement of Frank E. Morris, President, Federal Reserve Bank of Boston, in Panel No. 8, note 31 above, at 1192. See also Peter Fortune, "The Impact of Taxable Municipal Bonds: Policy Simulations With A Large Econometric Model," 26 National Tax Journal 29 (1973), providing further data on the Federal Reserve Bank of Boston Study. Another article by Peter Fortune, "Tax Exemption of State and Local Interest Payments: An Economic Analysis of the Issues and an Alternative," New England Economic Review (May/June 1973) 3, concludes that a 33% subsidy "is not likely to induce any use of taxable municipal bonds in the long run," while a 50% subsidy would "lead to almost a complete displacement of tax-exempt by taxable municipal bonds." On these assumptions, looking at the picture as of 1980, continuance of the present system of tax-exempt bonds (or adoption of a 33% subsidy since it would involve no basic change) would show an annual revenue cost of $9.3 billion to the Treasury and interest savings of $7.1 billion to state and local governments. The adoption of a 50% subsidy would show an annual *subsidy* cost of $11.1 billion to the Treasury and interest savings of $11.1 billion to state and local governments. While the assumed complete replacement subsidy of tax-exempt bonds by taxable bonds under a 50% subsidy would increase federal costs by $1.8 billion, it would increase state and local interest savings by $4 billion. Further, the $2.2 billion windfall of high-tax investors under a tax-exempt system (and a 33% subsidy) would be eliminated. The Fortune article concludes that "An additional cost to the Treasury of about $1.8 billion seems a small price to pay for the elimination of the problems associated with tax-exemption."

A Statement by Harvey Galper in Panel No. 8, note 31 above, at 1176 reaches the same general conclusions. As does Mr. Morris, he sees little to be gained by limiting the subsidy to 33.3%. He states that at a subsidy rate above 48%, however, Treasury costs rise rapidly and little is gained in return, since commercial banks would have turned to taxable securities anyway.

33. Senate Committee on Banking, Housing and Urban Affairs, Municipal Capital Market Expansion Act [S.3215], S. Rep. No. 836, 92d Cong., 2d Sess. (1972).

34. See, e.g., remarks of Senator William Proxmire, in Senate Hearings, note 4 above, at 193–194.

35. The Committee had before it an estimated cost to the Treasury of $412 million.

36. See the following from Morris, note 10 above, at 50–51:

The basic short-coming of the various proposals which have been made to date is that the proposed Federal interest subsidy has been too small. Most of the proposals have fallen within a 20 to 40 percent subsidy range — largely because of what I consider an undue concentration on establishing a subsidy level which would provide a financial break-even point for the Treasury. It is not at all clear to me that, in an era in which the Federal Government is providing $27 billion in grants to state and local governments and in which there is widespread support for massive revenue sharing with no strings tied, the level of a Federal interest subsidy should be determined upon the basis of a narrowly conceived break-even point for the U.S. Treasury.

However, if the issue is to be decided on the basis of cost-benefit analysis, it should not be overlooked that there are two subsidies involved — the subsidy given directly in the form of an interest subsidy if the issuer chooses to issue taxable bonds, and the subsidy given indirectly if the issuer chooses to issue tax-exempt bonds. It is axiomatic that the larger the direct subsidy, the smaller will be the indirect subsidy; since a smaller volume of tax-exempt bonds would be issued. In measuring the cost to the Treasury, it is the combined costs of the two subsidies relative to the benefits *actually received* by state and local governments which is the relevant measure. In the framework of cost-benefit analysis, it seems clear to me that the direct interest subsidy should be large enough to avoid significant "wastage" in the subsidy given directly through tax exemption. Such a cost-benefit analysis would, in my judgment, support a 50 percent subsidy level.

If state and local governments had the option of operating either in the tax-exempt market or in the taxable market with a 50 percent interest subsidy, I believe that they would realize substantial interest savings; because such a dual market system would avoid the overloading of the tax-exempt market and, in so doing, it would also eliminate most of the "wastage" of the benefit of the subsidy given through tax exemption which such an overloading inevitably produces.

37. Apparently some investment bankers have led state and local government officials to worry that if taxable bonds replace tax-exempt bonds and *then* some day for some (unexplained) reason the subsidy legislation is repealed, the investment houses will have lost their know-how in marketing tax-exempt bonds and will not be able to assist state and local governments desiring again to issue such bonds. But experienced and objective observers believe, on the contrary, that investment houses could readily switch to selling tax-exempt bonds once more — it would not take long to exploit the renewed tax-exempt shelter. See also Fortune, note 32 above, at 38.

38. Presumably, given a 50% subsidy approach, the interest rate on any new tax-exempt bonds still issued would be around one-half that of taxable bonds.

39. The following are the recommendations made by panelists before the House Ways and Means Committee in 1973, Panel No. 8, note 31 above:

Frank E. Morris, President, Federal Reserve Bank of Boston (1198):

> With the passage of time and the maturing of outstanding issues, the tax equity aspect of tax-exempt bonds would no longer be a matter of public concern. From a cost-benefit point of view a 50% subsidy gets the highest marks. Our Capital Markets Model suggests that it would generate interest savings to state and local governments of around $350 million a year at a very modest cost to the U. S. Treasury — somewhere in the neighborhood of $50 million a year. Thus the interest savings to state and local governments would be about seven times the net cost of the program to the Federal Government.
>
> A major disadvantage of a 50% subsidy program is that it is likely to produce some considerable short-term disruption in the capital markets, since the bond underwriters would be forced over night to shift from marketing tax-exempt bonds to taxable bonds. I would not want to exaggerate the length of time or the extent of the problems the capital markets would encounter in making this adjustment, but there would inevitably be some short-term problems. I suspect that many state and local officials would prefer to see a taxable municipal bond market firmly established before the tax-exempt market were, de facto, eliminated.
>
> It is for this reason that my own preference at this juncture would be to establish a 40% interest subsidy on taxable municipal bonds. This will establish the taxable municipal bond market on a firm and continuing basis. With a strong taxable market firmly established, the Congress could then move to a 50%

subsidy program without running the risk of creating short-term instability in the financing of state and local capital projects.

Harvey Galper, The Urban Institute (1190):

[Although] the subsidy at 48% is still contributing to total equity and to reducing state and local interest payments it is doing so at increasing costs. Furthermore, the sum of the marginal increase in equity (reduction in incomes) and the reduction in municipal interest payments is almost identical to the increase in net Treasury costs.

We should not take this to mean that the subsidy should be set at exactly 47.99%. Certainly our results do not lend themselves to this kind of precision. If 48% seems to represent the outside limit to the subsidy, there may be compelling reasons, not included in our model, to stop well short of 48%. For one thing, taxable and tax-exempt bonds are not perfect substitutes even at the same after-tax yields. As a result, investors including commercial banks may switch out of tax-exempt securities before a precise break-even point is reached. Similarly, differential effects for different maturities of municipal debt may effectively eliminate the tax-exempt market in the longer end of the maturity spectrum while tax-exempt short-term debt is still issued. If one objective is to maintain a viable tax-exempt market for all maturities, we have another reason for a slightly lower subsidy. In light of these considerations, I would recommend a subsidy in the 40–45% range. Our research indicates that moving beyond this will purchase relatively little in the way of equity or gains to state and local governments in return for the higher Treasury costs.

Wallace O. Sellers, Vice President, Merrill Lynch, Pierce, Fenner and Smith, Inc. (1221):

I have selected the rate of 33–1/3 percent because I feel it reflects a favorable relationship between taxable and tax-exempt yields and one which supplies positive benefits where they are of most use, in the long end of the market. It would allow both markets to coexist, keeping check on one another. Thus, it preserves for the issuers a meaningful option. . . .

A much higher rate of subsidy would rapidly erode the existing tax-exempt market by moving virtually all long-term debt to the taxable bond sector. Rather than easing and stabilizing conditions in the long-term municipal bond market, it could subvert that market and create overnight a very large and untested supply of taxable municipal obligations. Such bonds would be unfamiliar to the major taxable bond investors and, I believe, might glut the market and force up rates on taxable issues to a much greater degree than expected.

Peter Fortune, who has studied this area with the aid of an econometric model of U.S. capital markets, has concluded (note 32 above, New England Economic Review at 19):

A 33 percent subsidy rate will have no effect on the form of municipal debt in the long run but it will shelter the tax-exempt interest rate from the volatility imparted to it by monetary policy. Thus, this low subsidy rate will deal with the short-run marketing problem but it will have little, if any, effect on the long-run problems of efficiency and tax equity. Furthermore, since this low subsidy rate will induce little (if any) use of taxable bonds it will result in very little additional interest savings for municipalities or additional cost to the Treasury. A 40 percent subsidy also promises little long-run impact on the efficiency and tax equity problems, although it is better in these respects than a 33 percent rate since it will induce some use of taxable bonds in the long run.

An effective taxable bond option — one which eliminates the problems cited above — is likely to require a subsidy rate in the range of 45–50 percent. Our estimates suggest that a 50 percent subsidy rate will almost eliminate issues of tax-exempts, thereby eliminating the marketing, efficiency, and tax-equity problems of tax-exemption. It will do this while raising the interest savings of municipalities by roughly 70 percent, and the costs to the U.S. Treasury by a *maximum* of 20 percent, compared to the interest savings and Treasury costs which will be experienced if only tax-exempt municipal bonds are issued.

Mr. Fortune also states (note 32 above, National Tax Journal at 39):

> Our results suggest that while the costs to the U.S. Treasury are higher for a 40% rate than a 33% rate, they might well be *lower* for a 50% rate than a 40% rate. This outcome will occur if commercial banks behave discontinuously and withdraw completely from the tax-exempt market when a 50% rate is allowed. Banks might well behave this way since at a 50% subsidy rate the yield advantage for tax-exempts is eliminated for purchasers with tax rates of 50% or below. In short, if the political decision reduces to a choice between a 40% rate and a 50% rate the latter might provide the most equity with the most benefit to state-local governments and the least cost to the U.S. Treasury.

40. Interest rates vary depending on the various maturities for state and local bond issues. See the paper of Wallace O. Sellers, in Panel No. 8, note 31 above, at 1199. Short-term maturities, less than one year, generally carry an interest rate about 40% to 50% of the rate on U.S. Treasury note yields. The exemption here offers little tax advantage to commercial banks and is reasonably efficient, though it does offer tax advantages to a 70% bracket individual. As maturities lengthen, the interest differential decreases, being around 30–40% for maturities from 5 to 10 years, and 20 to 30% for maturities from 20 to 30 years. Hence the recommendation in the text, using only a 40% rate for maturities over five years.

41. The Boston Seminar, note 26 above, so thought. See also S.3215, note 33 above, continuing the industrial development bond non-tax-exempt, and hence non-subsidized, status. At some point, however, some of the still tax-exempt, and hence eligible for direct assistance under the taxable bond approach, industrial development bond categories need reappraisal. An example is the rapidly growing category of tax-exempt industrial development bonds to finance the acquisition of pollution control equipment by private companies; see *New York Times,* Oct. 22, 1972, p. F14. Care would have to be taken that the arbitrage bond rules are properly drawn to prevent subsidies being paid on bonds issued to take advantage of arbitrage swings between the interest rates on subsidized taxable bonds and those on Federal Government and agency bonds. The Treasury has proposed, note 30 above, new legislation to deal with arbitrage problems in relation to tax-exempt bonds and this proposal would have to be coordinated with any taxable bond subsidy.

42. As time passed, the value of outstanding tax-exempt bonds would rise, giving windfall gains from scarcity to their holders. These gains could well be taxed as ordinary income through legislative change. Further, consideration should be given

to making the interest on new federal issues taxable by state and local governments.

43. The assistance, however, may not be efficiently distributed. See J. Maxwell, *Financing State and Local Governments,* rev. ed. (Washington, D.C., Brookings Institution, 1969), 193:

> The benefits derived by state and local governments from the issuance of exempts accrue more to governmental units in high-income areas than in low simply because the former units issue more debt [per capita] . . . . Regarded as a subsidy, therefore, exemption is inefficient. And even though the exemption may not be more valuable to governmental units with high credit ratings than it is to those with low, the exemption is not distributed according to need.

For a discussion of the effect of the exemption on the allocation of capital between state and local governments and other sectors, see Ott and Ott, note 9 above.

44. This would also be true for development bank approaches, where the assistance would appear in the accounts of the particular agency.

45. Healy, note 7 above, at 8–9.

46. On the constitutional issue, see generally Comment, "Intergovernmental Tax Immunities: An Analysis and Suggested Approach to the Doctrine and its Application to State and Municipal Bond Interest," 15 Villanova Law Review 414 (1970).

47. 115 Cong. Rec. 23,745–23,747 (1969).

48. State and Local Fiscal Assistance Act of 1972, Pub. L. 92–512, 92d Cong., 2d Sess. (H.R. 14370); see House Ways and Means Committee, State and Local Fiscal Assistance Act of 1972, H.R. Rep. No. 1018, 92d Cong., 2d Sess. (1972); Senate Finance Committee, Revenue Sharing Act of 1972, S. Rep. No. 1050, 92d Cong., 2d Sess. (1972); Conference Report, S. Rep. No. 92–1229, 92d Cong., 2d Sess. (1972).

49. Other methods of giving assistance that are sometimes grouped under "revenue sharing" did involve federal tax changes of a tax expenditure character, such as the proposal of the Advisory Commission on Intergovernmental Relations and others for a credit against federal tax for state and local income taxes. See S.2483, 91st Cong., 1st Sess., printed in 115 Cong. Rec. 17,193–17,196 (1969).

50. E.g., House Committee on Ways and Means and Senate Committee on Finance, 91st Cong., 1st Sess., U.S. Treasury Department, Tax Reform Studies and Proposals (Comm. Print, 1969) (hereinafter cited as Treasury Tax Reform Studies) at 206; Hearings on H.R. 13270 [Tax Reform Act of 1969] before the Senate Finance Committee, 91st Cong., 1st Sess. 561 (1969).

51. Henry J. Aaron, *Shelter and Subsidies* (Washington D.C., Brookings Institution, 1972), 72, discussing the treatment of *property taxes* in relation to revenue sharing; see also the discussion in this chapter under Housing. The deduction for state and local *general sales taxes* is in essence a tax expenditure that benefits consumption. At the rate levels involved, it does not seem a needed accommodation in federal-state tax relationships. The deduction for state and local *general income taxes* is primarily a tax expenditure that is based on the need for accommodation, since without the deduction the combination of income tax rates would be quite high. If the tax expenditure accommodation for *income taxes* is to remain, states relying more heavily on the general sales tax will presumably oppose any downgrading of the tax expenditure for *general sales taxes.* However, the allocation of general revenue sharing under the State and Local Fiscal Assistance Act of 1972 (H.R. 14370) can favor those states that utilize the income tax (§106).

The Committee Reports on the revenue-sharing legislation recognize the importance of the deductions of these taxes as an aid to state and local governments, along with the exclusion of state and local bond interest, but do not further pursue the matter.

Senate Finance Committee, Revenue Sharing Act of 1972, S. Rep. No. 1050, 92d Cong., 2d Sess. Pt.1, at 10.

52. See generally Paul R. McDaniel, "Charitable Contributions: An Analysis of the Tax Reform Act" (pts. 1–3), 3 Non-Profit Report, Jan. at 16, Feb. at 1, March at 14 (1970); John M. Skilling, Jr., "Charitable Contributions," 23 Tax Lawyer 481 (1970); John Y. Taggart, "The Charitable Deduction," 26 Tax Law Review 63 (1970); John H. Myers, "Charitable Contributions," 4 Indiana Legal Forum 217 (1970).

In addition to the text items, the Act made extensive changes in the rules governing the conduct and activities of private foundations and both tightened and extended, to churches and social clubs for example, the tax on the unrelated business income of tax-exempt organizations.

For a Symposium discussion of the effects of the Act on charitable giving in general — the consensus was that of no lessening of gifts — and on the programs and operations of foundations, see *Tax Impacts on Philanthropy* (Princeton, Tax Institute of America, 1972).

53. There are other new approaches in this area, such as new requirements for deductibility where the charitable donee has a life interest or a remainder interest, designed to ensure that funds are really going to charity.

54. Examples are section 306 preferred stock, goods held in inventory, and capital assets held for less than six months.

55. Two other provisions, Code §§1231(b)(1)(C) and 1221(3)(B), adopted in 1969, now treat these as ordinary income items.

56. There are exceptions, as where the foundation in turn distributes the amount of the contribution within 2.5 months after the close of the year or where it is an operating foundation.

57. If the gift involves an ordinary income item, the deduction generally is measured by the tax basis, usually the cost, of the item. (Code §170(e) states that the deduction should be reduced by the gain which would have been ordinary income if the taxpayer had sold the property; in the case of "section 306 stock," where all the gain would have been taxable on sale, there would thus be no charitable deduction). If the gift is of a capital asset, then the deduction is the value of the gift reduced by 50% of the appreciation, which is roughly the equivalent of allowing a deduction only for the cost.

58. See, e.g., letter of President Kingman Brewster of Yale, in 115 Cong. Rec. 26,202 (1969), arguing that since the donor of appreciated securities can withhold his gift and thereby escape a tax on the appreciation (assuming the appreciation were to be subject to a tax if the gift were made), it is not contrary to tax equity to exempt the appreciation if the gift is made. This argument could equally apply to the tax on the sale of the asset. Also, it overlooks the fact that without the gift and the consequent deduction it effects, the tax due would be larger and would have to be paid in some manner. If we assume it would have been paid through funds raised by a sale of the appreciated asset, so that the appreciation would be taxed, the case for non-taxation when a gift is made does not stand up.

In their literature to donors, the colleges do recognize the additional benefit provided by the non-taxation of the appreciation in value when a contribution of appreciated property is made. See, e.g., How to Plan Your Giving to Harvard (1970), 9–10:

> But if you give [appreciated securities] to Harvard, you will not be treated as having realized a gain. There will be no capital gain tax. And the *full* appreciated value of the securities is deductible from your taxable income (subject, of course, to the percentage limitations previously described). There is thus double benefit in giving appreciated long-term securities.
> Let us suppose that you own 100 shares of stock now worth $100 per share

($10,000) which you bought more than six months ago at a cost of $20 a share ($2,000). If you sell these securities in order to provide cash for a gift to Harvard, you will ordinarily have to pay a maximum tax of 25 percent (if your aggregate long-term capital gain in that year does not exceed $50,000) on the profit. This will amount to $2,000, leaving you $8,000 to give to Harvard. If you are in the 50 percent tax bracket, the charitable deduction of $8,000 will result in an actual saving on your income tax of $4,000. Making the gift this way means that the government gets $2,000, Harvard gets $8,000 and the cost to you is $6,000.

Now, instead of selling the stock and giving the proceeds to Harvard, let us suppose you give the stock itself. You will have made a gift of $10,000 instead of only $8,000, and there will be no capital gain tax due. The $10,000 gift will result in a saving on your income tax of $5,000. If you consider, as some people do, that the true value of a security in your hands is its market value less the *potential* capital gain tax, then you may consider that the net cost to you is only $3,000 — this is the net value in your hands, $8,000, less the income tax saving of $5,000.

To repeat, if you are contemplating a gift to Harvard it will always be to your advantage, no matter what your income bracket may be, to give long-term appreciated securities rather than to sell them and give an equivalent amount in cash.

For a criticism of the exemption of the appreciation in value, see William D. Andrews, "Personal Deductions in an Ideal Income Tax," 86 Harvard Law Review 309, 371–372 (1972).

59. For the proposal, see House Committee on Ways and Means Report, note 4 above, at 80–83. This Treasury proposal fell under the combined assault of colleges, state and local governments, and oil companies. Colleges had two targets: allocation of the contributions deduction between taxable and exempt income and inclusion of the appreciation element of gifts as an item of exempt income for the purpose of this allocation (and also for the minimum tax). The oil companies were opposed to including percentage depletion and intangible drilling expenses in determining exempt income; the state and local governments were opposed to including tax-exempt bond income. To each his own tax expenditure! See also Chapter VIII.

60. Here, as elsewhere, the classifications in the Treasury Tax Expenditure Budget are accepted. Some, of course, may differ as to these classifications. For a different viewpoint on the classification of charitable contributions, see, e.g., viewpoint of Professor Andrews, note 58 above, at 344 and following, discussed in the Appendix to Chapter I and comments of Professor Boris I. Bittker, in Taxation and Education (Proceedings of Special Conference of American Alumni Council, Feb. 7–8, 1966) 29, and in *Tax Impacts on Philanthropy,* note 52 above, at 145, though his view presumably stems from his belief that there really is no concept of "net income" under an income tax but only a long series of pragmatic legislative judgments, e.g., Boris I. Bittker, "A 'Comprehensive Tax Base' As a Goal of Income Tax Reform," 80 Harvard Law Review 925 (1967); Boris I. Bittker, "Accounting for Federal 'Tax Subsidies' in the National Budget," 22 National Tax Journal 244 (1969). But see Stanley S. Surrey and William F. Hellmuth, "The Tax Expenditure Budget — Response to Professor Bittker," 22 National Tax Journal 528 (1969), and the Appendix to Chapter I.

See also Paul R. McDaniel, "An Alternative to the Federal Income Tax Deduction in Support of Private Philanthropy," in *Tax Impacts on Philanthropy,* note 52 above, at 171, and also Paul R. McDaniel, "Federal Matching Grants for Charitable Contributions: A Substitute for the Income Tax Deduction," 27 Tax Law Review 377

(1972), supporting the characterization of the charitable deduction as a tax expenditure item rather than a proper part of an income tax structure.

61. An interesting and important aspect of this view of the deduction is involved in the controversy over the status under the income tax of contributions to privately supported segregated schools. See the discussion of this matter in Chapter II.

62. See Edward H. Rabin, "Charitable Trusts and Charitable Deductions," 41 New York University Law Review 912, 922 (1966):

> It has been argued that the system of allocating funds via the deduction is undemocratic because it subsidizes "much more heavily the charities favored by the wealthy as distinct from those appealing primarily to the poorer contributors."

quoting William Vickrey, "One Economist's View of Philanthropy," in *Philanthropy and Public Policy,* (New York, National Bureau of Economic Research, 1962), 31, 54. See also Bernard Wolfman, "Federal Tax Policy and the Support of Science," 114 University of Pennsylvania Law Review 171, 176 (1965): "Affluence more than interest, ingenuity, or worthiness determines the extent of the federal support [for science through tax provisions]."

63. Statement combines 1971 distribution of revenue loss from charitable deduction, 1970 number of taxpayers with itemized deductions, and 1968 amount of itemized charitable deductions. See also comments of Henry J. Aaron, in *Tax Impacts on Philanthropy,* note 52 above, at 211.

64. If the donor were subject to the 10% minimum tax, he would be short $6.50, and save $106.50 through the gift. If he is also an executive seeking to save his 50% maximum marginal rate on compensation, he would be short $15.50 under the mechanics of that provision, since a capital gain can push some compensation into the 70% bracket, and the gift would save him $115.50. If the donor's capital gains would be subject to the 25% rate on the first $50,000 of gains, the gift is worth $95. If state income taxes are applicable, the saving to the donor can be larger, since the state as well as the Federal Government is giving up its tax. See generally 115 Cong. Rec. 37,496–37,504 (1969) (the debate on the proposal of Senator Edward M. Kennedy, which was defeated, to include the appreciation element in a charitable gift as a preference under the minimum tax).

In the course of the debate Senator Russell B. Long said (37,502):

> Mr. President, some of us on the Finance Committee have for years been concerned about the fact that it has been possible for someone to make money by giving something away. We have been very much concerned about the point that it was possible in years gone by for someone to give away something that is worth $1,000 and achieve a tax savings of $1,200 or $1,400.
>
> Generally speaking, of course, one is talking about persons who are in a high-income tax bracket and who are giving away appreciated property. That is a problem to which the Senator addresses himself.
>
> Under the bill reported by the Finance Committee, I am happy to say that we achieved everything I have been trying to do along that line for years. Under the committee bill it no longer would be mathematically possible for anybody to make anything by giving something away. He is giving something of himself when he gives something, under this bill.

This, however, is not the result under the 1969 Act, as the text indicates. But even assuming the Senator were right, what is the logic of his position (one which was echoed by the colleges) that the treatment is wrong if the donor obtains a saving of over 100% of the gift but is satisfactory if the saving is 100% — why should a taxpayer obtain a deduction for a painless gift — or in turn a gift where the saving is less than 100%?

64–1. The American Council on Education (ACE), in Hearings on General Tax Reform, House Ways and Means Committee, 93d Cong., 1st Sess. (1973) defends the present situation in this fashion:

> It is sometimes asserted that a donor, under certain circumstances, can profit financially by making a gift. We have carefully examined this contention and believe it to be without foundation.

This statement then refers to the following material:

> The fact that gifts reduce net worth no matter what the tax bracket may be illustrated by considering the balance sheets before and after gift and tax payments of a taxpayer with the following assumed conditions:
> 1. Taxpayer is in the 70% bracket.
> 2. Taxpayer owns securities with a cost of $100,000 and a fair market value of $500,000. He gives these securities to a qualified organization.
> 3. He has $1,000,000 of other assets at cost with a fair market value of $1,500,000.
> 4. He has sufficient other income subject to tax so that he may obtain full benefit of the contribution. Assume he owes $400,000 in taxes before the contribution.
>
> The balance sheets would be:

Estimated Current Value
Balance Sheets

	Before Gift	After Gift
Other assets	$1,500,000	$1,500,000
Securities	500,000	–0–
Total Assets	$2,000,000	$1,500,000
Liability for taxes	$ 400,000	$ 50,000*
Net Worth	1,600,000	1,450,000
Total Liabilities and Net Worth	$2,000,000	$1,500,000

(*$400,000 of previous liability minus 70% of $500,000 contribution.)

> The general statement of the decline in net worth is that the decline will equal (1 minus tax rate) times the current value of the gift.

But this balance sheet ignores the potential tax liability inherent in the appreciated securities and assets. Their total appreciation is $900,000, which at a 35% tax rate on this appreciation means a potential tax liability of $315,000. If this potential tax liability is added to the $400,000 current tax liability, then the balance sheet *before the gift* would show a net worth of *$1,285,000* instead of $1,600,000. Certainly a responsible tax lawyer or accountant would have to inform the individual of the potential tax liability inherent in the appreciated securities and assets.

Now we can see what really happens when he gives the $500,000 appreciated securities to charity. This gift eliminates $350,000 of current tax liability. It also eliminates the $140,000 of potential tax liability inherent in the securities themselves, leaving the individual with a potential tax liability of $175,000 on the other assets and a remaining current tax liability of $50,000, or a total of $225,000. His net worth *after the gift* is now *$1,275,000*. This is only *$10,000* less than before the charitable gift — and yet he has given away *$500,000!* Clearly, the $500,000 charitable contribution actually cost him only $10,000.

We can go a step further. Suppose the cost of the securities had been only $50,000, so that their inherent potential tax liability was $157,500. Then the net worth of the individual *before the gift,* taking potential and current tax liabilities of $732,500 into account, would have been *$1,267,500*. Now a gift of the $500,000 securities would eliminate $350,000 of current tax liability and also $157,500 of potential tax liability, leaving a potential tax liability of $175,000 on the other assets and a current tax liability of $50,000. The net worth *after the gift* is therefore *$1,275,000*, or *$7,500 greater* than before — despite the gift of $500,000. In this situation the gift has actually increased the individual's net worth. The difference between the two situations lies in the relationship of the cost of the securities to their present value, and hence in the resulting appreciation in value and consequent potential tax liability inherent in the securities. If the appreciation is sufficiently large, the gift, by both effecting a payment of current taxes and eliminating the potential tax liability inherent in the securities given away, can actually increase net worth. But even where the relationship of cost to value is such that net worth is not actually increased, the large gift has only a minimal effect on the individual's net worth — as stated above, in the ACE example itself a $500,000 gift cost the individual only $10,000!

The balance sheet set forth by the ACE and the argument the ACE bases upon it thus leave out a crucial element, i.e., the potential tax liability inherent in the appreciated securities and assets. The ACE presentation thereby glosses over the ability of the individual through the deductible stock gift both to eliminate potential tax liability inherent in the securities themselves and current tax liability. The gift enables the individual to rid himself of low basis securities having an inherent high potential tax liability and also pay his current tax liability at the same time — and that is why such a gift is either practically painless as in the ACE example or can actually increase his net worth.

See also note 58 above.

65. See Chapter VIII.

66. See note 64 above as to the $6.50 and $15.50. If his capital gains are subject to a 25% rate, he pays $5 and the Government $95.

67. The text relates to taxpayers who itemize their personal deductions, including the charitable deduction. If a taxpayer is using the standard deduction, then his charitable gifts do not per se reduce his tax. This is another peculiar aspect of the tax expenditure approach — it conditions Government financial assistance to charities largely on whether the contributor is a homeowner, the owner of a car, the purchaser of significant consumer goods on credit, ill, etc. — all factors which can lead to itemization of personal deductions. See McDaniel, Tax Law Review article, note 60 above, at 383.

68. Hearings on H.R. 13270 [Tax Reform Act of 1969] before the Senate Finance Committee, 91st Cong., 1st Sess. 2207 (1969).

69. Idem. at 2168–2171; 115 Cong. Rec. 28,943–28,944, 37,502–37,504 (1969).

70. Higher education clearly relies on the gifts of the wealthy, as compared with other charitable institutions. Thus the Peterson Commission (Commission on Foundations

and Private Philanthropy) survey showed that wealthy donors made 45% of their charitable contributions to higher education, though overall 17% of charitable gifts went to education. See McDaniel, Tax Law Review article, note 60 above, at 391.

71. The standard deduction is increased by the 1969 Act to 15% of income, with a maximum deduction of $2,000, and the minimum standard deduction (low-income allowance) increased by the 1971 Act to $1,300. In 1973 it is estimated that 62% of taxpayers will use the standard deduction, compared to 55% before the 1969 Act; see House Ways and Means Committee, Report on Revenue Act of 1971, H.R. Rep. No. 533, 92d Cong., 1st Sess. 16 (1971).

The Treasury had proposed in 1968, note 50 above, at 194–197, that, along with an increase in the standard deduction, the charitable deduction be allowed together with the standard deduction, but that only the aggregate of gifts in excess of 3% of adjusted gross income be deductible, whether the taxpayer was using the standard deduction or itemization for the other personal expenses. The charities opposed this proposal without, one gathers, giving the matter much thought. But the arithmetic of the proposal is in their favor, since under it more people would be eligible to deduct contributions than are eligible under the present treatment (i.e., no 3% floor and the charitable deduction absorbed by the standard deduction), once the standard deduction is increased as it was in 1969. See also Joseph A. Pechman, *Federal Tax Policy* (Washington, D.C., Brookings Institution, 1971), 84, suggesting a 2% or 3% floor for the charitable contributions deduction.

72. In the second item of the proposal, assume the person is in the 70% bracket and is contributing today $10,000. In the third item, assume the person is in the 70% bracket, 35% capital gain rate, and is contributing $2 million of fully appreciated stock. (See the text discussion earlier, at notes 64 and 66.) In the fourth item, assume the person is in the 70% bracket and is contributing $3.3 million to a foundation. If the $3.3 million contribution were in fully appreciated stock, then in the fourth item the translation to the direct expenditure route would be a contribution of $2.2 million of stock and a Government payment to the foundation of $1.1 million (since the charitable contribution deduction is reduced by one-half of the appreciation).

73. McDaniel, Tax Law Review article, note 60 above at 390–392, points out that the "pluralism" which many rely on to defend the charitable deduction is really operative only for the upper-income individuals in the country. There is a wide pluralism in *contributions* to philanthropy with about 60% of the contributions coming from donors in adjusted gross income brackets under $15,000. But the *tax pluralism* — the allocation of the Government funds embodied in the charitable deduction — is largely confined to the brackets above $20,000, and probably higher than that. It is *their* gifts that direct most of the Government assistance. See text at note 63 above. Moreover, since only about 38% of taxpayers itemize their deductions and thus explicitly obtain the charitable deduction, the outer range of tax pluralism extends to only a distinct minority of contributors. McDaniel therefore concludes that "the argument for pluralism only for upper-income individuals has a decidedly elitist caste to it."

74. McDaniel, Tax Law Review article, note 60 above at 381, states that the total amount of charitable contributions in 1970 by living persons was about $14.3 billion. But $3.8 billion of this amount — the tax revenue involved in the charitable deduction — in effect represented Federal Government matching funds triggered by the contributions. He says it is this $3.8 million of Government funds that the charities were fearful of losing as a result of the various proposals made in 1969.

75. The text discussion here reflects papers by Professor Paul R. McDaniel of Boston College Law School, note 60 above. See also a prior paper of his, "Alternatives to

Utilization of the Federal Income Tax System to Meet Social Problems," 11 Boston College Industrial and Commerical Law Review 867, 875–77 (1970). See also Laurence Stone, "Federal Tax Support of Charities and Other Exempt Organizations: The Need for a National Policy," 20 Southern California Tax Institute 27, 47 (1968). See especially Professor McDaniel's reference to the matching system used in England, under which for taxpayers above a certain income level gifts are matched by the Government if the donor agrees to make gifts for seven years, with the Government's share dropping as the taxpayer's income level drops. This arrangement seems not to have been consciously designed from the standpoint of support for philanthropy but rather to have grown out of the treatment generally under the British tax law of covenants to assign income. See also Royal Commission on the Taxation of Profits and Income, Final Report, Cmd 9474, Ch. 7 (1955), and other references to the English system, cited in McDaniel, note 60 above.

76. Professor McDaniel's papers, note 60 above, contain a discussion of the "incentive effect" of the present deduction, with references to prior discussions, and he concludes that it is limited in scope, having most effect in the highest brackets, and in any event is highly inefficient. He applies these judgments in estimating the expected reduction in the amounts of private gifts going to charity under the matching proposal. See also the comments of Henry J. Aaron, note 63 above.

77. Professor McDaniel discusses the effect on higher education, noting that prior studies show that the tax deduction incentive has an effect on high-income individuals and in turn on the institutions they support, among which educational institutions are very prominent. See Michael K. Taussig, "Economic Aspects of the Personal Income Tax Treatment of Charitable Contributions," 20 National Tax Journal 1, 16–17 (1967), stressing the need for further study of this area. If so, the tax support for educational institutions is purchased at a high overall cost. See Rabin, note 62 above, at 919. The conclusions in these studies seem supported by the legislative lobbying in 1969, in which the educational institutions led the effort to defend the existing tax provisions. Professor McDaniel concludes that the effect on higher education of his matching schedule is likely to be only slightly, if at all, adverse, especially since matching of gifts of donors in lower brackets would help in offsetting any real decline in private giving in upper brackets.

78. Professor Aaron, note 63 above, defends the matching proposal, saying that certainly the burden rests on those who support the present deduction to defend the upside-down matching under that deduction and the difference between itemizers and non-itemizers.

Professor Bittker in the same Symposium argues against the matching proposal, resting strongly on its possible unconstitutionality under the First Amendment since the matching would also apply to religious giving; *Tax Impacts on Philanthropy,* note 52 above, at 148. But his case here is quite weak. The decision in *Committee For Public Education v. Nyquist,* 93 S.Ct. 2955 (1973), noted in Chapter II, has strong indications to the effect that in the context of a mechanism to support philanthropy generally, with the lack of controls indicated in the matching proposal and not singling out religion, the coverage of religious organizations under the mechanism would not be barred by the First Amendment. This is also the indication of the *Walz* case, especially as it is explained in *Nyquist.* If this is not so, it seems hard to understand why the present tax deduction for contributions to churches can withstand attack. Indeed, Professor Bittker in response to questioning at the Symposium, note 52 above at 223, indicated he thought that a tax law which granted a deduction *only for religious gifts* would presumably be unconstitutional under the First Amendment. This indicates that since the present deduction with its broader scope, but still granting a deduction for religious giving, is apparently accepted as constitutional under the First Amendment, presumably a direct matching plan of equal breadth should likewise be constitutional. For under Professor Bittker's response — and indeed under the decision in *Nyquist* treating a tax deduction to parents of children in non-public schools in the same way as a direct grant to parents — it is not a *deduction* as compared with a *direct grant* that saves the present Code, but rather the present emphasis on *philanthropy in general* with religion only one of the many recipients benefited.

For an earlier discussion, see Herbert J. Korbel, "Do the Federal Income Tax Laws Involve an 'Establishment of Religion'?" 53 American Bar Association Journal 1018 (1967).

79. Waldemar A. Nielson, *The Big Foundations* (New York, Columbia University Press, 1972).

80. Budget of the United States, Fiscal Year 1973, Special Analysis I, 128.

81. American Association of Fund-Raising Counsel, Inc., Giving USA (1972), 36. One study of 1970–1971 gifts to higher education indicates that, out of a total of $1.5 billion, 95% of all gifts were less than $5,000 but these produced only 24.9% of the total. Of the gifts from individuals, which came to half of the total ($763 million), about $572 million came in gifts over $5,000. In turn, about $335 million of those gifts were in the form of property, almost always securities. In total, appreciated assets appeared to account for around $354 million of the total $763 million given by individuals. American Council on Education, Patterns of Giving to Higher Education II (1973).

82. For a study of "Government philanthropy," see Frank G. Dickinson, *The Changing Position of Philanthropy in the American Economy* (New York, National Bureau of Economic Research, 1970); this does not go beyond 1959 and hence does not cover recent innovations such as Government direct assistance to the arts.

83. For a general discussion of Government aid to higher education, see Charles Schultze, *Setting National Priorities, the 1971 Budget* (Washington, D. C., Brookings Institution, 1970), 70; "The Corporation and the Campus: Corporate Support of Higher Education in the 1970s," 30 Academy of Political Science, No. 1 (1970–1972); Statement of Roger Bolton, Hearings on Economic Analysis and the Efficiency of Government before the Subcommittee on Economy in Government of the Joint Economic Committee, 91st Cong., 1st Sess. 261–276 (1969); Kermit Gordon, *Agenda for the Nation* (Washington, D. C., Brookings Institution, 1968) 256.

84. The funds provided and mechanisms used in the higher education legislation in 1972 indicate that Congress is willing to structure federal aid on a general purpose basis to be used by the institutions at their discretion.

McDaniel notes, Tax Law Review article, note 60 above at 392–393, that 70% of the funds received by higher education from living individuals are restricted as to use, and states:

> If this be the case, the control argument is not one over the fact of control, but over who will exercise the control over the federal share. Apparently colleges and universities are more comfortable with control imposed by wealthy donors than by Congress or the Department of Health, Education, and Welfare.

85. See Rabin, note 62 above, at 920–925; Wolfman, note 62 above, at 181–186.

86. See testimony of Peter G. Peterson, on behalf of Commission on Foundations and Philanthropy, in Hearings, note 68 above, at 6053, 6140.

The Report of the Association of American Universities stating "the case for preservation of tax incentives to giving for higher education," "Tax Reform and the

Crisis of Financing Higher Education" (May 1973), essentially rests on the values of higher education and the need for funds if those values are to be preserved. It thus concludes (at 37–38, footnote omitted):

> Both practical and philosophical considerations compel retention of the existing tax incentives for private support for charity in general and higher education in particular. There is strong evidence that proposals to limit the income, gift and estate tax deductions now afforded for individual gifts to charity would seriously reduce those gifts, particularly large individual gifts which have proven so important to institutions of higher education. Congress has recognized that the nation's institutions of higher education constitute a "national resource which significantly contributes to the security, general welfare, and economy of the United States." To conserve this resource, any funds depleted through changes in the tax laws must be replaced from other sources. However, none of the tax reform proposals has answered the pivotal question of how revenues lost to higher education would be replaced as would be required by the national interest.
>
> The present charitable deduction is time-tested and has the virtue of certainty; donors, their attorneys and university officials know the system and its potential for financing higher education. Other ideas for direct subsidies, matching grants and the like are unknown quantities likely to produce new inequities with absolutely no guarantee that they would raise the same revenue for higher education as the present system. They would be susceptible to proof and perfection only after long and intensive trial and error. There is too much at stake to overthrow our traditional support of private charity through the charitable deduction. No less than the vitality and independence of higher education are in the balance.

This of course is a statement of the need for financial assistance rather than reasoned support for the unfairness and inefficiencies in the present tax expenditure. It really answers only the first question in the reconsideration of any existing tax expenditure: Is Government financial assistance required? But an affirmative answer, as we have seen, is only a step that leads to the search for alternatives rather than a stamp of approval for the existing tax expenditure.

Certainly we should not embark on new tax expenditure assistance for education. Proposals for a tax credit to parents of children in elementary and secondary private schools should not be adopted; they are unwise as well as unconstitutional. See Chapter II. Nor should the proposals for a tax credit for costs of higher education be adopted. See John K. McNulty, "Tax Policy and Tuition Credit Legislation: Federal Income Tax Allowances For Personal Costs of Higher Education," 61 California Law Review 1 (1973).

87. The Fourth Annual Report on National Housing Goals, transmitted to the Congress on June 29, 1972, H.R. Doc. No. 319, 92d Cong., 2d Sess. 41–42 refers to two other tax incentives as aiding the residential mortgage market:

> The Federal Government also encourages the provision of housing credits through the tax system. Mutual savings banks and savings and loan associations are allowed tax deductions for additions they make to their bad debt reserves, additions that are considerably in excess of actual losses. Since these thrift institutions are heavy lenders on residential properties, the effect of such special

tax deductions, which are higher than deductions allowed ordinary businesses for bad debts, is to encourage residential lending activity. It is estimated that this tax preference reduced Federal revenues by $400 million in 1971.

Real estate investment trusts are exempt from the "corporate" income tax on distributed earnings if 90 percent or more of their ordinary income is distributed and if certain other conditions are met. This means that distributed earnings are taxed only once as part of the personal income of shareholders.

Mortgage investment trusts, a specialized form of real estate investment trust, use proceeds from security issues and from short term borrowing to invest in mortgage loans. In 1971 these trusts acquired $1.8 billion of housing construction loans and $.3 billion of long-term residential loans. The special tax advantages represent substantial incentives for the creation of these financial institutions that supply funds to the mortgage market. It is estimated that for 1971 mortgage investment trusts and equity real estate investment trusts together distributed $530 million to shareholders and that the special tax treatment afforded these trusts reduced Federal revenues by $140 million.

The tax assistance provided to mutual savings banks and savings and loan associations is listed as a tax expenditure. The real estate investment trust is not listed, and its status, along with those of other entities which are allowed similar treatment for distributed earnings, is discussed in the Appendix to Chapter I.

Two other items should presumably be considered as tax expenditures in the housing area: (1) the "rollover" provision for sales of residences under which a gain on the sale is not taxed if the sales proceeds are invested in another residence but instead is held in suspense through a carry-forward of the basis of the residence sold (Code §1034); (2) the exemption from tax of the gain, not to exceed a ratio based on a sales price limit of $20,000, on the sale of a residence by a person aged 65 or over (Code §121). The latter provision, when adopted in 1964, was estimated to involve an annual revenue loss of $10 million. For a recent discussion of the area, see Horst G. Wolff, "The White Paper: Tax Treatment of Principal Residences," 18 Canadian Tax Journal 263 (1970).

88. Annual Report of Secretary of the Treasury, Fiscal Year 1968, at 329.

89. See the discussion of imputed rent on owner-occupied homes in the Appendix to Chapter I.

90. Aaron, note 51 above, at 62. A summary appears in Henry J. Aaron, "Federal Housing Subsidies," in The Economics of Federal Subsidy Programs, Part 5 – Housing Subsidies, Joint Economic Committee, 92d Cong., 2d Sess. 571 (1972). See also Statement of Martin David, in Hearings on H.R. 13270 [Tax Reform Act of 1969] before the House Ways and Means Committee, 91st Cong., 1st Sess. 4273 (1970); Statement of Roger F. Miller, idem. at 1965.

91. Aaron, note 51 above. The tax expenditure items involved, mortgage interest and property taxes (and this is the case also for imputed rent), while roughly a constant percentage of income up to about $15,000, then become an increasing percentage. See also Richard B. Goode, *The Individual Income Tax* (Washington, D.C., Brookings Institution, 1964), 123; tables in Chapter III on income distribution of tax expenditures.

92. Since homeowners as a class do not elect the standard deduction, this means that their property tax and interest deductions are sufficient, along with other personal deductions, to lift them above the standard deduction level. There apparently are no reliable data on the number of homeowners electing the standard deduction. Those who do elect are probably in the low-income group and have lesser amounts of mortgages outstanding, such as some elderly individuals.

The homeowners will still of course receive the benefit of the exclusion of imputed rent.

The standard deduction is viewed as a tax expenditure item under Health, Labor, and Welfare in the Tax Expenditure Budget, since its level is roughly determined by reference to the aggregates, in the brackets affected, for the itemized personal expense deductions all of which are classified as tax expenditures. It is not viewed as a rate reduction or as a part of the progressivity of the rate structure. (The low-income allowance — formerly the minimum standard deduction — is part of the rate structure in that, along with the personal exemptions, its function is to determine the starting levels of the income tax with incomes below those levels in effect receiving a zero rate.) Viewed as a tax expenditure, and considering that its size in large part reflects the amounts spent on mortgage interest and property taxes by homeowners in the brackets involved (see CCH 1972 Stand. Fed. Tax Rep. ¶8226), the standard deduction, while lessening inequality between homeowners and renters in those brackets still — because it is a deduction — provides for greater Government assistance to middle-income groups in meeting their expenses for housing shelter, either owned or rented, than for the lower-income taxpayers and the poor.

The 62% figure in the text is an estimate for 1973; see House Ways and Means Committee Report, note 71 above.

93. *New York Times,* Oct. 24, 1969, at 18, col. 5. To the same effect, see Statement of Anthony Downs in Hearings, note 83 above, at 276, 284–285.

94. See Fourth Annual Report on National Housing Goals, note 87 above, at 47–48.

95. Hearings on President's 1963 Tax Message before the House Committee on Ways and Means, 88th Cong., 1st Sess. 47, 226 (1963).

96. Code §§56–58 (minimum tax), §163(d) (limitation on interest deduction).

97. In the case of the mortgage and property tax payments, the income tax rate brackets assumed are 70%, 19% and 0%, respectively.

98. National Housing Act of 1934, §235, 12 U.S.C. §§17–152 et seq. See Charles L. Edson, "Sections 235 and 236 — The First Year," 2 Urban Lawyer 14 (1970).

99. Title V, Emergency Home Finances Act of 1970, 84 Stat. 450. The Conference Report on this item appears at 116 Cong. Rec. 24,946 (1970).

See also 118 Cong. Rec. E7894 (daily ed. Sept. 14, 1972) commenting on a proposal adopted in the House Committee on Banking and Currency to establish a pilot program of direct Government loans to "credit-worthy" moderate-income families who cannot obtain mortgage loans at "reasonable rates of interest." The family income limit under the program is $13,000, and the maximum mortgage amounts would range from $22,000 to $28,000. This measure was not enacted in 1972.

100. *New York Times,* Dec. 19, 1971, at 1, col.5.

101. Staff of the Joint Economic Committee, The Economics of Federal Subsidy Programs, 92d Cong., 2d Sess. 152 (1972). The direct programs, though not the amounts, are described in the Fourth Annual Report on National Housing Goals, note 87 above, at Appendix B, page 39. See also Henry B. Schechter, "Federal Housing Subsidy Programs," in The Economics of Federal Subsidy Programs, Part 5 – Housing Subsidies, Joint Economic Committee, 92d Cong., 2d Sess. 597 (1972).

The figure for the tax expenditures for housing does not include the exclusion of imputed rent from home ownership. Inclusion of such imputed income would raise the total assistance under the tax system to $15 billion; see Joseph A. Pechman and Benjamin A. Okner, "Individual Income Tax Erosion By Income Classes," in The Economics of Federal Subsidy Programs, Part 1 – General Study Papers, Joint Economic Committee, 92d Cong., 2d Sess. 13, 23 (1972).

102. Special Analysis M, Budget of the United States, Fiscal Year 1973. The tax assistance is mentioned, apparently as an innovation, in the Fourth Annual Report on National Housing Goals, note 87 above.

103. The Treasury estimates, see Chapter III, place the amount at 40% for mortgage

interest and 50% for real property taxes, or a combined 44%. The combined percentage is placed at 40% in the Fourth Annual Report on National Housing Goals, see text at note 94 above. Pechman and Okner place these combined benefits, and imputed rent, at 56%, note 101 above, at 34. See also Paul M. Dodyk, "The Tax Reform Act of 1969 and the Poor," 71 Columbia Law Review 758, 782 (1971).

104. See National Urban Coalition, Counterbudget (1971) 317, suggesting a deduction limitation of $500 on mortgage interest and $300 on property taxes. Perhaps a limitation approach and confinement of the deductions to the principal residence might appeal to Congress, but the limits are not likely to be severe.

105. It is interesting to note that the proposals to allow a credit against federal income tax for local property taxes extend to both homeowners and renters. See, e.g., Senate Amend. No. 881, 91st Cong., 1st Sess. (1970), proposed to H.R. 17550; 117 Cong. Rec. S19,223–19,229 (daily ed. Nov. 20, 1971) (credit for elderly renters adopted in Senate in 1971 Revenue Act, rejected in Conference).

Proposals to provide a federal credit against income tax for elderly persons, whether property owners or renters, for state and local property taxes paid would obviously be unfair in the case of those with insufficient income tax payments to absorb the credit, unless the credit were made refundable in those situations. See Statement of Hon. George P. Shultz, Secretary of the Treasury, in Hearings on General Tax Reform before the House Ways and Means Committee, 93d Cong., 1st Sess. (April 30, 1973) suggesting a refundable credit. Such a refundable credit is really a grant. There is no need to link this expenditure to the income tax, and clearly it should be a direct expenditure item legislated and administered as part of our housing programs. Even cast as a direct expenditure, such a proposal is of dubious merit. See Statement of Henry Aaron, in Hearings on S.1235, Property Tax Relief and Reform, before the Subcommittee on Intergovernmental Relations, Senate Committee on Government Operations, 93d Cong., 1st Sess. (1973); Henry Aaron, "What Do Circuit Breaker Laws Accomplish," in Conference on an Agenda for Property Tax Reform, The Lincoln Foundation, Hartford, Conn. (May 21, 1973).

106. Thus, assume a standard deduction equal to 15% or 20% of adjusted gross income. If that deduction were eliminated on simplification grounds because nearly all taxpayers were using it, then, to preserve the status quo vis-a-vis itemized deductions, only itemized deductions in excess of 15% or 20% of adjusted gross income should be allowed. The Congress would then face the question as to whether the revenue saved by these steps should be used to reduce tax rates, used for direct assistance to homeowners and renters (and for other activities encompassed by the itemized deductions and the standard deduction), or used in some other fashion. A decision to reduce rates, or use the revenue in some other fashion, would in this sense be a decision to cease tax expenditure assistance for these activities.

107. Other issues are of course present. For example, any restriction on a deduction for interest paid in connection with a residence would have to cope with problems of allocation or tracing — what about the individual who doesn't borrow on his house but does borrow on his securities to buy a house? What about the individual who borrows on his house to buy securities or for other pursuits? Compare the issues under §265(2) relating to interest paid to carry tax-exempt bonds. But the increasing attention being paid to the deduction for personal interest, e.g., §163(d), will in the end require the development of further technical expertise in these matters. See Chapter VIII.

108. *Crane v. Comm'r*, 331 U.S. 1 (1947); *Parker v. Delaney*, 186 F.2d 455 (1st Cir. 1950), *cert. denied*, 341 U.S. 926 (1951). See D. Nelson Adams, "Exploring the Outer Boundaries of the Crane Doctrine; An Imaginary Supreme Court Opinion," 21 Tax Law Review 159 (1966).

109. See Chapter IV for a discussion of tax shelters, including the real estate shelter. See also William S. McKee, "The Real Estate Tax Shelter: A Computerized Expose," 57 Virginia Law Review 521 (1971).

110. Note 50 above, at 438–458.

111. Code §167(j) and (k) and amended §1250, resulting from Tax Reform Act of 1969, §521.

112. C. Willis Ritter and Emil M. Sunley, Jr., "Real Estate and Tax Reform: An Evaluation of the Real Estate Provisions of the Tax Reform Act of 1969," 30 Maryland Law Review 5, 26 (1970). The model there utilized indicates that, for an individual in the 50% tax bracket, the pre-1969 rules provided a 20.9% present value return on investment in commercial real estate under a typical situation. The post-1969 return is about 17.7%, with a major part of the reduction due to the change in accelerated depreciation and the balance to the strengthening of the recapture rule.

113. Paul Taubman and Robert H. Rasche, "Subsidies, Tax Law, and Real Estate Investment," in Economics of Federal Subsidy Programs, note 9 above, at 343. The authors state (343–344):

> [T]he true depreciation of office buildings in the first year is less than one-tenth of that allowed under straight line depreciation. Indeed, true depreciation for office buildings falls short of that allowed by the straight line method for each of the first 45 years of the office building's useful life. We calculate that on a before tax basis, the straight line depreciation allowed by the law yields a subsidy of 18 percent of the purchase price while double declining balance adds approximately 10 percent more.
> . . .
> The tax depreciation rules lead to extra investment in office and in apartment buildings and to a reduction in the useful lives of buildings. For example, if true depreciation were allowed, office buildings investment would decline by 3 percent and useful lives would rise by 10 percent. In the apartment building sector investment would change more and useful lives less.
>
> Our major policy conclusions are that the depreciation allowed for office and apartment buildings should be made slower than straight line. Reverse sum of the years digits would be about right.

See also their earlier study, Paul Taubman and Robert H. Rasche, "Economic and Tax Depreciation of Office Buildings," 22 National Tax Journal 334 (1969).

114. Ritter and Sunley, Jr., note 112 above, at 45.

115. Idem at 15–27. Recapture, of course, is not a complete remedy for excessive depreciation, since it does not offset the benefit of the deferral of tax permitted by the deduction for the excessive depreciation (idem at 9 n.18, 47) and cannot even reach that deferral where the property is not sold. But a strong recapture rule is better than doing nothing about the excessive depreciation. See Chapter VIII.

116. The depreciation benefits, and weak recapture, had provided real estate with the equivalent of a 9.3% investment credit. For commercial buildings, the 1969 Act changes in depreciation and recapture rules were the equivalent of removing a 3.7% investment credit, thus leaving the equivalent of a 5.6% credit. Emil M. Sunley, Jr., "Changes in Depreciation and Recapture — Impact on Real Estate Investments," 38 Appraisal Journal 524 (Oct. 1970).

The Congressional discussion in 1971 on restoring the 7% investment credit, limited as before to machinery and equipment, did not indicate that its non-application to commercial and industrial real estate was due to the tax expenditure assistance already being accorded to that real estate. Rather, the discussion indicated that the policy considerations underlying the restoration of the credit extended only to machinery and equipment and not to real estate.

117. For example, see Ritter and Sunley, Jr., note 112 above, at 26, indicating that changes of one or two points in the interest rate can have an effect on the rate of return similar to that of the tax expenditures.

If tax expenditures are eliminated for commercial buildings and an investment credit is retained for machinery and equipment, then the question would arise whether to extend that credit to investments in commercial buildings. (The credit is presently available for certain *equipment* in buildings.) The issue here would turn on whether the policy basis for the credit, that of encouraging economic growth through an incentive to invest in machinery and equipment, applies also to investment in commercial buildings. The original proposal in 1961 for an investment credit did cover commercial buildings, but the credit as adopted did not apply to such buildings since the interested lobbies were more concerned in preventing the recapture principle from being applied to the sale of buildings than in obtaining the credit; such recapture was considered by the Treasury to be a prerequisite to a grant of the credit.

118. See Taubman and Rasche, in Economics of Federal Subsidy Programs, note 113 above. The authors state (343):

> [For apartment buildings, in] the first year, true depreciation is less than one-fourth of that allowed under the straight line method and true depreciation does not exceed the tax allowance until after the passage of 40 years. The straight line tax depreciation method confers a subsidy of 14 percent while accelerated methods can double this. In both industries a reverse sum of the years digits method would approximate true depreciation.

See also the quotation in note 113 above.

119. As a result, under the model used, note 112 above, the present value rate of return on an investment in residential real estate (not low-income housing) was decreased only from 20.9% to 20.1%, a reduction of about 4%, due to the tightening of the recapture rule.

120. See Ritter and Sunley, Jr., note 112 above, at 38–39, indicating that the investor benefit resulting from this difference in recapture rules is not significant and impliedly, is an unnecessary complication.

121. Idem at 29–42, indicating the change may have a limited attraction to investors, since the "rollover" technique requires the seller to accept a lower tax basis for depreciation on the second project.

122. For a criticism of the rehabilitation provision at the time of its adoption, see Statement of Charles Davenport, Hearings on H.R. 13270 [Tax Reform Act of 1969] before the Senate Finance Committee, 91st Cong., 1st Sess. 4903 (1969). Ritter and Sunley, Jr., note 112 above, at 37, point out that the rehabilitation provision is equivalent to a 19% investment credit for the 70% bracket taxpayer [a 14% credit for the 50% bracket taxpayer], a 5% credit for the 20% bracket taxpayer, and a zero credit to the nontaxpayer — these credits indicate the benefits of the rehabilitation provision as compared with the benefits of 200% declining balance depreciation! See also Emil M. Sunley, Jr., "Tax Incentive for the Rehabilitation of Housing," 39 Appraisal Journal 381, 384 (July 1971). Also discussion in the text later.

123. The Fourth Annual Report on National Housing Goals, note 87 above, at 51–52, describes the tax benefits for rental housing in these terms:

Notes to Chapter VII

Federal tax laws have been structured to encourage investments in rental housing. Through provisions authorizing deductions from taxable income (interest expense, State and local taxes, depreciation) and distinctions of income (capital gains), the Federal Government has made investment in real estate properties in general and rental housing in particular relatively attractive.

Since 1954, an important source of "earnings" for many real estate investors has been the tax savings that arise from application of the tax losses, created each year by property operations, against the other taxable income of the investor. These tax losses come about principally because accelerated depreciation and interest cost deductions, when added to operating expense and property tax deductions, appreciably exceed rental income, especially during the early years of operation.

Accelerated depreciation and interest cost deductions loom importantly in tax loss calculations because of the leverage effects the investor can take advantage of. Real estate properties are usually financed by a mortgage loan covering about two-thirds to 90 percent of the project cost, with the owner's equity providing the remaining 10 to 33 percent. Yet, the owner is permitted to depreciate the entire cost of the building, including the portion financed by the loan. And, a larger loan increases interest cost deductions, while decreasing the amount of equity funds that have to be furnished by the investor.

Further tax benefits accrue to the investor when he sells his property. Subject to the rules governing recapture of "excess depreciation" (in excess of straight line depreciation), the gains he makes from such a sale are taxed at a rate which is no more than one-half of his ordinary tax rate (the tax bracket of the taxpayer).

Moreover, provisions of the 1969 Tax Reform Act improve the tax incentives for housing investments relative to other real estate investments. For new non-residential buildings, the 1969 Act reduced the degree of accelerated depreciation (depreciation faster than straight line depreciation) to a maximum of 150 percent declining balance (150 percent of straight line depreciation calculated on a basis equal to the value of the building minus the cumulative depreciation taken in prior years). For new residential properties, the 1969 Act retained the more favorable 200 percent declining balance or "sum of the years-digits" method of depreciation (the numerator of the fraction used for calculating depreciation equals the remaining useful life of the asset and the denominator of that fraction is the sum of all the year's digits corresponding to the estimated useful life of the property). In the case of acquisitions of existing properties it ended accelerated depreciation for non-residential properties, which now can be depreciated only on a straight line basis, while reducing accelerated depreciation for residential properties to 125 percent declining balance, provided that the remaining economic life of the property is 20 years or more. It is estimated that in 1971 the revenue cost (for new rental housing only) of allowing depreciation methods for tax purposes which are more accelerated than straight line depreciation was $530 million.

Residential housing, especially low and moderate income housing, is also favored under "recapture" provisions in the 1969 tax legislation. "Recapture" refers to taxing, at the full, ordinary rate, that part of an investor's capital gains (from the sale of his property), which derives from his use of accelerated depreciation instead of straight line depreciation. Under the 1969 legislation, owners of low income rental housing receive the same recapture treatment as previously prevailed, i.e., a one-percent reduction in the recapture for each month the property is held beyond 20 months. For other residential properties, the phase-out of recapture of existing depreciation begins in the 101st month after property acquisition and for non-residential properties there is no phase-out of recapture at all. Thus, here too the tax treatment tends to encourage investment in residential over non-residential properties.

Finally, as mentioned earlier, special tax treatment for real estate investment trusts resulted in reduction of Federal revenues of $140 million. Since many of these REIT's are equity trusts and invest at least some of their funds in income-producing residential properties, the special tax benefits they receive may be viewed as incentives to the provision of rental housing.

Thus, the Federal Government through the aids and incentives described above plays a very important role in helping the Nation to achieve its housing objectives. This assistance is so diverse and so widespread that it touches all groups in our society — property owners in every income range, lenders and borrowers.

There could be added to the above description the ability of real estate owners to exchange appreciated real property for other forms of real property, whether similar in use or not, without the requirement of a tax at that time on the appreciation (the tax basis of the first property is carried over to the second property). Also, transfer payments made to tenants, such as HUD rent supplement payments, are not includible in the income of the tenants.

124. For a discussion of tax assistance to real estate, and a range of viewpoints, see Panel No. 4, Tax Treatment of Real Estate, Panel Discussions on General Tax Reform, House Ways and Means Committee, 93d Cong., 1st Sess. 507 (1973). See also Statements of various real estate trade associations defending the present system, and Statement of George H. Deffet, president of a building company, attacking the present tax expenditures, in Hearings on General Tax Reform before the House Ways and Means Committee, 93d Cong., 1st Sess. (March 26, 1973).

125. The rehabilitation tax benefit on its adoption was estimated to cost the Treasury over $400 million during the initial five-year term, and if retained after 1974 would result in an annual $330 million revenue loss. In comparison, the 1970 budget contained a recommendation of $84 million in direct assistance through a rehabilitation loan fund; see Ritter and Sunley, Jr., note 112 above, at 37. The revenue loss is that of five-year amortization compared to accelerated depreciation, and thus does not measure the entire loss on tax assistance to rehabilitated housing.

These revenue loss figures for rehabilitation may be compared with the Treasury's estimated loss of $250 million in 1969 from accelerated depreciation on new rental housing, indicating that in 1969 the weighting of tax assistance for rehabilitation was quite sizable relative to new construction. Yet apparently only about 5% of housing units assisted under HUD's section 236 and rent supplement programs are rehabilitations, and in 1970 HUD had reduced by 50% its estimate of substandard units to be rehabilitated; see Sunley, Jr., note 122 above, at 388. The Treasury has since revised these revenue loss figures, more than doubling that for new rental housing (to $600 million for 1972) and reducing the loss for rehabilitation to $165 million at the end of the transition period. The lower estimate resulted from the considerably lesser level of actual rehabilitation activity compared with anticipated rehabilitation.

126. House Report, note 4 above, at 165–167; Senate Report, note 8 above, at 211–215.

127. See generally Schultze, note 83 above, at 83–94; Special Analysis M, Budget

of the United States, Fiscal Year 1973; Fourth Annual Report on National Housing Goals, note 87 above, 48–51; Schechter, note 101 above.

128. Moreover, the investor with a 10% equity interest has a better after-tax rate of return than one with a 20% interest — and this in a provision designed to encourage equity investment! See the calculations in Ritter and Sunley, Jr., note 112 above, at 26.

129. The syndication fees run around 20% of the capital contribution of the investors, but can go up to 30% or so.

130. The adequacy of this return is indicated by the fact that the HUD subsidies being sought by developers exceed the available funds. If the developer does not do his own construction, then about 5% of construction costs, or about one-third of what the investors put in, must go to the builder as his profit.

For a general description of this syndication process, see Stanley S. Surrey, William C. Warren, Paul R. McDaniel, and Hugh J. Ault, *Federal Income Taxation, Cases and Materials* (Mineola N.Y., The Foundation Press, 1972, 1973) vol.1 at 421, vol.2 at 98; Statement of Jerome Kurtz in Panel No.4, note 124 above, at 553; Statement of Paul R. McDaniel, in Panel No. 6, "Minimum Tax and Tax Shelter Devices," Panel Discussions on General Tax Reform, House Ways and Means Committee, 93d Cong., 1st Sess. 697 (1973); Lewis R. Kaster, "Subsidized Housing: Facts Versus Tax Projections," 26 The Tax Lawyer 125 (1972). See also James E. Wallace, "Federal Income Tax Incentives in Low- and Moderate-Income Rental Housing," in The Economics of Federal Subsidy Programs, Part 5 – Housing Subsidies, Joint Economic Committee, 92d Cong., 2d Sess. 676, 678–683 (1972); Paul R. McDaniel, "Tax Shelters and Tax Policy," in National Tax Association-Tax Institute of America Symposium on Tax Reform (1973).

131. Under FHA regulations, the annual cash distributions may not exceed 6% of the difference between the cost of the project and the mortgage — which comes to 6% of 11.11% of the mortgage. In actual practice this works out to about 4% of the funds invested by the investor-limited partners.

132. The whole structure and investment policy of the new National Corporation for Housing Partnerships is pivoted on the tax assistance. This Corporation, established in 1970, is designed to attract equity capital from business interests to be used in cooperation with local groups to produce housing in volume for low- and moderate-income families. The Corporation acts as the sole general partner in the National Housing Partnership, and the business concerns making investments become shareholders in the Corporation and partners in the Partnership. The equity investment in the housing projects is made by the Partnership, and the tax benefits to the investors flow through the Partnership interest. The prospectus of the Corporation stresses the tax benefits and in effect actually describes the real estate tax shelter. There is really something wondrous in fashioning this $42 million investment venture, aimed at major corporate and financial institutions, around tax rules that were never designed for the purpose and therefore distort the entire investment process in this field. See First Annual Report of the National Corporation for Housing Partnerships, Senate Committee on Banking and Currency, 91st Cong., 2d Sess. (1970); Prospectus regarding National Corporation for Housing Partnerships and the National Housing Partnership 12, 20 (1970). See also Edson, note 98 above, at 26.

There are a number of other such partnership ventures being formed, under which the limited partnership will invest in a number of housing projects. The management fee in these situations is linked to tax deductions created for the investors. These ventures are registered with the S.E.C. See, e.g., American Housing Partners, E.F.

Hutton & Company, Inc., prospectus dated August 31, 1971. There are also nonregistered, limited partnerships involving only investment in a single project, marketed on a private placement basis. The S.E.C. apparently may look at several offerings of a developer to see if on an integrated basis they constitute a public offering requiring registration, a practice which may induce more of the publicly marketed type partnership that invests in a number of projects.

133. See the Statement of Jerome Kurtz, note 130 above at 566–567:

> The developer of this §236 project has developed two assets — an apartment project which produces a limited cash return and a stream of tax benefits. It is clear that of the two the tax benefits are the far more valuable asset to our investor. Since the total return to a 50% tax bracket taxpayer is 20.2% under our example and since the cash flow is limited to 6% which, absent tax advantages, would be worth only 3% after taxes, the tax benefits provide 17.2% out of the 20.2% return, over 85% of the return to our investor is attributable to the Internal Revenue Code and less than 15% to the Housing Act. . . .
>
> The project itself is of little interest to the investors. The cash return is fixed by law. It cannot be sold or refinanced for a very long time. In fact, the example assumes the project will be disposed of for no cash in 20 years. The investor, therefore, assumes there is practically no chance of appreciation or increased income. In fact, a §236 project is frequently not viewed in the market as a real estate investment at all, but rather as a purchase of tax losses. The only important economic fact of concern to the investor is that the project will not be foreclosed at an early date because that would cause an early recognition of gain and a consequent reduction of the projected yield.

134. See Sunley, Jr., note 122 above, at 387, n. 16; the calculation is for a 50% bracket taxpayer. See also Nathan S. Betnun, Tax Shelters for the Rich to Rehabilitate Housing for the Poor, master's thesis in City Planning, M.I.T., November 1971, describing in detail an actual project in the Boston area, and giving examples of after-tax rates of return in the range of 25% for a 50% taxpayer and 50% for a 70% taxpayer.

135. See Sunley, Jr., note 122 above, at 387; Betnun, note 134 above, at 23.

136. Indeed HUD at times seems not even to recognize the assistance provided by the tax benefits. Thus, in a study prepared by HUD "which attempts to add together all Federal assistance which goes to 'urban areas,'" the tax expenditure items are not mentioned. 116 Cong. Rec. 23,942 (1970) (remarks of Congressman Jeffery Cohelan). The Office of Management and Budget also does not recognize this tax expenditure assistance — there is no mention of it in Special Analysis M, Budget of the United States, Fiscal Year 1973, describing federal housing programs. But see the Fourth Annual Report on National Housing Goals, note 123 above, which does describe this tax assistance.

137. The matter may be put another way:

> There are also new provisions in the Tax Reform Act designed to provide greater tax incentives for investing in the so-called limited dividend housing programs under sections 221 and 236 of the Federal Housing Act. These programs are designed to produce low income housing by limiting the investors' return to 6 percent and thus maintaining rents at low levels. Opponents of any changes in the tax laws relating to accelerated depreciation argued that the tax benefits to the investor were taken into account in arriving at the 6 percent figure. This argument may be correct but, if so, it is certainly difficult to ascertain the

rational basis for the limited dividend provisions. For, if the tax benefits were determinative, why is a 6 percent return proper for the 30 percent taxpayer, who gets less tax benefit and hence a lower profit margin, as well as for the 70 percent taxpayer who derives a greater tax benefit from the depreciation deduction? In other words, one wonders if opponents of any change really believe that Congress consciously adopted the principle that taking into account the tax benefit plus the statutory 6 percent, the 70 percent bracket taxpayer is entitled to a higher rate of return than the 30 percent bracket investor.

Paul R. McDaniel, "Alternatives to Utilization of the Federal Income Tax System to Meet Social Problems," 11 Boston College Industrial and Commercial Law Review 867, 894–895 (1970).

138. The calculation in the text covers the net tax benefit from accelerated depreciation (i.e., the tax benefit of the excess early depreciation less the tax detriment of the later underdepreciation compared with straight line depreciation and less the capital gains tax occasioned by the basis reduction resulting from the net excess depreciation, taking account of the timing advantage provided through the excess early depreciation), and the present value of the net tax benefit from the expensing of construction interest and taxes (i.e., the tax benefit of the expensing in the first year less the tax detriment of the later underdepreciation compared with the capitalization of the items and less the capital gains tax occasioned by the basis reduction resulting from the noncapitalization, also taking the timing factor into account). It should be noticed that these calculations assume straight line depreciation as a benchmark. An investor, however, probably regards straight line depreciation as a benefit in itself, when compared with the slower schedule of amortization payments on the mortgage loan. Also, a study shows straight line depreciation to be more rapid than true depreciation; see note 118 above.

Sale after 20 years becomes advisable since the tax aspects have "turned around," as interest and depreciation deductions decline, tax savings disappear, and taxable income in excess of cash flow from normal operations appears. Sale before 20 years requires HUD permission. At the end of 20 years, the mortgage is only about 15% paid off, so that the investors have had large depreciation deductions over 20 years but still "own," in the sense of equity money in the building, only 15% of the building, and the institution that provided the loan still has an 85% interest.

See the example of such a housing project in Stanley S. Surrey, William C. Warren, Paul R. McDaniel and Hugh J. Ault, *Federal Income Taxation, Cases and Materials* (Mineola, N.Y., The Foundation Press, 1973) vol.2 at 98. see also Wallace, note 130 above, at 683–689, and McDaniel, note 130 above.

139. The HUD programs for rent supplements and section 236 interest subsidies (and also minor amounts for private rental housing assistance and homeownership assistance) are budgeted at $1.3 billion for fiscal 1972 and $1.8 billion for fiscal 1973. Budget for the Fiscal Year 1973, Special Analysis M, at 203. The revenue cost of the tax benefits allocable to this subsidized rental housing is probably considerably under $200 million and would not rise in future years at the rate at which direct assistance will increase. The revenue cost of accelerated depreciation on subsidized rental housing is about $150 million for fiscal year 1972.

140. The Senate Finance Committee appears to be interested in the answer to these questions, for its Committee Report on the Tax Reform Act of 1969 states:

Another problem with the present depreciation provisions is that they provide the same tax incentive to all real estate construction. This, in fact, tends to discriminate against the less profitable investments, particularly low income housing. In the 1968 Housing Act, the Congress expressed its desire to . . . eliminate the shortage in this area, and, in part, based the incentive program thereby provided on the existing tax incentives. These circumstances suggest the need for maintaining the existing incentives for low income housing until the programs can be reevaluated.

S. Rep. No. 552, 91st Cong., 1st Sess. 212 (1969). And the Treasury, perhaps recognizing that the recommendation for tax expenditure assistance to rehabilitation of low- and moderate-income housing was not one of its better moments, said:

> [We] are concerned with the continued heavy reliance upon tax incentives as a means of achieving our national housing goals, and believe that consideration should be given in the near future to other additional methods of doing so.

Hearings on H.R. 13270 [Tax Reform Act of 1969] before the Senate Finance Committee, 91st Cong., 1st Sess. 615 (1969).

141. See Betnum, note 134 above.

142. Robert H. Kuehn, Jr., "Limited-Dividend Sponsorship: The Limitations and the Dividends," (Cambridge, Mass., Housing Economics, Nov. 1971) compares these two routes.

Some community developers are seeking to retain a tax-exempt status even when they act as the general partner in the limited partnership, owning and operating the housing. Others assume that they will be considered as taxable entities in that role.

143. See in general, "Failed Federal Housing — The United States as Slumlord," New Republic (Dec. 11, 1971), also in 117 Cong. Rec. H12,392 (daily ed. Dec. 13, 1971).

144. See text at note 15 above; the numbers are rounded off. For estimates of "commissions" paid in other tax shelters, see McDaniel, NTA-TIA Symposium article, note 130 above (equipment leasing, 12% "commission" to bank lessor; oil drilling, 34% "commission" — 23% to investors and 11% to promoters, underwriters, and so on).

145. The proceeds presently received by the developer in the tax shelter syndication are includible in his income for tax purposes. Hence it would be appropriate to include in income any direct subsidy devised as a substitute for the tax shelter fee. This inclusion should not cause a problem in structuring the direct subsidy. Tax-exempt organizations acting as developers might have to treat the subsidy as unrelated business income and therefore also taxable.

The suggestion of a direct HUD payment to the developer is in some quarters met by the response that the developer would be engulfed in red tape. But this response overlooks, first, that the developer is already required to deal with HUD, red tape or not, to obtain the present HUD direct assistance on the mortgage; and second, the developer today to obtain his fee must become engulfed in the tax shelter syndication process, a process that certainly has its own red tape. Another aspect of this "red tape" response is that some wastage and inefficiency are a concomitant of Government programs. Perhaps — but we at least know that considerable wastage and inefficiency are *automatically* built into the tax expenditure assistance and the tax shelter process. The suggestion also evokes the reply: "What, give every developer, good or bad, a Government check!" But this response overlooks the fact that the present tax expenditure assistance goes to every developer, good or bad. Further, the suggestion produces the response that the presence of the investors in the tax shelter is a salutary control on the developer. But this control comes down to the developer's desire to maintain a good reputation that will permit syndication of future projects. Under the suggestion, the developer would also have to maintain a good reputation, to obtain HUD contracts.

If it were desired to keep the Government's assistance to the developer within the tax system, then instead of a direct subsidy the developer could be given a tax credit in the same amount as the subsidy. The credit should be refundable, to permit developers with losses and hence no tax liability and tax-exempt organizations to use the credit. The credit should also be includible in income. See McDaniel, NTA-TIA Symposium article, note 130 above.

146. Wallace, note 130 above at 691, also makes and discusses this direct subsidy approach; see also McDaniel, note 130 above.

Where a community group is the developer, then it can end up as the owner of the housing. Where a private developer is involved, it can continue as the owner or it can sell the housing to a nonprofit group, tenants' association, or the like. The ownership aspect of the limited partnership in the present tax shelter mechanics is thus not an essential function. Indeed, the basic problem in these low-income projects is that of providing continuous effective management, and the tax shelter arrangement does not aid in solving that problem and probably hinders it because of the tension it can create between tenants and investors.

147. The Treasury proposal in 1973, see note 30 above, to eliminate tax shelters for passive investors, in real estate as well as other activities, would appear to have the effect of ending investment by individuals in subsidized rental housing. Hence, it would seem to force the search for a direct subsidy as an alternative, since otherwise such housing would not be built unless banks or other corporations take over such investment. This aspect is not considered in the proposal. The proposal is considered in Chapter VIII.

Of course, the entire present method of HUD subsidization of low-income housing can be questioned. For example, some writers in this area believe that the present subsidies should be scrapped and instead housing allowances be paid directly by the Government to low-income families. See, e.g., Aaron, note 51 above, at 167. See also Housing Subsidies and Housing Policy, Report of Subcommittee on Priorities and Economy in Government, Joint Economic Committee, 93d Cong., 1st Sess. 23 (1973). If this method were used, presumably the question whether the developer still needed a subsidy would be considered. But, in any event, the present tax assistance should be abandoned, whatever method of direct subsidy is finally chosen to assist low-income families in obtaining housing. The §236 subsidization was suspended early in 1973 so that the matter could be studied by HUD.

148. HUD, of course, faces problems in exercising this determination, as news articles on its efforts to push integrated housing into suburbs indicate. E.g., *New York Times*, Sept. 3, 1970 at 39, col. 1. But the leverage that federal assistance possesses to achieve such steps is recognized. See *New York Times*, Aug. 29, 1970, at 10, col. 2, discussing attitudes of the U.S. Civil Rights Commission on this matter.

149. Indeed, freedom of choice for equity investors subsidized by tax assistance means a stress on white tenant-housing located in the suburbs, preferably for elderly or moderate-income tenants, since the investors at whom the tax subsidy is aimed will generally seek housing locations which they believe will produce the least risk, the lowest maintenance costs, the highest prospective residual values, and so on. The developer in turn will seek the less risky projects so that he can obtain the best price from the investors. Under the tax subsidy the rewards for risk-taking by the developer are upside-down; the greater the risks, the less the investors will pay for the tax benefits and hence the less the developer's profit. Since the Treasury tax subsidy is a constant

that does not vary with the risk, because it is a function of total cost and consequent accelerated depreciation benefits, the tax subsidy encourages this search for such low-risk enterprises. See Statement of Jerome Kurtz, note 130 above, at 568. It is an ironic aspect of the present tax expenditure-tax shelter assistance to rental housing that it operates to induce as little equity investment as possible. Since the tax assistance is geared to the cost of the building and is thus a fixed amount once that cost is determined, the investor will seek the highest debt financing to be obtained so as to keep the equity investment low. Any increase in the amount of the equity investment does not increase the amount of the tax assistance. Also, since the tax subsidy is a function of cost, it encourages the developer to build for the highest cost within a range of workable rents, and therefore offers no incentive to achieve economies in building once the HUD closing is final. See Statement of George H. Deffet, note 124 above. Any direct subsidy would have to be structured to avoid such a disincentive to economical building.

150. The estimated revenue loss of $150–200 million on accelerated depreciation on subsidized rental housing is under one-third of the $600 million revenue cost of accelerated derpeciation on all rental housing; see Chapter I. More than five-sixths of the new rental units started in 1971 and 1972 in structures of five or more units were in non-subsidized housing.

151. A good deal of tax assistance to non-HUD subsidized rental housing operates through the same tax shelter syndication process as in the case of subsidized housing. This is because the developers of non-subsidized housing, as in subsidized housing, do not have enough income of their own to absorb the tax expenditure deductions accorded to rental housing. Their mortgages are pushed to as high a level as the proposed rent structure on the housing will permit. The consequent deductible interest component of the mortgage debt plus accelerated depreciation and other tax benefits total an amount larger than the net rents, and "tax losses" result. The developer must therefore look to tax shelter syndication of those tax losses for his profit.

152. The text is a paraphrase of conclusions in a Paper by Paul Taubman, based in turn on the paper by Taubman and Rasche, note 113 above.

153. See Statements referred to in General Tax Reform Hearings, note 124 above.

154. Statement of George H. Deffet, note 124 above. Presumably straight line depreciation, plus the expensing of construction interest and taxes and of pre-opening costs, is a satisfactory shield against tax liability.

155. Another needed study, not in the tax field, is why the Government should be providing an interest subsidy to private lenders rather than itself directly providing the mortgage funds, since the present route is quite costly to the Government. See Betnun, note 134 above, for an illustration. Also, Housing Subsidies and Housing Policy, note 147 above, at 8.

CHAPTER VIII: REFORM MEASURES TO MODERATE TAX EXPENDITURE ABUSES

1. The Canadian 1971 reform legislation incorporates a similar proposal relating to a loss created by depreciation on the rental of real property under which the loss may reduce other rental income but not nonrental income. Ministry of Finance, Summary of 1971 Tax Reform Legislation (1971), 51. The Canadian legislation, section 20(1)(a) of the Income Tax Act, allows depreciation on one real estate asset to be applied against

income from other real estate. This is not necessitated by technical considerations, and proper policy would seem rather to proceed by treating each real estate property separately. Under this approach, presumably a group of buildings in the same area, covered by the same mortgage and built within the same period would constitute one property.

2. House Committee on Ways and Means and Senate Committee on Finance, 91st Cong., 1st Sess., U.S. Treasury Department; Tax Reform Studies and Proposals (Comm. Print, 1969), 15–16, 152–163 (hereinafter cited as Tax Reform Studies). The Nixon Treasury recommended, and the final 1969 Act adopted, a different and less effective approach which retains the initial deferral of income. For the history of the 1969 developments in this area, see Charles Davenport, "A Bountiful Tax Harvest," 48 Texas Law Review 1 (1969); Charles Davenport, "Farm Losses under the Tax Reform Act of 1969: Keepin' 'Em Happy Down on the Farm," 12 Boston College Industrial and Commercial Law Review 319 (1971).

The tax reform bill of Representative James C. Corman, H.R. 1040, 93d Cong., 1st Sess. (1973), 119 Cong. Rec. H44 (daily ed. Jan. 6, 1973) follows the initial Treasury suggestion as to farm losses (§307) and adopts a similar approach for intangible drilling oil expenses and other deductible exploration expenses (§202). See also Alan W. Perry, "Limited Partnerships and Tax Shelters: The *Crane* Rule Goes Public," 27 Tax Law Review 525, 540 (1972).

3. The farm proposal excepted cases where the net income from farming is computed by normal business methods of accounting with the use of inventories and proper capitalization of preparatory and development costs. Under such accounting, the "tax losses" that characterize the tax expenditure for farming would not arise. This exception is also contained in the 1969 Act provisions aimed at farm losses, see Code §1251(b)(4)(A).

The text is simply restating the concept of a tax expenditure. The application of the text suggestion does place stress on proper rules of accounting based on financial accounting (or book accounting) as contrasted with special tax rules. See Appendix to Chapter I.

4. The Treasury in April 1973, taking note of the growing Congressional knowledge of the facts of life about tax shelters and consequent tax reform interest in this area, recommended a limitation on the use of tax shelter losses against unrelated income. See Statement of Treasury Secretary George P. Shultz in Hearings on General Tax Reform before the House Ways and Means Committee, 93d Cong., 1st Sess. (April 30, 1973). However, the proposal applied only to individuals. Also, while for tax shelter equipment leasing, it applied lease by lease and for commercial buildings it applied building by building (several buildings on the same tract operated as a unit were treated as a single property), for oil activities it applied on an industry basis by aggregating all oil properties. Likewise, for residential real estate it aggregated all rental and sales income. For farm activities, while the proposal applied on an industry basis, it could come into play if there were a significant overall increase in tax shelter farm deductions. This latter aspect seems a compromise position between the asset approach and the industry approach.

The Treasury proposal included in the items whose use would be restricted, the excess of accelerated depreciation over straight line depreciation both for real estate and leased machinery and equipment, and the expensing of construction costs for real estate, but did not include the investment credit nor the ADR class lives. The non-inclusion of these items makes the proposal incomplete in its coverage of tax expenditure deductions.

5. See Statement of Paul R. McDaniel in Panel No. 6, Minimum Tax and Tax Shelter Devices, Panel Discussions on General Tax Reform, House Ways and Means Committee, 93d Cong., 1st Sess. 697 (1973).

6. McDaniel Statement, note 5 above. He suggests either turning accelerated depreciation into an increased investment credit, that would be refundable, or converting unusable depreciation into a tax refund that would be repayable without interest over the life of the property. Also, since a direct subsidy would be includible in income or reduce the depreciable basis of the asset, such an investment credit would require similar treatment if it were to parallel a direct subsidy. See also Paul R. McDaniel, "Tax Shelters and Tax Policy," in National Tax Association-Tax Institute of America Symposium on Tax Reform (1973).

7. As an example, suppose a rental building involved a dollar cost of $4 million, of which $3.4 million represented borrowed funds and $600,000 represented funds of the investor. The text suggestion could be carried out by allowing the accelerated depreciation of the tax shelter (i.e., depreciation faster than economic loss) to be computed on the basis of $4 million and taken until the deductions under that depreciation equaled $600,000. Thereafter, further depreciation deductions would be allowed, in similar fashion, only as equity was built up through repayment of the loan. Under this approach, a taxpayer could not obtain a "tax loss" in excess of his own investment. He could, however, still secure a rapid write-off of his own investment since it would be offset in the early years by the accelerated depreciation based on the leverage as well. A stricter approach would be to permit depreciation on the basis of only the $600,000 equity plus any loan repayments as they occur.

For recommendations using the approach here suggested see Statements of Jerome Kurtz and Adrian DeWind, in Panel No. 4, Tax Treatment of Real Estate, Panel Discussions on General Tax Reform, House Ways and Means Committee, 93d Cong., 1st Sess. 553 and 520 (1973). Mr. Kurtz said (571):

> An alternative or even an additional approach which has been suggested to limit the tax shelter aspects of a real estate investment is to limit the effect of leveraging. This can be accomplished either by treating the equity investment as being the basis of the property for depreciation purposes or by permitting depreciation with reference to the entire property, but limiting the aggregate losses to the cash investment. The first suggestion is justified principally by the fact that if the equity alone is depreciated at straight-line rates, the total allowable depreciation will approximate a "reverse sum of the years digits" method and thereby get close to true economic depreciation as determined by Taubman and Rasche. . . . On the other hand, decline in value of a building should be reflected first in the equity portion because that is the portion first at risk. Therefore, if straight-line depreciation is allowable generally it would seem appropriate to permit it on the entire property but to limit aggregate losses to the equity. If we are unwilling to limit depreciation generally to less than straightline, it nevertheless seems appropriate to limit aggregate losses to equity because the marketplace has made a determination of the true economic decline of a building by the way it is financed. In other words, if a lender is willing to make a loan secured primarily by the property, then a market determination has been made that the value of the property will not be less than the remaining balance of the mortgage at any given time. This determination would seem the best indication of economic decline and provide an objective basis for limiting losses.
>
> In most cases with a normal amount of equity investment and straight-line depreciation this limitation will not have much impact. However, it would have

substantial importance if any type of accelerated depreciation is to be continued.

A corollary to limiting losses to equity would be a requirement that mortgaging of a property for an amount in excess of basis would produce income to the extent of such excess at the time the loan is put on the property. This income element would then be added to the basis of the property.

In addition to the fact that limiting deductions in this way would bring depreciation deductions more in line with the economic decline of the building, it is difficult to justify deductions in excess of investment because the taxpayer is not running any substantial risk of incurring those excess losses. If such an approach were to be adopted it should be applied in all cases in which loans are secured by real estate, whether or not the taxpayer has any liability for such loans. To differentiate between a no liability mortgage and a mortgage with personal liability would produce widely disparate tax results in situations where there is little or no economic difference.

See also §502 of the Corman bill, note 2 above, and Statement of Kenneth A. Goldman in Panel No. 6, note 5 above, at 855. For differing viewpoints, see other Statements in that Panel, especially the Statement of Milton A. Dauber, at 719, and in Panel No. 4 above.

For a discussion of these approaches, see Perry, note 2 above at 537–540. Perry also discusses, at 547, the question whether a limited partner should be able, as under present law, to include in his basis for depreciation any partnership non-recourse borrowing for which no partner is liable. Perry concludes that as long as a single owner can so utilize borrowing leverage, a limited partnership should similarly be able to do so unless one adopts the pragmatic approach that since most tax shelter activities involve more than a single owner a restrictive approach limited to partnerships would have a dampening effect on tax shelters. See §313 of the Corman bill, note 2 above, applying a limitation in the partnership situation. McDaniel, in Panel No. 6, note 5 above, defends the denial of tax leverage benefit to a limited partnership by saying that if the partners seek the limitation of liability that comes with operation in limited partnership form they should not be able to use the tax leverage of the liability, but instead should be regarded as are stockholders in a corporation that incurs the liability. He recognizes, however, that this approach would shift many tax shelter operations to corporations, especially banks and other financial institutions.

The text discussion is here confined to the treatment of borrowed funds in connection with the use of tax expenditure assistance. The question of the appropriate technical treatment of borrowed funds under the income tax proper also merits exploration. But the consequences of the present rules are by far more serious in the tax expenditure area, and correction here can appropriately come before any wider exploration of the subject.

8. If there is a borrowing not secured by any particular assets, then the basis of all assets of the taxpayer should be reduced, with a consequent tax if after reduction there are still some borrowed dollars remaining. The order of reduction of basis — i.e., which assets come first for this purpose — could be prescribed, e.g., appreciated assets before other assets, securities before a residence.

Study would be required to determine the efficacy of the text proposal in the case of financial institutions, such as banks or insurance companies, or other corporations able to borrow on the strength of their general credit.

A much more limited approach in the real estate area would be, on a refinancing of the debt, to include in income any mortgage proceeds in excess of basis, or at least to the extent of depreciation previously taken. In effect, this applies a recapture approach to mortgage proceeds. See Statements of Kurtz and DeWind, note 7 above.

9. William Vickrey, "Tax Simplification through Cumulative Averaging," 34 Law and Contemporary Problems 736 (1969).

10. Vickrey, note 9 above, at 738, 741–742:

> Conceptually, cumulative assessment amounts to considering all previous payments on account of income tax on income reported for years included in the cumulation period as interest-bearing deposits in a tax guarantee account. The interest at an appropriate rate credited to this account during the last year plus the net taxable income from other sources for the current year are then added to the cumulated taxable income as of the previous year to get the cumulated taxable income for the period to date. The total tax due on this total income for the period is then obtained from a tax table appropriate to the number of years covered by the period, in exactly the same way as a tax is now computed for a single year. The tax currently due is the amount necessary to bring the balance in the tax guarantee account, including accrued interest, up to the level of this total tax due.
>
> . . .
>
> It may at first seem odd that a taxpayer should be permitted to write off his investments as rapidly as he pleases, especially as this treatment can, under present law, be considered the equivalent of exempting from income tax an amount equal to the normal rate of profits on the value thus written off. Here, however, owing to the fact that the interest factor is explicitly taken into account by allowing interest to be accumulated on early tax payments, postponement of tax by early write-off amounts simply to borrowing from the government at the stipulated interest rate. Provided that the rate of interest is maintained in suitable relation to market rates of interest, the taxpayer merely borrows from the government through tax deferment rather than from private lenders; the liquidity of the taxpayer may be enhanced, but his ultimate tax burden is not reduced.
>
> For example, if under the present law a taxpayer subject to a thirty percent marginal rate manages to postpone $10,000 of income for one year, say by arranging a sale on January 2 instead of December 31, his tax bill for the earlier year will then be reduced by $3,000. If he invests this $3,000 for one year at say eight percent, he will realize $3,240. He will, with respect to the second year, have to pay a tax at thirty percent not only on the $10,000 of income postponed, but on the $240 of interest earned, or a tax of $3,072, but even so he will wind up $168 better off. Under cumulative assessment, on the other hand, paying the $3,000 tax in the earlier year increases the balance in the tax guarantee account by $3,000, and if eight percent is used as the rate of interest credited to this account, equivalent to what could be earned on the outside, the $240 credited to this account and included in cumulated income just balances the $240 that the taxpayer could have earned by postponing tax and investing the amount himself. The cumulative income at the end of the later years is the same in either case, as is also therefore the cumulative tax. The tax payment in the second year will be $3,240 higher, and the taxpayer will wind up equally well off in either case. Investment in early tax payments is made just as profitable as outside investment of funds obtained by deferring taxes, for such a case.
>
> Of course, if the taxpayer has opportunities for investment that yield a higher return than the rate of interest currently being credited on the tax guarantee account, he will be able to gain from postponing his taxes. But this gain is essentially no different from the gain he could realize by borrowing from any

other source at the given rate of interest. The only effect of cumulative averaging is to offer a new source of borrowed funds, which may provide an improvement in the liquidity position of the taxpayer. To the extent that this takes place, it may well be considered a desirable improvement in the efficiency of the over-all capital market. However, the enhancement of liquidity provided by cumulative averaging is likely to prove considerably less substantial than might appear on the surface; a taxpayer who shows a potential lender a ledger with assets written down for tax purposes may expect his line of credit to be somewhat shorter than if his books showed the full value. Even if the lender is fully aware of the market values and is prepared to rely on them, he will have to take into consideration the potential liability for the deferred taxes. Therefore, borrowing by tax deferral may, to a considerable extent, be at the expense of ability to borrow from other sources.

11. Vickrey, note 9 above, at 745.
12. See in general Carl S. Shoup, *Public Finance* (Chicago, Aldine Publishing Co., 1969), 325; Vickrey, note 9 above, at 745–750.
13. Senate Committee on Finance, Tax Reform Act of 1969 [H.R. 13270] S. Rep. No. 552, 91st Cong., 1st Sess. 127, 129–130 (1969):

> The committee also modified the House bill to provide an interest charge to cover the tax payments by the income beneficiaries which are deferred by the use of accumulation trusts. This interest charge is based on the additional income tax which the beneficiary would have paid if the income originally had been taxed to the beneficiary instead of the trust. The committee believes that this interest charge is necessary because, otherwise, the deferral of the payment of the additional tax (i.e., from the time the income is taxed to the trust until the time when the remainder of the tax is paid on the accumulation distribution by the beneficiary) amounts, in effect, to an interest-free loan to the beneficiary by the government.
>
> . . .
>
> As indicated above, the committee amendments also modify the House bill to provide an interest charge to cover the tax payments by the income beneficiary which are deferred (to the extent the taxes may exceed those paid by the trust) by the use of accumulation trusts. This charge is to be the equivalent of what in the average case would be a 6-percent rate: namely, a 3-percent rate which may not be taken as an income tax deduction. It is based on the amount of tax payable by the beneficiary over and above the tax which was paid in the earlier years by the trust. When an accumulation distribution is made and the beneficiary uses the exact method to compute the tax, the 3-percent simple interest is imposed on each year's additional tax multiplied by the number of years of tax deferral involved (from the year earned until distributed).

14. The present Code in the treatment of mortgage insurance companies contains a provision that meets the problem of deferral. Under that provision the companies are allowed deductions for reserves required under state laws to meet severe economic losses resulting from economic deterioration of a depression character. The deductions reflecting this pessimism would produce large tax savings. However, the provision requires that the income taxes so saved must be invested in special federal bonds that do not carry interest. The reserves required by the state are thereby funded, but the deferral does not involve any present benefit. See Chapter IV, note 46.

15. See discussion of recapture in Chapter IV.

16. See discussion in Chapter VI.

17. The application to corporations of these approaches is considered later.

18. See discussion in Chapter IV.

19. Interest attributable to a trade or business or to property held for the production of rents or royalties is excepted from this alternative arrangement, and can be deducted along with the standard deduction, Code §62(1) and (5). This rule requires a tracing of the loan proceeds; e.g., interest on a rental real estate mortgage is not so deductible without a showing that the mortgage funds were used in business or in connection with the rental property, *United States v. Wharton,* 207 F.2d 526 (5th Cir. 1953).

20. Tax Reform Studies, note 2 above, at 15. See also discussion therein at 142–152 and further examples.

21. Tax Reform Studies, note 2 above, at 143.

22. Tax Reform Studies, note 2 above, at 15.

23. House Committee on Ways and Means, Tax Reform Act of 1969 [H.R. 13270], H.R. Rep. No. 413, 91st Cong., 1st Sess. 80–81 (1969).

24. The reasons stated by the Senate Finance Committee, note 13 above at 113, relate largely to the matter of the minimum tax, which is discussed later.

For descriptions of this history, see Charles Davenport and Kenneth A. Goldman, "The Minimum Tax for Tax Preferences and the Interest Deduction Limitation under the Tax Reform Act of 1969," 16 Wayne Law Review 1223 (1970); Mortimer Caplin, "Minimum Tax Preferences and Related Reforms Affecting High Income Individuals," 4 Indiana Legal Forum 71 (1970).

25. For a case stating a similar principle in the allocation of these items between domestic and foreign sources of income for the purpose of foreign tax credit computations, see *Grunebaum v. Comm'r,* 420 F.2d 332 (2d Cir. 1970).

26. The Treasury Tax Reform Proposals had not covered, on grounds that were technical and not substantive, intangible drilling expenses and accelerated real estate depreciation, as to which I and others in testimony before the House Ways and Means Committee urged extension of coverage to those items, nor farm tax losses which under the Proposals were covered directly; see Caplin, note 24 above, at 80.

27. The House Bill was estimated to yield $460 million, House Report, note 23 above, at 83.

28. The new form of minimum tax proposed by the Treasury in April 1973 (see Statement of Treasury Secretary Shultz referred to in note 4 above) took a different approach for these personal expense deductions. It considered the deductions as tax preferences to be combined, in structuring a minimum tax base, with certain income excluded under other tax preferences. In some situations, as where there is no excluded income and personal deductions are large, the suggested new minimum tax would be more severe than an allocation of deductions proposal. In other situations, as where there are both excluded income and personal deductions, the allocation of deductions proposal could be more severe. This new form of minimum tax is discussed later in the chapter.

29. See House Report, note 23, at 9. See Hearings on H.R. 13270 [Tax Reform Act of 1969], before the House Committee on Ways and Means, 91st Cong., 1st Sess. 5518 (1969), indicating that after charitable contributions, largely on returns using the unlimited deduction, the deduction for non-mortgage interest far exceeded the other itemized deductions. See also Chapter III.

30. Section 265(1) disallows any expense, including those incurred in trade or business, which is allocable to any wholly exempt item other than interest, and any expense (deductible under §212) incurred by an individual in the production of

nonbusiness income, including interest, so allocable. Section 265(2), referred to in the text, covers individuals and corporations, and both business- and nonbusiness-exempt interest.

Section 265 of course has a built-in tracing problem: for example, if a taxpayer with a portfolio of taxable and tax-exempt securities borrows money to invest in a business or to buy a house, is the indebtedness "incurred to carry" the tax-exempt obligations within the meaning of the section? Presumably not. See in general, Dale F. Jeffers, "The Investment-Interest-Deduction Limitation Under Section 163(d) in Light of 265(2) Cases," 38 Journal of Taxation 38 (1973).

31. See generally Daniel I. Halperin, "Capital Gains and Ordinary Deductions: Negative Income Tax For the Wealthy," 12 Boston College Industrial and Commercial Law Review 387, 389 (1971).

32. Interest and taxes, being expressly deductible, need not be capitalized under the Code. The Code does permit capitalization, §266, of such carrying charges at the taxpayer's election. In nonfarm situations other carrying charges must be capitalized. See *Schultz v. Comm'r*, 50 T.C. 688 (1968), *aff'd mem.* 420 F.2d 490 (3rd Cir. 1970). The Regulations permit current deduction in the farm area.

The 1969 Act requires expenditures attributable to the planting and maintenance of citrus or almond (1970 amendment) groves incurred before the third year after planting to be capitalized, §278. But the section is flabby and offers many avenues of escape, e.g., any allocable interest and taxes are not covered (Regulations, §1.278–1(a)(2)(ii)), trees replacing those destroyed by disease or freeze are not covered.

The 1971 Canadian tax reform required the capitalization of carrying charges (e.g., interest and taxes) on undeveloped real property, and this presumably includes the construction of a building, Ministry of Finance, note 1 above, at 51; section 18(2) of the Canadian Income Tax Act.

33. The suggestions made earlier, regarding the treatment of borrowed funds generally, see text preceding note 8, would reduce escape in the text situations.

34. House Report, note 23 above, at 72–73.

35. Senate Report, note 13 above, at 305–306.

36. Until 1972, excess investment interest was a tax preference for individuals under the minimum tax, discussed later.

37. The disallowed interest so carried forward can be deducted only against one-half of future investment income, so that use of the full carryforward depends on the receipt of investment income twice the carryforward amount. In effect, the allowed deduction against non-investment income of one-half the interest in the earlier year is recouped in later years if there is investment income, since one-half of the later investment income is really taking the place of the non-investment income that was earlier offset.

38. Staff of the Joint Committee on Internal Revenue Taxation, General Explanation of the Tax Reform Act of 1969 (1970), 98. The genesis of the compromise one-half approach appears to be in the Senate treatment of farm losses. See Halperin, note 31 above, at 399–402.

39. See Halperin, note 31 above, at 392.

40. The interaction under this section of the interest deduction and capital gain is, in general, as follows:

(1) In the year the interest would otherwise be deductible, any capital gain of that year offset by the interest (after the offset of the $25,000 floor and investment income of the year) is treated as ordinary income. This treatment in effect carries out the concept that interest allocable to capital gain is not fully deductible; i.e., the interest becomes fully deductible only by eliminating the capital gain character of the gain itself.

(2) Any remaining interest of that year is allowed only to the extent of one-half. The

disallowed one-half is carried forward, to be offset against one-half of investment income. If there is capital gain in a future year, any remaining disallowed interest to be carried forward is reduced by the excluded portion of the capital gain. This produces the same effect as in the year the interest first arose, except that the mechanics of the interaction here reduce the interest deduction rather than change the character of the gain.

41. The following comments are from Halperin, note 31 above, at 405–407:

> [Capital deduction] reduces the benefit of the deferral by allowing only one-half of the deduction in the initial year. For these reasons it is preferable to recapture; but the question naturally arises whether this partial disallowance can be supported when accounting principles, for example, would permit the deduction, such as interest, to be taken when incurred. It is submitted that allowance of only one-half of the deduction can be justified (even if it would be admitted for the sake of argument that a full disallowance would be improper or undesirable) because of the fact that it achieves symmetry with the taxation of only one-half of LTCG [long-term capital gain]. Thus, it seems that the capital deduction approach should be preferred to recapture when:
>
> (1) it is reasonably certain that the taxpayer's purpose in entering the transaction is to realize a long-term capital gain, or
>
> (2) it is likely that this is the taxpayer's purpose and general accounting principles would suggest that the expenditure be disallowed in full (capitalized).
>
> Since only one-half of LTCG is subject to tax, it is only reasonable to allow just one-half of expenses to be deducted when a taxpayer intends to produce only capital gain income. If, contrary to the taxpayer's expectations, ordinary income is in fact realized, the full amount of the deductions becomes allowable when such realization occurs. The capital deduction approach also would seem to be proper when the transaction results in a loss in that it permits one-half of the loss to be deducted, thus corresponding to the amount of income that would be taxable if the transaction had produced LTCG. For example, if the taxpayer's costs in raising a breeding animal were $140, the deduction would be limited to $70. If the animal were sold for a LTCG of $100, $50 would be taxed. The net loss for tax purposes, $20 ($70 – $50) is one-half of the economic loss of $40 ($140 – $100).
>
> It may be noted that if the $140 were capitalized, the sale would result in a capital loss of $40. Since a capital loss can generally be used only to offset a capital gain, the tax value of the loss is only $20 since a LTCG of $40 would produce only $20 of taxable income. In effect, therefore, the capital deduction approach reaches the same eventual result as would be reached if the expense were required to be capitalized and taken into account in computing capital gain or loss, while at the same time allowing the proper portion of the deduction to be claimed in the year the expense is incurred.
>
> . . .
>
> The author would support the use of the capital deduction approach for investment interest for the first of the two reasons given above. The provision would seem to apply principally to investors in the stock market and in vacant land. The dividend income to the former would almost certainly be less than the cost of borrowing; the latter, of course, have little or no current return unless the property is developed. Both are hoping that the purchased assets will appreciate in value and produce LTCG. Hence, their costs are clearly capital costs.

It may be noted that the investment interest provision would also apply to lessors of realty or personalty under a net lease resulting in current tax losses (those with gains are not troubled by the investment interest provision). Because of the inadequacies of section 1250 in achieving recapture, and the appreciation potential in most realty, it would seem that real estate investors with current losses would ordinarily be seeking capital gain on sale rather than future rent increases. Therefore, the provision properly applies. Equipment lessors, who have to contend with section 1245, may have a better case on this ground although they hardly would seem to be abused by the tax law; their plight will not be pursued here although it may be noted that since accelerated depreciation is not taken into account in computing investment expenses, equipment lessors may perhaps have enough net investment income to permit the deduction of interest paid.

In the farm area, it is more difficult to assert that the eventual goal is capital gain. The capital gain abuse has generally been limited to breeding livestock and trees. Efforts to distinguish other farm operations from these would be difficult, particularly where there is an integrated business. Moreover, a breeder could realize substantial ordinary income, and the trees could be retained until they bear fruit which is then sold for ordinary income. Nevertheless, the capital deduction approach can be supported on the second ground set forth above — the immediate deduction on the cash basis is improper, and, in light of the real capital gain potential, effective measures to deal with it are needed. Since it is hard to object to the validity of requiring capitalization of costs, this milder approach is clearly justified. . . .

It is not intended to suggest that capitalization of costs or denial of LTCG on sale would not be a better solution to some of the problems discussed herein, but until this millennium is achieved, it is the author's view that the capital deduction approach is worthy of serious consideration in what should be the continuing effort to deal with the double benefit of ordinary deductions and capital gains. Moreover, there should be a strong presumption in favor of this solution, as compared to recapture, whenever it appears that the transaction is clearly intended to produce capital gains; or, if capital gains is less certain, if it can also be established that the immediate deduction is not in accord with ordinary accounting principles.

42. The provision is discussed generally in Davenport and Goldman, note 24 above. See also Arthur I. Gould, "Trends in Tax Planning for Real Estate Investments," 50 Taxes 732 (1972).

43. The definitions are such that any leverage on an oil shelter is not covered, since the shelter operation would be regarded as the business of drilling for oil, and leverage on rental housing and some rental commercial property (an office building with a number of tenants) is not covered, since this also is a trade or business activity and not brought in through the coverage of property subject to a net lease.

44. As to tracing problems, see Jeffers, note 30 above. See also Chapter VII, note 107. Other tax systems have to face these tracing problems. Canada in general allows a deduction only for interest on funds borrowed to earn income from a business or property, and excludes personal interest expense; §201(c), Canadian Income Tax Act. The United Kingdom follows this same course, but also includes a borrowing for a residence; §§130 and 52–63, U.K. Income and Corporation Taxes Act, ch.10.

45. This is Case 7, set forth in Tax Reform Studies, note 2 above, at 92.

46. The revenue estimate for the Code provision is $20 million. Staff explanation,

note 38 above, at 101. Since this was also the estimate for the stronger House Bill provision, it appears that the estimators were not aware of the later changes. The proper estimate was probably around $10 million.

The Corman bill, note 2 above, would reduce the floor to $5,000 and eliminate the one-half approach (§304). Senator Edmund S. Muskie, in his tax reform proposals, would eliminate the one-half approach, reduce the floor to $10,000, and extend the provision to oil and real estate shelters, 119 Cong. Rec. S1050, 1056 (daily ed. Jan. 23, 1973).

47. Hearings on H.R. 13270 [Tax Reform Act of 1969] before Senate Committee on Finance, 91st Cong., 1st Sess. 576–577 (1969).

48. Senate Report, note 13 above, at 305–306. See also Halperin, note 31 above, at 403–404.

49. Such a limitation is also an appropriate structural part of the interest deduction under a basic income tax that does not consider accrued but unrealized appreciation in value to be income. Under such a tax, a proper structural question is how the interest deduction should be shaped. Another proper structural question is how borrowing should be treated when the taxpayer holds such appreciated property; see the text discussion preceding note 8. If the borrowing were taxed, then the consequent gain would be available to offset prior disallowed interest, as would any other realized gain.

If tax expenditure assistance did not exist and if accrued but unrealized gains were taxed, then an interest deduction limitation would not generally be needed. Thought would still have to be given, however, to borrowing to buy consumer durables or residences since imputed income is not taxed; also, if capital losses could not be offset against capital gains (even while both were included at 100%) because of the timing of loss problem, there presumably would be a similar problem of the timing of the interest deduction. The present limitation on the interest deduction is similar to the required carryforward of excess capital losses.

The text discussion equally applies to interest borrowed in connection with business activities involving these same escape paths. It also has relevance to certain corporate activities, since the interest deduction can also cause tax escapes in the corporate area, and more study should be given to this aspect. Thus, a corporation may obtain a full deduction for the interest on funds borrowed to invest in the stocks of other corporations although only 15% of the dividends from those corporations are includible in the income of the recipient corporation because of the inter-corporate dividend deduction. This situation is a factor in lowering the effective tax rate on mutual savings banks. See Chapter III, note 70.

The Treasury April 1973 proposal for a new minimum tax, note 28 above, would eliminate the limitation on the interest deduction in the belief that the treatment of interest under that new minimum tax adequately covers the problems in this area. But the adequacy of the new proposal is far from clear, and the better course is to seek expansion and improvement of the present limitation.

50. The proper interrelationship between the two deduction provisions would have to be worked out. The House Bill in 1969 first applied the allocation provision and then reduced the amount of interest expense that would be disallowed under that provision by the amount of interest disallowed under the limitation provision. In essence, the intent was to apply the provision which produced the greater disallowance of investment interest. It would seem that the reverse procedure would be feasible; i.e., apply the limitation on investment interest and then apply the allocation proposal, feeding into it only consumer interest and any other interest not characterized as investment interest or trade and business interest.

51. Tax Reform Studies, note 2 above, at 93–94, Cases 8–11.

52. Tax Reform Studies, note 2 above, at 13–14, 134–135.

53. The history is described in Kenneth R. Biederman, Gary A. Robbins, and Emil M. Sunley, Jr., "A Comparison of the Various Proposals for a Minimum Tax and Allocation of Deductions," 1971 Proceedings of National Tax Association 148; Davenport and Goldman, note 24 above; and Caplin, note 24 above. See also Richard D. Hobbet, "Transitional Mechanisms to Facilitate Tax Reform," 34 Law and Contemporary Problems 819 (1969), and Discussion by Martin H. David of paper by Biederman et al, above, at 242.

54. The Tax Reform Studies, note 2 above, at 133–134, gave this explanation for not including deferral items:

> In order to maintain a simple structure for the minimum tax, relatively minor items of excluded income — for example, sick pay and the dividend exclusion — would not be included in the expanded base. For similar reasons, tax preferences which represent a *deferral of tax,* rather than an *exemption from tax,* would be excluded in defining the expanded income base. In these deferral cases, a tax will eventually be paid assuming adoption of the proposal for including in income the appreciation on property at the time it is given away or transferred on the death of the owner.

The explanation is not satisfying since it does not cope with the benefits of tax deferral, and later related testimony included deferral items. See note 26 above.

55. Hearings on H.R. 13270 [Tax Reform Act of 1969] before House Committee on Ways and Means, 91st Cong., 1st Sess. 5050–5051, 5060–5065 (1969).

56. House Report, note 23 above, at 77–79.

The estimate of revenue increase was put at $85 million, similar to that under the Nixon Treasury proposal, compared with $420 million under the Johnson Treasury proposal. The main difference seems to be due to the effect on capital gains of the Johnson Treasury proposal, since in general that proposal raised the effective rate on such gains to 35% whereas the Nixon Treasury proposal and House proposal left the rate at 25%. See text discussion later.

57. Senate Report, note 13 above, at 112–113.

58. The $30,000 is applied against the preferences, and then the difference between the regular tax and the preferences as reduced is carried forward. If the preferences are less than $30,000, then the entire regular tax would be carried forward. But presumably any unused part of the $30,000 is not applied to increase the carryover.

59. Biederman et al, note 53 above, place the estimated revenue at $222 million from individuals and $333 million from corporations.

60. 118 Cong. Rec. S14,522 (daily ed. Sept. 11, 1972). There is a discussion of the minimum tax at S14,518–14,532 in connection with an unsuccessful attempt to strengthen the tax.

The minimum tax on *individuals* in *1970* (apparently $117 million) was paid by 19,000 persons, with an aggregate of $4.5 billion of preferences. Of that total, $3.7 billion represented the excluded half of capital gains; accelerated depreciation or amortization on real estate, $250 million; percentage depletion, $210 million; excess investment interest, $200 million; stock options, $130 million. The minimum tax on *corporations* was $218 million, of which about $104 million came from oil, mining, and related industries, with the balance scattered among primary metal industries, railroads, and savings and loan associations. Remarks of Honorable Edwin S. Cohen,

Undersecretary of the Treasury, before the Tax Forum of U.S. Chamber of Commerce, Nov. 29, 1972; Edwin S. Cohen, "The Administration's Tax Priorities," Tax Foundation, Inc. Conference (January 1973).

In *1971* the minimum tax on *individuals* produced $164 million, paid by 23,889 individuals on a total of $3.96 billion of preferences. Of those individuals, 1614 reported they had no adjusted gross income, but they had an average of $104,106 each in income from the tax preferences covered by the minimum tax. News Release of Senator Walter F. Mondale, April 15, 1973, using data from Preliminary Statistics of Income for Individuals for 1971.

61. For an enumeration of these and other weaknesses in the minimum tax, see Statement of Martin Ginsburg, in Panel No. 6, note 5 above. He states that an individual with $300,000 of income could have around $131,000 of tax preferences and still pay no minimum tax. His computation uses a formula set forth in Note, "The Minimum Tax for Items of Tax Preferences. . . Movement toward A Comprehensive Tax Base?" 41 University of Cincinnati Law Review 365, 386–387 (1972).

62. The Statements of Martin D. Ginsburg, Kenneth A. Goldman, and Paul R. McDaniel, in Panel No. 6, note 5 above, all contain recommendations for strengthening the minimum tax, largely along parallel approaches.

63. The Corman bill, note 2 above, uses a floor of $12,000; the Muskie proposal, note 46 above, uses a floor of $2,000. The Treasury has indicated that a floor of $20,000 would increase estimated 1972 revenue from individuals under the tax from $180 million to $220 million, and the number of individual taxpayers from 30,000 to 55,000; a floor of $15,000 would increase individual revenue to $250 million and taxpayers to 75,000. Remarks of Undersecretary Cohen, note 60 above. McDaniel, note 5 above, urges a $5,000 exemption structured to phase-out at $10,000 of preferences.

64. For a taxpayer in the 50% bracket, out of a total of $100 income, $67 of taxable income will shelter only $33.

65. The upside-down effect or reverse progression of the present provision is of course wrong, i.e., for a 70% bracket taxpayer, $59 of taxable income shelters $41, but for a 50% bracket taxpayer it takes $67 of taxable income to shelter $33. See Davenport and Goldman, note 24 above, at 1252 and subsequent.

66. See Remarks of Undersecretary Cohen, note 60 above, disapproving the supplementary approach on the ground that a supplementary tax simply waters down the preferences involved, and if that is the objective it is "far simpler to whittle down those particular incentive provisions directly rather than indirectly by a separate tax on the allowed preferences." Query, however, if this is the right political judgment. The Corman bill, note 2 above, uses the supplementary approach since it would eliminate the subtraction of the regular tax. It retains the 10% rate.

The Statements in Panel No. 6, note 5 above, urging a strengthening of the minimum tax, all apparently recommend a straight supplementary approach, which would drop the subtraction of the regular tax. See Statements of Paul R. McDaniel, Kenneth A. Goldman, and Martin D. Ginsburg, at 697, 855, and 879. These recommendations may be influenced by the belief that, whatever may be the most appropriate form of minimum tax, the supplementary aspect of the present tax may indicate that the best approach pragmatically to strengthening the tax lies in staying with a supplementary approach. There is support for this belief in the close vote in the Senate on the amendment of Senator Edward M. Kennedy, in connection with the Public Debt Limit legislation, to eliminate the subtraction of the regular tax; the amendment was tabled by a vote of 49–47, see 119 Cong. Rec. S12,178–12,185 (daily ed. June 27, 1973).

67. Thus, the basic defect of the present minimum tax lies not in its subtraction of the regular tax, but in its use of a low and flat rate, 10%. Those corrective proposals

that move to a progressive rate are therefore to be preferred. Further, a progressive rate on the total economic income without subtraction of the regular tax (i.e., the initial Treasury approach) is to be preferred over the technique that first allows for subtraction of the regular tax and then adjusts the rates of the minimum tax, since this latter route, even though using progressive rates, produces an upside-down effect; see note 65 above.

The Corman bill, note 2 above, uses a 10% rate with no subtraction of the regular tax. The Muskie proposal, note 46 above, uses a 10% to 20% rate, retains the subtraction of the regular tax but eliminates the carryforward of excess regular tax.

A matter to be explored is the appropriateness of a carryover technique in this area. The Johnson Treasury minimum tax proposal did not involve a carryover, and each year stood on its own footing. The Nixon Treasury proposal and the House Bill minimum tax had a five-year carryforward of the disallowed preferences. The present Code provision has a seven-year carryforward of excess regular tax. It would appear that under the concept of a minimum tax each year should be considered by itself, and the averaging inherent in carryovers is not advisable. See David, note 53 above. However, with a minimum tax at high rates, some averaging may be proper.

68. The Statements in Panel No. 6, note 5 above, recommending a strengthening of the minimum tax, note 66 above, use rates of 7 to 35%, as a *supplementary* tax, without subtraction of the regular tax from the total of tax preferences, which would put the total tax on capital gains at 52.5%, or a little less depending on the floor used. McDaniel points this out, while the other Statements leave it to inference.

The operation of the present *maximum* tax can, under certain conditions, produce a rate of 45.5% on the capital gains of an individual in the 70% bracket who has earned income that would be subject to the 50% maximum rate were it not for the offset of the untaxed portion of the capital gains. In effect, the loss of the 70%-50% differential under the maximum tax where preference income exists, means an increase in tax of 20% on preference income. In this sense, the maximum tax preference offset provision is considerably stronger than the 10% minimum tax with its subtraction of the regular tax. Thus the present minimum tax increases the capital gain rate of a 70% taxpayer to 36.5%; the maximum tax increases it to 45% (and to 45.5% if still subject to minimum tax).

A supplementary tax with a top rate of 35% may still produce a higher total tax than an alternative tax with a top rate of 50% in cases in which there are regular income items in addition to the tax preference items, since under the alternative tax the regular items shelter some of the preference items but do not do so under the supplementary tax.

A variation of the text approach is a minimum tax structured so that its relationship to the basic rate structure is in itself progressive. The minimum tax could start at 20% of the bottom 14% basic rate, go to 40% of the 30% basic rate, and rise to 80% of the top 70% basic rate, giving a minimum tax rate scale of 2.8% to 56%, as an alternative tax.

69. See the discussion in Chapter IV.

70. Ibid.

71. The present provision does not distinguish between exclusion and deferral items, presumably because the rate is only 10%. It thus is more favorable the longer the deferral. The deferral aspect was mentioned in the Senate Report, note 13 above at 117:

> Certain items subject to the 5-percent minimum tax, such as accelerated depreciation, involve tax deferral and not permanent escape from taxation. The committee is aware that in these instances some case could be made for providing

adjustments to basis to avoid double taxation. For example, the fact that accelerated depreciation in excess of straight-line depreciation is subject to a 5-percent minimum tax might be advanced as grounds for some increase in the basis of the property involved. However, the committee concluded that, as a practical matter, it would be best not to provide for such basis adjustments under a 5-percent tax since such adjustments would complicate the minimum tax. Moreover, the fact of deferring tax for an extended period of time is itself a tax preference for which the 5-percent tax is a moderate charge.

See discussion in Davenport and Goldman, note 24 above, at 1255–1257. The House provision, and the Nixon Treasury proposal, did not distinguish between the two types of preferences, relying apparently on the carryforward to remove the problem in the case of shorter deferrals.

72. There are other factors which a reasonable approximation avoids; e.g., the taxpayer may not be in the same marginal rate bracket in each year of the deferral; interest and earnings rates and hence exact discount rates may differ during the years of deferral.

The same problems with deferral-type preferences exist under an allocation of deductions provision. If itemized deductions are allocated to a deferral-type tax preference deduction, so that some of the itemized deductions are disallowed, then if the deferred income is later included, the disallowed portion should be restored. Restoration would in effect produce deferral of itemized deductions to match the deferral of income.

73. McDaniel, in Panel No. 6, note 5 above, suggests a 7–35% rate scale for individuals and a 20% rate for corporations, as a *supplementary* tax. Whether such a supplementary rate is stronger than a 28.8% alternative rate depends on the effective rate under the regular tax. In most cases, the supplementary approach would give the higher total tax. Goldman, in Panel No. 6, note 5 above at 855, would restrict the minimum tax to individuals.

The other indirect restraints are not applicable to corporations: they do not have personal expense deductions, so the allocation of deductions proposal is not relevant, and it is probably not really feasible to distinguish their investment interest expense from their trade or business interest expense, so the limitation on the deduction of investment interest is also not relevant.

74. The April 1973 Treasury proposal for a new minimum tax, note 28 above, involves another variation. This proposal would add to adjusted gross income four exclusion preferences — percentage depletion in excess of basis, the excluded one-half of capital gains, compensation earned abroad, and the bargain element in stock options. This would give an expanded adjusted gross income. From this would be subtracted investment expenses not in excess of investment income, the personal expense deductions for extraordinary medical expenses and casualty losses, the personal exemptions and a $10,000 floor. The resulting figure is divided by two to give the minimum tax base. This base is then subjected to the regular tax rates. The individual would pay the higher of his normal tax or this minimum tax.

This proposal is in part a throwback to the Nixon Treasury proposal for an alternative minimum tax in 1969. As for its coverage of exclusions, it is hardly worth the effort. The mechanics would not increase the tax on capital gains, and the stock option, compensation earned abroad, and percentage depletion items are minor indeed. The items in the present minimum tax that involve deferrals of income, such as the deductions for intangible drilling expenses or accelerated depreciation, were omitted because they were dealt with — inadequately to be sure — under another proposal, see note 4 above.

The bite of the proposal comes in its effect on the deductions for personal expenses, such as charitable contributions, state and local taxes and mortgage interest (except extraordinary medical expenses and casualty losses, defined as expenses in excess of 10% of expanded adjusted gross income). This approach is the first of the minimum tax proposals to consider these expenses as tax preferences. However, the treatment is erratic. If there are excluded income preferences, then $1 of included income shelters $1 of excluded income, with one-half of the remaining excluded income being taxed at regular rates and all the personal expense deductions disregarded. If there is no excluded income, then $1 of included income can in effect absorb 50 cents of personal expense deductions and the remaining 50 cents is disregarded. Such a structure requires more analysis to determine its operative effects, and its comparison with the allocation of deductions concept. On initial study the proposal seems distinctly less preferable than the allocation of deductions concept to deal with the personal expense deductions. Also, the treatment under the proposal of excess investment interest, which is to consider the excess of investment expenses over investment income as an excluded deduction in computing the minimum tax base, and then to eliminate the present section 163(d) limitation on the interest deduction, requires further study to compare its effectiveness with the present limitation and the expansion possibilities of that limitation.

The proposal extends only to individuals and leaves the corporate minimum tax untouched.

The proposal, together with the tax shelter proposal, note 4 above, was estimated to raise $800 million additional income — $1 billion gross less $200 million because of the repeal of the present minimum tax. Apparently the minimum tax by itself was considered to raise $500 million gross.

75. Presumably the limitation on interest would first apply and then the allocation of deductions proposal in computing the regular tax. Then the minimum tax would be computed (for which all the deductions would be allowed since the preferences are included) and its amount compared with the regular tax. As to the relationship between minimum tax and allocation of deductions, see Tax Reform Studies, note 2 above, at 139.

76. House Report, note 23 above, at 208–209.

77. Senate Hearings, note 47 above, at 560.

78. Senate Report, note 13 above, at 309–310. The reasons given were:

> The committee questioned whether it was appropriate to single out earned income for preferential exemption from the top marginal tax rates while still imposing a much higher tax on income from other sources, particularly when a given taxpayer might benefit from the 50 percent limit on earned income and still make use of tax preferences to minimize his tax on other income. Questions can also be raised as to whether a reduction in the marginal rate on earned income by so substantial an amount as provided by the House bill is consistent with the progressive rate structure for individuals.
>
> For the reasons indicated above, the committee deleted this provision of the House bill. It has, however, provided uniform rate reductions for all tax brackets in a manner which is in keeping with the progressive rate system.

79. Code §1348. The long-run revenue loss was estimated to be $170 million.

80. See Tax Reform Studies, note 2 above, at 17–18, 172–174.
81. The provision also excludes certain deferred compensation from the definition of earned income. See Caplin, note 24 above, at 101–102.
For a comparison of the effectiveness of this offset for tax preferences under the maximum tax with that of the minimum tax on the same preferences, see note 68 above.
82. Tax Reform Studies, note 2 above, at 18.
83. The House Ways and Means Committee adoption of the maximum tax and its Treasury support appear in part to be based on a belief that the provision would reduce the search for tax shelters and other preferences. The House Committee Report states, note 76 above:

> The 50-percent limit on the tax rate applicable to earned income was adopted not as a tax relief measure but to reduce the pressure for the use of tax loopholes. Your committee concluded that one of the most effective ways to prevent the use of any remaining tax avoidance devices and to forestall the development of new methods of tax avoidance is to reduce the incentive for engaging in such activities by reducing the high tax rates on earned income. . . .
> Your committee concluded that a 50-percent limit on the tax rates applicable to earned income would substantially reduce the incentive to engage in otherwise unprofitable operations and reduce the time and effort devoted to "tax planning" at the expense of pursuing normal business operations.

However, in practice the provision appears to have the effect of adding still another variable to the calculations involved in tax shelters, executive compensation arrangements, and like pursuits, with many an executive and professional person still participating in these tax reduction activities. The variables do become more complex and result in the accounting firms and investment houses specializing in advice in these areas to turn to computer analysis. Moreover, since an individual electing the maximum tax must forego the averaging provisions, he is pushed to seek tax shelter or other tax reduction activities. On tax shelters and the maximum tax, see Hugh Calkins and Kenneth E. Updegraft, Jr., "Tax Shelters," 26 The Tax Lawyer 493 (1973).
84. A 50% maximum effective rate, or a reduction of top marginal rates, would reduce taxes currently being paid by taxpayers with very large amounts of dividends and no preferences, but with very large asset holdings having significant accrued but unrealized appreciation in value. Their advantage would lie in the deferral of tax on that appreciation. If there is a significant number of these taxpayers, then the problem requires some solution before they are to be benefited by a reduction in marginal or effective rates.
85. A problem arises, of course, if the Treasury, even though it has the requisite information, does not make it public. The Securities and Exchange Commission is moving toward a rule that would require corporate reports subject to its jurisdiction to indicate why the provision for federal income tax expense varies from 48% of book profits. Such a rule, properly implemented, would make data on corporate use of tax expenditures available to the public, and perhaps even more readily available to the Treasury than its corporate tax return data. But the problem would remain as to public information on the use of tax expenditures by individuals. Congressional tax committees could secure such data from the Treasury and make them public, without having to disclose the particular individuals involved.

Index

Aaron, Henry J., 4, 147, 233, 324 (note 5), 329 (note 33); on reform of tax system, 344 (note 15); on revenue sharing, 370 (note 51)

Abatement: least-cost, 156; uniform, 158, 165; technologically feasible, 158; regressive cost of, 167

Accelerated depreciation, 102, 310 (note 12), 315 (note 21); as incentive for investment, 348 (note 35); on new rental housing, 386 (note 125). *See also* Real estate

Actual income, vs. taxable income, 51

Adelman, M.A., 307 (note 67)

Adjusted basis, 113

After-tax profit, 104

Aged, the, special tax benefits for, 2, 67, 127–128, 152; credit for property taxes of, 135; personal exemption for, 179; direct assistance for, 200, 353 (note 60)

Agriculture, 207; as tax shelter investment, 63; continuance of tax preferences in, 186–187; substitution of direct expenditures in, 199–200. *See also* Farm activities

Alcohol tax, 26–27

Almond groves, 117

American Automobile Association, 194

American Chamber of Commerce, 184

American Council on Education, 227, 374 (note 64-1)

American Housing Partners, 387 (note 132)

American Law Institute, 29, 182

Andrews, William D., ix, 20, 27, 287 (note 12), 288 (note 15), 289 (note 16), 289 (note 20), 291 (note 31)

Apartment buildings, depreciation of, 384 (note 118)

Appreciation, accrued, 287 (note 8); on property used as charitable deductions, 55, 224, 268, 299 (note 6), 371 (note 58); on property transferred at death, 304 (note 47); and interest deduction, 402 (note 49)

Art works, gifts of, 224

Asset Depreciation Range System, 32, 34, 109, 188–189, 317 (note 29)

Association of American Universities, 378 (note 86)

Ault, Hugh J., ix

Automobiles, taxes on, 222

Back-door financing, 147, 333 (note 53)

Bad debt reserves, 77, 79; reduction in, 177, 190

Barnes, Peter, 312 (note 19)

Barr, Joseph W., 283 (note 3), 307 (note 69), 325 (note 7)

Bennett, Wallace F., 333 (note 53)

Biederman, Kenneth, R., 327 (note 17)

Bittker, Boris I., 285 (note 1), 287 (note 10); on civil rights and taxes, 293 (notes 11, 16, 17); on matching proposal, 377 (note 78)

Black Watch Farms, Inc., 312 (note 17)

Blacks, effects of tax programs on, 40; *Green v. Kennedy,* 40–42; *McGlotten v. Connally,* 42–46

Blind, the: special tax benefits for, 2, 67, 127; direct assistance for, 200–201

Borrowing: and leverage, 111–113, 251, 395 (note 8); limits on deductions of interest from, 402 (note 49). *See also* Investment credit

Boston Federal Reserve Bank, 216; Seminar on State and Local Finance, 216, 369 (note 41)

Brewster, Kingman, 371 (note 58)

Brinner, Roger, 352 (note 54)

Brookings Institution, 29

Budget, Bureau of, and tax expenditures, 144

Budget deficit, and income tax surcharge, 1

Buildings (other than rental housing): as tax shelter investments, 63; excess depreciation on, 188. *See also* Apartment buildings; Commercial buildings; Real estate; Rental housing

Bureaucracy, and payment of subsidies, 131–133

Burger, Chief Justice, 297 (note 23)

Burns, Arthur F., 358 (note 76)

Canadian tax reform, 392 (note 1), 399 (note 32), 401 (note 44)

Capital expenditure, as current expense, 101

Capital gains, 351 (note 52); individual, 25; tax incentives for, 34, 35; deductions of, 54–55, 95; and tax shelters, 63, 113–117, 118; of high-income taxpayers, 64; corpo-

fits for, 177; industrial and commercial, 237–238, 253; limiting scope of deductions on, 248. *See also* Homes; Houses

Recapture of capital gains, 115–117, 237, 253

Reform, tax. *See* Tax reform

Regulatory taxes, 155–174

Rehabilitation, housing; amortization of costs of, 34, 63; relative benefits of, 37–38; tax incentives for, 127, 152, 177

Rehnquist, Justice, 298 (note 23)

Religious organizations, and taxes, 295 (note 22), 377 (note 78)

Rental housing: support for, 232, 236–246; luxury and middle-income, 238–239; 245–246; low and moderate-income, 239, 245–246; tax expenditures for, 239–241; direct government assistance for, 242, 244–246; private investment in, 242–244

Replacement of tax expenditure by direct assistance, 175; tax expenditure analysis, 176–180; assessment of programs under tax expenditures, 180–181; classification of tax expenditure items, 182–208

Reporting of income, on individual tax returns, 55–56

Research and development: tax relief for, 78–79; tax incentives for, 127

Reserve ratio test, 349 (note 35)

Retail sales tax. *See* Sales tax

Retirement income credit, 67, 68, 128

Reuss, Henry S., 59

Revenue Act of 1962, 175

Revenue Act of 1964, 175

Revenue Act of 1971, 26, 27, 175, 178

Revenue and Expenditure Control Act of 1968, 2

Revenue sharing, 222, 370 (note 49)

Revision, tax, defined, 30. *See also* Tax reform

Ribicoff, Abraham, 133, 327 (note 20)

Roberts, Marc, 170–171

Romney, George, 233

Rosebush tax shelter, 109, 139, 318 (note 30)

Rosow, Jerome, 304 (note 49)

Rural areas, business investment in, 128

Sale of tax benefits, 106–107

Sales tax, 26, 27; coverage of, 20, 288 (note 13); to tax consumption, 21; and revenue sharing, 370 (note 51)

Savings and loan associations, 75, 80; tax incentives for, 127, 190

Schools, church-affiliated, tax aid to, 298 (note 24)

Schultze, Charles L., on pollution control,

339 (note 7), 340 (notes 8, 9, 11), 341 (notes 12, 14, 16)

Securities, gifts of, 224, 227, 229

Securities Industry Association, 217

Segregated schools, tax benefits to, 40–42

Seigel, Stuart E., ix

Self-employed person, 65; incorporation of, 303 (note 38)

Sellers, Wallace O., 368 (note 39)

Senate Banking Committee, on taxable local bond subsidies, 218

Senate Finance Committee: on household expense deductions, 202; on minimum tax, 271–273

Shanahan, Eileen, 329 (note 35)

Shipping: deferral of tax on companies in, 80, 200, 353 (note 59); operations in, 309 (note 9)

Shoup, Carl S., 122–123

Shultz, George P., 217–218, 284 (note 9), 298 (note 24), 329 (note 37), 393 (note 4)

Sick, the: special tax benefits for, 2, 128; exclusion of pay for, 192

Simons, Henry C., 12–13, 20–22, 285 (note 4)

Single persons: new rate schedule for, 178; vs. married, tax treatment of, 182, 343 (note 13)

Sloan v. Lemon, 294 (note 20)

Social clubs, 45, 294 (note 18)

Social programs, fostered by tax incentives, 131, 147

Social security, exclusion of, 67, 68, 94, 128

Special tax rate, 93

Standard deduction, 61; increase in, 177, 187, 376 (note 71); effect of on charities, 227, 375 (note 67); and homeowners, 380 (note 92)

State and local bonds: tax exemptions for, 32, 56–57, 62, 77, 177, 194, 268, 270; alternatives to present system, 216–222; relation of commercial banks to, 361 (n10)

State and local governments, aid to, 209–222; efforts to alter, 210–211, 212; affirmative aspects of, 211–212; lobbying for, 212; events since 1969 related to, 212–222; federal assistance, 215, 221–222; by taxable bonds, 216–220; and revenue sharing, 222; and state and local taxes, 222

State and local taxes: as deductions, 35, 127, 255, 299 (note 7); possible substitution of subsidies for, 204; and subsidized taxable bonds, 222

Stern, Philip M., 305 (note 58)

Stewart, Richard B., ix

Stock investments: capital gains from, 62;

Index

Taxable bonds: for state and local governments, 216–222; amount of subsidy for, 218–220

Timber industry: special tax treatment for, 2, 75, 79; as tax shelter investment, 63; effective tax rate for, 80; direct grants for, 199–200

Training provided by employer, 34

Transfer payments, 68, 325 (note 50)

Travel and entertainment, as expense deduction, 287 (note 9)

Treasury Department, 29; on tax incentives, 150–152; tax expenditure study by, 176; on taxable local bond subsidies, 217; on interest deduction, 265–266; on minimum tax, 268–269, 276–277; on maximum tax, 280–281

Treasury Tax Reform Studies and Proposals, 50–56, 176, 255; on excluded income, 53–54; on corporations, 74; on capital gain, 196; on real estate, 237; on farm income, 248; on maximum individual income tax, 304 (note 47; on minimum tax, 403 (note 54)

Trusts: income accumulated in, 182; charitable, 223; family, 252, 343 (note 10)

Tuition: and tax grants, 47–48; tax credits for, 152

Unemployment benefits, 94, 128, 201, 290 (note 26)

Unionized industries, fringe benefits in, 67

U.S. Conference of Mayors, 216

Unreported income: interest on state and local bonds, 55; losses in a tax shelter syndicate, 55

Urban Development Bank, 215

Urban Development Corporation, 213

Uses of Tax Expenditure Budget: for revision and reform, 30–31; economy in government expenditures, 31–33; tax simplification, 33–35; evaluation of present tax expenditures, 35–39; evaluation of proposed tax expenditures, 39–40; evaluation of effect on constitutional issues, 40–48; effect on tax process, 48–49. *See also* Tax Expenditure Budget

Value-added tax, 20

Vanik, Charles, 308 (note 71)

Veteran's benefits and services, 208; tax benefits for, 67; direct benefits for, 203

Vickrey. William, 373 (note 62), 396 (note 10)

Wall Street Journal, 313 (note 19)

Walsh, Albert A., 331 (note 43)

Walz v. Tax Commission, 295, 296 (note 22), 377 (note 78)

Water Pollution Control Act, 173

Ways and Means Committee: on income tax surcharge, 1; on tax expenditure budget, 143; on interest deductions, 262–263

Wealthy, the: benefits to from tax expenditures, 36–37; individuals paying no tax, 54–60, 301 (notes 19, 21). *See also* High-income taxpayers

Welfare, individual as recipient of, 67–68; exclusions benefitting, 94; hiring of recipients of, 202, 357 (notes 67, 68)

Welfare-training projects, 34–35

Western Hemisphere Trade Corporations, 79, 80, 127, 184, 307 (note 65), 325 (note 5)

White, Justice, 297 (note 23)

Withholding of tax on wages and salaries, 98

Work incentive programs, tax incentives for, 152

Workmen's compensation, 201

418